An Island Archaeology of the Early Cyclades

Cyprian Broodbank uses comparative island archaeology to present the most up-to-date analysis of early Cycladic culture and to reinterpret a vital phase in early Aegean history. He traces the development of Neolithic and Early Bronze Age societies in these islands from first colonisation through to their incorporation, three millennia later, in the world system of the Minoan palaces and the wider eastern Mediterranean. The archaeology of the Cyclades is rich and well documented, allowing Dr Broodbank to reformulate early Cycladic history and deploy detailed examples that question established approaches in island archaeology. He shows that islanders can actively define their cultural spaces and environments, and that island communities are linked by complex relations to the non-insular world. This book will provide many new perspectives and challenges for island archaeologists and Mediterranean specialists alike.

CYPRIAN BROODBANK is Lecturer in Aegean Archaeology at the Institute of Archaeology, University College London.

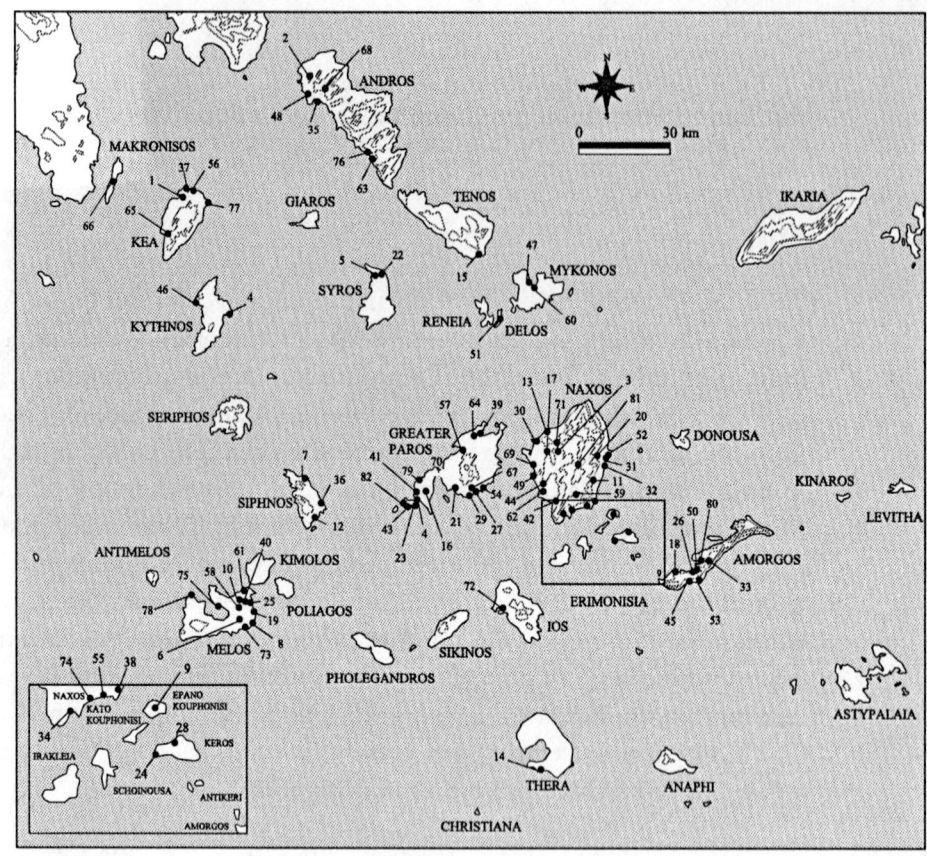

Key to sites		Avdeli	20	Kouphi	40	Phyrroges	62
		Avyssos	21	Krassades	41	Plaka	63
Agia Irini	1	Chalandriani-Kastri	22	Lakkoudes	42	Plastiras	64
Agia Marina	2	Cheiromylos	23	Livadi	43	Poisses	65
Agioi Anargyroi	3	Daskaleio-Kavos	24	Louros Athalassou	44	Provatsa	66
Agios Ioannis	4	Demenegaki	25	Markiani	45	Pyrgos	67
Agios Loukas	5	Dokathismata	26	Maroula	46	Rethi	68
Agios Panteleimon	6	Drios	27	Mavrispilia	47	Rizokastellia	69
Agios Sostis	7	Gerani	28	Mazareko	48	Saliagos	70
Agios Theodoros	8	Glypha	29	Mikri Vigla	49	Sangri	71
Agrilia (Kouphonisi)	9	Grotta-Aplomata	30	Minoa	50	Skarkos	72
Agrilia (Melos)	10	Kampos tis Makris	31	Mt Kynthos	51	Skouries	see 4
Aïlas	11	Kanaki	32	Moutsouna	52	Spathi	73
Akrotiraki	12	Kapros	33	Notina	53	Spedos	74
Akrotiri (Naxos)	13	Karvounolakkoi	34	Panagia	54	Sta Nychia	75
Akrotiri (Thera)	14	Kastri (Andros)	35	Panermos	55	Strophylas	76
Akrotirion Ourion	15	Kastri (Syros)	see 22	Paoura	56	Sykamias	77
Antiparos cave	16	Kastro	36	Paroikia	57	Vani	78
Aphendika	17	Kavos	see 24	Pelos	58	Vouni	79
Aplomata	see 30	Kephala	37	Phionda	59	Xylokeratidi	80
Arkesini	18	Korphi t'Aroniou	38	Phtelia	60	Zas cave	81
Asprochorio	19	Koukounaries	39	Phylakopi	61	Zoumbaria	82

The Cyclades, showing sites mentioned and coastlines as they existed in the fifth to third millennia BC. Contours at *c.* 160, 330, 660 and 1000 m.

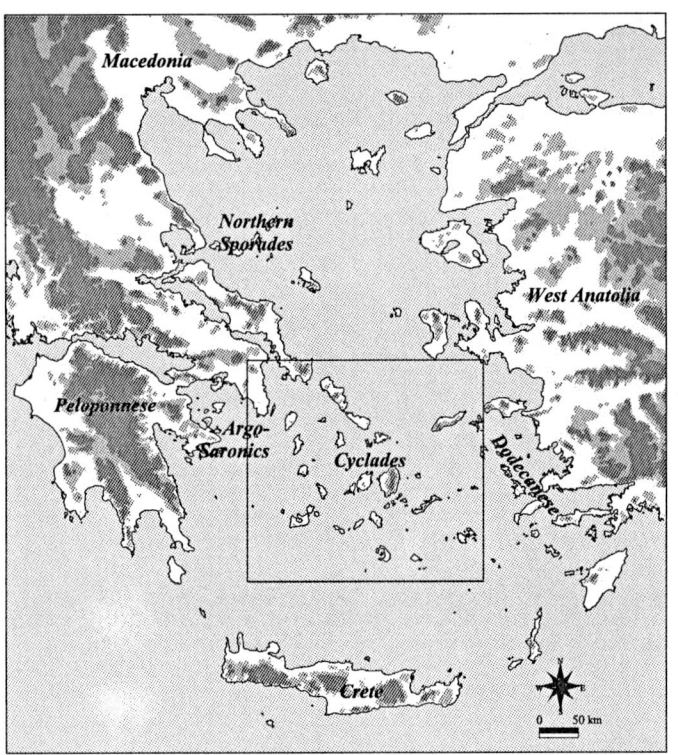

Key to sites	
Agia Photia	1
Agios Kosmas	2
Agios Petros	3
Agios Stephanos	4
Archanes	5
Asine	6
Askitario	7
Asomatos	8
Chamaizi	9
Chrysokamino	10
Cyclops cave	11
Emporio	12
Eutresis	13
Franchthi cave	14
Gournia	15
Heraion	16
Iasos	17
Kalythies cave	18
Karystos cave	19
Kastri (Kythera)	20
Kiparissi cave	21
Kitsos cave	22
Knidos	23
Knossos	24
Kolonna	25
Lavrion	26
Lefkandi	27
Lerna	28
Limantepe	29
Mallia	30
Manika	31
Miletus	32
Mochlos	33
Mycenae	34
Myrtos	35
Palaikastro	36
Palamari	37
Paximadi	38
Pefkakia	39
Petras	40
Phaistos	41
Plakari	42
Poliochni	43
Poros	44
Pyrgos cave	45
Raphina	46
Tharrounia cave	47
Thebes	48
Thermi	49
Tiryns	50
Troy	51
Tsoungiza	52
Vasiliki	53
Ziros	54

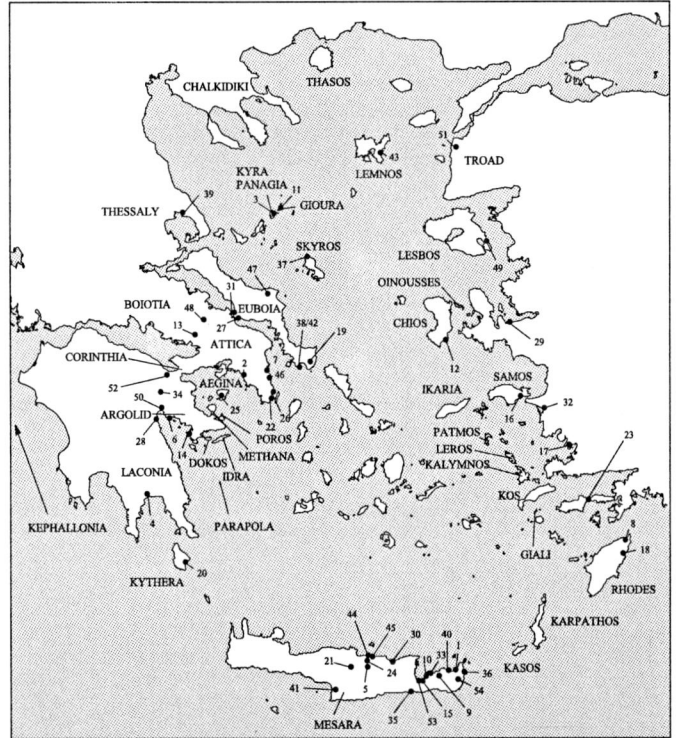

The Aegean, showing the main regions and sites mentioned.

An Island Archaeology of the Early Cyclades

CYPRIAN BROODBANK

PUBLISHED BY THE PRESS SYNDICATE OF THE UNIVERSITY OF CAMBRIDGE
The Pitt Building, Trumpington Street, Cambridge, United Kingdom

CAMBRIDGE UNIVERSITY PRESS
The Edinburgh Building, Cambridge CB2 2RU, UK
40 West 20th Street, New York NY 10011-4211, USA
477 Williamstown Road, Port Melbourne, VIC 3207, Australia
Ruiz de Alarcón 13, 28014 Madrid, Spain
Dock House, The Waterfront, Cape Town 8001, South Africa

http://www.cambridge.org

© Cambridge University Press 2000

This book is in copyright. Subject to statutory exception
and to the provisions of relevant collective licensing agreements,
no reproduction of any part may take place without
the written permission of Cambridge University Press.

First published 2000
First paperback edition 2002

Typeface Monotype Plantin Light 10/14 pt.   *System* QuarkXPress™

A catalogue record for this book is available from the British Library

Library of Congress Cataloguing in Publication data
Broodbank, Cyprian.
An island archaeology of the early Cyclades / Cyprian Broodbank.
    p.   cm.
Includes bibliographical references and index.
ISBN 0 521 78272 4
1. Cyclades (Greece) – Antiquities.   2. Greece – Antiquities.   3. Cyclades
(Greece) – Civilization.   4. Island people – Greece – Cyclades.   5. Bronze
Age – Greece – Cyclades.   I. Title.
DF221.C93   B76 2000
939′.15-dc21   00-024174

ISBN 0 521 78272 4 hardback
ISBN 0 521 52844 5 paperback

To my mother and father
Who taught me how to live

To Valasia
For life

CONTENTS

List of figures		*page* x
List of tables		xiv
Acknowledgements		xv
List of abbreviations and dating conventions		xviii
	Prologue: islands of 'prehistory'	1
1	Whither island archaeology?	6
2	Cycladic approaches	36
3	Islands, people and seafaring	68
4	The dawn treaders	107
5	Cultures of colonisation	144
6	Small worlds	175
7	Which islands in the stream?	211
8	Paint, paddles and the politics of value	247
9	Ulysses without sails	276
10	An altered archipelago	320
11	The emergence of Minoan dominance	350
12	Cycladic archaeology as island archaeology	362
	References	368
	Index	402

FIGURES

	The Cyclades	*Frontispiece*
	The Aegean	*Frontispiece*
1	Chronology, terminology and major synchronisms	xix
2	Ways of visualising islands and islandscapes	24
3	The Mediterranean, south-west Oceania and the Caribbean	39
4	Maximum seaward visibility from land in the Mediterranean	40
5	The Cyclades and select other island clusters	42
6	Recent work on early Cycladic sites and landscapes	49
7	An exploration index for the early Cyclades	52
8	The price of esteem: Daskaleio-Kavos looted	59
9	The descent of Cycladica	61
10	A critique of proportionality in Cycladic figurines	62
11	Painted decoration on Cycladic marble figurines	63
12	The Cyclades as a *kyklos* around Delos	69
13	Six Cycladic islandscapes	72
14	Island size in the Cyclades	73
15	Inter-island distance in the Cyclades	75
16	Three-dimensional computer-generated view of the south-east Cyclades	76
17	Rainfall and hydrology in the Cyclades and rainfall in surrounding areas	77
18	Inter-annual fluctuation of rainfall on Melos	79
19	Cycladic geology and mineral resources	80
20	The composition of faunal assemblages at early Cycladic sites	82
21	Currents and winds in the Cyclades	93
22	Agricultural tasks and the sailing season in the Aegean	95
23	Early Bronze Age Cycladic boat depictions	98
24	Daily travel range in the early Cyclades	103
25	An experimental reed-boat and its Cycladic voyage	104
26	Model phases for the settlement of an island	109
27	The sinking of Cycladia	112
28	Part of Sta Nychia obsidian quarry on Melos	114
29	Mesolithic sites in the Aegean	115
30	Aegean islands colonised in the Neolithic and Early Bronze Age	118
31	Saliagos and its environs	119

32	Kephala and its environs	119
33	Neolithic Cycladic flaked-stone points	121
34	Neolithic sites in the Cyclades	122
35	North-east Melos showing the location of Neolithic sites	124
36	Axes of entry into the Cyclades for short-range colonising groups	132
37	The high island chain: Samos, Ikaria and Naxos	134
38	Expansion model for colonisation of the Cyclades from Attica and Euboia	135
39	Target/distance analysis for colonisation of the Cyclades from the south-east Aegean	136
40	Expansion model for colonisation of the Cyclades from the south-east Aegean	138
41	Microlocations of Saliagos culture sites	147
42	Kephala cemetery	150
43	Distribution of Grotta-Pelos culture and other contemporary sites	151
44	A typical Grotta-Pelos cemetery: Lakkoudes on Naxos	152
45	Final Neolithic copper flat axe from the Zas cave	160
46	Distribution of select later Neolithic prestige objects found in the Cyclades	161
47	Distribution of Neolithic light-on-dark pottery in the southern Aegean	162
48	Mt Zas	165
49	Elements of the proposed Grotta-Pelos exchange culture	168
50	Distribution of Grotta-Pelos culture marble vessels	169
51	The diversity of anthropomorphic figurines from the early Cyclades	172
52	Terrell's proximal point analysis for the Solomon islands	182
53	Proximal point analysis for the Cyclades	184
54	Naxian worldlets	188
55	Changing maritime orientation in the Cyclades	189
56	Remote and parochial zones in the Cyclades	192
57	Islands with Grotta-Pelos culture sites compared with the PPA 1 network	199
58	Corbelled graves at Chalandriani cemetery on Syros	200
59	Corbelled grave distribution compared with PPA 4 network	201
60	Painted, incised and stamped-and-incised pottery of the Early Bronze II Cyclades	203
61	Pedestal-based jar variants and their distributions	204
62	The creation of a south-east Cycladic islandscape: interaction and material culture	208
63	Chalandriani-Kastri	213
64	Hedgehog figurine from Chalandriani cemetery	216
65	Agia Irini	217
66	Grotta-Aplomata	219
67	Daskaleio-Kavos and Kavos North	224
68	Part of the so-called 'Keros hoard'	226
69	Marble vessels from sanctioned archaeological work at Daskaleio-Kavos	227

List of figures

70	Kavos North	231
71	Quantitative fabric analysis of the surface material from Daskaleio-Kavos	233
72	Pottery import levels at selected Cycladic Early Bronze II sites	234
73	Provenance of imports at Daskaleio-Kavos	235
74	Painted pottery from Daskaleio-Kavos	236
75	Nodes of intense communication in the Cyclades	239
76	Islandscape seen from Daskaleio-Kavos	242
77	Syros: settlement pattern and the islandscape seen from Chalandriani-Kastri	243
78	Similar figurine heads with different decoration	248
79	Equipment for body decoration and modification from burial contexts	250
80	Greenstone symbolic crucible from Amorgos	251
81	Symbols of maritime travel, navigation and swiftness	252
82	Marble harpist figurine said to come from Keros	254
83	The ideology of fighting: a hunter-warrior figurine and a 'silvered' dagger	255
84	Areas favourable to the organisation of longboat activity in the Cyclades	257
85	One-day travel ranges from major Early Bronze II island centres	261
86	Number of grave goods per grave in the Agioi Anargyroi cemetery	264
87	Early Bronze II Cycladic distributions of marble figurines and painted pottery	266
88	Skeuomorphism seen in clay jugs	271
89	Two island trading systems compared: the Cycladic and Siassi networks	274
90	Major sites of the Early Bronze II Aegean	280
91	Distribution of obsidian finds in the southern Argolid	281
92	Selection of large Early Bronze II Aegean settlements	282
93	The Early Bronze II Aegean as a margin of the Near Eastern world system	284
94	Major maritime routes of the Early Bronze Age Aegean	289
95	Two Cycladic metal-processing landscapes: Agios Sostis and Skouries	295
96	Distribution of talc ware	296
97	Chrysokamino and its environs	299
98	The main sites involved in long-range Kampos group trade	300
99	Kampos group bottle	301
100	Distribution of select inter-regional trade objects of earlier Early Bronze II	305
101	Cycladic imports at Knossos, Crete, in Early Bronze II	307
102	Principal Kastri group shapes	310
103	Distribution of Kastri group pottery in the Aegean	312
104	Distribution of fortified sites in the Cyclades	314
105	Fortified settlements: Kastri, Mt Kynthos and Panermos	315
106	Changing patterns of Early Bronze Age Cycladic long-range interaction	319
107	Phylakopi I culture rock-cut tombs at Phylakopi	323
108	Duck vase found on Amorgos	324
109	Distribution of later Middle Bronze Age Cycladic sites	327

List of figures   xiii

110	Two major Middle Bronze Age Cycladic settlements: Phylakopi and Mikri Vigla	329
111	Distribution of Phylakopi I culture sites	330
112	Phylakopi I	331
113	The Early Bronze III 'gap'	332
114	Proximal Point Analysis 5	339
115	Design on a Minoan seal illustrating a sailing ship	342
116	Images of the new shipping in the Cyclades found at Phylakopi	344
117	Model for the transformation of settlement in the south-east Cyclades	348
118	Phylakopi I culture pyxis from the Agios Loukas cemetery	349
119	Distribution of duck vases in the Aegean	352
120	Three major Aegean interaction zones at the start of the Middle Bronze Age	355
121	Dendritic pattern of maritime trade centred on palatial Crete	357
122	Middle Minoan imports from palatial Crete found at Phylakopi	358

TABLES

1	Island demography in the early Cyclades	*page* 90
2	Iconographic features of longboats and other canoes	98
3	Performance parameters and functions of longboats and other canoes	102
4	Ranked size/distance scores for Cycladic islands	130
5	Large Cycladic cemeteries and their burying populations	178
6	Percentage of points with different degrees of seafaring orientation in each PPA	190
7	Relative popularity of painted, incised and stamped-and-incised decoration	202
8	Pottery shapes with painted decoration at four investigated Cycladic sites	205
9	Painted motifs at the investigated Cycladic sites	206
10	Two rich south-east Cycladic burials of Early Bronze II date	265
11	Phylakopi: nomenclature, diagnostics, culture attributions and dates	322
12	Comparative boat performance for canoes and sailing ships	345

ACKNOWLEDGEMENTS

> I am debtor both to the Greeks, and to the barbarians; both
> to the wise and to the unwise. ROMANS 1.14

John Cherry enabled a man who loves islands to become an archaeologist who could also analyse them, Todd Whitelaw brought method and a wealth of advice to temper the excesses of islomania, Andrew and Susan Sherratt ensured that island research never became insular, and Chris Chippindale drove me to prove that an early Cycladic history might be written. To these teachers, and likewise to Peter Warren, I owe the best part of my education in archaeology. Among many scholars working in the Cyclades who have shared their thoughts with me, it is a particular pleasure to thank Jack Davis, Angelika Douzougli, Olga Hadjianastasiou (Filaniotou), Mariza Marthari, David Wilson and Kostas Zachos. Among other Aegeanists, Jeremy Rutter and Paul Halstead have always been more than generous with their advice and encouragement, and the overall development of the ideas about islands that are elaborated in this book owes a profound debt to the intellectual examples set by John Terrell, Chris Gosden and Nicholas Purcell.

The doctoral dissertation from which this book derives was researched under the ever-stimulating and exacting supervision of John Cherry, and for shorter periods under Colin Renfrew and Henry Hurst. I thank them all for their support and cajoling, and the first in particular for bearing the brunt of the task. I further thank Joan Oates, without whose staunch support at a critical juncture this research might never have been completed. Likewise to my examiners, Todd Whitelaw and Chris Gosden, I express my warm gratitude, and apologise for spoiling their Christmas preparations. Since I started my research, the following institutions have provided a range of research environments that have all contributed in diverse ways to the final product: at Cambridge University, the Faculty of Classics, King's College and Girton College; at Oxford University, University College and the Ashmolean Museum; at London University, the Institute of Archaeology, University College London; and in Greece, the British School at Athens. The last two institutions (including the Fitch Laboratory of the British School) I thank in particular for providing the peace and time to complete this book. For encouragement in my fieldwork I am grateful to several scholars, but above all to Colin Renfrew, Christos Doumas, Lila Marangou and Photeini Zapheiropoulou, for kindly inviting me to study the pottery recovered in 1987 from the remarkable site of Daskaleio-Kavos on Keros. It is through their generosity that I draw upon the 1987 material in this book. Although my interpretations do not always accord with their own, I remain extremely grateful for the honour of being able to differ from an informed position. For ensuring that the pottery study proceeded smoothly and happily I thank Olga Hadjianastasiou (Filaniotou), Daphni Lalagianni and the ever-friendly guards at the Naxos Archaeological Museum. For permission to study other material, further thanks extend to Elizabeth Schofield and David Wilson (Agia Irini), Colin Renfrew and Photeini Zapheiropoulou (Phylakopi), and Katie Demakopoulou (material from Chalandriani-Kastri in the National Museum, Athens).

I further thank the following for creative discussion, advice and information: Christos Agouridis, David Anthony, Robert Arnott, Lis Bacus, Robin Barber, George Bass, John Bennet, Kiki Birtacha, Lucy Blue, Electra Boli, Jeremy Bond, Warwick Bray, Ann Brown, Tristan Carter, Susan Colledge, James Conolly, Tracey Cullen, Peter Day, Hayat Erkanal, John Evans, Lesley Fitton, Vasso Fotou, Noel Gale, Ian Glover, Yiannis Hamilakis, Sue Hamilton, David Harris, Jon Hather, Jan Hekman, Stephen Held, Nicolle Hirschfeld, Valasia Isaakidou-Broodbank, Richard Jones, Patrick Kirch, Bernard Knapp, Olga Krzyszkowska, Kurt Lambeck, Sandy MacGillivray, James McGlade, Sean McGrail, Sturt Manning, Ezra Marcus, Toula Marketou, Manolis Melas, Lena Mendoni, Jennifer Moody, Georgia Nakou, Vivek Nanda, José Oliver, Clive Orton, Yiannis Papadatos, Edgar Peltenburg, Catherine Perlès, Cemal Pulak, Daniel Pullen, Curtis Runnels, Vasif Sahoglu, Yiannis and Efi Sakellarakis, Adamantios Sampson, Guy Sanders, Chris Scarre, Louise Schofield, Stephen Shennan, Peggy Sotirakopoulou, Christiane Sourvinou-Inwood, Zofia Stos-Gale, Tom Strasser, Laurie Talalay, Jeremy Tanner, Robin Torrence, Riza Tuncel, Peter Ucko, Tjeerd van Andel, Sarah Vaughan, Kaddee Vitelli, Sophia Voutsaki, Ruth Whitehouse, James Whitley, and many of my students at the Institute of Archaeology, University College London, 1993–99.

I would like to express my gratitude to several people who contributed much to the later stages of this book's gestation. First among equals must come Jessica Kuper, Frances Brown and the staff of Cambridge University Press for their patience, perseverance and faith in the final outcome, as well as the two readers for the Press who recommended this text for publication. For constructive comments on advanced drafts I equally thank Andrew Bevan, John Cherry, Jack Davis, Paul Halstead, Vicky Jackson, Georgia Nakou (also for compilation of the index), Todd Whitelaw and David Wilson. Individual credits for the figures are given in the captions where appropriate (unless otherwise stated all photographs were taken by the author), but I owe a more general and heartfelt thanks to three stalwart people for their preparation of many of the figures, namely Andrew Bevan (computer graphics), Stuart Laidlaw (photographs) and Dorella Romanou (line drawings), as well as to Maria Papaconstantinou for help in Athens, and to Sven van Lokeren, Anna Stellatou and

Valasia, who were in on it at the very end. Quotations are reproduced with kind permission of the following publishers: University of Pittsburgh Press for Odysseus Elytes' *To Axion Esti* translated by E. Keeley and G. Savidis; Faber & Faber and Farrar, Straus & Giroux for Derek Walcott's *Omeros*; Faber & Faber and Harcourt for T. S. Eliot's *Four Quartets*; and Faber & Faber and Random House for W. H. Auden's *On this island*.

It should be noted that this book went to press just before three relevant major works became available. The first of these is Peggy Sotirakopoulou's final publication of the Neolithic and Early Bronze Age material from Akrotiri on Thera (Sotirakopoulou 1999). The second is Joseph Maran's magisterial analysis of the late third millennium BC on the Greek mainland and in the Cyclades (Maran 1998). The third is Georgia Nakou's outstanding DPhil thesis 'The end of the Early Bronze Age in the Aegean: material culture and history' (Nakou 2000). Susan Sherratt's comprehensive and innovative publication of the Ashmolean Museum's Cycladic material (Sherratt in press) was made available in manuscript form through the author's generosity, but it did not prove possible to provide final page numbers for citations in this book.

ABBREVIATIONS AND DATING CONVENTIONS

The following abbeviations are used (see also fig. 1):

Aegean-wide periods:

LN	Late Neolithic
FN	Final Neolithic
EBA (EB I, II, III)	Early Bronze Age (Early Bronze I, II, III).
MBA	Middle Bronze Age
LBA (LB I, II, III)	Late Bronze Age (Late Bronze I, II, III)

Regionally specific:

EM I, IIA, IIB, III	Early Minoan I, IIA, IIB, III (Crete)
MM IA, IB, II, III	Middle Minoan IA, IB, II, III (Crete)
LM I, II, III	Late Minoan I, II, III (Crete)
EH I, II, III	Early Helladic I, II, III (southern Greek mainland)

Dates, centuries, millennia and other time-spans are given in calendar years BC or AD unless specified as uncalibrated radiocarbon years bp (before present).

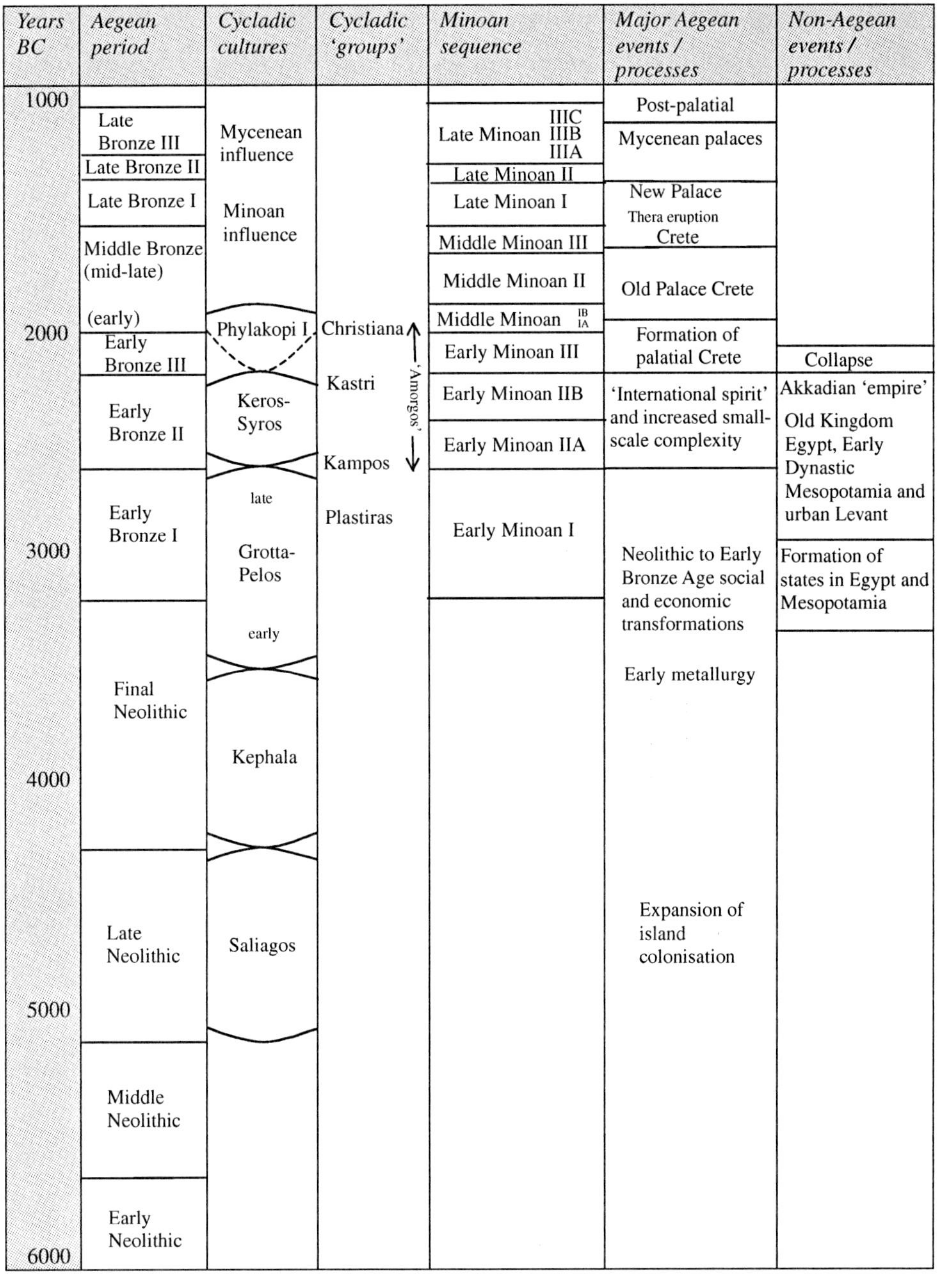

Years BC	Aegean period	Cycladic cultures	Cycladic 'groups'	Minoan sequence	Major Aegean events / processes	Non-Aegean events / processes
1000	Late Bronze III	Mycenean influence		Late Minoan IIIC / IIIB / IIIA	Post-palatial	
	Late Bronze II			Late Minoan II	Mycenean palaces	
	Late Bronze I	Minoan influence		Late Minoan I	New Palace / Thera eruption / Crete	
	Middle Bronze (mid-late)			Middle Minoan III		
	(early)			Middle Minoan II	Old Palace Crete	
2000	Early Bronze III	Phylakopi I	Christiana	Middle Minoan IB / IA	Formation of palatial Crete	Collapse
			Kastri	Early Minoan III		Akkadian 'empire'
	Early Bronze II	Keros-Syros	'Amorgos'	Early Minoan IIB	'International spirit' and increased small-scale complexity	Old Kingdom Egypt, Early Dynastic Mesopotamia and urban Levant
			Kampos	Early Minoan IIA		
	Early Bronze I	late Grotta-Pelos	Plastiras	Early Minoan I	Neolithic to Early Bronze Age social and economic transformations	Formation of states in Egypt and Mesopotamia
3000						
	Final Neolithic	early			Early metallurgy	
4000		Kephala				
	Late Neolithic	Saliagos			Expansion of island colonisation	
5000						
	Middle Neolithic					
6000	Early Neolithic					

Fig. 1 Chronology, terminology and major synchronisms for the Neolithic and Early Bronze Age Cyclades, with the later Bronze Age sequence simplified (see also further discussion in chapter 2). Adapted from Demoule and Perlès 1993, Manning 1995, Renfrew 1972 and Warren and Hankey 1989.

Prologue: islands of 'prehistory'

> The real life, and the history, of the early Cycladic civilization
> is still almost blank and therefore perplexing.
> *Greece in the Bronze Age,* EMILY VERMEULE

This book is about ways of understanding islands and islanders in the deep and more recent past. In particular, it explores the dynamics of those Mediterranean (specifically Aegean) island communities that, during the Neolithic and Early Bronze Age, inhabited an archipelago that we know as the Cyclades. Through this exploration, it offers a new interpretation of the archaeological record of the earliest three millennia of settlement in these islands. But this book also advocates a rethinking of the premises, agendas and methods of island archaeology as a world-wide analytical domain. It argues the need to move beyond current interpretative paradigms, largely characterised by adaptive models and simple, static concepts of insularity, to develop more complex and culturally driven perspectives that recognise the extent to which islanders have consciously fashioned, and refashioned, their own identities and worlds. Once this is fully acknowledged, it follows that assumptions common to much island archaeology have to be qualified, if not set aside. For instance, individual islands are no longer necessarily the ideal units for analysing island societies. Equally, island material culture assumes a more active, constitutive role in island life than has generally been realised. Inter-island and island–mainland relations, explored within the context of maritime culture, provide insight not only into movements of things and people, but also into insular definitions of centrality and marginality, as well as ideologies and ideas about value in a given matrix of island communities. Such a rethink seems crucial for the field's future. For although island archaeology has proved outstandingly successful in the last few decades, in terms of both fieldwork and theory-building, if it fails to embrace more sophisticated perspectives as its data improve, there can be little hope of it realising its potential as a vehicle for writing island history, and illuminating the enormous spectrum of island societies that have existed at different points in time and space across much of the pre-modern world.

Looking at the Cyclades, the need for a new interpretation is readily apparent. Early Cycladic archaeology as a coherent discipline has just celebrated its centenary. Yet despite the stream of information now emerging from these islands, despite the success in ordering new and older data into systems that satisfy a desire for taxonomic hygiene, and notwithstanding the appearance of several major studies, Vermeule's words (1964: 58, cited above) still ring true more than a generation after they were written. The early Cyclades remain essentially islands of 'prehistory' as far as our understanding of them goes. 'Prehistory' is, of course, the label applied by convention to the entire period in the Aegean prior to adoption of the alphabet, and certainly this book cannot constitute history as it might normally be imagined. There are no written accounts to draw upon, local or externally observed; we snatch glimpses of meaning in symbols only rarely and through the darkest of glasses; we sense people as actors and the creators and users of things, but their details elude our pursuit; we deal of necessity in time-slots centuries long; and gaps in our knowledge dictate that many facets of island life have to be passed over with barely a word. But if the sleight of terminology that places these islands in the purdah of prehistory can be overcome, and history's analytical remit extended to cover activities and change among people throughout the world, it indeed becomes possible to envisage a history for the Cyclades in remote antiquity, before broader Mediterranean rhythms engulfed them. One aim of this book is therefore to write some first passages of an early history for a group of islands that have hitherto been in effect without one.

What is lacking in most existing studies of the early Cyclades is not so much an adequate amount of evidence, however incomplete the data may be, but rather a fruitful conceptual framework for formulating the fundamental questions that need to be asked, and rendering intelligible the answers received. Many archaeologists have grown to doubt whether the early Cyclades really witnessed a 'civilisation' in the sense implied by Vermeule. But what remains missing is a sense of the structure of Cycladic societies and culture, both their 'interior architecture' and their relationship to the world beyond, that might enable us to give convincing meanings to the objects and observations that accumulate, to account for the complexities of past lives and present data, and to explain the patterns that we think we discern. Clearly, the choice of framework is vital. It must be axiomatic that until the *kind* of history that needs to be written is established, we can neither hope to decode much of these islands' past, nor appreciate how their particular past might be made of wider significance. So, to summarise the task, how might we set out to write an interpretation of early Cycladic archaeology that is more specific, more general, and more convincingly explanatory than its predecessors?

By now it should be apparent that the approach proposed in this book is that early Cycladic history is essentially *island history*, and that the most promising way to comprehend it is through the perspectives and techniques of island archaeology, albeit an island archaeology rather different in emphasis from much of that practised to date. Initially, this idea may seem absurdly obvious. Yet once its implications are realised, it forces us to reshape our basic approach to the Cyclades, as indeed to any island group.

It demands an examination of how the unusual, complex and ambiguous attributes of insularity have influenced the course of history in these islands. More specifically, it encourages a structure of enquiry centred around a series of key questions about people on islands that are common to island archaeology all over the world. Why did people go to islands? How did they choose to live after arrival? How were people's lives shaped by, and how did they reshape, in physical but also cognitive terms, the islands that they inhabited? What kinds of interaction took place between island communities, and also between islanders and other, non-insular communities? How did external contacts affect the cultures of islanders? How and why did island societies 'end' – if indeed they did? Issues of another kind arise, moreover, concerning the congruence, and arguably causal relationships, between patterning in human life on islands, and that attested by insular fauna and flora. Consider, for instance, the manifold possibilities raised by just one observation, made in the earlier twentieth century AD on the Cycladic island of Andros: 'Northern Andros alone has, or had till recently, the mainland rabbits, woolly dogs, and Albanian settlers; elsewhere, there are hares, smooth haired dogs, and Greeks of approximately pure strains' (Myres 1941: 140).

Thinking more particularly about some of the issues that face archaeologists in the Cyclades, an island archaeological perspective may prove a healthy remedy for the chronological obsession evident in much literature on these islands, by encouraging the investigation of Cycladic societies as communities distributed in space, and specifically in island spaces dispersed over the sea. History demands time as one of its dimensions of analysis, and there will be ample opportunity to look at changes through time, not least in the activities and relations of people in space – what Terrell and Welsch (1997: 549) term the perspective of 'temporal geography'. But we would do well to place an equal emphasis on what Foucault (1986: 22) describes as 'epoch[s] of simultaneity . . . juxtaposition . . . of near and far, of the side-by-side, of the dispersed . . . the world . . . of a network that connects points and intersects with its own skein'. Spatial analyses of island archaeological questions are therefore central to this book, with the emphasis being placed just as much on how island people fashioned island spaces as vice versa.

In pursuit of such insights, a series of simple spatial models will be constructed to explore and simulate activities such as colonisation and interaction, and to see how informatively they correlate with known archaeological distributions. Such strategies have long been common practice in Pacific archaeology, as attested by explorations of language genesis (Terrell 1981), voyaging (Irwin 1992; Irwin *et al.* 1990; Levison *et al.* 1973), and colonists' survival prospects (Black 1978; McArthur *et al.* 1976), but, with a handful of exceptions, their strategic potential in the Cyclades has remained untapped.

Given the Cyclades' intricate configuration, the complex frameworks of island space offer a promising context in which to explore the remarkable diversity of these islands' material culture. This diversity, which is seldom sufficiently acknowledged, was memorably captured by Vermeule in a sketch of two islands' burial assemblages: 'Syros . . . with its dolichocephalic skulls, fondness for frying pans and spiral ornaments, and indifference to covered toilet boxes, presents another aspect from Amorgos with its incised wares, huge idols, and interest in copper weapons' (Vermeule 1964: 47–8). Why are there such notable differences between the grave goods on islands only a few dozen kilometres apart? Why are early Cycladic assemblages, if sometimes broadly predictable, at other times bewilderingly variable, to a degree that plays havoc with our traditional definitions of an archaeological culture? To what extent was this diversity a reflection of the effect of physical separation on different communities of islanders? Or, conversely, to what extent was it the relatively conscious material expression of ideas and beliefs about the world that once emanated from those 'dolichocephalic' crania?

Such windows onto the Cyclades, opened more or less at random, are intended simply as an invitation to the fuller analysis that follows in this book. The first priority, however, is to establish the intellectual framework for island archaeology. This is the aim of chapter 1. Chapter 2 turns to the Cyclades, explaining why they are a promising archipelago in which to study island life, comparing them schematically to other island groups, placing their Neolithic and Early Bronze Age (EBA) in the wider history of the eastern Mediterranean and the Near East, summarising our current state of knowledge, introducing the chronology and culture sequence (fig. 1) and outlining the paradigms that have dominated study to date. Chapter 3 introduces early Cycladic environments, resources, landscapes, subsistence options, demographics, sea conditions and seagoing technology; it sets out some basic parameters, but also draws attention to the substantial degree of variability, and argues that although the islanders' activities were subject to certain constraints, the borders of the possible were in fact susceptible to a considerable amount of cultural negotiation.

The next eight chapters (chapters 4–11) each investigate a separate issue and highlight a range of periods, places and material in the Cyclades and also neighbouring areas. Chapter 4 asks what, if anything, can be inferred about pre-colonisation activity from the Pleistocene onwards, and uses configurational and archaeological data to ask where and why the first settlement horizons developed during the Neolithic, probably around the end of the sixth millennium BC. In chapter 5, the contrasting material cultures of several early settlement horizons are argued to relate to alternative ways of inhabiting these islands. In chapter 6 we move into the Aegean EBA (the late fourth and entire third millennia BC). Network models are developed to explore local interaction patterns, to ask how these relate to cultural perceptions of travel and isolation, and to shed light on observed features in material culture. Chapter 7 analyses several prominent settlements of the mid-third millennium BC, and identifies them as island communication centres that played a major role in maritime trade and the production and conspicuous consumption of prestige objects. In chapter 8 the dynamics of these centres are examined further, by an investigation of maritime ideology and strategies of social differentiation, display and the manipulation of value. Chapter 9 turns to long-range EBA interaction between the Cyclades and the Aegean rim, particularly evident during EB II, and the wider question of the Aegean's relations at this point to the distant world of archaic states and empires in the Near East. Chapter 10 concentrates on the obscure period that follows, examining the collapse and transformation of Cycladic societies at the end of the third millennium, during a period of sweeping changes across the Aegean and much of the Near East. This 'island ending' is pursued further in chapter 11, which explores how the Cyclades became realigned, early in the second millennium BC, in the orbit of the emergent palatial states of Minoan Crete, a point taken to mark the end of early Cycladic history. Chapter 12 draws together the argument, and indicates some ways forward for future research.

The structure of this book is designed to allow the reader to move up, down and across spatial and temporal pathways as freely as is compatible with coherence. There is a diachronic element in most chapters, and the overall sequence of chapters can be read to tell a long-term history, if one (it is hoped) that remains alert to the pitfalls that attend all archaeological narrative (Terrell 1990). Equal emphasis is laid, however, on another form of investigative mobility, namely lateral movement between places. As will be seen in chapter 1, the comparative suitability of linear versus tangled, net-like histories in island settings is a debated issue. Yet, to pre-empt slightly, these approaches are not mutually exclusive. In the Cyclades, some of the most fascinating material-rich snap-shots of social practices would assuredly be missed if we attempted to over-simplify the multitude of paths, webs and vortices that comprise early Cycladic history. But equally, it would be perverse, when looking at phenomena such as the movement of metals, the introduction of exotic drinking habits, or the events of the late third millennium BC, to ignore the fact that these islands' intricate local histories were fashioned in the shadow, at first faint, but increasingly solid, of the early states and empires of the Near East. This book sets out to achieve a balance that will allow the texture of cultural diversity at different times and in different places in the Cyclades to emerge, whilst simultaneously drawing attention to a larger trajectory within the *longue durée* of the Mediterranean.

1

Whither island archaeology?

> There are no more deserts, there are no more islands. Yet the
> need for them makes itself felt.
> *Minotaur, or The Halt at Oran,* ALBERT CAMUS

Camus' islands and deserts are metaphors for solitude, but his words are likely to strike chords with many people who study island societies. Islands still exist, of course, as do islanders who trace their descent from settlers in the remote or recent past. But with the modern world's expansion in the last few centuries across the deserts of the sea, island societies as once-distinctive ways of living have become increasingly rare. Some islands have profited as the stepping-stones in continent-based maritime networks of commerce and power, as did those Mediterranean islands in the sixteenth century AD aptly described by Braudel (1949: 136) as 'la flotte immobile de Venise'. For the vast majority of islands, however, modernity has brought chronic social, economic and ecological exploitation and disintegration, plus an off-loading of continental escapism and violence best captured by the name 'Bikini'. It is only a superficial paradox that as islands the world over have been transformed, often past recognition, their role in Western culture as settings for political utopias, nostalgic idylls and savage fantasies has been affirmed in literature and art. But the demise of countless island societies in recent times and the persuasive, if often contradictory, cultural metaphors that surround them, make it now hard to conceive what living on islands might once have been like. This chapter examines island archaeology as a means, and (as will be seen) often the only sustainable means, for shedding light on the islanders of the pre-modern world.

Island archaeology emerged as a defined field during the 1970s, its birth being often dated to a well-known article by Evans on 'Islands as laboratories for the study of culture process' (1973). Since then, it has generated an impressive range of ideas and analytical techniques, often inspired by island biogeography and island anthropology, that are theoretically applicable to islands anywhere. Books like Kirch's *The Evolution of the Polynesian Chiefdoms* (1984), Terrell's *Prehistory in the Pacific Islands* (1986), Irwin's *The Prehistoric Exploration and Colonisation of the Pacific* (1992), Keegan's *The People Who Discovered Columbus* (1992) and Spriggs' *The Island Melanesians* (1997), plus countless monographs and articles, are testimony to island archaeology's achievements – as well as to its relative dominance by Pacific scholarship of a high calibre. This spate of research has established that although islands were among the last parts of the globe to be settled, island life has nonetheless been an essential feature of our species' history for at least the last 40,000 years (Gamble 1993: 214–40). But as the field expands, and despite demonstration of an encouraging capacity for paradigm shifts within specific island theatres (Terrell *et al.* 1997), there is a serious danger that island archaeologists will cease to remind themselves of some crucial basic questions. What is island archaeology? Why is it done and why does it matter? And is it being done in the most appropriate, productive and innovative ways?

As the first theorists were quick to point out, one of the most striking features of islands is their diversity (e.g. Evans 1973: 517; Terrell 1977a: 62), and this demands a good measure of plurality in interpretative approaches too. But a more critical glance suggests that whilst much of the wild-growth of ideas has been fruitful, some may be a more mixed blessing. If island archaeology is to become as rigorous, challenging and creative as it should be, there is arguably a need to think harder about when and why specific approaches are properly applicable. It has to be recognised, too, that ultimately many of the basic 'hows' and 'whys' of the subject are inextricably linked to still under-resolved questions concerning the nature of insularity, and whether islands should be considered good analogies for the rest of the world, or distinct places without sustained parallels elsewhere. On a rather different note, island archaeology would also do well to ponder the implications of wider sea-changes in archaeology since the 1980s, notably in approaches to landscapes and material culture. Current island archaeology therefore stands at a crossroads. Given this fact, it is best to begin an exploration of the field by standing some distance back, and asking simply what we think we know about the past of islands, in the most general sense, and how we claim knowledge of it.

Islands and history

The abundance of island history

Modern nostalgia and dreams of a virgin paradise foster two common mistakes about pre-modern islands and islanders, delusions that can be termed 'edenic equilibrium' and 'pristine seclusion'. Sharp observers have long been aware that neither will bear close comparison with what is actually known of island life, but both reward a glance at this stage, not only to establish what island archaeology is not about, but also because they may easily creep back into our thinking via the back door of unguarded assumptions. Examination of their deficiencies, moreover, can help to establish some important initial points about history on islands, and its articulation with the histories of continents.

Taking edenic equilibrium first, a realisation of the extent of islands' undoing in recent times should not lead to the presumption that earlier islanders necessarily lived in a perfect balance with their environment. Island environments and ecologies undergo a constant flux even without human intervention (Whittaker 1998: 27–31), and indeed the concept of species turnover is central to the science of island biogeography (MacArthur and Wilson 1967). The arrival of people invariably quickened the tempo. Contemporary with the early human occupation levels on many islands is evidence for anthropogenic alteration of the ecology and environment of land, coast and sea, with a consequent rise in disequilibrium (Amorosi *et al.* 1997; Burney 1997; Flannery 1994; Kirch and Hunt 1997; Kirch and Ellison 1994; Rackham and Moody 1996; Steadman 1995; Whittaker 1998: 228–56). Grove (1995) argues that the more perceptive early European visitors to small islands such as Mauritius and St Helena, where the damage became most rapidly visible, were well aware of the degradation caused by their compatriots' island-altering activities, and it would surely be perversely chauvinistic to deny such an awareness to the anonymous people who long before had manipulated the biota on innumerable islands from Mangaia to the Balearics. It is likely, in other words, that islanders have always been conscious of their role as world-makers in terms of the transformation of their environments.

Equally against the existence of an edenic equilibrium is the clear evidence that island societies have enjoyed dynamic histories. Even before the beginnings of island archaeology, ample hints already existed. Classical Greek historians such as Herodotos described an Aegean sea that was alive with busy, volatile island societies. When Cook entered the Pacific, he quickly realised from the spread of Polynesian dialects over vast areas, and the residual knowledge of sailing directions for distant islands along routes no longer used, that people had once voyaged in different ways from those observed in the period of contact. As will shortly become apparent, testimonies from this period and its aftermath are problematic in several ways, but overall there is little doubt that even within this narrow time-slice, the Pacific was no Gauguinesque dream-world, but a hive of people engaged in history-making. The vying chiefdoms of Hawaii, the drama of crescendo and collapse on Easter Island, the rise of political and ceremonial centres at Pohnpei and Lelu in Micronesia, and the violent encounters between Melanesian communities and intrusive Polynesian groups are simply a handful of examples. As this time-slice in the Pacific was a quite random sample from the islanders' viewpoint, there is every reason to presume that this plenitude of history was entirely typical of the preceding millennia, however much the individual structures may have altered. In the last two to three decades of the twentieth century, overwhelming archaeological confirmation of the truth of this extrapolation has emerged, as will be seen later in this chapter.

The delusion of pristine seclusion can apply to contact between islands, but has a wider significance in relation to contact between islands and the world beyond them. The last great island encounters, in the Caribbean and Pacific, were head-on collisions between peoples separated by cosmological and technological chasms (Greenblatt 1991; Meleisea and Schoeffel 1997; Sahlins 1985, the last criticised in Obeyesekere 1992, with a rejoinder in Sahlins 1995). The casualty figures, e.g. most of the indigenous population of the Caribbean annihilated within a generation or so of Columbus' landfall (Moya Pons 1992), make it easy to excuse a conceptual tendency to polarise islands' options between extremes of seclusion and integration, purity or death. But in fact such polarisation can be seriously misleading. Even in the Pacific and Caribbean theatres, the picture is more nuanced and complex than it initially appears to be. There is evidence for earlier, non-disastrous and (at least for some islanders) plausibly advantageous links with people and places on the surrounding continental rims, contacts that extended well beyond the obvious fact that the first islanders came from somewhere else. Contacts between the Caribbean islands and the American mainland are likely (Alegría 1983: 154–5; Watters 1997). In the Pacific, links are attested between Island South-East Asia and south-west Oceania (Ambrose 1988; Bellwood and Koon 1989), between the Aleutians, Alaska and possibly north-east Asia (Corbett *et al.* 1997), as well as between eastern Polynesia and South America, the latter indicated by the dispersal of the sweet potato (Hather and Kirch 1991) and supported by computer simulations that demonstrate the probability of Polynesian landfalls on the coast of the Americas (Irwin 1992: 99–100; *contra* Heyerdahl 1952). At this juncture, it is worth emphasising that Sahlins' dissection of the meeting between the Hawaiians and Cook (Sahlins 1985), which contrasts world-views structured by utterly different, mutually incomprehensible principles, is essentially a classic essay in extreme cross-cultural encounter *per se* (cf. Fagan 1998), and probably does not describe a scenario at all typical of many islander–mainlander meetings in the past. Interestingly, in this respect, Spriggs (1997: 187–222) suggests that in eastern Melanesia, a less sequestered part of the Pacific at the period of European contact, the indigenous peoples' reactions to the first of the Europeans were preconditioned by prior clashes with the crews of Polynesian canoes.

Moreover, it is important to remember that in other island theatres, such as the Indian Ocean, north Atlantic and Mediterranean, where integration between islanders and mainlanders began in general much earlier, more tentatively and with less extreme technological distinctions distinguishing the participants, there was probably never any one horizon of encounter that represented as vertiginous a jump as those experienced in the Pacific or Caribbean during the first phases of contact with Western navigators. In the Mediterranean, in particular, sustained, often multi-directional extra-insular contacts seem, with very few exceptions, to have been a feature of island life from the start, and although we can detect signs of severe shocks to island systems during phases of rapid increase in their integration with the wider world (as will be seen in chapters 10 and 11), the options in terms of contact or seclusion can seldom have been starkly phrased.

What kinds of history?

In general, therefore, island and mainland histories are interlinked, if at some times intimately and at others quite distantly. How we go about exploring this dynamic is crucial, as one group of Pacific archaeologists have indeed recently recognised: 'giving up the notion that islands are isolated worlds may achieve little if we are unsuccessful at finding out how people, places and events "on the outside" have influenced – sometimes decisively, sometimes not – what people "on the inside" thought, did, and accomplished' (Terrell *et al.* 1997: 175). We can, perhaps, conceptualise the external contacts of islands in terms of a sliding scale, with the two terminals representing (a) complete independence and (b) complete integration with the outside world (the latter terminal being that around which most islands currently cluster). Islands at any given point on the scale might move in either direction, of their people's volition or under compulsion, although the aggregate trend through time has certainly been towards integration. Movement along this scale need not be smooth or gradual, and there is nothing to prevent an island from remaining in the same place on the scale for a long time, and subsequently moving rapidly in either direction. Nor is there any reason why the constituent communities on an island, or even individual islanders, need all occupy the same point on the scale at any given time (a matter to which we shall return later in this chapter). It is difficult to say whether this freedom of manoeuvre is now largely a thing of the past, in other words whether islands and islanders are ever likely to break free to a significant degree from their present status as closely integrated adjuncts and satellites of continental systems.

The relationship between islands and the outside world is equally relevant to the intriguing question as to whether island histories are qualitatively different from those of mainlands, not in the internalised sense that all cultures, insular and non-insular, tend to see history through their peculiar prisms, but rather in terms of the manner in which we do best to conceptualise and analyse them. In particular, it may indicate a way forward in a current debate between those who advocate the exploration of island history mainly in linear, narrative, often phylogenetic, terms (Bellwood 1987; Kirch 1984; Kirch and Green 1987), and those who prefer 'reticulate', i.e. net-like, approaches that emphasise history as something that works through a mesh of local, dense, often recursive links, rather than as an onward march (Dewar 1995; Terrell 1988; Terrell *et al.* 1997). Though reticulate forms of explanation are far from unique to islands (Bellwood 1996), it is striking that several of their strongest advocates are island scholars. Terrell (1988), for instance, argues that the Pacific's past matches Darwin's metaphor of a 'tangled bank' better than the more familiar evolutionary model of a branching tree. In contrast to the pursuit of origins down the dimension of time, he recommends that we move between paths and across time, generating a multiplicity of histories in the place of a grand narrative and aiming 'to discover what creates, maintains or changes similarities and differences among people' (Terrell 1988: 645). Dewar (1995) develops similar ideas in the context of Madagascar. Such reticulate models are indeed attractive and apposite in many island contexts, given that islands are scattered, diverse places where overarching order is relatively rare, where hierarchies are as liable to be flat as vertical, where histories are prone to diverge, converge and blur with bewildering frequency, and where any single narrative, or equally an evolutionary model of division and differentiation, is bound to gloss over and flatten the detailed dynamics and variability of island culture.

Yet despite their attractions, there is little to be gained, and something to be lost, by insisting upon exclusively reticulate models in the writing of island history. This is not simply because certain islands at certain times have witnessed discrete episodes of rapid rise in social complexity and hierarchy that invite sequential analysis, for example Minoan 'state formation' (Cherry 1984a) or the establishment of chiefdoms in Polynesia (Kirch 1984), in the latter case regardless as to whether phylogenetic processes were in fact involved. The need to supplement reticulate models is also felt as soon as it is remembered that most island societies were in contact with mainland regions whose history can be informatively (if far from exclusively) analysed in terms of large-scale, long-term trajectories, sometimes of a world-systemic nature, with which island history has to be articulated. Island archaeology will require reticulate and linear approaches if it is both to remain sensitive to the peculiar dynamics of island lives, and at the same time provide convincing accounts of how these dynamics were meshed with other patterns, often quite different in nature and scale, beyond the insular sphere.

This vision of islands as places rich in history raises one final point. Among the bad jokes that mainlands have played on islands, one of the worst yet most recent is the reference to much of their past as 'prehistory'. It will be clear by now that their expanse of 'prehistory' lies 'before history' only if we privilege the written word (Wolf 1982). Given that the advent of literate navigators as harbingers of world history has marked a change, and in many circumstances a catastrophic one, for the people at the receiving end, the arrival of what we call history must frequently have spelt an end to indigenous history for the islanders involved. Beckett's portrait of colonialism in the Torres Strait islands (1988), or the 'humanitarian' prohibition on the Siassi traders' risky traditional long-range voyages (Keegan and Diamond 1987: 66–7) are but two salient examples of a common theme. To relegate contemporary islanders to a twilit 'posthistory' would be a mistake, given the qualified optimism that has recently started to be expressed about the future for at least the Pacific islanders (Hau'ofa 1993; Nero 1997; Spriggs 1997: 286–91; Terrell 1998). It would, moreover, fly in the face of the fact that many islands have experienced long and eventful cycles of history since their incorporation in the wider world, notably those, such as the Mediterranean and north Atlantic islands, that were drawn in earliest, while for those islands that remained empty until the age of global navigation (e.g. the Atlantic outposts and some Indian Ocean islands), the advent of history itself correlates with the spring tide of world history. But for people studying the lives of islanders in the deep past, or even on the threshold of the present in regions where world history arrived late, the term 'prehistory' is best avoided, save as a conscious irony. Plenty of island history has certainly existed. The question now is how to access it.

Island archaeology as island history

How can pre-modern island history be explored? The answer put forward here is that for most islands during most of their past, island archaeology is in effect the only viable means of doing so. To sustain this claim, however, it is necessary to examine several other possibilities, primarily oral histories, ancient written sources and, more recently, navigators' or ethnographers' reports.

Pre-modern oral and written sources

It is salutary to acknowledge how rarely it is possible to gain access to an island history of any time-depth through the islanders' own words. Oral history is notoriously liable to reworking, and indigenous islanders' historical accounts have proved very hard to integrate with Western analytical traditions (Linnekin 1997: 14–20). Even Garanger's excavation of the purported graves of Roy Mata, his retinue and other long-dead culture heroes of Vanuatu (Garanger 1972) does not so much prove the truth of local oral history as demonstrate that it grows out of, and weaves together, past events in ways that can curate some startlingly accurate details over long periods of time; how much is accurate, and how much tactically reworked by generations of telling, is still uncertain. Equally, few island societies used writing until relatively late in their history. Very few cases of indigenous island scripts are known from around the world, and most, if not all, developed during periods of increasing integration with continental societies – for instance 'Hieroglyphic' and Linear A on Crete in the second millennium BC (Olivier 1986), the latter spreading to adjacent islands, contemporary Cypro-Minoan on Cyprus (Merrillees 1995), and the Irish Ogham script (Edwards 1990: 103–4); Easter Island's *rongorongo* is a possible exception (Fischer 1997). Exogenous writing systems spread into the west Mediterranean islands only with Greek and Phoenician expansion in the first millennium BC, and into the islands off Eurasia's Atlantic fringe during the Roman empire. Further zones of island literacy developed in Ceylon and Island South-East Asia in the first five centuries before and after Christ. Thus written evidence is strikingly circumscribed, temporally and spatially, in contrast to the literary silence lying over the deeper past of islands, and over the Caribbean and most of the Pacific until the arrival of the Western navigators.

The same limitations attend ancient written testimony from external, non-island sources. The earliest examples come from the Mediterranean and Near East. There are several references to islands in Egyptian and Near Eastern texts of the second millennium BC (Cline 1994: 109–28; Knapp 1996), but these are restricted to a few very terse texts referring to Cyprus, the Aegean and Bahrain, mostly dealing with trade, diplomacy or warfare, plus some propagandistic and ritual texts designed for home consumption. In the first millennium BC the sources improve, producing narrative history and, by the end of the millennium, *periplous* texts describing in detail the routes, sea-marks and ports of the Mediterranean and Indian Ocean (e.g. Casson 1989). East Asian sources start to hint at islands stretching out into the Indo-Pacific at about the same time. Such continental writings can provide splendid details or vignettes of island life within the regions that they cover, but again the limits are apparent: geographically limited scope, externally driven agendas, ethnocentric perspectives and a bias towards islands that were on, or over, the brink of wholesale incorporation into extra-insular structures. Even in the Aegean, the area most richly documented by the Greek and Roman authors, textual sources work best when used in close conjunction with archaeology (Snodgrass 1987: 36–66).

Contact period testimonies and ethnographies

A third potential category of information comprises the testimonies of recent eye-witnesses to island societies, such as the navigators of the contact periods, and the ethnographers and others who followed. In the Mediterranean, ethnographies relate, of course, to a late, generally highly integrated phase of island life, and the rich tradition of ethnography in Island South-East Asia (e.g. Sopher 1965; van Leur 1955) should not disguise the fact that here too the region had long been integrated into the Indian and Chinese worlds by trade (Chaudhuri 1985, 1990) and undergone subsequent disruption and reorganisation by the Portuguese and Dutch. This is not to deny the importance of Mediterranean and Indian Ocean sources, but if the aim is to explore societies further from the somewhat familiar terminal of integration, we need to turn elsewhere. In the Caribbean, the period of early contact is poor in sources, apart from Columbus' journal (1492), scraps of navigators' reports, and passages of Las Casas' history (1951). In part this is because the indigenous population was extinguished so quickly, but it is also due to the subsequent encounter with the Aztec and Inca, who provided the Spanish with a far more compelling imperial 'other' to document and destroy. Similar problems attend any study of the *guanche* people of the Canaries, encountered slightly earlier during exploration of the so-called 'Mediterranean Atlantic' (Chaunu 1979: 106). European reactions to Caribbean and Canary islanders veered between compassion for innocents and contempt for savages, but little thought was apparently given to the possibility that such people had enjoyed an eventful past. Moreover, Greenblatt's analysis of the discourse of such encounters makes a compelling case that they meant utterly different things to the different parties involved, and indeed that there was no true dialogue at all, but merely cultures talking past each other (Greenblatt 1991). His conclusion serves as a warning as we turn to the Pacific, the last and largest world of islands to be 'discovered' by the West, and one that has generated a voluminous corpus of navigators' reports, ethnographies and anthropological literature, which at least ostensibly provides glimpses into something tantalisingly close to the pre-contact past.

Melanesia and Micronesia were known to people outside Oceania earlier than is widely recognised (Meleisea and Schoeffel 1997). Their western fringes had probably experienced sporadic visits by South-East Asian traders from an early date. Spriggs (1997: 223–43) offers a thought-provoking analysis of the Spanish reports of brief encounters with Melanesians in the sixteenth and early seventeenth centuries AD, and speculates on the invisible horizon of epidemic that may have swept the islands in their wake. Further north, the Manila galleons' routes brought Micronesians on Guam into disastrous contact by the later seventeenth century. A trickle of reportage continues through the seventeenth-century Dutch explorers, and swells in the eighteenth century into a spate covering much of the Pacific, with the voyages of Bougainville, Carteret, Cook and other navigators soon to be followed by conquest and a consequent mass of colonial-period records.

But such records must be handled cautiously. Greenblatt's warning is relevant here too, and in addition it is now recognised that the 'golden age' of ethnography and anthropology in the Pacific, of Malinowski in the Trobriands (Malinowski 1922), Mead on Samoa (Mead 1928) and Firth on Tikopia (Firth 1936), was not the epoch of pristine societies that such scholars imagined it to be (and which the points made above suggest never existed), but one transformed by explorers, traders, colonial officials and missionaries (Linnekin 1997). The fundamental problem, as Deetz (1991: 6) and Wolf (1982: 4–5) stress, is that the very fact of contact altered indigenous societies. Spriggs' suggestion that even the briefest of Spanish contacts may have triggered a wave of disease that devastated parts of Melanesia at a time when no one from Europe was present to bear witness has already been noted. Other studies of contact's aftermath emphasise the rapidity of island reorientation. Kirch and Sahlins (1992) argue persuasively that the emergence of a unified native kingdom in Hawaii was encouraged by the activities of European and American adventurers, and that it marked a deviation from pre-contact processes rather than their culmination. At the opposite end of the Pacific, and the scale of action, an analysis of obsidian artefacts from the Admiralty Islands suggests to Torrence (1993) that lithic production underwent a shift in the first phase of sustained contact to production for an incipient collectors' market. In both these examples the proximate agents of change were the same islanders who had met the first Europeans (or at least their close descendants), yet island life had already been reworked by the world-system in which these islands had become involuntarily entangled.

This is not, of course, to argue dogmatically against the usage of navigators' reports, ethnographies and anthropological studies in the reconstruction and analysis of island societies. Some of the earliest contact reports are as close as one can hope to get to snap-shots of a world not yet transformed, even if taken through lenses of uneven clarity and range. They can make useful reference points, as is demonstrated by Irwin's diachronic work on Mailu, a Papuan island trading centre, where they serve as a fair, if slender, anchor to the immediate pre-colonial past (1974, 1985). Such information can also be useful in illustrating the diversity of island cultures that have existed, so long as explicit recognition is given to the contact- or colonial-period context, and also the fact that some classic anthropological interpretations have been subjected to major revision, for example Malinowski's analysis of the *kula* (Leach and Leach 1983). Moreover, it should not be forgotten that an island's integration is a fascinating field in its own right, exemplified by Kirch and Sahlins' work in Hawaii (1992), or Deagan's in the Hispanic Caribbean (1995). What such warnings do insist upon is that recent accounts cannot be seen as an investigative avenue of any depth into the island past, both because of the post-contact contamination factor, and for one last profound, if very simple, reason.

This reason is the fact that, as Pacific island archaeologists in particular have come to realise, using recent accounts as the basis for talking about the past has the effect of freezing islanders in an unchanging state that denies their past the potential to be substantially different from the ethnographic present (e.g. Kirch 1990: 128–30; this limitation is far from being restricted to island contexts). This is a fatal criticism of the desirability of attempts at island palaeoethnography, a strategy defined by Keegan (1992: 224) as making a 'portrait of a past society built up from traditional ethnographic categories'. Such portraits achieve little beyond a replication of those in the handbooks. They can never extricate their subjects from the ranks of 'the people without history' (Wolf 1982), nor contribute to archaeology's endeavour to provide some intimation, however imperfect and fugitive, of how different much of the past must have been from anything that we, in the present, are ever likely to witness or experience.

The argument returns, fortified, to the initial proposal concerning the centrality of island archaeology in the writing of island history. It should come as no surprise that the first major steps in this direction have been made in the Pacific, where the wealth of contact-period and colonial reports creates a challenging bench-mark in the present, and the virtual absence of earlier texts, together with the problematic nature of oral tradition, dictates that island history from the mid-eighteenth century AD back into the Pleistocene must be island archaeology, or essentially nothing at all. Since the 1970s, Pacific archaeologists have started to plumb this time-depth and have come up with remarkable results. Contact-period structures have been revealed as merely recent configurations among a vast spectrum of alignments that have come and gone over the millennia (for examples: Allen 1977; Allen and Gosden 1991; Irwin 1977, 1983, 1985; Kirch 1986, 1990; Kirch and Hunt 1988; Lilley 1988; Spriggs 1997; Terrell 1986; Wickler 1990). Although this research draws on interdisciplinary data, it shares a firm archaeological perspective as its focus. Notwithstanding those parts of the world where texts come into play earlier, the Pacific revolution confirms island archaeology's potential as the only avenue into most of the past on the majority of islands and, not insignificantly, as the means for writing some very unusual kinds of history indeed.

Insularity: what is an island?

If island archaeology is to generate island histories worthy of their subjects, it would do well to take a more searching look at insularity as a phenomenon. What is an island? Even this apparently innocent question is less simple than it seems. Most people would probably identify a watery surround as the defining feature of a 'true island', with subdivisions into oceanic, continental shelf and non-marine islands often advocated (Whittaker 1998: 7). But other spaces surrounded by something else also qualify for quasi-insular status. The most obvious are 'habitat islands', what Braudel termed 'islands that the sea does not surround' (1972: 160–1). Large-scale examples include oases, lakes, montane valleys, *Inselberge*, inhabitable fragments of the Arctic (Fitzhugh 1997) and those 'islands of the interior' that Veth (1993) identifies in Australia's arid zone. On a small scale, almost any circumscribed area is effectively a candidate. Williamson (1981) cites experiments in simulating insular conditions in environments as varied as mangrove trees and buckets of water. On another level, it is a commonplace that islands are an abiding source of metaphor. What is less often noted is the range of conditions that the metaphor can be deployed to signify. To take three scattered examples, when the Jacobean poet John Donne wrote that 'no man is an Island' (Meditation XVII), he meant something different from Abu-Lughod (1989: 13) when she depicts medieval Eurasia as an 'archipelago of towns' and both in turn imply something different again from Tilley (1994: 166–9, 200) describing a Neolithic enclosure on Hambledon Hill in England as an 'island of death'. Apparently, therefore, islands do not mean the same thing to all of us, even when they are just metaphors, and not really islands at all.

Yet even among true, water-girt islands, insularity can be understood in many different ways. This is in part a function of the enormous diversity of islands: large and small, high and low, solitary and clustered, offshore and in deepest ocean, to mention but a few of the main dimensions of variability. We can start by distinguishing between *analytical islands*, regions where it is unlikely that pre-modern inhabitants considered themselves islanders, but where insularity is important when analysing flows of people, animals, plants, diseases, or indeed cultural innovations, and *perceived islands* whose insularity was readily experienced by their occupants. An excellent example of the first category is the fragmenting landmass of Gondwana, later Pleistocene Sahul, and now Australia, New Guinea and their satellites, whose insular status was fundamental to the long-term evolution of fauna, flora and people (Flannery 1994); to this category could be added Greenland and the American continent at Holocene sea-levels. Perceived islands are too numerous to list. But even this distinction must admit a grey area. Within this lie what Held (1989a: 10) has named *matchbox continents*, sub-continental islands that are large and self-contained enough to act, under some circumstances, as land-masses in their own right. Potential candidates include Madagascar, Japan, Ceylon, Britain and the larger South-East Asian,

Melanesian, Caribbean and Mediterranean islands. An indication that such ambiguities are not unique to our own time can be found in Herodotos' statement, in the fifth century BC, that Sardinia is the 'biggest island in the world' (Book I: 170; Book VI: 1), an assertion of interest because it is wrong even in terms of the size of those water-girt land-masses known in his day – Sicily is considerably larger, and presumably its proximity to Italy compromised its insular status in Herodotos' eyes.

A closer look at perceived islands suggests that even this category is open to cultural negotiation and therefore variation. For example, certain islands that were too large to be taken in at a glance before aerial travel were long ago recognised as islands as a result of voyages of circumnavigation. Thus, the native Cubans described their homeland to Columbus (1492: 59) as a place that required more than twenty days to paddle round. At a subtler level, islanders' views of their insularity and its significance can be domains of active social contention and manipulation. Eriksen (1993) explores a telling example from contemporary Mauritius, whose people either affirm or deny that they are islanders, depending on what they want to say about their identity. A similar rhetoric underpins the current debate over Britain's place in the European Union. Although pre-modern examples of this contentiousness will naturally be hard to prove, far-travelled Cubans, ambivalent Mauritians and confused Britons demonstrate that even the most apparently straightforward categories of insularity are in fact fuzzy, and ones that both islands and islanders cross between, as views and knowledge change.

As the example of circumnavigation has already hinted, seafaring culture (or its absence) plays a key role in defining perceptions of insularity. This issue requires more attention, for what makes true islands interesting is not so much that they are surrounded by another element, but rather that element's nature and what people are able to do with it. Evans (1973: 517–18) observed that water is a different sort of surround from those around the quasi-islands, because for true islands, the sea's role can vary from that of insulator to hyper-conductor. Attitudes towards the sea are culturally variable. They may define the threshold of the unknown at the surf-line, or create almost frictionless highways over the ocean. As Gosden and Pavlides (1994: 170) rightly put it, 'just as the land can be made and remade by human influence, so can the sea'. In fairness, Pétrequin (1993: 45) hints that such a reworking of barriers is not exclusive to true islands: mountains can act as highways as well as dividers, because their emptiness serves to free travellers from the social negotiations that entangle movement in more populated lowlands. But the retort must be that, for true islands, the sea and its mediation by seafaring culture amplify the ambiguities and the flexibility of expression to a unique degree (see Dewar 1997 for an affirmation that the sea-girt status of Madagascar, one of the world's largest islands, was decisive for the development of its long-term history).

This variation in attitudes to the sea, so crucial to the meaning and impact of insularity in a given context, repays consideration at a range of scales. Between large regions there is palpable variation, witness for instance that seen at a global level in the distance of colonising ventures from continental margins (Keegan and Diamond 1987: 52–7), or contrast the contact-period Tasmanian islanders' reluctance to venture far from the shore (Jones 1977), with many Polynesian groups for whom the sea was no barrier at all (Finney 1994; Terrell 1986: 72). But a similar degree of variation can also be seen within regions and communities. Examples of a specialisation in sea-going that certain islands have fostered (sometimes amounting to maritime monopolies at their neighbours' expense) are recorded in Melanesian ethnography, the Siassi traders being a classic case (Harding 1967), and are common in medieval to early modern Mediterranean history – the Balearics, Kastellorizo and Aegean islands like Idra and the Oinousses all enjoying such status at various junctures. Within communities, variation in knowledge of the sea is illustrated by the status often accruing to experienced navigators (Helms 1988: 86–7; Lewis 1972). Finally, to compound this complexity, it should be recalled that although maritime activity in a given region is liable to be partly conditioned by certain long-term constants, such as geographical configuration and sea conditions, it is also a profoundly cultural practice, and therefore likely to be subject to contingent variation through time.

So what, then, is an island? 'An island', Perec parries (1987: 280), 'is an area surrounded by shores.' This elusive answer is quoted only slightly in jest. For given the multiple ways in which insularity can be defined and experienced, it is surely wisest to give up pursuing the will o' the wisp of an all-embracing formula, and make a virtue of the multiple layers and ambiguities within insularity that have been touched upon above. This emphatically should not imply the abandonment of rigorous analyses for a morass of relativism. Islands are far too interesting, important, and rich in pertinent data for that to be desirable or indeed possible. But it does suggest that an awareness of the degree to which insularity is culturally constructed, open to multiple meanings in a given context, historically contingent, and therefore liable to change, is essential if we are to develop an archaeology of islands that is as sophisticated as its subject demands.

Revisiting some insular stereotypes

The conclusion that insularity is a changeable attribute and one that can operate, at least on certain levels, as a social strategy or way of thinking, allows us to advance beyond some of the cruder stereotypes that have restricted the study of islands, and replace them with more complicated pictures in which the role of human agency is more prominent. Take, for a first example, the question as to whether islands are predominantly bounded and closed systems, as many have advocated (Evans 1973; Fosberg 1963: 5; Goldman 1957; Goodenough 1957; Sahlins 1957; Vayda and Rappaport 1963), open ones receptive to outside ideas, as is also asserted (Kirch 1986, 1988; Kirch and Yen 1982), or torn between the poles of involution and cosmopolitanism, and archaism and innovation, as Braudel has proposed (1972: 149–50). As the above discussion of island history has already implied, the answer is in fact 'all and none of these', or (better still) 'it depends when, how, and for whom'. It can now be appreciated that what decided where an island lay on the continuum between closure and openness at any one time was to a large degree the decisions or customs of its islanders and those of people in the outside world.

Braudel's superficially attractive vision, in particular, exaggerates the extent to which islands have been tugged between the terminals of the scale, and underestimates the extent to which they have fluctuated subtly around the middle of the range. Another over-simplification is surely his image of large islands as involuted mini-continents with 'stagnant centres' (Braudel 1972: 150–1), a characteristic earlier noted by Myres (1941: 139) in the case of Archaic-to-Classical Crete. For at other times, the same island can behave quite differently, as is shown in the Cretan context by the extent of the island's Minoan, Phoenician, Roman and Venetian trade networks. We should, parenthetically, also beware of 'stagnation' as a concept, as it may disguise plenty of reticulate history. To take another example, Aboriginal Australia's slight take-up of external innovations (e.g. dingos, Polynesian-style fish-hooks in the east, and outrigger canoes on the coast opposite New Guinea) was not a product of the island continent's physical closure as such – indeed these introductions, plus the visits by Island South-East Asian sea-slug collectors (Flood 1995: 258), demonstrate that its coasts were permeable – but rather of the cultural closure of Australian societies to most exotic things and ideas. The issue was not one of availability but of decisions to adopt or reject innovations (Lemonnier 1993; van der Leeuw and Torrence 1989). It would be naive to say that Aboriginal Australia was stagnant; its history was simply configured in a manner unfamiliar to Western eyes.

A sharper focus also begins to emerge on the factors lying behind the 'esoteric efflorescence' of extravagant monument-building that Sahlins (1955) first identified on certain isolated islands, of which the two most oft-cited examples in the archaeological literature are Easter Island and Malta in the Temple (principally the Ggantija and Tarxien) periods (Evans 1977; Renfrew 1973a: 147–66). In fact, these cases reflect very different forms of isolation. Easter Island, although frequently cited as a good example of an isolate, is a unique case, the exception that proves the rule of a predominantly cultural definition of closure. For there is simply no parallel for an island with long-term habitation, yet without inhabited neighbours and (after total tree-felling) entirely devoid of the means to build boats with which to travel elsewhere. Easter is *sui generis*, an analogy for nothing except the Earth's ecosystem, humanity's only other truly bounded world that cannot be left for any greater distance than the equivalent of an offshore paddle, at which point the analogy starts to become as horrifying as it is enlightening (Bahn and Flenley 1992). Malta is different. Although in Mediterranean terms Malta is small and relatively distant from other land, recent work has demonstrated that throughout most phases of the island's early settlement, *except* the Temple periods, the island maintained contacts with neighbouring areas (Stoddart *et al.* 1993: 7). Rather than inevitable closure leading by degrees to efflorescence, what seems more plausible is closure agreed upon or imposed, as presumably one element in a set of social strategies that *enabled* colossal monument building. Whatever happened on Malta happened not because the island was intrinsically isolated, but because it was far enough from other land, in Neolithic terms, to make itself isolated if its islanders (or at least some decisive people on the island) wished it to be so. Suggestions that isolation was created by internal social change, rather than creating it, are now being proposed for late pre-contact Polynesia (Terrell *et al.* 1997: 165) and the matchbox continent of Madagascar as its interior become thickly settled after the destruction of the Indian Ocean trade by the Portuguese (Dewar 1997), and may also be relevant to inward-looking societies on Bali.

Thinking of insularity as a cultural construct also sheds intriguing light on some of the processes that commonly occur during the formation of an island society and, at the other end of island history, under conditions of rapid incorporation by continental powers. Both subjects are too extensive to be more than touched upon here, but a few salient points can be made. One concerns the role of 'founder effects', a term coined by Mayr (1954) as an evolutionary concept, but borrowed by anthropologists and others (e.g. Vayda and Rappaport 1963: 134–5) to explain why island societies commonly lose elements of the parent culture from which they originate, and why some features that are retained deviate in unusual ways. In many cases, this undoubtedly can be explained as a result of the constituents of the sub-sample of a parent population that the colonists comprised, from genuinely irreparable loss of people, skills and knowledge in transit or after landfall, or from cumulative forgetting in conditions of slight external contact. But it is worth considering that, in some instances, loss of cultural traits, deviation, and the curation of archaisms were strategies through which island identities were created and sustained by people who remained aware of how things were done elsewhere. These alternatives will always be hard, and often impossible, to discriminate archaeologically, but the latter explanations assuredly deserve more attention than they have received. An intriguing example in this respect comes from the early period of agricultural settlement on Cyprus, known as the aceramic Neolithic. Several salient characteristics of its well-explored seventh millennium Khirokitia phase, such as archaising round-house architecture, absence of cattle and pottery, and marked paucity of imports (despite inter-visibility with the Anatolian mainland) have been taken to demonstrate the isolated state of the first farmers and their descendants (Cherry 1985: 26–7). Recently, however, evidence has emerged of an antecedent late ninth- to eighth-millennium phase, contemporary with the late pre-pottery Neolithic of the Levant, in which imported obsidian is much more common and cattle were probably also present (Briois *et al.* 1997; Guilaine *et al.* 1995; Simmons 1998). These new data imply that the idiosyncrasies of the Khirokitia phase resulted from decisions made well after the inception of farming, and that the distinctive island identity that these idiosyncrasies reveal was forged at least in part via a rejection not only of mainland contacts (as in the case of Temple period Malta) but also of mainland traits, including some already introduced to Cyprus (e.g. cattle) and others developing in mainland areas with which the islanders had trade contacts (e.g. pottery production).

Turning to islands' ultimate incorporation by continental systems, one common factor is that this has tended to occur when islanders lost control over the definition of their own insularity. Fosberg (1963: 5) portrays islands as enjoying 'protection from outside competition and consequent preservation of archaic, bizarre, or possibly ill-adapted forms' leading to 'extreme vulnerability, or tendency towards great instability when isolation is broken down; and tendency to rapid increase in entropy when change has set in'. For island ecologies this may be correct, but for island societies this picture is far too simple. What mattered for an island society was not that it managed to isolate itself (often difficult and, in many instances, apparently not desirable), but that it could determine on whose terms cross-cultural interaction took place. Examples of flourishing interaction over extended periods between islands and continental areas were commonly possible because superior seafaring allowed the island societies concerned to interact on their own terms, and often at points of communication located in continental territory. Once continental powers started to intensify their own long-range seafaring activities, as started to happen fitfully from the second millennium BC in the Mediterranean, throughout the first millennium AD in the Indian Ocean, and (in the form of European navigation) during the middle to late second millennium AD in the Atlantic and Pacific, island societies became increasingly unable to define and maintain their own insularity, save in resistive terms, and thereby lost the ability to control much of their own history.

The analysis of islandscapes

A more flexible approach to insularity, and one that incorporates the sea and maritime culture as components of its definition, also prompts reconsideration of the best way to approach island landscapes and seascapes, or in effect *islandscapes*. The evidence that islanders have regularly changed the ecological face of islands was noted earlier. But an examination of the many dimensions of insularity implies that islandscapes are liable to have been reworked by islanders in other ways too. The physical properties of islands, such as size, location, configuration and topography provide general constraints and openings, a point to which we will return below when assessing the relevance of island biogeography to island archaeology. But this does not deny the fact that conditions on most islands were sufficiently generous to allow people to define their surroundings in multiple ways. There are likely, in other words, to be plenty of opportunities for island culture to act back on the physical framework, with different islanders ordering it into a range of patterns at different times. As Gosden and Pavlides (1994: 169) have put it, 'individual island landscapes respond to the connections in which they are enmeshed and the demands that these networks create'. In colonial contexts unsustainable patterns were sometimes forced on islands by newcomers with alien political, ideological or economic agendas, as is nicely illustrated by the Norse settlement of the north Atlantic islands (Amorosi *et al.* 1997) or the counterfeit Europes imposed on temperate islands and continents across much of the world over the last few centuries (Crosby 1986).

A revision of the assumptions that island archaeologists bring to the exploration of islandscapes is more than timely, given the recent loss of innocence in landscape studies in and beyond archaeology, itself one element of post-modern geography (Soja 1989). Landscape seen as a usefully ambiguous category (Gosden and Head 1994), as a constructor of, and yet also constructed by, individual and collective memory (Bradley 1993; Küchler 1993; Schama 1995), as imbued with many contested meanings (Bender 1993; Cosgrove 1984), and as experienced by passage through it (Tilley 1994): all of this range of possibilities have manifest applications in the diverse, counter-intuitive, Alice-through-the-looking-glass world of islands. Yet save for Gosden and Pavlides' short paper and Patton's call for an 'island sociogeography' (1996), the potential has so far gone unrecognised. What, then, might a new approach to islandscapes involve?

First, the diversity of ways in which islanders perceive land and sea, together with the physical diversity of islands themselves, argues that there is no intrinsic reason why unitary islands should be the primary blocks from which island people constructed their worlds – nor, equally, through which we do best to analyse them. MacArthur and Wilson's *The Theory of Island Biogeography* (1967), a book to which the argument will return shortly for other reasons, contains a statement that has subsequently become something of a catechism for island archaeologists: 'In the science of biogeography, the island is the first unit that the mind can pick out and begin to comprehend' (MacArthur and Wilson 1967: 3). Despite the beguiling simplicity of this proposal, and its continuing relevance in island biogeography, no such assumption can in fact be made when analysing human societies on islands. In island archaeology, the identification of the island as the primary unit is simply an imposed view: the most obvious unit that *we* can pick out. But 'the island' is just one point on a spectrum of potentially relevant frameworks ranging from a patch of coast to entire island groups, and beyond; it may prove to be of special relevance in a particular spatial, temporal, social or political insular context, but equally it may not.

Empirical observation could indeed have told us this long ago. Thinking simply of topography, among dense archipelagos of high islands (a common insular setting), the difficulty in crossing a rugged interior can easily bring adjacent coasts of different islands closer to each other than each is to the far side of its own island. Equally, in a clusters of very small islands, interdependency may render the cluster as a whole more significant than its individual constituents. But it is also apparent that social formations, as well as the definition of political and ritual territories, need not be congruent with the limits of an individual island. Terrell (1977a: 66–9) warns against assumptions of island homogeneity and demonstrates the converse among people on Buka and Bougainville. In the Caribbean, Atajazido phase pottery styles suggest that, among the larger islands, the foci of group identities lay not within the islands, but on the straits between them (Rouse 1977: 7). In Polynesia, society on larger islands commonly split into ramages. Others (e.g. the Hawaii chain) were contested territories, and small islands were often grouped into wider chiefdoms, like the Marquesas, Cooks and Tuamotus (Kirch 1984). In the Archaic and Classical Aegean, two of the Cyclades spawned several independent polities (four on Kea, three on Amorgos), island cults such as those of Delos and the Kalaureian Amphyctyony on Poros acted as the centre of networks incorporating both islands and a mainland fringe, and major island cities off the Anatolian coast, such as Rhodes and Samos, controlled extensive lands on the mainland opposite (Fraser and Bean 1954; Shipley 1987), an economic symbiosis of island and mainland that more or less survived until the imposed boundaries of the twentieth century AD. On the margins of Neolithic Europe, Maltese temples aligned themselves on Sicily, although the latter lay over the horizon (Stoddart *et al.* 1993: 16–17), and in Jersey, activity at La Houe Bie can be understood in terms of the landmark's visibility from France (Patton 1991). This list of examples is necessarily selective, and could be extended considerably.

A second point concerns the angle of vision that we adopt when visualising and analysing islandscapes. Maps are one way of representing islands, but islanders would see things differently. Indeed a cartographic presentation, in which islands appear as a scatter of discrete points of land in the sea ('the first unit that the mind can pick out and comprehend') gives priority to the one viewpoint that no ancient islander could ever have experienced (fig. 2). Maps are hard to avoid using, but they do not inform us of the raking, sea-level views that made up the islanders' own perception of islandscapes, and which must have heavily influenced how they put these together. Helms (1988: 24–8) makes the point that this oblique vision, that divides the islandscape into land, coast, sea, horizon and sky (three broad bands and two liminal zones), may even encourage a similar cosmological division. Also significant is the fact that islanders (as indeed most people before the expansion of modern cartography) employed mental maps to locate distant points, in which travelling time, direction and landmarks were remembered in sequence, the *periplous* tradition mentioned earlier being essentially a commitment of this sequence to writing (Frake 1985; Lewis 1972). Navigation under such conditions is in large part an art of memory, drawing upon experience, inherited knowledge, stories (both 'real' and mythic) about the things that have happened along the way, and names given to places as a result of their history. Difficult as it is to address such issues in the context of early island societies, and impossible as it is to abandon maps as a mode of representation, if we aim to draw more than superficial pictures of the island societies of antiquity, we will have to take such factors into account as fully as possible.

An island archaeology of the early Cyclades

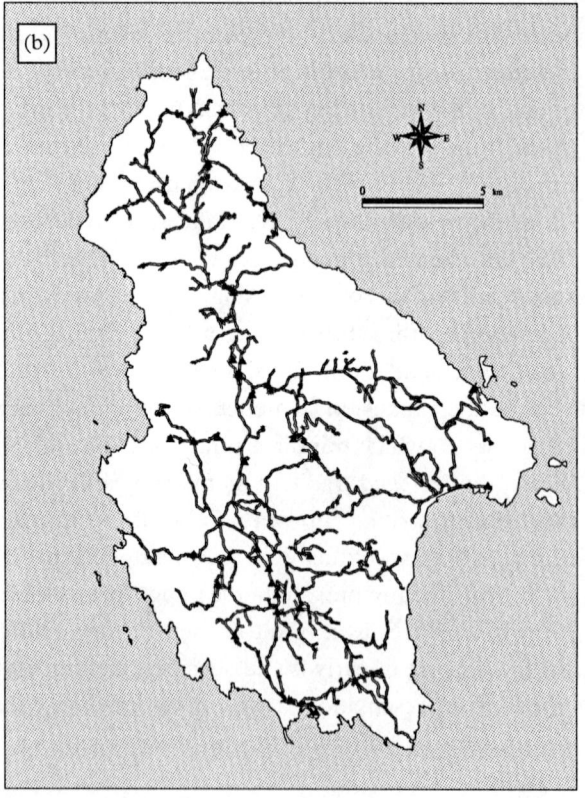

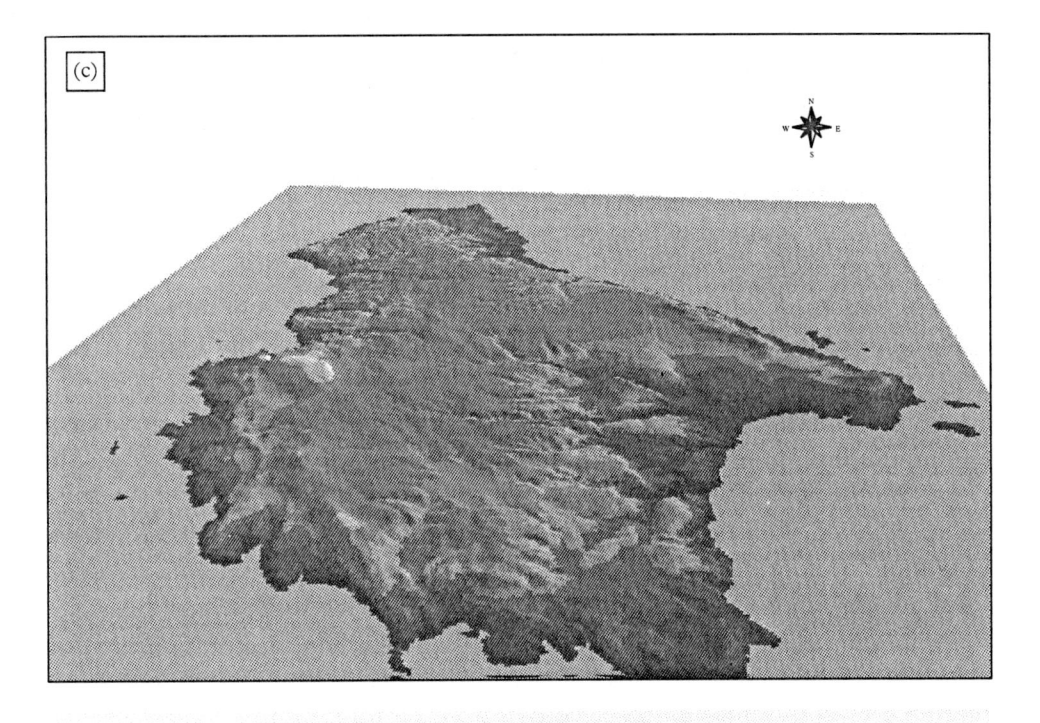

Fig. 2 Ways of visualising islands and islandscapes – Kythera in the south-west Aegean: (a) Venetian map, 1572, (b) twentieth-century AD map, (c) three-dimensional view derived from digital elevation model, (d) sea view from the east. (a) by permission of the British Library.

Do island laboratories exist?

The conclusions drawn so far in this chapter cast severe doubt on the plausibility of the concept of islands as laboratories for the study of cultural process, an influential idea in island archaeology since Evans' seminal paper (1973). The idea that islands can be informative places for understanding processes at work elsewhere in the world is at least as old as archaeology itself. Grove (1995) believes that the origins of conscious environmentalism go back to those Europeans of the seventeenth and eighteenth centuries AD who saw what was happening to the ecology of tropical islands under early colonial exploitation, and made a leap of inference to what must be happening less perceptibly on continents as well (in an intriguing aside, he postulates that long voyages in cramped ships heightened such an awareness, as the ships in effect comprised habitat islands in themselves). It is also well known that Darwin's observation of the Galapagos fauna sowed certain of the seeds of *On the Origin of Species by Means of Natural Selection* (1859). By the end of the nineteenth century, anthropologists were advocating the study of islands as a means of shedding light on wider issues in cultural evolution (Kuklick 1996). A more recent example is Vayda and Rappaport's essay on island cultures (1963). In a manner that now seems little short of extraordinary, Vayda and Rappaport explicitly cast out large, well-connected islands, in order to buttress their claim that society on a 'normal' (i.e. small, isolated island) was analogous to 'a Neolithic village surrounded by hostile neighbours and an ethnic minority living in a ghetto' (1963: 133). As Terrell *et al.* (1997) eloquently point out, this tendency in anthropology was part of a wider misplaced faith among social scientists in the 'myth of the primitive isolate'.

The emergence during the 1970s of the island laboratory analogy in archaeology took its cue from ideas such as those of Vayda and Rappaport, but it was also influenced by the parallel paradigms of anti-diffusionism and systems theory, then dominant in archaeology, which emphasised internal dynamics over external stimuli and analysed societies as bounded units – in effect as metaphorical islands. In addition, a dose of disciplinary self-justification for the nascent field of island archaeology can be detected. Why practise island archaeology? Because the definable boundaries of islands make them ideal places for observing general features of human behaviour with a clarity lacking under continental conditions. In short, interesting as islands are in their own right, they deserve study mainly because they enable us to understand mainlands better.

There are serious problems with this approach. Apart from the dubiousness of identifying individual islands as secure units for analysis, we have seen much evidence to suggest that islands were seldom isolates (however greatly their degree of external relations varied). As a leading Pacific archaeologist has put it, 'Polynesian society was commonly less insular than its islands. We should be wary of regarding islands as laboratories' (Irwin 1992: 206; also Terrell *et al.* 1997: 168–71). If this can be stated for

Polynesia, the implication for many other islands can hardly be in doubt. Moreover, it is not demonstrable that the cultural processes on the tiny handful of islands that have come close to total closure at some point in their history do in any useful sense exemplify wider social processes. On the contrary, we have seen that Maltese society closed itself off when it wanted to be different from the rest of the world, and the laboratory on Easter Island created a Frankenstein monster that can hardly be taken as a general social type. The closer we get to laboratory conditions, the more these alter the nature of the processes under study, a paradox with an extensive literature in the hard sciences. A further objection is that the flat hierarchies and reticulate relations typical of so many island societies contribute precious little to some of the most essential issues in mainland archaeology. In this context, it might be noted that a global roll-call would reveal island archaic states to be fairly rare, and early island empires even rarer (if they ever existed). Polynesian chiefdoms were never in fact the analogues for societies from Wessex to Cahokia that they were once deemed to be (Peebles and Kus 1977; Renfrew 1973b). A cynic might add that if island societies had resembled the societies of at least certain mainlands more closely, many might be in a rather more robust state today.

With the benefit of hindsight the island laboratory can be seen as an interesting idea that was very much a product of the intellectual climate of its time, and which has probably insuperable problems in its application. It is therefore odd that it continues to be regularly invoked by archaeologists as a justification and strategy in the analysis of islands (e.g. Fitzhugh and Hunt 1997, where the ambivalence is fairly apparent), with choices of fieldwork location particularly often explained with reference to the natural boundedness of the chosen island. Another hardy aspect is the suggestion that island groups are ideal places to conduct comparative experiments in adaptation and differentiation among discrete island populations that share an original common culture. This possibility was broached by Evans (1973: 519) and was later explored by him in a Mediterranean context (1977: 13). In the Pacific, the most important application is Kirch's (1984) and Kirch and Green's (1987) model of 'adaptive radiation' from a postulated ancestral Polynesian society as colonisation spread across the Pacific, which makes the claim that cumulative phylogenetic differentiation is the principal reason why contact-period Polynesian societies differed from each other so markedly. In the dense islandscapes of the Mediterranean, the hope that individual islands, and the societies on each island, could ever be seen as discrete units is particularly forlorn. But even in the Pacific, as Irwin's warning (cited above) states, such assumptions are likely to crumble in the face of the reports of long-range links in the remembered past, as well as recent experimental canoe voyages that demonstrate the relative ease of contact between central Polynesia and its outer fringes (Finney 1994). With such solid reasons to cast doubt on the island laboratory's viability as an analytical concept, at the very least the onus should now be placed on its continuing exponents to demonstrate its suitability and relevance – rather than baldly assume it – in a given island context.

Island archaeology and island biogeography

No attempt at rethinking the premises, agendas and practices of island archaeology can avoid considering the role of island biogeographical concepts in illuminating patterns of human activity on islands. Historically, island archaeology's debt is a real and lasting one. Much of the pioneering theoretically driven research during the 1980s was in large part inspired by island biogeographical models (e.g. Cherry 1981; Held 1989a, 1989b; Keegan and Diamond 1987; Terrell 1986), and the deployment of such models to interrogate data was one of the means by which a lasting degree of first-level order was brought to an ever-increasing quantity of empirical information. This book reveals the continuing debt at several junctures, notably during the exploration of the influence of islands' *geometric properties*, i.e. size, distance and configuration, on colonisation and post-colonisation life (Keegan and Diamond 1987: 58–65), as well as in the construction of spatial models, based on the physical frameworks of land and sea, to explore, at an heuristic level that will require much cultural overlay, how people may have settled and moved round in the Cyclades. If carefully handled, there is no reason why analyses of island space that begin with such generically biogeographical premises should not be compatible with acknowledgement of the fact that culture, society and politics can make and remake specific islandscapes. Indeed, to strike this balance is to highlight the often overlooked middle ground between crude geographical determinism and assertions of a wholly culturally relative construction of space, on which the development of a mature new generation of island archaeology is likely to depend.

What calls for serious thought is not whether ideas influenced by biogeography have any place in island archaeology (they palpably do), but how the two fields relate to each other, now and in the future, and how best to define sensible rules governing the limits of concepts drawn from the former for explaining phenomena in the latter. Both fields are likely to develop and reform themselves, a process within island archaeology that is covered in this chapter, but which is equally true of island biogeography, where MacArthur and Wilson's seminal idea (1967) has been subjected to much subsequent modification (Whittaker 1998 for recent discussion). New developments in both fields will sometimes create mutual overlaps of interest and at other times open up distance.

Current trends indicate one respect in which the two fields seem set to drift apart and another in which they will definitely converge. The former concerns their utility as analogues for continental processes. In archaeology, islands are problematic analogues for non-insular processes. But in island biogeography the increasing sub-division of the earth's ecological zones and habitats into smaller parcels under the impact of human activity is liable to make all biogeography in effect island biogeography before too long (Quammen 1996; Whittaker 1998: 192–227). The latter concerns the convergence that is increasingly apparent in the analysis of species turnover on islands. Compelling cases of anthropogenic island extinctions and introductions are furnished by recent research in the Mediterranean (Reese 1996; Schüle 1993; Simmons 1991, 1999; Vigne 1987; Waldren 1994), far Oceania (Steadman 1995) and Australia, Papua New Guinea and Melanesia (Flannery 1994; Flannery and White 1991). In the latter region, it has become clear not only that people have been environment-alterers and prodigious 'future eaters' for many millennia, but also that in Melanesia the earliest islanders were responsible for all subsequent species inflow of terrestrial mammals from the size of a rat upwards, and thereby for knock-on effects throughout the ecosystem. The stark implication of such studies is that as soon as people arrived, the ground-rules for island biogeography changed drastically, and that this change had often occurred a very long time before any biogeographers came onto the scene. There is accordingly a pressing need for further investigations of such 'encultured' island biogeographies (Crosby 1986 provides a masterly global overview whose scope encompasses both continents and islands).

So much for delineating some probable outlines of a future relationship between these twin domains of island research. What of the appropriate limits when applying island biogeographical concepts in island archaeology? These are in fact commonly a matter of degree, with excessive applications tending to damage the contribution of concepts that in a more nuanced form have much to recommend them. It is best to see island biogeographical parallels as neither an irrelevance nor a universal solution but, in Cherry's words, as a 'useful exploratory strategy' (1990: 146). Three key points about the transfer of ideas between the two fields reward closer scrutiny at this juncture.

1 What islands mean for island people versus island fauna and flora

Clearly there are high-level similarities between human and animal/plant life on islands, in so far as both alike face challenges in getting to islands and establishing themselves, both have the ability to alter, sometimes radically, the face of their new homes and may equally find their habits altered by them, and both may experience local extinctions. Set against this is the major difference that island people, through maritime culture and a high degree of consciousness of the surrounding islandscapes, can decide the meaning and import of a given island setting to a unique (albeit not infinite) degree. To give a simple example, the survival chances of a small population of animals or plants on a small, remote and ill-favoured island are essentially determined by the reproductive and dispersive capacities of each species and stochastic factors such as the sex of off-spring and the vagaries of weather. Turning to people on an equivalent island, the range of possibilities is broader. Such adversity could create a vulnerable population liable to succumb to even a fairly mild run of bad luck, especially if the technology for off-island communication is inadequate (the tiny population of *Bounty* mutineers on Pitcairn is a good example, prior to its 'rescue' by outside shipping). But other islanders under similar circumstances might invest in seafaring and succeed in establishing a central role and consequent security for themselves. It is precisely because of this variability that in island contexts the association between physical remoteness, isolation, marginality or centrality is so irreducibly complex. An additional observation takes us back to earlier thoughts concerning the importance (or rather the lack of it) of the unitary island. The island remains a useful unit of analysis for many species in island biogeography, but for human islanders its relevance has to be proved rather than assumed. To summarise, interactions between people and islands are vastly more changeable, unpredictable and recursive than those between animals or plants and islands. If human beings are, at one level, another island-living species, they are certainly a profoundly unusual one, and the skilful application of island biogeographical concepts to human life on islands will depend on sensitivity to the questions asked and the kinds of answers expected.

2 The spatial scale of analysis and resolution

In tandem with the question of degrees of similarity, questions of scale and resolution can be considered. For instance, is the aim to establish high-level generalisations about island societies and island biota at a global scale or to examine the intricacies of human, animal and plant life in a single archipelago? This point is best exemplified by looking at colonisation, a key theme for island biogeographers, and one that has also enjoyed considerable attention from theoretically inclined island archaeologists (Cherry 1981, 1984b, 1990, 1995; Held 1989a, 1989b; Irwin 1992; and Keegan and Diamond's 1987 global survey of 'Colonization of islands by humans: a biogeographical perspective'). Island biogeography's premise that dispersal patterns are influenced by an island's geometric properties has encouraged analyses of human colonisations using similar criteria. At a comparative level (Held 1989a: 14–15; Keegan and Diamond 1987) and within macro-regions like the Mediterranean and Caribbean (Cherry 1981; Keegan 1992: 48–64) impressive general parallels have be identified. People do indeed often settle larger, closer islands first and most successfully, and intervening stepping-stone chains often speed things up. But in contrast to the remarkably regular impact of area and distance demonstrated in certain studies of island fauna (Diamond 1972; Diamond and Mayr 1976), such patterns in human island colonisation tend to display a great deal of 'noise' (Cherry 1981: 52, 56). Some of this noise is attributable to the gaps in the data, but the quantity and resilience of the anomalies argue that although geometric properties do influence human colonisations they seldom explain the whole story. Limitations are often increasingly exposed when focusing in on a specific context. Recent examples are Bowdler's (1995) study of Aboriginal activity on Australia's offshore islands, where minimal association was found between the islands' geometric properties and their history of use, and B. Bass' (1998) study of the Early Neolithic in the Adriatic islands, where geometric properties likewise seem of less import than resource wealth and location on movement routes. In chapter 4, both some consonance with and substantial deviation from geometrically derived expectations will be seen in the Cyclades. Clearly, a range of cultural and resource-oriented factors specific to each regional and temporal context condition and, in certain cases, override the predictions of island geometry.

3 The precision and utility of analogies

Despite the popularity of analogies between particular island biogeographical and island archaeological phenomena, there has been strikingly little discussion of how seriously these should be taken. In fact, such analogies regularly comprise the weakest and most superficial transfers between the fields. One example that encounters problems once it is looked at in more detail is the observation that people and animals alike display great variability in their readiness to travel across water. Among animal species, consummate swimmers, fliers and rafters contrast with species incapable of even modest crossings (e.g. Diamond 1977), ostensibly rather as Tasmanians differed from Polynesians. But whilst the variability among animals is anatomically based and differentiates between species, that between people is a result of variations in culture and technology that may be culturally transitory. Diamond and Keegan's (1984) suggestion that specialised island-colonising animal species (termed 'tramps' and 'super-tramps') find parallels in highly proficient human colonists begs the question as to what we learn from this beyond the fact that big oceans have selected for species and people adept at moving around them. What does thinking of Polynesians and Oceanic ants as super-tramps tell us about the one in relation to the other? In fact, the parallel is less than perfect, given that super-tramp fauna are deemed to be so specialised that they find it hard to adapt to continental conditions, whilst Polynesians made a spectacular success (albeit not against human competition) of settling the quasi-continental island of New Zealand. If we are to prove that such analogies are more than trivial, we need to ask what grounds they are based upon, what they really tell us, and how much weight of inference they can sustain.

In drawing this discussion together, it should by now be apparent that, however many genuine and important insights island biogeography can provide, it does not offer anything approximating to a complete paradigm for understanding island societies. An agenda for island archaeology set out in terms of biogeographical issues of dispersal, adaptation, radiation, competition and extinction is manifestly over-reductive, and will encourage a minimalist vision of island life. There is, in short, rather more to living on islands than getting there and managing not to die out.

A few issues concerning cultural perception have been thoughtfully addressed by scholars working in a biogeographical tradition, a prominent example being Keegan and Diamond's interesting concept of *autocatalysis* (1987: 67–8), which postulates that certain configurations of islands and coasts reward increases in people's seafaring skills and experiments in island settlement in a manner likely to lead to spectacular take-offs in colonising sequences (see chapter 4). But post-colonisation culture (and colonisation is, after all, only the beginning of island-based life) more commonly gets short shrift in biogeographically inspired interpretations. For example, when Diamond surmises that: 'Perhaps man's rapid behavioral response capability offsets his slow genetic responses imposed by his long generation times and lets his social systems track the environment rapidly but also very "noisily" (i.e. with much non-adaptive variation)' (Diamond 1977: 259), one might be forgiven for not immediately realising that the 'noise' referred to is culture. Some aspects of island culture may indeed be interpreted as adaptive strategies (although there are typically different, comparably adaptive, ways of living in most islands), but at a more general level the problem is that many elements of island culture give no sign of being particularly adaptive, and call for radically different forms of explanation. If portraits of islanders painted in a biogeographical light are weak on culture, they are equally thin on history. The fullest attempt at such a portrait is represented by Keegan's writings on the pre-Columbian Bahamas (Keegan 1985, 1992, 1995), which portray islanders as optimisers given cultural substance through comparative ethnography and contact-period information. The result is enlightening in certain respects, but it is ultimately two-dimensional. For example, Keegan sacrifices a historical perspective to avoid association with traditionalist studies of the region's culture sequence (Keegan 1992: 224). But trading a release from such strictures for the loss of island history is a poor bargain, and there is really no need for the historical baby to go out with the typological bathwater. For the brightest future surely lies in the development of an island archaeology (informed by island biogeography as and when appropriate) that explores how island space, environment, time and culture can be most convincingly woven together into island history.

Expanding the horizons of island archaeology

What would an island archaeology informed by the ideas and perspectives advocated in this chapter look like, and how could we go about practising it? The best way to answer this is by demonstration, and that is what this book attempts to do for the Cyclades. But first let us consolidate the points established, and consider how to make them work in terms of methods, fieldwork and material analysis.

A first observation is that there is surely no longer any need to justify island archaeology. Island archaeology is worth doing because islands exist in profusion, and because their archaeology is undeniably fascinating. This is reason enough, as Pacific archaeologists seem the readiest to recognise. Or if there must be a justification, let it be that island societies as they once existed have all but vanished, and that archaeology is our only avenue into most islands' past for most of the time. This also reminds us that island archaeology must aim to produce essays in island history of sufficient subtlety and complexity to capture their subjects' protean natures. Islands are tricky, changing places. In the past, they were seldom absolutely isolated from the rest of the world nor fully integrated in it. Rather, the majority moved around between these extremes, often performing bewildering manoeuvres in the central stretch of the range. Not all islanders in a given society necessarily occupied the same part of the range in any given moment. What we analyse as islands, and what were seen as such by islanders, are not always the same thing. Islands have a physical existence, but they are also made and remade by people. Sea and land combine to create islandscapes, which are seldom congruent with unitary islands. Insularity, furthermore, is a form of social identity, and a cultural strategy that islanders manipulated until continental peoples found a means of imposing definitions upon them. And even when that happened, insularity might reinvent itself as a resistant identity, and may yet re-emerge in robust health if the opportunity arises. Islands are slippery as metaphors. They are neither entirely different from the rest of the world, nor exactly like it. If islands are difficult to use as metaphors, they are frankly dangerous to use as laboratories. Seldom is the analogy apt, and even if its aptness can be proven in a given case, the experiment's results may not be widely applicable. Island archaeology should neither shun island biogeography nor be in intellectual thrall to it. At one level, the two fields will converge as the anthropogenic nature of much change in island biota grows apparent. Beyond this, they are likely to continue to identify parallelisms worthy of exploration; what matters is that we devote enough energy to asking when, where, why and at what level these are significant. Any temptation to allow the perspectives of island biogeography to write the overall agenda for island archaeology must be resisted, for there is much about island societies that biogeography can shed little light upon.

How might all this translate into practice? *First, when formulating research it is unwise to assume that the unitary island is necessarily the ideal unit of analysis, despite its apparent circumscription by the sea.* This applies to the design of field surveys in particular. If practical reasons dictate that a single island be selected, an alertness to the probability that, in innumerable different ways, this island will comprise either more or less than the area most relevant to the islanders and issues under analysis is essential. There are implications, too, for the ways in which maps, and models based on maps, are used. Their usage cannot easily be avoided, but it is possible to remain aware of the assumptions that they are liable to import into the reasoning. They represent the one perspective that is not the islanders' own, and force the division of space into discrete island units. Further, a really rich insight into a given islandscape will never be gained if overhead analyses are not supplemented with a phenomenological approach to what might be described as 'being in the island world'. Despite the difficulties that attend attempts to understand landscapes through ancient eyes, considerable progress towards this goal can be made by standing where we know that islanders stood, populating the landscape as we know that they populated it, and modelling movement across land and sea along routes and over ranges that the distribution of artefacts and likely performance of seacraft give us reason to believe that they followed.

Second, we need an archaeology of the sea to match that of the land. This does not simply mean maritime archaeology as it is currently defined (though this will play a part), but an archaeology of the dynamics of maritime culture at a given period. Models need to be built for how the sea was used, by whom, for what objectives, over what distance, at what cost, and how often. This is no easy matter, but there are strategies for gaining insight. What can be learnt from the parameters of boat technology in terms of the performance and social implications of seacraft? What do subsistence remains tell about exploitation of the sea? To what degree, and where, were people, raw materials, objects, styles and symbols moving over water? Can the sea-paths along which these moved be discerned? What does our understanding of life on the land in a given context suggest about the necessity and frequency of sea-crossings for various kinds of people? Last, but not least, what do the gaps in the terrestrial evidence suggest – not the gaps that are likely to be the result of lacunae in detection, or loss of archaeological data, but those that hint that a land-based perspective is missing an integral part of the overall pattern. A pioneering exploration of this approach is Gosden and Pavlides' suggestion that the Lapita phenomenon in south-west Oceania reflects a *colonisation of the sea*, as much as the land, reflecting mobile groups for whom the coast was a point to touch on periodically in the course of maritime movements (Gosden and Pavlides 1994: 168–9).

The third and fourth points are derivative of the first two, but they benefit from separate emphasis. *The third is the need to look hard at material and other clues relating to social interaction or its absence, for this will tell us about the fashioning of insularity in islands.* Patton (1996: 33) explores the ways in which the possibilities inherent in sea movement may boost the role of exchange networks as a way of linking up or closing off islands. It is important to go as far as possible beyond generalisations about the presence and absence of interaction, and to ask who took and received what from whom, in what quantities, and by what means. This naturally demands an awareness of the various models of trade and exchange in archaeology and economic anthropology, but it also requires the detailed, context-sensitive exploration of different archaeological sites. Again, the need to focus on gaps in the evidence is apparent: what was moving, but also what was not moving, even in times when other things were? And if periods of apparent isolation are identified, precisely how do these seem to have been created, and why? Such matrices of variability need to be kept in the forefront of our minds.

Fourth, and last, *we need to bring the pot styles and other material texture of the island past back in, not just as markers of periods or archaeological culture groups, but as signifiers of island social practices*, whether our interpretations emphasise the social significance of style in a passive and reflective sense, in an active and constituting one, or as something that can switch between these (Conkey and Hastorf 1990). Comparatively little has been done by way of analysis of early trans-insular distributions of style, with the exception of research in the Caribbean (Rouse 1977: 7) and on Lapita (Spriggs 1990;

also a recent survey in Ambrose 1997). This task, in tandem with other detailed investigations of material culture, will be no easy undertaking, but if we do not make the effort in strict yet also imaginative ways, we will stand little chance of realising the extent to which, in the history of islands, it is just as interesting to see what people have made of islands as what islands have made of people.

2

Cycladic approaches

> Where fairer Tempes bloom, there sleep
> Young Cyclads on a sunnier deep.
> *Hellas,* PERCY BYSSHE SHELLEY

The Neolithic and EBA Cyclades are an ideal theatre for island archaeology in general, and in particular for exploring the perspectives outlined in the preceding chapter. There are several reasons why this is the case. One factor that may surprise archaeologists accustomed to bemoaning the limitations attending current archaeological knowledge of the early Cyclades is the quantity of data available and the longevity of the tradition of research. There is certainly a lot that remains unknown, in terms of lacunae in island coverage and study of specific kinds of material and sites. Equally certainly, a lot more could be done with what is known. But despite these caveats, it is a peculiarly under-recognised fact that the early Cyclades constitute one of most intensively researched and archaeologically data-rich island clusters in the world, and one of the very few that can occasionally provide sufficiently dense clusters of data to allow examination of material culture in frameworks more ambitious than chronology and taxonomic affiliation. This range of information, and its gaps, is investigated later in this chapter. For the moment the point to stress is that with the data now available, and a carefully chosen arsenal of questions, there is a great deal of interest that can be explored. Moreover, the time-span of slightly over three millennia that encompasses the later Neolithic and EBA periods in these islands (*c.* 5200–2000 BC) provides a generous scope for analysis, equivalent in Pacific history to the entire period from the start of the Lapita horizon to the arrival of the European navigators. During this extended period of time, many different ways of living in the Cyclades were practised by island societies, communities and individuals.

The early Cyclades are also of special interest because a remarkable number of the conceptual problems attending investigation of ancient islands apply to them. Some of these, such as the nature of Cycladic islandscapes, are dealt with in chapter 3, but others can be outlined here. For example, the recent growth in tourism and subsidies (a classic example of extreme integration, yet without which most islands would probably be experiencing abandonment) has ensured a high-profile modern presence that makes it hard to conceive how these islands operated under different regimes. In particular, the ferry routes that condition most contemporary movement between islands slice through ancient maritime networks like motorways through Aboriginal songlines. The current configuration is, moreover, only the latest of many that separate us from these islands' early past. In between lie four millennia of intense interaction with the cities, states and empires of the Mediterranean: the Greek nation-state, the Ottoman empire, Venice and Genoa, Byzantium, Rome, the Hellenistic kingdoms, Classical Athens, the city-states of Iron Age Greece, and the Mycenaean and Minoan palace-states of the later Bronze Age. The veils that separate us from these islands' early history are thick and complex. Equally significant is the fact that the Cyclades' proximity to important extra-insular regions demands that, even in the Neolithic and EBA, their history must to a degree be linked to other histories in the Aegean and beyond. Lastly, a mention must be made of the contemporary popularity of an idealised, nostalgic view of the early Cyclades as a world of unravished insular purity, the result of a modern exaltation of the EBA islanders' marble anthropomorphic figurines as pristine art forms. This last intriguing, and archaeologically not uninfluential, phenomenon is returned to later in this chapter.

One final reason why an island archaeology of the early Cyclades is an attractive prospect is that it can help to shift the global balance of island archaeological research away from its present heavy bias in favour of the Pacific. Although, in the wake of the pioneering studies by Cherry (1981, 1984b, 1985, 1987, 1990), a number of analyses have been undertaken in the Mediterranean (Bass 1998; Bellard 1995; Broodbank 1999; Held 1989a, 1989b; Malone 1999; Patton 1996; Stoddart 1999; Stoddart *et al.* 1993), the region's potential remains comparatively under-realised. In tandem with advances in other island theatres, Mediterranean island archaeology should contribute far more to the pool of ideas relevant to the comparative study of islands. This is important, not only because there is a real danger that, if island archaeology continues to be dominated by Pacific-orientated agendas and methods, its applications elsewhere will become little more than the transmission of ideas developed for the Pacific and mechanically imposed on different data sets, but also because it remains to be seen whether a comparably stimulating programme of island archaeology conducted in different sorts of island locations might not diversify the intellectual topography of the field as a whole. The closely packed nature of many Mediterranean islandscapes, and the necessity of a glance over the shoulder to the extra-insular world even in the course of the most involuted island analyses, are immediately suggestive of major differences. Likewise distinctive (if by turns advantageous and a handicap) is the fact that for the early Mediterranean there is no relevant ethnographic baseline. Consequently, there is little option but to start with a blank slate and no prior expectations. In short, there are clearly several respects in which Mediterranean island archaeology should differ from that practised in the Pacific, or indeed other regions. How sustained these differences prove to be, and what they contribute to an expanded understanding of the history of islands in general, will emerge, it is hoped, through the course of this book.

This chapter's aim is to take a closer look at some of these themes, in order to gain a more precise appreciation of how analysis of the early Cyclades relates to wider frameworks, and what information and general research traditions already exist. First comes a necessarily brief comparative analysis of island configuration, which examines how the Mediterranean, the Aegean and the Cyclades compare as physical arenas with other island worlds. This is followed by a sketch of the macro-history of the Aegean, east Mediterranean and Near East during the time-span of this analysis. The remaining sections of this chapter ask what information exists and what remains lacking for the early Cyclades, introduce the regional terminology and chronology, examine the main interpretative paradigms adopted to date, and set out the few examples of explicitly island archaeological analysis that have been undertaken in these islands to date.

The Mediterranean and the Cyclades in comparative insular perspective

As many archaeologists have stressed, and as was intimated above, the Mediterranean islands could not be more different in their configuration from those scattered across the central, east and south Pacific (e.g. Evans 1977: 12–13; Davis and Cherry 1979: 3), nor from the thinner scatters in the Indian Ocean west of South-East Asia, and in the central-to-south Atlantic. Three other major island-studded regions of the world are different again. In Island South-East Asia the principal islands are massive (Sumatra is almost half the length of the Mediterranean, whilst Borneo could land-fill one of the latter's principal basins), and the block of large islands in the Philippines has no Mediterranean analogy. The islands running from Taiwan via Japan to the Kuriles form an immensely long offshore chain enclosing more or less empty inland seas. The islands of the north Atlantic are comparatively few in number, dominated by large islands, and in the west separated by long distances. Much better comparisons for the Mediterranean can be found in south-west Oceania and the Caribbean (fig. 3). Knapp (1990: figs. 2–4) reminds us that the area of the Lapita complex and the later, ethnographically famous island traders of Melanesia is similar in size to the eastern half of the Mediterranean. Brotherston (1992: 10) describes the pre-Columbian Caribbean as the Mediterranean of the Americas, a central sea linking together mainland regions from Florida to the delta of the Orinoco. In terms of their range of islands, all share a similar spectrum of small, medium, and a few large islands, high and low islands, and singletons versus clusters. All three regions, moreover, were major cradles of island culture.

A longer look will reveal, however, that although the Mediterranean resembles south-west Oceania and the Caribbean to some degree, it possesses distinctive features that make it something of a unique case, as recognised by Braudel (1972: 148–60), and in the context of island archaeology by Evans (1977: 13–15). Climate, of course,

Cycladic approaches

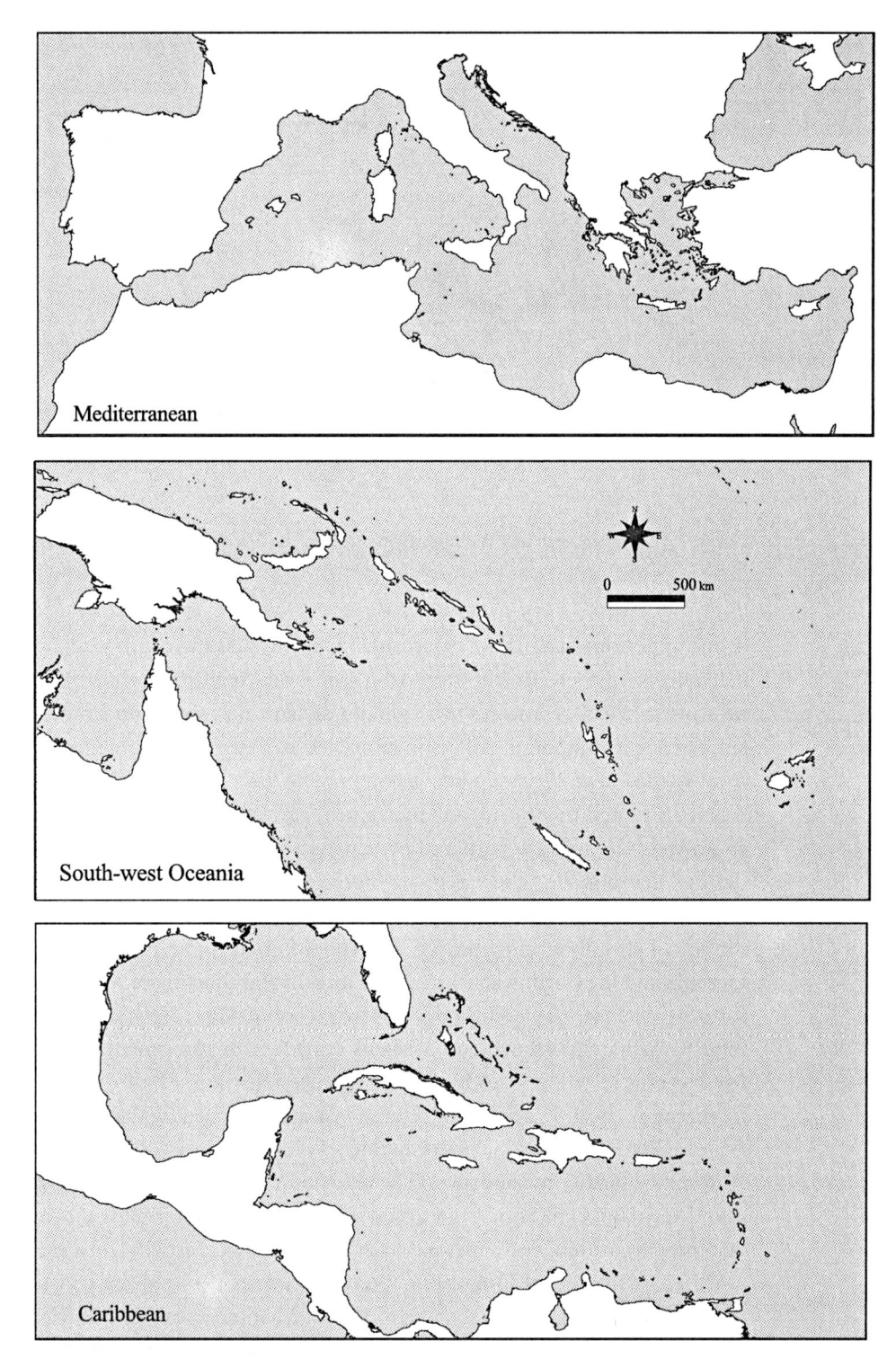

Fig. 3 The Mediterranean, south-west Oceania and the Caribbean at the same scale, illustrating comparative configuration of islands and mainland regions.

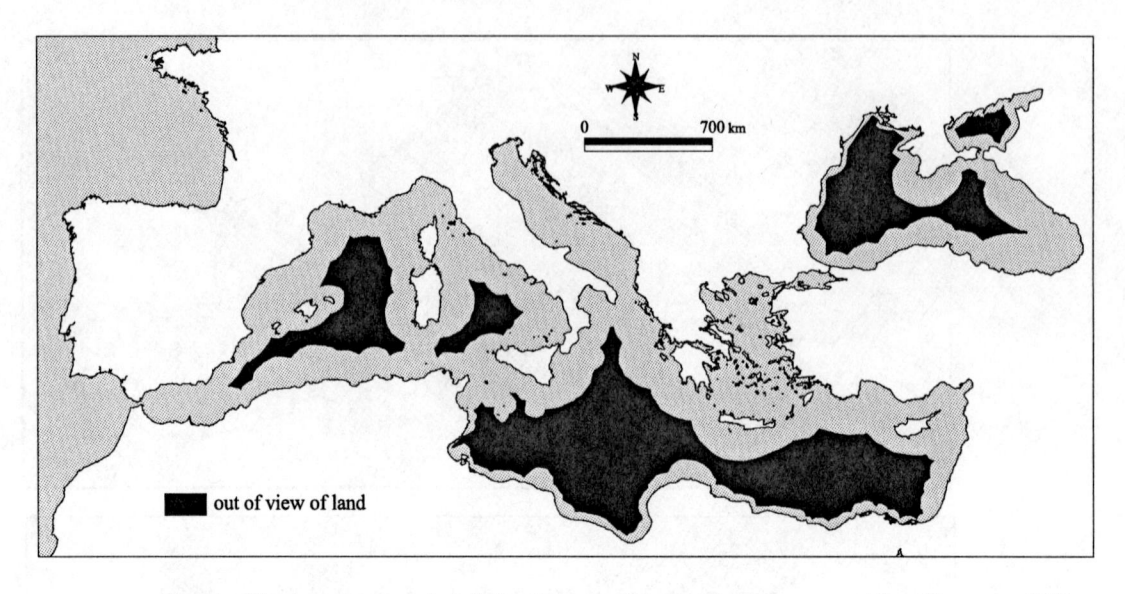

Fig. 4 Maximum seaward visibility from land in the Mediterranean. After Chapman 1990: fig. 59.

is one important distinction. South-west Oceania and the Caribbean are tropical and generally well watered in contrast to the semi-arid Mediterranean. Similarly, the slightness of the Mediterranean's tidal regime dictates narrower opportunities for coastal subsistence. Configurational distinctions are also evident. Although the size range of most islands in all three regions is comparable, the former two have more groups of tiny islands, and there is no Mediterranean equivalent of Cuba. The Caribbean and south-west Oceania are bordered by expanses of empty ocean on several flanks, 'sea deserts' that bounded these regions more effectively than did their coastal rims and that, unlike the latter, were not a source of external influence on the islands within until the rise of ultra-long-range seafaring. In addition, the pattern of islands in south-west Oceania and the Caribbean is markedly more linear than in the Mediterranean. In the former two areas, easy points of access from the outside are few, and long island chains tend to define subsequent inter-island corridors of movement, in contrast to the Mediterranean, whose islands are usually accessible from several directions and which, furthermore, occupy a series of separate theatres defined by the east Mediterranean, Aegean, Illyrian–Ionian, Sicilian Channel, Tyrrhenian and west Mediterranean basins. Whilst the linearity in south-west Oceania and the Caribbean encourages cumulative island-to-island expansion on a grand scale, in the Mediterranean there is scope for colonisation within each theatre to have remained partially discrete until linked together by the rise of long-range interconnections between the constituent basins. Other observations include the fact that most Mediterranean islands fringe the deeply crenellated northern coasts, leading to a high degree of inter-visibility in optimal weather conditions with mainland areas as well as with each other (fig. 4), and the degree to which many islands are juxtaposed with peninsulas so attenuated that they live up to their etymology as 'almost islands'. This last feature entails the partial erosion of the mainland–island division in certain regions, particularly the southern tip of Italy, the Illyrian coast and above all the Aegean.

It is therefore a commonplace (but no less important for it) that Mediterranean islands are potential stepping-stones from everywhere to everywhere else, and that they become enmeshed in complex multi-directional links with each other and the mainland. Plausible corridors of movement can indeed be identified in such profusion, and along so many potential axes, that to establish which routes mattered at which time is often impossible by geographical intuition alone, and instead demands an examination of the period-specific archaeological (or other) evidence of contacts.

Within the Mediterranean, the configuration of the Aegean is equally distinctive. Allusion has been made to the fact that the erosion of island–mainland distinctions is nowhere more common in the Mediterranean than in the Aegean. If an island the size of Crete might be seen as a quasi-continent, conversely much of the coastal Peloponnese, Attica, Chalkidiki and the east Aegean littoral are quasi-insular in their configuration. A second feature is that the Aegean comprises an inland sea within the much larger inland sea of the Mediterranean, being enclosed on three sides by mainland coasts and on the fourth by Crete, which affords only limited access to the open sea to its south. In this respect the Aegean resembles the Adriatic and Tyrrhenian, yet its islands are greater in number and their configuration is more complex. The Aegean is unusual in Mediterranean terms, too, for the numerical dominance of smaller islands over large ones, as opposed to the pattern of big islands with small satellites in the west (i.e. the Balearics, Sardinia–Corsica plus the Elba group, and Sicily plus the Maltese, Lipari, Egadi and Pantelleria–Lampedusa clusters); Cyprus in the east is unusual in its solitude. In the Aegean, there are only four large islands (Crete, Euboia, Rhodes and Lesbos) and none of these is centrally located relative to the main clusters of smaller islands. Such a compact, island-crowded sea, fringed by mainlands on three sides and the comparatively giant island of Crete on the fourth, is more or less without close geographical parallels in or beyond the Mediterranean. It should come as no great surprise, either, that one of the Aegean sea's ancient Greek epithets has given us the modern word 'archipelago'.

The Cycladic islands form the central cluster within the southern Aegean. Fig. 5 compares them with some other archaeologically or anthropologically prominent island groups. Within the Aegean, their size is typical of all but a handful of islands, ranging from Naxos (430 sq km) and Andros (380 sq km) down to minute uninhabited rocks. Cycladic geography and environment are examined in more detail in chapter 3, during an exploration of the micro-diversity that qualifies their homogeneity as a group, but some generalised points can be made here. First, the Cyclades are the Aegean islands most distant from mainland shores. The majority of the other islands either hug the mainland, as do the Argo-Saronics, Kythera, Thasos, most of

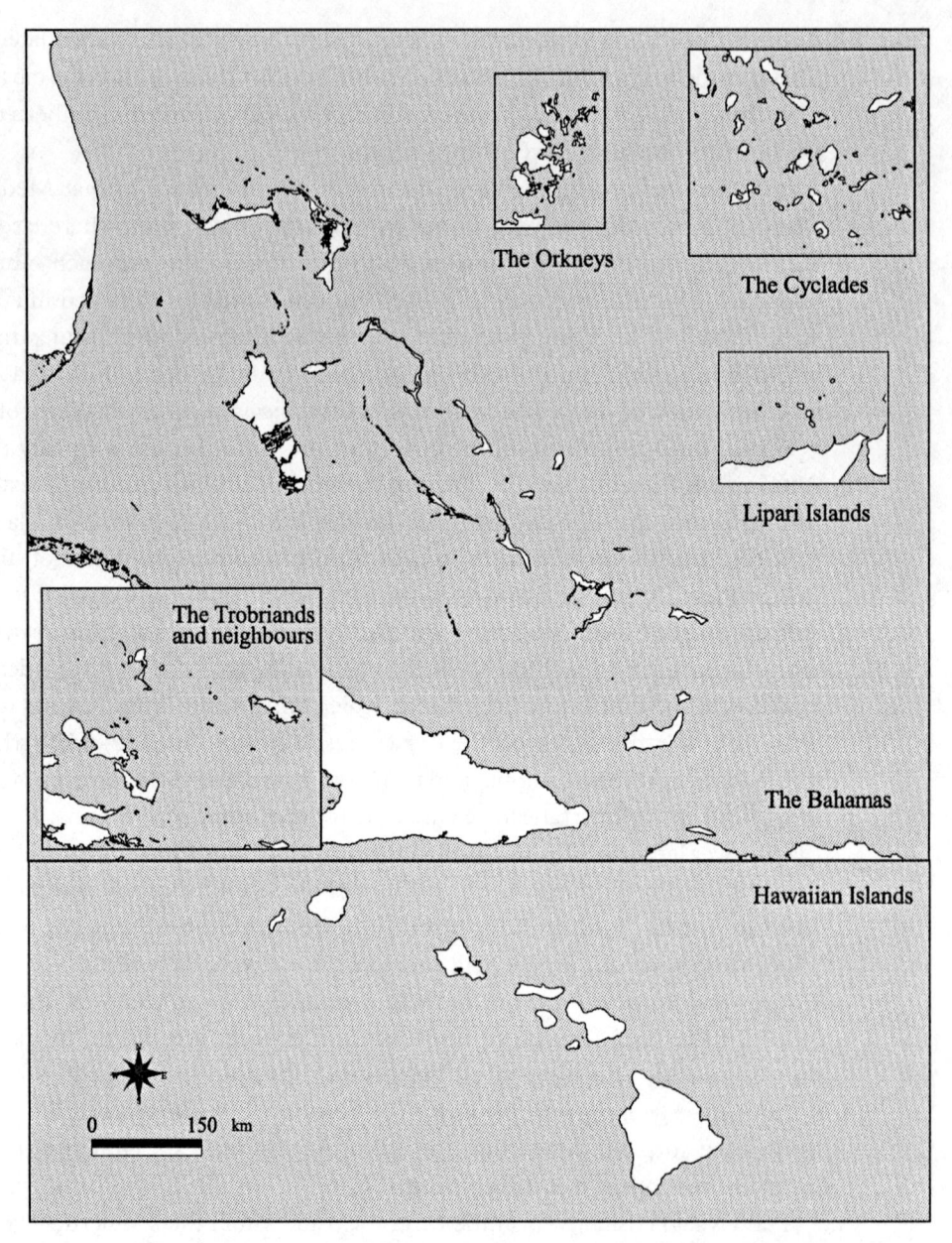

Fig. 5 The Cyclades and select other island clusters at the same scale, illustrating comparative configuration and size.

the Dodecanese, and the other islands lying off the coast of Anatolia, or are aligned seaward to a lesser degree, as in the case of the northern Sporades. Second, their roll-call of some thirty substantial islands and many more islets makes the Cyclades the most numerous and complicated cluster in the Aegean. Third, their location places them both on the edge of everywhere *and* at the centre of the whole, a deeply ambivalent position that must shed light on their chequered history. In this sense, at least, the Cyclades are quintessential examples of a Mediterranean island. For comparative purposes, then, the Cyclades can be visualised as a distinct subset (islands in the Aegean) of another distinct subset (the Aegean within the Mediterranean) of a third distinct subset (the Mediterranean among island-studded seas). At each level there are both similarities to be drawn out and idiosyncrasies and distinctions to be highlighted. This way of conceiving the Cyclades should encourage a simultaneous exploration of the unique patterning of early history in one island group, and the situating of Cycladic archaeology within the wider study of islands as a whole.

The Cyclades as islands in Aegean and Near Eastern macro-history

If it is inadvisable to interpret the Cyclades without paying enough attention to the fact that they are islands, it is equally unrealistic to write about them as isolates abstracted from surrounding history. One general reason is that the dynamic between islands and what lies beyond is an interesting aspect of island life. A more particular reason is that these particular islands were exposed from the beginning to ways of doing things in the surrounding small-scale societies of the Aegean and also, from a comparatively early stage, among emergent larger-scale societies, at first in the distant and refracted form of the early Near Eastern cities, states and empires, but later, and much closer, in the guise of the first Aegean palace-states on Crete. Hence the requirement throughout this analysis to maintain a dialectic between the investigation of internal Cycladic patterns and the locating of such patterns within larger, sometimes world-systemic, contexts. As A. G. Sherratt has succinctly put it, we need 'both to chart these processes of growing uniformity and to recover the locally unique patterns and structures that they overwhelmed' (Sherratt 1995: 25). In other words, whilst our main emphasis in this book is on the rediscovery of some of the locally unique island micro-patterns and structures that must have once existed in the early Cyclades, the presence of powerful actors in the wings of the Cycladic arena, or further off-stage, should not be forgotten.

The Cyclades share with the rest of the southern Aegean archipelago, Cyprus and Bahrain the distinction of being the first of the world's islands to become closely integrated into major continental systems. They therefore anticipate a process that has been accelerating through recent millennia, reaching its crescendo over the last few hundred years. As intimated above, the beginnings of this shift in the Aegean can be placed early in the second millennium BC, with the rise of the first palace-states on

Crete (Cherry 1984a; Warren 1987; Watrous 1994: 720–53). Palace-states such as Knossos, Phaistos and Mallia created the first substantial, inter-regional asymmetries in Aegean economic and political power, the palatial centres of production and consumption differing by an order of magnitude from the smaller, local structures that had hitherto existed, and realigning much of the southern Aegean into their cultural, economic and possibly political orbit. The end of the third millennium BC and the early second millennium BC also produce the first definite evidence for direct maritime interaction between the Aegean and the eastern Mediterranean centres. From this time onwards, societies in the Cyclades were shaped by, as well as in a limited way reshaping, a maritime trade network extending from Egypt to the Aegean, and later as far as the Adriatic and Tyrrhenian basins, where other local island worlds were in turn transformed (Sherratt and Sherratt 1991). As Renfrew (1972: 195) and Gamble (1993: 240) have recognised, the pivotal period around the start of the second millennium BC divides the later Cyclades from their earlier island past, and therefore forms the end-point for this book. Chapters 10 and 11 examine the island ending that took place around this time, an unusual one from a comparative perspective in so far as it was a series of island-based centres (albeit on the outsized, quasi-continental island of Crete) that forced change on another system of islands. The present aim is instead to look further back into the history of the regions surrounding the Cyclades during the Aegean's preceding, pre-palatial, millennia. For although the Cyclades in earlier times occupied positions much further from the integration terminal on the scale of island–mainland relations, their history was still far from independent of wider processes.

An overview of the early Aegean

Around the end of the Pleistocene, the Aegean saw a transition from late Upper Palaeolithic to Mesolithic hunter-gatherer societies, similar to that around much of the Mediterranean littoral. An increased emphasis on maritime resources is attested as sea-levels started to rise from their lowest glacial stand. Mainland finds from the Franchthi cave, in the Argolid, of obsidian from the Cycladic island of Melos provide the earliest definite evidence for seafaring in the Aegean, at a time when sea-levels were still well below present levels and inter-island distances consequently shorter (Perlès 1987: 142–5; Renfrew and Aspinall 1990). Neolithic communities comprising small farming villages first appear at the start of the seventh millennium BC, with a particular concentration on the plains of Thessaly (Demoule and Perlès 1993; Andreou et al. 1996). There is as yet no agreement as to whether these primarily reflect demic advance or the local adoption of agriculture and an agricultural ideology (Halstead 1996a; Hodder 1990; van Andel and Runnels 1995; Whittle 1996: 37–71). The crops cultivated at this stage were cereals and pulses, alongside animal husbandry of sheep, goat, cattle and pig, augmented to a very slight degree by wild food acquisition.

Over the next three-and-a-half millennia, there are abundant signs of small-scale complexity in Neolithic social organisation and craft production, as well as long-range interaction exemplified by the movement of exotic flints and *Spondylus* shell ornaments within and beyond the Aegean (Perlès 1992). There is also growing evidence of island colonisation during the Neolithic, and especially the LN (*c.* 5200–4200 BC) and FN (*c.* 4200–3200 BC), to which periods the first Cycladic settlements are securely dated (Broodbank 1999; Cherry 1990). By the FN this process can be seen as one part of a more general settlement expansion into marginal areas of the Aegean (Halstead 1994), a process that continued in the EBA. Metal objects start to appear by the LN, initially as exotica deriving from the precocious early Balkan centres of metallurgy, but by the FN Aegean metal-working is sufficiently well attested for the period to be viewed as, in effect, a Chalcolithic (McGeehan Liritzis 1996; Nakou 1995; Zachos 1996a). The principal metals attested at this period and throughout much of the (in fact strictly misnamed) EBA are copper, usually alloyed deliberately or accidentally with arsenic, plus gold, silver and lead. Tin, a non-Aegean metal, and therefore the advent of true tin-bronze, is a feature of the later EBA. This technological overlap between a final Stone Age with metals and an EBA partly devoid of true bronze underscores the gradual nature of the transition from the Neolithic to EBA, which occupied the later fourth millennium BC. Gradual as it was, however, this shift nonetheless marked the start of a cumulative transformation in Aegean societies.

The EBA (*c.* 3200–2000 BC) is marked by widespread changes, the majority of which are best attested during EB II (*c.* 2700–2200 BC). Renfrew's *The Emergence of Civilisation: The Cyclades and the Aegean in the Third Millennium BC*, a book central to early Cycladic research, provides the classic summary of changes in society, economy and technology prior to the formation of the first palace-states (Renfrew 1972: 225–475). These include a sharp increase in settlement density in the southern Aegean, the rise of local centres of wealth and power, such as Troy, Lerna, Manika and pre-palatial Knossos, the intensification of inter-regional exchange (in which the Cyclades played a key role), and increased circulation and deposition of metal objects. Renfrew stressed the social impact of the adoption of Mediterranean polyculture at this date (i.e. the addition of the olive and the vine to the Neolithic repertoire), though the extent to which these crops were cultivated before the palaces has been questioned (Hamilakis 1996; Hansen 1988; Runnels and Hansen 1986). An alternative, or complementary, model is that the transformation correlated with a 'secondary products revolution' through the FN–EBA period (Sherratt 1981; also van Andel and Runnels 1988: 242), entailing the adoption of the ox-plough complex, a new exploitation of sheep for wool and the consumption of dairy products, the latter two arguably associated with the growth of pastoralism. The former should have had most impact in the lowland plains and in areas of emerging social hierarchy, whilst the latter two are held to have facilitated expansion into marginal regions. Some knowledge of the ox-plough in the EBA is attested (Pullen 1992), but the question of wool, dairy products and pastoralism is still problematic (Cherry 1988; Halstead 1996b). It therefore remains unclear, in short, precisely what combination of factors most satisfactorily explains the changes evident in the EBA.

But what is now amply evident is that the outcome was not a smooth transition to state-level societies across the entire southern Aegean (Cherry 1984a). For in EB III (c. 2200–2000 BC) the social trajectories of the different parts of the Aegean diverged starkly (Manning 1994). Collapse horizons characterise the southern Greek mainland and north-east Aegean, the southern Aegean islands enter a complicated, obscure period of apparent hiatus, realignment and shifting foci, and only on Crete are the first signs seen of a cluster of social, economic, political and ideological changes that culminated in state formation by the start of the second millennium BC.

The early Aegean and the Cyclades within the wider world

Whatever the Aegean's debt to the Near East in terms of agricultural origins, it is clear that the Neolithic Aegean belonged to a broad, although regionally nuanced, continuum of Neolithic and Chalcolithic societies extending from Anatolia to the southern Balkans. In metallurgical terms, it lies between the main Balkan/Pontic and Near Eastern nuclei of innovation, but overall it is hard to see a strong external dynamic influencing Aegean societies until close to the transition to the EBA. At this point Aegean historiography splits profoundly. Since Childe (1957) portrayed the Aegean as civilised by diffusion from the Orient, two paradigms have been proposed to explain the relationship between the EBA Aegean and the outside world. Renfrew (1972), in explicit reaction to Childe, advocated a model of systemic internal growth that stressed the limited case for links between the pre-palatial Aegean and the Near East, exploring the explanatory potential of internal processes of positive feedback between the several sub-systems of a largely independent Aegean system, notably through his 'subsistence/redistribution' and 'craft specialisation/wealth' models. In contrast, the Sherratts (Sherratt 1993a, 1993b; Sherratt and Sherratt 1991) have eloquently urged a world-systemic explanation, in which large-scale socio-economic transformations were wrought by long-range flows of raw materials, goods, customs and ideologies between *core* areas (massive urban centres of advanced production and consumption that were initially confined to Mesopotamia and Egypt), *peripheries* that supplied raw materials and became structurally altered in the process, and extensive *margins* into which fragments of core and periphery culture tended to escape (often with their meanings scrambled in the process), but which lay beyond range of direct intervention. The 'big history' of the Bronze Age Aegean can be summarised, the Sherratts suggest, in terms of a transition of status from margin (most if not all of the pre-palatial period), via periphery (latest pre-palatial to first palatial – a short and unclear phase), to core (the main palatial age) as this world-system expanded down the axis of the Mediterranean and into temperate Europe. This itself was but the westward aspect of an expansion that moved northward towards central Asia, eastward overland across the Iranian plateau and southward by maritime and riverine corridors into Arabia and Africa beyond the Nile's first cataract.

Without engaging in the debate over the precise application of world-systems analysis in the ancient world (Frank and Gills 1993), the term 'margin' does accurately summarise the position of the EBA Aegean relative to a Near East that, by the second half of the fourth millennium BC, had witnessed the emergence of archaic states in tandem with its urban and secondary products revolutions. Potential connections could develop via the Anatolian land-bridge or the sea-routes along Anatolia's south and north coasts, the southern sea-route connecting the Aegean to the Levant (itself the crossroads of Mesopotamia, Anatolia and Egypt), and the northern route linking the Aegean to the Black Sea interaction sphere (Anthony 1996; Chernykh 1992: 54–97; Price 1993). By roughly 3500 BC, Uruk-period colonists from Mesopotamia had infiltrated the southern part of the central Anatolian plateau (Algaze 1993). Over the next 1500 years this region functioned episodically as a supply zone for the cities of the Mesopotamian alluvium and the so-called 'empire' of Akkad of the later third millennium BC (Marfoe 1987: 28–9). Evidence of substantial social change on the Anatolian plateau is attested throughout the third millennium, and by the end of this period urban centres had sprung up over much its area (Joukowsky 1996: 141–84). Central Anatolia lies midway between Sumer and the Aegean, and it is not hard to envisage how Near Eastern activities and their impact on plateau societies could have sent ripples of ideas, demands for materials, escaped technologies and stray objects down the river valleys and coastlines of western Anatolia as far as the Aegean, there to be adopted, ignored or reworked according to the vicissitudes of local social context (Mellink 1986: 139–41; Nakou 1997). During the third millennium, and especially in EB II, the Aegean evidence comprises small amounts of inflowing exotic objects, metals, social practices and technologies (chapter 9). This pattern was superseded in turn by a new and different dynamic, driven by the direct long-range maritime contacts with the east Mediterranean that were forged by emergent Cretan palatial elites at the very end of the third millennium BC and during the first centuries of the following millennium, and which rapidly led to the Aegean's integration within the expanding Near Eastern world-system.

The weight placed on the data concerning the Aegean's external contacts during the third millennium BC therefore relates closely to the model of change being promoted. Renfrew (1994: 10) dismisses them as 'exotic knick-knacks', while Sherratt and Sherratt (1991: 367–8) see them as the durable tip of a deeper connection involving invisible (because recyclable or perishable) materials, perhaps ultimately grounded in the first trickle of Aegean metals eastward. A position allied to the latter model is to suggest that the scale of transfer was indeed small and the mode indirect, but its impact on the societies of the Aegean 'margin' disproportionately large (e.g. Nakou 1997), a position that this island history will largely endorse. Such interpretative ambiguity resembles that observed in other island worlds on the fringes of emerging continental systems.

Several phases of Melanesian history provide parallels. Whether elements of the Lapita complex can be associated with the expansion of the Island South-East Asian Neolithic is still debatable (Spriggs 1997: 67–107; Terrell and Welsch 1997), but in the late first millennium BC fragments of South-East Asian bronzes at island centres like Lou (Ambrose 1988) match the discovery of eastern cylinder seals at Aegean nodes such as Mochlos and Poliochni. Moreover, a suggestive parallel might be drawn between the intensification during EB II of Aegean island trade networks (analysed in chapters 7–9) and that detected in Melanesian networks some 1000–500 years ago (Allen 1977: 394–5; Spriggs 1997: 152–86), at a time when the South-East Asian and Chinese commercial sphere reached its greatest extent, trading at least as far as western New Guinea for sea-slugs, sandalwood, slaves, birds of paradise and sago (Denoon 1997: 154) – all archaeologically invisible perishables that warn us against too naive an interpretation of the often scanty surviving traces of contact between islands and distant world-systems in other regions of the world. Certain similarities could also be claimed with the pre-Columbian Caribbean. Both the Aegean islands and those in the Caribbean maintained contacts with the continental rim, via which exotic objects and ideas could expand into the islands, but in both cases the islanders can have possessed only the faintest, most refracted knowledge of the huge centres of power that lay beyond the mountains – the distance from the Bahamas to Tenochtitlan being equivalent to that from the Cyclades to Sumer. Frustrating as it is to attempt to establish the extent and significance of contacts through such elusive clues, it is surely wisest to recognise the broader setting of all these island theatres, not only as an antidote to the tendency to analyse islands as isolates in a manner that denies vital dimensions of their history, but also because in each case it is plausible that more distant processes did have an impact on island lives that is not clearly expressed in the durable archaeological remains.

An outline of knowledge and lacunae in the early Cyclades

The previous section has only sketched an outline of the wider context of early Cycladic history, but it is enough to highlight several periods of decisive importance and to allow Cycladic evidence to be situated within the poles of the current debate. What, now, of the archaeological information available? The first investigations in the early Cyclades, much of which focused on investigation of EBA cemeteries, go back to the pioneers of the later nineteenth century, such as Bent (1884), Dümmler (1886), Tsountas (1898, 1899) and the British team that excavated the settlement of Phylakopi with precocious care (Atkinson *et al.* 1904). After a lull in the first half of the twentieth century, a new phase of fieldwork and synthesis developed in the 1960s and 1970s, largely thanks to the work of Caskey (e.g. 1971a, 1972), Doumas (e.g. 1972, 1977), Renfrew (e.g. 1965, 1967, 1969, 1972) and Zapheiropoulou (e.g. 1967,

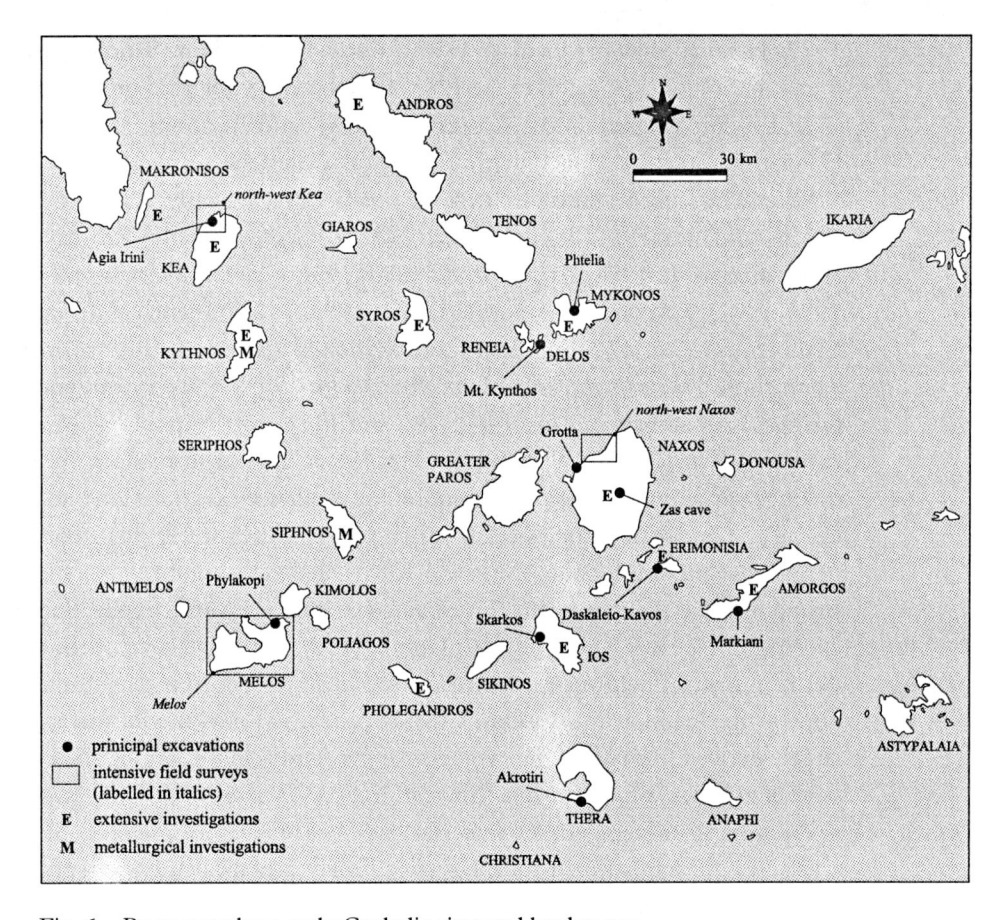

Fig. 6 Recent work on early Cycladic sites and landscapes.

1975). This in turn has triggered a veritable explosion of research over the last quarter of the century (fig. 6), involving excavations, intensive surveys, extensive explorations, plus a wide range of material studies and provenance analyses. Davis' comprehensive survey of recent research in the Aegean islands (1992, 2000) obviates the need for a full recital here. It suffices briefly to highlight the salient elements, not least in order to assess the strengths of current data and identify the enduring lacunae.

Our knowledge of early Cycladic settlement patterns has been improved greatly by intensive field surveys in Melos (Cherry 1982a; Renfrew and Wagstaff 1982b), Kea (Cherry *et al.* 1991) and Naxos (Erard-Cerceau *et al.* 1993), as well as a substantial amount of extensive investigation in Amorgos (Marangou 1984, 1994), Andros (Koutsoukou 1992, 1993), Ios (Marthari 1997: 365, 1999), Kea (Galani *et al.* 1987; Georgiou and Faraklas 1985, 1993; Mendoni *et al.* 1998), Kythnos (Hadjianastasiou 1998), Makronisos (Spitaels 1982a), Mykonos (Sampson 1997), Naxos and the Erimonisia (Barber and Hadjianastasiou 1989; Fotou 1983; Hadjianastasiou 1989, 1993; Zapheiropoulou 1967), Pholegandros (Hadjianastasiou 1996) and Syros (Aron

1979; Hekman 1994; Marthari 1998). Early metal-mining landscapes, including mines and slag heaps dated to the EBA, have been investigated on Siphnos (Wagner *et al.* 1980; Wagner and Weisgerber 1985) and Kythnos (Gale *et al.* 1988; Hadjianastasiou and MacGillivray 1988; Stos-Gale 1998).

Several new excavations also deserve mention, particularly at Phylakopi on Melos (Evans and Renfrew 1984; Renfrew 1982a), Grotta and the Zas cave on Naxos (Hadjianastasiou 1988; Zachos 1990, 1994, 1996b, 1999), Skarkos on Ios (Marthari 1990, 1997), Markiani on Amorgos (Davis 1992: 752–3; French and Whitelaw 1999; Marangou 1994: 470–1), Phtelia on Mykonos (Sampson 1997; Tsakos 1992), Akrotiri on Thera (Sotirakopoulou 1986, 1990, 1993, 1996, 1999), and cemeteries on Naxos (Lambrinoudakis 1990: 26) and the nearby Kouphonisi islands in the Erimonisia cluster (Zapheiropoulou 1983, 1984). The excavations at the Zas cave are unique in providing a long-term stratigraphic sequence (Zachos 1999) and substantial faunal and botanical samples (Halstead in prep. for the former) that span most of the period covered in this book. Daskaleio-Kavos on Keros, another small member of the Erimonisia, has recently been reinvestigated by intensive surface collection and limited excavation (*Annual Report* 1986–7; Doumas *et al.* nd; Whitelaw nd). In tandem with this new wave of fieldwork, another significant step forward is the imminent publication of the Ashmolean Museum's major collection of Cycladic material, which is largely derived from early archaeological explorations in the islands and contains substantial numbers of key objects (Sherratt in press).

Progress in the analysis of material has been equally impressive. Studies of the Cycladic lithic industries include Torrence's analysis of the acquisition, production and distribution of Melian obsidian (Torrence 1982, 1984, 1986), the EBA picture now being expanded and reinterpreted by Carter (1994, 1998, 1999), the first typologies of island lithics (Cherry and Torrence 1984; Torrence 1979, 1991), and several marble characterisation programmes of an, unfortunately, as yet inconclusive nature (Herz and Doumas 1991; Manti 1993). No less important is the major programme of lead isotope analysis of Cycladic metal ores and EBA objects (Gale and Stos-Gale 1981; Stos-Gale 1989, 1993, 1998; Stos-Gale and Macdonald 1991), building on the foundations laid by Renfrew (1967) and Branigan (1974). Although this programme's methods and results are not without their critics (Budd *et al.* 1995; Knapp and Cherry 1994; Pernicka 1995), there is no doubt that, in conjunction with the information from investigation of mining and processing sites, the outlines of metal exploitation and supply are clearer than they have ever been. Detailed studies of pottery assemblages have been undertaken for the settlements of Mt Kynthos on Delos (MacGillivray 1980), Agia Irini on Kea (Wilson 1987, 1999; Wilson and Eliot 1984), Phylakopi on Melos (Evans and Renfrew 1984), Akrotiri on Thera (Sotirakopoulou 1986, 1990, 1993, 1996) and Daskaleio-Kavos on Keros (Broodbank 2000). Petrographic analysis of pottery fabrics is also underway (Vaughan 1989, 1990; Vaughan and Wilson 1993). Lastly and, as will soon become evident, controversially in certain instances, the recent aesthetic appreciation of EBA Cycladic marble figurines has generated a burgeoning literature on these objects (Doumas 1983a; Fitton 1984; Getz-Preziosi 1987a, 1987b; Renfrew 1991; Thimme 1977), augmented by the first substantial study of the islands' stone vessels (Getz-Gentle [formerly Getz-Preziosi] 1996).

This is the positive picture. On the negative side must be admitted an ignorance of the contextual associations of much of the tomb material, despite the invaluable work of Doumas (1977) and Papathanasopoulos (1961/2) in this respect, the virtually complete absence of any physical anthropology, a generally poor grasp of subsistence practices and gender roles, and in effect no archaeology of the household (although excellent preservation at the newly excavated site of Skarkos promises an imminent start). Last but not least is the difficulty in interpreting patterns that is created by the still extremely uneven amount of research undertaken in different parts of the Cyclades.

This last problem needs to be faced squarely, as it profoundly affects efforts to establish the reality, or otherwise, of patterns observed in the known data. As Cherry (1979: 23) once put it, 'the real stumbling block seems to be not so much a lack of data as our inability to assess the reliability of the data that we *do* have'. Nor is it simply a matter of contextualising the data that are known, for the interpretation of lacunae is no less critical. It is important to have some idea as to whether apparent gaps echo actual features of ancient distributions, or merely reflect where archaeologists have yet to look properly. Moreover, if our interpretations are to be more than play-things dancing to the rhythm of each discovery as the flow of information increases, it is vital to have some means for assessing the importance of data as they appear, and identifying their place in wider distributions of material and activities. A vast quantity of objects and information has emerged from sources that range from modern fieldwork, through excavations by the first pioneers, to purchase or other testimony by early travellers, chance finds and (increasingly) looting. Some archaeological projects look specifically for early remains; others encounter them as basal deposits at sites chosen for their later importance; many items surface on the art market with no better provenance than what Chippindale christens the catch-all island of 'Sounds-possible-os' (1993: 702). Specific and subtle factors may also be at play; for example objects looted from Daskaleio-Kavos on Keros are now said to be spirited out through Naxos but, as Getz-Preziosi (1987a: 133) points out, finds made in the nineteenth century may have been removed to Amorgos, as Keros at that time belonged to an Amorgian monastery, thereby creating a false provenance for such objects by the time they appeared in front of the scholarly world. Certainly, the number of early finds said to come from Amorgos is suspiciously high (Sherratt in press). In this situation it is far from immediately apparent which patterns should be taken seriously, which treated with caution and which dismissed as figments of uneven exploration.

A useful means for assessing the reality or otherwise of gaps in the distribution is to estimate an approximate index of exploration for each island, based on the amount of

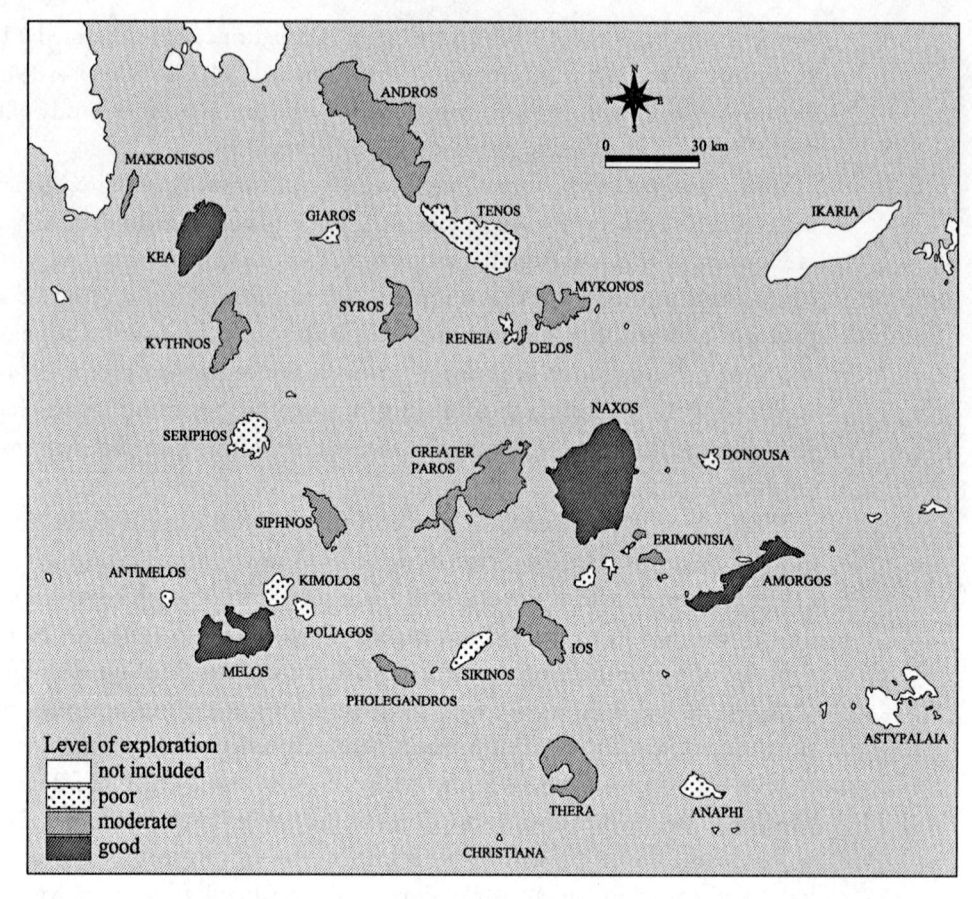

Fig. 7 An exploration index for the early Cyclades. The criteria for inclusion in the first category are the excavation of a multi-period settlement and/or a large amount of field survey, usually of the intensive type. The second category comprises islands with a one-period excavated settlement and/or a lower but substantial level of field survey. Islands that have had little or no formal exploration, or from where rumoured finds are unsubstantiated, are categorised as Poor.

fieldwork relating to the early periods. Fig. 7 categorises islands as Good, Moderate or Poor. There is no suggestion that islands in the first category are devoid of future surprises, and there is a degree of fuzziness to the categories (for example on the large island of Andros the north-west has been well investigated but the rest of the island is much less known; and on Thera the smothering of the earlier land surface by a mid-second-millennium BC volcanic eruption produces special conditions that restrict most of our knowledge to the Akrotiri excavations). Yet this approach does allow distinctions to be identified. Out of the fourteen major islands, which comprise almost 90 per cent of the surface area of the Cyclades, four qualify as Good, eight as Moderate and only two as Poor. The smaller islands are less well explored, with six in the Moderate category and the remainder poorly known. To look on the positive side, an effective working sample of roughly half the islands will allow inferences to be made about a substantial number of the Cyclades and permit some cautious extrapolations to islands that have been little investigated. Equally encouraging is the fact that the islands in the Good and Moderate categories include a range of sizes and are widely distributed. On the less positive side, in terms of island-counts comparatively little is known about roughly half the Cyclades. The worst blind-spots comprise Tenos, Seriphos and many of the smaller islands.

Early Cycladic chronology and terminology

A similar consideration of strengths and weak points in early Cycladic chronology (cf. fig. 1) is necessary and also revealing. Renfrew's work (1965, 1972), together with Doumas' ordering of the cemeteries (Doumas 1977), first clarified the culture sequence. Although some amendments to their system have been made, and differences of several centuries separate the long and short EBA absolute chronologies (Manning 1995: fig. 2; Warren and Hankey 1989: 121–7), their framework remains robust and forms the basis for the system used today. Renfrew identified five 'cultures', defined in Childe's terms by regularly observed assemblages, and named after type sites that might be settlements or, especially in the EBA, cemeteries (Renfrew 1972: 66, 75–6, 135–95; also Evans and Renfrew 1968). The earliest of these, the *Saliagos* culture, correlates with the LN. The later *Kephala* culture falls within the early FN. The *Grotta-Pelos* culture is something of a misnomer (although an enshrined one) best used as a convenient shorthand for two sub-phases that cover the later FN and the entire EB I, thus emphasising the gradual nature of the shift from Neolithic to EBA in the Cyclades. The *Keros-Syros* culture equates with EB II. The *Phylakopi I* culture is of primarily MBA date (Rutter 1983), but elements of it are probably to be anticipated in EB III. Renfrew and others (Bossert 1960; Doumas 1976a, 1977; Zapheiropoulou 1984) also identified more confined 'groups', those not subsumed in the wider cultures being *Plastiras, Kampos, Kastri, Amorgos* and *Christiana*. Controversy continues over the chronological details of this schema (MacGillivray and Barber 1984; Manning 1995). Rather than rehearse these in the abstract, however, a more constructive approach is to investigate them as contextualised problems in the course of our exploration. For if the social significance and distribution of the material being disputed is taken into account, it is often possible to reconfigure a controversy in a manner conducive to its resolution.

If this island archaeology of the Cyclades is to address and explain the texture of material culture to any serious degree, it will be important to understand what such clusterings of the data can tell us, and what they should not be manipulated into saying. Renfrew's intention was to affirm a distinction between assemblage-orientated constructs (i.e. the cultures and groups) and the system in use for chronology (LN, FN, EB I–III). Despite criticism from traditional archaeologists who prefer an Early

Cycladic (EC) I–III nomenclature for the EBA (Barber 1987; Coleman 1979a, 1979b, 1992: 266; Renfrew 1979 for a response) this strategy is still the most appropriate practical way of dealing with the data clusterings detected. Arguments that these cultures are redundant because early Cycladic culture was 'demonstrably a unity' (Barber 1987: 25) are far from valid. It will become apparent in the course of this book that although the Cyclades can be treated as a fairly defensible, if fuzzy, geographical group for purposes of analysis, their culture demonstrably was *not* a unity. The culture names are accordingly used in the argument when a particular type of assemblage is being referred to. Otherwise the Aegean time periods form the framework of reference (i.e. LN, FN, EB I–III material).

However, it has to be acknowledged that several of the cultures and groups are problematic in other respects. One trouble stems from their tendency to become reified into absolute entities laden with overly specific spatial and chronological associations, instead of remaining pragmatic, flexible, first-order organisations of the data, as their creators intended. Equally, it is all too easy to forget to ask what sort of activities lay behind the clusters in the data, and how these might explain the degree and character of any coherence that is observed. Such questions will in fact produce diverse answers in different cases. In the interests of clarification, some of these answers are outlined here.

In chapters 4 and 5 it is suggested that the Saliagos, Kephala and Grotta-Pelos cultures are roughly descriptions of the material cultures of early settlement in different parts of the islands. Inter-dependence of the first low-density networks of settlements over limited areas probably explains why these constructs have maintained an archaeological coherence within a specific area of distribution. The EB II Keros-Syros culture, as defined by Renfrew, is a more diffuse and intriguing entity. It is the only culture with an approximately pan-Cycladic distribution, yet unlike the above three, it comprises not only common forms like so-called 'sauceboats' and pedestal-based collared jars, but also rare, prestigious, symbolically charged objects of wider Aegean distribution, such as the (again so-called) 'frying pans', painted or stamped pots, metal weapons and jewellery, and folded-arm figurines, that do not reflect the overall material in settlements, nor indeed necessarily in cemeteries. It is hard to attribute many small EB II sites to a Keros-Syros culture thus defined without appending qualifications listing the elements that they lack. Moreover, the Keros-Syros culture was defined in the first instance from what will emerge as two of the most remarkable sites in the Cyclades: Chalandriani-Kastri on Syros and Daskaleio-Kavos on Keros, in other words from what can now be recognised as exceptions rather than norms. Rather than a culture *sensu* Childe, the Keros-Syros culture reflects a nexus of trade items, prestige symbols and social practices, used as a common currency for diverse communities, analogous to the Beaker phenomenon of prehistoric western Europe or, in Terrell's view, the no less perplexing Lapita complex (Terrell 1989). 'Keros-Syros' as a cultural term is therefore employed sparingly to refer to a prestige culture that settlements took part in to varying degrees; otherwise sites are referred to simply as 'EB II'. Although it is starting to be possible to identify EB II regional style zones, it would be unwise to propose new groupings at this juncture, before publication of the full assemblages from sufficient sites. A discussion of the significance of the Phylakopi I culture, a late development in terms of this book's time-frame, can be deferred until chapter 10.

Lastly, the original 'groups' also reflect different, and in some cases scrambled, phenomena. Renfrew (1984a: 50–3) himself argues that the Kampos group contains elements of disparate significance, one a typological change in pottery forms, the other associated with status claims; a trading or even ethnic dimension could be added, given the material's links to Crete and the east Aegean (Day *et al.* 1998; Warren 1984: 58–60; Zapheiropoulou 1984; see chapter 9). As the Plastiras group comprises marble forms contextually disassociated from pottery (Renfrew 1984a: 44), prestige displays may again be suspected. The Kastri assemblage is largely about new ways of drinking, and cannot be discussed in the same breath as the very indistinct range of closed shapes comprising the Amorgos group (*contra* Renfrew 1972: 535). What additional light can be shed on the social meanings lying behind these groups will be seen in later chapters.

Sense and sensibility in Cycladic archaeology

Within what frameworks of explanation have scholars approached the early Cyclades? The rest of this chapter explores three principal types that between them cover the main archaeological traditions in early Cycladic studies. With apologies to Jane Austen, the first two can be called *sense* and *sensibility*. The third (discussed in the final section) is island archaeology. The first includes the most influential archaeological interpretations that have been expounded to date. The second ventures into realms that, though at first glance barely archaeological, raise ethical matters that are becoming far too pressing for archaeologists to ignore. The third comprises the immediate antecedents of this book.

Sense

We start with sense. But what is meant by it? Several answers are relevant in the present context. For example, 'making sense' embraces the programme of empirical work undertaken to define material and order it chronologically and relative to the rest of the Aegean. But another usage is equally apt. This is 'common sense', which itself bifurcates into two strands. One is the assumption that the sense to be made of the early Cyclades is one common to that of other areas, both adjacent and further afield. The other employs the term in its idiomatic usage, namely the assumption that it is possible to grasp how things once were in the early Cyclades by recourse to experiences and modes of explanation that appear common-sensical to us. These usages between them encompass the approaches adopted by the two major works of synthesis that we need to address: Renfrew's *The Emergence of Civilisation: The Cyclades and the Aegean in the Third Millennium BC* (1972) and Barber's *The Cyclades in the Bronze Age* (1987).

The Emergence, although now dated in many respects, remains one of the most stimulating explorations of social change in the early Aegean. Renfrew's *explanandum* was the rise of 'Minoan–Mycenaean civilisation', and in pursuit of this the net he cast was an explicitly pan-Aegean one. Evidence for each change was drawn from different parts of the Aegean, the implication being that data deriving from each area were more important as illustrations of pan-Aegean themes than as a means of delineating intra-Aegean differences within the EBA. This is not the place to debate Renfrew's case in depth (cf. above; also van Andel and Runnels 1988), although we should note Cherry's (1983, 1984a) point that palatial institutions were initially limited to Crete, leaving other areas of the Aegean (including the Cyclades) as effectively 'null cases'.

More immediately relevant is the impact of Renfrew's aims and methods on his interpretation of the Cyclades, for as palatial society did not emerge in these islands, his pursuit of the pan-Aegean level of explanation inevitably lessens the resolution on what was actually going on in the Cyclades themselves. Certainly *The Emergence* made great strides in defining the culture sequence and detected important features of the Cycladic archaeological record, such as the modest number of Neolithic relative to EBA sites, the limited size of most settlements, the impact of metals in the EBA, the distribution of the prestige artefacts in the cemeteries, the symbolic investments attested by cemeteries and figurines, and the central position of the Cyclades in wider Aegean trade. Yet what is peculiarly missing is any sense that the Cyclades are *islands* as opposed to merely one more region of the Aegean, and that as such they should prompt interesting questions *distinct* from those asked of other areas. In his discussion of assemblages, for example, there is little consideration of how the Cyclades were colonised, and what impact this had on their material culture; of why regional groups and rich burials appear in certain places, and what position these occupied in the pattern of islands; or of how the sea and land might shape societies differently from the mainland and equally Crete. The pursuit of generalisation obscures that which is specifically insular, and in the final assessment the entire Aegean is presented as simply one instance of the rise of complex societies as a universal phenomenon (Renfrew 1972: 500–2). Therefore *The Emergence,* though a landmark in so many ways, is simultaneously much more, and decidedly less, than a truly satisfactory study of what lies behind the archaeology of the Cycladic islands.

Barber's *The Cyclades in the Bronze Age* (1987) is a very different book, but it too does not provide a satisfying account of early Cycladic history. Its time-range takes in the entire Bronze Age, with a short treatment of the Neolithic. Discussion of the EBA amounts to a descriptive survey of material culture from a typological and chronological viewpoint, plus a brief summary couched in the language of progress, which concludes that the islands led 'a charmed course' through the EBA (1987: 140). The problem is that this fails to get underneath the artefactual surface of the past to discover what might actually have been going on. Moreover, the opinions on island life that are offered are informed by a contemporary and potentially misleading conception of common sense.

Three examples can serve to illustrate this. First, Barber argues that the timeless environment of the Cyclades until mechanisation has preserved ancient ways of life, and that traditional island agriculture has changed relatively little since antiquity (1987: 18–19). Halstead (1987a) provides a trenchant criticism of assumptions of continuity between traditional and ancient practices, assumptions that seem particularly fragile in the present context, given that the extent and significance of olive and vine cultivation before the second millennium BC remain unresolved (e.g. Runnels and Hansen 1986), and that donkeys (for transport) have yet to be positively identified in the Cyclades before the LBA (Gamble 1979: table 1). At a more fundamental level, this approach fails to account for the profound differences that exist between the settlement patterns of the fifth to third millennia BC and those of the earlier part of the twentieth century AD. If so little had changed, why are early Cycladic sites so often located in now-deserted islandscapes?

A second example concerns the exploitation of Melian obsidian. Here, Barber criticises Torrence's conclusion that obsidian was *not* controlled and marketed by the nearby centre of Phylakopi, as the first excavators had assumed (Bosanquet 1904), but was instead open to access by all comers (Torrence 1982: 220–1, 1984: 61–2, 1986: 169). His concern is that Torrence's criteria for recognising control (e.g. workshops, extraction tools, guard-houses and perimeter walls) are unrealistic and project 'the expectations of the modern mind onto an ancient situation' (Barber 1987: 118). His doubts about Torrence's criteria are not unreasonable, but the charge of inappropriate modernity cuts both ways. For regardless as to whether her points ultimately convince us, Torrence's painstaking analysis led her to a conclusion that was radically different from her starting assumptions, and undeniably alien to modern, monopoly-orientated, mind-sets. Torrence may, if she is right, have touched on something of the otherness of ancient behaviour, but Barber, by insisting that control of the obsidian sources was of obvious advantage to Phylakopi, has failed to escape a modernist commercial mind-set himself.

Our third example is revealing in terms of maritime culture. Barber (1987: 18) comments that 'seamanship is endemic to island life'. This contrasts interestingly with a statement by another Cycladic scholar, coincidentally also published in the same year:

> Although they had boats that were well suited for travelling the Aegean water-ways, it is likely that most of the islanders were, as they are now, more at home on land than on water. In the Cyclades, although one is almost always aware of the presence of the surrounding sea, the landscape is one of hills and highlands, and with the exception of the fishermen, merchants and middlemen who hug the perimeters of the islands and maintain outside contacts, Cycladic people have essentially always been uplanders in spirit, with neither great fondness for nor familiarity with the sea about them. (Getz-Preziosi 1987a: 5)

Both are plausible statements, both make good common sense, both are bound to have been right in certain places and at certain times, but both assuredly cannot be right for the same people, in the same place and at the same time. This variance in time and place matters crucially, as will be emphasised repeatedly in future chapters, and it is for precisely this reason that a searching 'archaeology of the sea' is so necessary.

In conclusion, common sense (in either form) does not get us very far. It is, as Geertz (1975) once put it, a cultural system. Whilst Renfrew generalises outwards from the islands' archaeological record, Barber generalises about the islanders themselves. It is ironic that both these leading Cycladic scholars have adopted approaches that in effect confirm the Cycladic islanders in the category of people without history. The thrust of this book is not, of course, that Cycladic archaeology is 'non-sense', but that it reflects particular forms of insular sense to which archaeologists must be attentive. But before turning to this path, what about sense's more familiar opposite? What of sensibility?

Sensibility

The irruption of sensibility into early Cycladic archaeology is a recent phenomenon that began with modern aesthetic appreciation of a select element of material culture, namely the marble figurines produced by the islanders in the EBA. The story is well known of the 'discovery' of these figurines, along with African, American and Oceanic culture, by twentieth-century Modernists such as Picasso, Brancusi, Moore and Modigliani. Also well documented is the consequent transformation of these figurines' status from crude curiosities into prized works of art worth enormous sums. These developments have been the subject of a recent investigation by Gill and Chippindale (1993), who trace the intellectual and archaeological implications of current esteem for Cycladica to their at best dubious, and at worst disastrous, conclusions. Three consequences of this esteem invite exploration. The first concerns the archaeological record, the second, Cycladica's role in contemporary culture, and the third, the formation of an alternative agenda for the archaeology of the early Cyclades in some recent scholarly circles.

The most catastrophic impact of esteem for the figurines has been the wholesale looting of Cycladic sites since the 1950s, including countless cemeteries and a particularly large deposit of prestige goods at Daskaleio-Kavos (fig. 8). Gill and Chippindale may exaggerate when they claim that Cycladic archaeology is on the way to becoming an impossible field, as the figurine-poor settlements remain relatively untouched, but it is beyond dispute that the looting of the cemeteries has led to irreparable losses of cultural and skeletal material, and concomitant lost opportunities for the archaeology of Cycladic death-rituals. Some 90 per cent of all figurines now known are without secure context, rendering typologies (e.g. Renfrew 1969) of necessity provisional beyond allocation of basic types to broad time bands, and any analysis of regional

Cycladic approaches

Fig. 8 The price of esteem: Daskaleio-Kavos looted. Courtesy of Todd Whitelaw.

variations problematic (Broodbank 1992). Because marble-working cannot be dated with any confidence, another inevitable result has been the infiltration of the corpus by an unknown number of fakes. Moreover, the figurines' fate threatens to encompass other Cycladic material. In a sense this happens anyway, as robbing a cemetery wrecks the entire assemblage. But, in addition, a worrying parallel can be drawn between the recent recognition of a heterogeneous range of early Cycladic artefacts as art, including marble vessels (Getz-Gentle 1996) and even obsidian blades (Renfrew 1991: 55), and Steiner's shrewd observation (1994: 110–21) about the West African art market, in which he documents the incremental inclusion of more everyday objects like slingshots in the saleable definition of art objects, as the supply of masks and figures, the initial stimulus to Western identification of the local material culture as art, dries up. Motivations may differ, but the implications of archaeological writing on Cycladic material of unknown provenance have rightly become the focus of critical debate (Renfrew 1991: 21–4; cf. Broodbank 1992; Cherry 1992a: 140–4; Elia 1993; Renfrew 1993a). It is striking how slowly an awareness of the problematic nature of such links between scholarship and the art world has emerged. For example, the first major exhibition catalogue of Cycladic art (Thimme 1977) opened with a sequence of scholarly essays and concluded with the advertisements of antiquities dealers, the two discretely quarantined by the images of the (thereby contested?) objects themselves.

It is equally striking to explore the modern cultural ramifications of this fashion for deracinated pieces of 'primitive art in civilised places' (Price 1989). One frequent assertion is that Cycladic figurines occupy a central place in the ancestries of later Greek and Western art (Renfrew 1991: 168–87; Walsh 1993). Sporadic cases of the curation of figurines rediscovered in antiquity are intriguing, with examples from later Bronze Age Cycladic sites (Davis 1984a; Sotirakopoulou 1998: 157–65) and Classical Greece (Getz-Preziosi 1987a: ix), as well as the EBA marble vessels, or kandiles, hung in Greek churches from the Middle Ages onwards (Getz-Gentle 1996: 5). Yet although Cycladica never quite vanished, there is nothing to indicate their formative role in Greek Archaic and Classical figural art, let alone all that followed. Notwithstanding this, the wish to identify and name Cycladic artists (Getz-Preziosi 1987a), apart from enhancing the value of their alleged creations, surely reflects a desire to associate Cycladica with the birth of the European ideal of the artist as an individual genius. Again, the contrast with Western expectations of African art is informative, for in Africa, as Steiner (1994: 104) shows, what the West desires is the anonymous pulse of a primal creator; objects whose makers are known by name are deemed inauthentic. Additional ramifications include the manner in which the possession of figurines constitutes cultural capital, and acts as a signifier of elite social and aesthetic status. This has led to the construction of pedigrees of modern ownership (Gill and Chippindale 1993: 650–1), further indication of the extent to which figurines' social biographies have been subject to drastic 'path deviation' (Appadurai 1986: 16–29; Kopytoff 1986). As might be expected, in response to Cycladica's establishment as a symbol of aesthetic discernment and social status, an inverse consumer-driven process is becoming increasingly apparent: the descent of Cycladica through commodification and the adoption of figurines as pop-icons (fig. 9). From the originals, through tasteful replicas, to tourist junk and even soap bars, Cycladica are spiralling rapidly down-market into kitsch.

We can identify several ways in which the rise of 'sensibility' presents in effect an alternative, influential and, in certain respects, profoundly disturbing programme for Cycladic studies. This is most obvious in the programme of scholarship focused on the figurines, and in particular the work of Getz-Preziosi (1977, 1987a, 1987b) on the identification of carvers, or 'masters', and the systems of proportionality within which they purportedly worked. The aim of identifying individual carvers is not intrinsically unreasonable as part of the search for the individual in prehistory (Hill and Gunn 1977), and it is likely that objects by the same hand do indeed exist in the known corpus. Their identification and provenance *if feasible* could tell us much about how these otherwise rather mute objects were produced and used. But as Cherry (1992a: 142–4) and Morris (1993: 41–7) have stressed, the paucity of detail on the Cycladic figurines makes them particularly inappropriate objects for the application of Morellian method, and it is not surprising that to date there remain no agreed criteria for the identification of individuals (Renfrew 1991: 110–16). Similar problems attend certain formal analyses of figurines, where the identification of canons of proportion has been criticised on methodological grounds (fig. 10) (Gill and Chippindale 1993: 641–7; Cherry 1992a: 140–4). The pursuit of such issues has, ironically, won more attention than a modest yet revealing practical replication of the

Cycladic approaches 61

Fig. 9 The descent of Cycladica: (a) marble folded-arm figurine, (b) Goulandris Museum of Cycladic Art in Athens, (c) accurate replica for the mantelpiece, (d) cheaper derivatives for sale in a tourist boutique in Plaka, Athens, (e) Cycladic soap available on Naxos.
(a) courtesy of the British Museum.

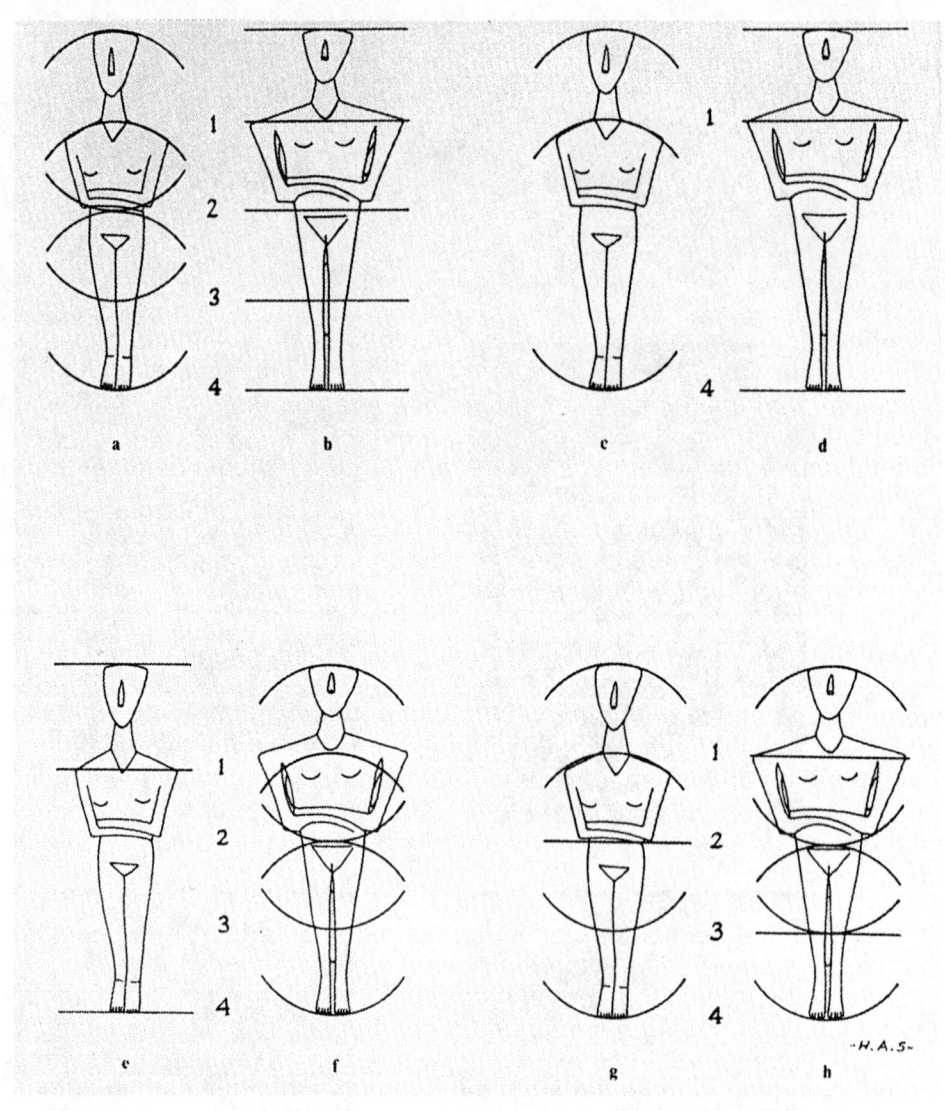

Fig. 10 A critique of proportionality in early Cycladic figurines as offered by Gill and Chippindale (1993). (a) and (b) illustrate Getz-Preziosi's contention that a four-part division determines the layout of two figurines, defined by equally spaced compass-drawn curved or straight lines. (c) and (d) retain only those lines that demonstrably, precisely correspond to specific anatomical features (in both cases shoulders), thereby weakening the case for an overall canon of proportion. (e) and (f) swap the figurines; to retain the correspondence with the shoulder in (e) the line has to be lowered, violating the canon, and in (f) the curved lines miss most of the significant bodily divisions. (g) and (h) explore the flexible option of allowing both straight and curved lines in a single figurine, but still the correspondences with prominent features on the figurines are not compelling. Drawing by Arthur Shelley for Gill and Chippindale 1993: fig. 1, reproduced courtesy of the authors.

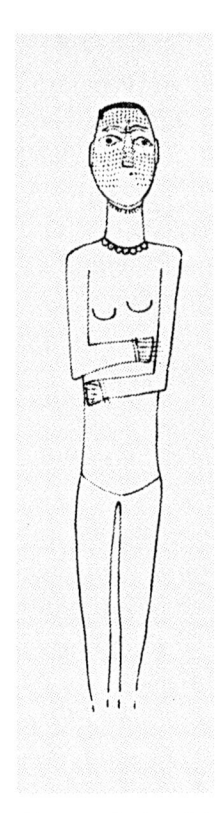

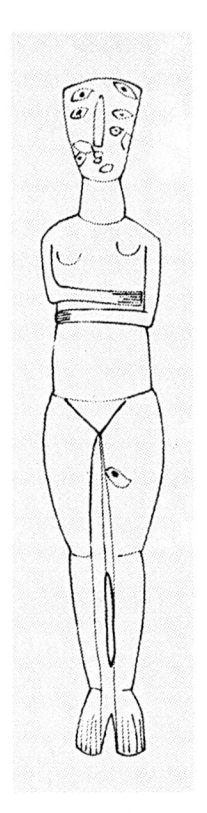

Fig. 11 Painted decoration on Cycladic marble figurines (not to scale). *Left:* as evident from visible traces. *Right:* as revealed by ultraviolet reflectography and computer enhancement. After Getz-Preziosi 1987a: fig. 29 and Hendrix 1998: fig. 16 respectively.

pragmatic realities of production, which demonstrated that only a moderate amount of skill and time was required to fashion at least the simpler kinds of Cycladic figurine (Oustinoff 1984). It would be foolish to deny the possibility, even the likelihood, that the marble figurines, along with other objects in marble, metal and pottery, were regarded during the EBA as finely crafted, symbolically charged and perhaps sensuous objects, but it must be doubted whether modern connoisseurship and geometry provide us with a plausible means to access such ancient experiences.

It can also be argued that the Modernists' exaltation of the figurines' perceived purity of form focuses on the wrong features of these objects when it comes to trying to decode their significance. For most Cycladic figurines have suffered a double loss of information, of which destruction of context is only the first. Despite the Modernists' fascination with the clean contours of white marble, their appreciation of these figurines reflected a chance collision of taphonomic process and taste, for the Cycladic figurines were originally decorated with red and blue designs painted in cinnabar and azurite. The residues of decoration have often been scrubbed off in recent times, either accidentally or in the unfortunate pursuit of purity. But as fig. 11 shows, the traces that do remain indicate bodily tattoos, hair, facial details and jewellery, and the most detailed study, which employed ultraviolet reflectography and computer enhancement techniques, has produced truly extraordinary results, including one figurine with multiple 'eyes' painted over the face and thigh (Hendrix 1998). One can speculate about appreciation during the EBA of the gleaming qualities of marble, but what seems certain, given the hints of diversity in decoration that survive as traces or ghosts, is that decoration encoded more of the meanings that once imbued these objects than did the blank outlines that survive. Obsession with the whiteness of these figurines also makes us forget that the women or men who carved them, and whose small skeletons we find hunched up in their tombs, were surely burnt a deep brown in skin colour by life-long work in the sunlight and salty air; and that forgetting is perhaps pregnant with many of the misconceptions that surround the status of Cycladica today. When we do recall this discrepancy, and try to conjure up an image of the early islanders behind the artefacts by reconstructing the tattooed faces of the figurines, the marble forms start to become more alive as people, but as people deeply distanced from ourselves.

One could argue that the emergence of this parallel, aesthetically driven branch in Cycladic studies, partly abstracted of necessity from the archaeology of the islands and centred on a cult of the marble figurine, is simply a harmless, albeit to many minds unconvincing, foible, despite the negative feedback loops leading from appreciation to desire, and onward to valuation, demand and finally looting. Yet the pervasiveness of sensibility as an explanatory paradigm should not be underestimated. First, there is the danger that early Cycladic culture will become at least in part formulated by the modern museum and collection, conforming to Modernist aesthetics and to a nostalgic Western stereotype of insular purity that has little to do with the archaeology of the real islands out there in the Aegean. Bourdieu's phrasing could hardly be more apposite when he identifies the 'world of art . . . a sacred island systematically and ostentatiously opposed to the profane, everyday world of production' (1977: 179). Second, figurines dominate much of Cycladic scholarship, as well as popular perceptions, where they are the 'chief icon, and indeed the logo' of the islands' early cultures (Getz-Gentle 1996: xix–xx), and this can all too easily lead the rugged, splintered Cycladic archipelago to be transfigured into a cradle of art. Chapter 7 will demonstrate how most interpretations of Daskaleio-Kavos, a crucial site for the early history of the Cyclades, have been dominated by efforts to explain its unusually numerous figurine finds, to the virtual exclusion of alternative approaches. Third, assertions of a unifying creative spirit in the early Cyclades (Renfrew 1991) distract from the reality of cultural diversity that will be repeatedly encountered in the course of the coming chapters.

To summarise, of course the figurines matter, as does every element of island material culture, and something can be gleaned about their roles from those with known contexts, and some of the formal characteristics of certain others. But this can only happen if they are seen as objects of their time, not ours, and if the idea of civilisation is prevented from distracting us from the prosaic realities of early life in the Cyclades. We asserted earlier that whatever did happen in these islands during the EBA, it was not an 'emergence of civilisation' in the sense that this can be used for the rise of Knossos or Mycenae. Now we have seen how Modernist aesthetics seek to foist the concept of 'art-as-civilisation' upon them. Sensibility is, in fact, just as deceptive a path into the early history of the Cyclades as are the varied formulations of sense.

The first generation of island archaeology in the Cyclades

Let us now turn away from sense and sensibility, and towards island archaeology as an investigative and explanatory framework. Davis and Cherry's introduction to their edited volume of *Papers in Cycladic Prehistory* (1979) demonstrated the first awareness of this framework's potential in a Cycladic context. Drawing upon the ideas of Braudel, the early island biogeographers, and island archaeologists working elsewhere, Davis and Cherry identified many of the issues that remain central to this day. How coherent and homogeneous are, and were, the Cyclades as a natural and cultural unit? What range of relations did these islands have with surrounding regions? In what ways did the rigours of the environment shape the lives of their inhabitants? Davis and Cherry also argued for the particular virtues of the Cyclades as a cluster of fairly small islands, close enough, one to the other, to provide good conditions for analysis of interaction, and yet diverse enough to prompt comparisons. Despite this, only a few papers in the volume took up the challenge. One (Cherry 1979) dealt with visitation, colonisation and demography, and two explored spatial patterns of second-millennium BC trade (Davis 1979) and animal exploitation (Gamble 1979) in the context of Minoan influence. Davis looked at the effect of geographical configuration on the formation of island culture, and the so-called 'western string' of islands (Thera, Melos and Kea), that he argued was preferentially connected to trans-Cycladic maritime routes, has the distinction of being the first spatial model developed for the Cyclades. Subsequent island archaeology in the Cyclades has explored three avenues, and has remained associated with a small handful of scholars.

The first avenue elaborates the post-EBA spatial approaches initiated by Davis in 1979 (e.g. Davis 1980, 1982a, 1984b; Davis and Cherry 1990; Schofield 1982). One of the most stimulating examples is Davis' diachronic analysis of the location of Delos (1982a). In addition to using cross-cultural analogies (for instance with Cozumel, the sacred sea-trader island of the Maya), this paper was innovative on several accounts. It employed graph-theoretical techniques to substantiate the hypothesis that Delos' central location relative to the cities of the Ionian Amphyctyony explains its prominence during the Archaic period. In doing so it established that Delos' centrality was contingent on a specific wider pattern of political and cultural alignments in the southern Aegean, and that centrality within the Cyclades had, in this case, to be understood in a partially *non*-insular context. It invited comparison with other periods, such as the early LBA, when Cretan-orientated networks encouraged a different pattern and Delos' importance was much reduced, or the subsequent Mycenaean period, when a zone of culturally similar settlements extended from southern Greece through the islands to the western coast of Anatolia, at which juncture finds on Delos clearly indicate another flourishing period. Davis' strategy foreshadows in many respects several approaches adopted in this book.

A second avenue of island archaeological thought has followed up the issue of island colonisation. Cherry's studies of the 'pattern and process' in island colonisation throughout the Mediterranean have opened an entire field for investigation (Cherry 1981, 1984b, 1985, 1987, 1990). Chapter 4 looks at Cherry's analysis in more detail; for the present, the point to stress is that the results for the Cyclades reflect a trade-off, gaining from the broader pan-Mediterranean perspective in terms of comparative analysis, but losing in terms of a satisfactory level of resolution regarding island-to-island sequences in the Cyclades themselves (Bellard 1995 reaches a similar conclusion concerning the smaller members of the Balearics). This is more than a matter of mere nit-picking detail, as the Cyclades' configuration makes them one of the most complex and interesting theatres for island colonisation in the Mediterranean, and understanding the manner in which they were settled is critical for any convincing interpretation of their early material culture. In tandem with analyses of colonisation, Cherry's work also touched on other issues in island life, notably the subsistence strategies chosen by settlers in the face of an inimical environment, and the role of maritime trade and exchange in enabling settlement to take off (1985: 28, 1987: 25–6). These ideas, similarly, indicate promising directions to which we will return.

The third avenue is represented by two interdisciplinary field projects on Melos (Cherry 1982a; Renfrew and Wagstaff 1982b) and Kea (Cherry *et al.* 1991). Their aim was to explore the association over time between settlement patterns, political structures and external relations. Both mark major advances in the theory and practice of regional analysis. Yet although they focused on two Cycladic islands, they tell us relatively little about how the Cyclades operated as an island cluster. One reason for this, encouraged by the practical constraints of fieldwork, is that both advocated the paradigm of islands as bounded, naturally defined areas for investigation – in short, islands as laboratories (Renfrew and Wagstaff 1982a: 2; Cherry 1982a: 13; Cherry *et al.* 1991: 9–10). As was argued in chapter 1, this is more a statement of faith than a reflection of the realities of islandscapes and social geography. The alternative model on offer in both studies is that of dependency on extra-Cycladic power centres, such as Minoan Crete and Classical Athens (Cherry *et al.* 1991: 4–9; Renfrew 1982a; Wagstaff and Cherry 1982a). These alternatives fostered a polarisation of the options: either a self-sufficient system defined by the coast, or a regime of world-systemic integration. If an island's articulation with outside powers is the focus of interest, this polarisation may not appear to matter too much. But by overlooking intermediate spatial scales of analysis, such as integration within intra-Cycladic networks, it creates problems for interpretation of those periods when regimes of strong external manipulation did not exist, as is in fact the case for the entire period that concerns us in this book. As will be seen in the next chapter, the early Cyclades were thoroughly dependent on each other for survival, and neither island boundedness nor external dependency is really helpful as a model for understanding their dynamics. Instead, closer attention to the central part of the range on the sliding scale of island–mainland relations will be essential if we are to fulfil the clear promise of these first experiments at undertaking island archaeological analyses in the Cyclades.

3

Islands, people and seafaring

> What shall we tell you? Tales, marvellous tales
> Of ships and stars and isles where good men rest.
> *The Golden Journey to Samarkand*, JAMES ELROY FLECKER

Some assessment of the main structuring elements and variables of island life during the Neolithic and EBA is an important preliminary task for any island archaeological analysis of the Cyclades. This chapter identifies and explores three essential themes. The first is the variegation in islandscapes, environments and resources. The second is generalised ways of living, including subsistence, community size, island demography, and their implications for interaction between islanders. The third is movement, and in particular the opportunities and restraints of maritime travel, as reconstructed from sea conditions and evidence of seacraft. Although there is a danger that such broad-brush overviews may flatten the diversity specific to different times and places, it is helpful at this stage to establish the general parameters within which variability can subsequently be investigated. The central point that should emerge in this chapter is that insularity in the early Cyclades needs to be understood as a dynamic rather than static condition.

If the explicit aim of this chapter is to put forward some initial ideas about how Cycladic island societies might have operated in remote antiquity, its implicit twin is to render these islands 'other', by stripping away misleading later influences on the ways in which we visualise them. A partial deconstruction of the island cluster itself is a good place to begin. On the map, the Cyclades appear a justifiable group in so far as they are defined on most sides by much wider stretches of sea than those separating one island from the next. This makes it reasonable at a strategic level to select them as a region for analysis. But even this point requires qualification. One exception is the northern edge of the Cyclades, where a gradual transition from mainland to island is provided by the Attic and Euboian peninsulas, which are effectively as well as etymologically 'almost islands' – in Euboia's case all the more so because this nominal island is even now barely separated from the mainland, and may have been joined for part, if not all, of the time-span under discussion (Kambouroglou *et al.* 1988). A rather different exception is found on the south-east fringe of the Cyclades, facing Astypalaia and the little stepping-stones of Levitha and Kinaros, with these three islands being as much Cycladic outliers as parts of the Dodecanese. Astypalaia's

Islands, people and seafaring

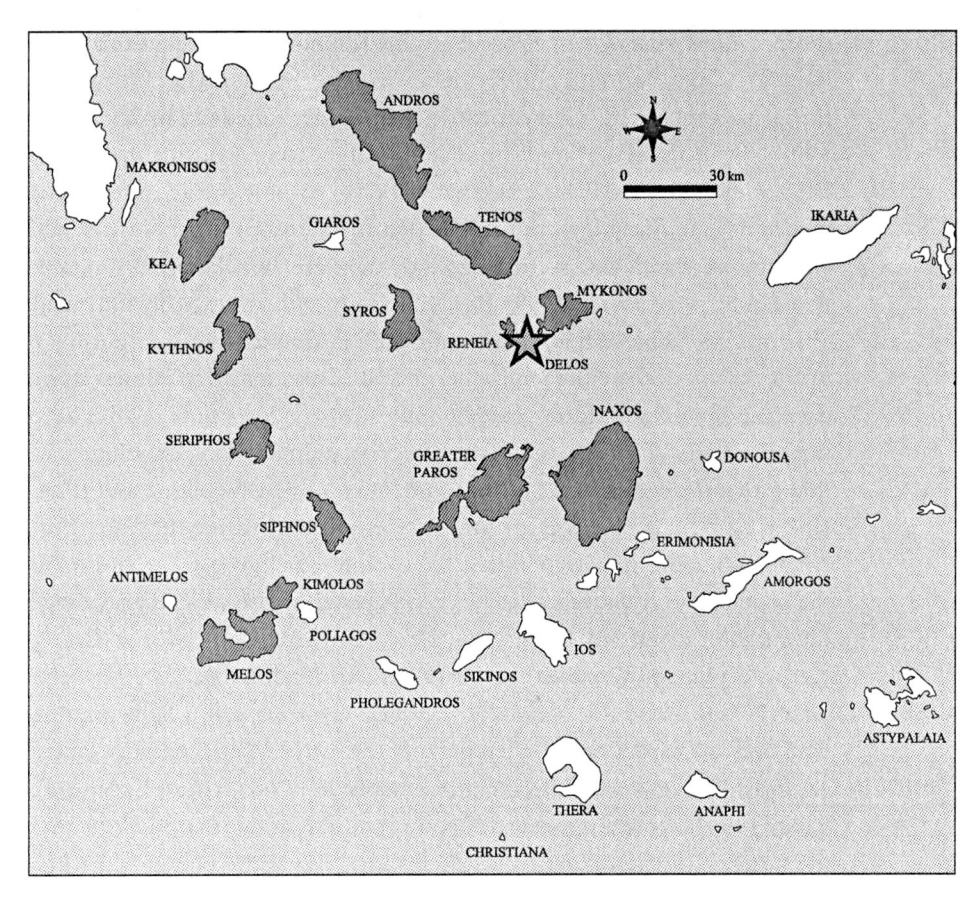

Fig. 12 The Cyclades as a *kyklos* around Delos, according to the ancient geographer Strabo (Book X). This sacred geography not only differs from the modern roll-call of islands, but also matches imperfectly with the major politico-ethnic division of the Classical period into a numerically dominant 'Ionian' sphere and a few southern 'Dorian' outliers in the form of Melos and Thera.

exclusion from the Cyclades is in fact simply the result of a diplomatic blunder in the 1830s (Myres 1941: 145). These two blurred edges, or permeable boundaries, will repeatedly emerge as areas of special interest.

It is also worth recalling that the current name for this island group reflects a specific sacred and ethnic geography of the first millennium BC. The poet Kallimachos was one of many who imagined the islands forming a *kyklos* around the Ionian centre on Delos: 'Asteria [Delos], island of incense, around and about you the isles have made a circle and set themselves about you as a choir' (Hymn 4, 301). Interestingly, this *kyklos* excluded several islands that are currently numbered among the Cyclades (e.g. Ios, Thera, Anaphi and Amorgos) but were then known as the Southern Sporades, the 'scattered islands' (fig. 12). Prior to the first millennium BC, we have no idea whether the Cycladic islands were identified and named as a group. Nor can the antiquity of the individual islands' names be ascertained, although the names of a few other Aegean islands – Chios, Lemnos and Kythera – may be mentioned in Linear B records of the thirteenth century BC (Bennet 1997: 519; Coldstream and Huxley 1972: 33; Renfrew 1998 speculates on the linguistic affiliation of the islands during the second millennium BC). Although there is little alternative but to employ the accepted names for convenience, it is important to remember that the subject of this book is actually a set of anonymous islands that were ordered by their Neolithic and EBA inhabitants in ways that can be reconstructed only by archaeology and contextually informed modelling.

In order to achieve this, as was intimated in chapter 2, it is important to banish the overlay of modern settlement patterns and communication routes. In particular, the contemporary road-, ferry- and air-routes largely determine relative accessibility and the periodicity of travel to and from different points among the islands, with the result that it requires a concerted effort to understand why Neolithic and EBA settlements, and in particular places of prominence, are found where they are. For example, in chapters 6 and 7 it is argued that the overall social geography and travel network of the south-east Cyclades has to be reconfigured before we can grasp the logic behind the location of an EB II centre at Daskaleio-Kavos on the now-deserted island of Keros, a place now passed at dusk, without landfall, *en route* between Naxos and Amorgos. Because the people of the early Cyclades left a light impression on their land, this is a harder task than in parts of the world where cognitive landscapes can be explored through earth-altering monuments, as in north-west Europe (Bradley 1993; Tilley 1994) or certain western Mediterranean islands (Patton 1996: 89–111). Given the absence of such clues, the search must instead be conducted with reference to where people lived, to traces of connecting sea-paths, and to points of prominence that may have served as foci of long-term memory and activity, such as caves, obsidian and metal quarries, and distinctive seamarks that bear signs of the islanders' presence. Much of the cultural significance of the islandscapes of the Cyclades was probably created by the islanders' journeys across the sea, activities that unfortunately have left no direct mark of their passage.

Islands of diversity

Physical islandscapes

Careful modern observations can nonetheless reveal quite a lot about the physical nature of Cycladic islandscapes, since their overall outlines have altered little in the last seven millennia, save for localised shoreline shifts, vegetation changes, and the denudation of hillslopes and consequent deepening soil on the valley floors. Taking shoreline changes first, a combination of eustatic data, high-precision curves for postglacial sea-level rise and modelling of crustal rebound demonstrates that the Cyclades had reached roughly their modern form by the later Neolithic (see chapter 4). The generally steep coasts permit little lateral displacement with subsequent small-scale fluctuations in sea-level. The only two significant differences were a land-bridge between the current islands of Paros, Antiparos and Despotikon (Bent 1884: 47; Morrison 1968), creating a big island of *c.* 250 sq km that can be christened *Greater Paros*, and a larger (*c.* 100 sq km) Thera than has existed since the mid-second-millennium BC eruption (Heiken and McCoy 1984).[1] Turning to vegetation, it is likely that the Cyclades were never fully forested, but high maquis, with woods and smaller stands of trees in better-watered or sheltered areas, can be tentatively reconstructed before the start of widespread clearance (Bintliff 1977a: 537–8). Pollen analysis on Naxos hints at a reduction in tree cover in the EBA (Dalongeville and Renault-Miskovsky 1993) and a new geomorphological study at EBA Markiani on Amorgos also indicates vegetation disturbance (French and Whitelaw 1999). In the LBA (by which time extensive tree-felling might be anticipated), large beams were still used for house construction at Akrotiri (Doumas 1983b: 51–3), although these could have been imported from other islands, or conceivably even further afield.[2] Turning to soil movement, the evidence from Markiani indicates that early clearance and grazing did trigger soil movements off slopes and onto the valley floors, but the impact of this, although potentially considerable for farming activity and localised landscapes, can have had little effect on the overall topography of the islands.

This general stability of island form means that contemporary insights into the manner in which the Cyclades break up and regroup as physical islandscapes is able to provide at least some introduction to the complexity of these islands as arenas for island life. According to the Classical Greeks, Delos was once a floating island that cruised the Aegean, and when one enters the Cyclades by sea the islandscape is indeed mercurial. The map states that a cluster of islands lies ahead, each named and plotted, but the eye's testimony is different: part of one island's coast passes close on the left, another island is well defined as a solid grey block ahead, a scrap of something else lies further off at the edge of the haze (an island, or two islands, or maybe just a cloud?), this last vague form looking as if it might be Syros, but not located quite where Syros was expected to materialise, and where Naxos should be there is nothing but empty horizon. Visibility varies enormously, from days when even adjacent islands are barely inter-visible, to others of extreme clarity (occasionally aided by atmospheric refraction), when islands

---

[1] A few areas of extremely localised submergence are known, for example at Grotta on Naxos (Lambrinoudakis 1979; Papathanasopoulos 1981), but although these affect the survival of sites in the immediate vicinity, they have no impact on overall configuration.

[2] More recent data also serve to illustrate the potential for tree growth in certain areas of the islands. There was woodland on Naxos during the nineteenth century AD (Dugit 1874: 82–4, 303 cited in Bintliff 1977a: 537, and further attested by relict woodland avifauna (Watson 1964: 214)). Stands of valonia oak exist on Kea, Tenos and Naxos, and pine, plane, cypress, oak and maple grow on several of the larger islands (Rackham 1978; Watson 1964: 25). The existence and exploitation of valonia oaks on Kea is documented since the Middle Ages, and may well be considerably older (Bennet and Voutsaki 1991).

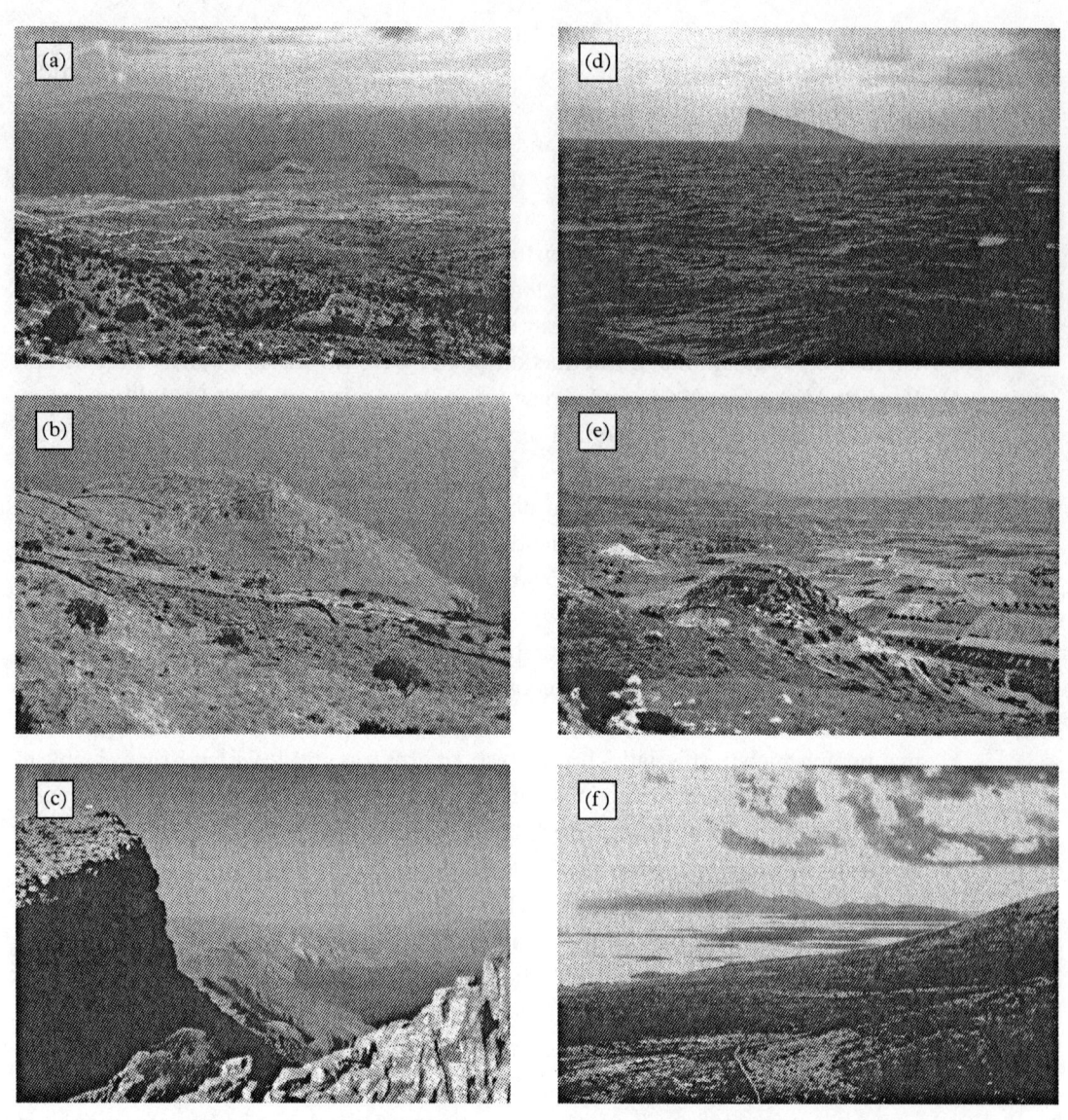

Fig. 13 Six Cycladic islandscapes: (a) eastern Naxos with Donousa on the horizon, (b) south-west Andros, (c) south coast of Amorgos, (d) islet near Kythnos, (e) Melos, inland plain with the Pelos settlement on the knoll-top, (f) south-east Naxos with Keros and Epano Kouphonisi in the background.

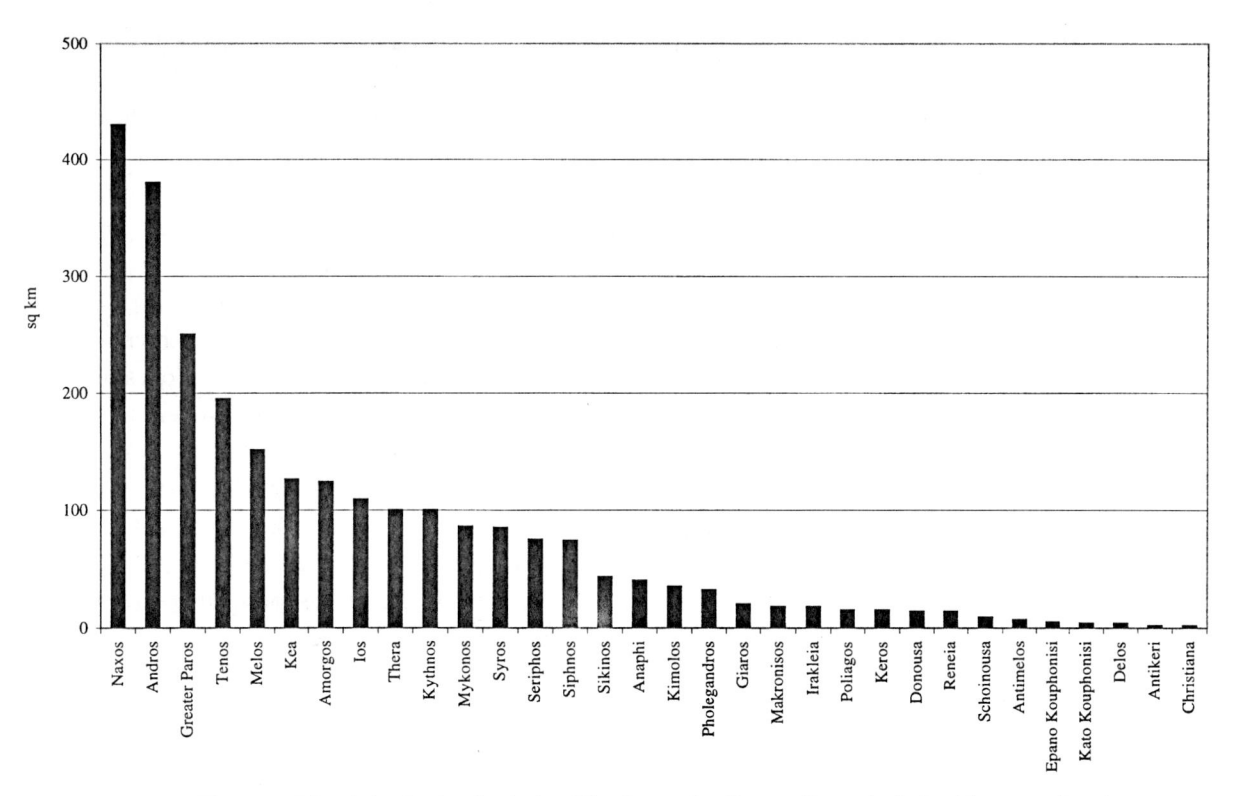

Fig. 14 Island size in the Cyclades. The figure for Greater Paros is derived by summing the areas of modern Paros (196 sq km), Antiparos (35 sq km) and Despotikon (8 sq km) plus an additional approximate 10 sq km for submerged areas. The estimate for Thera prior to the mid-second millennium BC eruption is derived from the reconstruction in Heiken and McCoy 1984.

are unveiled on every side, breaking the sea like dolphins' backs and superimposed behind each other in bewildering numbers. A familiarity with the Cyclades increases the ability to name and predict, but it does not alter the fact that our experience of them is made up of innumerable patchy collages of land and sea. Even if the intact outline of an island is visible, what is really seen, of course, is half an island, its contours massed into a form unique to a specific viewpoint. The images of Cycladic islandscapes in fig. 13 complement this brief attempt to conjure up some of their salient characteristics.

But a more analytical approach can also capture certain of the ways in which a mosaic of micro-diversity is generated over the Cyclades. The islands are the peaks of a much larger drowned Pleistocene island and its satellites (see chapter 4). This explains the basic form of many islands, dominated by a high central ridge, with corrugated valleys sloping gently or abruptly down to rocky shores punctuated by small coves and less frequent larger bays. But these drowned peaks vary considerably in their geometry and configuration, as well as environment and resources. Starting with the former (fig. 14), ranking individual island area reveals four large islands (Naxos,

Andros, Greater Paros and Tenos), a more numerous group in the 75–150 sq km range (Melos, Kea, Amorgos, Ios, Thera, Kythnos, Mykonos, Syros, Seriphos and Siphnos), and a tail of smaller islands and islets that extends beyond the limits shown, to include myriad fragments of rock emerging from the sea. The four largest islands comprise roughly half the total land area of the Cyclades, and the middle-sized group take up most of the remainder, leaving the numerous smaller islands to share something like a tenth of the total. The small islands include singletons but also form pairs such Delos and Reneia, and in one case a more complex cluster known as the Erimonisia (comprising Irakleia, Keros, Epano and Kato Kouphonisi, Schoinousa and the Antikeri). Some small islands tend to become the satellites of larger ones (e.g. Donousa, Christiana, Giaros and many of the tiniest islets), but others under favourable conditions link larger islands together.

Maximum altitude for each island, which has implications for ecological zoning and rainfall, relates fairly regularly to island area, with the peak of Mt Zas on Naxos (at $c.$ 1000 m the highest point in the Cyclades) rising above the largest of the islands (NB all reconstructions of the vanished volcanic cone of Thera are speculative). Yet the topography of a few islands, notably Mykonos, Kythnos and Melos, is lower-lying than might be anticipated from their size. Island shape also modifies the effect of size and altitude. For instance, much of the land on slender Amorgos comprises steeply sloping coast, making it a less attractive prospect than size alone indicates. Conversely, it is the broader shape of Naxos, as much as its sheer size, that explains the existence of its major inland valley systems, a distinctive niche more or less restricted to this island, which provide shelter from the winds and act as soil traps, both reducing soil loss into the sea and probably smothering some of the early settlements in the island's interior.

Inter-island configurational factors are equally important. Distances between the islands are modest, in so far as it is possible to travel between almost any two islands without a crossing of over 25 km, if indirect routes are allowed. Yet a finer analysis of inter-island distance reveals several sub-clusters (fig. 15), notably a compact group in the north-east, another in the south-east with ragged edges, and a long string of islands between Makronisos and Melos. The close proximity of Andros to Tenos and, to a less marked extent, Naxos to Greater Paros means that the four largest islands in fact create two even larger masses. Another significant variable is the distance between each island and a mainland. The extremes are, on the one hand, Thera, Christiana, Ios and the islands of the Erimonisia (all some 150–180 km distant) and, on the other hand, the offshore island of Makronisos (3 km distant) followed by Kea and Andros (the latter if Euboia can be considered as effectively a mainland).

Taken together, these configurational variables generate a remarkable amount of diversity. A few islands emerge as overall anomalies, for example Andros on account of size, proximity to the mainland and virtual fusion with another island. Others share similarities. But overall the conclusion must be that, at least from these perspectives, there is really no such thing as a typical island that represents the Cyclades as a whole.

Islands, people and seafaring

Fig. 15   Inter-island distance in the Cyclades (isobars at 5, 10, 15, 20 and 25 km).

Moreover, once observed more closely, islands begin to break up as individual entities. This is caused by four principal characteristics of the Cyclades. The first is that distances between islands are commonly less than the length of individual islands. Until the effectiveness of land and sea movement has been examined, the full significance of this cannot be assessed, but it raises the possibility of closer linkages between people at the extremities of different islands than between an island's internal population. This is most applicable at the hearts of the north-eastern and south-eastern sub-clusters (fig. 16), and least so for Amorgos, Seriphos, Siphnos, Syros and Thera, therefore making the latter islands in configurational terms the closest approximations to unitary islands in the Cyclades. Second, the upland interiors and radiating ridges usually block visual contact between different coastal zones within an island (and impede contact on foot), but except in poor atmospheric conditions the facing coastal zones of adjacent islands are inter-visible. Third, the rugged topography fragments arable areas into a few small plains and, more commonly, tiny patches of land, creating habitat islands that also turn attention towards external links, as most

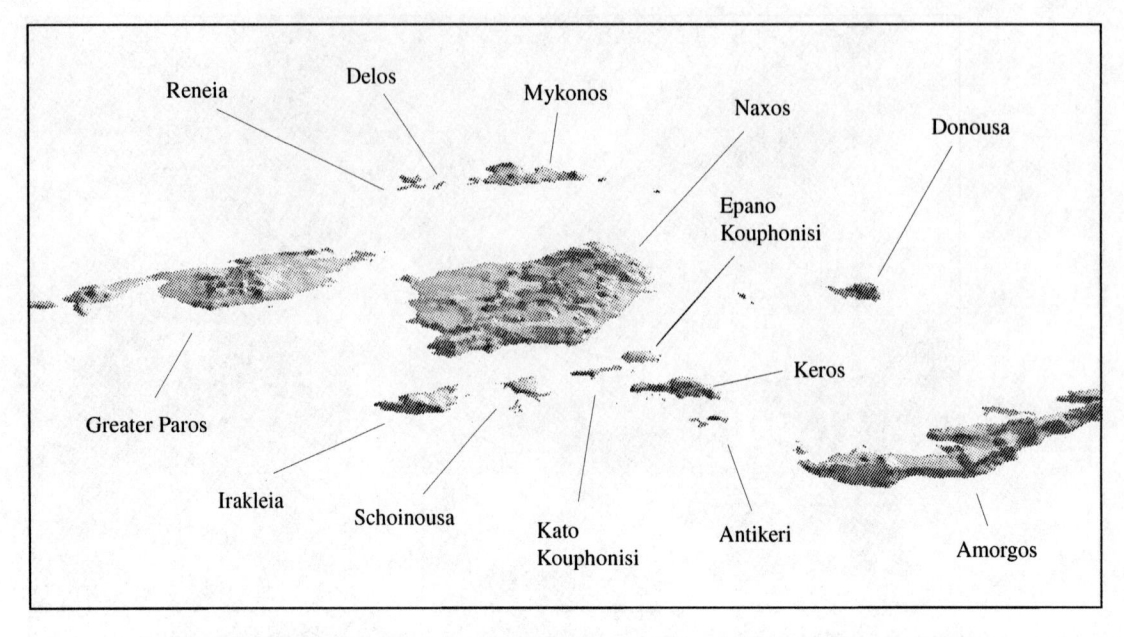

Fig. 16 Three-dimensional computer-generated view looking north-west from Amorgos across the Erimonisia to Naxos, with Greater Paros and Mykonos in the background. Vertical distances are exaggerated threefold.

lie along the coasts. The fourth factor concerns some of the smaller islands, which are so densely packed that they seem like exploded pieces of a larger unit. In at least some regions of the Cyclades, these factors mean that individual islands dissolve into a graded continuum of land and sea.

Environments and resources

Chapter 2 drew attention to an ambiguity in the Cyclades' location – potentially both marginal to each other part of the Aegean and central to the Aegean as a whole. The Cyclades are ambiguously marginal and central in other respects too, being climatically and environmentally marginal for farming, yet central in terms of their desirable lithic and metallic resources. Starting with the former, variability is again encountered within the general picture. Overall, the Cyclades have precious little arable, especially under the 10–15° slope that allows farming without investment in terracing, and, at least on the strength of the evidence from Markiani and north-west Kea, terracing does not seem to have been practised until well after the end of the EBA (French and Whitelaw 1999: 173–5; Whitelaw 1998). The larger islands tend to possess more arable, with farmland on the smallest islands limited to minute scraps that present a particularly marginal prospect (Halstead and O'Shea 1982: 94 for the inverse

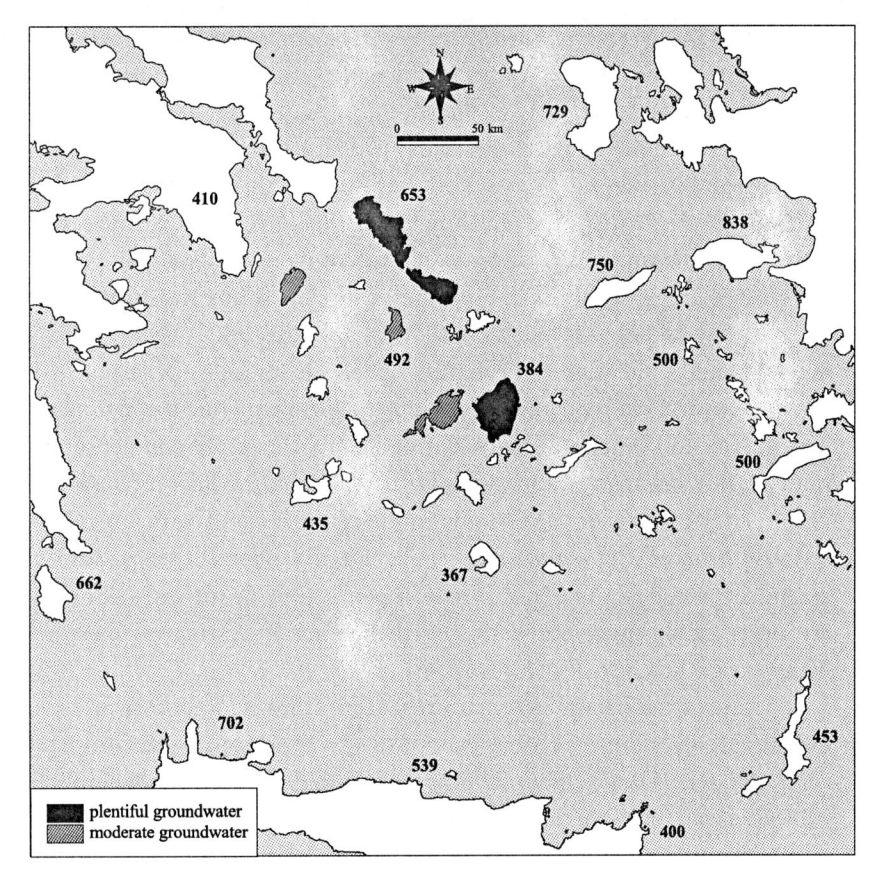

Fig. 17 Rainfall and hydrology in the Cyclades and rainfall also in surrounding areas (rainfall measurements in mm; the figures for Patmos, Kos, Ikaria and east Crete are approximate). Note that the Cyclades lie in a rain-shadow in every direction save the northeast. Data from Naval Intelligence Division 1945, Papalas 1992, Wagstaff and Gamble 1982 and Watson 1964.

relationship between land area and inter-annual variation in harvest yields). But the ratio between island size and arable area is not straightforward. Coastal plains and inland valleys on Naxos give this island a total arable area far out of proportion to what even its large size would lead us to anticipate. To contrast two islands of similar size, whilst relatively little of Kea can be cultivated without terracing, the gentler contours of Melos encourage wider cultivation. Varied topography also creates substantial variation within islands, such as the distinction on Syros between the wild, precipitous north and the lower, much more fertile south.

Fresh-water resources vary greatly (fig. 17). It is still uncertain whether climate regimes identical to modern conditions applied in the Aegean during the later Neolithic and EBA, or whether the earlier part of this period was slightly wetter

(Bintliff 1977a: 51; Rackham 1972: 303; Rackham and Moody 1996: 38–9; Wagstaff and Gamble 1982: 96–7). Yet in relative terms the Cyclades have the distinction of being one of the worst parts of the southern Aegean for rainfall, with average levels halving between the east Aegean island of Samos, via Ikaria to Naxos. Because orographic rainfall takes effect at altitudes of 600–700 m (Watson 1964: 16), the higher islands have the best chance of catching what rain there is. Andros and Tenos capture the most, thanks to their position in the path of the prevailing weather from the north, with the more modest rainfall on even the highest southern islands explained by the fact that few rain-clouds reach them. The other extreme is occupied by Thera in the far south, and small islands throughout the Cyclades. Springs nuance the picture and can create veritable miniature oases in their vicinity. They are abundant on Andros, Tenos, Kea and much of Naxos, in the latter case amply compensating for modest rainfall. But on many other islands, most notably Melos, Thera and Mykonos, ground-water is scarcer, combining in the case of islands with low rainfall to present serious threats of drought, and the small, cliff-girt islands of Giaros and Antimelos are essentially waterless. The problems of water supply facing the drier southern islands are only slightly ameliorated by a higher summer dewfall on these most seaward members of the Cyclades (Myres 1941: 145).

What turns the data about water resources from static observations into dynamic factors that must have become part of the reckoning and decision-making of many early islanders is the element of temporal unpredictability. Rainfall in the Cyclades is subject to wild inter-annual fluctuations (fig. 18), and the less frequent tectonic events to which the islands are prone can open or destroy springs instantaneously, with drastic results for areas dependent on such water sources. Concentrating on rainfall, the small size of most rain-clouds suggests that variation between islands in any one year might be great, and that the relative average annual rainfall of different islands may not be reflected in their relative actual rainfall in a sample year. Certainly, microvariation is evident within islands. A spring or summer storm can drench one valley and leave its neighbours dry. Depending on exactly when the rain falls, it may either save or destroy crops (Whitelaw 1991b: 451). If contemporary conditions do resemble those in the Neolithic and EBA, fig. 18 indicates that islanders on Melos could expect droughts sufficient to threaten the crops at least once a decade, and none of the islands is entirely free of danger in the long-term. If conditions were rather wetter in the earlier part of the period, the incidence of drought would have been less, but in relative terms the same phenomenon of chronic short-term rainfall fluctuation across the Cyclades would not have been greatly altered.

A final, crucial, dimension of physical variability concerns the lithic and metallic resources known to have been exploited by Neolithic and EBA people (fig. 19). The Cycladic islands can be crudely categorised into marble-dominant, schist-dominant and volcanic geologies, although most islands in fact have a range of rock types.

Fig. 18 Inter-annual fluctuation of rainfall on Melos. After Renfrew and Wagstaff 1982b: fig. 9.4.

Specific, sought-after lithic resources are distributed unevenly. Workable obsidian is restricted to two outcrops at Demenegaki and Sta Nychia on Melos (Torrence 1982), volcanic rocks for grind-stones can be found on Melos, Thera and Anaphi, and emery exists only on Naxos. Most islands, save Melos, have some marble, but the best sources are located on Naxos and Greater Paros. Clays are diverse, with the palest-firing clays associated with the volcanic islands of Melos and Thera.

In Aegean terms the Cyclades are rich in small metalliferous deposits, and much progress has been made in establishing those used from an early date, both by the direct identification and dating of mines and slag heaps, and through lead isotope analysis. A combination of these approaches has demonstrated that Siphnos produced silver, lead and possibly some copper, although there is no evidence for exploitation of the modest gold deposits that were mined there in the first millennium BC (Gale and Stos-Gale 1981; Wagner *et al.* 1980; Wagner and Weisgerber 1985), and that Kythnos was an important copper source (Gale *et al.* 1988; Stos-Gale 1989, 1993, 1998). Mining and processing sites on these islands have been dated by radiocarbon and thermoluminescence dating to the EBA (Stos-Gale 1998: table 1; Wagner *et al.*

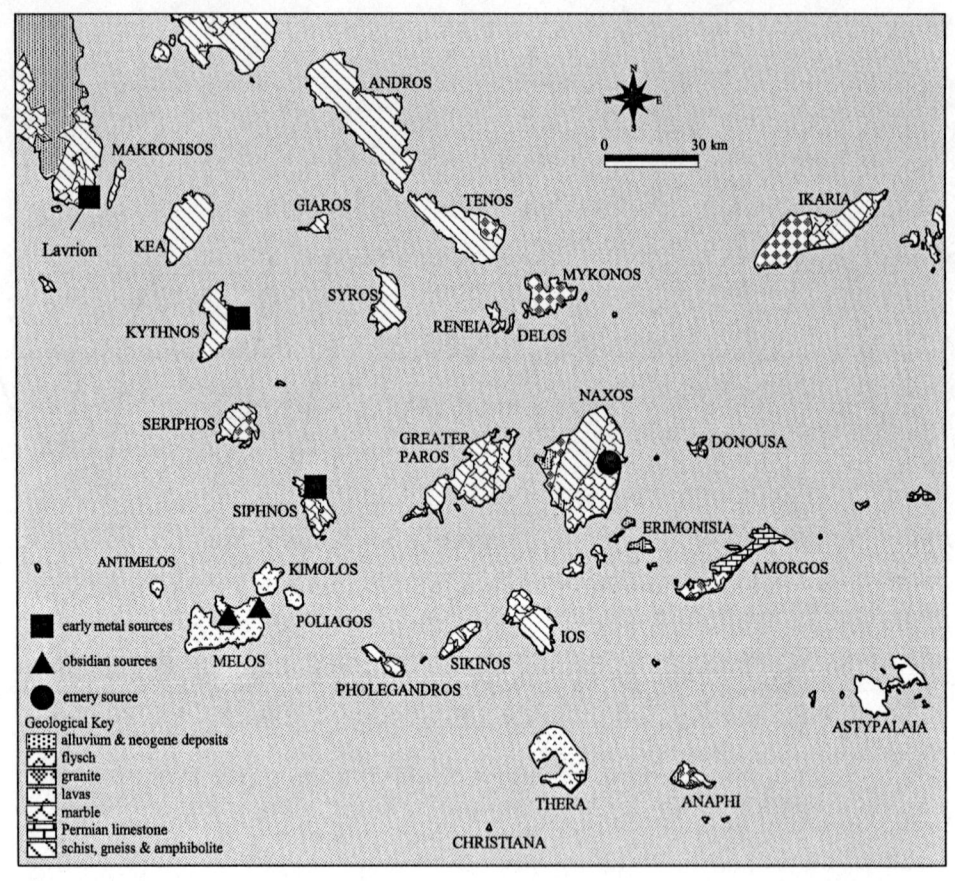

Fig. 19 Cycladic geology and mineral resources. After Higgins and Higgins 1996: fig. 15.1 with additions.

1980: 73–5), and in the former case a few FN sherds near the mines could indicate earlier extraction. Just beyond the north-west Cyclades, at the almost insular tip of Attica, lie the larger polymetallic deposits of Lavrion, which were also exploited by the EBA (Spitaels 1984). Several other islands possess minor metal sources (Stos-Gale and MacDonald 1991), but Seriphos is the only one for which possible evidence for early processing (of copper) has been forthcoming (Stos-Gale 1993: 124); early mining on Kea is deemed unlikely (Gale 1998). This pattern of apparently selective usage of the range of metal sources that were potentially available, whether or not they were actually known, is paralleled by the situation in central Europe (Shennan 1999: 361). In the Cyclades, the western islands (and by extension Lavrion) emerge as a distinctive zone in terms of their range of exploited metal ores and, equally, their obsidian sources. They contrast in this respect with the eastern Cyclades, a factor that may have shaped people's perceptions of the western sector of the archipelago.

Ways of living in the early Cyclades

Subsistence and storage strategies

Such an island setting, environmentally marginal overall but with much subtle variation and micro-diversity engendered by configuration and climate, is likely both to select for certain overall survival strategies and to allow room within these for plenty of different ways of doing things, according to local ecology (the particular niche occupied) as well as cultural factors (specific traditions, customs or choices). Social and cultural diversity over time and between locations in the early Cyclades should therefore come as no surprise, and whilst some of this diversity may reflect genuinely different approaches to environmental challenges, and some reflect variable responses to perceptions of risk, much is liable to reflect disparate lifestyles and traditions that were of fairly equal merit in terms of ensuring people's survival. This book advocates looking at variability and specific histories, but precisely because most of the remaining chapters emphasise these dimensions, it is as well at this juncture to stand back and frame the domains of cultural choice with broader parameters. Although, as seen in chapter 4, some terminal Pleistocene to early Holocene hunter-gatherer activity in the Cyclades can be assumed before the first Neolithic settlement, the present discussion focuses on the options open to agricultural groups. Cherry (1981: 60, 1985: 20), drawing on the work of Halstead (1981a), has set out some of the strategies available to groups farming in marginal island environments. These include crop diversification, increases in storage, supplementary exploitation of wild foods, exchange networks to buffer against bad harvests, changes in community size and/or location, and increased mobility (see also Gallant 1991). These possibilities could, of course, be taken up and combined in different, culturally specific manners, and also to different degrees. Their investigation therefore serves as an informative pathway along which to begin an exploration of the underlying dynamics of life in the early Cyclades.

How might these strategies have operated in the early Cyclades? For individual households or communities, it would be advantageous to cultivate a variety of crops in discrete micro-environments, so as to guard against the failure of any one crop (Forbes 1976; Whitelaw 1991b: 451). Overall, however, the suite of domesticates found in the early Cycladic settlements is no wider than elsewhere in the Aegean. The first settlers in the Cyclades basically transplanted the mainland 'package' wholesale, a transfer similar to that witnessed elsewhere among the Aegean islands, and which contrasts with the staggered introduction of agriculture into several west Mediterranean islands (Cherry 1990: 173–91). In the Cyclades, excavations at Neolithic and EBA settlements such as Saliagos (Higgs *et al.* 1968; Renfrew, J.M. 1968), Kephala (Coy 1977; Renfrew, J.M. 1977), Zas (Halstead in prep; Zachos 1999), Phtelia (Sampson 1997) and Phylakopi (Gamble 1982; Renfrew, J.M. 1982) all reveal a preponderance of sheep and goat with small numbers of cattle and pig

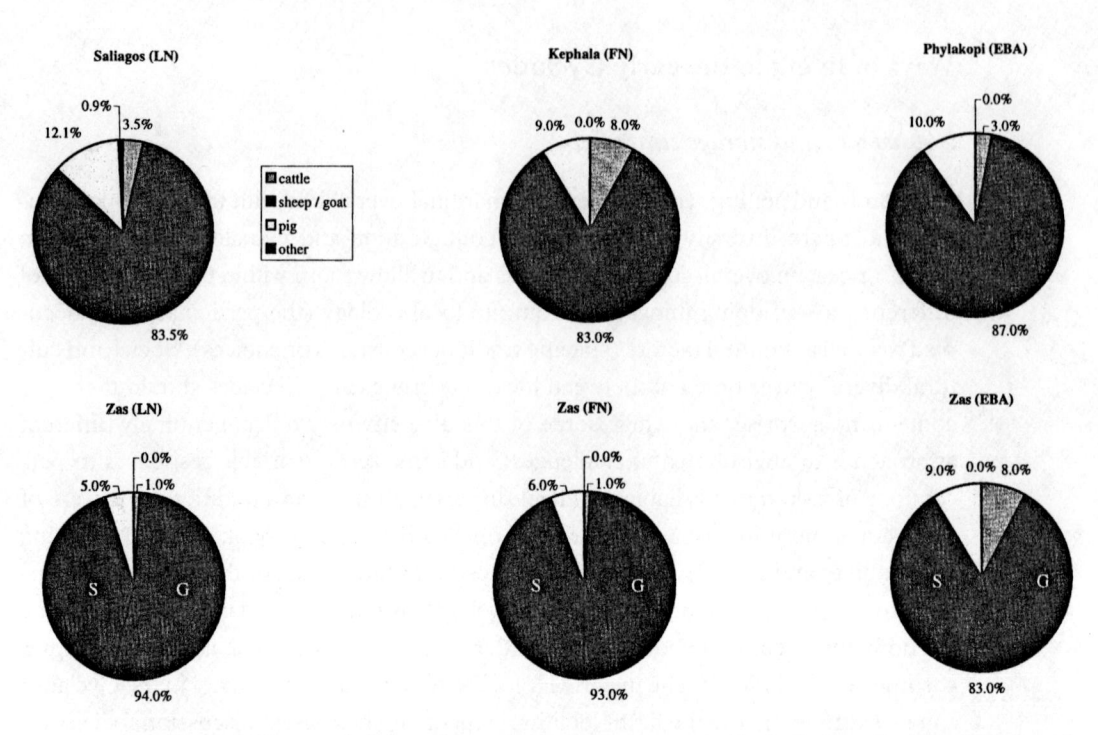

Fig. 20   The composition of faunal assemblages at early Cycladic sites. Data from Halstead 1996b: table 1.

(fig. 20). At Zas, where sheep and goat have been successfully distinguished, the latter predominate, a pattern that may be typical of more marginal areas in the southern Aegean (Halstead 1996b). The principal cereal crops are barley and wheat, with pulses also reported at Zas and Phtelia (in large quantities at the former site (Zachos 1999: 156–7)). The faunal information, which is the better documented, matches information from Knossos on Crete (Jarman 1996; Jarman and Jarman 1968), Agios Petros on Kyra Panagia in the Northern Sporades (Efstratiou 1985: 54), Emporio on Chios (Clutton-Brock 1982) and the Kalythies cave on Rhodes (Halstead and Jones 1987).

The most significant potential expansions of this agricultural package within the period that concerns us are the exploitation of domestic animals for secondary products and the cultivation of the olive and the vine. The actual occurrence and significance of these changes are the subject of ongoing debates among Aegeanists (see chapter 2), to which the Cycladic data contribute only modestly (NB once again the purported developments are far from unique to the Cyclades). The ox-drawn plough would have had a minimal relevance in the Cyclades, given the limited amount of arable land and the high grazing demands of plough oxen, and most island agriculture probably took the form of small intensively hoed fields throughout the Neolithic and EBA (Halstead 1994). But dairy products could have provided a useful, even decisive, dietary supplement, and grazing by goats or sheep is an advantageous way of exploiting the rougher landscapes of the Cyclades, which are suitable for little else. Plausible as this proposal is, locating such practices within overall subsistence strategies and identifying them in the archaeological record has proved to be less easy than might initially be imagined.

The widespread appearance in the FN of open vessels with perforated rims known as 'cheese-pots' (Sampson 1987: fig. 43a) is assumed to indicate processing of dairy products, but proof through faunal analysis that herds were indeed kept for dairy products as well as meat has encountered methodological obstacles (Halstead 1998). Moreover, milk extraction could be integrated into island economies either through the practice of small-scale mobile pastoralism, a popular concept with Aegean prehistorians but not supported by early Aegean faunal data (Halstead 1996b), or through increasing the role of stock-breeding within mixed farming economies, i.e. alongside continued meat consumption, in which case its zooarchaeological detection would be extremely difficult (Halstead 1998). The stability in patterns of animal exploitation throughout the LN–EBA period at Zas cave argues against pastoralism as separate practice, but cannot decide either way concerning the model of small-scale dairying within a mixed farming economy (Halstead in prep; cf. Zachos 1999: 160–1). One relevant factor for communities in the miniaturised environments of the Cyclades, where extensive hillslopes closely hem in arable areas, is that there might be little call for mobile herding practices beyond the grazing of flocks at a relatively short distance from the fields. Longer-range movement of animals, if it occurred, might be best explained instead in terms of deliberate interbreeding between small, local community flocks (Halstead 1996b: 35).

The jury remains out over the issue of olive and vine cultivation in the Cyclades during the EBA, and is likely to remain so until the question is resolved by macrofossil evidence, phytolith identification or residue analysis. The claimed identification at the start of the last century of olive oil in an EB II juglet from Spedos on Naxos has become something of a factoid in the literature (Stephanos 1906: 88; cf. Hansen 1988: 45), and should not be given weight unless confirmed by modern techniques. *If* correct, the fact that the container was a tiny vessel covered in silver foil would raise the question as to whether olive oil should be seen as part of an overall diversification of the subsistence economy, or as a high-status liquid – unless higher-status perfumed oils were already produced at this stage (Shelmerdine 1985 for the later palatial perfumed oil industry). The frequency of vine-leaf impressions on EB II pot bases implies a greater degree of familiarity with the plant than is revealed by a single grape pip from Zas (Zachos 1990: 31), and the simultaneous increase in drinking vessels, some of designs that certainly do not originate in the Cyclades, may argue for imported fashions in the consumption of alcoholic liquids, with wine being a reasonable guess (see chapter 9). In summary, the Cyclades produce equivocal evidence for diversification, but nothing to suggest a divergence from practices that are equally likely (or unlikely) elsewhere in the Aegean.

Storage strategies are critically important, given that in a marginal environment agricultural over-production for a small-scale surplus is the only means of minimising shortfalls if the harvest is damaged or fails (Halstead 1989; Sahlins 1972). If a surplus materialised, it could be physically stored against a year of drought, blight or accident, or deployed socially, either to cement bonds with other communities through feasting, gift-giving and other ceremonies, or to build up social capital. Social storage strategies create a milieu of mutual obligation between communities, allowing each to request help from neighbours in adversity (Halstead 1981a; Halstead and O'Shea 1982), but over the long-term can also start to create net winners and losers (Halstead 1988). Social storage is a particularly attractive way of buffering against disaster in regions like the Cyclades where environmental micro-diversity makes it likely that the fortunes of the individual communities participating in a social storage network would vary in a given year. But it should be stressed that in such environments social storage represents not a monolithic strategy but a spectrum of behaviour. In particular, the extent of networks and energy invested in them would be likely to vary with the anticipated frequency of crop disasters within each micro-region. For example, communities in the most clement areas would need to request help least frequently, leading either to less intense involvement in such networks or, if the network also incorporated less favoured environments, to long-term accumulations of social credit at their less fortunate partners' expense.

In the early Cyclades varied combinations of physical storage and social storage can be envisaged, augmented by storage on the hoof in the form of domestic animals. There is also one possible instance (as is argued in chapter 7) where the regular (as opposed to dearth-driven) acquisition of staple foods via maritime exchange might be inferred. Cherry (1987: 35–6) remarks that social storage forms a convincing rationale for the paraphernalia of exchange and the ceremonial equipment that abound in the material culture of the early Cyclades, and this theme will be explored in detail in chapter 5. The evidence for the physical storage of crops largely comprises storage jar finds and suggests an orientation on the individual house. No signs of communal storage facilities have been found, save for a possible small silo at Saliagos (Evans and Renfrew 1968: 18, 81). A chlorite schist model of a multi-chambered structure, found in Melos, has been interpreted as a granary (Renfrew 1972: pl. 15.1; Renfrew, J.M. 1982: 156), but there are no full-sized parallels known to date, and the identification seems questionable given the model's equal resemblance to the small, cellular, fortified settlements of the later EBA (see chapter 9). Household storage, or at any rate very localised forms of organisation, should not be surprising in the patchy environment of the Cyclades, as the generally small pockets of arable do not encourage generation of a large surplus, and bulk movement of staples could have been achieved only through heavy investment in transportation at a time when, as will be seen below, transport options were decidedly narrower than in later Cycladic history.

The key role of agricultural buffering is further underlined by the slight room for manoeuvre afforded by wild food resources in the Cyclades. Terrestrial wild foods are of particularly limited potential. Their proportions in the Neolithic and EBA faunal material are negligible, with the LN–EBA levels at Zas producing only a few bones from hare, fox, wild cat and bird species (Halstead in prep). Of particular interest, given the possible anthropogenic introduction of fallow deer as a food source to several other Aegean islands in the Neolithic (Halstead 1987b: 75), is the minimal incidence of this species among the Cycladic Neolithic faunal assemblages. Only a few deer bones were identified at Saliagos during a re-examination of 50 per cent of the material (Bökönyi 1986: 90; cf. Higgs *et al.* 1968), a few are also reported at Phtelia (Sampson 1997: 9–10), and none was found at LN–EBA Zas (Halstead in prep; a few fragments from mixed later levels are noted). It is interesting to speculate whether this dearth is a result of the small sample of sites investigated, or whether it reflects the greater difficulties in transporting sufficient numbers of deer into the Cyclades, in comparison to big offshore islands like Rhodes, where their presence is best attested (and to where some animals may have swum). The scantier archaeobotanical evidence indicates the gathering of wild fruits in areas protected enough to allow the plants to grow; pistachio, plum and fig were found at Zas (Zachos 1990: 31). Wild greens are a very likely, if undemonstrable, addition.

The role of marine resources is hard to assess, not least because wet-sieving has not been regularly practised. Neolithic Saliagos, which was wet-sieved, has produced a range of molluscs, fish (including a substantial quantity of tunny bones), and even a small, presumably beached, whale (Renfrew, J.M. *et al.* 1968: 119; Shackleton 1968), although the tunny's level of contribution to the diet has been recently recalculated and somewhat down-graded (Rose 1986). For the EBA the evidence shrinks to mere hints; Gamble (1979: 125–7, 1982: 171) considers marine food to be of slight importance at Phylakopi, although a few fish-hooks have been found in tombs (Powell 1996: 138–58), and analysis of human bone from Daskaleio-Kavos suggests a marine element in the diet (Doumas *et al.* nd). Patton (1996: 6) argues that for small islands the favourable coast-to-interior ratio would allow most inhabitants access to the safety net of marine food, but the point is that it remains uncertain how substantial that net actually was in the Cyclades. The Mediterranean is relatively poor in marine life compared to oceanic environments (Powell 1996: 12–15), and the tunny shoals that are the largest single resource move at unpredictable times along changeable routes (Gallant 1985: 27–9, 53). If such shoals were to be exploited as more than irregular windfalls, communities would have had to make investments of time and labour to intercept them – a strategy further examined in chapter 5. Overall, as Gallant (1985) and Powell (1996) concur, it is likely that most fishing was a small-scale, episodic and largely littoral activity that comprised a dietary supplement and back-up but seldom, if ever, a mainstay.

An outline of settlement types and distribution

What of the settlements themselves? The chapters that follow examine the extent, layout and populations of particular settlements in more detail, but these can be anticipated by a general overview. Some salient features are clear. First, all early Cycladic settlements were fairly small. Prior to the end of the third millennium BC there was probably none that extended over much more than a hectare, or whose population mounted higher than the low hundreds, and the vast majority of settlements were markedly smaller. Therefore variability in settlement size is about degrees of smallness. For the sake of clarity we can categorise the main types of community that will be encountered as:

1 *Farmsteads* of one or two households (i.e. about 5–10 people)
2 *Hamlets* of up to about ten households (i.e. about 11–50 people)
3 *Villages* of over ten households (i.e. about 51–300+ people)

Several points follow from this. One is that most communities could subsist on minute areas of arable land. Research into ancient crop yields (Halstead 1981b: 317–18; Gallant 1991: 82–7) indicates that a family-sized community could be supported on 3–6 hectares and even a substantial village would only need a few square kilometres. Another corollary is that all early Cycladic communities should fall in the category somewhat misleadingly termed 'egalitarian', i.e. typified by face-to-face relations and lying below cross-cultural thresholds for ascribed stratification (Forge 1972). Such social diversity and inequality as existed is likely to have approximated to the kinds of small-scale complexity outlined by Allen (1984) and Price and Brown (1985) in which social roles, authority and prestige would be personal, achieved and temporary, although the precise manner in which societies were structured in different areas and times assuredly varied. This must cast serious doubt on Renfrew's interpretation of the richest EBA Cycladic graves as proof of 'chiefly' personae (Renfrew 1972: 377). Social formations akin to chiefdoms are extremely unlikely to have existed in the early Cyclades.

Other implications also follow from the small size of the Cycladic communities. If local hierarchies (as opposed simply to differences in size) are to be argued for, the scale of the differences will need to be remembered, and the size of different settlements accurately assessed. In addition, the majority of communities will have been dependent on exogamy for reproduction, and therefore will have had kinship bonds with other communities through marriage alliances, with more extensive lineage networks developing between groups of small segmentary communities. There must also have been a marked degree of settlement instability at the lower end of the size range, partly as such communities fissioned, but also as they failed. It will be seen that the smaller types of early Cycladic settlements, i.e. the farmsteads and hamlets, have a tendency to wink on and off in the landscape. There are likely to be several reasons for this, including shifting interaction networks and, as has been recently argued, poor land-management practices leading to localised degradation of arable (French and Whitelaw 1999), but the stochastic influences of small-scale demographics must surely have played an important part too.

Early Cycladic settlements are typically dispersed across the landscape. This is a common feature of settlement in marginal regions, but in the Cyclades is also a result of the small, scattered patches of farmland, as well as of a general tendency for settlements to fission rather than expand. This pattern has gradually emerged through identification of settlements and cemeteries since the late nineteenth century. It was first formally proposed for Melos (Cherry 1979, 1982a: fig. 2.3), but is also amply documented on Naxos and the Erimonisia (Doumas 1977: fig. 2; Erard-Cerceau *et al.* 1993; Hadjianastasiou 1993: fig. 1), Amorgos (Marangou 1984: 99–100 and fig. 1, 1994), Ios (Marthari 1999) and Syros (Hekman 1994: fig. 8), and there are strong indications that it holds good for most other parts of the Cyclades too. The only possible anomaly so far identified is north-west Kea during the EBA, where there is little settlement beyond the village-sized site of Agia Irini (Cherry *et al.* 1991: 219). There is, of course, plenty of important variation to be explored in subsequent chapters. Not all early Cycladic societies tried to live in the same sectors of the landscape to the same degree, and accordingly they distributed themselves rather differently. In those cases where a community occupied a particularly favourable niche or a key node in interaction networks, modest population build-ups will be observed that may have acted as a centripetal vortex on surrounding demography. In this context, it is apposite to recall that although dispersal is an oft-cited way of risk-spreading, risk appraisal can be perceived and resolved at a range of social scales. Maximum dispersal minimises the risk to the aggregate population, but leaves each community individually vulnerable. It would not be surprising if risk perception at the individual or family level sometimes favoured movement into a somewhat larger community, despite the fact that from an aggregate viewpoint this would increase the risk of catastrophic failure affecting a larger proportion of the overall population.

Island demography

Having established a rough grasp of community size and distribution, let us turn to overall early Cycladic demography. There have been three main attempts to estimate population levels. The first, by Renfrew (1972: 249–53), generated figures of 3000 people during the Neolithic and 34,400 in the EBA, but was conducted before reliable intensive survey data became available, and these figures have been revised drastically downwards by Cherry (1979: 37–43; Wagstaff and Cherry 1982b: 137–8) and Nevett (1988), in both cases using data from the Melos survey as the basis for calculation. An estimation of Neolithic demography is still premature, although the overall figures were probably lower than in the EBA. But for the latter period, Cherry's calculations suggest population densities in the order of 0.5–1.5/sq km for EB I and 1.5–3.0/sq km for EB II, indicating population growth through time but nonetheless generating modest Melian population figures in the low hundreds, and by extrapolation pan-Cycladic populations of only a few thousand. Unlike many areas of the Pacific at the period of contact with the West, in the Cyclades under-population, rather than saturation, emerges as a key feature. We may start to think of people as a scarce resource, especially if the people sought in any given context had to be of a particular sex, age, lineage or role. By way of a comparison with some other contemporary populations, estimates of about 1290–1940 people for EBA Knossos (Whitelaw 1983: 339) imply that there were about as many people living at this major site as there were on the whole of Naxos (at higher densities) or the entire Cyclades (at the lowest density), and there must have been considerably more inhabitants in a contemporary fourth- to third-millennium BC Mesopotamian city like Uruk than there ever were early Cycladic islanders.

There are obvious uncertainties in these calculations, common to all exercises in palaeodemography (Hassan 1981). For example, it is probable that localised population dynamics in different parts of the Cyclades oscillated in innumerable ways as a result of differing colonisation horizons and diverse social and environmental factors; even the most general trends of population growth probably did not operate synchronously or at the same rate throughout the islands. But if we take Cherry's densities to be reasonably reliable in terms of their orders of magnitude and tabulate the derived populations for each Cycladic island, some revealing results are obtained (table 1). Although there is little hope of establishing the exact population of an individual island at a given time, the ranges displayed in table 1 indicate the probable options, and often it is possible to make an informed guess as to which part of the range is most likely in a given context. Moreover, they prove useful in ruling out certain possibilities and highlighting others.

The figures in table 1 underscore the high degree of island interdependence, and further undermine the status of the unitary island as a domain for analysis. Taking cross-cultural estimates suggesting that 300–500 people is the minimum number needed to maintain long-term populations and endogamous networks among small, dispersed groups (Adams and Kasakoff 1976; Jones 1976; MacCluer and Dyke 1976; Williamson and Sabath 1984; Wobst 1974), it transpires that at the lower end of the range of population densities *no* island, with the possible exception of Naxos and Andros, could have been self-sufficient, and even at the highest density only four islands lie comfortably above the threshold range, and well under half the islands enter it. Naturally, even in cases where an island is potentially self-sufficient, it is not necessarily the case that its people in fact operated in this way, rather than creating outward looking sub-groups that linked up instead with neighbouring islands. Moreover, it must be remembered that the above cross-cultural figures are minima. Real kin-group marriage networks in the Cyclades probably did not mechanically conform to a simple format of minimally sized groups of 300–500 people. Such groups often expand further before dividing. For example, in the Torres Strait islands a colonial-period population of about 4000–5000 was divided into five or six kin-based groups of about 900 people apiece, each occupying a few of the islands (Harris 1979: 83). The larger the populations of kin-groups in the early Cyclades, the more their distribution would, of necessity, have been trans-insular.

The case of the smaller islands is particularly interesting. Demographically, they are revealed to be in a chronic situation, and must have constituted 'commuter islands' in the language of island biogeography (Keegan and Diamond 1987: 59), in other words places that were heavily dependent on external linkage for long-term survival. Records from the early twentieth century AD are informative in this respect. Then, the population of the Antikeri numbered just seven people, and twelve lived on Keros (Naval Intelligence Division 1945: 483–4). In World War II, Donousa starved when its regular boat link was cut (Rougemont 1990: 205). Having said this, however, it is worth anticipating chapter 7 to raise the counter-case of Daskaleio-Kavos on Keros, a substantial village-level settlement by early Cycladic standards, that certainly contained a population larger than the 8–45 people predicted for the entire island in table 1, or indeed the early twentieth-century figures. Without going at present into the reasons for this anomaly, it should be stressed that far from losing their overall validity as a result of such occasional mismatches, the population ranges in table 1 provide the essential background expectation that allows anomalies to be identified, contextualised, and perhaps ultimately explained.

Exchange and mobility

Of Cherry's list of survival strategies cited earlier, only exchange and mobility are left to consider. By now it should be transparently clear that both are fundamental to life in the early Cyclades. One or the other has been implicated in practices of cultivation and herding, in the possible acquisition of new crops and accompanying ideas about their usage, in social storage networks, in exploitation of wild resources and in the biological reproduction not only of individual settlements but of entire island populations. It could be added that one or the other would be essential for procuring the unevenly distributed lithic and metallic resources of the Cyclades. Other kinds of interaction aiming at more elaborate social and cultural goals should also be included. In short, we need to envisage a virtually ceaseless movement between individuals, communities and islands, simply in order to keep life going and information flowing in the Cyclades. This movement must have been made up of many different rhythms, including those of the female and male life-cycles, the agricultural calendar, fluctuations in climate over several different time-scales, migrations of fish, seasons for ceremonies, and consumption rates of non-local materials. We can anticipate variation too in the spatial range and intensity of these oscillations. Some might be mapped

Table 1. *Island demography in the early Cyclades, as generated by likely occupation densities of 0.5–3.0 persons per sq. km. Few islands attain populations that could become self-sufficient demographic pools and marriage networks of about 300–500 people. Projected populations that fall within this range are underlined, and those that exceed it are printed in bold. The islands of Giaros and Antimelos are waterless and therefore effectively uninhabitable*

Island	Size (sq km)	Population at range of densities per sq km					
		0.5	1.0	1.5	2.0	2.5	3.0
Naxos	430	215	430	**645**	**860**	**1075**	**1290**
Andros	380	190	380	**570**	**760**	**950**	**1140**
Greater Paros	250	125	250	375	**500**	**625**	**750**
Tenos	195	97	195	293	390	487	**585**
Melos	151	76	151	227	302	378	453
Kea	126	63	126	189	252	315	378
Amorgos	124	62	124	186	248	310	372
Ios	109	55	109	164	218	273	327
Thera	100	50	100	150	200	250	300
Kythnos	100	50	100	150	200	250	300
Mykonos	86	43	86	129	172	215	258
Syros	85	43	85	128	170	213	255
Seriphos	75	38	75	113	150	188	225
Siphnos	74	37	74	111	148	185	222
Sikinos	43	22	43	65	86	108	129
Anaphi	40	20	40	60	80	100	120
Kimolos	35	18	35	53	70	88	105
Pholegandros	32	16	32	48	64	80	96
(Giaros)	20	(10)	(20)	(30)	(40)	(50)	(60)
Makronisos	18	9	18	27	36	45	54
Irakleia	18	9	18	27	36	45	54
Poliagos	15	8	15	23	30	38	45
Keros	15	8	15	23	30	38	45
Donousa	14	7	14	21	28	35	42
Reneia	14	7	14	21	28	35	42
Schoinousa	9	5	9	14	18	23	27
(Antimelos)	7	(4)	(7)	(11)	(14)	(18)	(21)
Ano Kouphonisi	6	3	6	9	12	15	18
Delos	4	2	4	6	8	10	12
Kato Kouphonisi	4	2	4	6	8	10	12
Antikeri	2	1	2	3	4	5	6
Christiana	2	1	2	3	4	5	6
Total Cycladic population:		1292	2583	3875	5166	6458	7749

out over long distances or impressive time-spans, but much seems likely to have resonated within far tinier worlds. Exogamy, by way of an example, surely often involved neighbouring communities. The extent of social storage networks is also liable to have varied, not only with the specific environmental niche occupied but also with the scales of disaster that they set out to buffer against. Quite circumscribed networks might suffice to cope with normal micro-regional fluctuations in climate and fortune, but buffering against occasional more regional failures would demand wider networks (in the event of the rare, deadly droughts that scythe the entire Aegean, the crisis would be so general and deep as to overwhelm such networks).

Much of the remainder of this book involves an exploration of the dimensions of interaction and movement in the early Cyclades as seen through the archaeological record, aiming to draw out its extraordinary variability in purposes, extent, time-scale, contents and participants. Indeed, it is no exaggeration to state that if the primary social and cultural factors that shaped this variability can be identified and explored, we will have come very close to understanding one of the central dynamics of early Cycladic history. Archaeology can provide rich and varied windows into these issues, but there are other forms of interaction that can only be inferred, and surely others too that we cannot even guess at. To indulge a brief analogy, this section ends with a passage from Columbus' diary, in which he relates an encounter with a canoeist in the straits between two islands in the Bahamas:

> And being midway between these two islands . . . I found a man alone in a canoe who was crossing from Santa Maria to Fernandina and he had with him a piece of their bread about the size of a fist and a gourd of water and a piece of brown earth powdered and kneaded into a mass and some dried leaves [i.e. tobacco], which must be something they value highly because I was brought some on San Salvador as a present. And he was carrying one of their baskets in which he had a string of glass beads and two blancas. (Columbus 1492: 39)

Foodstuffs, raw materials, social stimulants, prestige exotica already in circulation four days after Columbus' landfall, and (not least) the news of strange arrivals; such, and much more, it will be suggested, was the stuff of interaction in the early Cyclades.

Moving around in the islands

Terrestrial movement

If such interaction is to be modelled with any accuracy, it is necessary to find out about the major means of moving around the early Cyclades, and to assess the opportunities and constraints that these entailed. For terrestrial movement the options are constrained. For most, if not all, of the Neolithic and EBA, human portage was the best mechanism for moving things overland, and a not ineffective one thanks to the modest size of the islands. In Cycladic terrain a person might in one day carry a load of 20–30+ kg over a distance of about 20 km as the crow flies, a rate capable of traversing all islands in at most a couple of days. It is uncertain exactly when, and to what extent, the first equids were introduced to supplement or partly replace human portage. The arrival of the first small equids (probably donkeys) in the Aegean at present dates to the late EBA (Crouwel 1981: 32–5; Gejvall 1969: 35–7; von den Driesch and Boessneck 1990: table 16), but in the Cyclades there are as yet no identifications from stratified levels earlier than the LBA (Gamble 1979: table 1), although, given the paucity of Bronze Age faunal studies in the islands, more substantial evidence is desirable. The wheel and cart make a later arrival in the Aegean than the first equids, dated to the start of the second millennium BC on the strength of the evidence from Crete (Crouwel 1981: 54). In the Cyclades, these technologies would find little application in much of the islands' terrain. Although equids create the potential for a change of gear in overland transport networks, the constraint that they and pedestrians alike share in the Cycladic islands is the obvious one: neither can cross between islands without seacraft. As a result, even if the first equids did appear within the timescale of our analysis, their impact would be more limited than that which Whitelaw *et al.* (1997: 273) propose for Crete, where a possible arrival in EB II (albeit not yet directly proven) may correlate with the sudden increase observed in the movement of bulky pottery vessels overland. In the Cyclades, it is the sea and the maritime technology with which islanders were able cross it that constitute the most crucial variable for the analysis of movement within the whole island cluster.

Sea conditions and their implications for island life

The sea, as suggested in chapter 1, is an integral part of islandscapes, and the Cycladic seas prove just as variable as the terrestrial environments. Agouridis (1997) provides an expert description and interpretation of Aegean seafaring conditions. As so often, there is a need to balance overall trends with equally significant short-term fluctuations. The main currents and prevailing northerly winds (fig. 21) are prominent among the former. Equally important is the Mediterranean's open season for navigation, which runs from May to September, as opposed to the closed season running from November to March, with April and October as intersticial months (Casson 1971: 270–92). These factors influence patterns of movement at a generalised level. Prevailing currents and winds enable identification of the axes of movement that are most likely to be enhanced or opposed, particularly for long journeys requiring steady runs of weather. Equally, the timing of the open season suggests that most maritime activity took place between May and September, and probably all such activity that involved prolonged periods at sea.

Yet other phenomena cut across this grain, creating a more complex mixture of opportunities and impediments. The powerful Etesian winds, or *meltemia,* can close

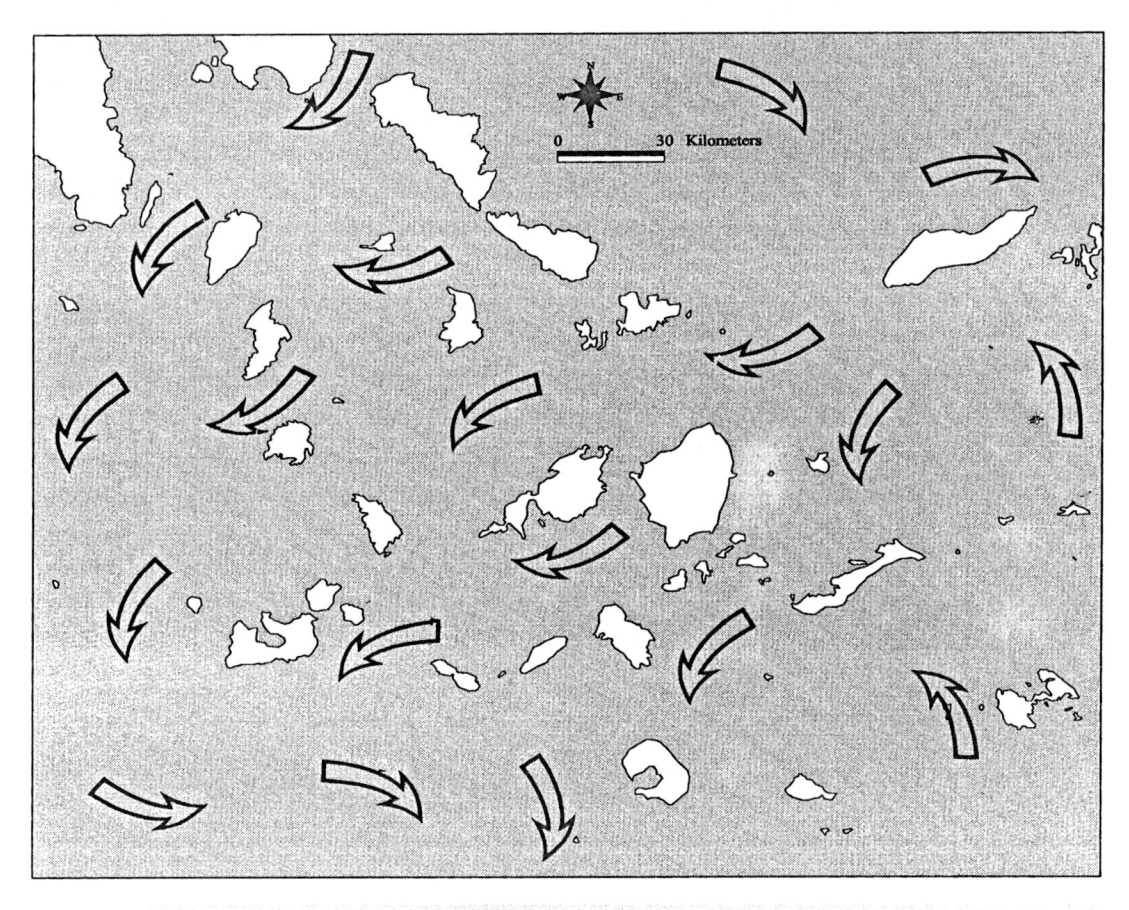

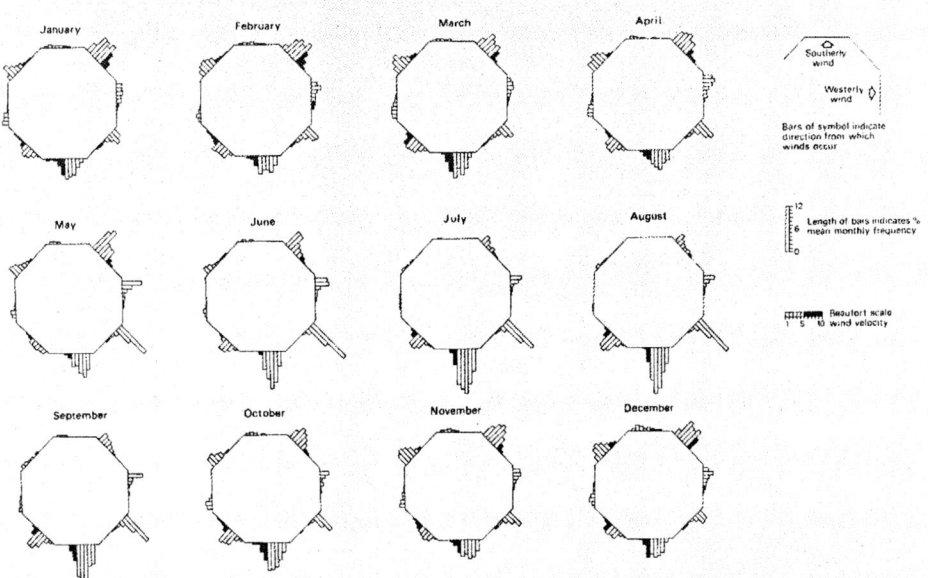

Fig. 21 Currents and winds in the Cyclades. *Above:* main summer current flows. *Below:* wind-roses for Melos. After McGeehan-Liritzis 1988: fig. 1, and reproduced from Renfrew and Wagstaff 1982b: fig. 9.3 courtesy of Malcolm Wagstaff, respectively.

the sea for days on end during 'open' July and August (though boats travel fast downwind as they abate), whilst the 'Halcyon days' of January are a short window of opportunity in the middle of the 'closed' period (Agouridis 1997: 5–6). Still briefer fluctuations are of equal significance, including the regimes of morning and evening offshore and onshore breezes, the fact that winds create surface currents that commonly override deep current flows for shallow-draft craft, and the sheer degree of variation in daily wind direction and intensity, which may in practical terms invite or thwart any given passage at any time of the year (Georgiou 1993: 361). Lastly, to balance the opportunities of sea travel are its manifest dangers, with rough coasts, reefs, and high-frequency waves (Agouridis 1997: 4) added to the changeability of the weather outlined above. Even the shortest of coasting trips or inter-island hops are never entirely risk-free, and all longer journeys are intrinsically risk-full. In short, the Cycladic seas can in turns both enable and constrain sea travel, and impact differently at different temporal and spatial scales.

Unpredictability is therefore of the essence, and has implications for seafaring. For short journeys movement in any direction should have been possible, at least if people were prepared to wait a few days. Longer journeys taking in several locations, and especially those crossing open seas (what can be termed *voyaging*), would involve much closer attention to the prevailing patterns. All journeys would be prone to delays or diversions by adverse weather, often with little warning, and longer-range journeys could easily spin out far longer than anticipated. This renders it very probable that embedded in even the most specifically motivated sea-travel was a range of other potential activities, such as social interaction, resource procurement and manufacturing. The selfsame variability in conditions makes it unlikely that prevailing currents and winds would determine the locations of maritime centres (*contra* McGeehan Liritzis 1988); instead, it is more likely that social geography in combination with technological parameters for early seafaring defined such centres and fashioned the sea-paths linking them. At another level, the risks inherent in sea travel must have served to enhance the reputations of people, objects and information that travelled across the sea, and likewise encouraged the cultivation of sophisticated seafaring skills in the fields of navigation, boat handling and weather prediction, for in such tricky seas, increasing expertise is the only viable risk-minimisation strategy, apart from the alternative of opting to travel by sea as little as possible. Given that maritime activity was crucial to most movement in the Cyclades, and that it also represented a potential avenue to glory, the development of an advanced maritime culture amongst some islanders is to be expected – although not, as we shall see, always in the same places, nor among the same proportion of the population.

The restricted duration of the sailing season also implies the need for a degree of time- and labour-allocation to reconcile the demands of the agricultural calendar with seafaring activities (fig. 22). This should not greatly affect short journeys involving

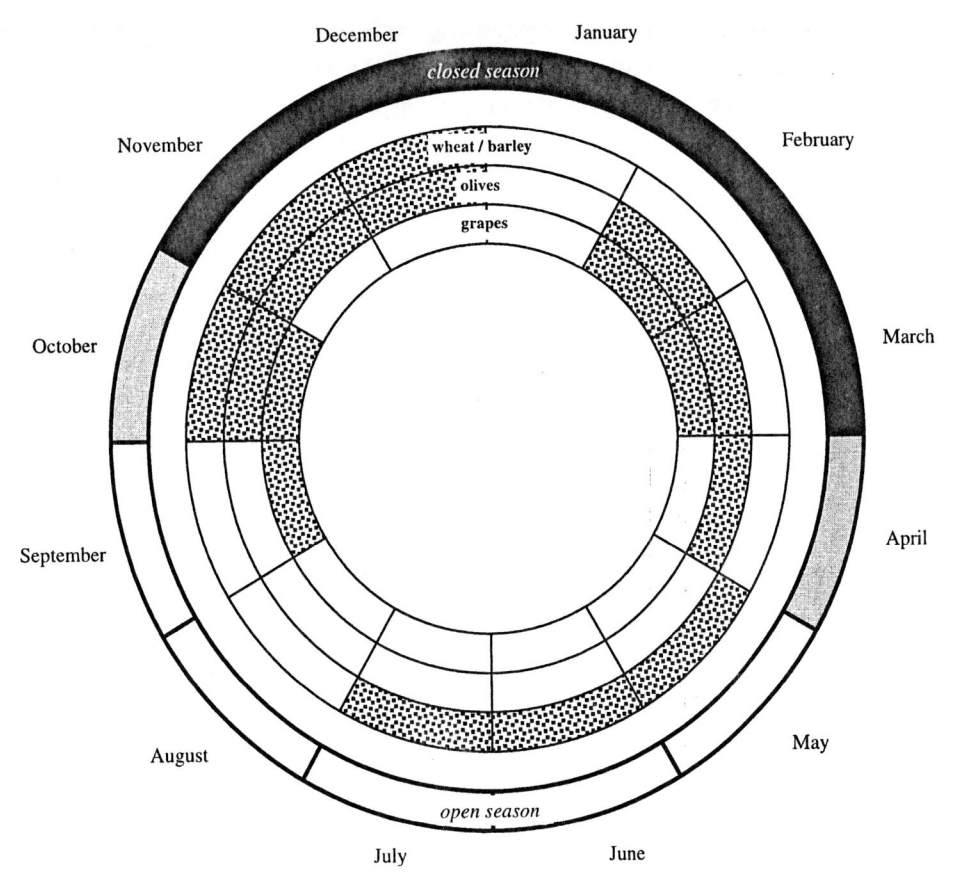

Fig. 22 Agricultural tasks and the sailing season in the Aegean. Note that the earliest date and extent of olive and vine cultivation remains open to debate.

brief, if never entirely predictable, absences, but it does have major implications for the dynamics of long-range voyaging. It was suggested above that longer voyages should belong between May and September, with April and October as marginal months. But how does this match with the rhythm of agricultural tasks? Hoeing and cereal sowing in the Mediterranean take place in October to December, the harvest occupies May through to July, and the grape-picking and wine-making fall in September and October (if vines were indeed cultivated to any degree); the olive (again if relevant to this period) is less problematic, as its main labour requirement is in the early winter, therefore in the closed season for voyaging (cf. Halstead and Jones 1989; Wagstaff and Augustson 1982: fig. 10.7). The windows for voyaging without conflict with agricultural demands are the marginal month of April (olives excepting), August, and September (vines excepting). To complicate matters, August voyages operate in the teeth of the *meltemi* season.

Various responses to this fairly tight scheduling situation can be postulated. One possibility is that long-range voyaging was limited in duration (and therefore distance) to absences of one month, or at most two. Another is that long-range seafaring and the agricultural duties that coincided with the sailing season became gender- or age-specific activities, in order to enable longer absence at sea for certain people. In the light of the fact that both the harvest and seafaring would draw heavily upon the labour of the young adult component of the population, the gender-specific option is more likely, and long-range voyaging may have been a strongly gendered practice. Another possibility is that certain communities might commit themselves sufficiently to wealth accumulation through voyaging and other maritime activity that they could afford partially to neglect their agricultural productivity and make good their shortfall through trade. The last two solutions imply at least seasonal specialisation in seafaring at the level of individuals in the community (however selected), or at the level of the community itself.

The evidence for early Cycladic seacraft

As Braudel (1972: 102) reminds us, 'we . . . have to measure these expanses of water in relation to human activity; their history would otherwise be incomprehensible if indeed it could be written at all'. To do this reliably requires a knowledge of seacraft. In many early societies seacraft comprised the largest pieces of technology in existence (Muckelroy 1978: 3), but such craft are not just machines for crossing water. They are cultural objects as well. Access to them will determine the limits of experience for any islander, will establish channels of communication, will define isolation, and can also act as an instrument of power or coercion. Shedding light on such issues in the early Cyclades will require information about boat types, their performance and the manners in which they could stitch this scatter of islands together. As mentioned in chapter 1, not until the termination of the third millennium BC is there evidence for deep-hulled sailing ships in the Aegean, best illustrated by the depictions on Cretan seals (Basch 1987: 95–106; Wachsmann 1998: 99; Yule 1980: 165–6). This horizon is discussed in more detail in chapter 10. If the case rested on iconography alone, the reality of this horizon as one of earliest incidence might be queried. But as such ship types only started to venture from the Nile up the Levantine coast in the mid-third millennium BC (Marcus 1998: 35–58; Wachsmann 1998: 9–18), and as Cretan direct contacts with the east Mediterranean took off only at the close of this millennium, the genuine absence of such seacraft in the earlier Aegean seems very probable. Evidence for the quite different seacraft that plied the Aegean during the EBA, Neolithic and still earlier periods comes in four forms.

Finds of island materials, notably obsidian, on the mainland, and early traces of people's presence in the islands, tell us only that the means existed for crossing the sea from an early date. The earliest evidence is analysed further in chapter 4, and suffice to note here that, by the beginning of the Neolithic, seacraft must have been sturdy enough to transport breeding populations of Neolithic domesticates, including cattle, to Crete (Broodbank and Strasser 1991: 241). Study of available tools for boat construction is also of limited assistance – after all, the Pacific was conquered by a technology built with stone and shell tools, and (*contra* Renfrew 1972: 356, 491) in the Aegean metal tools would not have been an essential for boat-building until the demand for complex joinery required in the construction of the sailing vessels that appear at the end of our period. More promising, but still hard to evaluate, are the possible remains of an EBA wreck off the island of Dokos on the edge of the southern Argolid (Papathanasopoulos 1976, 1990; Papathanasopoulos *et al.* 1992). Although the possibility that the remains are those of a sunken settlement or the result of landslip can be more-or-less discounted, no physical remnant of a hull survives, and in these circumstances it is not certain that the considerable quantity of material on the seabed came from a single boat, as opposed to being a palimpsest created by the material lost or dumped from boats over an extended period, in what was clearly a protected anchorage.

This leaves the corpus of two- and three-dimensional representations of seacraft from the Aegean, which number among the earliest images of seacraft known in the world. To date, most study of this corpus has concentrated on questions of boat design (Basch 1987: 76–89; Johnston 1985: 7–11; Johnstone 1988: 60–4; Roberts 1987; Wachsmann 1998: 69–82). Several attempts have been made, however, to integrate the information derived from the images into wider social interpretations (Broodbank 1989; Renfrew 1972: 356, 358, 455; Runnels 1985a: 42–3). The full range of boat representations is discussed in full elsewhere (Broodbank 1989: 327–9; see Marangou 1991 for the clay models of monoxyla, or simple dug-outs, at Neolithic sites in northern Greece, most of which represent river or lake craft).[3] In terms of dating, all the representations, save for the monoxyla, date to EB II. The Cycladic examples are most numerous, comprising images incised on the so-called frying pans, rock-pecked images and lead models (fig. 23). The majority of frying pan images are strikingly

---

[3] The report of depictions of seacraft with sails on a sword from the notorious 'Dorak treasure', which is claimed to have been excavated in north-west Anatolia, are excluded from this analysis on the grounds that the authenticity of the Dorak material has never been adequately substantiated. Basch (1987: 91–3) gives a thoroughly sceptical expert assessment of the boat depictions and the mixed iconographic sources that they reflect.

[4] A recent restudy of the three lead models now in the Ashmolean Museum, Oxford, casts doubt on the genuineness of these objects (E.S. Sherratt, pers. comm.; in press). The reason is that whilst the balance of nautical opinion favours interpretation of the high end of the vessels depicted on the frying pans as a representation of the stern-post, the high end on the lead models is clearly fashioned as the prow. As most frying pan depictions come from graves excavated at the end of the nineteenth century by Tsountas at Chalandriani on Syros (Tsountas 1899: 85–90), their status is beyond doubt. In contrast, the lead boat models surfaced several years later on the Athenian antiquities market, with no better provenance than a claimed association with a grave on Naxos. The suggestion is that the models reflect a modern misreading of the frying pan images.

Table 2. *Iconographic features of longboats and other canoes*

Attribute	Small canoe	Longboat
Iconographic profile	Low and scattered	Selectively high (Chalandriani)
Context of 2-D image	Crude rock pecking	Finely crafted (?) ritual vessel
Material of model	Clay	Metal (if genuine)
Further elaboration	None	Fish totem and trailing 'banners'
Symbolic association	None	Sun/star, vulva and (?) waves
Activities depicted	Loading animal? (everyday)	At sea (if stamps are waves)

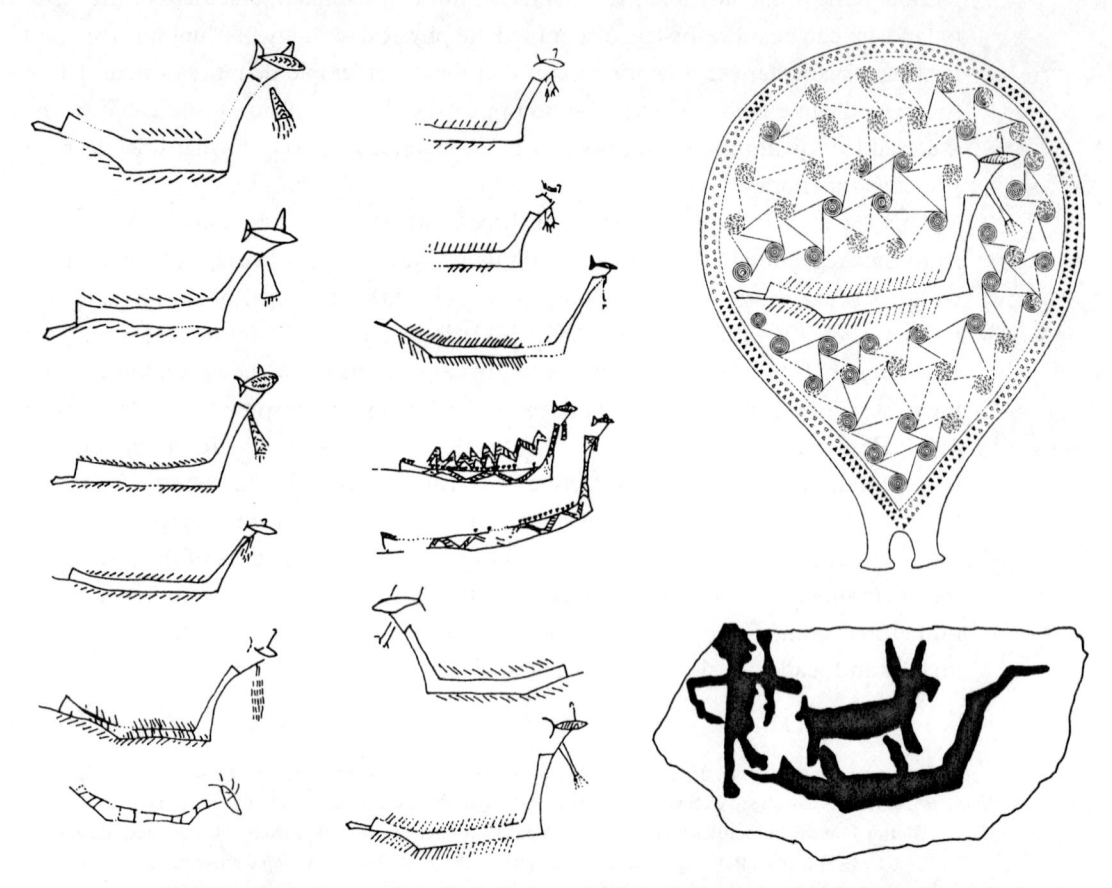

Fig. 23 Early Bronze Age Cycladic boat depictions (not to scale). *Left:* longboats depicted on frying pans. *Right above:* example of frying pan with image of longboat. *Right below:* rock-pecking showing a small canoe with a person and quadruped, from Korphi t'Aroniou in southern Naxos. After Coleman 1985: fig. 5 and Doumas 1965: fig. 4; frying pan reproduced courtesy of the Fitzwilliam Museum, drawn by Norman Rayner and Richard Nicholls.

concentrated in the Chalandriani cemetery on Syros, the clearest of the rock-peckings come from Korphi t'Aroniou in southern Naxos, and the lead boats are all without sound provenance.[4]

These representations enable two types of seacraft to be reconstructed, both of which are generically canoe-type vessels (table 2). The first is a large, although slender, 'longboat', either an extended dugout or a more fully clinker-built vessel (Basch 1987: 85–8), with an angled hull for speed and a tall post surmounted by a fish totem at what is almost certainly the stern (Roberts 1987), and powered by a large number of paddlers. Ignoring the most myriapodic depictions, a minimum vessel of some 15–20 m length with a crew of perhaps twenty-five people can be reconstructed (Broodbank 1989: 328–9). Even longer boats and larger crews are feasible, and are well paralleled in Maori New Zealand (Best 1925), the Pacific Northwest (de Laguna 1972: 340–1; Waterman and Coffin 1920: 12–17) and the Caribbean (Columbus 1492: 31, 105). The second type of canoe is a much more modest craft with a small crew, judging from scrappy indications of rowlocks, lack of decoration, and only the high post resembling the longboat. This surely represents a small, simple dugout or dugout-derived vessel, probably a general type of small craft used throughout the Neolithic and EBA. Although the smaller canoe seems likely to be a very ancient vessel type, in the case of longboats it is harder to decide whether the iconographic horizon in EB II indicates a real innovation at that time, or whether their first use predated their depiction, with the images instead signalling a rise in cultural prominence during EB II. The case for the cultural significance of longboats in EB II is made in chapter 8, but it should be noted that the carpentry needed for any planking in a longboat's construction is unlikely to have exceeded the capabilities of the copper flat axes that are now attested at the Zas cave as early as the FN (Marangou 1990: cat. nos. 2–3), although the first metal saws, attested in the later EBA (Marangou 1990: cat. no. 71; Renfrew 1972: 328), would naturally have facilitated construction.

It is unlikely that these canoes represent the entire range of seacraft in existence in the early Cyclades, for ethnographic studies demonstrate the typically wide range of types encountered (e.g. Bowdler 1995: fig. 7; Haddon and Hornell 1936–8; Waterman and Coffin 1920). Intermediate kinds of canoe probably existed, as perhaps did inshore rafts, although the latter's seaworthiness and utility would have been slight in Cycladic conditions. It is unlikely, however, that we need fear the existence of iconographically invisible types of craft with very different *performance capabilities*. This is important with regard to the possibility of an earlier use of the sail, for although no iconographic trace of a mast or sail is attested before the end of the third millennium BC (cf. note 3 above), this absence of evidence cannot be taken as definitive evidence of absence with so limited a number of images. But what can be emphasised is that a sail will transform performance only if it is stabilised either by constructing wider-hulled, keeled vessels like those that are seen at the end of the third millennium (involving major changes in boat-building traditions), or by adding outriggers (a tradition unknown in the ancient Mediterranean). Ethnographic accounts of the small sails mounted on Maori war canoes (Best 1925: 177–90) and (after contact with Westerners) on Pacific Northwest vessels (Drucker 1951: 85–6; de Laguna 1972: 341) emphasise their limitations, not the least being that they could only be mounted if travelling downwind, when they acted as an ancillary boost to the paddlers. In the changeable Aegean the most that we might expect of a hypothetical sail mounted on a canoe would be a modest extension of a vessel's speed with a following wind. A recent experiment at crossing the Aegean in a dugout canoe with a small sail erected, at least when the wind permitted it without threatening to capsize the craft, has revealed travel capabilities that are in no sense superior to those deduced below for paddle-only canoes (Tichy nd).[5]

Of more import is the likelihood that the iconographic emphasis on the longboat over-represents this craft relative to humbler types, and that smaller canoes were in fact the everyday craft used for most maritime movement in the early Cyclades. The cultural reasons *why* specific kinds of boats were depicted at specific places in the Cyclades cannot be addressed at this point, but the differences between depictions of longboats and small canoes seen in table 2 provides strong hints that longboats were deliberately distinguished. Over-representation of spectacular, high-status craft is in fact a problem throughout the Aegean Bronze Age. Probably the best approximation to a balanced view is a miniature wall-painting from the LBA West House at Akrotiri on Thera (Doumas 1992a: fig. 38), which shows skiffs meeting an incoming fleet – itself a reflection of the unusual breadth of 'realistic' matter permitted in this illustrative genre, and even this omits trading vessels. Small, unglamorous, hence overlooked craft seem in fact to have outnumbered the handfuls of large, prestigious high-visibility boats throughout much of the Mediterranean's history (Braudel 1972: 107).

If under-depicted small canoes were in all probability the work-horses for most maritime communication in the islands, what were the functions of the large canoes, or longboats? Taking into account their more prominent and elaborate iconography, their large crew, and excellent ethnographic parallels from the Maori and Pacific Northwest (e.g. Best 1925; Waterman and Coffin 1920: 14–17), it can be suggested that longboats were special-purpose prestige craft used for warfare, raiding and high-status activities such as ceremonial processions and (arguably; cf. chapter 9) long-range voyaging (Broodbank 1989: 335–6, 1993: 327). Although they could certainly carry cargo, they are superfluously labour-intensive for everyday shuttling and too

[5] The craft, a 6.2 m dugout carved from a single trunk, and with the sail mounted in the middle of its length, took seventy hours at sea, spread over two weeks, to complete a 230 km journey from Samos via the north-east Cyclades and Euboia to Attica. The average speed of 3.3 kmh was exceeded up to a maximum of 4.5 kmh. Neither of these figures outstrips the cruising speeds estimated for the early Cycladic longboats, and the average speed is barely higher than that proposed for the small canoes.

slender to handle bulk cargoes beyond the capabilities of a few smaller canoes. In addition, for small-scale societies they represent so serious a demographic risk in terms of their potential loss at sea, that a commensurate expectation of gain through their usage might be anticipated. Lastly, and again with reference to island demography, it is striking that if such vessels had crews of at least twenty-five people, and perhaps considerably more, it cannot have been at all straightforward to organise longboat-related activities; far from being a generalised phenomenon, they need to be associated with particular practices, places and forms of island culture (see chapter 8).

The performance of early Cycladic seacraft

With a clearer grasp of the types of vessel involved, it is possible to draw conclusions about the general capabilities and limitations of early Cycladic seacraft. This in turn will allow a series of major parameters for maritime movement in the early Cyclades to be put forward. A combination of experimental archaeology with broadly analogous boats (Johnstone 1988: 112; Tzala 1989), calculations based on the hull remains of ancient vessels (McGrail 1988, 1990) and ethnographic data (de Laguna 1972; Drucker 1951; Glazier 1991; Haddon and Hornell 1936–8; Keegan 1992: 49–51) enable the principal features of early Cycladic canoe performances to be estimated.

First, as such craft require no harbour facilities beyond a beach to draw up on, they could be used from any point on the coast not fringed with cliffs. Second, despite accounts of Pacific canoes operating in heavy swells, there are obviously limits due to the modest freeboard and open construction, and the choppy, short-frequency waves of the Aegean would present substantial problems in rough weather for Aegean seacraft, not least if such craft were in part plank-built and liable to 'hog', or arch and buckle, as Wachsmann (1998: 74) argues. Third, as an allied point, canoes do not respond well to travelling into wave-lines or head-winds of any magnitude, needing to zig-zag to make even slow headway. Fourth, they have a limited capacity for bulky cargoes because of both low freeboard and stability; smaller canoes could carry a few people, livestock or storage vessels, or a quantity of smaller objects, whilst ethnographic records suggest that longboats acting as barges with reduced crews might shift a ton or so in very calm conditions (de Laguna 1972: 340; with a full crew there would be little room for bulk cargoes). The limitations on cargo must have helped to select for dispersed social storage practices as opposed to regionally centralised storage of foodstuffs in the Cyclades, for medium-sized container jars that could be stowed easily, and for low-bulk/high-value prestige goods. Flexible in terms of where they could be beached, but unable to go to sea at all on many days, and able to transport only a modest cargo, Cycladic canoes present a radically different set of navigational opportunities and constraints from those familiar in the islands today.

In terms of speed and effective range they also belong to another world. When using

Table 3. *Performance parameters and functions of longboats and other canoes.*

Attribute	Small canoe	Longboat
Size	About 4–6 m?	About 15–20+ m
Crew	About 1–4	About 25+
Labour intensiveness	Low	High
Maximum speed	About 5 km per hour	About 10 km per hour
Daily range	About 20 km	About 40–50 km
Cargo capacity	About 50–150 kg	1 ton as barge (inoperable at sea?) Low with full crew at sea
Construction input	Low	High
Ethnographic use	General purpose craft	War canoe and high-status vessel

comparative data, a problem is faced in distinguishing between optimal performance, derived from hull form or known from observed sprints, and the overall distance that could be covered at a sustainable speed. Big canoes, analogous to the early Cycladic longboats, are reported to attain maximum sprint speeds of 4–6 knots or about 7–10 kmh (Best 1925: 189; Keegan 1992: 60; McGrail 1988: 45), but although some quite spectacular feats might be possible under very favourable conditions, it would be unrealistic to translate this into a typical day's journey of about 100 km. An average daily range of some 40–50 km for a longboat with a full crew and a negligible cargo is probably fairly accurate on the basis of Pacific data (Broodbank 1989: 333). Allowing for some night paddling, it is backed by the claim of the Ragged Islanders to Columbus that they could reach Cuba (about 100 km distant) in one of their large canoes in a day and a half (Columbus 1492: 57). For small and/or heavily laden canoes, the practical range should be set considerably lower. Alden (1979: 175) states that travel in small canoes is about 33 per cent slower than walking on flat ground, and an average of 15–20 km per day was covered in the Aegean by an experimental 6 m reed-boat, or *papyrella*, powered by five or six paddlers on a voyage from Attica to Melos (Tzala 1989). The daily range for small canoes is accordingly set at about 20 km. Interestingly, this is about the same as that for overland portage. Together with canoes' modest cargo capacities, this similarity suggests that for local traffic land and sea transport were equivalent in range and bulk, and evenly balanced alternatives for intra-island transport where coasting travel was feasible, although of course they differ in that sea travel involves higher risks and more skill. Table 3 summarises the performance parameters of the two main types of canoe.

Scaling early Cycladic maritime space

Many implications of the above analysis will become apparent during the course of this book, but one intriguing issue that commands our attention straight away is how

Islands, people and seafaring

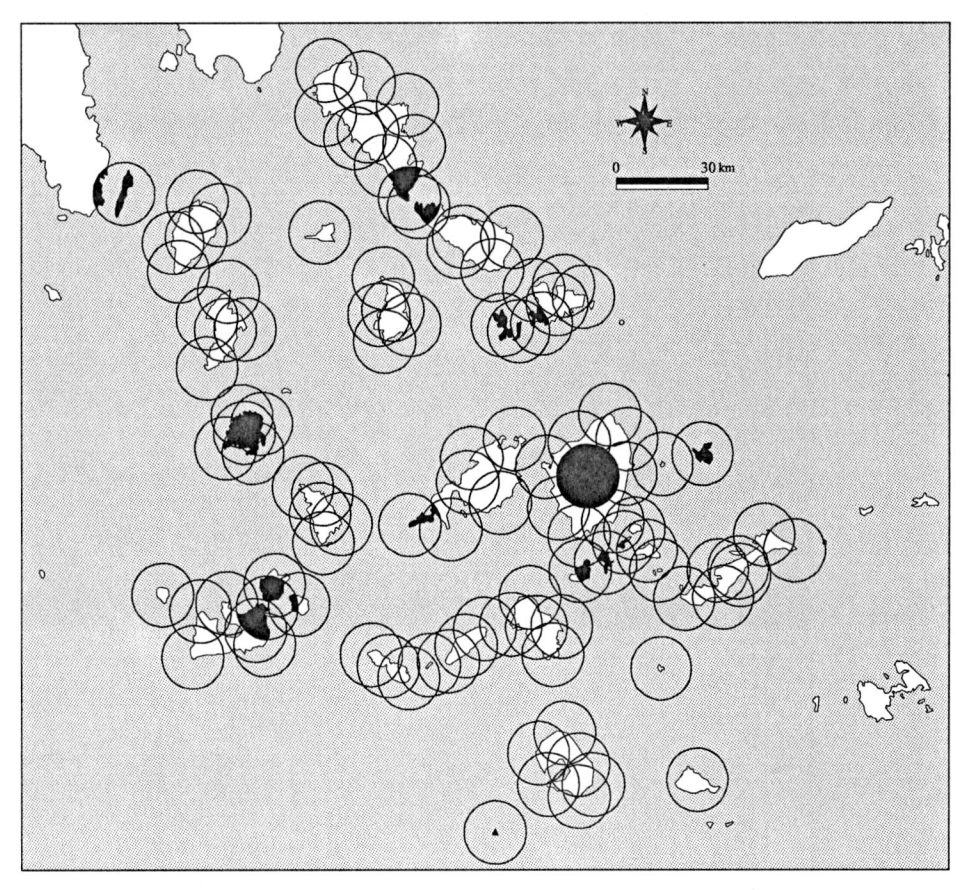

Fig. 24 Daily travel range in the early Cyclades based on a 10 km radius for a there-and-back journey. Circles are taken from the centres of all islands and the corners of larger ones. Shaded examples illustrate the diversity of terrestrial and maritime islandscapes encountered in different parts of the Cyclades.

canoe speed and range affected the experienced scale of early Cycladic space. Fig. 24 shows the range in a small canoe, or on foot, of a one-day 10 km there-and-back journey from points on each island. Circles that touch indicate points that can be connected within the range of a day's one-way journey. This experiment provides some idea of the scope of local interaction by boat, on foot, or indeed by a mixture of both these. Although in later chapters it will be demonstrated that many factors affected the degree to which people travelled, this daily range offers provisional clues as to where we might expect island communities in regular contact to form. The islands in contact at the 10 km there-and-back range make up a series of small groups or chains. The 20 km distance of a day's one-way journey creates fewer, larger groups. Thera, Christiana, Anaphi, Syros and Giaros remain cut off, however, and several other islands hover at the limits. It would be unwise to interpret these thresholds too precisely, but at least they start to identify potential areas where people would either have

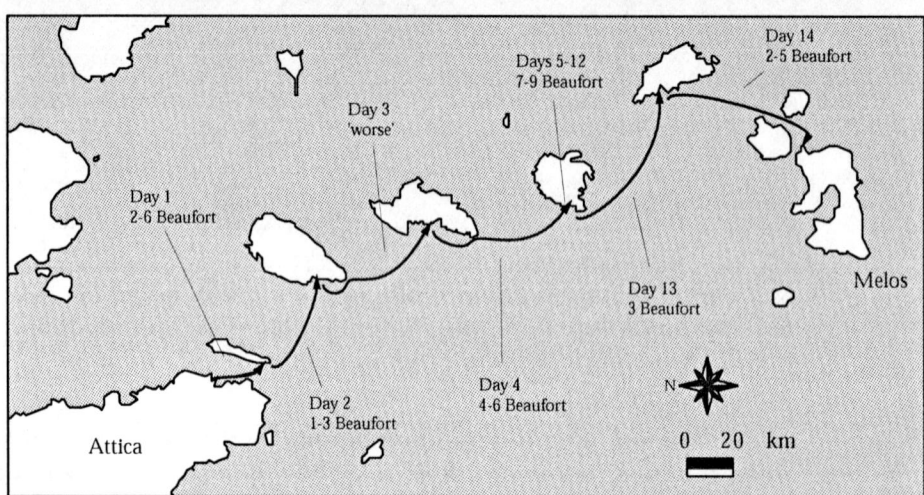

Fig. 25 An experimental reed-boat, or *papyrella*, and its two-week Cycladic voyage from Lavrion to Melos. Photograph courtesy of Catherine Perlès; data from Tzala 1989.

to work harder to keep in touch, or slip into a state of relative isolation. Fig. 24 also provides insights into the diversity of the local terrestrial and maritime islandscapes that people in different parts of the Cyclades would have experienced in their short-range interactions, from the land-locked horizons of central Naxos, through inter-island examples, to many others dominated by sea.

But surely the most surprising fact is quite simply how extensive the Cyclades seem. Setting aside the potential for faster longboat voyaging, in terms of everyday small craft the Cyclades as a whole appear to be roughly a week's journey in length, assuming a perfect run of days favourable to seagoing in a particular direction. In fact such runs are rare. Fig. 25 shows the day-by-day progress of the *papyrella* voyage mentioned earlier, which undertook such a traverse in a small paddled craft. Despite a minute freeboard, the flow-through construction allowed waves of 1.5 m and winds of Beaufort Scale 5–6 to be ridden, but under worse conditions the craft had to be brought ashore (Tzala 1989: 15–16). The journey took seven days of paddling time, but equally significant is the fact that it lost seven more days to rough seas. In other words, the Cyclades took in effect not just a week, but a fortnight, to cross, implying a month for a return journey. Combined with the length of the sailing season and the demands of the agricultural calendar, the complex of factors that must have surrounded long-range voyaging across or beyond the Cyclades starts to become apparent.

This prompts one last, intriguing exercise. It is frequently stated that the Aegean is a frogpond in comparison to the Pacific or Caribbean. But this is not the whole story. If we aim to pursue a contextual approach to islandscapes, sea distances will possess only limited meaning as absolute measurements, and gain much of their significance in the light of travelling time. When thinking about early Aegean distances in comparison to those of the Pacific in particular, we would do well to introduce some scaling ratios. For the pre-contact Pacific, at least as far back as the Lapita phase, sailing canoes, albeit with varying rigs, were the main means of long-range maritime movement. Gladwin (1970) and Lewis (1972) suggest that about 100 sea miles (about 170 km) was the limit of a one-night island-to-island crossing for a sailing canoe of the late pre-contact period, and Irwin (1992: 44) concludes that long-range canoes could cover about 100–150 sea miles (about 170–250 km) in a 24-hour run. Put against the Aegean estimates of some 20 km a day in smaller canoes and 40–50 km in longboats, the implied scaling ratio is in the order of between 4 and 8 to 1. Whether this should enjoin us mentally to shrink the Pacific or expand the Aegean is a matter of perspective and preference (and both are stimulating exercises). This ratio also makes some comparative patterns appear in a different light.

For if this scaling ratio is applied to the Cyclades, these islands become similar in terms of travelled distance to the Solomons, and the Aegean as a whole would equate to Melanesia from the Manus group to Fiji, plus parts of southern Micronesia, in other words to approximately the extent of the Lapita zone. One corollary of this is that the dispersal ranges of Melanesian and Melian obsidian, which appear ostensibly so very different, become more comparable than they at first appear. Knapp's parallel, cited in the previous chapter, between the eastern half of the Mediterranean and the southwest Pacific (Knapp 1990: figs. 2–4) in fact becomes apposite only with the second-millennium BC expansion of the new long-range sailing ships across the former. Even as late as the Renaissance the Mediterranean was 66–80 days long (Braudel 1972: 365), and before the spread of sailing craft it must have been unimaginably vast. The pre-Columbian Caribbean, whose canoe technology was comparable to that of the early Cyclades, is in fact a better direct analogy for the Mediterranean before sailing craft than is south-west Oceania, and, interestingly, contact period accounts of the Caribbean suggest that it too was divided into a series of largely distinct worlds, much as can be envisaged for the several basins of the pre-second-millennium Mediterranean. Clearly, further factors need to be taken into account. One is the high degree of inter-visibility in the Aegean, which is not subject to cultural stretching. Maritime risk is a more ambiguous issue, for although oceanic voyaging is a dangerous enterprise, one of the most treacherous features of Aegean seafaring is the ubiquitous presence of rugged coastlines and reefs. Speculative as these comparisons may be, they serve their purpose if they enhance our respect for the activities of early seafarers in the Aegean, and for early Aegean distances across a sea that is now shrunk to the size of a postage stamp by modern shipping and air travel.

4

The dawn treaders

> From morn
> To noon he fell; from noon to dewy eve,
> A summer's day; and with the setting sun
> Dropped from the zenith like a falling star,
> On Lemnos the Aegean isle.
> *Paradise Lost,* JOHN MILTON

The earliest horizon of colonisation in the Cyclades is the most obvious point at which to begin an island history. But in reality it is not that simple. For understanding what came before colonisation is essential if the circumstances of first settlement are to be put in context. Moreover, the term 'colonisation' itself stands in need of clarification, as a variety of practices and intentions can be intended by it. Only once these questions have been explored can we move on to analyse the first settlement horizons of the LN and FN, the reasons why people started to live in these islands, and the insights afforded by configurational perspectives and modelling of expansion routes, in order to understand the processes by which the Cyclades were transformed from an empty archipelago into one occupied by resident communities. Cherry's work excepted (1981, 1985, 1987, 1990), Cycladic archaeologists have seldom addressed such questions. Indeed, the first excavators of a Cycladic Neolithic settlement, that at Saliagos, hardly considered how people got there, assuming a development from an earlier, undiscovered phase in the islands (Evans and Renfrew 1968: 82–91). Yet the colonisation of islands should, like any form of small-scale migrational activity, be accessible to analysis (Anthony 1990), and a combination of approaches will allow us to generate a range of ideas about the ways in which communities may have started to emerge in the Cyclades. Chapter 5 develops this line of enquiry further by interpreting the varied archaeological signatures of the early horizons as indications of different ways of living in the islands within the parameters established in chapter 3.

The meanings of colonisation

Cherry's pioneering research on the colonisation of the Mediterranean islands will be taken as a blueprint to elaborate and, in several respects, rework. Despite ongoing changes in colonisation dates (cf. Cherry 1981 and 1990 for the Mediterranean as a whole), much of his paradigm remains robust. There is manifestly a patterning to island colonisation that, at a generalised level, relates to island size, distance from a mainland, and configuration. Cherry was equally right to emphasise the fact that the first island settlements post-dated by many millennia the earliest indications that islands were being explored and their resources exploited. A third lasting contribution is his proposal that colonisation, although certainly purposive, tended to involve quite short-range moves by small groups of settlers previously living in adjacent areas, rather than waves of immigrants from far afield. Some of the movement parameters proposed in the previous chapter are relevant to this third issue. For in contrast to Pacific or Caribbean domesticates, the Aegean farming 'package' was bulky and vulnerable at sea, and one day's travel, or about 20 km at laden canoe speeds, must have been a common maximum for uninterrupted crossings (so, considering also seasonal constraints, Milton probably got the time-scale right in the lines that head this chapter, despite the unlikely mode of entry). Somewhat longer uninterrupted colonising crossings should have been feasible in favourable conditions, although after two days at sea animals can become difficult to handle (Case 1969: 180), and any reliance on a run of steady weather in the Aegean is risky. An upper threshold can therefore be set at two days plus a night at sea, or about 50–60 km with some night paddling. This distance in fact brings all the Aegean islands into colonising range from other land.

On the other hand, there are several ways in which Cherry's models need to be modified if a better resolution on Cycladic processes is to be realised. For example, his focus on high-level comparison operates at the expense of context-specific exploration. It allows little opportunity to explore colonisation as a cumulative, historical process in which each event shaped the next in often unanticipated ways, and in which the overall pattern is our *post hoc* rationalisation of a palimpsest of actions in reality driven by the short-term decisions of individuals or groups. It can also be argued that there must have been considerable variability in the purposiveness as well as the range of colonisation episodes, from localised shifts that were probably never considered significant events, to others where fairly ambitious decision-making may be inferred. One instance of the latter is likely to have been the colonisation of Crete early in the Neolithic (Broodbank and Strasser 1991); other instances are highlighted in this chapter. And lastly, Cherry's assertion that the first Cycladic settlements were small and fairly isolated will be shown to stand in need of serious revision (Cherry 1981: 60–2, 1985: 23–8).

As indicated above, some preliminary matters of definition are also in order, starting with 'colonisation' itself. Purcell (1990: 56), writing of Greek colonisation in the first millennium BC, argues that the term can be misleading because it obscures the many antecedent activities and movements that led to a permanent population transfer to a new area (see also de Angelis 1998). Smith (1995) criticises the assumptions that are introduced when deploying the term in the Pacific. Gosden (1993: 24) reconfigures the very idea of colonisation by visualising it as a form of spatial reworking, involving the creation of new nodes, and as one end of a spectrum of ways of using

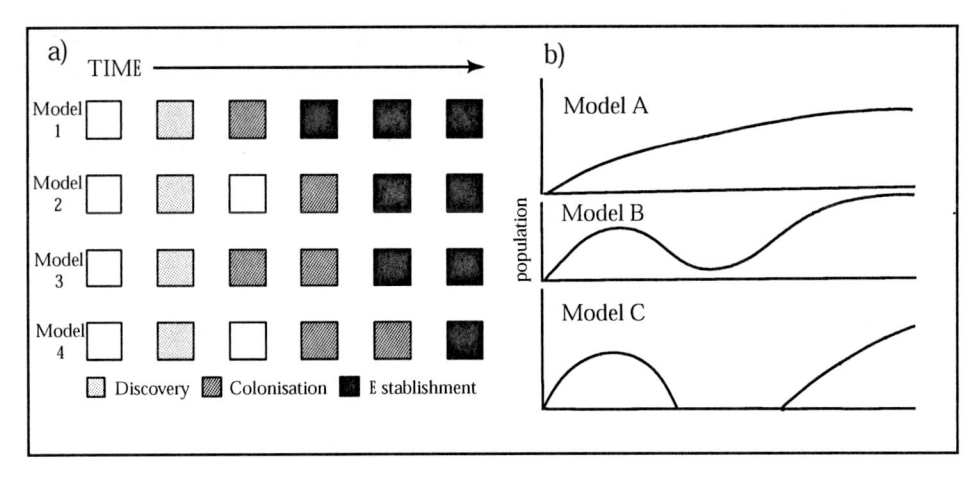

Fig. 26 Model phases for the settlement of an island. *Left:* Graves and Addison's four sequences, exploring relative rates for the transition from discovery to colonisation and establishment. Model 1: discovery, colonisation and establishment succeed each other rapidly. Model 2: discovery precedes colonisation by a significant period of time; colonisation is quickly followed by establishment. Model 3: discovery is quickly followed by colonisation; establishment occurs significantly later. Model 4: Significant periods of time separate discovery, colonisation and establishment. *Right:* Stanley Price's hypothetical three trajectories for an island's population in the aftermath of colonisation. Information from Graves and Addison 1995: table 2 and after Stanley Price 1977: fig. 3, respectively.

islands. And at a practical definitional level for islands archaeologists, Cherry distinguishes between:

> the earliest *occupation* of an island (i.e. the point at which it has become the principal provider of a group's subsistence requirements and the focus of its residential pattern throughout the year), and its earliest *utilisation* (i.e. short-term or seasonal visits to procure resources, or even accidental, unsuccessful colonisation). (Cherry 1990: 198)

Even this distinction leaves some ambiguity. For should unsuccessful colonisation be grouped with deliberately short-term visits? A failed settlement, however brief, is as appropriately categorised by what it attempted as by how long it survived – it depends whether one is interested in people's intentions, or their impact upon, and duration in, a given island. Graves and Addison (1995: tables 1 and 2), building on Irwin (1992: 42–100), set out further distinctions for eastern Polynesia that clarify this problem, *mutatis mutandis*, for other islands. They distinguish between *colonisation*, which is defined as 'placement of human settlements on discovered islands', and *establishment*, defined as 'occupation of an island by a population of sufficient size (i.e. one that has passed the threshold at which catastrophic accidents or reproductive bottlenecks would be likely to affect its long-term viability)'. They use this distinction to define four model sequences for an island's settlement (fig. 26 left). Likewise, Stanley Price (1977) has outlined three hypothetical trajectories in the case of Neolithic Cyprus:

(1) colonisation followed by logistic growth, (2) colonisation, expansion and subsequent decline without abandonment, and (3) colonisation, collapse and recolonisation (fig. 26 right).

How well do these ideas and sequences work for the Cyclades in particular? Some qualifications need to be made. Defining discovery as 'exploration which results in successful identification and location of an island or set of islands' (Graves and Addison 1995: table 1) is unrealistic in the inter-visible Aegean and better replaced by 'exploration involving landfall and reconnaissance'. Moreover, the modest populations derived from the previous chapter's exercise in early Cycladic demography argue that if too stringent a definition of establishment is applied to individual islands, the majority will never qualify as anything more than contingently colonised, yet obviously many did succeed in sustaining communities over considerable periods of time. The problem here is that Graves and Addison take the individual island as the unit for analysis, whilst the key to sustaining communities in the early Cyclades lay in the maintenance of inter-island networks. In other words, the concept of establishment is really relevant to networks of communities in wider patches of islandscape, not to the individual islands. In addition, Graves and Addison's models 1 and 3 are inapplicable in the Cyclades, owing to the extended period that elapsed between discovery/reconnaissance and colonisation. Their models 2 and 4, however, which emphasise the variable time-spans that separate the first attempts at colonisation from the establishment of viable populations, prove useful in helping to understand the Cycladic archaeological record. Likewise, Stanley Price's models prepare us to anticipate varied colonising trajectories in different parts of the island group. To summarise, 'colonisation' can be retained as a convenient short-hand term as long as we remain alert to the range of things that it can signify, and the variety of antecedent and subsequent activities that bracket it.

Pre-Neolithic activity and the sinking of Cycladia

The previous chapter argued that the Cyclades are in many respects not an easy place to live in. The zero option is therefore not to colonise, and to exploit their resources from afar. And indeed, although people have occupied these islands to varying degrees for much of the last 7000 years, there are clear signs that the Cyclades – or to be strictly accurate, a changing configuration of islands that occupied their area of the Aegean at different Pleistocene sea-levels – received earlier visits by mainland-based groups, apparently without colonisation, for almost as long a period again.

Melian obsidian found in late Upper Palaeolithic levels dating to the eleventh millennium uncalibrated years bp (roughly the eleventh millennium BC) at the Franchthi cave in the southern Argolid constitutes the earliest evidence of a human presence in the Cycladic region (Perlès 1987: 142–5; Renfrew and Aspinall 1990). The obsidian continues through the Mesolithic strata at Franchthi, and from the start of the

Neolithic is encountered at early farming sites across much of the Aegean. In the maritime regions surrounding the Cyclades, the case for an even earlier start to hunter-gatherer seafaring and visitation of islands is growing, informed by an increasingly refined knowledge of sea-level stands, and therefore the status of currently insular areas, during the last glacial (Fairbanks 1989; Lambeck 1996; van Andel 1989, 1990; van Andel and Shackleton 1982). The very earliest indications of sea-crossings are Middle Palaeolithic tools found on Kephallonia in the Ionian islands just west of the Aegean (Kavvadias 1984) and unconfirmed reports of tools on Skyros in the Northern Sporades (Cherry 1981: 44), in both cases best interpreted as residues of visitation rather than colonisation. The former sea-crossing would have been negligible at low sea-level stands, but the latter can never have been less than about 20 km. In fact, these dates and distances should not come as a surprise, for sea-crossings of 60 km or more to Pleistocene Sahul and Melanesia, and a remarkable 200–230 km crossing to later Pleistocene Manus in the latter area, are amply confirmed (Irwin 1992: 18–30; Spriggs 1997: 23–42). Moreover, the encircling, dense configuration of Aegean coasts and islands favours experiments in seafaring by creating ideal maritime 'nursery' conditions (Irwin 1989: 168, 1992: 5). The reduced distances generated by glacial sea-levels would have rendered the Aegean even more favourable to such experiments when seafaring began, despite the lower temperatures and buoyancy (Jameson *et al.* 1994: 212), with subsequent sea-level rises plausibly serving to enhance the development of nascent navigational skills.

Although this very extended pre-colonisation phase in the Cyclades remains obscure, some insights can be gleaned. Like other major drops in sea-level during the Pleistocene, that during the last glacial maximum at *c.* 18,000 bp (uncalibrated) created a large island with several satellites in the place of the Cyclades. This island will be named *Cycladia*. Recent improvements in the documentation and calibration of eustatic change combined with sophisticated modelling of crustal rebound have enabled Lambeck (1996) to generate a remarkably precise reconstruction of the topography of Cycladia and the degrees by which it drowned towards the end of the Pleistocene (fig. 27). At the lowest sea-level stands, Cycladia was an insular land-mass of slightly more than 6000 sq km, with extensive lowlands at its centre and apparently a lacustrine depression between the uplands that were later to become Mykonos and Naxos. Off its coast lay expanded versions of Amorgos, Anaphi, Thera, the Melos group, Siphnos, Seriphos and Kythnos, totalling maybe in the region of another 1500 sq km. Kea and Makronisos were parts of the mainland, which lay only some 5 km to the north-west of Cycladia. Despite its large size, however, Cycladia's expanses of lowland were vulnerable to rising seas, and it was rapidly reduced at the close of the Pleistocene. By the start of the Holocene, Cycladia had vanished save for the modern islands, most still with a narrow halo, a few small land-bridges, and a more substantial tract of land between Greater Paros and Naxos. The physical form of the Cycladic region was therefore altering throughout the late glacial millennia, and sometimes fairly rapidly.

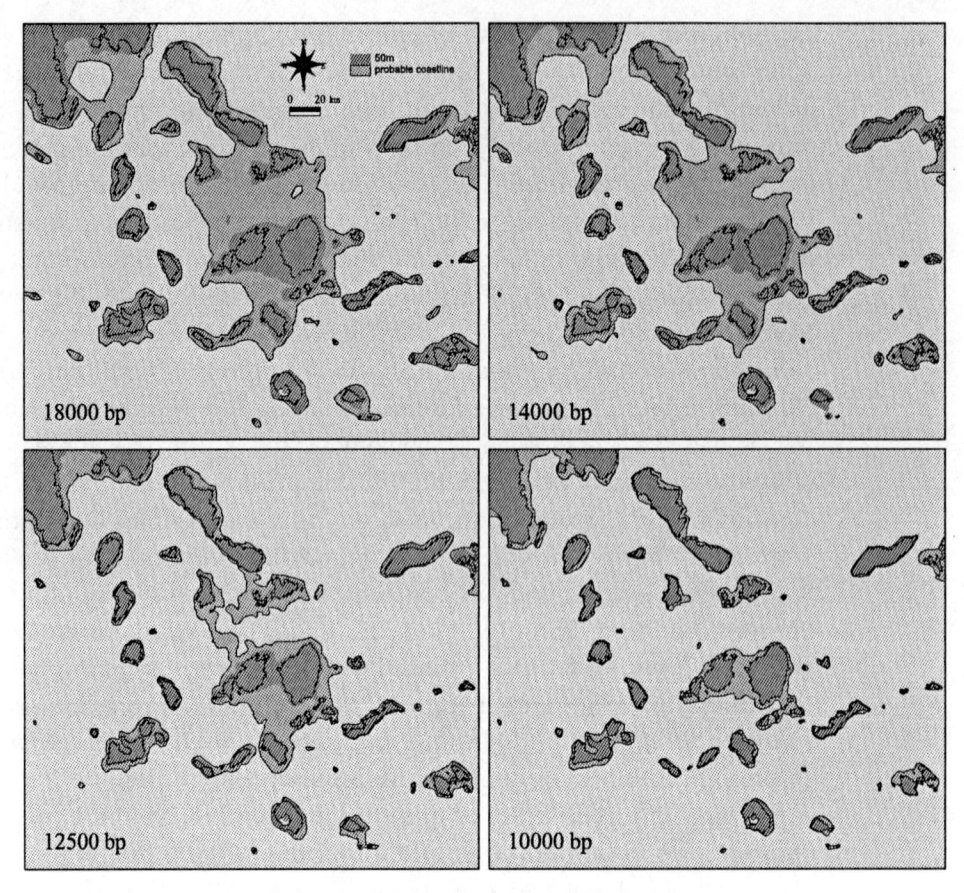

Fig. 27 The sinking of Cycladia. After Lambeck 1996: fig. 6.

There is no archaeological evidence for Pleistocene colonisation of Cycladia, despite the indications late in the period of visits to the obsidian quarries. Cherry (1981: 59) and Evans (1977: 14–15) have argued, surely rightly, that the smaller Mediterranean islands would have been too marginal to support communities before the advent of agricultural economies. This argument loses some of its force, however, if it is recalled that at their maximum extent, Cycladia and its satellites were some three times larger than all the Holocene Cyclades lumped together. Moreover, in terms of subsistence, an endemic dwarfed megafauna developed on Cycladia, as also on a number of other Mediterranean islands, during the Pleistocene, descended from full-sized ancestors who had swum the straits – the dwarfing being surprising given the small water-gaps that separated the fauna from mainland predators. Bones of dwarf elephant have been found on Naxos, Seriphos, Melos and Delos, and possibly dwarf deer on Amorgos (Dermitzakis and Sondaar 1978; Held 1989b: 116).

On several other large Mediterranean islands with endemic fauna, sites with ephemeral occupation by late hunter-gatherer groups around the time of the Pleistocene–Holocene transition are starting to emerge (Cherry 1990: 193), although the case for substantially earlier Palaeolithic occupation (as opposed to visitation to islands such as Kephallonia and perhaps Skyros) remains emphatically unproven (Cherry 1992b). The stability of residence implied by such sites is unclear. They seem to represent more than seasonal visitation, but only barely colonisation and certainly not, on current evidence, establishment. The most striking example known to date is the Akrotiri-*Aetokremnos* rock shelter on Cyprus, where careful excavation has revealed chipped stone artefacts in association with the bones of over 500 dwarf hippopotamus, several dwarf elephant and many bird species, all dated to the eleventh millennium bp (Simmons 1991, 1999: 208–9), and therefore crudely contemporary with the earliest obsidian at Franchthi. Analogous sites are attested on Corsica and Sardinia (Cherry 1990: 173–84). On Crete, the Aegean's largest island, such sites have not been detected to date (Lax and Strasser 1992; Reese 1996), although speculation continues (with good cause) to the effect that this prominent land-mass across the southern boundary of the Aegean was known and perhaps visited from an early date (Rackham and Moody 1996: 1–2; Runnels 1995: 728).

In the light of the above horizon, how is the absence of evidence for a human presence on Cycladia, especially at the end of the Pleistocene, best interpreted? Given that the island was two-thirds the size of Cyprus, it might ostensibly have sufficed to support pre-Neolithic communities on a short-term basis *if* the Pleistocene megafauna were still thriving. Despite the fact that the majority of Cycladia is now submerged, the remains of such communities may yet be discovered, although it should be stressed that no finds have been forthcoming from promising locations like the Antiparos and Zas caves. But alternatively, and maybe more plausibly, the absence of evidence may reflect a genuine absence of occupation. There are several reasons why this might have been the case. For one thing, fig. 27 indicates that there was little of Cycladia left by the end of the Pleistocene, save for the enduring mountains. Another relevant factor is the date at which the Pleistocene fauna vanished. In contrast to Cyprus and several of the western Mediterranean islands (Cherry 1990: fig. 9) there is simply no proof from the Cyclades that any dwarfed megafauna survived into the later Pleistocene. If these animals did go extinct earlier than elsewhere, the topography of Cycladia could be in part to blame. Proximity to the mainland is one factor, and indeed Watson (1964: table 6.18) reports a low level of species endemism by Mediterranean standards. But it is also relevant that during a succession of previous inter-glacials, Cycladia would have repeatedly shrunk and fragmented, losing the majority of its land area and splitting up faunal populations, thereby rendering each more vulnerable to demographic collapse at the same time as these populations were coping with climatic shifts. In this sense Cyprus and the other sizeable Mediterranean islands represent a better prospect, being both further from mainland predators and remaining intact, if slightly reduced, as the sea-levels rose.

Considerably more confident judgements can be ventured concerning the degree to which the late Pleistocene and early Holocene islandscapes in the area now occupied

Fig. 28   Part of Sta Nychia obsidian quarry on Melos. Courtesy of Robin Torrence.

by the Cyclades were known to at least some mainland-based groups. Cherry (1981: 45) was the first to point out that the discovery of the Melian obsidian sources, high on the cliffs of an island off the south-west tip of Cycladia (fig. 28), is only credible if understood as the archaeologically visible residue of a much more extensive maritime exploration of the Aegean. He and van Andel and Shackleton also emphasised that during the last glacial maximum, a journey to Pleistocene Melos along the line of Cycladia's western satellites demanded sea-crossings of only a few kilometres (Cherry 1985: 22; van Andel 1989 and Shackleton 1982: fig. 2). Concerning seafaring technology at this early period, almost any floating contraption would suffice for such crossings with the aid of on- and offshore breezes. Light-weight reed-boats similar to the experimental craft mentioned in chapter 3 might have been most suitable for mobile groups with small, water-resistant cargoes (Johnstone 1988: 56–60; Tzala 1989). A less minimalistic assessment of the capabilities of the earliest Aegean seafarers and seacraft might also be entertained, however, given that the experimental reed-boat managed several crossings between the modern Cyclades. For early procurement routes between Franchthi and Melos, an alternative to the long, indirect coastal journey to a jump-off point in Attica would have been a direct journey made up of 20–35 km hops along the chain of then-larger Pleistocene islets in the open sea between the Argolid and Melos.

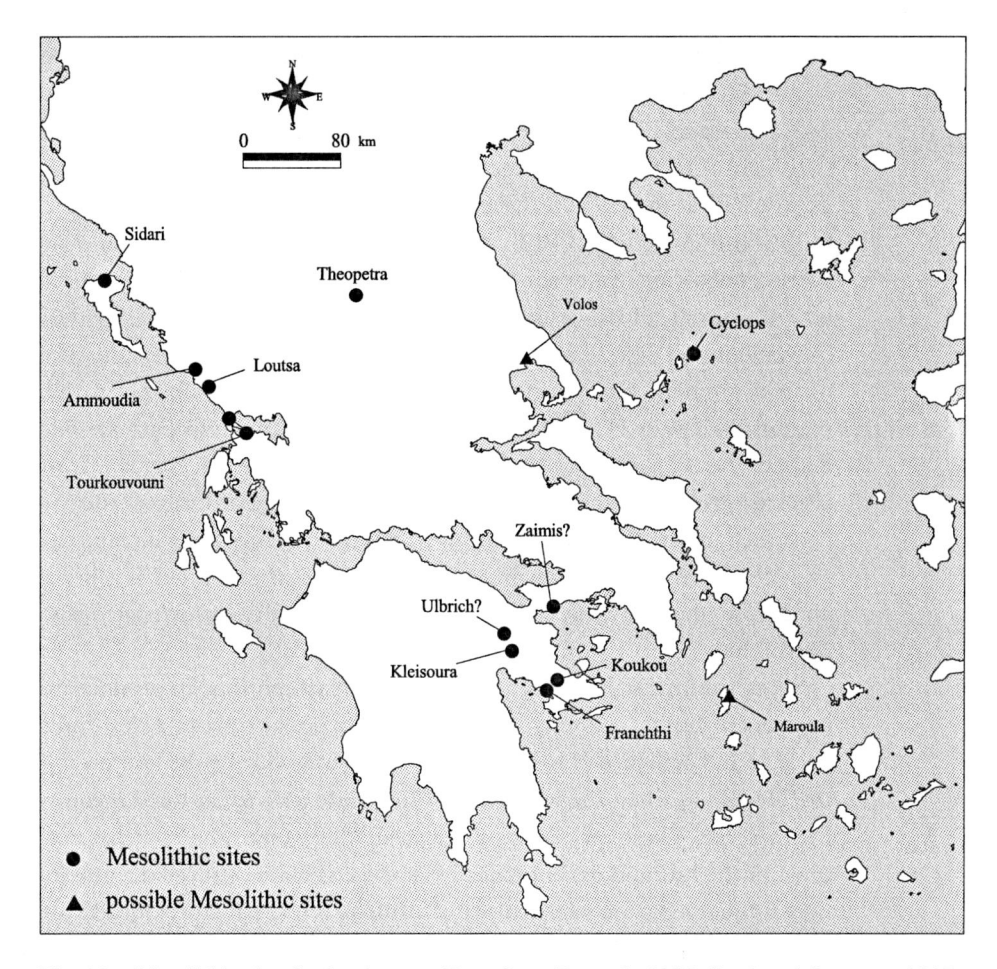

Fig. 29 Mesolithic sites in the Aegean. Data from Runnels 1995: fig. 9 and Sampson 1998.

Particularly for the Aegean Mesolithic, a strong maritime orientation may be one of the reasons why the terrestrial picture appears so wanting (Runnels 1995: 719–26). As fig. 29 shows, the Aegean distribution of Mesolithic sites is patchy, and impossibly thin in terms of the networks of people needed to keep even known communities going for any length of time (Halstead 1996a: 299–300). Much of the problem must simply be failure of site detection, but it is worth speculating that part of the Mesolithic population may have been moving around the maritime Aegean for some of the year, somewhat akin to those people who, according to Gosden and Pavlides (1994), 'colonised the sea' in early Melanesia. At Franchthi, the Mesolithic levels see the addition of large, if fluctuating, quantities of tunny to the diet (Payne 1975), although whether this represents distant fishing or local windfalls is obscure, and likely to remain so, given that changing water temperatures and coasts may have altered the locations of nutrient-rich upwellings that attract the fish, and that the possible lack of a sea connection between the Aegean and the Black Sea until well into the Holocene may suggest that Pleistocene and early Holocene tunny behaviour and migration routes did not resemble the modern pattern (van Andel and Shackleton 1982: figs. 2–3; Ryan and Pitman 1998 argue a date of *c.* 5500–5600 BC for the linking of the two seas). On the small, precipitous island of Gioura in the Northern Sporades, excavations at the Cyclops cave have recently revealed deep Mesolithic strata dating to the ninth millennium BC, containing large amounts of fish bones as well as a few pieces of obsidian (Sampson 1996, 1998). It is hard to imagine how this focus of activity on Gioura could have emerged, save as one element of a wider pattern of maritime movement and exploitation, and the fact that the highest point on Gioura is, at 570 m, a prominent sea-mark in the northern Aegean is unlikely to be coincidental (Agouridis 1997: 21). Such hunter-gatherer movement implies an extensive knowledge of the sea and the means of surviving far out in the Aegean. It must also have involved prolonged absence from the mainland. If the progress of the *papyrella* voyage described in chapter 3 is anything to go by, groups from the mainland could have been away for months, departing and returning on a seasonal cycle. It is hard to escape the conclusion that the earliest long-range seafarers in the Aegean date back at least to the Mesolithic.

So, to summarise, although the Cyclades may continue to produce no evidence for permanent hunter-gatherer occupation, they could start to reveal indications of the passage and activities of such people, in particular during the last few millennia before the Neolithic, when the incidence of maritime activity in the Aegean was clearly on the increase. These will surely never be anything other than patchy, not least because most of the lowland and practically all the coastline of Cycladia and its satellites are now submerged. Low archaeological visibility is also a factor; indeed even at the obsidian quarries on Melos any typologically distinctive residue of pre-Neolithic procurement has been swamped by later debitage. But the recent revival of work at the controversial site of Maroula on Kythnos may prove to be of interest. Claims of a Mesolithic date for the lithics and ochre burials originally reported by Honea (1975) met with a scepticism that was eminently reasonable, given the dubious nature of the published information (Cherry 1979: 27–32; Cherry and Torrence 1982: 34; Perlès 1990a: 125–6), but the first report of the renewed investigations seems to concur with the identification of the site as Mesolithic in date (Sampson 1998: 21). It must be hoped that full publication of the data will resolve this issue in the near future. Maroula lies on one of the obsidian routes to Melos, and a small scatter of lithics plus a few burials are not unreasonable as the traces of comings and goings over the millennia along a route of inferred movement.

If this sketch of maritime activity in the Cyclades and the Aegean before the Neolithic has captured anything of the ancient picture, it may also shed light on certain aspects of the Aegean's transition to the Neolithic (Broodbank 1999). It is actually very difficult to explain the transference of a Neolithic way of life (whether involving mobile farmers or the movement of domesticates and ideas) from Anatolia across the Aegean to mainland Greece and Crete without postulating some antecedent information network criss-crossing the sea and islands, equivalent to the scouting that Anthony (1990) sees as a necessary precursor to population transfer. Such networks could also explain the transmission of crucial knowledge such as the location of the obsidian sources. Pre-Neolithic maritime networks probably formed a thin skein compared to the networks of the Neolithic and EBA that are investigated in the following chapters. Yet this glimpse of the latter's antecedents makes us much better prepared to interpret the later signs of a very different pattern of activity in the Cyclades, namely the first attempts by Neolithic people to inhabit these islands on a permanent basis, and to domesticate their long-known and sporadically visited islandscapes.

An introduction to the Cycladic Neolithic and its historiography

The discovery and first interpretation of the Cycladic Neolithic

The archaeology of Neolithic settlement in the Aegean islands has, as seen in fig. 30, witnessed rapid recent advances (Broodbank 1999; Cherry 1990: 158–73; Davis 1992). The colonisation of Crete remains the earliest event known, but an early sequence can also be discerned in the Northern Sporades. The LN and FN sees a marked increase in colonisation in the south-east Aegean (with possible instances of pre-LN pottery on a few of the larger, offshore islands) and at least some members of the Cyclades. Most islands off the coast of the southern Greek mainland appear to have been settled during the FN and EBA. Although the details change yearly, the picture emerging seems to be one of a series of discrete spurts followed by hiatuses, the timing of each triggered by localised factors, and its extent circumscribed by the sharp increases in sea-crossing distances once a given cluster had been settled (Broodbank 1999). Within the Aegean islands as a whole, the Cyclades emerge as relative late-comers, in terms of both their colonisation dates and the fact that few of the data have been known for more than a few decades. Despite this, the Cycladic Neolithic has enjoyed a lively historiography.

Scraps of Neolithic material have emerged from the Cyclades since the start of the twentieth century, for example in the form of sherds of pre-Bronze Age date on Naxos and Greater Paros, unspecified material on Tenos, stone axes said to come from Melos, and steatopygous figurines purportedly from Naxos and Amorgos (Karo 1930: 131–5; Levi 1925–6: 203; Renfrew 1972: 507–9; Weinberg 1951). But secure definition of Neolithic phases only began in the 1960s. The overall culture sequence shown in fig. 1 requires elaboration at this point. Renfrew defined the Saliagos culture, mainly characterised by its light-on-dark painted pottery and distinctive lithic repertoire, through excavations with Evans at the eponymous settlement (Evans and Renfrew 1968) supplemented by surface material at Mavrispilia on Mykonos and

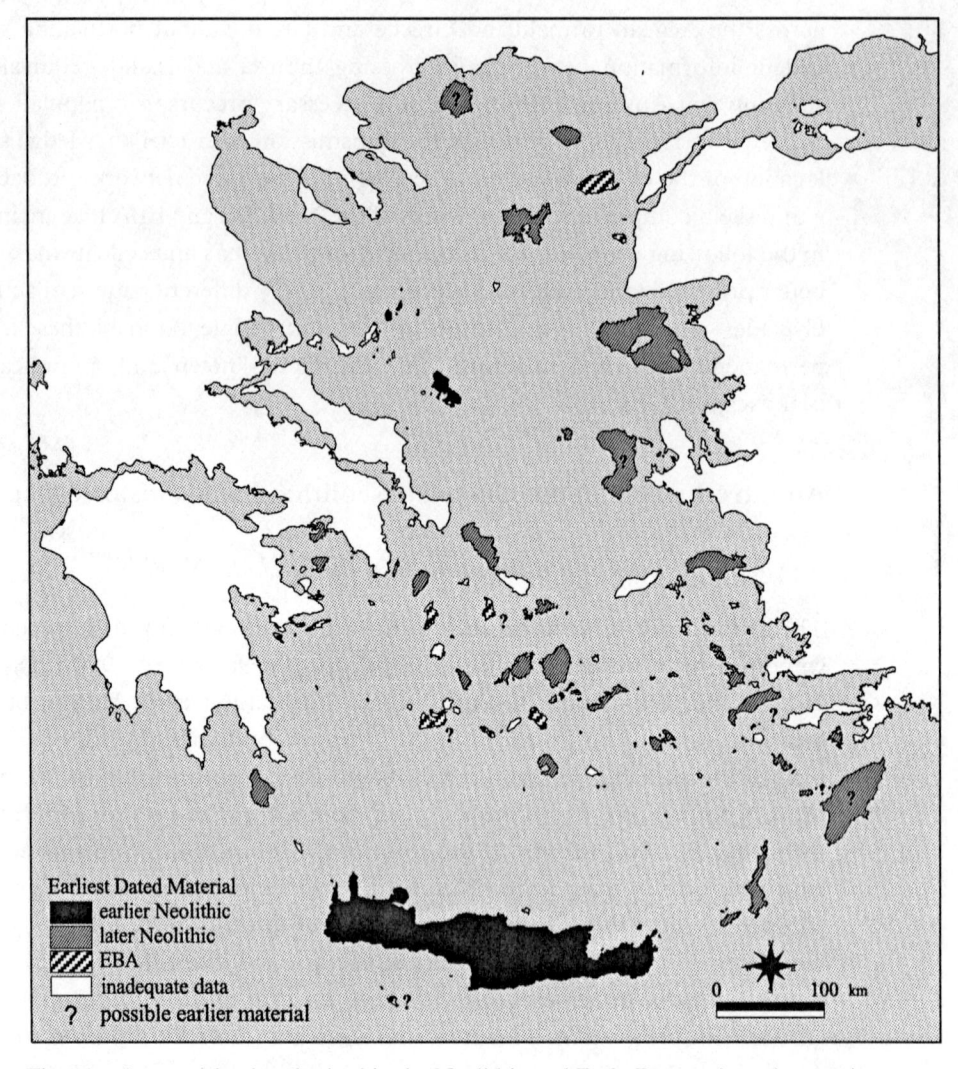

Fig. 30 Aegean islands colonised in the Neolithic and Early Bronze Age; the quasi-continental island of Euboia is not included. Data from Broodbank 1999: table 1.

other sites such as Agrilia and Vouni on Melos and Greater Paros respectively (Belmont and Renfrew 1963). Saliagos is now an islet in the strait between Paros and Antiparos (fig. 31), but was originally a knoll on a slender isthmus of southern Greater Paros. The Saliagos radiocarbon dates, when calibrated, indicate occupation during the fifth millennium BC (Evans and Renfrew 1968: 144), and therefore place the assemblage in the Aegean LN. Excavation by Coleman (1977) of an early FN settlement, dating to the first half of the fourth millennium BC, at Kephala on Kea (fig. 32) prompted Renfrew to define a Kephala culture, distinguished by pattern-burnished pottery typical of the Aegean FN (Renfrew 1972: 75–6). Similar material was identified at the Keian sites of Paoura and Sykamias (Coleman 1977: 156–8). A third

The dawn treaders

Fig. 31　Saliagos and its environs, as seen from the modern island of Antiparos with Paros in the background. The site is located on the smaller, uninhabited islet in the middle distance, once part of an isthmus crossing the modern straits.

Fig. 32　Kephala and its environs, with Makronisos and Attica on the horizon. Traces of the settlement extend over much of the prominent headland. The cemetery is located overlooking the narrow neck of land at the entrance.

breakthrough was the demonstration that the mainly EBA Grotta-Pelos culture started in the later FN and continued through EB I (Renfrew 1972: 166). A detailed consideration of this last horizon is deferred until chapter 5.

The next stage in the exploration and interpretation of the Cycladic Neolithic was dominated by a series of closely argued papers by Cherry, which offered a critical appraisal of Neolithic settlement in the Cyclades prior to the Grotta-Pelos culture, based on the information then available and the data emerging from intensive field survey on Melos (Cherry 1979: 32–7, 1981: 61–2, 1985: 24–7; Cherry and Torrence 1982: 33–4). His and Torrence's research (Torrence 1979, 1982, 1986, 1991; Cherry and Torrence 1984) also paid close attention to the lithic industries, which were primarily executed in Melian obsidian (fig. 33). Cherry emphasised (1) that of the then-known Saliagos culture sites, only Saliagos and Mavrispilia had yielded diagnostic pottery and therefore definitely represented permanent settlements, (2) that scanty or stray finds should not be given undue weight when assessing an island's colonisation dates, (3) that all the Neolithic sites found by the Melos survey were lithic assemblages that might imply nothing more than seasonal visits for obsidian collection or fishing, thus questioning whether Melos was in fact colonised before the Grotta-Pelos culture, and (4) that the tanged and barbed-and-tanged projectile points, which Renfrew identified as Saliagos culture diagnostics, were common on mainland Greece too, and could, in the islands, reflect visiting mainlanders as plausibly as resident islanders.[1] Cherry further stressed the lack of external comparanda for Saliagos' ceramics, and for evidence of continuity into the Kephala and Grotta-Pelos cultures. This revised image of the Neolithic depicted a largely unsettled archipelago, periodically visited by outside groups and relieved by a mere handful of small, short-lived settlements, in sharp contrast to the major phase of Grotta-Pelos settlement expansion at the end of the Neolithic and into the earlier EBA.

Recent advances

Subsequent fieldwork has since increased our resolution on the Cycladic Neolithic substantially. But despite the increase in the data, there has been little rethinking of the models deployed to examine the processes at work and the possible patterns

---

[1] As was first demonstrated by Diamant (1977). Subsequently, Runnels (1985b: 386) has documented a few finds of such points in EBA levels at Lerna in the Argolid. The absence of comparanda for such finds at other EBA sites in the Cyclades and on the Greek mainland, together with the existence of later Neolithic levels at Lerna, makes it likely that these finds are kick-ups, and accordingly the projectile points are interpreted here as later Neolithic diagnostics. The large numbers found at the LN Saliagos culture sites, and the smaller numbers at FN sites (Torrence 1991: table 7.1) indicate that they probably belong predominantly in the former period, but when found as surface finds it is obviously impossible to be certain as to the precise date.

The dawn treaders

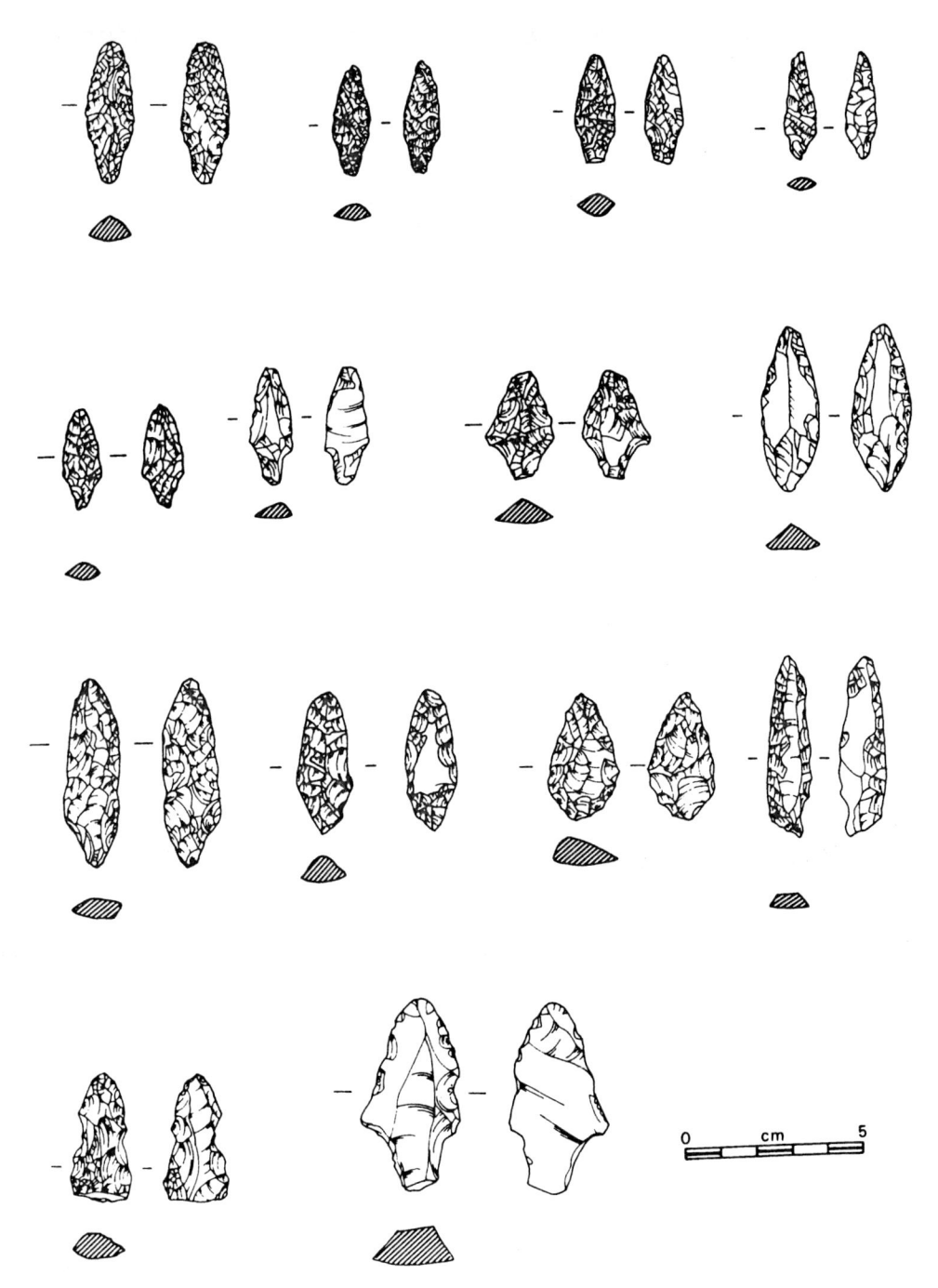

Fig. 33 Neolithic Cycladic flaked-stone points. Reproduced from Renfrew and Wagstaff 1982b: fig. 3.1, courtesy of John Cherry.

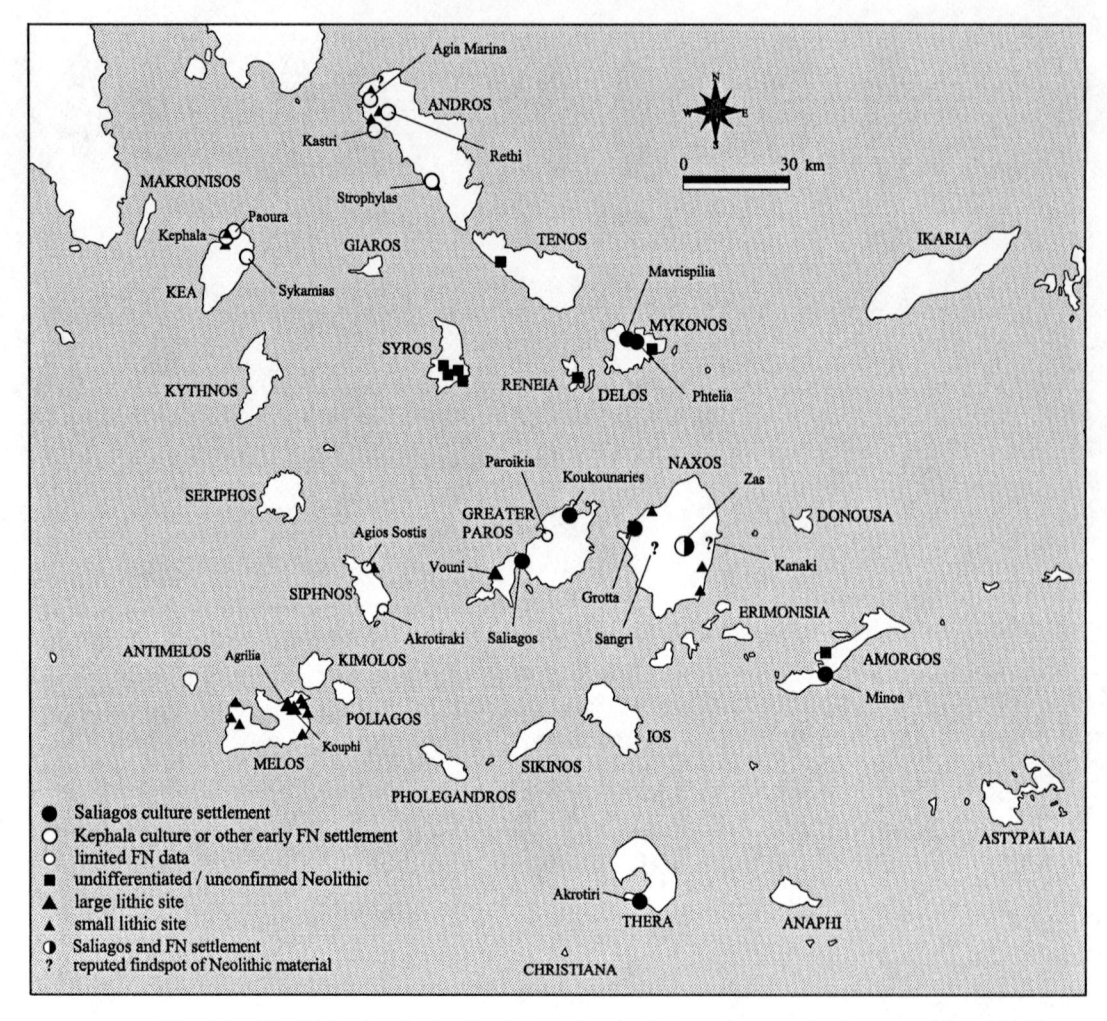

Fig. 34 Neolithic sites in the Cyclades (Grotta-Pelos culture and other transitional FN to EBA sites are not shown).

emerging. Before turning to these, however, it is useful to review what the last decades have revealed at an empirical level about these islands' Neolithic phases. Fig. 34 shows the extent of current information. Although, significantly, no pre-Saliagos culture horizon has been found, the number of LN and FN settlements and find-spots is rising steadily.

The stratigraphy of occupation levels at the Zas cave on Naxos is of crucial importance, and provides the only substantially complete sequence known to date, with a series of radiocarbon dates forthcoming (Zachos 1990: 30, 1994, 1996b, 1999). The basal stratum (Zas I) contains Saliagos culture material. Zas I is succeeded by two FN strata, the earlier (Zas IIa) with pattern-burnished pottery and other material contemporary with, but distinct from, the Kephala culture, and the later (Zas IIb) including rolled-rim bowls typical of the early Grotta-Pelos culture. Overlying this is an EB I stratum (Zas III) with later Grotta-Pelos material, after which a stratigraphic break is defined before a late EB II stratum (Zas IV). In addition to Zas I, further Saliagos culture settlements have been excavated at the multi-period site of Grotta on Naxos (Hadjianastasiou 1988) and Phtelia on Mykonos (Sampson 1997; Tsakos 1992), with hints of further settlements in the form of pottery finds at Akrotiri on Thera, Minoa on Amorgos and Koukounaries on Greater Paros (Schilardi 1990, 1991; Sotirakopoulou 1986, 1990). Some small lithic sites on north-west Andros could indicate LN activity, but there is no convincing indication of settlement until the FN (Koutsoukou 1992, 1993), and much the same can be said of Kea (Cherry *et al.* 1991: 165; Torrence 1991: 191–2).

The evidence for the FN has improved too, notably through intensive surface explorations at Kephala and Paoura (Whitelaw 1991a). On Andros several settlements, notably Kastri, Rethi, Agia Marina and Strophylas, are dated to this period by surface material (Koutsoukou 1992, 1993), the first of these having particularly good parallels at Kephala in terms of material and location. New excavated data include Zas IIa and the level overlying the Saliagos culture material at Phtelia (Sampson 1997: 11). Pattern-burnished sherds have been identified on Greater Paros at Paroikia (Overbeck 1989a: 5, cat. no. 1) and at sites on Siphnos such as Agios Sostis (Gropengiesser 1987: 34, 44). Agia Irini I on Kea, the basal material of an important multi-period site, is dated later than Kephala, either to late FN or early EB I (Cherry *et al.* 1991: 166; Wilson 1999: 6–7, 227).

Set against such relatively unproblematic material, and the indisputable growth in the number of attested settlements, several other bodies of data remain difficult to evaluate. These include further Neolithic sites of unspecified date, claimed on the basis of surface finds on Mykonos and nearby Reneia (Sampson 1997: 11–12), Syros (Hekman 1994: 70 and fig. 8, using the report of Aron 1979) and Amorgos (Marangou 1994: fig. 1). An optimistic viewpoint might, rightly or wrongly, embrace these as further settlements, but some degree of caution is required until more supporting data are available. The claim of Neolithic material on Reneia is particularly important, as it would constitute the only exception to a general avoidance of small islands by settlers in the Cyclades until the period of the Grotta-Pelos culture.

Several of the lithic find-spots found by surface investigations are also hard to interpret. These range from intensively investigated sites to barely documented chance finds. The lithic sites on Melos and Kea that have been examined in detail are mainly small scatters (Cherry and Torrence 1982: 24; Torrence 1991: 189–91). Many can be best interpreted as evidence of off-site activities. Some, especially those in coastal areas unsuitable for farming, could indeed be look-out points, perhaps for fish, a particularly good example being the cache of a massive stone axe and an obsidian nodule weighing 5 kg, together with a scatter of obsidian tools and debitage, at Cape Vani in Melos (Cherry and Torrence 1982: 25–6). But the absence of pottery at such sites, or at least

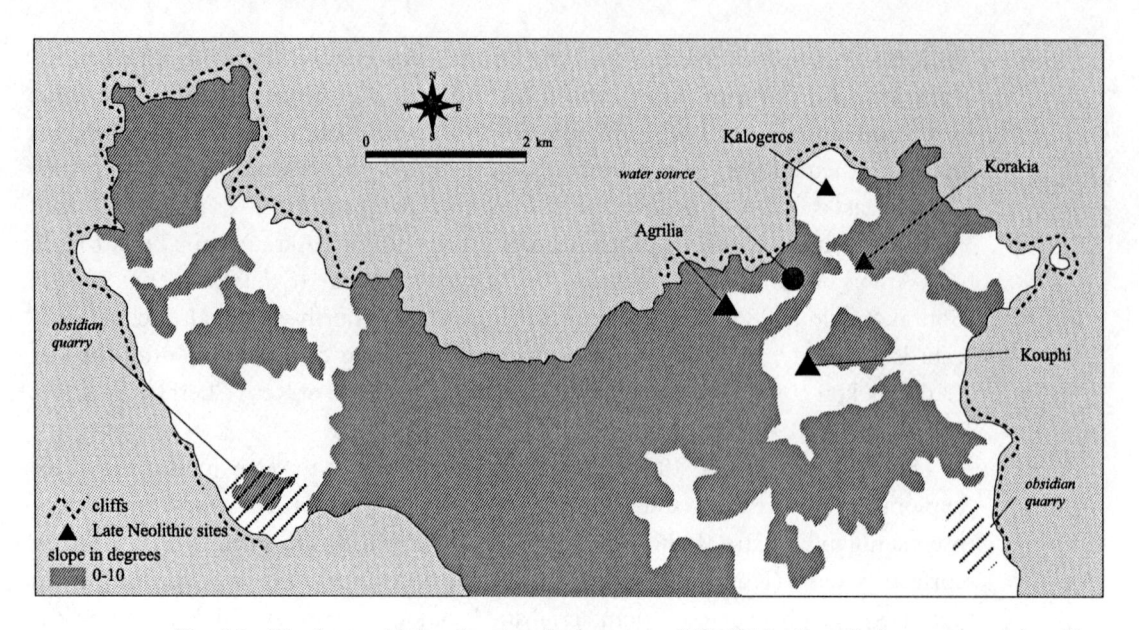

Fig. 35 North-east Melos showing the location of Neolithic sites relative to potential arable land, water, look-out points and obsidian quarries. After Renfrew and Wagstaff 1982b: fig. 9.5.

diagnostic early pottery, need not in all cases be decisive, for Neolithic pottery often preserves few diagnostics when exposed on the surface, and more research is needed into the deterioration of low-fired Neolithic ceramics before it can be stated with certainty that all the Cycladic lithic sites have always lacked pottery (Whitelaw 1991a).

This raises another order of question concerning the interpretation of a limited number of much larger lithic scatters of Saliagos culture date, namely Agrilia (6.9 ha) and Kouphi (2.8 ha after mining) on Melos, and the less thoroughly investigated site of Vouni on Greater Paros (Cherry and Torrence 1982: 24–8; Evans and Renfrew 1968: 74–5). These assume a particular prominence not only because of their impressive size, but also because their interpretation by Cherry as the palimpsests of visitation to the same locations by non-resident groups over an extended period forms part of his argument that Melos was not permanently settled until the period of the Grotta-Pelos culture. There is no positive evidence to contradict this interpretation, and if correct it provides an interesting picture of non-resident practices on a regularly visited island. But it is at least worth entertaining the possibility that these sites may instead represent the eroded remnants of settlements, albeit perhaps 'failed' ones of limited duration. The locations of Agrilia and Kouphi could support either scenario (fig. 35). Their position within north-east Melos puts them in easy reach of one of the island's few water sources, *and* the obsidian quarries, *and* the most likely landfall zones for colonising groups moving through the islands. Neither site is plausible as a fishing look-out, and indeed Agrilia is a poor second in this respect to the nearby Kalogeros headland, on which a small lithic scatter was found (Cherry 1982b: 296–7). Lastly, a lot or little can be made of the fact that Agrilia and Kouphi are adjacent to pockets of arable land (Bintliff 1977a: 539; Nevett 1988: 26). The issue is an open one, and the alternatives need to be exercised.

Emergent patterns?

What does the current information concerning later Neolithic settlement in the Cyclades appear to be telling us? Cherry's original scepticism about the degree and coherence of Neolithic settlement undoubtedly needs to be heavily qualified. At least in some parts of the Cyclades (but how wide an area?) there is increasingly solid evidence for settlement and some signs also of continuity into the EBA. Whilst caution in identifying Neolithic settlements must be observed, it might be suggested that an approach to low-grade data which discounts 'isolated single artefacts without context or mere handfuls of pottery without corroborating data of other kinds' (Cherry 1981: 48) may, despite its admirable rigour, generate a deceptively minimalist impression in the context of a very unevenly investigated archipelago. The extent to which recent fieldwork has swelled earlier hints from scanty finds on Naxos, Greater Paros and Amorgos is indeed striking. Naxos is a particularly good illustration of this transformation. At the beginning of the 1980s its Neolithic finds comprised a figurine from Sangri, bone spatulae from Zas and reports of pre-Bronze Age material at Grotta, all in retrospect promising signs, but insufficient to affirm colonisation by Cherry's criteria. Fig. 34 show that in the intervening period Naxos has emerged as a linchpin of the Cycladic Neolithic (a conclusion underscored by further analyses in the course of this chapter). It might be noted that several of the Cyclades remain as under-explored to this day as Naxos was before the 1980s.

But what of the patterns currently emerging from distributions of Neolithic sites in the Cyclades? One feature of the current data is the concentration of definite Saliagos settlements in the south-east Cyclades, and especially on Naxos. By contrast, there is at present no indisputable evidence for Saliagos culture settlement as opposed to visitation in the northern or western Cyclades, despite intensive surveys on Kea and Melos. On Kea and Andros the first definite settlements date to the early FN, although a few lithics on both islands might indicate some LN activity (Koutsoukou 1993: 100–1; Torrence 1991: 191–2). On Melos the first indisputable settlement evidence is the Grotta-Pelos horizon, although the alternative interpretation of the largest lithic sites should be borne in mind. *If* this pattern even partially reflects actual processes, it would suggest that the first Cycladic islands to be colonised were not those closest to the mainland, but rather a cluster of large-to-medium islands located far out to sea in the south-east Cyclades.

The degree of continuity is another issue of interest. The stratigraphy of Zas and Phtelia, together with a few pattern-burnished sherds on Greater Paros (despite the termination of occupation at Saliagos itself at approximately the beginning of the FN), indicates some form of continuity on Naxos, Mykonos and probably Greater Paros. To date, however, no post-Saliagos, but pre-Grotta-Pelos, culture material has been found on Thera and Amorgos. It is unclear whether this reflects simply a failure to detect such material, or a caesura in these islands prior to the Grotta-Pelos expansion. On Kea, the present data cannot demonstrate continuity of occupation from Kephala and Paoura to Agia Irini I (but equally cannot rule it out), and on north-west Andros there are in fact fewer EBA than Neolithic settlements, although some possible transitional sites exist (Koutsoukou 1993). On Melos, the chronological significance of several small lithic sites categorised as typologically transitional Neolithic-to-EBA is unclear (Cherry and Torrence 1982: 31).

Such differential patterning presents a challenge. Is it a result of several distinct sequences of early colonisation in different parts of the Cyclades, or simply a chance reflection of patchy fieldwork? With data from such diverse sources as a well-stratified material trap like Zas cave, a handful of extensively excavated open sites, several more sites known from small soundings or kick-ups, sites explored by intensive survey and others known only through casual investigation, plus stray finds going back to the start of the century, interspersed with continuing gaps in terms of island coverage, it is hard to answer this question. It would certainly be unwise to assume that the current state of knowledge will be any more impervious to revision in the coming years than has been the case in the past. But there are also grounds for optimism, and in the remainder of this chapter it is suggested that a lot can be learned about the processes that may have been at work by constructing colonisation models. Our exploration of the data and their lacunae urge two important attributes of such models. First, they must be designed in a way that allows them to retain their relevance as the data increase in unpredictable ways. Second, they need to explore the likelihood, hinted at in the data, that different parts of the Cyclades had divergent histories of colonisation. For example, Naxos and Melos may both have been important places during the Saliagos culture, but were they important in the same kinds of way? In order to achieve this, an interrogative approach to modelling will be necessary – one, in short, that asks when, where and why the first attempts to people the Cyclades most probably originated.

Contexts for the early colonisation of the Cyclades

Some motivational models

Early on in this chapter it was suggested that the option of not colonising the Cyclades was perfectly viable and, under certain circumstances, decidedly wise. Faced with the archaeological evidence that during the later Neolithic certain people started to reject it in favour of settlement, the question 'why colonise?' is a real and indeed forceful one. Several models have been put forward to explain why people may have started to do so. All quite rightly explore human strategies within an essentially static topographic framework, for one basic corollary of the fact that the Cyclades and their immediately surrounding region had reached roughly their modern form early in the Holocene is that changing coastal environments cannot have played a role in encouraging their settlement akin to that in the Indo-Pacific (e.g. Birdsell 1977; Thiel 1987; Broodbank 1999 for discussion of a small number of Aegean islands outside the Cyclades where Holocene shoreline change may be relevant to colonisation history). Although they differ in their particulars, these models likewise share a preference for explanations of the transition from visitation to colonisation that stress the role of incremental shifts in specialist activities. As will become clear, the explanatory power of such models must in fact be questioned. For in the final analysis, colonisation in the Cyclades is not likely to have developed out of such activities. It involved fundamentally different choices and decisions relating to risks and advantages, and instead owed its origins to decisions made in a few key areas to use certain islands or patches of islandscape in a new and substantively different manner. If there was a gradual element in the start of Cycladic colonisation it is to be found less in the shift from one set of activities to another, and more in the role played by the fuzziness of the distinction between insular and non-insular landscapes, and between Cycladic and non-Cycladic islands, in eroding the spatial transition in the particular regions where the first settlement horizons arose.

Several forms of maritime activity have been put forward as practices that might have culminated in colonisation. These can be summarised as Scenarios 1–3, of which the first may have a variant, Scenario 1B.

Scenario 1 Mineral resource acquisition leads to settlement.
Mainland groups had collected Melian obsidian for millennia. Over that time, as Renfrew (1984a: 42) has put it, 'some occupation is to be expected'. Patton (1996: 145) also suggests a link between ideologies of obsidian collection and those of settlement. A variant, Scenario 1B, would envisage similar processes resulting from prospection for, and exploitation of, the metalliferous sources in the western Cyclades, principally on the islands of Siphnos and Kythnos.

Scenario 2 Fishing leads to seasonal occupation and then to settlement.
The large quantity of fish bones, including pelagic species such as tunny, at Mesolithic and Neolithic Franchthi has been interpreted as a sign of seasonal fishing expeditions, perhaps in association with obsidian-collecting voyages, although the earliest evidence of obsidian pre-dates that of fishing at Franchthi (Renfrew and Aspinall 1990: 269). Bintliff (1977a: 117–22) was the first to argue that early island settlements may have concentrated at locations where fish were known to shoal.

Scenario 3 Seasonal pasturage on offshore islands leads to settlement.
Movement of flocks to summer grazing on islands is known ethnographically, and the EBA rock-pecking of a boat at Korphi t'Aroniou in Naxos portrays an associated

quadruped (fig. 23). Cherry (1985: 20) has suggested that similar practices could have led gradually to the settlement of some Aegean islands.

Scenario 1 is problematic for several reasons. Cherry (1979: 26–8) long ago argued that obsidian procurement had a negligible impact on colonisation because the source island of Melos, on the strength of the intensive survey data, was not an initial focus for colonisation as opposed to visitation. Although possible alternative ways of interpreting a few of the island's LN lithic sites were aired above, no case can be made for colonisation over the six preceding millennia of procurement. Procurement clearly could continue for an extremely long time without triggering settlement, even though it must have boosted the pool of knowledge about the Cycladic environments that was available to potential settlers. Perlès' (1990b) analysis of Melian obsidian in mainland contexts helps to explain why obsidian collection did not lead directly to settlement. In the earlier Neolithic, the small amounts of obsidian found at mainland sites, combined with their uniform reduction technology and an absence of raw blocks, indicates that obsidian was being supplied by itinerant groups of voyagers, quarriers, knappers and distributors (a continuation of the pre-Neolithic pattern), in short task-specific groups that were unlikely to be diverted to the idea of settling down. Black (1980) makes the point, in the case of a similar fishing hypothesis for early settlement of the Galapagos islands, that if only single-sex groups were involved in special-purpose voyages, long-term settlement could never take off for the simplest of reasons. Perlès contrasts the earlier Neolithic pattern with a dramatic shift in the southern Aegean during the LN, marked by a great increase in the quantity of obsidian arriving on the mainland, a wide range of reduction techniques and the first arrival of raw blocks. She argues that this reflects a movement away from specialist procurement towards an opening up of access to the quarries as the Cyclades started to be colonised. But this interesting and well-documented shift was surely a consequence, and not a cause, of colonisation. It is easy to imagine how a web of island settlements providing watering stops, food and chances for interaction would transform conditions of procurement, making travel to the sources easier, but much more difficult for traditional specialised groups to control effectively.

Similar points can be made with regard to Scenario 1B, although as the metal-rich islands have not been intensively surveyed, the details of the relative chronology of metal exploitation and settlement cannot be determined with confidence. Kythnos and Siphnos do not stand out at present as major centres of Neolithic activity save for a few FN sherds on the latter island (although future research may always change this) and, conversely, those islands with the good evidence of Neolithic occupation are not those with metalliferous deposits that were exploited at an early date. More decisively, as the earliest Aegean metallurgy dates to the FN, Scenario 1B cannot explain the start of Cycladic colonisation a millennium earlier, although the presence of the ores could have subsequently become an additional stimulus to expansion into the western Cyclades.

Scenario 2 runs into equal difficulty in explaining the shift from special-purpose groups to permanent settlers, and encounters additional problems too. As mentioned in chapter 3, the Mediterranean is not rich enough in marine life for fishing to act as more than a dietary supplement. Distant trips from mainland bases to intercept pelagic species are a plausible strategy, if a risky and time-consuming one, especially in the pursuit of tunny shoals, which move fast along changeable routes at unpredictable times. The quantity of fish bones in each stratum at Mesolithic and Neolithic Franchthi varies considerably (Gamble 1979: 125–6; Payne 1975: 128–9; Rose 1986), suggesting that fishing played an irregular role in subsistence, and it is quite possible that the peaks reflect sporadic windfalls on occasions when the fish shoaled in nearby bays rather than the fruit of regular long-range expeditions. Taking these points together, fishing seems too irregular and secondary a food-gathering practice to have acted as a main stimulus to island settlement (although it was undoubtedly an ancillary option for people once they had – for quite different reasons – already settled in the Cyclades).

Finally, what of Scenario 3, the seasonal movement of herds? In chapter 3 the absence of evidence for mobile pastoralism in the early Aegean was discussed. Most of the islands used in this way in the recent past were small places where animals could be safely corralled, suggesting that this scenario is unlikely to help to explain settlement of larger islands and, for understandable reasons, most of the distances over which herds were transferred were relatively short. Small, offshore Makronisos is the one plausible Cycladic candidate for such a pre-colonisation strategy, but its earliest site at Provatsa (Lambert 1973), although dated to the Neolithic by Hope Simpson and Dickinson (1979: 210), has been redated to the EBA by Spitaels (1982a). Certainly, stock-raising and a certain amount of movement of animals for breeding or grazing must have been a key feature of life in the early Cyclades (cf. chapter 3), but this is again a rather different issue from the role of seasonal island grazing as an initial stimulus to colonisation.

A configurational perspective on the beginnings of colonisation

Let us instead explore a different avenue of enquiry. Among the limitations of all the above scenarios is their slight ability to predict successfully *where* colonisation should have first occurred. Yet the 'where' question, if properly addressed, can produce useful perspectives on the 'why' and 'when' questions. The currently available data suggest an empirical answer: namely in the south-east Cyclades, with colonisation in the north beginning slightly later, during the FN. But we have also seen that, given the uneven level of archaeological investigation, such patterns need more searching interrogation if they are to bear inferential weight. For these reasons, a predictive strategy drawing on features of island configuration is advisable. To date, such attempts at prediction have not had much success in shedding light on processes in the Cyclades, not least

Table 4. *Ranked size/distance scores for Cycladic islands, with distance measured from the nearest mainland (including Euboia as a mainland).*

Island	Score
Andros	31.7
Kea	6.7
Makronisos	4.5
Tenos	3.9
Naxos	3.6
Kythnos	2.6
Greater Paros	2.2
Syros	1.4
Melos	1.4
Seriphos	1.2
Mykonos	1.0
Siphnos	0.9
Ios	0.8
Thera	0.6
Giaros	0.5
Kimolos	0.4
Sikinos	0.3
Anaphi	0.3
Pholegandros	0.3
Reneia	0.2
Irakleia	0.1
Poliagos	0.1
Keros	0.1
Donousa	0.1
Schoinousa	<0.1
Antimelos	<0.1
Delos	<0.1
Ano Kouphonisi	<0.1
Kato Kouphonisi	<0.1
Antikeri	<0.1
Christiana	<0.1

because, as Cherry observed (1981: 50), the complexity of the cluster and the multitude of stepping-stones renders straightforward island-to-mainland measurements simplistic, a point illustrated by table 4, which shows that island size and mainland distance scores predict that the islands off the coast of Attica and Euboia should be the first settled, a prediction that does little to illuminate the strong Saliagos culture presence in the south-east Cyclades, among some of the islands furthest from mainland regions.

What is needed is a way of looking at colonisation origins and expansion that is sensitive to configurational detail, and dynamic in its ability to model sequences. Two island archaeological concepts developed for other theatres are extremely useful in this respect. One, introduced in the discussion of the origins of Aegean seafaring, is Irwin's concept of island nurseries, whereby experimentation in travel between, and living on, islands is encouraged by a favourable configuration of mainland and islands (Irwin 1992: 31). The second, and allied, concept is that of autocatalysis, a form of cultural chain reaction or 'pull' factor that helps to explain impressive inter-island colonisation sequences (Keegan and Diamond 1987: 67–8). Autocatalysis is most liable to originate in favourable nurseries, and to take off under conditions where a scatter of accessible but progressively more challenging islands extending out to sea serves to draw colonists outwards (e.g. on a grand scale the inverse gradation of overall island size and distance from Island South-East Asia to Easter Island). In such circumstances, islanders' perceptions of accessibility exhibit a tendency to stretch as successive colonisations succeed. The resultant ideologies of expansion, and the prestige accruing to successful seafarers, explain why some colonists take higher risks and occasionally overreach themselves, although Irwin (1992: 62–3) criticises this last aspect of autocatalysis on the grounds that few colonists deliberately adopt strategies that are likely to incur high casualties. Applied to the specific configuration of the Cycladic islands and surrounding regions, such concepts enable a series of new explanatory scenarios to be proposed.

Bearing in mind the colonising distances discussed at the start of this chapter, there are two axes of viable short-range entrance into the Cyclades (fig. 36). One enters from the north, starting from the extremities of Attica and/or Euboia and involving short one-day crossings. The other enters from the south-east Aegean islands of Ikaria and Astypalaia, and perhaps Patmos, Leros and Kalymnos via the stepping-stone islands of Kinaros and Levitha. This south-eastern axis demands longer crossings on the order of 30–50 km into the Cyclades, representing substantially more than a day's crossing at laden canoe speed. Other potential axes are much less plausible in terms of their length and implied durations (e.g. 78 km from the southern Argolid, 101 km from Cape Malea, 84 km from Chios and 110 km from Crete). Concentrating, therefore, on the likely Attic-Euboian and south-east Aegean entry points, several striking points emerge.

First, both areas qualify, albeit to different degrees, as nurseries. In the former case, a square of sea is semi-enclosed by Euboia, Attica, Andros and Kea. Given that this area is one of the starting points for the route to Melos, long-term experience of its conditions and the strong currents that pass through it is likely to have built up over the millennia as the seas rose and gradually sundered the straits that now divide the islands from the mainland. Kea must often have acted as a long-stop landfall for craft caught by the westward currents. More spectacular, however, is the south-eastern Aegean region, which possesses the most intricate coastal and island configuration in the entire Aegean. With its slender peninsulas, screen of protective islands parallel to the coast, short hops to large, fertile islands such as Samos, Kos and Rhodes, and

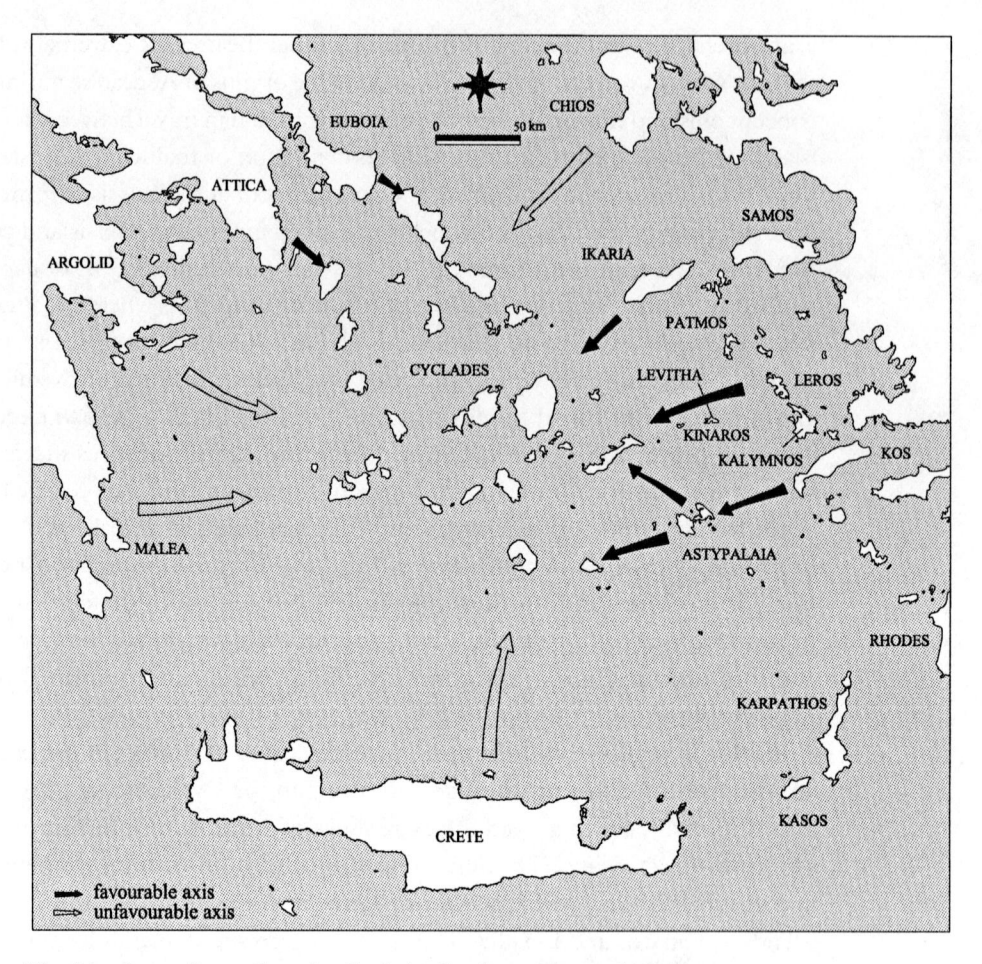

Fig. 36 Axes of entry into the Cyclades for short-range colonising groups.

strings of smaller, more distant and progressively more testing islands extending out to sea, this zone comprises not only a perfect nursery but also ideal conditions for large-scale autocatalysis.

Second, and crucially, in both areas the border between the Cyclades and non-Cycladic regions becomes indistinct as soon as modern categorisations are set aside. In the case of the Attica–Euboia–Kea–Andros zone, the two peninsulas are quasi-insular in terms of coastlines, Andros and Kea are conversely two of the larger Cyclades, and the topography and climate of southern Attica and Euboia are more or less indistinguishable from the northern Cyclades. In this region, the transition from mainland to island life may have been so elided as to be barely perceptible. In the south-east Aegean, a similar continuity from the non-insular to the insular is seen along the west Anatolian coast, but more immediately relevant is the fact that inter-island distances do not delineate a hard eastern edge to the Cyclades. Astypalaia lies equidistant between Kos and Amorgos, and the distances that separate Ikaria and

Astypalaia from the Cyclades are equivalent to the internal distances within the south-east Aegean that divide Karpathos from Rhodes. In terms of topography and climate, two pathways traverse this region. The first is a chain of large, high, well-watered and often cloud-topped islands, made up of Samos, Ikaria and Naxos, which exhibits a high degree of inter-visibility (fig. 37). The second is the scatter of less large and more arid islands comprising the central Dodecanese, Astypalaia and Amorgos. Therefore to ask why people first colonised the Cyclades may well be to misphrase the question. Rather, the settlement strategies of people living just beyond the fringes of the Cyclades started to push them over non-evident borders in the course of a continuum of expansion that incrementally brought areas of the Cyclades into the realm of settlement. We can now turn to the dates and dynamics of such events.

Spatial modelling of Neolithic expansions into the Cyclades

Likely processes in the jump-off zones of Attica–Euboia and the south-east Aegean are suggestive and contrasting. In southern Attica and Euboia, the picture is of little occupation prior to the FN, when a spate of small settlements relatively rapidly filled in the landscape. Central Euboia has plenty of earlier Neolithic, but in the drier south the only pre-FN site is the Karystos cave, in contrast to nineteen FN to EBA open-air sites in the Paximadi peninsula alone (Keller and Cullen 1992; Sampson 1981: 92, 145). The Attic evidence is patchier, owing to modern settlement, but a major FN horizon is again attested (Immerwahr 1971; Lohmann 1993: 111–14; Spitaels 1982b; Theocharis 1953/4: 66), preceded by LN in the south at the Kitsos cave (Lambert 1981). Much the same pattern is seen in the southern Argolid and Methana, two more dry peninsulas jutting into the central-southern Aegean (Jameson *et al.* 1994: figs. 4.11–13; Mee and Taylor 1997: 42–51, though in Methana settlement expansion did not take off until the EBA), as well as on the Saronic Gulf island of Aegina (Walter and Felten 1981: 10–11). Indeed, as noted earlier, this settlement expansion and the infilling of marginal regions is a widespread phenomenon in the FN Aegean. If the FN horizon in southern Euboia and Attica is as secure as it seems to be, little, if any, island settlement along this northern axis is to be expected at an earlier date. Yet once the expansion did take off within the peninsulas of southern Attica and Euboia, it should have exerted a 'push' effect on small, fissioning groups, encouraging them to settle land that was accessible but slightly further afield, and at some point to extend this strategy to patches of territory that were truly insular.

The picture in the south-east Aegean islands is very different. Roughly sixty LN and FN sites are currently known on large and small islands alike (cf. fig. 30) (Furness 1956; Melas 1985; Sampson 1984, 1987, 1988a), supporting the observation that the area was excellently suited to generating extensive inter-island colonisation sequences. The level of documentation varies, but many of these sites were clearly settlements. Looking at islands likely to act as jump-off points into the Cyclades, five LN sites have

Fig. 37 The high island chain: Samos (*above*, seen from Ikaria with a Classical tower in the foreground), through Ikaria (*middle*) to Naxos (*below*). Clouds gathered over the mountainous centres of these islands would enhance their prominence from afar.

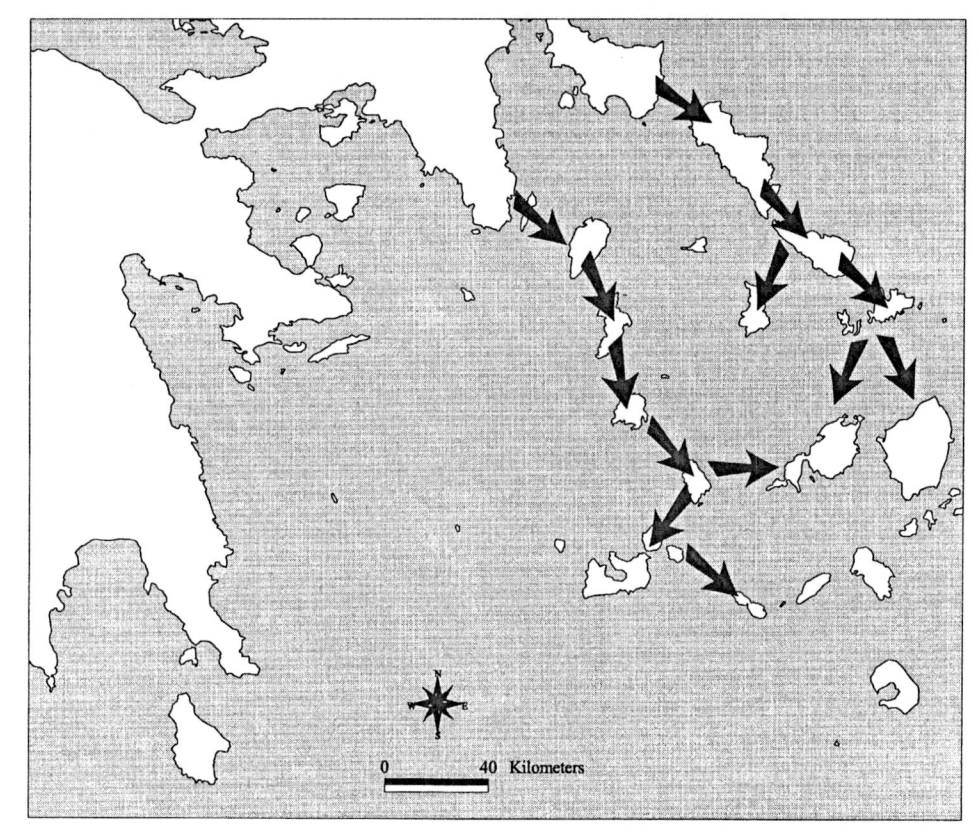

Fig. 38   Expansion model for colonisation of the Cyclades from Attica and Euboia.

been identified on the key midway island of Astypalaia (Sampson 1984: fig.7), and although Ikaria remains almost as frustratingly under-explored as it was in the 1980s (Cherry 1981: 52), several Neolithic axes have been found (Papalas 1992: 11). The documented LN settlements on surrounding Samos, Chios, Mykonos, Naxos and Amorgos make a LN phase on Ikaria extremely plausible. The general conclusion must be that colonisation reaching into the Cyclades along the south-east axis could be expected as early as the LN, and might well prove to be fairly ambitious in its scope.

The ground is now prepared for modelling expansions along each axis. The sequences starting from Attica and Euboia are relatively straightforward and involve crossings within the one-day threshold, aided by the prevailing winds from the north (fig. 38). Makronisos and Kea are the first landfalls from Attica, and Andros from Euboia. From here parallel routes develop, separated by the wide sea channel running down the centre of the northern Cyclades and the inhospitable nature of the intervening island of Giaros. One route runs down the western Cyclades, and the other proceeds effectively as an overland expansion down the length of Andros and Tenos, and by sea to Mykonos plus its satellites, and Syros. Beyond these points, colonisation might fan out in a variety of ways across the southern Cyclades.

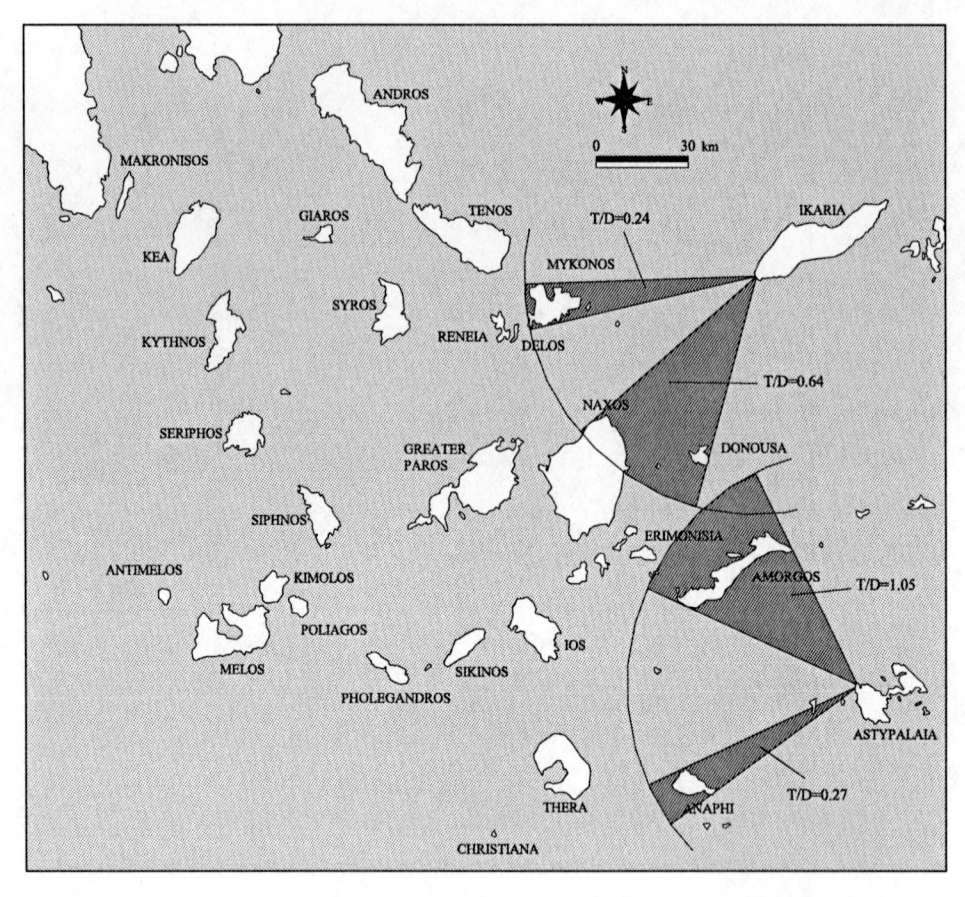

Fig. 39 Target/distance analysis for colonisation of the Cyclades from the south-east Aegean, up to a maximum crossing range of 60 km.

Potential expansions from the south-east Aegean involve longer initial crossings well over the one-day distance threshold, and brave the notoriously rough Ikarian sea, although with the direction of the prevailing winds and currents largely favourable. The circumstances are therefore unusually challenging in Aegean terms, and reward more detailed modelling of probabilities. In particular the calculation of target/distance (T/D) ratios can clarify which islands might be first settled (fig. 39). These ratios estimate the comparative accessibility of different islands or island chains by dividing the proportion of the horizon that they occupy as a target seen from a relevant departure point by their distance from that point. The higher the score, the more accessible the target, providing a first probabilistic measure to which other factors such as prevailing winds and currents can later be added (Held 1989a: 13–15; Keegan 1992: 59; Keegan and Diamond 1987: 61). In the Neolithic and EBA Aegean, where a long prior tradition of island visitation can be inferred, and where levels of island inter-visibility are high in good weather conditions, T/D ratios are in general less useful than in areas where long-range over-the-horizon voyaging is basic to colonisation sequences. But the conditions of comparatively long crossings across particularly unpredictable seas pertaining to the south-eastern route into the Cyclades make them helpful as a measure of the relative frequency and likelihood of landfalls over the long-term, and consequently of access routes into the Cyclades from the islands to their east.

From Astypalaia the favoured island is Amorgos (T/D = 1.05). From Ikaria, the favoured target is Naxos and its small satellites (T/D = 0.64), with Mykonos in second place (T/D = 0.24); Naxos is further favoured by prevailing northerly winds, and is also the clear favourite when prominence on the horizon is considered, as much of low-lying Mykonos is invisible from afar at sea-level (Agouridis 1997: table 1). These scores are higher (and therefore in T/D terms easier) than several other crossings within the south-east Aegean to islands where the presence of Neolithic settlements proves that people did colonise, for example Kos to Astypalaia (T/D = 0.42) and Rhodes to the Karpathos group (T/D = 0.62). This implies that although the south-eastern route into the Cyclades was undoubtedly difficult, it involved no colonisations any more difficult than others in the same region of the Aegean that certainly were undertaken around the same time. Such impressive, high-risk crossings should occupy the more conscious end of the spectrum of colonisations in the early Aegean, in contrast to those from the northern entry points to the Cyclades. Indeed, the ideal conditions for autocatalysis in the south-east Aegean render very plausible the development of a maritime colonising ideology that might place a lower cultural value on the risk than on the opportunities of a potentially wild passage downwind towards the high seamark of Mt Zas on Naxos or the rugged profile of Amorgos. If the scaling ratios proposed at the end of chapter 3 are applied to the Ikaria–Naxos crossing, it transpires that this crossing is equivalent in range (though not inter-visibility) to Pacific voyages of c. 200–400 km, distances that took people from the Solomons to Santa Cruz, Vanuatu and New Caledonia.

The consequences of a south-east Aegean expansion into the Cyclades can be explored by building a simple simulation model based on suitable parameters. Fig. 40 shows a simulation of inter-island expansion, starting with bridgeheads on Naxos and Amorgos and operating through a sequence of time-frames (TFs). Behind each TF must of course be imagined a much messier process of pioneer settlements, shuttling, stops, starts and local retreats. The central role played by Naxos comes out clearly, not just as the probable target from Ikaria, but as the focus of both subsequent paths of expansion. Once settlement on Naxos is consolidated, the next predicted stage is the colonisation of a compact group of other large and medium islands in the south-east Cyclades (Greater Paros, Mykonos, Ios and Thera), from which the pathways radiate into the northern and western islands. The undeniably striking parallels between the earlier TFs and the distribution of currently known Saliagos settlements now prompt us to enquire to what extent these simulations can shed light on the early Cycladic archaeological data.

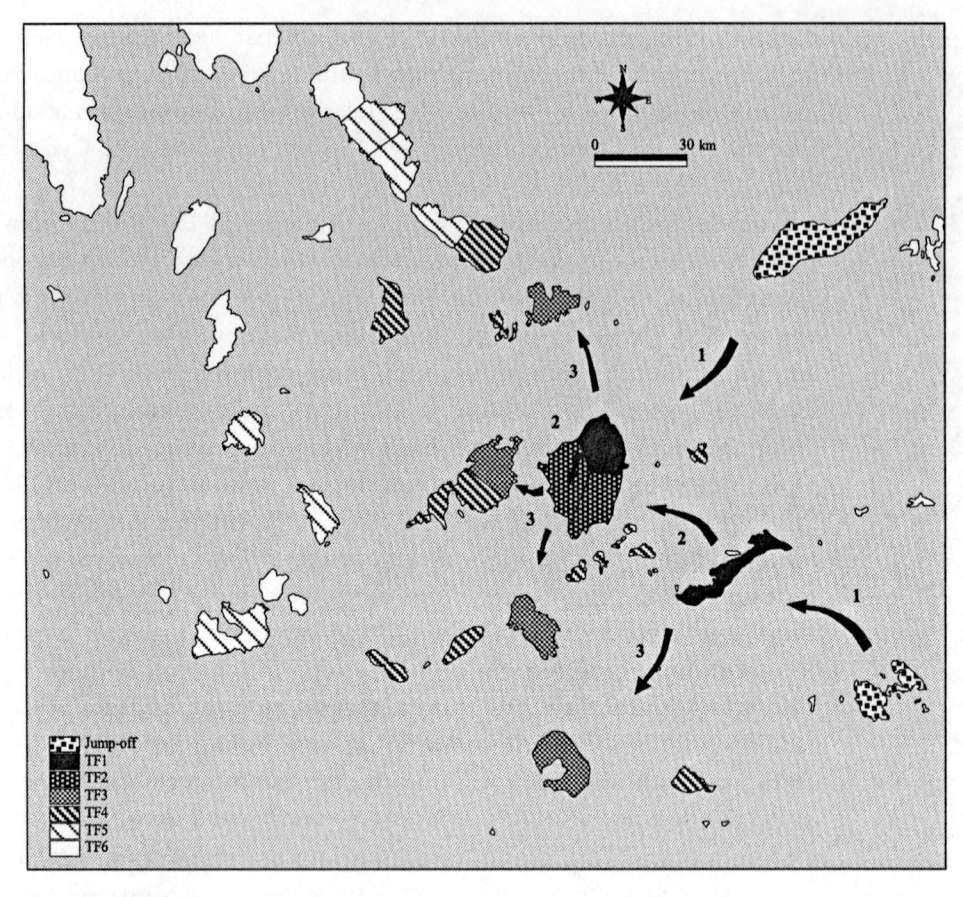

Fig. 40 Expansion model for colonisation of the Cyclades from the south-east Aegean. In each time-frame (TF) all already colonised areas expand into the nearest empty area, up to a maximum range of 60 km. In order to create approximately equal areas, islands in the average Cycladic range of 75–150 sq. km are treated as single areas, but larger Naxos and Andros are divided into three areas apiece, and Greater Paros and Tenos into two. The smaller members of the Cyclades (those below 75 sq. km) are deemed ineligible for colonisation until all larger targets within range have been colonised (this reflects a bias in Neolithic Cycladic settlement towards larger islands that is discussed more fully in chapter 5). If an empty area is targeted by two or more colonising areas simultaneously, the expansion of the more distant one(s) is redirected to the next most accessible target(s). When no more targets lie in range, an area ceases to colonise. Given the short range of most crossings, winds and currents are ignored. Arrows indicate expansion axes during the important opening TFs.

Taking into account the results of this exploration of colonisation dynamics in the south-east Aegean, there is good reason to suggest that the first settlement horizon attested in the Cyclades, namely the LN Saliagos culture, represents an extension of its eastern neighbours' impressive expansion sequences. Naxos, Amorgos and Mykonos would be the first islands settled from such a direction, and their total of five definite Saliagos culture settlements, and a considerable number of other find-spots of Neolithic material, should come as no surprise. On Naxos, the landfall zone should be the eastern coast (fig. 13a), an area that has been comparatively little explored to date, but which has produced stray Neolithic finds in the form of a white-on-dark jar from Kanaki and an axe near Moutsouna (Zachos 1990: 32). There should be more Neolithic material to be found there, perhaps beginning earlier than the first occupation at Zas, to the west, pushing colonisation back into the later sixth millennium BC and perhaps raising the possibility of an immediately pre-Saliagos phase. The model of expansion out through the Cyclades from these bridgeheads cannot yet be compared in detail with the available data. On the other axis of approach, the first expansions modelled along the routes through the northern Cyclades correlate well in timing and distribution with the FN horizon seen on Kea and Andros.

So far, the data and the models correlate reasonably convincingly. Beyond the landfall islands, however, multiple interpretative pathways as well as expansion routes open up. To predict that expansion might continue in a certain way is not to affirm that it did. People might, for example, quite simply decide not to expand any further for a considerable length of time. Moreover, as colonisation did eventually move deeper into the Cyclades and away from the initial bridgehead zones, the possibilities of discerning colonisation paths diminish, and indeed a complex process of people filtering in from diverse islands within the cluster is more than likely. Another point worth airing is the fact that as the south-east Aegean expansion into the Cyclades appears to have started a millennium before the Attic-Euboian one, it is in theory possible that most of the cluster was settled by the former expansion before the latter had a chance to have much effect, although the present patchiness of the record throughout the LN and FN makes this currently seem unlikely.

The picture in the northern Cyclades is particularly obscure and defies effective comparison with the simulated expansions, owing particularly to lack of reliable data for Kythnos and Tenos. The most that can be ventured is the setting out of hypothetical options. It may be that communities on Kea and Andros did continue the practices that had made islanders of them in the first place, expanding over the later fourth millennium down the short hops of the northern Cyclades, and perhaps explaining the FN material on Siphnos (though this island could just as plausibly have been reached from Greater Paros) and some of the purported Neolithic sites on Syros. On the other hand, the first settlers might have opted not to extend further into the attenuated lines of islands to their south, but to remain part of the compact Attic-Euboian zone. A literal interpretation of the lack, to date, of proven cultural links on Kea between the early FN Kephala culture settlements, late FN/EB I Agia Irini I and EB II Agia Irini II–III (Coleman 1977: 107), could prompt a suggestion that the first Keian communities failed to maintain a long-term hold, and that Kea underwent more than one colonisation phase before an island population became firmly established

(Cherry *et al.* 1991: 226, 474). Only a substanti al number of radiocarbon dates or the seriation of excavated assemblages from several early Keian sites is likely to produce conclusive answers to this particular question.

Suggestions can be made regarding expansion from the islands of the south-east Aegean. The hints of a conscious colonising ideology with ambitious horizons make it unlikely that settlement would fizzle out after the first bridgeheads. Indeed, the Saliagos settlements not just on Naxos, Amorgos and Mykonos, but also on Greater Paros and Thera, represent decisions to form new communities across a patchwork of islands and narrow sea-gaps in the south-east Cyclades, much as the first TFs in fig. 40 predict. In this light, the likelihood of Saliagos culture settlement on Ios seems high. The apparent lack of evidence for Saliagos culture settlements beyond the south-east Cyclades is less easy to evaluate. Once people had crossed the Ikarian sea, there would be nothing in terms of spatial challenges to stop them spreading throughout the Cyclades. Among the several predicted expansions out of the south-east Cyclades, one promising candidate must be from Mykonos to the large island of Tenos, and perhaps to all but contiguous Andros. Whether the south-eastern expansion extended further westward is uncertain but, returning to Melos, where much of the debate over colonisation dates began, it is intriguing to note that, according to our expansion models, this island is one of the last major islands to be colonised along *either* axis of entry. One reason why the Saliagos culture as a settlement horizon remained open to criticism for so long was therefore the fact that the best data were being generated on an island which was unlikely to be an initial focus of settlement. Concerning the large lithic sites of Agrilia and Kouphi, if these are indeed not settlements (as Cherry believes), Melos provides the only strong confirmation from an intensively investigated Cycladic island that Saliagos culture settlements did not extend over the entire group, despite the fact that the island was known and visited. If they represent settlements, perhaps failed ones, these sites mark the end of a line of expansion that should reach back to the Anatolian coast.

What of the apparent lack of evidence for continuity between the Saliagos culture and later horizons on some of the south-eastern islands, particularly Amorgos and Thera? This may simply reflect a current gap that future discoveries will fill. Chapter 5 suggests that it may also be an artefact of shifting settlement strategies rather than genuine failure to maintain a long-term presence. But, at least in heuristic terms, it is worth exploring at this juncture a more pessimistic possibility. If the Saliagos settlements were to be seen not as signs of a major expansion sequence but as a limited overspill on the edge of the south-east Aegean, a model might be proposed in which, at least in some parts of the Cyclades, populations never attained a sufficient level to be immune in the long-term to a demographic crash or sudden climatic crunch. Put another way, this would imply that Saliagos culture colonisation did not everywhere lead to establishment, in the sense coined by Graves and Allison, although here it is necessary to recall that the overall establishment of Saliagos culture settlement is most appropriately considered in terms of its network of communities over a wide tract of islandscape rather than by the fate of individual islands. Such a 'bridge too far' model cannot be assessed to a reliable degree until far better data are available concerning the numbers, size and precise contemporaneity of the Saliagos culture settlements. But a few possible scenarios can be sketched to explore what might have happened under severely adverse conditions. For example, people on Naxos, Amorgos and Mykonos could draw upon links back to the south-east Aegean, i.e. the 'rescue effect' in the terminology of island biogeography (Brown and Kodric-Brown 1977), although if the fairly small, arid island of Astypalaia was in trouble too, Amorgos loses this advantage. In terms of island environment and size, communities on Naxos and Greater Paros (either separately or together as the major block of land in the south-east Cyclades) would be best placed to survive, and to act as a refuge for people from the outlying islands in any phase of settlement recession. Combining location, size and environment, Naxos emerges, as so often, as the focal point. Whatever reality future archaeological discoveries favour, simulation within a spatial framework once again enables us to think about the multiple possibilities and diverse trajectories that are subsumed within the processes that we have problematised as Cycladic colonisation.

The spatial approach to colonisation: an appraisal

This chapter has tried to demonstrate that the marriage of data and island archaeological modelling can be a fruitful one, even in the context of an unevenly investigated cluster. After millennia of specialist exploitation that appear to have contributed little besides knowledge to the later process of island settlement, early colonising movements into the Cyclades started at different times in two transitional zones where the edges of the Cyclades were negotiable, in one instance resulting in a probably thoroughly conscious series of jumps to quite distant islands, and in the other a more incremental expansion through a quasi-insular and insular zone. The implication is that colonisation started through sequences that did not acknowledge the over-arching process to which we have devoted this chapter. It can be hazarded that subsequent expansion through the islands was equally a result of diverse context-specific decisions at varying scales, the current data implying that a long period elapsed before the archipelago was fully settled. The smoothed long-term pattern could well hide several discrete phases of expansion separated by pauses, with the starts and stops determined partly by configuration, but also by the motivations of the colonising actors, and their perceived fulfilment. Varied compliance with Graves and Addison's Model 2 (rapid progress from colonisation to establishment) and Model 4 (a substantial passage of time elapses between colonisation and establishment) might be expected, perhaps with the large islands in the south-east Cyclades corresponding to Model 2, and other islands closer to Model 4. If subsequent collapses did occur in parts of the Cyclades, variation between a complete local failure and more subtle temporary recessions could be anticipated, although in no instance are the data yet good enough to distinguish these. And, much as it is misleading to assess a colonisation horizon by the barometer of an individual site, it is unwise to interpret the record of any single island, however well explored, as illustrative of the Cyclades as a whole. Everything tells us that islands, and other groupings within the islandscape, varied greatly in their early histories, and that this is not just a result of uneven fieldwork.

Models stimulate exploration in other respects too, for instance by highlighting counter-intuitive patterns. One might expect the nearest Cycladic islands to the mainland to be settled first, but modelling has shown why this might not have been the case. Likewise, big islands might at first sight be expected to be settled before smaller ones, but models have enabled us to appreciate why (for example) Mykonos might be colonised before far larger Andros. Modelling can also sharpen the focus of future field strategies for investigating the Cycladic Neolithic, by identifying important lacunae in the data (cf. Cherry 1981: 56). In addition, the spatial framework now exists to answer questions such as 'Where are we to find evidence of the Cycladic Early Neolithic?' (Renfrew 1984a: 42). If such a phase exists, it is most likely to be found on Naxos or Amorgos, but the likelihood of it existing at all is best explored by looking at processes at the points of entry into the Cyclades. So far, neither shows signs of a dynamic and expansive earlier Neolithic. If, on the other hand, an earlier phase does materialise in the Cyclades without contemporary evidence at the points of entry, we will need either to look harder at the archaeology of those areas, or to expand the range of our explanatory scenarios for island colonisation in the early Aegean.

A last observation concerns the relationship between the methods and processes witnessed in this chapter and island biogeography. This chapter is, unsurprisingly, that in which reference and resort to techniques and ideas derived with island biogeography is most apparent. It is also that where the 'island', as destination, target, stepping-stone and unit of archaeological investigation, is of necessity most foregrounded, although it may be suspected that if a finer grain of analysis were practical, this prominence would be reduced somewhat (e.g. was 'Kea' colonised, or the coastal landscape of Kea facing Attica, Makronisos and Euboia?). However, although similarities have been affirmed, such as the importance (up to a point) of island size and distance, and the crucial role of stepping-stones, several substantial differences have equally emerged. The keys to understanding the earliest colonisation horizons have turned out to be the interaction between configuration and culture in the south-east Aegean, plus the cultural perception of the northern axis of entry as a patchwork of peninsulas, islands and sea. Colonists seem to have displayed marked variation in their decisions as to when, why, where, how much and how far to settle. Comparison with Watson's study of the biogeography of Aegean avifauna, one of the few of its kind for the Aegean islands, is instructive in this context (Watson 1964; see also Simberloff and Levin 1985). Watson (1964: 218–19) identifies the sea gap between the eastern Aegean and the Cyclades, which groups of people almost certainly did cross to settle the Cyclades, as a major barrier for dispersals of avifauna, reptiles and plants. He also states (1964: 155–6) that some of the Naxian avifauna have been prohibited from expanding to other islands by the latter's poorer environments, whilst for human colonists Naxos seems to have acted as the base for further expansions. People could clearly manipulate and perceive the Cyclades in many different ways that greatly exceeded the scope of island fauna. So far this variety has been explored by looking for clues in the incidence and patterning of early settlement horizons. In the chapter that follows, the focus moves to the range of cultural practices witnessed during these first horizons, in order to elaborate a series of perspectives on the lifestyles and social structures of the first Cycladic islanders.

5

Cultures of colonisation

> Sparse the earth beneath your feet
> so that you have no room to spread your roots
> and keep reaching down in depth
> and broad the sky above
> so that you can read the infinite on your own
> *To Axion Esti*, ODYSSEUS ELYTES

An archaeology of island colonisation should offer more than an explanation of spatial patterning. This chapter therefore looks at different cultural approaches to living in the Cyclades during the first two millennia of their settlement. In doing so, the timeframe of analysis shifts forward, leaving behind pre-colonisation activities and bringing into view the Grotta-Pelos culture, a major horizon of settlements and burials that starts late in the FN and continues throughout EB I (*c.* 3500–2700 BC). This extended duration serves to remind us that colonisation was a very protracted process, with some of the most marginal areas of the archipelago first being settled, as a result of changing living strategies, only some 2000–2500 years after the pioneer Neolithic communities began to move into the Cyclades. It will also enable this chapter to act as a bridge between the Neolithic and the fuller exploration of the EBA that occupies the remainder of this book.

A recurrent theme will be that colonisation and subsequent interaction within and beyond the Cyclades engineered a shift in perceptions of these islands, from places on the edge of everywhere else (therefore effectively an internal frontier and wilderness) to ones at the hub of a region of now enhanced significance, namely a southern Aegean whose seas, islands and coastal rims became enmeshed through people's networks to a degree that was altogether new. How settlement, travel, exchange, style and symbolism affected this in the Cyclades is a question that requires a detailed consideration below. But the key point to emphasise is that the first Cycladic people, far from being engaged primarily in a struggle to survive, began at an early date to fashion and redefine their islandscapes as well as the status of their islands in relation to the world around them. A continuing discourse between the Cyclades and surrounding areas helps to explain the fact that several overall trends seen in Cycladic societies, economies and culture during the later Neolithic and earliest EBA are insular refractions of wider Aegean processes. Moreover, although this chapter concentrates of necessity on the Cyclades, this should not distract from the wider implications for Aegean societies of the emerging networks of island people and culture in the seas that lie between the south-east Aegean, southern Greece and Crete. Without this transformation, some of the Aegean EBA's most crucial developments, especially those associated with intensified maritime exchange and interaction, are unlikely to have developed in the forms and to the degrees that they did.

Domesticating islandscapes from the Saliagos to Grotta-Pelos cultures

Saliagos culture settlement and subsistence strategies

Settlement size, settlement distribution and food-producing practices in the Saliagos, Kephala and Grotta-Pelos cultures define an informative initial analytical focus. The evidence is patchy, but still sufficient to indicate several distinctive ways of integrating people and resources within the overall parameters of early island life set out in chapter 3. A comparison between such structures identifies their differences and prompts the question as to whether they represent simply alternative ways of living in the islands, or whether one was in any definable sense superior to the others as a means of settling the Cyclades, bearing in mind the need to ask some searching questions about the categories of 'success' or 'failure' that tend to be imposed on colonisation horizons, and to consider what the islanders involved were actually setting out to do, or not to do.

A closer look at the Saliagos culture settlements proves particularly rewarding. Earlier doubts about the size and longevity of Saliagos itself (Cherry 1985: 24) belong to the phase of scepticism concerning this horizon that new work has made a thing of the past. In fact the Saliagos culture open settlements that have been investigated to any extent are substantial by Aegean Neolithic standards. Saliagos is now an islet of about 0.7 ha. Signs of habitation were recovered from all the trenches, and walls eroding into the sea show that the settlement was originally larger (Evans and Renfrew 1968: 3). At Grotta a part of the site has also been lost to the sea, but material is known at several locations (Hadjianastasiou 1988: 11–12, 1989: 207, 209). Phtelia too has suffered from erosion and also quarrying. It appears to be large, assuming that available information relates to both the Saliagos and early FN levels (Sampson 1997: 6). At Mavrispilia the scatter extends over several hectares (Belmont and Renfrew 1964: fig. 1), although this area will have been expanded by the erosion of material. The specific significance of the large lithic sites of Agrilia, Kouphi and Vouni depends, of course, on whether they represent special purpose sites associated with visitation, or relics of settlement. Given the size of the best-documented Saliagos settlements, and likely Neolithic population densities, their populations should have been at least in the order of 70–150 people, and, given the reduction of site area through erosion at several sites, perhaps even larger.[1] The small number of Saliagos culture open settlements that have been explored in detail therefore represent the remnants of substantial village-sized communities. There is no reason to assume that the same is not the case for other Saliagos culture settlements, like Minoa in Amorgos or Akrotiri in Thera, although only future work can substantiate or falsify this assumption.

Moreover, the available radiocarbon dates and stratigraphy indicate that Saliagos settlements were not only relatively large, but also long-lived. The radiocarbon dates for Saliagos itself indicate a duration of c. 200–400 years (Evans and Renfrew 1968: 90, 144), a longevity that is supported by the depth of the stratigraphy, which includes several building phases, and the diachronic change in the pottery and lithics. At Grotta and Phtelia the stratigraphy is thick (Hadjianastasiou 1988: 11–12; Sampson 1997: 3–6), and Phtelia's material spans the LN and the early FN, in both cases also arguing for a fairly long lifespan. The same may be true of Zas, with its stratigraphic sequence through the later Neolithic into the EBA, but the special circumstances inherent in a cave site, in terms of its fixed location in the landscape and the conditions of stratigraphic accumulation, make it hard to compare with the open settlements.

At least some Saliagos culture settlements were therefore substantial, long-lived places, but the overall distribution of settlements indicates that they were widely spaced (cf. fig. 34). The only exception is the two adjacent sites of Mavrispilia and Phtelia on Mykonos, whose exact chronological relationship has yet to be clarified. A degree of infilling of this pattern can be anticipated as archaeological prospection advances, but it may not fundamentally alter the impression that although people at this time *visited* a lot of the islandscape (as is attested by the many small lithic sites), they were a lot more particular about where they actually *resided*. In this respect, the scattered nature of the settlements distinguishes the Cyclades from Neolithic Thessaly and other areas of dense Neolithic occupation. For example, all the currently known Saliagos culture settlements in the south-east Cyclades, spread out across their exploded fragments of land, are equivalent to the numbers of Neolithic sites packed into a small patch of the Thessalian landscape (Demoule and Perlès 1993: 368). This

---

[1] Renfrew (1972: 251), in his analysis of Aegean demography, suggested population densities in the order of 200 people per hectare for the Neolithic and 300 per hectare for the EBA. Although the regional population totals that he derived from these densities are now regarded as exaggerations by a large margin (cf. chapter 3), the error lay mainly in the average settlement size that Renfrew took as his working estimate, rather than the density ranges themselves. In the light of subsequent detailed analyses of a small number of Neolithic and EBA sites (Whitelaw 1983, 1991a), a population range of 100–200 people per hectare in the Neolithic and 200–300 in the EBA is used in this book. The best confirmation of the EBA level remains the case of the densely packed EB II settlement of Myrtos Phournou Koryphi on Crete (Warren 1972a; Whitelaw 1983) which contained five or six households suitable for a nuclear family apiece within an area of about 0.09 ha. Assuming an average family size of five people, this generates a community of 25–30 people, or about 280–330 people per hectare, a figure for a closely packed EBA site that matches encouragingly with the upper end of Renfrew's range. Examination of Neolithic settlements in the Aegean confirms that they are in general less densely occupied than EBA Myrtos (e.g. Evans 1994; Sinos 1971; Whitelaw 1991a).

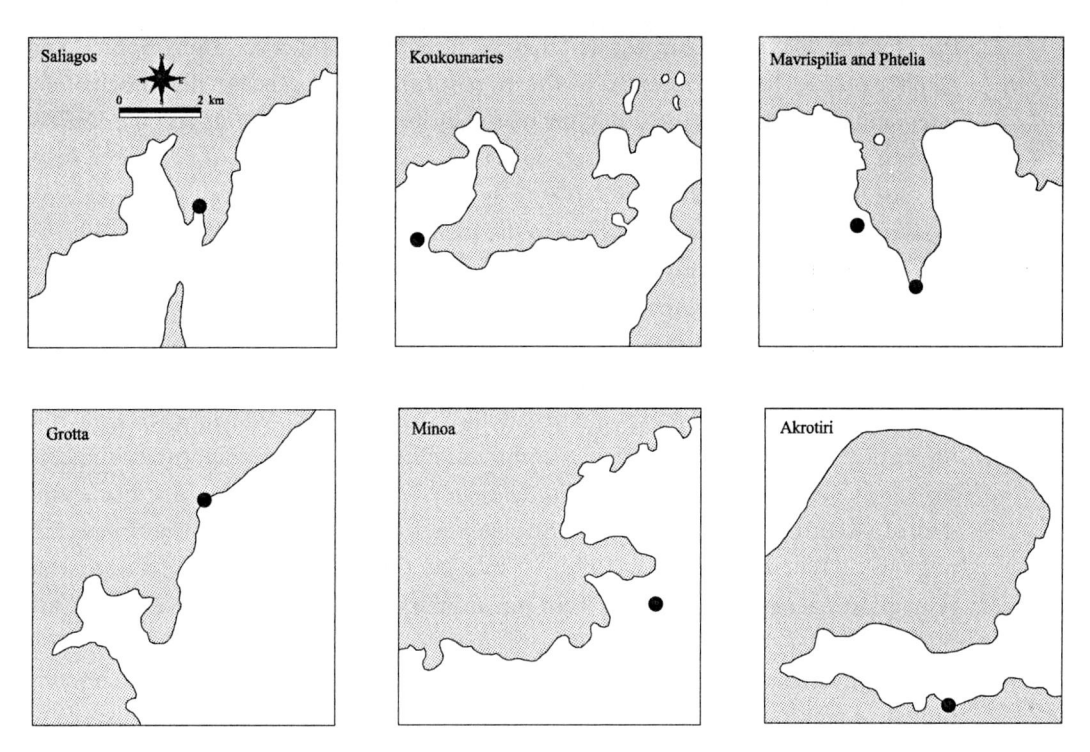

Fig. 41 Microlocations of Saliagos culture sites, showing a preference for location in proximity to deep bays.

must have had implications for the nature of the social relations between Cycladic communities. More immediately, a look at the specific micro-niches that the Saliagos culture settlements occupied in the islandscape provides one possible explanation for this apparently wide spacing.

The sample is small but shows a marked preference for environmentally clement niches, even on islands that are not known for their environmental clemency. All are on medium or large islands, several are close to good water sources (Evans and Renfrew 1968: 5; Halstead in prep; Hadjianastasiou 1988: 11; Sampson 1997: 11) that would have enabled spring-fed gardening (Jameson et al. 1994: 342–3; Johnson 1996), and most are situated on knoll-tops or bluffs dominating major bays and the flat valley lands at their head (fig. 41). If this pattern does reflect real preferences, it is interesting in several respects. First, it may turn out to possess some predictive power in terms of detecting further Saliagos settlements (for example there is a lot of fertile, well-watered arable land around Sangri on Naxos, the long-known findspot of a Neolithic figurine). Second, the comparative rarity of such niches in the Cyclades might suggest that one constraint on the distribution of Saliagos settlements was quite simply the finite number of suitable locations that existed. The observation that Saliagos communities preferred medium and large islands over smaller ones (which assumes that the individual island was indeed an important perceived unit), might therefore be adapted to suggest that they preferred niches that for topographical and climatic reasons largely occurred on the more substantial islands, but that much of the intervening islandscape, including the marginal areas on large islands and the entirety of most small islands, was left unsettled.

The location of several of the settlements around bays may also reflect strategies to maximise the contribution of fishing to the food supply, both as a small-scale activity and by occasional bonanzas when fish shoaled in the bay, as Evans and Renfrew (1968: 79–80) envisaged for the community at Saliagos. Although in chapter 3 fishing was presented as an episodic activity as opposed to a regular mainstay, and in chapter 4 fishing expeditions were considered an unlikely trigger of island colonisation, neither of these cautionary remarks should negate the possibility of an ancillary, seasonal role for fishing within some Cycladic communities. The wet-sieving programme at Saliagos showed that this community exploited marine resources to a considerable degree (Renfrew, J.M. et al. 1968; Shackleton 1968). The report of very few fish remains at Phtelia (Sampson 1997: 9) may be premature, as most of the marine remains at Saliagos came from refuse pits on the edges of the settlement. There are other hints that the Saliagos culture communities did attempt to increase their sea-harvesting efficiency. Small LN lithic sites situated on coastal bluffs are often interpreted as look-out points for tunny, and make sense in terms of local networks of observation points set up by people based in the islands to improve their chances of intercepting shoals, rather than hoping that they would pass near the settlement. Among the Saliagos culture lithics, the large ovates might have been mounted as the heads of tunny spears, and the much more common barbed and tanged projectile points could have been used as harpoon tips as well as arrowheads. A terrestrial dimension to this strategy might also have existed, with the few bones of fallow deer at Saliagos perhaps indicative of long-range hunting, or even a trade in carcasses, rather than regular local herd management, and inland finds of projectile points suggesting the hunting of small mammals.

To summarise, one settlement strategy in Saliagos culture times may have been to locate a favourable niche for farming and fishing, settle it at the village level, and detach specialist procurement groups seasonally to expand the community's wild food supply. The limited number of such niches in the Cyclades itself implies that Saliagos expansion episodes took the form of discrete jumps rather than accretional advances. If Saliagos culture subsistence did indeed rely upon a set of practices that assumed village-level communities, this may suggest that relatively large groups of people relocated in each expansion episode, rather than small splinter groups that gradually built up into villages in their own right. In other words, people may have colonised in groups that conformed to culturally constructed ideas about the right size of a viable community, and targeted places perceived as appropriate for such communities to inhabit (Williamson and Sabath 1984). Whether such a tradition in the Saliagos culture is best attributed to antecedent history, in other words to cultural attitudes fashioned in more environmentally clement parts of the south-east Aegean, or whether it reflected a means of living tailored for the Cyclades, is at present hard to establish. On the one hand, if the major axis of expansion ran through Samos and Ikaria to Naxos, the legacy of experience would have been one of life on big, well-watered islands. On the other hand, plenty of the smaller south-east Aegean islands were settled in the later Neolithic (see fig. 30), in contrast to the situation in the Cyclades, and an axis of entry through the central Dodecanese would certainly have introduced colonising islanders to marginal environments. Whilst many south-east Aegean sites are located on coastal bluffs (Melas 1985; Sampson 1987), it is striking that projectile points are rarer than in the Cyclades (Melas 1985: 140 for finds on Karpathos and Kalymnos). Quite how the strategies used by the Cycladic colonists emerged out of this potential mixture of prior histories and the environmental conditions within the Cyclades will remain obscure until comparable data exist.

Comparing Saliagos culture strategies with those of later horizons

Comparing Saliagos culture settlements and those of the early FN is difficult, given that detailed knowledge of the latter is limited to two Keian sites, of which one (Kephala) has been both excavated and intensively surveyed but the other (Paoura) only explored by intensive survey, and the Zas IIa stratum of similar date, with some support from the provisional reports for Phtelia, as well as the surface data from Andros and other Keian sites. Several observations can nonetheless be made. The open settlements again appear to be villages or large hamlets often situated on coastal bluffs. Whitelaw (1991a: 208, 214–15) estimates the settlement extent of Kephala and Paoura at 0.7 ha and 1.75–2.0 ha respectively; on Andros, Kastri is comparable in size and Strophylas may be larger (Koutsoukou 1993). The population of Kephala has been estimated at about fifty people by Coleman (1977: 111), or thirty-five to fifty by Whitelaw (1991a: 207–8). Extrapolated to Paoura, these figures suggest a population of about 100–150 for the latter site. Kephala and Paoura are, however, poorly situated for access to the best arable in northern Kea, in contrast to the settlement that would emerge at the end of the Neolithic and exist through much of the Bronze Age at Agia Irini. Their locations might instead reflect a desire for long-range inter-visibility, not least with FN sites in southern Euboia, or considerations of defence; Koutsoukou (1993) makes the same observation about the FN settlements in Andros. So although generic similarities can be identified with the Saliagos culture communities, certain differences are also starting to become apparent.

Kephala, in particular, contrasts in other ways with Saliagos culture settlements. There is no evidence for wild meat resources (Coy 1977: 132), although without wet-sieving the contribution of smaller marine and land fauna cannot be assessed. A decline might be supported by the fact that Kephala has far fewer projectile points than do the Saliagos culture sites. Another contrast is the possible evidence of dairying in the form

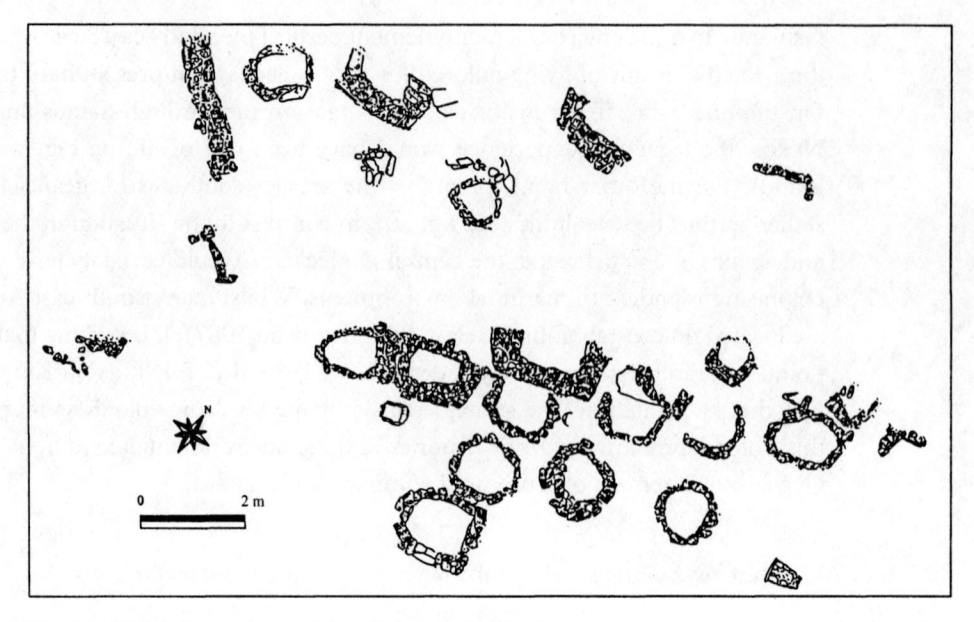

Fig. 42 Kephala cemetery. After Coleman 1977: plate 8.

of the cheese-pot fragments found at Kephala (Coleman 1977: plates 37, 88). One last, very striking, difference is the institution of a community cemetery at the entrance to the site (fig. 42), comprising, along with that of Tharrounia in Euboia (Sampson 1992: 86–91, 1993: 223–40), one of the earliest of its kind in the southern Aegean and a notable innovation, given the apparent absence of cemeteries in the Saliagos culture horizon, and the sporadic incidence of archaeologically visible disposal of the dead in much of the Aegean Neolithic (Cavanagh and Mee 1998: 6–11). Talalay (1991) sees the Kephala cemetery as signalling new claims to resources. Whatever the precise reasons for the initiation of the Kephala cemetery, it anticipates practices associated with the disposal of the dead that are central to subsequent dynamics in the Cyclades, and indeed much of the southern Aegean during the EBA.

A shift from the Saliagos culture way of life is most marked in the signature of the Grotta-Pelos culture sites, both settlements and cemeteries, dating to the late FN and EB I. Fig. 43 highlights the extremely large number of Grotta-Pelos sites identified, the southerly emphasis in terms of well-documented sites, and the extent of the islandscape that was settled. Whether the southerly emphasis reflects an ancient pattern or is merely a product of uneven investigation is uncertain, and will depend on the results of further investigation among the northern islands (cf. Renfrew 1984a: 43; also chapter 6). But it is striking that although this distribution overlies the main area of known Saliagos culture settlements, it represents a radically different way of living in the islands. First, Grotta-Pelos settlements were widely dispersed over large and small pockets of arable alike, and provide the earliest solid evidence for colonisation of smaller islands, notably in the Erimonisia (Renfrew 1972: 521;

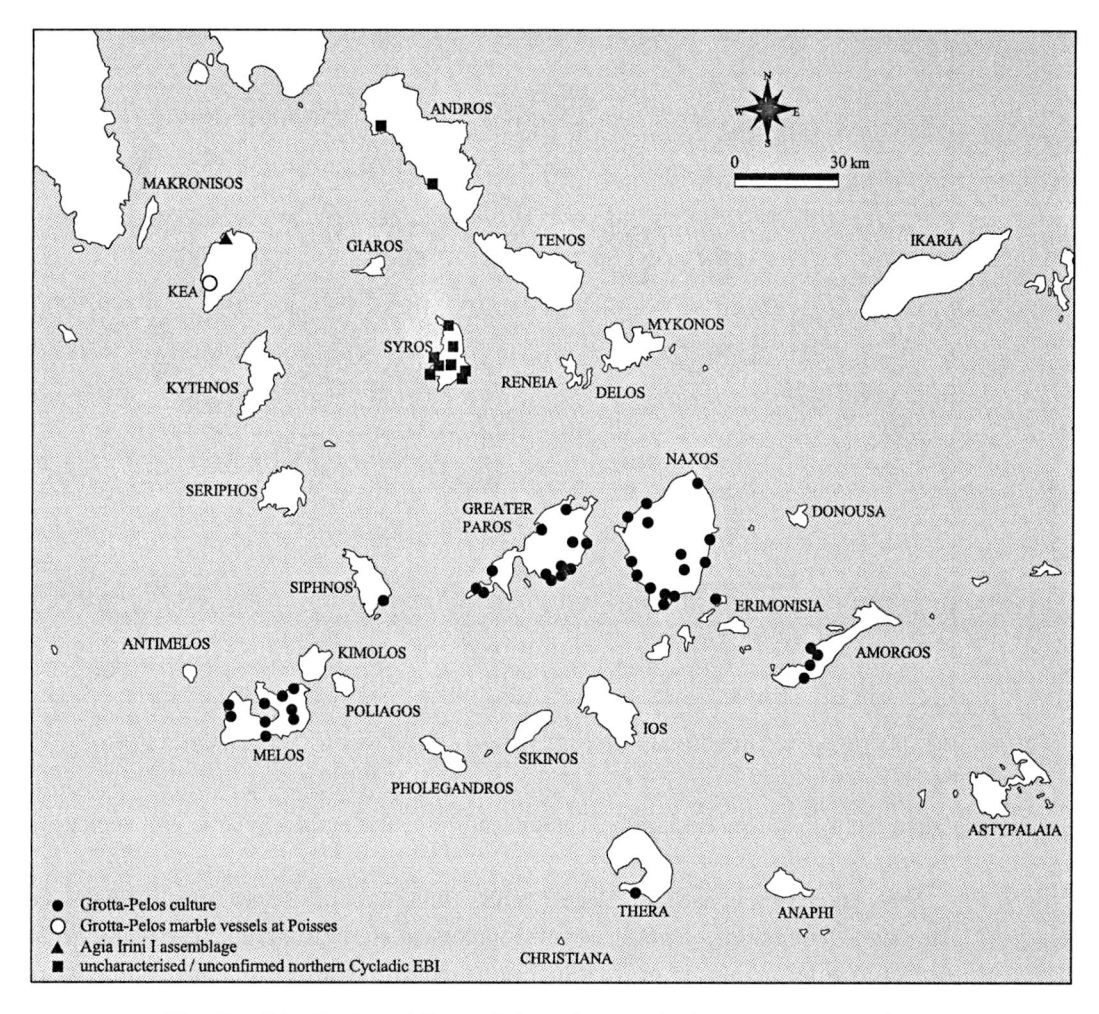

Fig. 43   Distribution of Grotta-Pelos culture and other contemporary sites.

Zapheiropoulou 1967: 381). Second, although the faunal and botanical evidence for Grotta-Pelos subsistence practices is unfortunately minimal, projectile points disappear at this juncture. Third, the Grotta-Pelos settlements represented tiny human groups, mainly short-lived farmsteads of one or two families. This last point, which has substantial implications, requires rather fuller justification.

Few Grotta-Pelos settlements have been extensively excavated, but recent work at Markiani on Amorgos suggested a Grotta-Pelos occupation area of much less than the site's EB II size of 0.25 ha (French and Whitelaw 1999: 153, 162). The surface scatters at the Grotta-Pelos sites on Melos average well under a hectare (Cherry 1982b), a small size that is striking not least because Aegean erosion conditions tend to generate surface scatters that exceed the original occupation areas to a considerable degree. This image of very modestly sized communities is corroborated by an examination of the many small cemeteries for which the Grotta-Pelos culture is well known, and

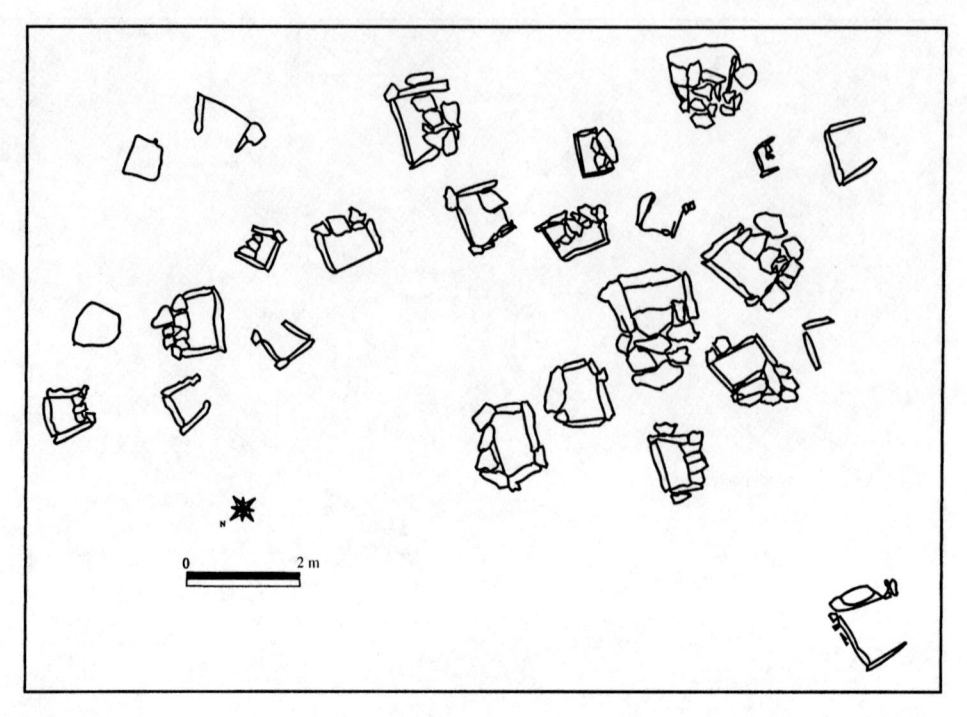

Fig. 44   A typical Grotta-Pelos cemetery: Lakkoudes on Naxos. After Doumas 1977: fig. 14.

which from this time become a regular feature of the early Cycladic archaeological record.

The cemeteries consist of largely single inhumations in cist graves (fig. 44). Although the amount of physical anthropological study undertaken remains negligible, gross distinctions in grave dimensions indicate that different age cohorts were buried (Doumas 1977: figs. 19–28; Tsountas 1898: 142–3). Men and women have also been identified (Doumas 1977: 55). Different kinds of people were therefore receiving formal burial. Several examples of convincing cemetery–settlement pairs are known (Doumas 1977: 29; Wagstaff and Cherry 1982b: 137–8), suggesting that each of the cemeteries belonged to a single community. Yet despite the strong indications that the Grotta-Pelos cemeteries represent a substantial proportion (if not virtually all) of the population of the adjacent settlements, the number of graves that they contain is modest. The majority total only ten to twenty graves, the three exceptions being Kampos tis Makris (ninety) on Naxos, and Krassades (fifty) and Pyrgos (fifty-eight) on Greater Paros (Doumas 1977: 29). These figures may be inflated for the hypothetical non-inclusion of some people (in particular neo-natal deaths), and it must be accepted that parts of most cemeteries have been lost to erosion or robbing, which may explain the occasional find of a single grave (Doumas 1977: 31). But however generously these various factors are allowed for, a comparison of cemetery size with the twenty of so deaths expected of a pre-modern nuclear family over a century

(Bintliff 1977b: 83–4; Whitelaw 1983: 336) argues that no Grotta-Pelos burying community can have comprised more than one or two families over a century or two (see also Broodbank 1989: 322–5; Cherry 1979: 40; Doumas 1977: 31). If this is the case, as it certainly seems to be, the individual Grotta-Pelos farmsteads must have come into being and faded out again every few generations.

Explaining the variability in settlement strategies

What can be deduced from a comparison between the diverse archaeological signatures outlined above? The most stimulating contrasts can be drawn between the very different Saliagos and Grotta-Pelos cultures, with the Kephala culture sites occupying a midway position (village-orientated, yet with less of a hunting element and initiating formal burial?). Moreover, a contrast between Saliagos and Grotta-Pelos allows us not only to draw out their differences, but to explore ways of understanding the transition from the one to the other, and thereby to shed light on the obscure early FN of the south-east Cyclades, after the end of the Saliagos culture settlements and preceding the floruit of the Grotta-Pelos culture.

Several contrasts can be summarised and their implications explored. First is the difference in settlement size. In terms of demography, this means that counting dots on the map for each culture is meaningless, as the population of a single Saliagos culture village should be equivalent to many Grotta-Pelos farmsteads. It is salutary to note that the thirty-five or so Grotta-Pelos settlements estimated for Melos from the survey data (Cherry and Wagstaff 1982b: 138) should reflect an aggregate population no larger than a couple of Saliagos villages. Given the further point that many of the Grotta-Pelos sites cannot have been contemporary with each other, estimating regional populations becomes an exercise in the counter-intuitive. Second, different kinds of community mobility can be discerned. Saliagos settlements appear to have acted as the stable residential foci from which task groups would move out for limited durations to exploit the resources of the islands. In contrast, the Grotta-Pelos settlements must have been shifting around the islandscape within the span of human memories. In the former horizon a close association is seen between a given community and a specific location (or even territory?), but in the latter, communities must have consisted of changing scatters of temporarily settled points in the islandscape. Third, at least the higher population estimates for individual Saliagos culture villages suggest that there would have been room for manoeuvre between endogamous and exogamous alliances (although even such a village could not have been self-sufficient overall in this respect), whilst in the Grotta-Pelos farmsteads exogamy must have been largely the rule. As a fourth contrast, it is tempting to explain the Grotta-Pelos culture's investment in cemeteries as a means of claiming association with a tract of land through burial of the ancestors, at a time when in reality this association was more temporally fragile and open to dispute than in the established shadow of a larger Saliagos culture village.

Seeing the Saliagos and Grotta-Pelos horizons as alternative ways of living in the Cyclades invites us to look at the centuries of the early fourth millennium, which separate them, as a period of structural transformation between the two, and thereby to offer an alternative to the partial hiatus that the present archaeological record ostensibly suggests in the south-east Cyclades (as was explored in chapter 4). In fact, similar problems in identifying transitional sites and levels, and tracing culture sequences, are encountered elsewhere in the fourth-millennium BC Aegean (Manning 1995: 168–70; Renfrew 1989), and the scale of the lacuna argues that a broad approach to the phenomenon is needed. One convincing explanation for the low visibility of settlements is that it was associated with reduced community size and permanence, itself linked to an increase in stock-breeding as part of the mixed farming economy or (less probably) through small-scale pastoralism. Halstead (1996b) outlines why decreases in community size would allow people more room to distance themselves from the heavy dependence on crops seen in village settlements, and take on a flexible mixture of farming and small-scale herding.

Explaining the patchy FN record in the south-east Cyclades as a result of changes in ways of living rather than a partial collapse of settlement is attractive for a number of reasons. An alternative to models of demographic crisis or sudden climatic catastrophe (although neither should yet be rejected as possible scenarios) is the dissolution of the traditional Saliagos culture villages and the dispersal of populations into smaller, lower-visibility settlements that spread across the islandscape, opening up the small arable interstices between the best niches, the sea and the mountains. Rather than the Grotta-Pelos sites representing an effective recolonisation following a partial desertion, they may reflect a resurgence in archaeological visibility following a poorly understood phase of social restructuring. What the surface signature of the first new settlements might be is as yet unknown, but the Zas IIa and IIb strata, plus the uppermost level of Phtelia, promise to provide some diagnostics. Other Naxian data hint at such a transition, for example a few cheese-pots at Grotta (Hadjianastasiou 1988: 19), and a couple of jars with red-crusted decoration of FN type, one with an EBA pedestal-based form, found at Kanaki and another, unknown, site (Zachos 1990: 32). These jars are particularly intriguing because their intact condition argues that they were tomb finds, and thereby hints at the existence of cemeteries on Naxos antedating those of the Grotta-Pelos culture. If so, the earliest phase of the Naxian burial record is currently missing, and the beginning of cemetery use in the south-east should correlate with the Kephala cemetery in the north, the Grotta-Pelos cemeteries instead marking a later increase in visibility as diagnostic objects started to be more frequently placed in the tombs. In Greater Paros hints of such a transition can be detected in material such as a rolled-rim bowl combining later FN form with earlier FN pattern-burnished decoration (Overbeck 1989a: 5, cat. no. 1). It may even be relevant that the latest level at Saliagos itself was restricted to a small area of the site (Evans and Renfrew 1968: 22). This transitional phase will certainly reward further exploration; and at the northern end of the Cyclades, the potential for explaining the slightly later obscure post-Kephala culture succession on Kea in these terms is tantalising, if empirically deadlocked by the current state of the data, with the excavated assemblages being restricted to Kephala and Agia Irini I.

These thoughts force us to confront the question as to whether the Saliagos and Grotta-Pelos cultures reflect simply different ways of living (with the Kephala culture as something of a half-way house?), or whether one was better suited to surviving in these islands (if criteria can be agreed for judging this). A rogue variable in this context is the unconfirmed possibility that, between the Neolithic and the EBA, Aegean climates gradually became drier and therefore changed the ground-rules (chapter 3; a long-term process not to be confused with a disastrous short-term crunch, such as a severe run of drought years). At one level, whether or not the climate was changing, an increased emphasis on stock-based and possibly dairying subsistence economies, in conjunction with a shift to small, farmstead-sized communities, would have provided the islanders with a wider range of options in terms of where to settle. It is decidedly tempting to associate such a shift with the expansion of settlement into the environmentally more marginal parts of the Cyclades. The declining incidence of projectile points through the fourth millennium might be taken to indicate that hunting and fishing was a strategy that was readily down-graded once an alternative became culturally accepted, although until further wet-sieving has been undertaken this can only be tentatively proposed.

Yet, conversely, Saliagos settlements practised another way of life for roughly a millennium, with at least Saliagos itself enjoying a longevity unrivalled in the Cyclades until the rise of a handful of big settlements in EB II (see chapter 7). It is hard to deny that the Saliagos culture was a manifest success in its own terms, and a perfectly viable way of living in the Cyclades. Any limits to its expansion, whether across the Cyclades as a whole or in intra-regional terms (regarding patches of islandscape left unsettled), are best investigated for the insights they provide into what people thought was worth doing in the fifth millennium BC. In terms of their approaches to risk, the two horizons also differ, but again with no obvious advantage lying with either. Saliagos settlements represent, in effect, a small number of precious eggs placed in large baskets chosen for their safety, whilst Grotta-Pelos settlements represent a great number of individually expendable eggs distributed in small baskets of variable quality. The first combination makes for low endemic risk but a major catastrophe if anything goes badly wrong, the second for a constant medium-level risk to each settlement balanced by high collective security for the wider whole, with much more of the overall islandscape being settled, as opposed to utilised, but many individual areas often abandoned at any given time. Both succeeded in reproducing Cycladic communities over very long periods of time.

Lastly, how did the fact that the Cyclades are islands mediate the impact of these changes, at a generic level so widespread in the Aegean? For one thing, the switch from village to farmstead was an extreme one, with smaller communities apparently replacing larger ones across a variety of islandscapes. What appears to be observed is a shift in a whole nexus of practices, and in relations between people and environments. A parallel can be drawn with the 'tramping' settlement strategy identified by Diamond and Keegan (Diamond 1974; Diamond and Keegan 1984; Keegan and Diamond 1987: 73–4) in the context of tropical island horticulturalists, in which moving on becomes preferable to intensification at a given location. Certainly there are differences, not the least being that the stimulus to move onward for tropical horticulturalists is embedded in the practice of swidden gardening, whilst the stimulus in the Cyclades would be a new belief that shifting, centrifugal residence networks were preferable to more focused centripetal ones. But the parallel underscores how altered attitudes and practices could lead to very different patterns of island settlement. Lastly, and most crucially, in most other parts of the Aegean the environmentally marginal areas settled during the FN remained marginal, and in certain cases people subsequently retreated from them (for a recently documented example see Branigan 1998a on the Ziros region of eastern Crete). But in the Cyclades, as will become clear, island configuration and maritime networks created a quite different outcome, whereby, once settled, certain environmentally marginal areas started to became central points in the cultural islandscape, turning the world of the Neolithic Cyclades inside out.

Dialogues in the islands

Implicit in the processes outlined above is the need for communication between people, islands and the world beyond. In the later Neolithic, the Cyclades shifted from a silent, secret world penetrated by specialist mainlanders to a space full of voices. Analysis of movement, exchange and stylistic interaction is therefore an essential complement to the analysis of shifting community structures and practices just undertaken, and once again the view of the Neolithic settlements as insecure isolates will be seen to be in need of revision. It is now widely acknowledged that the later Neolithic saw an increase in the amount of maritime activity in the Aegean (Demoule and Perlès 1993: 403; Nakou 1995: 6), but what has not been investigated is the way in which settlement in the Cyclades contributed to the generation of such maritime networks. Concerning Aegean Neolithic trade, Perlès (1992) has usefully proposed three principal varieties: (i) utilitarian (e.g. obsidian), (ii) local/social (e.g. pottery) and (iii) ritual/prestige (e.g. figurines, stone vessels or jewellery). Clearly, Neolithic trade was far from simple or uniform, and indeed the complexities of value systems and contexts of exchange events were surely more intricate than even Perlès' categorisation allows. We will look first at obsidian and those other shiny minerals, known as metals, that rose to prominence in the later Neolithic. We then turn to the circulation of social and prestige items, and to patterns of stylistic interaction. The focus will be on the Saliagos and early FN horizons, before exploring the Grotta-Pelos culture and the transition to the EBA in the final section.

Obsidian

By the time the Cyclades saw their first settlements, the procurement of obsidian was already an activity of immemorial antiquity. Perlès' case for a shift across the southern Aegean from specialised procurement in the earlier Neolithic to open access in the later Neolithic was cited during analysis in chapter 4 of practices triggering colonisation. It was argued that the sharp rise in the quantity of obsidian circulating in the latter period was a consequence rather than a cause of the first Cycladic settlements. Yet remarkably little is really known of the mechanisms that lay behind this enhanced accessibility, and equally of the social action behind the excellent case made for unorganised, expeditious quarrying that is documented by detailed survey of the Melian sources (Torrence 1982, 1984, 1986: 164–217). Did the Neolithic islanders become the dominant suppliers to the outside world, or catalyse a higher level of external access thanks to the network of stopping points that the new island communities represented? If the former, did they themselves take obsidian outside the Cyclades, or did their settlements act as locations where plentiful obsidian could be found by outsiders without the need to travel on as far as Melos? If the latter, to what extent did intervening Cycladic communities represent a help (e.g. victualling) as opposed to an impediment (e.g. protracted social negotiation, or outright hostility) to external procurement groups? In short, was open access to obsidian agreed or contested? And precisely how and where in the southern Aegean did procurement by direct trips to the quarries articulate with procurement through exchange?

Variability in the quantity and quality of obsidian utilisation in the later Neolithic Aegean suggests that there are no simple or uniform answers to these questions. Part of this variability is probably to do with geography and configuration. For maritime groups in the Cyclades and their fringes, obsidian was surely a less mysterious and generally more mundane material than in more distant Laconia or northern Greece, for example, where it continued to be a rarity into the later Neolithic (Carter and Ydo 1996: 161–5; Demoule and Perlès 1993: 395–6). Yet even within the maritime-orientated areas of the southern Aegean we can anticipate differentiation. For example, did Melian obsidian arrive in the same manner at the Kalythies cave on Rhodes (Sampson 1987) as it did at the Kitsos cave in Attica (Lambert 1981)? Given that the former's links to Melos lay via the Saliagos culture communities of the southeast Cyclades, whilst the latter's followed an ancient route that may have been fairly lightly settled, if not uninhabited, until late in the Neolithic, it seems unlikely. But what can be affirmed with little cause for doubt is that the burgeoning movement of obsidian meant that people in the Cyclades must have been frequently encountering strangers with different customs and possibly languages, whether in their own settlements, at the Melian quarries (which may have been settings for much cross-cultural interaction and information exchange), or beyond the islands. The effect of such encounters must have been to boost mechanisms for communication, through material culture just as much as speech, and equally to enhance definition of the cultural attributes that distinguished the people of the Cyclades from people elsewhere.

The few Neolithic Cycladic sites whose obsidian has been properly documented provide some hints as to the amount of the material moving around within the islands. Taking the weight of the obsidian from the trenches at Saliagos for which figures are available (Evans and Renfrew 1968: 48), and extrapolating to the surviving area of the site as a whole, it can be estimated that this community utilised about 1700 kg of obsidian. This is liable to be an underestimate, as the trenches concerned were shallow and the edges of the site are lost to the sea. Allowing Saliagos a life-span of 200–400 years, as the excavators suggest, it transpires that the community's consumption of obsidian was therefore at least 4.3–8.5 kg per year, and probably substantially more. This is not an enormous quantity (although for a single village it argues fairly profligate utilisation), but it does suggest the need for regular visits to the quarries, some three days' canoe journey distant. The weight of obsidian at Saliagos can be informatively compared with Torrence's estimate from surface material at the quarries that some 1.3 million kg of macrocores, the partially prepared nodules from which further knapping was done, left Melos over the three millennia of the later Neolithic and EBA (Torrence 1982: 212–13). Comparing these figures, it transpires that Saliagos consumed about 0.13 per cent of all the obsidian used in the Aegean during the above period. This may seem unimpressive until it is recalled that obsidian was dispersing to numbers of sites probably to be reckoned in the thousands over an extremely long period. If for experimental purposes we assume that macrocores left Melos at a steady rate through the later Neolithic and EBA, some 87,000 to 174,000 kg should have done so in the lifetime of the Saliagos settlement, of which Saliagos' own obsidian comprised about 1–2 per cent of the total. If other Saliagos culture settlements used obsidian to a similar degree, we might suggest that collectively they were not only prominent in the shorter-range acquisition of a substantial proportion of all the obsidian in circulation at any one time, but also that Saliagos settlements, or their people abroad, were a good starting point for non-Cycladic people seeking to obtain the material. The estimated number of pieces of obsidian that are now lying on the surface at Saliagos (99,400), Kephala (23,000) and Paoura (57,000) is also instructive (sources of data: Evans and Renfrew 1968: 48; Whitelaw 1991a: 202, 213). These figures cannot be ranked, as the degree of deflation at each site differs, and the shorter life-span of Kephala compared to Saliagos suggests the need for adjustments to achieve any insight into consumption rates. But clearly, the Keian FN sites also had access to large quantities of obsidian. In general, this scale of usage and discard in the Cyclades (and perhaps immediately adjacent areas) contrasts with the much more sparing levels attested elsewhere in the Aegean, for example the total of merely 1638 pieces of obsidian recovered by a diachronic intensive survey covering about 70 sq km of Laconia (Carter and Ydo 1996: 141). The Neolithic Cycladic figures also exceed the modest levels typical of individual EBA sites both in and beyond the islands.

Metals

Obsidian has been convincingly shown to have been of relatively low, if assuredly still variable, value in the early Aegean (Torrence 1986). Metals, on the other hand, can be demonstrated to have entered the system of the overall Anatolian–Aegean–Balkan region much higher up the scale (e.g. Renfrew 1986), and early exploitation of the Cyclades' metal sources is accordingly of particular interest in the present context. During the FN, metallurgy became an island activity for the first time, although its visibility remained sporadic for over a millennium (Nakou 1995: 3–9), and indeed only at the transition to EB II does a clear relationship between metal acquisition, production and power in the islands emerge (chapters 8, 9 and 10). FN sherds near the Agios Sostis silver/lead mine on Siphnos might optimistically be taken to indicate exploitation before the EBA usage that is established by radiocarbon and thermoluminescence dating (Gropengiesser 1987; Wagner *et al.* 1980: 73–5). Despite the fact that silver first becomes prominent in the Cycladic burial record much later, in the EB I–II Kampos group (Renfrew 1984a: 51–3), the existence of FN Aegean silver jewellery (Zachos 1996c) does suggest the use of at least one Aegean silver source by this time. Evidence of FN copper production comes from Kea, in the form of smelting debris at Kephala and Paoura (Coleman 1977: 3–4, 157–8), plus a crucible fragment at later Agia Irini I (Caskey 1972: 360). Further circumstantial evidence is the number of FN copper artefacts at Zas cave, including flat axes (fig. 45), pins and a dagger, although a small perforated gold strip, presumably an item of adornment, from the same site is probably an exotic northern import and may date slightly earlier (Zachos 1996b, 1999: 154). This mixture of tools, jewellery and weapons is entirely typical of the spectrum of uses of metal in the Aegean FN (Zachos 1996a, 1996c).

Despite our continuing ignorance of the degree to which Cycladic metal sources were in use by the FN, is seems likely that metal prospection, production and exchange created an additional theatre for encounters between different kinds of people in the fourth millennium BC. In this respect, Kea and its surrounding region defines a critical zone, incorporating the metal source of Lavrion and forming a gateway into the metalliferous islands of the western Cyclades. It is noteworthy that in addition to the Keian data, southern Euboian FN sites have also produced traces of metal-working (Keller 1982: 48; Spitaels 1982a: 43). One possible reason why Kephala, Paoura and the similar FN settlement at Plakari over the straits in southern Euboia were situated on defensible hilltops could perhaps be that their manufacture of coveted metal objects rendered them vulnerable to raids by people passing along the maritime route on which they lay.

Fig. 45   Final Neolithic copper flat axe from the Zas cave. Courtesy of Konstantinos Zachos and the Nicholas P. Goulandris Foundation – Museum of Cycladic Art.

Stylistic interactions

We have seen that procurement journeys are likely to have ensured that certain areas of the Cyclades enjoyed contacts with the outside world, with such contacts potentially ranging from peaceful encounters to aggression. But what of other dimensions of interaction? Saliagos provides evidence for exchange between the Cyclades and other areas, in the form of a few decorated sherds of Greek mainland type, foreign flints and several pieces of obsidian from Giali in the south-east Aegean (Cann *et al.* 1968; Evans and Renfrew 1968: 47–8, 82–3). To these can be added the gold strip from Zas, whose best parallels are objects at Aravissos in northern Greece and Varna on the Black Sea (Zachos 1996b: 88, cat. no. 304). The low incidence of these finds does not argue for intensive interaction, but the distances from which objects derived is startling. Exactly how communities in the Neolithic Cyclades acquired and circulated such exotica is beyond recovery. Exchange through prestige chains similar to those suggested for the Neolithic dispersion of *Spondylus* ornaments into the Balkans,

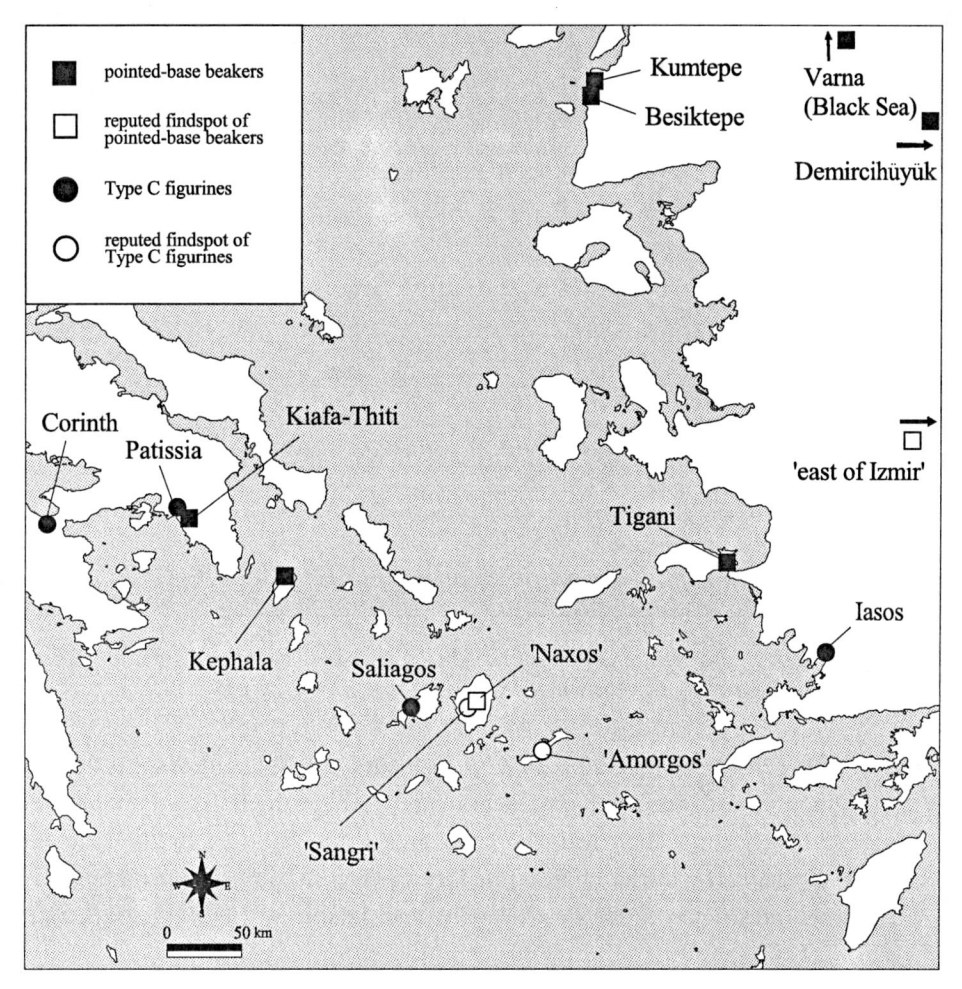

Fig. 46 Distribution of select later Neolithic prestige objects found in the Cyclades. Data from Getz-Gentle 1996: map 6 with additions and Talalay 1983.

alongside fairly broad interaction spheres, may be more plausible than directional long-range travel. But the very presence of exotica suggests that Cycladic people were interested in relating to the world beyond their islands by capturing such foreign objects as came their way.

The impression that the horizons of the Neolithic islanders were larger than their islands is strengthened by an examination of the elements of material culture that they shared with people in other regions. One example is the obsidian projectile point, which is equally at home in the Cyclades and on the Greek mainland (Cherry 1979: fig. 4; Diamant 1977). Fig. 46 plots further examples, comprising objects in Perlès' ritual or prestige class, namely LN figurines of Talalay's Type C (1983: 187, 1993: 66), and FN marble pointed-based beakers. In both cases the maritime bias of the distribution is marked. However, whilst the Type C figurines' distribution encompasses

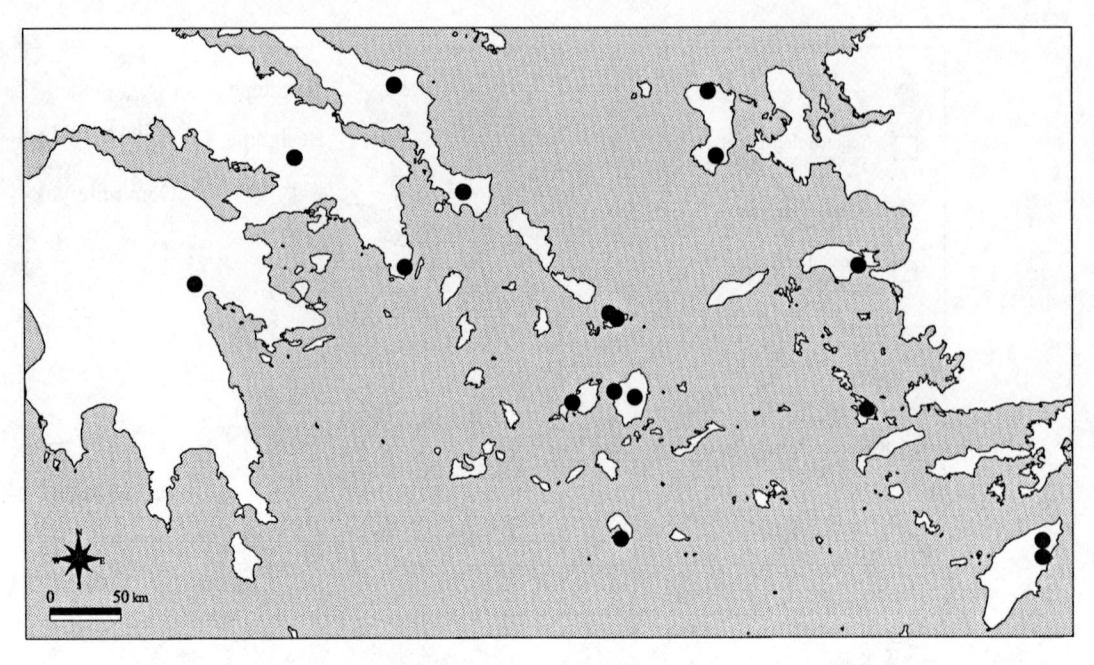

Fig. 47 Distribution of Neolithic light-on-dark pottery in the southern Aegean. Data from Sampson 1987: fig. 34a with additions.

the Cyclades and southern Greek mainland, the FN pattern shifts the axis of interaction towards the north-east Aegean and perhaps the Balkan–Pontic zone beyond. An indirect connection with the latter area is also attested by the manufacture in the Cyclades, by the late FN, of the Grotta-Pelos culture rolled-rim bowl, a form otherwise restricted to the north-east Aegean (Renfrew 1972: fig. 10.6; Sampson 1984: 242).

Stylistic interaction can be seen most clearly, however, in the pottery decoration of the Neolithic Cyclades, where there is also more certainty that the distributions seen are telling us about shared ways of doing things as well as about moving objects. It is now far more obvious than it was at the time when Saliagos was excavated that light-on-dark painted pottery, one of the Saliagos culture's principal traits, forms a style zone spreading from the eastern Aegean through the Cyclades to Attica and Euboia (fig. 47). Common motifs can be identified at widely separated sites, such as the superimposed chevrons on the bowl rims from Cycladic, south-east Aegean and Attic sites, and where large assemblages have been published the parallels extend to rarer motifs (for instance Kalythies and Saliagos share hatched and concentric rhomboids plus a range of branch designs). Although the unprecedented diversity of motifs on the pottery from Saliagos itself may be the result of sheer sample size from this relatively extensively excavated site, it also makes sense in spatial terms, given that Saliagos lies near the centre of the swathe of communities participating in this medium of stylistic communication. A case that Crete, too, was beginning to participate in

Aegean interaction at this time is made by Washburn (1983), whose symmetry analysis of Aegean Neolithic pottery decoration identified parallels between the design structures employed at Saliagos and those of the incised pottery at contemporary Knossos. Other innovations like weaving equipment appear at Knossos at around this time (Evans 1994: 14). If a Cycladic connection can be sustained, this would neatly illustrate the manner in which the colonisation of the Cyclades led indirectly but fairly rapidly to reworkings of culture and technology in the surrounding areas of the Aegean rim from a surprisingly early date.

The pattern of ceramic design interaction is different in the early FN, but again shows that Cycladic potters were regularly quoting styles of wider Aegean distribution, most notably pattern-burnished decoration, but also the applied red crusting seen on FN pottery (and occasionally also on the latest Saliagos culture pottery). The complexity of design is reduced in the FN to a simpler repertoire, in the Cyclades as elsewhere in the Aegean. However, the fact that there is early FN evidence from both the northern and south-east Cyclades allows us for the first time to explore how, at least in terms of their pottery styles, different areas of the islands were creating interaction spheres that tied them into different extra-Cycladic regions. Cycladic pattern-burnish aligns with two of the wider Aegean groups identified by Renfrew (1972: 77–9). At Kephala it takes the form of red-brown designs, and displays links with Attica and Euboia, whose overall material culture the Kephala assemblage closely resembles (e.g. Coleman 1977: 100–4; Keller 1982; Sampson 1984: 242). In the south-east Cyclades, on the other hand, the Zas IIa pattern-burnished pottery has affinities both with Kephala and with the distinctive black pattern-burnish of the eastern Aegean, especially Samos and the Troad. Overall, Zas lacks sufficient Kephala diagnostics (e.g. pottery scoops) to preclude its equation with the Keian–southern mainland group (Zachos 1990: 30, 1994: 103). In effect, what seems to be going on is the emergence of two linked but separate ceramic style zones emerging in different parts of the Cyclades, each relating to neighbouring non-Cycladic traditions, echoing different expansion routes into the Cyclades and developing their own dynamics, rather than the formation of a discrete pan-Cycladic entity. The material from settlements on intermediate islands such as Mykonos will surely in future help to explain such similarities as are attested between the assemblages at Kephala and Zas.

Standing back from the specific evidence outlined above, several conclusions can be drawn. First, the pattern of wide links in the first phases of island settlement makes good sense as a colonising strategy. Anthony (1990) stresses that migratory movement into new regions requires two-way information flows, and distributions of material that we should be able to detect. Kirch (1988) sees extensive exchange as crucial to Lapita colonisation sequences, and Gosden and Pavlides (1994) propose similar social strategies that enabled colonists to link together scattered settlements. In this light, large stylistic interaction spheres are actually a more plausible signature of the earliest settlement of the Cyclades than are assemblages without good comparanda, and the remarkable design complexity seen at Saliagos culture sites may indicate that messaging was at its most diverse and intensive when communities were first moving into the Cyclades, and needed to maintain contact with other groups both in and beyond the islands. If, as Vitelli (1993: xx) has postulated, Neolithic pots were often made by women, some of these links could have even resulted from medium- to long-range exogamous ties. A similar desire to maintain contacts during the FN expansion in the northern Cyclades probably explains the extremely close similarities between the material culture of Keian, Euboian and Attic sites, and perhaps the marked degree of inter-visibility between the Keian communities and others in southern Euboia.

But, second, there may well be more to the material culture of the first Cycladic communities than a need to keep in touch with ancestral homelands and each other. For what emerges at least in the south-eastern islands is a series of distinct material cultures that are not simply derivatives of external patterns, but which mark out combinations of traits and ways of doing things that fashioned identities specific to communities within the Cyclades, and which must have contributed to a growing perception of these islands as places at the centre of the Aegean rather than on its internal periphery. This implies that settlement in the south-east Cyclades probably did develop beyond a dependence on external points of origin in the course of the fifth millennium BC, and began to establish its own cultural dynamics. As the analysis of south-east Aegean and Cycladic Neolithic assemblages advances, it should become feasible to draw detailed comparisons between these regions, exploring changes in material culture and plotting differentiation as colonisation paths expanded. The material culture of communities on Ikaria and Astypalaia, just beyond the modern Cyclades, should be interesting in this respect. Already, some intriguing details in the Cyclades can be glimpsed, for example the fact that colonists moving in from the south-east Aegean nonetheless adopted the projectile point types and, later, red-crusted pottery decoration that are more typical of the western half of the Aegean. The association of Kephala's material culture with the mainland suggests, in contrast, that, at least at this stage, communities on Kea had yet to differentiate themselves substantially from their antecedents. Such patterns of selective adoption, reformulation and internal innovation must have become ever more complex over the last millennium of the Neolithic, as increasing numbers of islands were settled by people moving in from different directions, along different routes, using different strategies, and bringing with them initially quite different cultural traditions.

Third, it is worth considering the role of the Zas cave in patterns of Neolithic interaction and emerging identity. Final interpretation of the cave's usage must await the publication of the excavations, but although the case for habitation is strong (Halstead in prep; Zachos 1999) a case could be made that Zas was not only a locus

Fig. 48 Mt Zas dominates the landscapes of central Naxos and overlooks the routes that criss-cross the island's interior. The large Zas cave is situated high up in a steep gully below the peak, close to a spring and with good access both to upland grazing and to patches of arable land below.

of occupation during the fifth and fourth millennia BC. Neolithic ceremonial activity has been identified at several of the Greek caves (Perlès and Demoule 1993: 404–5), and although caves generally act as good material traps, it is notable that a striking array of prestige or symbolic objects has been discovered in the Neolithic levels at Zas. These include the already mentioned gold strip, which constitutes the larger of just two published pieces of gold from the early Cyclades, a number of copper tools, and further unusual finds such as carved bone bird heads, spatulae, and foliate obsidian spearheads (Marangou 1990: 34–8; Renfrew 1972: 509; Zachos 1999: 158–9). If Zas did enjoy some kind of symbolic role in the later Neolithic Cyclades as a place of ritual deposition, the cave's location on the upper slopes of Mt Zas is likely to have been relevant (fig. 48). Mt Zas, the highest peak in the Cyclades, is a prominent visual referent and seamark in the islandscapes of the south-east Cyclades, and overlooks the interior routes across Naxos. Speculatively, the deposition of prestige items at Zas cave, a fixed focus amid an expanding settlement geography, may have helped to define a regional identity for the Neolithic communities emerging in the south-east Cyclades.

The lady and the tramp: the formation of 'Cycladic culture' revisited

It remains to examine how the Grotta-Pelos culture, as seen in the southern Cyclades, represents a transformation of Neolithic cultural norms and patterns of interaction, just as its dispersed farmstead-sized settlements attest to a revolution in ways of living. This is of particular interest because it urges the need to revise our explanations of the origins of what is commonly regarded as 'Cycladic culture'. This loose cluster of EBA objects includes marble anthropomorphic figurines, marble vessels, certain distinctive pottery forms and other items including metal objects, that are commonly associated, at least in depositional terms, with funerary contexts. Its origin has hitherto been explained either in typological terms by descent from Neolithic prototypes (e.g. Renfrew 1969: fig. 4), which in no real sense *explains* the process and the convergence on a specific range of forms, or in metaphysical terms as the formulation of a new Cycladic aesthetic, as was explored in chapter 2's discussion of 'sensibility'. In fact, the promotion of figurines, specific vessel types and mortuary practices is better understood as an integral part of a broader refashioning of island lives through the course of the fourth millennium BC. It will soon become apparent that much of the evidence once again comes from the south-east Cyclades. Whether this region actually played a key role in generating the material culture that is now considered to be so distinctively Cycladic, with resultant practices and forms being subsequently translated to the remainder of the islands, or whether other, potentially different, local sequences remain to be discovered elsewhere in the islands, is at present hard to assess, but the latter scenario is a real possibility.

The definition of a new exchange culture

A key factor in explaining the transformation may be the emergence during the fourth and early third millennia BC of a new exchange culture and the material for marking such exchanges. Reasons for this can be sought in the sharp reduction of community size, which will have made each community much more dependent on its neighbours for social and biological reproduction, and in the expansion of settlement to inhospitable parts of the Cyclades. In the context of a shift from villages located in favourable niches to dispersed farmsteads often cultivating marginal areas, social storage networks should have taken on a more vital role than had perhaps hitherto been the case. As mentioned in chapter 3, Cherry (1987: 25–6) has suggested an association between social storage strategies and the rise in the numbers and range of objects and tokens that were suitable for exchange in the EBA Cyclades. Where this picture needs modification is in the dating of the first substantial island interaction to the EBA, and the assumption that the particular dense networks witnessed then were a necessary prerequisite for established settlement of the Cyclades (Cherry 1985: 28). In fact, as we have seen, the Saliagos culture communities created large interaction zones and participated in exchanges that brought them distant objects at a much earlier date. What was new in the Grotta-Pelos culture and its EBA successors was not so much the existence of island networks, but rather their nature, extent and intensity.

If the Neolithic to EBA transition marks not the start of Cycladic networks, but a change in their nature, what forms did this take? For one thing, a shift in emphasis is seen in the Grotta-Pelos culture from medium- and long-range links to local networks. In comparison to earlier Neolithic patterns, the Grotta-Pelos culture produces few signs of interaction beyond the Cyclades. In place of the complex Saliagos culture pottery decoration and the wide Aegean currency of light-on-dark painted and pattern-burnished designs, the decoration on Grotta-Pelos vessels reflects a local incised tradition without close external referents, and which is limited in terms of design almost to the point of uniformity. If style was indeed a form of communication in the early Cyclades, we might infer that the range and variety of the messages were altering profoundly.

But in contrast to the diminished horizons and decreased complexity of stylistic communication, the Grotta-Pelos culture may see an increase in the exchange of objects *within* the Cyclades. A selection of the most popular shapes is illustrated in fig. 49. The emergence of a regular range of marble vessels after the very sporadic evidence for Neolithic production may reflect an increasing demand for prestigious, but robust and durable exchange items. Marble vessels are found on many islands (fig. 50), including Melos, which is marble-less, and Thera and Kea, where the marble is not of the same quality as that of the vessels found. Easily the commonest shape is the kandila, a heavy pedestalled jar of which some 300 examples are now known (Getz-Gentle 1996: 12), followed by the beaker (descended from the FN type), lugged bowl and palette. The frequency of suspension lugs on all these forms (which would elevate the object to somewhere nearer to eye level and also preserve it from damage on floor surfaces) may well argue a prominent role for these objects. Their forms imply different practices, in the case of the beaker and bowl probably the functions of food (or drink) consumption abandoned at this time by the decorated pottery (see below). The kandila is the first of several Cycladic varieties of pedestalled jars with a collar neck and wide mouth, that are sadly of unknown usage and meaning. Grain residues from one kandila (Getz-Gentle 1996: 38) may imply a fermented beverage, which might suit the beaker too. Palettes were at least in some cases used for grinding the pigments employed in the decoration of marble vessels and figurines. More will be said about the latter objects, which form another feature of increasing prominence in material culture, later in this chapter.

Pottery exchange cannot yet be proven, owing to a lack of petrographic analysis of Grotta-Pelos assemblages, and, equally, may have been more common among Saliagos culture and early FN communities than is currently apparent. But several of the new Grotta-Pelos pottery forms are admirably suited for exchange, and the focus on pottery decoration shifts between the Saliagos and Grotta-Pelos cultures from

Fig. 49 Elements of the proposed Grotta-Pelos exchange culture (not to scale): (a) clay cyclindrical pyxis, (b) clay collared jar, (c) marble beaker, (d) marble kandila. All courtesy of the Ashmolean Museum.

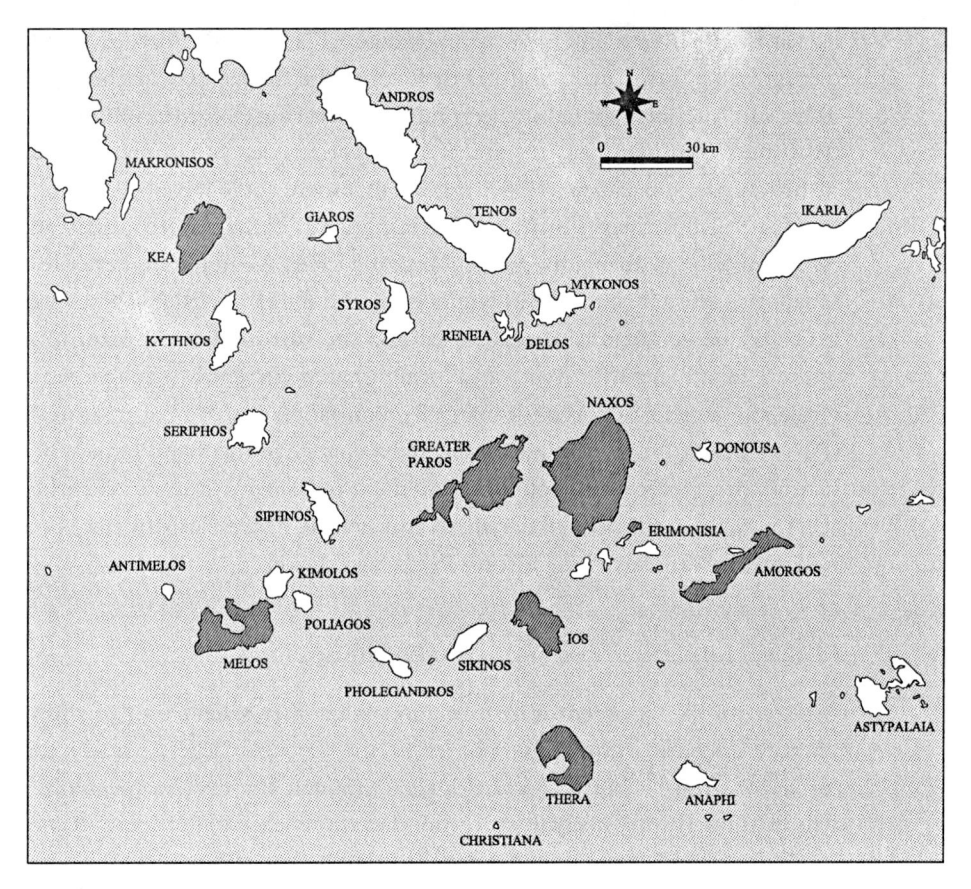

Fig. 50 Distribution of Grotta-Pelos culture marble vessels. Data from Getz-Gentle 1996: maps 5–7.

bowls to closed shapes, principally pyxides and collared jars, in short from food consumption vessels to small transportable containers. It is not known what the latter held, but a viscous substance of some value, such as honey or an unguent, would suit the form and size of the vessels well. Although the pottery has yet to be subjected to ceramic analysis, at least it, like the marble objects, is visible. Metal objects are in contrast an obvious missing element. These decline in archaeological visibility between the Neolithic cave deposits and a resurgence in EB II, largely associated with burials (Nakou 1995). This decline should not lead us to neglect the likelihood that metal goods were an important above-ground component of Grotta-Pelos exchange, for there is continuing evidence for production at this time, such as surface finds of lead at the site of Cheiromylos and copper slag at Avyssos, both on Greater Paros (Renfrew 1967: 4; Tsountas 1898: 176).

In summary, between the periods of the Saliagos and Grotta-Pelos cultures, Cycladic interaction networks appear to move from an emphasis on medium- and long-range communication through decorative style and the acquisition of exotica towards an investment in local exchange of a limited suite of standard, readily recognisable forms including the new container shapes and marble prestige vessels. This surely reflects something beyond the increasing circumscription of horizons that is witnessed in many islands and non-insular regions as populations became established, not least because we have argued that there could have been as many people in the big Saliagos villages on at least certain islands as there were farmstead dwellers on the same islands during the transition to the EBA. We might do better to visualise the change as one active means of engineering the shift from established villages engaged in elaborate contacts with each other and the surrounding Aegean, to an exchange culture of sufficient flexibility and locally shared currency to enable the dense small-scale interactions required for internal colonisation of marginal areas in the Cyclades. Part of this shift may also have reflected a change in the main domain of social interaction, from inter-household entertainment in Saliagos culture villages to gift-giving ceremonies, social storage networks and diverse expressions of status between individuals and families in the Grotta-Pelos farmsteads.

The increasing archaeological visibility of individuals

Related to this apparent transformation is another salient trait of the Grotta-Pelos culture and also subsequent phases of the Cycladic EBA, namely the increasing archaeological visibility of individuals. Although the precise meanings of this trait elude us utterly, it is likely to correspond in some sense to the creation and affirmation of different, and at least initially new, kinds of personae, roles, kin relations or even life histories. Clues that a change in this direction was going on can be found in the high frequency of individual burials, and the increasing number of anthropomorphic figurines.

So far, the Cycladic cemeteries have been portrayed in this book as a means of bolstering claims to resources, in this case land, at a time when traditional allocations were in dissolution and marginal arable land was in the process of becoming settled. However, the overwhelming predominance of individual burials in the early Cycladic cemeteries, the increasing use of the tombs as a depositional focus for objects, and the likelihood that most of the community were buried (including children to judge by the smallest graves), suggest that rather more than this was at stake. The detailed attention paid to individual people, at least at the time of their death, is particularly apparent in the precise yet varied statements implicit in decisions as to what things to bury with whom, contrasting not only 'rich' and 'poor' graves, but also specific combinations of objects (Doumas 1977: 58–64; see also chapter 8). The significance of most of these cultural choices is at present largely beyond recovery and may remain so, thanks in large part to the destruction of contextual associations through the looting of so many graves. There must be a strong probability, however, that the variability and patterns have much to do with the roles and achievements of the dead person. A nice example is grave 145 at the Akrotiraki cemetery in Siphnos, where a pyxis (a type mentioned above as an exchange object probably containing a valuable substance) was associated with an individual, at least in death, for he or she was found still clutching the vessel (Tsountas 1898: 74). Further instances of material-rich graves and cemeteries are given in chapters 8 and 9.

The apparent tension between a community's claims to land (expressed by the cemetery) and individual claims to social position and status (expressed in the single burial and its association with accumulations of prestige goods) is not as real as it first seems, given the small scale and short duration of Grotta-Pelos communities; the interests of the dead person, or their relatives, and those of the community would be more closely associated than in a larger settlement because much of the community is likely to have consisted of the deceased's immediate and extended family. Evidence for minor sub-divisions within the community can be adduced from the tendency for graves to be grouped in clusters within the cemetery, and later in the EBA for multiple burials to be deposited in a minority of graves (Doumas 1977: 31–4, 54–8), although it remains unclear whether these divisions were temporal (i.e. generational) or synchronous. The combined facts that cemeteries would not have been visible from afar in the islandscape, but that individual grave locations within them were marked for recognition at close range, and that low platforms for the performance of ceremonies were constructed on the edges of cemeteries (Doumas 1977: 35–6), illustrate the balance between the desire for a communal statement and the emphasis on individual members of the community. The contrast is extreme with the round and house tombs of EBA Crete (Branigan 1970, 1993, 1998b), which were prominent monuments used over long periods to emphasise real or fictive continuity in the burying community over many generations, but within which individuals were lost in the collective mass of inhumations. In comparison, the Cycladic cemeteries make less permanent statements about a community's place in the islandscape, but lay more emphasis on the continuing visibility of the individual.

More opaque in terms of its precise significance, but nonetheless indicative of a change from the prior Neolithic, is the broadly simultaneous increase in the number of anthropomorphic figurines, and the occasional appearance of anthropomorphic marble vessels. To add that the major deposition context for figurines shifts from settlement contexts in the Saliagos culture, via a position outside the tomb but within the cemetery at Kephala (Coleman 1977: 52, 68, 80, 90), to actual placement in the tomb during the Grotta-Pelos culture may be premature, given the limited archaeological investigation of Grotta-Pelos settlements, but the expansion of the funerary domain certainly provided an important new location for deposition of images of people. The figurines also alter in their appearance (fig. 51). Saliagos possessed two types with female attributes, the one steatopygous, the other violin-shaped (Evans and Renfrew 1968: 62–5). The latter forms the main Grotta-Pelos type, and a tradition of manufacture in the intervening centuries is commonly, and probably

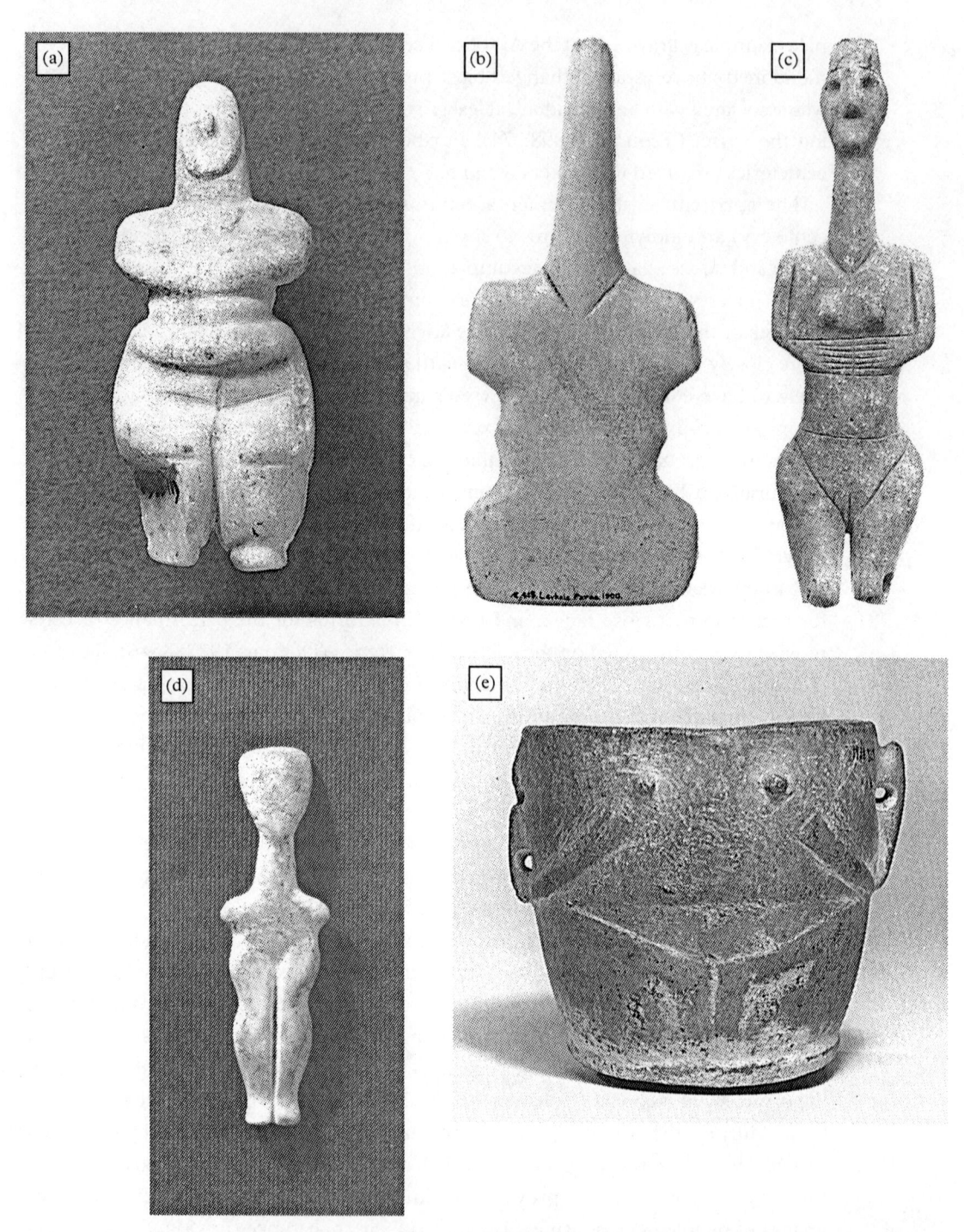

Fig. 51 The diversity of anthropomorphic figurines from the early Cyclades (not to scale): (a) Neolithic steatopygous type, (b) Grotta-Pelos violin-shaped, (c) Plastiras type with mend-hole in right leg, (d) Louros type, (e) anthropomorphic vessel. All courtesy of the Ashmolean Museum.

correctly, assumed. But the fourth millennium BC also sees the appearance of other figurine forms, including those at Kephala (Coleman 1977: plates 26, 71–3), an early plank-like folded-arm type in the FN levels at Zas (Zachos 1996d), and different types again at Phtelia (Sampson 1997: 8), several unprovenanced vessels with anthropomorphic features, and at some undefined point in the Grotta-Pelos culture (possibly as late as the third millennium BC) the Louros and Plastiras type figurines. This last type is of interest in that, unlike the great majority of figurines, which either bear explicitly female sexual characteristics or are unspecific in terms of gender, several of the Plastiras figures display male genitalia and sport a distinctive form of head-gear.

Some of these figurine types were probably intended to be generic and to form part of the general exchange culture of the islands. Even at this level, the emphasis on women, and female sexuality and procreative potential, is unlikely to be coincidental. It is to say the least striking that the boom in production of female figurines in the EBA coincides with the phase of maximum population dispersal in the Cyclades, between the preceding Neolithic villages and the nucleated settlements of the later Bronze Age (see chapter 10), in other words with the period when exogamy and competition for women would have been at its most pronounced (Broodbank 1992). But, as Knapp and Meskell (1997) point out, figurines need not always be assumed to represent generic types as opposed to specific individuals, especially if they display distinctive details. Some of the Cycladic figurines, particularly those with unusual forms or attributes, and those most elaborately decorated with paint, may well represent individuals and have played a part in defining a person's identity or marked a stage in their life. But whether the signifieds were individuals, generic types or a mixture of both does not alter the fact that the material culture of the Cyclades had started to express a particular emphasis on the attributes and characteristics of the islanders who created and deployed it.

Questions concerning both death rituals and figurines are revisited in chapter 8, when the EB II peak in the elaboration of the practices introduced during the Neolithic–EBA transition is examined. In concluding this chapter's exploration of early colonising cultures, it is worth reflecting on this nexus of individual burials and anthropomorphic figurines. Although both undergo several changes in form and deployment through the EBA, they remain important features of the two millennia that follow the Saliagos phase and precede the radically different world of the later Bronze Age. In addition, although both figurines and single burials are known from other contemporary cultural zones in the southern Aegean, nowhere is their prominence nearly as distinct as in the Cyclades.

It is tempting to suggest that some of the conditions particular to these islands may have encouraged these phenomena. One possibility is that the low populations and small size of settlements generated conditions in which decision-makers and community leaders comprised a fairly large proportion of the population, and in which individuals, whether marriage partners, labourers in the fields, herders, canoe crews or surviving children, were also a markedly finite, therefore highly valued, commodity. In addition, as larger village settlements dissolved and disappeared, the collective social regulation that they represented is liable to have been replaced by a more fluid, freed-up situation in which opportunities for individual achievement and, equally, failure were enhanced, and the old mechanisms to suppress it effectively lost. Coupled with settlement of new areas in the islands, these conditions point to a world in which people, whether dominant actors or desired resources, mattered a lot. Thus, for example, a funeral would provide an opportunity to remember a successful life, or mourn for an adult or child whose death could easily spell the demise of an entire settlement. Such explanations at least have the virtues of moving us beyond the mere recording of what were manifestly meaning-rich features of early Cycladic culture and practice, and of starting to open up windows onto the people whose history we are trying to illuminate.

6

Small worlds

> Let sea-discoverers to new worlds have gone,
> Let maps to other worlds our world have shown;
> Let us possess one world; each hath one, and is one.
> *The good-morrow,* JOHN DONNE

Braudel's observation that 'the Mediterranean has no unity but that created by the movements of men, the relations they imply and the routes they follow' (1972: 276) is certainly true of the complicated cluster of islands that we know as the Cyclades – although we have already realised the need to search for many, culturally defined unities rather than a single one, and for women just as much as men. Attention has focused so far on the manners in which colonisation created islandscapes in different parts of the island group, and how changes in settlement strategy implied diverse material and non-material ways of putting Cycladic worlds together. Yet as questions about colonisation start to fade in our wake, and the extensively settled, data-rich and culturally variegated Cyclades of the EBA come fully into view, different means of putting our observations about material culture distributions and social activity into specific explanatory contexts within the islands will need to be created. Without such means, it will be extremely hard to make much insular sense of these islands' archaeological records, and to plumb their real or apparent lacunae. This need, in effect, sets the agenda for the next few chapters.

An approach that operates at a range of spatial and social scales is adopted, for a single analytical framework is unlikely to provide anything approaching a well-rounded explanation of the patterns in Cycladic data. A thought-provoking article by Renfrew (1979: 61–3) recognises this problem and airs several potential factors that might have influenced the form of early Cycladic material cultures. His proposals were (1) local interaction (note that this was shown in chapter 5 to be a complex variable in itself), (2) expressions of group identity and (3) the creation of prestige symbols and activities for high-status people or groups. Among networks of small communities, dependent upon each other for reproduction and survival, the first and second factors are in fact likely to overlap heavily. In general, however, Renfrew's subdivisions serve as a reminder of the palimpsest of activities that is liable to lie behind the islands' archaeological record.

This chapter focuses on an exploration of local worlds within the Cyclades. In particular, it shows that a consideration of demographic conditions, in conjunction with variables such as configuration, environment and travel-range, suggests the existence of many changing local interaction networks, each of which created its own opportunities and challenges. This will enable us to grasp something of the social realities behind several features of the archaeological record. Archaeological information, of course, can only inform us about one surviving, durable sub-set of island culture, and much of what follows has hypothetical relevance to other, vanished forms of expression like language, dialect, dress, song and dance. The chapters that follow then extend the realm of analysis. Chapter 7 explores the rise of a restricted group of central communities, chapter 8 analyses manipulation of resources and the elaboration of a prestige culture at such sites, and chapter 9 investigates long-range voyaging beyond the Cyclades, which had a major impact on island culture, especially during EB II. Teasing apart the diverse phenomena that are nested within the aggregate data is a tricky, if rewarding, business, and in addition it should be noted that the subjects of these chapters represent far from discrete domains of enquiry. Each feeds back into the other, and our attention will have to switch repeatedly between diverse data sets, and different areas of the Cyclades, if we are to sense much of the texture of island culture.

Cycladic demography and the modelling of local interaction

How might we model local interaction networks and establish plausible theatres for the emergence of local identities in the early Cyclades? One strategy is to return to fig. 24 for information about which areas of the islands should be most intimately linked, and which most separated, given early Cycladic parameters affecting movement. This gives us some broad indications, and similar data have been put to good use in Micronesia to establish an association between the current distribution of mutually intelligible dialects and the range of a night's canoe voyage (Marck 1986). But in addition to its inherent reductivism, this would not explain why patterns of contact might expand, contract or otherwise change through time, nor does it acknowledge that perceptions of acceptable 'local' travel ranges might well differ and alter, especially in the maritime sphere.

Another possibility is to look at climatic variability between and within islands, and to model its impact on the likely extent of social storage networks as well as relative degrees of reliance upon them. This too can provide insights. It might be predicted that such networks would be most intensive and extensive in the more marginal areas of the Cyclades, in short among the smaller islands and several less favoured medium islands. Conversely, least investment in such networks might be anticipated in areas such as the Andros–Tenos block and parts of Naxos. However, this again does not provide much insight into diachronic changes, beyond the possibility that such networks might have spatially expanded through time if arable land was indeed progressively degraded in the course of the EBA (French and Whitelaw 1999). If information on climate change in the EBA Cyclades existed (which it does not), its impact might also be modelled, although the size of networks relative to each other should remain broadly proportional.

Another strategy is to investigate the effect of population growth as the Cyclades started to become more thickly settled. This promising investigative avenue is the main one followed here. Population growth is taken as the principal observed variable, and is used to build models of the consequent changes in temporal patterns of local interaction. Sea-crossing ranges and other environmental factors are taken as further variables to be introduced into these models in order to enrich them and highlight the range of cultural decisions that may have been open to islanders under different sets of circumstances. In chapter 3, an estimation of island demography revealed the relatively small numbers of people living in the Cyclades, and the generally high degree of island interdependence. The range of population densities in table 1 prompted comments on the demographic implications of different sections of this range for specific islands, and for the Cyclades as a whole. But it was stressed that this range also represents an approximate *sequence*, in other words that the numbers of people living in these islands increased through the EBA. Such a trend is hardly surprising for a group of islands following colonisation, or for newly colonised niches on partly settled islands. But given the importance of this point for the models that follow, the case for population increase in the EBA Cyclades deserves closer attention. For present purposes, the discussion is limited to the Grotta-Pelos culture (3500–2700 BC) and EB II phase (2700–2200 BC); the last few centuries of the EBA are an obscure period that requires separate resolution in chapter 10.

A crucial point to clarify is that the pattern of small, dispersed settlements seen in the Grotta-Pelos culture remains the overall norm during EB II. This is demonstrated by the surface data from several islands, including Melos (Cherry 1982a: fig. 2.3), Kea (Cherry *et al.* 1991: 71), Amorgos (Marangou 1984, 1994), Naxos and the Erimonisia (Doumas 1977: fig. 2; Erard-Cerceau *et al.* 1993; Hadjianastasiou 1993). The continuing small size of many settlements is also apparent from excavated examples such as Mt Kynthos on Delos (0.04 ha) (MacGillivray 1980), and Naxian settlements at Panermos (0.02 ha), Korphi t'Aroniou (0.08 ha maximum; estimate of the hilltop area) and Avdeli (Doumas 1965, 1972: 155, 1977: 29). At likely EBA occupation densities of 200–300 people per hectare, such settlements cannot represent more than a few families, or even single families in some instances.

The majority of the cemeteries tell a similar story. Of some eighty EBA cemeteries known in 1977, Doumas (1977: 31) listed just eight with fifty graves or more, although rumours of about sixty looted graves at Kapros on Amorgos, in addition to the twenty excavated at the end of the nineteenth century, may indicate another (Renfrew 1967: 6). Archaeological fieldwork has since produced a definite ninth example, with ninety-two graves after extensive robbing, at Agrilia on Epano Kouphonisi (Zapheiropoulou 1983; NB this cemetery is not to be confused with the Saliagos culture site of the same name on Melos). The increasing frequency of multiple inhumations in a single cist

Table 5. *Large Cycladic cemeteries and their burying populations. Adapted from Broodbank 1989: table 1.*

Cemetery	Burials (approx.)	Population 100 years	200 years	300 years	400 years
Krassades	50	13	6	4	3
Pyrgos	58	15	7	5	4
Karvounolakkoi	82	21	10	7	4
Kampos tis Makris	90	23	11	8	5
Agrilia	92	23	12	8	6
Agios Loukas	94	24	12	8	6
Phyrroges	100	25	13	8	6
Aphendika	170	43	21	14	10
Chalandriani	600–1000	150–250	75–125	50–83	38–63

during EB II does not greatly affect the overall figures, as (somewhat surprisingly) it occurs principally in the smaller cemeteries (Doumas 1977: 55–8; Fotou 1983: 28, 38, 42; Tsountas 1899: 83). Of the nine larger cemeteries (table 5), three are those of the Grotta-Pelos culture mentioned in chapter 5 (Kampos tis Makris, Krassades and Pyrgos), and finds of different periods from four others (Phyrroges, Karvounolakkoi and maybe Aphendika on Naxos, plus Agios Loukas on Syros (Barber 1981; Renfrew 1972: 518–19)) suggest that their size is attributable to a longer period of use, rather than a larger community. The only sustainable cases for community expansion are the *c.* 600–1000 graves at EB II Chalandriani in Syros, and perhaps the Agrilia cemetery of at least ninety-two plus graves, whose duration seems limited, given that it belongs to the Kampos group, an intermediate EB I–II horizon of short duration. Both the latter are sites to which we shall return (Broodbank 1989: 323–5 for fuller analysis of the case summarised here).

What *does* change in EB II is (1) the quantity of small settlements, (2) in some cases their longevity, and (3) the number of exceptions to the norm, both in the form of settlements that expanded from farmsteads to hamlets, and in the re-emergence of a small but high-profile category of village-level settlements after an apparent gap of more than a millennium. So whilst there was not a general drift to larger settlements, as Doumas once suggested (1972: 158, 1977: 31), there was some divergence of settlement types. Taking the first of these changes, on Melos the increase is only from six sites to eight within the survey area (Wagstaff and Cherry 1982b: table 11.1), but islands such as Naxos (Doumas 1977: 14; Renfrew 1972: 514–23; Zapheiropoulou 1990: 23), Syros (Hekman 1994: 65, fig. 8), Ios (Marthari 1999) and Amorgos (Marangou 1984: 99–100, 1994) demonstrate more marked rises. The Greater Paros cemetery record provides the only ostensible example of an inverse trend, with a peculiar dearth of EB II graves following an abundance of Grotta-Pelos ones (Renfrew 1972: 514–17), but it is proposed in chapters 7 and 8 that this reflects a decrease in the deposition of grave goods and consequent archaeological visibility, rather than an actual decline in population. The substantial numbers of EB II settlements on smaller islands also indicate an increasingly full occupation of the Cyclades. Examples are settlements on all the Erimonisia (Renfrew 1972: 520–1), and on Delos (MacGillivray 1980), and several sites on Pholegandros (Hadjianastasiou 1996). With the infilling of these small islands, the internal colonisation of the Cycladic islandscapes was effectively complete.

Turning to the second change, a case for increasing locational stability at some sites can be made on the basis of domestic architecture and cemetery finds. Architecture shows signs of rebuilding (Doumas 1972: 155–66; MacGillivray 1980: 7). Several of the larger cemeteries, as was stated above, contain material dating to more than one chronological period, especially on the long-settled island of Naxos; even the small Naxian cemetery at Agioi Anargyroi appears to span several periods (Doumas 1977: 100–20; Renfrew 1984a: 49). This implies that a larger proportion of the EB II sites in a given area can be considered genuinely synchronous than had hitherto been the case.

The third difference from the Grotta-Pelos pattern is the evidence that a limited number of larger settlements did exist in EB II. In some cases this involved a modest rise in the number of households, leading to hamlet communities. A well-documented example of this process is the increase in the settlement area at Markiani on Amorgos, where a late Grotta-Pelos farmstead was replaced by an EB II hamlet of about 0.25 ha, perhaps with an intervening period of abandonment (French and Whitelaw 1999: 153, 162). In a handful of cases, however, both the settlement and funerary records signal the re-emergence of substantial villages. Chalandriani-Kastri on Syros, Daskaleio-Kavos on Keros, Agia Irini II–III on Kea, Grotta-Aplomata on Naxos and Skarkos on Ios are at present the main examples of these distinctive if unusual sites, which are examined more fully in chapter 7. Suffice to note for the present that each represents a localised concentration of people that should be equivalent to several dozen small farmsteads.

Accepting the overwhelming evidence for an increase in population during the EBA, mainly manifested in a rising number of small settlements, some of which lasted longer, but also in the appearance of some larger settlements, we can start to address the task of modelling its effects in the early Cyclades. Demography abstracted from spatial settings allows only limited progress to be made. For example, it enables us to estimate into how many minimal demographic networks of 300–500 people the overall Cycladic populations generated in table 1 might divide. From a mere two to four networks for the entire Cyclades at the lowest density, the total rises to fifteen to twenty-five at the highest. This suggests that EBA Cycladic material culture should display increasing signs of sub-regional styles and local patterns of interaction through the course of time (the lowest figures surely also provide insights into the large style zones of the Neolithic). Given the regularity with which such trends have been observed in periods of demographic growth after colonisation in other island theatres, there is every chance of this being vindicated.[1] But the limitations are apparent. The estimates tell us nothing about how such patterns might have been distributed within the Cyclades, and (as pointed out in chapter 2), the 300–500 population range is a notional minimum that is really most helpful as a means of demonstrating that a given area could not be even potentially self-sustaining, and in no sense militates against the possibility that actual groups might have expanded further before dividing. What is therefore needed is a more specific and a more dynamic means of analysing interaction and the distributions of culture in Cycladic island space.

A proximal point analysis for the Cyclades

Questions of design for network models in island theatres

In these circumstances, modelling based on graph theoretical analysis provides a good way of simulating interaction networks in the Cyclades, and generating results that can shed light on archaeologically observed phenomena. Graph theoretical techniques have long been used to examine patterns in the Pacific. Early examples include Brookfield with Hart's work (1971), Irwin's analysis of Mailu (1974) and Terrell's analysis of the Solomons (1977b). Later examples include further investigations by Irwin (1983), by Hunt (1988) on Lapita, and two major studies by Hage and Harary (1991, 1996). Such techniques vary greatly in their complexity. The most sophisticated varieties can easily turn out to be a mixed blessing when investigating ancient island societies, because the virtual certainty that part of the data is missing can all too easily render apparently high-resolution analyses spurious, and because it is usually far from obvious precisely how to weight a complex range of variables appropriately. For this reason, Proximal Point Analysis (PPA), a simple and transparent technique, is used to construct models for the Cyclades. The complexity and nuancing will come instead in the questions asked of the patterns generated by this technique, and in the manner in which a range of potential constraints and opportunities for the EBA islanders of the Cyclades are then elaborated.

Put simply, PPA predicts patterns of connection between points distributed in space. Its assumption is that each point will connect with those points nearest to it (the number of links drawn is conventionally three).[2] Webs of these connections generate

---

[1] For instance the substitution of the extensive, relatively homogenous Lapita complex by later, more localised south-west Pacific cultures (Gosden *et al.* 1989: 578; Kirch 1990: 129; Spriggs 1997: 152–86).

[2] Networks could, of course, be drawn by using four or more connections, or possibly even fewer than three. The results would not, however, differ greatly from those that are generated by three connections, because the measurement is one of relative degrees of connection and much the same patterns and emphases emerge. This was tested at an empirical level by comparing the networks generated by three connections that are published here with others using four and five; the results were very similar.

networks. If the distribution of points is uneven, as it almost invariably is, some points will start to collect more than their minimum number of links by virtue of the fact that they represent the closest target for a larger number of other points. It is also important to grasp that PPA indicates *relative degrees* of connection, rather than absolute presence or absence. As PPA is a gravity model, its premise when modelling social interaction is that communities or other groups of people will interact most intensely with their closest neighbours. Although this is not likely to represent the entire truth about interaction in the early Cyclades, it was stressed in chapter 3 that it should have been a key feature of local demographic and social storage strategies (note furthermore that a gravity model is appropriate for maritime travel in the Cyclades because longer journeys would generally be riskier ones too). PPA has most often been used to explore centrality, by discovering which points in a network are best connected and through which most communications flow. For the Cyclades, this question is deferred until chapter 7, as centrality is crucial enough to merit separate attention. However, one of the great advantages of PPA is that as all the points can be evenly weighted and initially treated without assumptions about hierarchy, the technique can be used to pose a series of other equally pertinent questions about forms of interaction within a given network.

In order to get the most out of such analyses, we need to think carefully about how to generate and locate the points. Given a group of islands, there are three options:

1 Assign a set number of points to each island, to be placed within the island according to a fixed set of rules.
2 Use the location of known settlements to determine the placement of points.
3 Take what is known of general settlement patterns and simulate its extension across all islands through the placement of points, using similar rules to (1).

For several reasons, the third option is the most appropriate for the early Cyclades. The problem with Option 1 is that it produces a single, ahistorical network that may happen to capture a real interaction pattern, or superimposed fragments of several, but does not allow us to ask how actual settlement patterns in the islands might generate a particular network, nor how networks alter over time. Terrell's PPA of the Solomon Islands of Melanesia illustrates the problem (fig. 52). For unless it can be proved that the points do represent real distributions of people, what emerges is a study not of how islanders interact, but of how islands as geographical entities do, and it is not clear what the latter really means. Equally, the common decision to award three points to large islands and a single point to small ones creates a simplified dichotomy that often under-represents the largest islands, over-represents islets, and misses the important variability in between. In short, it is vital to decide to what extent our networks are meant to be configurational expressions of island distribution, or products of social geography. They should in fact combine elements of both, but circumspection is called for when

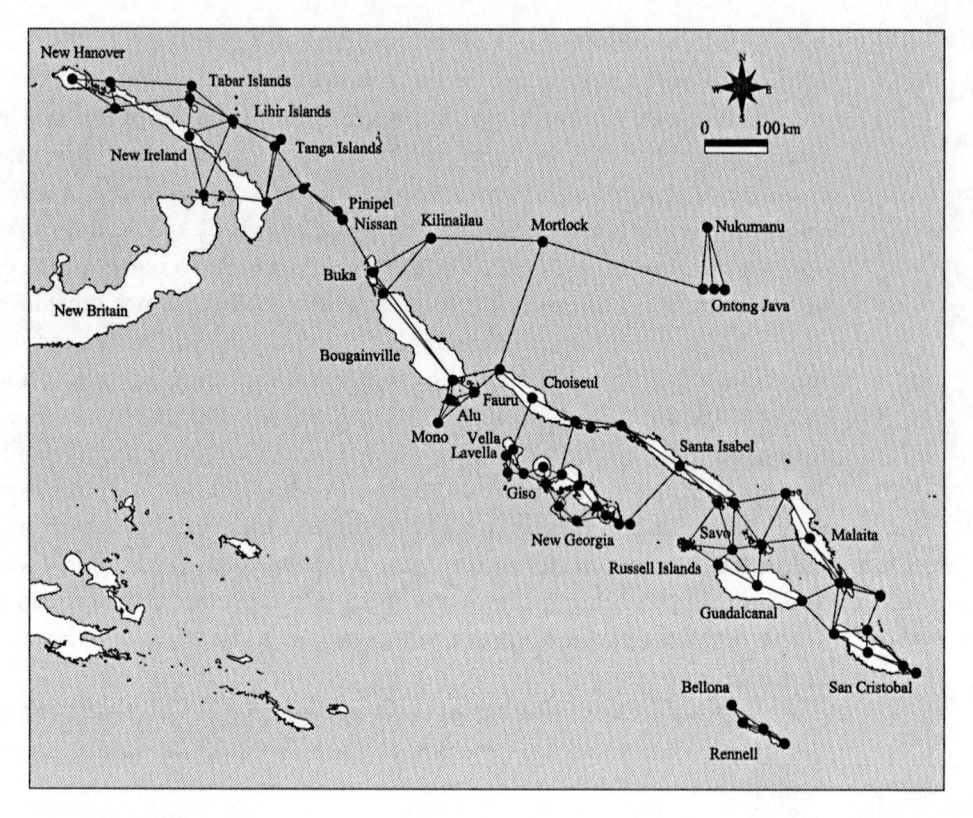

Fig. 52 Terrell's proximal point analysis for the Solomon islands. After Terrell 1977b: fig. 6.

putting them together. The problem is illustrated by the ambiguity inherent in Kirch's (1990: 120) approval of a PPA that indicated the geographical centrality of Mussau in western Melanesia (Hunt 1988: fig. 9.7) as part of an argument for diachronic shifts of centrality in the region.

The second option, that of using 'real world' data, is also problematic unless a fairly complete settlement pattern is known, for example from ethnographic sources, as in the case of Mailu (Irwin 1974), or from textual sources, as in Davis' investigation of Delos at the time of the Ionian Amphictyony (Davis 1982a). If such information is accessible, the scope for analysis is all but unlimited. But, as Hunt (1988: 136–7) points out, in archaeological conditions of uneven site detection and preservation, the disadvantages of working with real world data generally outweigh the benefits. To illustrate the point that networks based on real sites are drastically affected by the extent of archaeological knowledge, imagine the pitfalls of a comparison between such networks on intensively surveyed Melos and under-explored areas of the Cyclades. Another disadvantage is that networks have to be reworked every time that a new site is discovered. And lastly, the apparent realism of such networks may in fact be bogus if in fact all the settlements of a given period within a region were not synchronously occupied (so that the network will make communities talk to each other that in reality could not have done so), a problem of palpable relevance among the temporally unstable settlements of the EBA Cyclades.

These dilemmas can be surmounted in ways that actually enhance our insights if what is known of real settlement is used to inform *simulated* distributions of people in the islands. Moreover, if archaeological information suggests that increasing population was changing these distributions over time, its effects can also be simulated, generating a sequence of snap-shots of networks that model temporal shifts in interaction patterns as the numbers of islanders grew. Irwin's demonstration that the centrality enjoyed by the Mailu settlement varied with successive regional settlement horizons is exemplary in this respect. If a sufficient sensitivity to contexts and changes can be attained, PPA of island groups can transcend deterministic analysis, and develop into a relatively subtle tool for investigating the many ways in which culture and history may develop within, but also profoundly rework, the configurational features of a given islandscape.

Constructing a proximal point analysis for the Cyclades

How, then, should such a PPA for the EBA Cyclades be designed? Several factors in practice work to our advantage. First, the dispersed settlement pattern observed on most of the Cyclades means that a distribution of points evenly spread over the islands *is* a reasonable simulation of EBA reality, and one that can also be fairly extrapolated to islands whose archaeology is less well known. By way of contrast, this would not be the case during any of the later Cyclades' many phases of nucleation. The objection that this assumption smooths over local distinctions, such as the paucity of EBA settlements beyond Agia Irini in the 25 sq km of north-west Kea covered by intensive field survey (Cherry *et al.* 1991: 219, 228), is best addressed by acknowledging that such micro-variation relates to scales of spatial resolution below that which a PPA of the entire island group can practically access. Similar considerations argue that local topographical features and variations in the distribution of arable land should not greatly distort the analysis at the scale at which it is intended to operate, although a few of the larger, more fertile regions may be under-represented by this uniform treatment. Another objection, namely that the assumption of an even settlement distribution ignores the existence of a few demographically dense spots, namely the EB II villages, can also be countered. For such villages represent very localised population clusters and, moreover, it will become obvious in the next chapter that their emergence during EB II was largely a *consequence* of their position within networks, and is therefore best considered during elaboration of the models, rather than introduced as a starting variable. Lastly, the parameters for land and sea movement in the early Cyclades (cf. chapter 3) imply that there is no need to weight local land and sea distances significantly differently, and the fluctuation in wind direction is sufficient to allow all potential axes of local linkage to be considered equally viable.

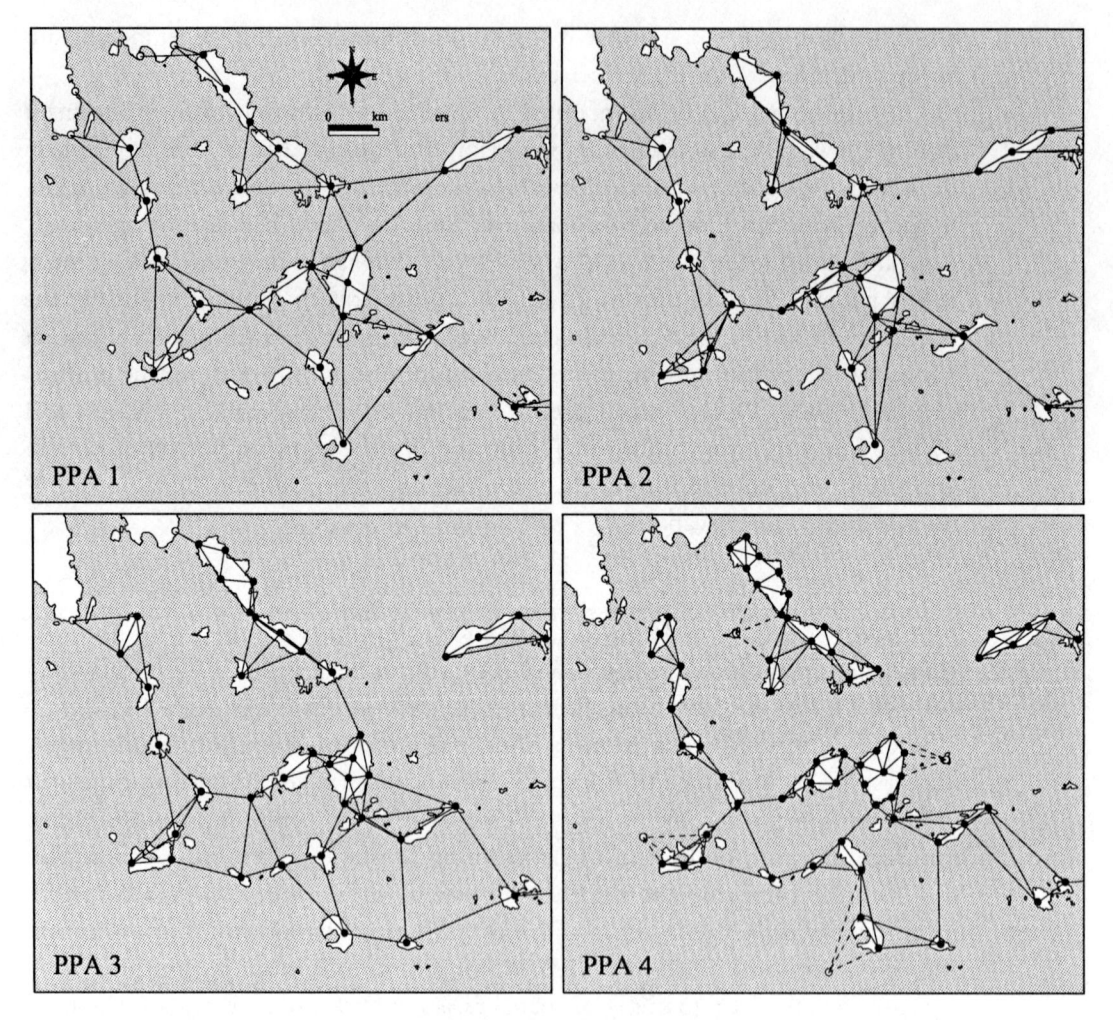

Fig. 53   Proximal point analysis for the Cyclades: PPAs 1–4.

Fig. 53 shows a sequence of PPAs (PPAs 1–4) that simulate local interaction in the Cyclades under conditions of demographic growth in the EBA. As quite a lot will be inferred from this model, its rules need to be set out in some detail. Points are allocated in proportion to island size, each being a surrogate for the settlements scattered over the area that the point represents. Placement is governed by uniform rules: one point at the centre of an island, two at the ends of its longest axis, three along this axis, four or more as suits an island's shape. Dense clusters of small islands have their combined areas treated collectively. Population increase is modelled by increasing the number of points in each PPA according to a simple set of rules. For PPA 1, one point is allocated per 150 sq km of island area, with islands below this threshold and residual areas on large islands allocated one point for any land area comprising 50+ per cent of this figure (any area under the 75 sq km threshold thereby generated is given no point). The reason for this starting level is that the resultant 75–150 sq km range covers the centre of the size spectrum for the Cyclades, so that the sequence starts with a single point on most of the islands. Population growth is simulated through generating more points by successively lowering the area per point to 100, 75 and 50 sq km (or 50+ per cent thereof, as above) in PPAs 2, 3 and 4 respectively (a PPA for one point per 125 sq km barely differed from PPA 1, and is not illustrated). By PPA 4 the number of points in the Cyclades has risen from an initial nineteen to fifty-four, simulating a two- to threefold population increase and turning the issue of how to distribute the points to our interpretative advantage. A final general feature of the model is that, in order to allow the networks to emerge without imposing *a priori* borders, Ikaria and Astypalaia are included, and although Attica and Euboia are not considered to require linkage into the islands, notional points along their coasts are allowed to operate as destinations for outward connections from the northern Cyclades.

Before beginning to explore some of the implications of this model, two further observations can be made. One is that the infilling of the Cyclades through progressive colonisation of the smaller islands is effectively simulated, although the area thresholds determine that, of the smallest islands, only the Erimonisia and Poliagos (lumped with Kimolos) come into play. This is not to deny that other extremely small islands were inhabited (they clearly were), but it underscores the fact that their tiny populations should have had a negligible impact on overall demographic patterns (note the alternative in the light of the above criticism of certain PPAs: if a point is allocated to tiny Christiana, roughly 2 sq km in area, 215 points should be placed on Naxos – a practical absurdity). Links for several small islands that will feature in the course of the next few chapters (Antimelos, Christiana, Delos, Reneia, Donousa, Giaros and Makronisos) are shown by dotted lines in PPA 4, in order to indicate their connections. It should be emphasised that such links are excluded from the main network analyses that follow, and that these small islands are not considered legitimate targets for linkage with other points.

The other observation is that this PPA-derived model probably can be grounded to an albeit crude degree in what we know of early Cycladic *absolute* as well as *relative* demography. If each set of four necessarily linked points were to be taken as equivalent to a minimum network of 300–500 people, it would follow that each point represents on average something in the order of 100± people. The range of point densities from one per 150 sq km (PPA 1) to one per 50 sq km (PPA 4) would therefore imply densities of population ranging from an initial 0.7 people per sq km to a final 2.0 people per sq km, both figures lying well within the range provided in table 1 and matching Cherry's suggested densities of 0.5–1.5 people per sq km for the Grotta-Pelos culture and 1.5–3.0 for EB II, as well as his estimation of a two- to threefold population rise in the EBA (Cherry 1979: 37–43, Wagstaff and Cherry 1982b: 138). An alternative approach, that takes into account the fact that a number of points are allocated to places that are up to 50 per cent smaller than the full qualifying area for each PPA, is to examine the increase in the total number of points in the Cyclades. This increase, from nineteen to fifty-four points, would simulate slightly less than a threefold growth in population, and in absolute terms an increase from about 2000 to 5400 people (again with the expectation of a slight under-estimation due to the small areas that fail to qualify), both falling comfortably within the ranges suggested by table 1 and the results of Cherry's calculations. The implications of this approximate ability to calibrate the PPA sequence are considerable, for it suggests that it will be defensible to use the sequence to explain salient features of the islands' settlement, local dynamics and material culture at different junctures in the EBA, an interpretative exercise to which we will return later in this chapter.

Implications of proximal point analysis for local island dynamics

It is instructive to start by taking PPAs 1–4 simply as a relative sequence that models the implications of settlement and population growth under early Cycladic conditions, and ask a series of basic questions, subsequently introducing additional criteria to nuance or develop the answers. Leaving centrality aside, four good questions to ask are:

1. How homogeneous or fragmented are the Cyclades at different stages in the sequence, and what sub-divisions can be identified?
2. How discrete is the individual island as an analytical unit in such networks?
3. How important are sea-links, and how does this importance vary across the Cyclades and through the sequence?
4. What can be determined about degrees of isolation in different areas of the Cyclades? Here 'Isolation' is taken to denote not a total absence of contacts, which is not feasible in the context of inter-visible exogamous communities, but two separate phenomena that shelter within this ambiguous term. The first is the relative difficulty of maintaining external contacts. The second is the kind of isolation that occurs where people create locally self-sufficient worlds with little need or opportunity for outside contacts; this is likely to occur only if a comparatively dense accumulation of people is involved.

Question 1 How homogeneous or fragmented are the Cyclades at different stages in the sequence, and what sub-divisions can be identified?

A starting observation is that external edges to the island group become better defined through the sequence, in the east as Ikaria breaks away, although Astypalaia maintains its role as a midway island, and in the north as population growth on Andros and Kea renders this region increasingly independent of Attica and Euboia. Within the

Cyclades, however, the process of increasing definition of discrete areas cuts the other way, with the trend shifting from a relatively homogeneous network in PPAs 1–2 to a number of increasingly sharply defined sub-clusters in PPAs 3–4. The emergence in PPAs 3–4 of north-eastern, south-eastern and south-western sub-clusters, plus a string of western islands, suggests that under these conditions the Cyclades (or rather the islands that we collectivise under this name) might not actually exist as a recognised group, at least in the sense that we understand them today. Moreover, although the sub-clusters in PPAs 3–4 quite closely match the divisions suggested by inter-island distance (cf. fig. 15), this correlation is less apparent at lower density PPAs 1–2. It is unlikely that this increasing fragmentation would be countered by social storage networks, for although the latters' absolute extents cannot be gauged, it was suggested in chapter 3 that their role would be less significant on large islands with a clement environment, and it is precisely these areas where the increase in point density causes the most spatial shrinkage in modelled demographic links; conversely the remaining islands, where social storage networks might be more important and extensive, generally retain wider links in PPAs 3–4.

Question 2 How discrete is the individual island as an analytical unit in such networks?

Chapter 3 demonstrated that topography helps to break up the individual islands in the Cyclades, and that low population levels must have turned people's attentions outwards to neighbours on other islands, and in chapter 4 it was noted that the establishment of populations is better assessed in terms of networks of mutually sustaining communities than in terms of a single island. PPA now allows us to refine these observations, locate them in spatial contexts, and demonstrate that the modelled demographic networks regularly ignore insular 'boundaries'. Indeed it is conspicuous that among all the networks there is not a single neat example of a self-contained and homogeneous island, i.e. a unit represented by four interlinked points on one island and with no external connections. Andros in PPAs 2–3 and Greater Paros in PPA 4 are the closest approximations. Instead, the networks delineate areas that either extend beyond the island (the most common pattern) or create sub-insular zones that break up an island into fragments (witnessed only on larger islands later in the sequence). The astonishing variety of small worlds that this can create is illustrated by the example of Naxos (fig. 54). Once again, there is no reason to think that island homogeneity would be more apparent if social storage networks were considered, given the ease with which small cargoes of staples and animals could be transferred to an adjacent area across the sea. These mosaics of land and sea effectively deny any hope of finding island laboratories in the early Cyclades, and confirm that archaeological analyses that are confined to a single island are likely be looking at more, or less, or probably both more and less, than the social islandscapes relevant to early Cycladic

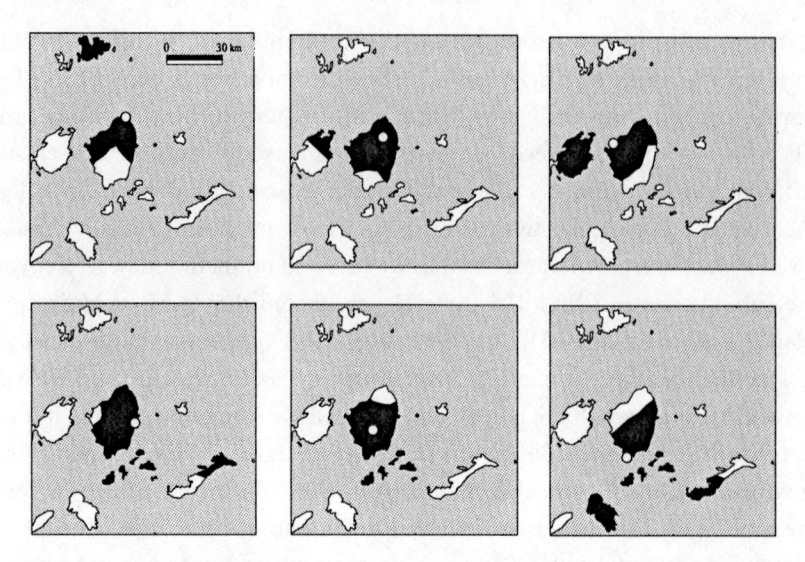

Fig. 54 Naxian worldlets as explored by the network connections of each point on Naxos to other areas of the Cyclades in PPA 3. The choice of Naxos in PPA 3 is simply one example among many potential illustrations of the complex trans-insular networks generated for the Cyclades.

people. They also indicate that naming cultural groups after islands (e.g. Amorgos group, Christiana group) is unfortunate, as it is most unlikely that the cluster of material phenomena that they are held to signify will in fact reveal a distribution largely, let alone wholly, centred on the said island.

Question 3 How important are sea-links, and how does this importance vary across the islands and through the sequence?

At this juncture it is useful to recall the antithetical claims of 'endemic seafaring' and 'uncommon seafaring' provided by Barber (1987) and Getz-Preziosi (1987a), quoted in chapter 2. The PPAs strictly tell us only about the maritime element in demographic networks, and there were obviously other reasons for people to go to sea. Let us start, however, with what the PPAs reveal, and then ask to what extent their picture needs reworking to bring in other seagoing activities. Fig. 55 represents for each point in PPAs 1–4 the number of outgoing links that connect to others overseas. Some intriguing patterns emerge. In PPA 1, the networks that bind the islanders together are essentially maritime, with almost all areas reliant to a large degree on sea connections. Through the course of PPAs 2–4, this situation is transformed as islands, parts of islands or island clusters become ever more self-supporting, and sea connections decline in importance. By the end of the sequence, most areas of the largest islands hardly use sea connections at all, becoming examples of what Baladié (1980: 214) calls 'islands with backs turned to the sea', most medium-sized islands

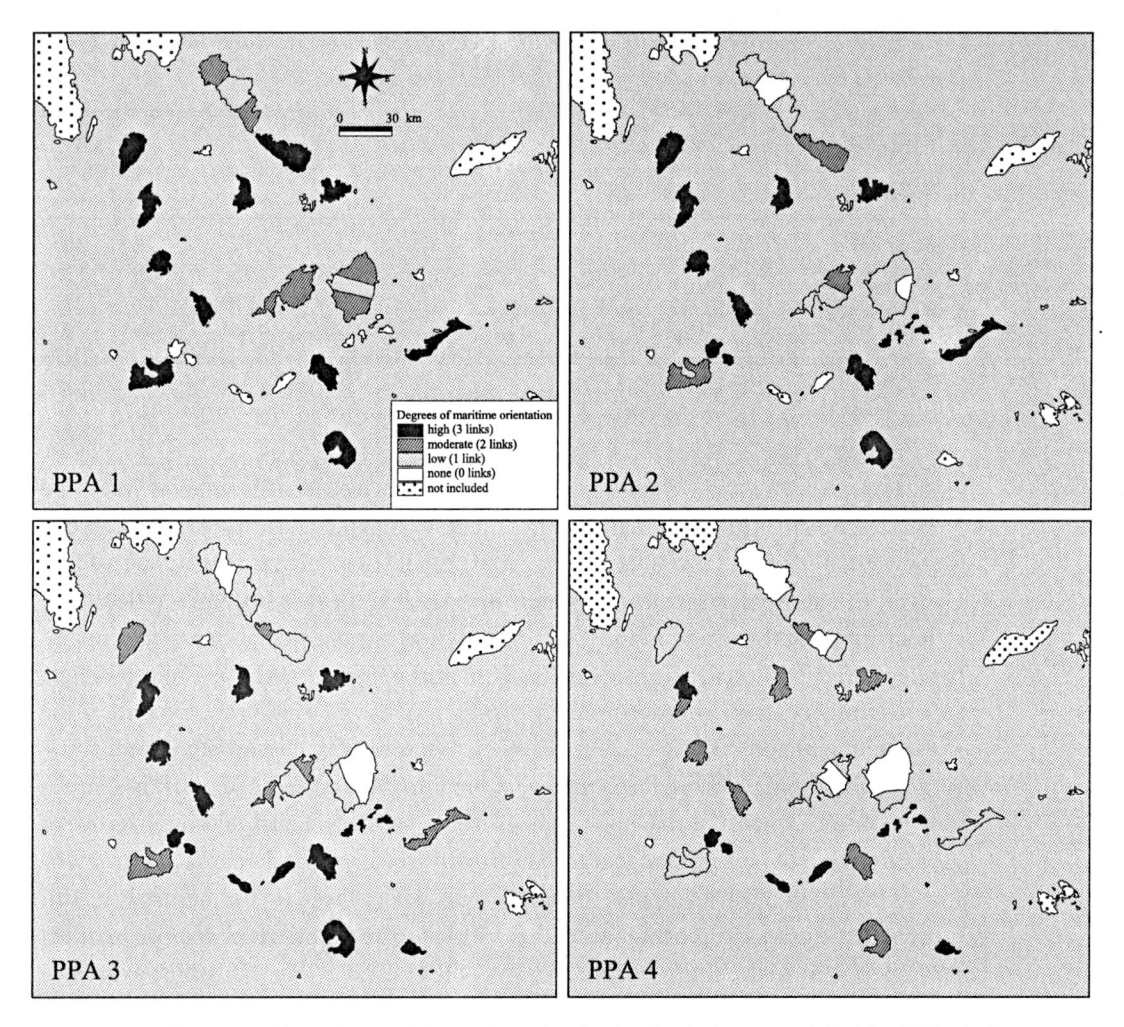

Fig. 55 Changing maritime orientation in the Cyclades as modelled by PPAs 1–4.

retain only moderate or low maritime linkage, and high levels of maritime connectivity are almost exclusively limited to the smallest islands. The transition from ubiquitous to concentrated maritime activity through PPAs 1–4 is brought out in table 6.

In addition to drawing attention to the increasingly sharp differentiation between landlubbers and seafarers, it can also be noted that through PPAs 1–4 the average length of maritime links reduces substantially, as a part of the general shrinking of horizons. Initially, most networks include sea-crossings markedly longer than the suggested approximately 20 km one-day threshold, but the mean length of maritime links roughly halves between PPAs 1 and 4, bringing all sea-crossings within this threshold in the configurationally denser areas of the Cyclades. Only for a few medium but mainly small islands are long connecting links still predicted by PPA 4, Anaphi being the most extreme case.

Table 6. *Percentage of points with different degrees of seafaring orientation in PPAs 1–4, as modelled by the number of outgoing points that cross the sea.*

Number of overseas links per point	PPA 1 No.	PPA 1 %	PPA 2 No.	PPA 2 %	PPA 3 No.	PPA 3 %	PPA 4 No.	PPA 4 %
Minimal (0)	0	0	3	12	6	17	16	30
Low (1)	3	16	7	27	8	23	18	33
Medium (2)	4	21	4	15	9	26	15	28
High (3)	12	63	12	46	12	34	5	9

An assessment of the degree to which this PPA-driven transformation might be overridden by other kinds of maritime practices is obviously necessary. In fact, it can be shown that the PPAs produce a fairly robust model of local maritime activity. First, it was argued above that social storage networks would be less important on the largest islands, implying that these islands' increasingly terrestrial orientations would not be greatly altered by such networks, and on all other islands the lower populations dictate some continued island interdependency throughout the EBA anyway. Second, if the assessment in chapter 3 was correct, fishing was a sporadic, commonly littoral activity, and EBA fishing is more likely to have fitted into local patterns of maritime movement than to redraw the maritime map of the Cyclades. Third, although growing populations might be expected to translate crudely into growing demands for the maritime importation of obsidian and metals to areas where these do not naturally occur, it would be naive to assume that this necessarily led to an undifferentiated rise in direct maritime access to the sources from all parts of the island group. For whilst aggregate demand should grow with increasing population, the frequency with which a small individual community needed to replenish its resources would remain relatively constant, and probably fairly low. Decreasing levels of maritime travel in most parts of the Cyclades are in fact more likely to have led to a concentration of resource procurement journeys in those few areas that did maintain an investment in sea travel. In other words, rather than rising total demand invalidating a model of declining overall seafaring activity, these divergent trends might have created a tension that those people who did still travel regularly by sea would be in an excellent position to exploit. This argument is taken up and expanded in the next few chapters.

To summarise, there are solid reasons to think that PPAs 1–4 do enable us to gain insight into the relative incidence of local sea travel in various parts of the Cyclades under different conditions, although long-range voyaging, of course, will need separate investigation. The choice between Barber and Getz-Preziosi is very much a question of 'when' and 'where'. Maritime activity seems far from being a cultural constant that can be invoked to 'explain' early Cycladic societies as a whole, and instead emerges as a shifting factor that might (if explored with sensitivity to context) help us to explain why particular societies or communities behaved in particular ways.

Question 4 What can be determined about degrees of isolation in different areas of the Cyclades?

Isolation is a thoroughly protean concept. It must be repeated that what is envisaged in the present context is a *relative* state. It is impossible to know whether the areas that can be identified as isolated had contacts with outsiders once a month, year or lifetime. But we can look at where forms of isolation are most strongly attested, and at what this tells us about aspects of island life in different parts of the Cyclades. It is also important to distinguish two different kinds of isolation. One of these involves a relative difficulty in maintaining an adequate set of contacts with outsiders. Areas in which this seems to apply we shall call *remote*. The other variety of isolation relevant in the present context is that which can develop in conditions where people are so closely packed and collectively self-sufficient that they have little incentive to extend their horizons beyond the immediate locality. Such areas we will term *parochial*.

The means of identifying such areas are provided by introducing further rules to the models. Isolation of either variety is considered to be potentially significant only in those areas that are represented by points with the minimum of three links to others. Within this group, all those points whose mean distance of linkage is over 20 km (i.e. above the one-day, one-way travel range) are identified as potentially remote, whilst all points for which this mean is 10 km or less (i.e. within a one-day there-and-back range) are considered potentially parochial. This focus on the extremes screens out the less interesting (for present purposes) places in the middle, whose three links average within the 10–20 km range. A final rule identifies as remote areas only those that need outside contacts more than outsiders need them, as identified by points at least one of whose three links represents a non-reciprocal connection, and adds that an area's remote status increases in extremity if this applies to two or three of its links. This approach generates a generally coherent set of results, indicating that certain parts of the early Cyclades might well have experienced substantially more isolation (of either kind) than others. How people in such areas reacted to these conditions is another matter, and one that will bring us back again to issues of cultural choice and decision-making.

Starting with remote areas, fig. 56 shows the potential candidates generated by PPAs 1–4, and the degree of remoteness defined by the number of non-reciprocal links. Occasional appearances in this category, e.g. Ios in PPA 1, southern Greater Paros in PPA 2, Seriphos in PPAs 2–3 or Mykonos in PPA 3, illustrate how particular areas can be temporarily linked in or cut off as networks shift, but perhaps should not be taken too seriously on an individual basis, given the potential for the odd freak result caused by the specifics of point placement. If we set these cases aside, we can

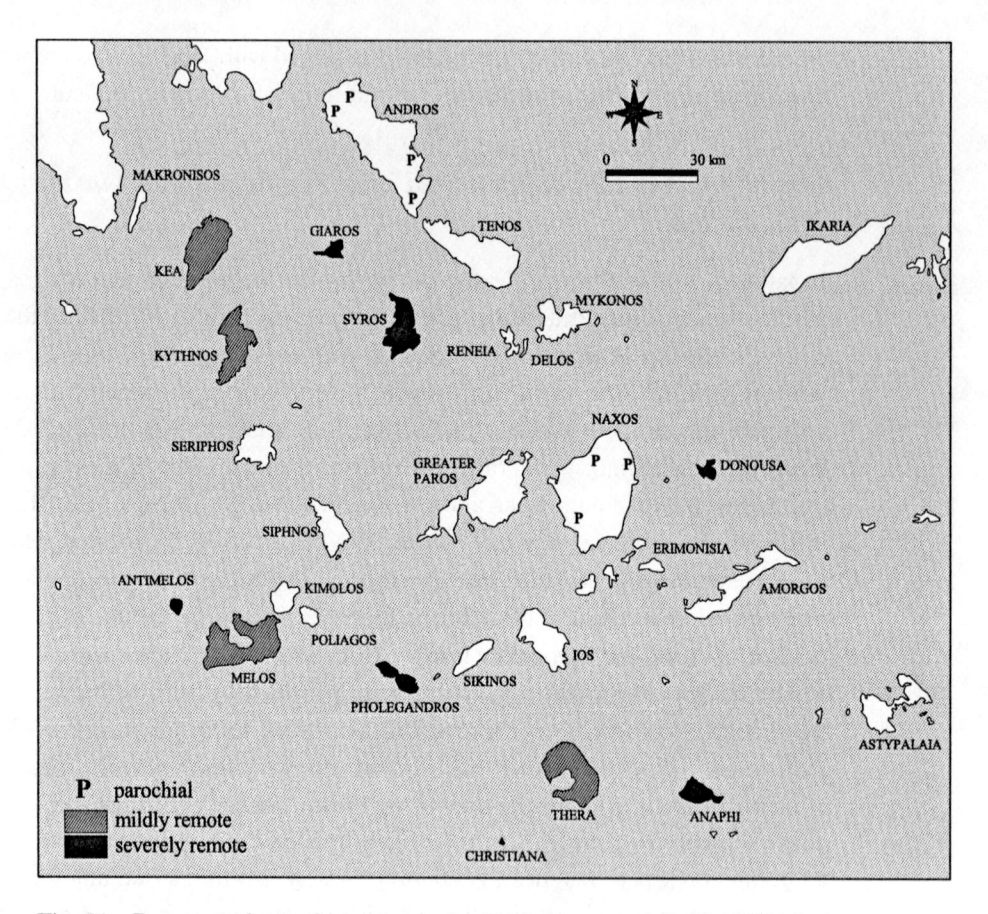

Fig. 56 Remote and parochial zones in the Cyclades as modelled by PPAs 1–4.

identify eleven islands that are vulnerable through much or all of their inclusion in the PPA (Astypalaia, outside the modern Cyclades, constitutes a twelfth). Most lie on the edges of the Cyclades, but Syros makes for a startling exception, and all comprise medium to small islands, including four that lie below the size threshold for inclusion even in PPA 4 (i.e. Antimelos, Christiana, Donousa and Giaros).

In terms of their degrees of remoteness, Kea, Kythnos, Melos and Thera are the most mildly affected, and a modest extra investment in maintaining contacts would in all likelihood overcome any potential problems. Melos and Kythnos can also be discounted on the grounds that they were visited by people seeking their mineral resources, which should have created other opportunities for interaction, and Kea's role at the entrance to the Cyclades from the north might argue for a similar dispensation.[3] By contrast, on the smaller islands of Anaphi, Antimelos, Christiana, Donousa,

---

[3] It is worth noting in passing a distinction between island people, for whom obsidian procurement trips probably overrode Melos' status as a remote area, and island birds, for which Melos remains one of the hardest of the Cyclades to repopulate after a local extinction (Watson 1964: 190).

Giaros, Pholegandros and even larger Syros the condition is so severe that, at least as modelled, it raises the possibility that the rest of the world had little or no need of these places. None of these seven islands has other means of attracting outsiders: all lack mineral resources known to have been used in the EBA, and all but Syros have arid environments and little arable land, that would not put them in a strong position with regard to social storage networks. In this last respect, Syros is in fact a more apparent than real exception, despite its better climate, because its closest neighbours are large, well-watered Andros and Tenos, where such incentives to forge links with communities on Syros are liable to have been minimal. Whilst such a grim predicament may not be unexpected in the case of the several smaller islands highlighted here, the identification of larger and superficially better-located Syros as one of the most marked and enduring remote areas in the early Cyclades is a surprise, and one that illustrates the rewards of an explicit contextual modelling of early Cycladic networks, as opposed to reliance upon our modern-day 'sensible' intuition.

It is interesting to speculate what the cultural responses to such a situation might have been on different islands. Long-term introversion is one possibility, but a rather unlikely one, as all seven of the most remote areas would need outside alliances if they were to survive a run of bad harvests, or to reproduce their populations over any length of time without violating likely incest taboos. More plausible options are (1) inhabiting such places only sporadically, if at all, or (2) committing additional effort to maintaining external connections despite a lack of reciprocal interest, which in island terms implies a deliberate investment in intensified sea travel. On the six small islands, the odds seem stacked in favour the former option, not least as their populations might not even reach a level that gave enough flexibility to intensify maritime travel, and their participation in social storage networks would have been on desperately unequal terms. These islands, and other obscure islets on the fringes of the Cyclades, must have been the internal ends of the EBA islanders' worlds. On larger and potentially populous Syros, on the other hand, local people might have stood a better chance of circumventing their remoteness by boosting maritime travel. Syros could prove to be a very interesting island indeed.

The definition of potentially parochial areas is no less intriguing but can be dealt with more briefly. Such zones emerge in parts of two islands (fig. 56), namely Andros and Naxos, and only in PPA 4, although an incipient tendency towards limited and very localised connections can be discerned in the same areas in earlier PPAs. The conditions that generate these zones are high populations in those parts of large islands that do not face towards other islands sufficiently close to broaden their network. The plausibility of both zones is increased by the fact that they are devoid of lithic or metallic resources to draw outsiders in, and that neither should have been heavily dependent on social storage. Braudel's description of such areas as introverted islands with stagnant centres (1972: 150–1) does scant justice to the complexity of the internal structures that they might generate. To speculate on the culture of such areas, it might diverge from more general practices, and elaborate localised ways of doing things. In archaeological terms, local EBA material might possibly have an idiosyncratic signature that we are at present less equipped to recognise, and might be poorer in the high-visibility items circulating between islands in the more open areas of the Cycladic networks. The relatively mild nature of such conditions in the Cyclades must, however, be stressed. In size, Andros is broadly comparable to Malta plus Gozo, that ultimate Mediterranean example of an island group whose people decided to turn in on themselves at one stage of their early history; but although the archaeology of EBA Andros may be anomalous in certain respects, as will become apparent, it is certainly devoid of megalithic temples.

A summary of what has been learnt

To summarise before comparing the modelled patterns with the archaeological picture, the likely complexity of local networks in the EBA Cyclades has been amply indicated. Strikingly, there has been little to suggest that the networks generated by modelling demographic growth through PPA analysis would be countered to a substantial degree by social storage connections. The main reason for this appears to be a close correlation between the largest islands and the best environments, which has meant that the densest populations developed in areas that needed to invest least in the latter networks, and the parallel associations between a continuing reliance upon more extensive demographic connections on most other islands, and such islands' equal need to continue to maintain social storage networks, owing to their less clement conditions. A third point has been that travel range is better introduced as an interrogative variable once the initial networks have been delineated than as a fixed element from the start. Altogether, if the model that has been built, adapted and explored has produced even roughly accurate simulations of the dynamics of local Cycladic EBA interaction, we can anticipate some very diverse social strategies and material cultures, as well as many shifts over the course of time.

Specific comments about various parts of the Cyclades can also be offered. One intriguing generalisation is that the most dramatic differences both between and within islands, as well as the most unusual islands (or parts of islands), have emerged in the eastern half of the Cyclades, where distinctions in island size and inter-island spacing are most pronounced and where networks, especially in the south-east, are at their most complex. In the western Cyclades, by contrast, the networks are more uniform and the islands resemble each other more (consider how little cause there has been to mention Kea, Kythnos, Seriphos, Siphnos, Melos, Kimolos or Poliagos, save to conclude that none makes an ultimately convincing candidate for remote status). Thus, to state that the western Cyclades, with the partial exception of the Melos group, are medium-sized islands with average environments, whose relatively wide, even inter-island spacing and linear configuration tend to favour stable, reciprocal relations of interdependence under EBA conditions, is not to be guilty of too serious an oversimplification. For the eastern islands, conversely, it would be impossible to begin to generalise in this way. This does not mean that the western islands are an uninteresting prospect, but rather that (their striking similarity aside) the most interesting things going on in them may relate to different scales and kinds of EBA activity, not the least of these being, of course, the exploitation of their diverse mineral resources.

Turning to more specific areas of the Cyclades, several further conclusions have also emerged. Andros is an unusual place. It is one of the few locations that almost works as a unitary island at one juncture in the PPA, it displays the strongest tendency to develop land-based networks and eschew maritime links, and it includes parochial areas. It both resembles and yet strongly contrasts with Naxos, its only rival in size. Naxos, too, has its parochial areas, but other parts of the island continue to enjoy some maritime links throughout the sequence, and whilst Andros looks in on itself, Naxos is instead prey to centrifugal connections that pull parts of it towards Greater Paros and the islands to its south. Perversely, Tenos, Andros' close neighbour, displays several tendencies more akin to Naxos, whilst Greater Paros (after a strong maritime orientation in PPA 1) displays in a less extreme form some traits seen on Andros. Syros is another paradox, located at the heart of the Cyclades, and yet the only major island with regular difficulties in maintaining external contacts, despite ever-changing networks around it. At the other end of the size spectrum, Anaphi, Antimelos, Christiana, Donousa, Giaros and Pholegandros cling on to the margins of the networks. But small island connections were not necessarily precarious, as a glance at the network positions of the Erimonisia, Makronisos, Delos, Reneia, Sikinos or Kimolos and Poliagos confirms. Apart from the western Cyclades, and solitary Thera in the deep south, this leaves Amorgos, Ios and Mykonos. These medium-sized, environmentally fairly harsh places in fact behave in similar ways, showing few signs of isolation and exhibiting links in several directions. Overall, the complexity is daunting, not least as the additional factors of centrality and longer-range interaction have yet to be addressed. But in another sense this complexity is encouraging, as it reveals the sheer diversity of the spatial contexts in which the settlements and material culture of the EBA Cyclades can be situated.

Network models and the archaeology of the EBA Cyclades

There are two ways in which the modelling undertaken in the preceding sections can inform an analysis of the archaeology of the EBA Cyclades. One way is to look at those areas of the islands that modelling indicates might be unusual in certain respects, and to investigate whether this can help to explain any distinctive features of the archaeological record in such places. Another is to use the PPA networks to shed light on distributions of material culture. Both assume that the sequence of PPAs 1–4 can be calibrated with different EBA archaeological horizons. Although it is unrealistic to expect each PPA to equate with a single chronological period, a rough calibration is justified, given the fact that the overall model was carefully designed to simulate EBA conditions, and that the numbers of points could be correlated reasonably with estimates of absolute population.

PPA 1 can be taken to correlate with a situation of fairly low-density settlement on the main islands, and little build-up on the smaller islands, in other words with the period from the end of the Neolithic through most of EB I. The fact that a PPA using a density of one point per 125 sq km (not shown in fig. 53) revealed almost no change suggests that the PPA 1 network reflects an enduring low-density pattern. PPA 4, the high-density final network with maximal small-island involvement, that results from the virtual tripling of the number of points in PPA 1, is correlated with EB II, possibly the later part of the period. Between these two distinctive networks, intermediate PPAs 3–4 should be best associated with later EB I and early EB II, although it would be unwise to force each into one of these chronological compartments too dogmatically. It is in fact essential to leave an element of flexibility in these equations, in order to allow for the probability of a time-lag in the population build-ups in different parts of the Cyclades, not least as a legacy of the temporal and spatial differences in colonisation history. Even at this level of generalisation, a perfect match between networks and data is not to be expected. For one thing, the patchiness of the current information dictates that, in some parts of the islands, the models simply constitute predictions that future fieldwork may confirm or deny. Furthermore, the further dynamics of centrality and long-range travel have still to be added in to complete the picture. Despite this, the present simulations enable us to make insular sense of existing information in a surprising number of cases.

Understanding isolation in the EBA Cyclades: predictions and data

The areas of the Cyclades that PPAs 1–4 predicted to be relatively isolated in one way or other form a good starting point. Archaeological data from the predicted remote areas do indeed suggest that people were aware of the predicaments of such places, and that this awareness often influenced decisions as to whether to live in them. On the small islands in this category, the evidence to date suggests that people either avoided them entirely, or inhabited them only sporadically. Antimelos and Giaros, both virtually waterless, have to date revealed no signs of inhabitation. Anaphi is to date also a blank, although settlement was certainly feasible, as the island was occupied in later antiquity. Traces of EBA settlement are reported on Christiana (Doumas 1976a; Sotirakopoulou 1993: 16–17), Donousa (Zapheiropoulou 1967) and Pholegandros (Hadjianastasiou 1996), in most cases datable to EB II. On larger, more fertile Syros, however, a different pattern is seen. Despite its poor location relative to local networks, this island was well settled and has long been known for its large EB II cemetery, settlement and fortified site at Chalandriani-Kastri (Hekman 1994;

Marthari 1998; Tsountas 1899). In this instance, people clearly did overcome the problems suggested by PPA. Possible reasons for this are put forward in chapters 7 and 8, in the context of a more detailed analysis of Chalandriani-Kastri and its role in the EB II Cyclades.

What of the inverse form of isolation, namely the parochial zones identified on parts of Andros and Naxos? It was speculated that here different forms of island culture might emerge, and ones that might be hard to detect archaeologically, either because of their unfamiliarity, or because they less frequently acquired the kinds of prominent inter-island exchange objects familiar to us – or, at least, less frequently deposited these in archaeologically visible contexts. The abnormally low maritime orientation of Andros, and to a lesser degree parts of Naxos, might likewise amplify tendencies to diverge from patterns of behaviour seen in the more open parts of the networks. In this context, the fact that little diagnostic material and few definite examples of EBA settlements have been identified on Andros (Koutsoukou 1993: 102), despite the island's size, clement environment, number of Neolithic sites, and increasing degree of exploration, could be explained by the parochialism and terrestrial orientation so evident in our modelling. An indication that low visibility may indeed be a problem in such areas is also provided by the conclusions of an intensive survey of north-west Naxos, also a region predicted by PPA to be a potentially parochial zone. This part of Naxos had long been noted for its striking paucity of EBA remains by Naxian standards, save for a small Grotta-Pelos cemetery at Akrotiri (Erard-Cerceau *et al.* 1993: 59). The survey proved that settlements certainly existed, but that (in the team's chagrined words):

> Ces observations suggèrent un habitat très dispersé, où les préoccupations défensives n'ont guère d'importance, et une économie essentiellement agricole, où la mer ne joue probablement qu'un rôle très secondaire: seuls deux sites . . . sont situés à son voisinage immédiat, et l'on utilise peut-être moins l'obsidienne de Mélos et plus les ressources locales (silex, chaille parfois et même quartz) qu'on ne l'a supposé jusque-là. On dirait bien que ce n'est pas ici qu'il faut chercher les hardis navigateurs dont les embarcations sont représentées sur les 'poêles à frire' de Syros ni les pirates que Minos, selon Thucydide, aurait pourchassés dans les îles. (Erard-Cerceau *et al.* 1993: 89)

Spatial distributions of material culture in the EBA Cyclades: predictions and data

But what of wider patterns in the distribution of material culture? The PPAs suggest that local EBA networks should have broken up the Cyclades to varying degrees and along different axes at different periods. In PPAs 1–2 the northern and southern islands are only slightly linked, and in PPAs 3–4 several sub-clusters become defined. The early north–south divide may indicate some reasons for our poorer knowledge of the northern Cyclades, given the degree to which southern, particularly south-eastern, material has dominated Cycladic scholarship through its quantity (not least in the high-profile burial sphere), becoming enshrined in definitions of cultural phases, and thereby moulding expectations about the form of the archaeological record. With the honourable exception of Chalandriani-Kastri, the only extensive excavations of EBA settlements in the northern islands have resulted from the serendipitous discovery of early material at sites excavated for their later significance (i.e. Agia Irini I–III under a later Bronze Age centre and Mt Kynthos under a Delian temple). There is every chance that a programme of research in the north will reveal assemblages that diverge from the familiar southern templates and diversify our conception of the culture of the EBA Cyclades.

The distribution of the Grotta-Pelos culture illustrates this situation. In chapter 5 Grotta-Pelos was interpreted as a cultural package that accompanied the expansion of tiny farmstead settlements from the end of the Neolithic. The overwhelming majority of sites belonging to this culture are located in the southern Cyclades. In the north, the only contemporary evidence comes from Kea, in the form of the basal material at Agia Irini I, which shows few affinities to the Grotta-Pelos culture (Wilson 1999: 6–19, 227), and two imported Grotta-Pelos marble vessels found at Poisses during road-building, plus a possible transitional FN/EB I site on Andros (Koutsoukou 1993: 101–2) and reports of sites of equivalent date, but undefined in terms of assemblages, on Syros (Hekman 1994: 65). Whatever went on in the northern Cyclades after the Kephala culture, we know next to nothing about it. The differences that can be seen between the northern and southern Cyclades might be explained by recourse to historical descent, given that at least some of the northern islands were settled from Attica and Euboia, rather than by Saliagos culture period or later expansion from the south. But, taking PPA 1 as a model of local networks at low population densities, it can be seen that a north–south division might well continue after colonisation, or indeed develop even if the historical descent hypothesis were proven spurious. If the *bona fide* Grotta-Pelos sites known to date are mapped onto PPA 1 (fig. 57), it transpires that their limit matches the extent of the main southern Cycladic network, with Seriphos and Mykonos acting as narrow filters that effectively segregate north and the south from much local interaction. In this light, the southern Grotta-Pelos culture distribution looks like the material culture of something in the order of a thousand islanders at any one time. These people were perhaps divided into two main sub-groups, the larger in the south-east and the smaller in the south-west, the two linked via western Greater Paros. Two or three contemporary sub-groups with a more-or-less unknown material culture could be expected in the northern islands.

For EB II, PPA leads us to expect shrinking interaction spheres and increasing differentiation, with potential foci developing in the north-east, west and south-west, as well as a series of complex possibilities in the south-east. Cycladic EB II assemblages do in fact display a marked diversity, to which the umbrella term 'Keros-Syros

Small worlds

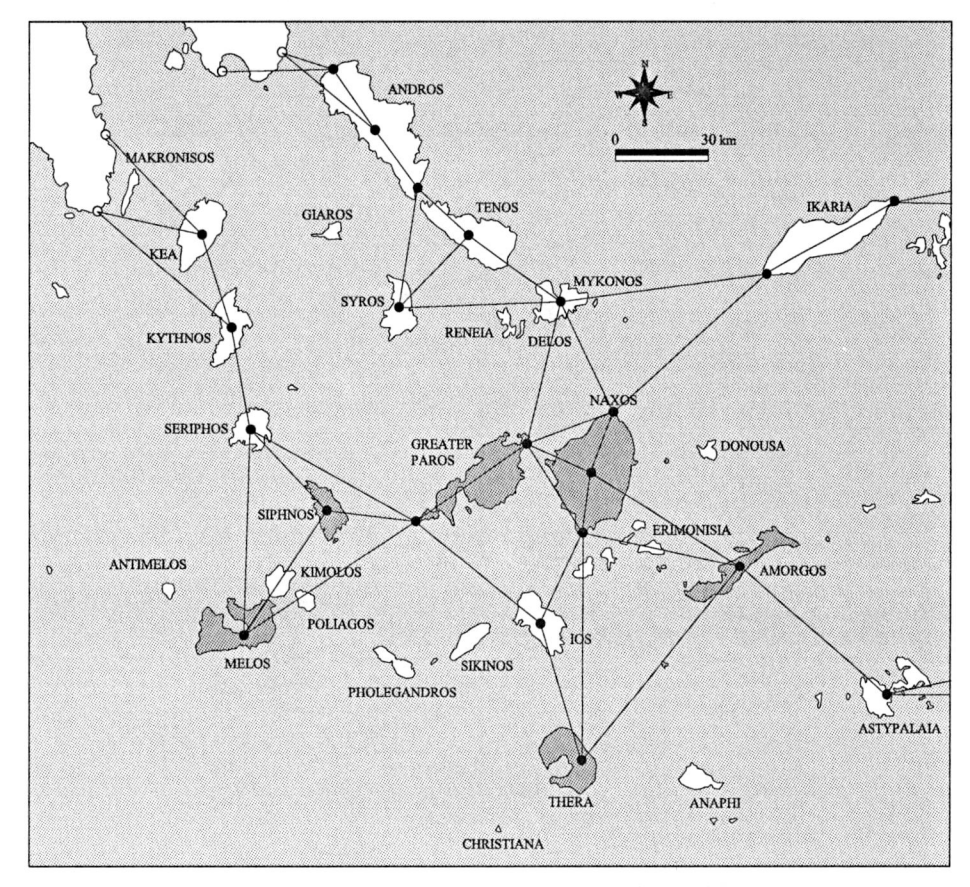

Fig. 57 Islands with Grotta-Pelos culture sites compared with the PPA 1 network.

culture' lends a fragile unity that can mislead at a local level. Adequate substantiation of this claim will be frustrated until the full publication of substantial numbers of assemblages allows archaeologists to penetrate beyond the veneer of uniformity that is created by the preliminary reports of a few widely disseminated types (cf. Davis 1992: 753–5). Already, however, there are numerous indications. Grave architecture is a good point at which to start because, unlike mobile objects, its distribution patterns cannot be blurred by physical exchange (Doumas 1977: 37–53). The corbelled graves of Syros (fig. 58), and probably also Mykonos (Belmont and Renfrew 1964: 397–8), exemplify a type of apparently limited incidence. These graves are unusual not only in their form, but also in the fact that the dead were often laid on their left side, an inversion of the norm in the south (Doumas 1977: 55; Tsountas 1899: 83). A plot of their distribution onto PPA 4 (fig. 59) shows why a distinct tradition might be shared between Syros and Mykonos and reveals the possibility that intervening Tenos may also have had graves of this type. Corbelled graves may be one element of a wider, at present little understood, northern tradition of built tombs, first seen at the

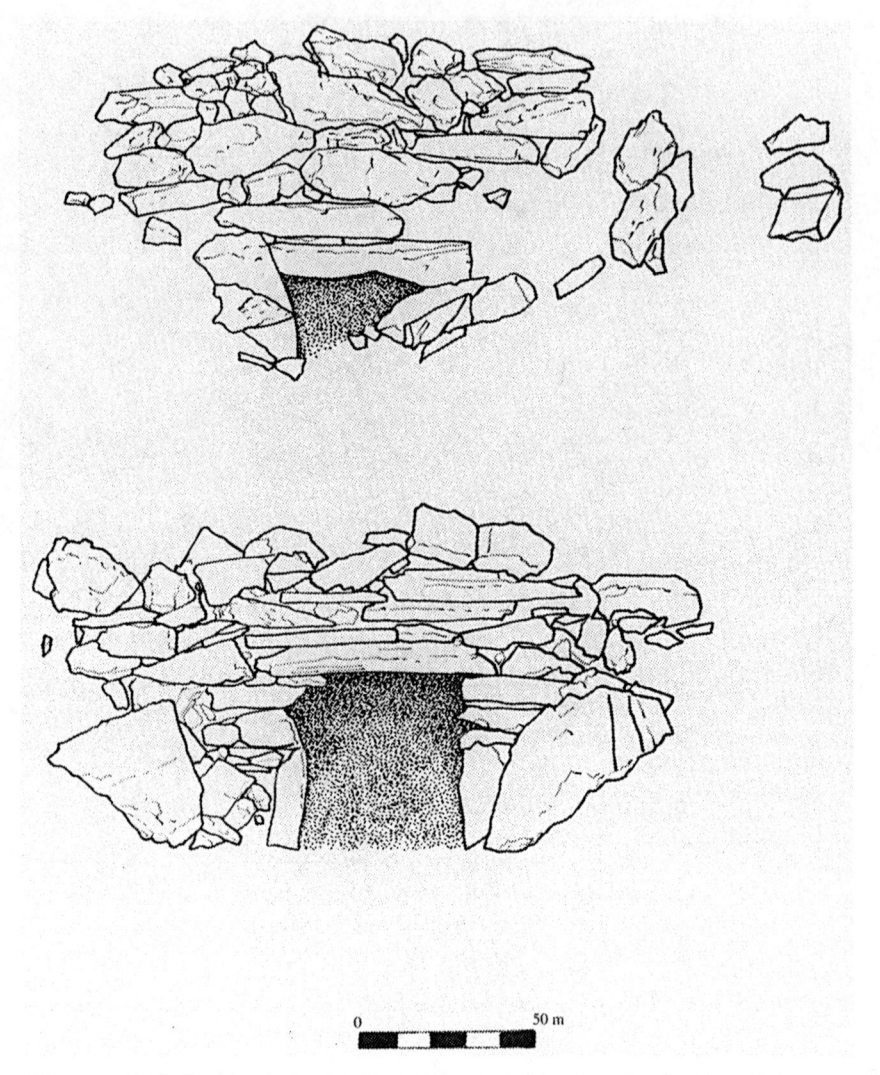

Fig. 58 Corbelled graves in the Chalandriani cemetery on Syros. After Hekman 1994: fig. 5.

FN Kephala cemetery and shared with the EB II corbelled tombs at Agios Kosmas in Attica (Mylonas 1959). Alternatively, the small number of cemeteries known in the northern Cyclades may suggest that formal burial grounds became a less regular trait in the EBA than in the southern islands. Once again, only more archaeological prospection in the north will tell.

Several other elements of EB II material culture also display signs of regional differentiation, despite the fuzziness created by intra-Cycladic trade. Even if we take Getz-Preziosi's figurine-carving 'masters' as merely analytical individuals (Cherry 1992a; Morris 1993; Redman 1977), it can be noted that only two are well documented from secure contexts on more than one island (Getz-Preziosi 1987a: fig. 53).

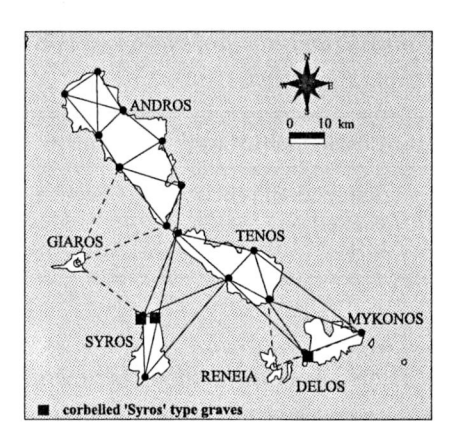

Fig. 59 Corbelled grave distribution compared with PPA 4 network.

Likewise, the figurines of an otherwise little-known 'pre-canonical' type discovered at Akrotiri on Thera may indicate a style local to the southernmost islands (Sotirakopoulou 1998: 134–8). At the rich Aplomata cemetery on Naxos, the number of figurines conforming to the slender 'Kapsala' type, and of figures seated on a backless stool, is certainly striking (Marangou 1990: 154–7, cat. nos. 159–63). More generally, the main varieties of folded-arm figurines – the Spedos, Dokathismata, Kapsala and Chalandriani types (Renfrew 1969: 15–18) – could reflect regional traditions of manufacture, although equally they could reflect chronological or symbolic distinctions. Among the marble vessels of open form, which predominate in EB II, there is a strong preponderance at Chalandriani in the north-east of bowls with ledge lugs and small cups with flaring rims or a pedestal base (Getz-Gentle 1996: 115, 123, 165) over the shallow bowls with rounded base and thickened rim that predominate at Daskaleio-Kavos on Keros and the southern Naxian cemeteries. At Aplomata, midway between Keros and Syros, a more balanced mixture of these vessel types is seen. The tantalising, yet confined, nature of these remarks is a depressing reminder of the irretrievable loss of information that has resulted from the wholesale looting of such objects from their cemeteries.

But pottery provides the best evidence of a trend towards regional differentiation in EB II. Although complete assemblages cannot to date be compared, there are already indications of how distinct such assemblages will prove to be. Wilson (1987, 1999: 228, 231) reports, for example, that the best parallels for Agia Irini II–III's local assemblage are with east Attica; imports from other Cycladic islands stand out as exotics. Similar distinctions are liable to emerge in the south as the assemblages from sites such as Akrotiri, Daskaleio-Kavos, Markiani, Phylakopi and Skarkos are published. At present, the best case for regional style zones comes from analysis of the decorated pottery, usually comprising vessels of fine or medium clay fabrics, such as pyxides, jugs, sauceboats, cups, frying pans and pedestalled jars, all forms associated

Table 7. *Relative popularity of painted, incised and stamped-and-incised decoration at Daskaleio-Kavos, Chalandriani-Kastri, and Phylakopi.*

Ranking	Daskaleio-Kavos	Chalandriani-Kastri	Phylakopi
1st	Incised	Stamped-and-incised	Painted
2nd	Painted	Painted	Stamped-and-incised
3rd	Stamped-and-incised	Incised	Incised

with social rituals, trade and burial. The stylistic distinctions between such vessels seem greater than those seen among storage vessels and other domestic shapes, and the high social profile that can be inferred for the decorated vessels (from their functions, the investment in production and decoration, and their frequent funerary deposition) makes it reasonable to use them to access local spheres of interaction and statements about identities.

The decorated pottery of the EB II Cyclades

Distinctions are apparent in the varying popularity of the main decorative modes, which in EB II comprise painted, incised and stamped-and-incised decoration (fig. 60), in the range of shapes decorated, and in the motifs. Information from four EB II sites permits a semi-quantitative analysis of this variation. These sites are Agia Irini II–III (Wilson 1999), Chalandriani cemetery (Tsountas 1899: 77–115), Daskaleio-Kavos (Broodbank 2000), and Phylakopi (Evans and Renfrew 1984). These sites are widely scattered across the Cyclades, each fortunately lying in one of the sub-clusters predicted in PPAs 3–4. Table 7 shows the relative popularity of each decorative technique at Chalandriani, Daskaleio-Kavos and Phylakopi. At Agia Irini the picture is complicated by the imports; stamped decoration is used on local hearths and occasionally on other shapes, but the stamped-and-incised vessels are non-local; there is a minor local painted tradition, but most of the painted pieces are again imports, and incised decoration is rare. It is very tempting to interpret these distinctions as indicators of self-conscious attempts at intra-Cycladic differentiation, and although the distinctions are at the moment site-specific, they probably reflect wider trends in the areas of the Cyclades to which each of the sites belongs. The overall rarity of stamped-and-incised decoration in the south-east islands (matching its rarity at Daskaleio-Kavos) supports this claim, with only tiny amounts being reported at Akrotiri (Sotirakopoulou 1990: 43) and virtually none known from the cemeteries of southern Naxos.

The designs decorating the pedestal-based jars provide the clearest examples of local differentiation within a single shape (fig. 61). Of the four types known, those with incised decoration cluster in the south-east, from southern Naxos via the Erimonisia

Fig. 60 Painted, incised and stamped-and-incised pottery of the Early Bronze II Cyclades (not to scale): (a) painted sauceboat from the Spedos cemetery on Naxos, (b) incised pedestal-based jar also from Spedos, (c) stamped-and-incised pedestal-based jar from the Chalandriani cemetery on Syros. All courtesy of the National Archaeological Museum, Athens.

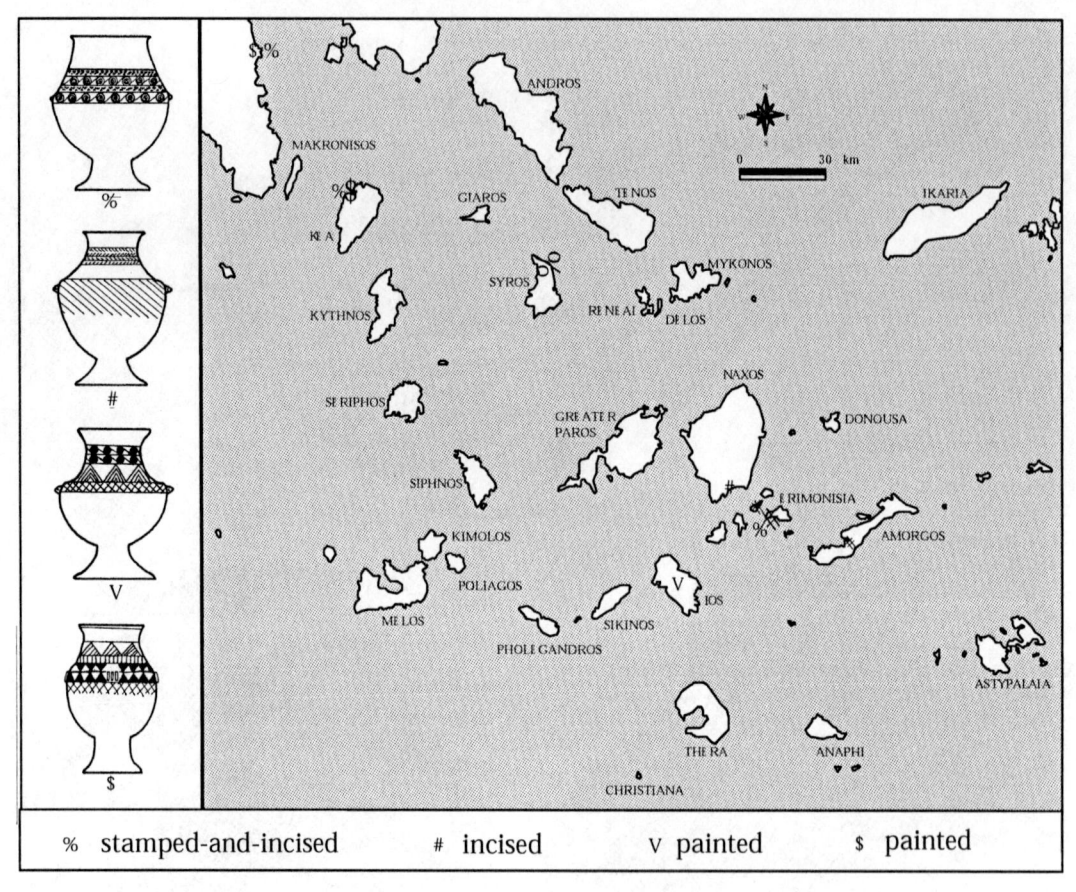

Fig. 61 Pedestal-based jar variants and their distributions (cf. fig. 60b–c for the incised and stamped-and-incised types).

to Amorgos, one painted variety is known at Agia Irini and the Attic site of Askitario, and another is attested by a single example, said to be from Ios and perhaps indicative of a variety local to the southernmost islands (Thimme 1977: 346, 355, cat. no. 385). The fourth type has a distinctive dark brown to black polished surface and stamped-and-incised decoration. It is found as a rare import from the east coast of Attica as far as Daskaleio-Kavos, but the large number of such vessels (and also of similarly decorated frying pans) at Chalandriani leaves little doubt that its home area of production lies in the north-east Cyclades. Interestingly, no variants have yet been identified in the south-west, or in the area of central-northern Naxos and Greater Paros.

An analysis of the diversity within the painted pottery further clarifies these style zones. Table 8 shows the popularity of different painted shapes at those sites for which the information is available. The sample is small, and inspection of the fabrics reveals a variety of clay types, with some of the outliers sure to be non-local. The differences and trends are sharp enough, however, to suggest that although the painted

Table 8. *Pottery shapes with painted decoration at four investigated Cycladic sites. The division of the Agia Irini pottery is due to the fact that this assemblage sub-divides clearly into local material and imports, each with a different shape range. Absolute quantities cannot be compared because the material from Chalandriani-Kastri comprises whole vessels, whilst that from other sites consists of sherds, and because the sites have been explored to varying degrees. Accordingly, popularity is defined as Common, Moderate or Rare.*

Shape	Chalandriani-Kastri	Daskaleio-Kavos	Phylakopi	Agia Irini (local)	Agia Irini (import)
Bowl/saucer	—	Rare	—	Common	Rare
Pedestalled bowl	Common	—	—	—	—
Pedestalled cup	Rare	Rare	Moderate	—	Moderate
Chalice	—	—	Rare	—	Rare
Pyxis	Common	Moderate	Rare	—	Rare
Pedestalled pyxis	Rare	—	—	—	—
Cylindrical pyxis	Rare	—	—	—	—
Multiple pyxis	Rare	—	—	—	—
Jug	Rare	Common	Rare	Rare	Rare
Juglet	—	Rare	—	—	—
3-spouted vessel	Rare	—	—	—	—
Sauceboat	—	Common	Common	Rare	Common
Triple sauceboat	—	Rare	—	—	—
Medium jar	—	—	Common	—	Common
Pedestalled jar	—	—	—	Moderate	—
Other jar	—	—	—	Moderate	—
Hedgehog	Rare	—	—	—	Rare

assemblage from each site is not entirely local, the majority is representative of material in the site's wider vicinity (here again Agia Irini forms an exception). Chalandriani's assemblage is dominated by pyxides and bowls on a pedestal base; painted sauceboats, supposedly a typical Keros-Syros type, are conspicuous by their absence. At Daskaleio-Kavos the most popular forms are jugs and sauceboats, with the similar finds from nearby Spedos underscoring this trend. Phylakopi's painted pottery comprises principally sauceboats and medium-sized jars with broad-streak decoration, the latter being the only example of painted decoration on vessels of coarser fabric. Agia Irini's local group is made up mainly of bowls and pedestal-based jars; the imports, many of which are thought to be Melian (Wilson 1999: 232), are mainly sauceboats and broad-streak decorated jars. The only forms common to all of the four sites are jugs, pyxides and a small class of pedestal-based cups, the first of these displaying considerable variety in terms of form, the second being a container probably for low-bulk/high-value substances, and the last probably being produced in Melos and widely dispersed across the Cyclades.

Table 9. *Painted motifs at the investigated Cycladic sites. Comments as for Table 8.*

Motif	Chalandriani-Kastri	Daskaleio-Kavos	Phylakopi	Agia Irini (local)	Agia Irini (imports)
Hatched triangle	Common	Present	Present	—	Present
Hatched band	—	Present	—	Present	Present
Cross-hatched triangle	Present	Common	—	—	Present
Cross-hatched band	—	Common	Present	Present	Present
Thick line cross-hatched band	Present	—	Present	—	Present
Cross-hatched zone, central dot	—	Present	—	—	—
Widely spaced cross-hatched net	Present	Present	Common	—	Present
Zone of parallel lines	—	Present	Common	—	Present
Linked crescent line	Common	Present	—	—	Present
Running linked circles	—	Present	—	—	Present
Horizontal chevron band	—	Present	Present	—	Present
Superimposed chevrons	Present	Present	Present	Present	Present
Oval chain	—	Present	—	—	Present
Oval chain and central dot	—	Present	—	—	Present
Bisected oval chain	Present	Present	—	—	—
Bisected lozenge chain	Present	Present	—	—	Present
Lozenge chain and central dot	Present	—	Present	—	Present
Pendent lozenge	—	—	Present	—	Present
Concentric lozenges	—	Present	—	—	Present
Bordered dotted line	Present	—	Present	—	Present
Fish	—	Present	—	—	—
Dog	—	Present	—	—	—
Star	—	—	Present	—	—
Chequerboard	—	—	Present	—	Present
Zig-zag line	—	Present	—	—	Present
Zig-zag zone	—	—	—	—	Present
Solid triangles	—	—	Present	Common	Present
Comb	—	—	—	—	Present

These distinctions are echoed by the popularity of different motifs at the main sites (table 9). There is plenty of overlap, owing partly to the presence of imports, but a preference is seen for crescents and hatched triangles at Chalandriani, tiers of densely cross-hatched triangles at Daskaleio-Kavos, plus Spedos (Papathanasopoulos 1961/2: plates A–C, 49), Akrotiri (Sotirakopoulou 1990: fig. 3a) and Amorgos (Marangou 1984: fig. 18), as well as rarer motifs like fish, dogs and circles, for cross-hatched netting and distinctive chequerboard and pendant lozenges at Phylakopi and among probable Melian imports at Agia Irini, and for solid triangles among the local Agia Irini vessels. Further regional styles of painted decoration must have existed, as is indicated by odd finds at several of the control sites that do not match with the geographically assigned varieties. Again, the area of the central Cyclades may still have much to reveal in this respect.

Within a decade or so (and perhaps sooner), it should be possible to undertake a far more sophisticated study of regional variation in EB II, drawing upon a wider range of material culture, expanding the sample of sites analysed, and filling in some of the ceramic blanks. But already there are solid indications among the decorated pottery that the concept of an overall Keros-Syros culture disguises regional trends that look very much like attempts at differentiation. The differences between Chalandriani and Daskaleio-Kavos, which are seen in all the above analyses, are particularly cogent in this respect, as material from these two sites played a key role in defining the Keros-Syros culture (Renfrew 1972: 528–33). Overall, there is a good match between stylistic groupings and the sub-clusters generated by PPAs 3–4, with the north-east, north-west, south-west and south-east repeatedly distinguished. In the south-east we have seen evidence to suggest that the area from southern Naxos to Thera can be treated as a single style zone, but contrary hints, too, that the most southerly islands could be distinct. As information grows, it will become feasible to investigate more thoroughly what material is widespread in a given sub-cluster, what defines tightly circumscribed micro-regions, and how the overlaps between distributions of different shapes are best explained. A better grasp should also be possible of the kinds of distances over which pottery moved. Already, the finds of north-east Cycladic stamped-and-incised pedestal-based jars as far afield as Attica and the south-east Cyclades, plus the probable Melian imports at Agia Irini, demonstrate that pottery movement was not restricted to local networks. To return to the question once posed by Vermeule (1964: 47–8), and cited in the Prologue to illustrate the differences between material culture on different islands, we may not yet have understood why the grave goods on Syros and Amorgos display the specific traits that they do, but we are starting to see why they may differ so much.

An introduction to one small world

So far this exploration of diversity in the islands' EB II material culture has worked, of necessity, by taking select types and looking at their distribution across the Cyclades. In one part of the Cyclades, however, the data are dense enough (or *almost* dense enough) to enable us to see patterns within a local islandscape. The area concerned is defined by southern Naxos, Amorgos, and the intervening Erimonisia (comprising Irakleia, Keros, Epano and Kato Kouphonisi, Schoinousa, and the two Antikeri), with Ios as a third, less-integrated, corner of a triangle surrounding the small islands at the region's centre. The extraordinary prominence during EB II of Daskaleio-Kavos, on Keros, ensures that this region will figure prominently again in the coming exploration of centrality.

Natural and cultural features confirm this area as a significant EB II islandscape (see front cover, figs. 13f and 76). Topographically, the massif of Mt Zas cuts southern

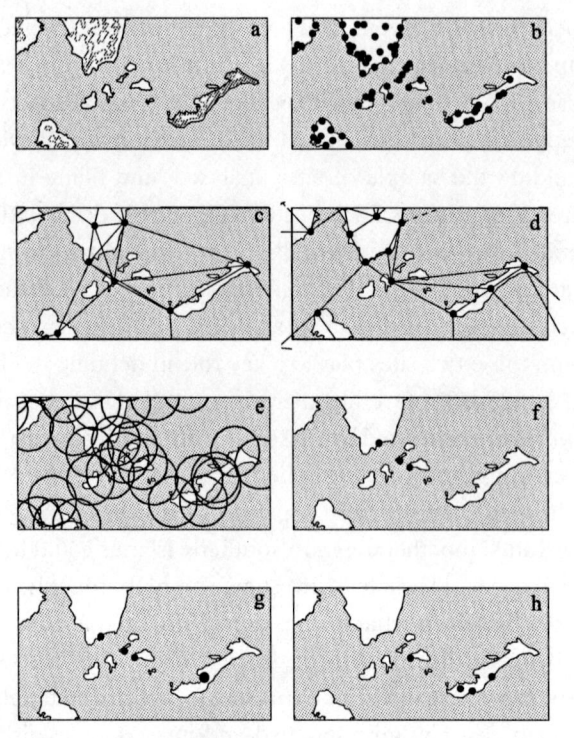

Fig. 62 The creation of a south-east Cycladic islandscape: (a) topography, (b) EBA sites, (c) PPA 3, (d) PPA 4, (e) 10 km travel range, (f) multiple-headed 'lamp' vessels, (g) pedestal-based collared jars with incised decoration, (h) jars in Amorgian schist fabric with herring-bone incisions.

Naxos off from the remainder of the island, turning it towards the south (Hadjianastasiou 1989: 206, 1993: 257). The environment of southern Naxos resembles the arid, marginal Erimonisia and rugged, razor-backed Amorgos, rather than the lusher conditions of central-northern Naxos. Water is scarce throughout this region and the barren ridges of southern Naxos and Amorgos are only thinly interspersed with small patches of arable, which resemble similar scraps in the Erimonisia. The eastern coast of Ios, framing this region's south-western border, has a similar topography and environment. There are signs that this region became an integrated cultural islandscape in the EBA, and that its coherence and prominence were contingent upon the prevailing conditions of dispersed settlement spread across large and small islands alike, and in particular on the densest phase of this settlement during EB II. This islandscape has never subsequently regained the status that it enjoyed in EB II. Earlier, too, during the Neolithic, it seems to have been a largely empty zone to be traversed or visited for fishing; a Saliagos culture settlement at Minoa on Amorgos is currently the only secure sign of occupation during the first phase of inhabitation in the Cyclades.

Fig. 62 explores this EBA islandscape, showing how thickly EBA settlement spread across it, and how closely islands were tied together by one-day canoe range and

EB II demographic networks. Interaction to sustain social storage links must have been an additional feature of crucial importance in this environmentally inimical part of the islands. It also shows the distribution of EB II pottery types as reflected by currently published material, mostly from grave contexts, plus data from the 1987 investigations at Daskaleio-Kavos. In the future, assemblages at Markiani on Amorgos, Panermos (a key site for defining material culture on southern Naxos) and more distant Skarkos on Ios will without doubt cast much additional light on the present patterns.

This approach to the material culture of the south-eastern corner of the Cyclades encourages a deconstruction of the so-called 'Amorgos group', a loosely defined range of material first identified by Renfrew (1972: 534–5). As is now becoming increasingly obvious, this construct conflates material ranging in date from the intermediate EB I–II Kampos group to the EBA–MBA transition. One component, the pedestal-based jar with incised diagonal decoration on the belly and collar (cf. fig. 61) is most at home in the Erimonisia, numerous fragments having been recovered at Daskaleio-Kavos. An example found at Xylokeratidi on Amorgos (Marangou 1984: fig. 17) is probably an import. These vessels are made in a distinctive sandy reddish-buff fabric that points to an origin in the Kouphonisia, which form a sandstone and marl pocket in the calcite- and schist-dominated geology of the area. Similar jars at Spedos differ slightly in their decoration (Papathanasopoulos 1961/2: plate 50 b–c). Although the Amorgos group is usually dated to the late EBA because some of its forms are found in association with late weaponry and pottery (Renfrew 1972: 534), these pedestal-based jars are clearly a local EB II type (Doumas 1988: 22). One EB II jar type that surely *does* derive from Amorgos is a variety of upright-necked jar in a schist fabric, decorated with incised herring-bone bands below the rim (Marangou 1984: fig. 12). Other components of the Amorgos group are nebulous; for example the group's purported presence on Melos and modern Antiparos (Doumas 1977: 25) is based on a jar with a sagging profile and a wide-mouthed jug, neither a sufficient criterion to determine the extent of a stylistic group, and several greenstone artefacts instead belong to an EB I–II transitional phenomenon in the south-east Cyclades (Getz-Gentle 1996: 185–90). The 'Amorgos group' should now be abandoned, to be eventually replaced by a more detailed analysis of overlapping patterns of production, style and exchange in the south-east Cyclades.

Two closing comments can be made. First, if even within this small area of the islands, where an unparalleled degree of at least semi-detailed resolution is attainable, microstylistic variation can be detected between Amorgos, the Kouphonisia and Spedos on Naxos, the enormous task and opportunity that awaits in the rest of the Cyclades can hardly be in doubt. The earlier prediction of some fifteen to twenty-five demographic networks by EB II is unlikely to tell us precisely how many localised style zones we should be looking for (given the likelihood of fuzzy overlaps and the certainty that other factors influenced the patterns of material culture distribution), but it may give us an heuristic idea about the orders of magnitude that can be anticipated.

Second, it is striking that PPA together with plots of canoe range and distributions of material culture traits combine to indicate that the geographical components of this small world were not all equally and directly connected to each other. On the contrary, the Erimonisia have emerged as the funnel for interaction between Naxos, Amorgos and, to a lesser extent, Ios. The implications of this observation for societies living on these little islands in the EBA, and especially EB II, form a central topic of analysis in the next chapter.

7

Which islands in the stream?

> Heureux qui comme Ulysse a fait un beau voyage
> *Les Regrets, Sonnet No. 31,* JOACHIM DU BELLAY

The previous chapter explored the local interaction networks that linked together or divided up the islandscapes of the EBA Cyclades. The main theme of this chapter and the one that follows is the role within such networks of a handful of relatively large, village-sized communities, that stand out from the majority of smaller settlements, and which date mainly if not entirely to EB II. These places established a prominent role in maritime trade and the production and conspicuous consumption, via burial, of prestige objects in pottery, marble, metal and other media. This prominence, it will be argued, made them major vortices of island life for the people living in and around them. From an island archaeological perspective, such places and the people in them pose a fresh set of questions about the relationship between, on the one hand, the physical framework of island configuration and, on the other hand, the manner in which islanders' activities constructed nodes of interaction and foci of social power out of the mosaics of land and sea that they inhabited. Equally informative in terms of island archaeology will be the role played by maritime cultures in fashioning the political economies and the forms of material expression that developed in and around these unusual communities.

The first tasks are to identify these places, examine their nature, document their activities, and consider any outlying claimants for inclusion in this category. With the empirical picture clarified, the proposal that most of these sites were located at the main communication hubs of EB II interaction networks is explored through the PPA models used in chapter 6, supplemented by other spatial scales of analysis as appropriate. Our exploration cannot, however, cease at this juncture, for to show why such sites were located where they were is not, of course, to provide an adequate overall explanation of their emergence and efflorescence. Chapter 8 accordingly examines their wider social, cultural and ideological context in the Cyclades, and the kinds of practices that created powerful communities in potentially advantaged places. Chapter 9 looks outwards, to the longer-range connections that such communities forged in and beyond the islands, and which were a decisive element in the dynamics of the so-called 'international spirit' of the EB II Aegean (Renfrew 1972: 451–5).[1]

---

[1] The interpretations that are offered in this chapter build upon and, where necessary, supersede earlier explorations in a similar vein (Broodbank 1989, 1993).

Owing to their high profile in the islands' archaeology, most of the places that will concern us have in fact already been encountered in previous contexts. *Daskaleio-Kavos* on Keros and *Chalandriani-Kastri* on Syros were introduced in chapter 2 as type sites of the Keros-Syros culture, and the looting of a large number of fragmentary figurines from a deposit at the former site illustrated the boomerang effect of modern appreciation of Cycladica. Daskaleio-Kavos featured again in chapter 3, this time because of its location on a deserted island that now lies far out of the stream, in contrast to its prominence in EB II – an observation suggesting that the ancient and modern islandscapes of the Cyclades differ profoundly. At the end of chapter 6, the small world of the Erimonisia, together with the adjacent areas of Naxos, Amorgos and Ios, at whose heart Daskaleio-Kavos is situated, had started to emerge as a vibrant EBA islandscape. Chalandriani-Kastri also made another appearance in chapter 6, as one of the indications that people on Syros manifestly did manage to overcome their predicted position of relative isolation within the north-eastern Cycladic networks. The other principal sites on which this analysis concentrates have hitherto figured more fleetingly: *Agia Irini* (Periods II–III) on Kea, *Grotta-Aplomata* on Naxos (Aplomata being the cemetery of the Grotta community during EB II), *Skarkos* on Ios, and a slightly earlier Kampos group cemetery, as yet without a well-documented accompanying settlement, at *Agrilia* on Epano Kouphonisi.

Identifying the major sites

Because of their differing degrees of preservation and exploration, the available information concerning each of these communities, as well as several other potential candidates, is only imperfectly comparable. Each therefore needs to be examined, in order to establish their basic similarities and isolate their individual features. Investigation of Daskaleio-Kavos is deferred until the salient elements of the other sites have been established. The reason for this separate treatment is that, alone among the large EB II sites, a radically different interpretation has been proposed for this site, to the effect that it functioned primarily as a cult centre, or pan-Cycladic sanctuary (Renfrew 1984b: 27–9, 1991: 50, 101, 186). This alternative view is best evaluated by drawing on the high-resolution information from recent intensive surface collection and limited excavations at the site, and comparing the picture that emerges with that for other sites, whose interpretation as large communities of the living is not disputed.

Chalandriani-Kastri

Let us start at Chalandriani-Kastri, in acknowledgement of its venerable position in the history of archaeological exploration in the Cyclades (fig. 63). The site is distributed over two imposing coastal ridges in north-east Syros, a rugged and agriculturally

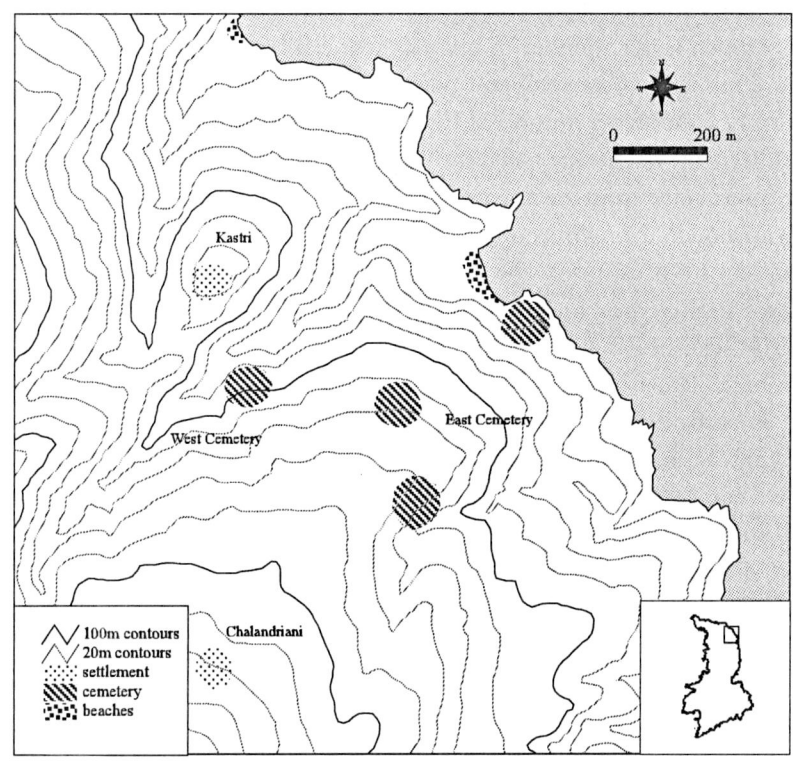

Fig. 63   Chalandriani-Kastri. *Above:* view looking north-east across the site to the outlines of Andros and Tenos. The Chalandriani settlement lies under and around the nearer buildings, with the cemetery on the lower slopes beyond; the fortified settlement of Kastri is situated on top of the precipitous hill in the middle distance. *Below:* plan of the same area. Photograph courtesy of Tristan Carter, plan after Hekman 1994: fig. 3 and Marthari 1998: fig. 1.

marginal sector of the island. The enormous Chalandriani cemetery comprises four discrete clusters of corbelled tombs, on the hill-top of Kastri is situated an excavated late EB II fortified settlement, and in the Chalandriani area an unexcavated earlier EB II settlement lies upslope of the cemetery. Chalandriani-Kastri therefore needs to be understood as an extensive site complex, with shifting foci of residence (and possibly also burial) during the earlier and later phases of EB II.

When Tsountas (1899: 77–115) and later Doumas (1977: 128–30) excavated in the cemetery, they estimated that it contained about 600 graves, with the graves in almost all cases containing a single burial. But a reanalysis of the earliest reports suggests that in the mid-nineteenth century the surviving total was nearer to a thousand graves (Hekman 1994: 48; Papadopoulos 1862: 225). Even at 600 graves, Chalandriani is well over three times the size of the Aphendika cemetery on Naxos, its closest documented rival. A previous attempt to assess the size of the burying community (Broodbank 1989: 324–5), using the total of 600 graves, a figure of twenty burials per family per century, and allowing for growth from a small founder group, but a taking a shorter duration for EB II than is advocated in this book, generated a peak population of about 100 people (see table 5). Given the likelihood of an originally much larger number of graves, balanced by a longer duration for EB II, this figure remains reasonable, and perhaps on the low side, if the community in fact flourished for only a portion of EB II, or if a significant proportion of the cemetery had been lost before the nineteenth century. In terms of the grave goods, analysis of the information from the grave groups recorded by Tsountas shows a marked degree of variation in the number and range of objects in each tomb (Doumas 1977: fig. 48; Renfrew 1972: 373–5). The concentrations of ceramic, marble and metal Keros-Syros culture types, including pottery frying pans, sauceboats, pedestal-based jars, marble figurines, marble vessels and metal tools and jewellery, are impressive.

The settlement that goes with the main period of inhumation at the cemetery has never been thoroughly excavated, but its location under the modern hamlet has recently been confirmed, and its extent estimated at probably over one hectare (Marthari 1998: 22). This confirmation is significant for two reasons. First, it indicates a village-level community to match the adjacent cemetery, and indeed a population of some 200–300+ people at the EBA population densities suggested in the last few chapters. Second, it effectively negates a recent argument by Hekman (1994: 52–3, 72) that the Chalandriani cemetery was the burial ground for a number of smaller, dispersed communities, and affirms the fact that Chalandriani represents an anomalous concentration of people. The settlement on the Kastri hill-top belongs to a late EB II occupation phase that overlaps with the latest burials in the cemetery. As Davis (1987: 33) has argued, Kastri was not a defensive refuge for a wider population, but rather the main residence for the whole community during the last phase of occupation in the area. The lack of stratigraphy suggests that this settlement was short-lived, which may in turn also indicate that the community was already past its demographic peak. Excavations by Tsountas (1899: 115–30) and Bossert (1967) revealed a settlement of about 0.5 ha, of which the upper half had totally eroded and the lower half was tightly packed with approximately ten small, irregular houses behind a double fortification wall, the inner line of which was covered by several small bastions. An EBA population density of 200–300 people per hectare generates a population for Kastri of about 100–150 people, a total similar to that derived if each of the ten surviving houses is taken to relate to a nuclear family of five, and the resultant total of fifty people is doubled to take account of the eroded part of the site. To summarise a necessarily involved analysis, an encouraging number of lines of enquiry converge on the conclusion that, although the Chalandriani-Kastri community surely fluctuated in size, an estimate of 100–300 people should bracket the true range.

Given the manifest importance of Chalandriani-Kastri, it is unfortunate that its material has not been studied to a degree that would allow the activities at the site to be explored in detail. Some crucial points can, however, be established. Kastri furnished excellent evidence for craft production in several media. This includes residues from silver and copper production, multiple-sided moulds for casting tools and weapons, a metal saw and other wood-working implements, obsidian tools, and a range of small grinders, much of this material being concentrated in a single room (Tsountas 1899: 124–6; Bossert 1967: 60–4). To the prestige goods in the cemetery can be added a silver diadem and several marble bowls at Kastri (Bossert 1967: fig. 5; Marthari 1998: 28; Tsountas 1899: plate 10). Furthermore, despite the lack of quantifiable data, there are ample indications that the site was widely connected in the Aegean. For example, Syros type stamped-and-incised pedestal-based jars, which are very common in the cemetery, are found as far afield as east Attica, Agia Irini and Daskaleio-Kavos (cf. fig. 61), a drinking hedgehog figurine (fig. 64), has comparanda at Agia Irini (Caskey 1972: 64), an unknown site on Naxos (Marangou 1990: 106, cat. no. 102), Manika in Euboia (Sampson 1988b: fig. 87; Sapouna-Sakellaraki 1991: plate 49, c–d) and Cheliotomylos in Corinthia (Wiencke 1986: 86, fn. 43), and an unusual three-spouted vessel from the cemetery (Zervos 1957: plates 185–6) is best paralleled at Kolonna on Aegina (Walter and Felten 1981: fig. 92). To this can be added the presence of tin-bronze alloys at Kastri (see chapter 9) and the suggestion from lead isotope analysis that some metal objects at Kastri were manufactured from non-Aegean copper sources (Stos-Gale et al. 1984).

One final and compelling piece of evidence underlines the special nature of the community at Chalandriani-Kastri, and its close connection with maritime activity. This is the fact that the entire properly provenanced corpus of Cycladic images of longboats, large canoes identified in chapter 3 as high-status seacraft used for warfare, raiding and perhaps prestigious voyaging, is made up of images incised on the ceramic frying pans buried in the Chalandriani cemetery (Broodbank 1989: 331–2). When it is considered that these labour-intensive craft represent not only a high-status activity, but also a unit of social mobilisation, the association of the images with one of the

Fig. 64 Hedgehog figurine from the Chalandriani cemetery. Courtesy of the National Archaeological Museum, Athens.

handful of larger settlements able to generate crews of at least twenty-five people is decidedly striking. The role of longboats in the maritime ideologies and strategies of EB II communities in the Cyclades receives fuller attention in chapter 8. For the moment, the images furnish additional evidence for a substantial community with a strong maritime orientation, and also provide potential insights into the means by which the members of one community on Syros were able, through an investment in large, fast canoes, to participate in the interaction networks of the north-east Cyclades on terms more advantageous than their relatively remote position in such networks would seem to predict. This convergence of locational, demographic and iconographic data transcends coincidence, and is a startling example of the distinctively insular sense that can be discerned in the fragments of data that make up the archaeological record of the early Cyclades.

Agia Irini

The record of preservation, exploration and data analysis at Agia Irini is different (fig. 65). The settlement is located on a small, low promontory jutting out into the deep,

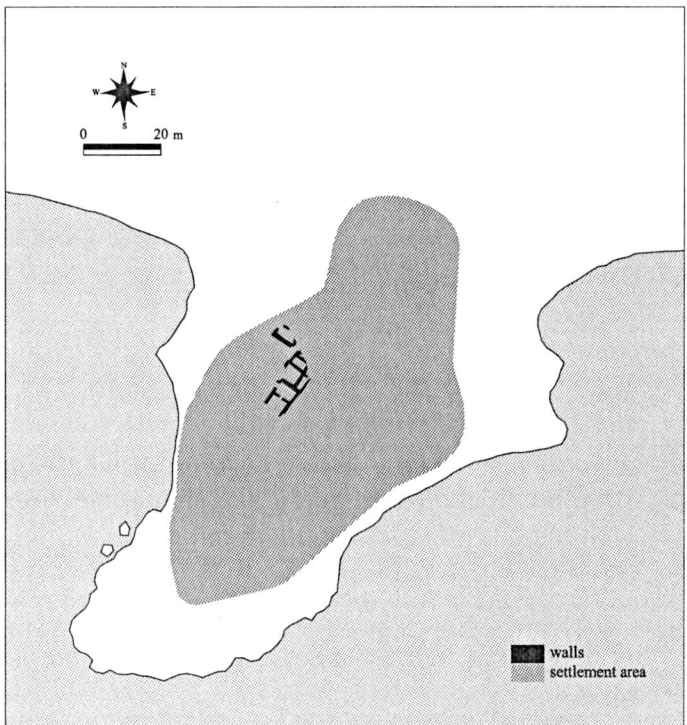

Fig. 65 Agia Irini. *Above:* view of the site, among the trees on the small peninsula jutting out into the bay of Agios Nikolaos. *Below:* plan of the site. Plan after original by Todd Whitelaw.

sheltered bay of Agios Nikolaos in north-west Kea, and lies close to good arable. Spatially and culturally, the site is peripheral to the Cyclades, being oriented instead towards east Attica (Wilson 1987, 1999: 228, 231). Agia Irini II–III, the settlements that concern us, overlie bedrock deposits of rather earlier date (Agia Irini I) and are followed by a hiatus in occupation before the first MBA settlement (Agia Irini IV). Agia Irini II belongs to the first half of EB II and Agia Irini III to late EB II, with architectural modifications and changes in the pottery indicating extended occupation, probably of several centuries' duration (Wilson and Eliot 1984). Traces of settlement have been found over most of the promontory, comprising an area of slightly less than one hectare (Davis 1984a: 20 fn. 17; Schofield 1998: 119). This area was densely occupied, to judge from repeated rebuildings, best witnessed in House D/E, a large structure that may have had two stories at some point in its life (Wilson and Eliot 1984: 83–5). Further evidence for numerous houses comes from the identification of fragments of at least sixty large 'key-hole' hearths, each of which seems to have been the focus of one house per building phase (Wilson 1999: 49; Wilson and Eliot 1984: fig. 4).

Taking an EBA population density range of 200–300 people per hectare, there is little doubt that Agia Irini was a substantial village, with a population probably in the order of 150–300 people.[2] An EB II cemetery has not been located (if it ever existed), but the forty-two EBA figurine fragments found in various stratigraphic contexts at the site are an eloquent index of the amount of prestige goods that the community must have possessed (Caskey 1971b, 1974; Davis 1984a). Moreover, it is established that about 30 per cent of the Period II pottery and 25 per cent of the Period III pottery was imported from Attica, Euboia, Melos, Siphnos, Syros and other locations that cannot yet be identified (Wilson 1987, 1999: 91, 231–9). Metallurgical finds are abundant, and the analyses indicate an exceptionally high degree of skill in the cupellation of lead to obtain silver (Gale *et al.* 1984: 406). Remains of a probable EBA pottery kiln were also discovered (Caskey 1971a: 372).

Grotta-Aplomata

Another important community is likely to have flourished at Grotta-Aplomata (fig. 66). This cannot be conclusively proven, owing to the same mixture of coastal erosion,

---

[2] Davis (1984b: 18) has proposed a much higher range of about 780–1250 people for the comparably sized MBA and early LBA settlements at Agia Irini, based on Wagstaff and Cherry's estimate for contemporary Phylakopi (Wagstaff and Cherry 1982b: 139–40). He considers this a heuristic maximum for EBA Agia Irini II–III. The inflated nature of the latter estimate is discussed in chapter 10. In the present context, it can be noted that the figures thereby generated for EBA Agia Irini imply occupation densities radically higher than those that are now corroborated by available analyses of houses and households in the EBA Aegean (cf. Whitelaw 1983: 332–3), and by the consistency that was attested above at Kastri between population estimates derived from the number of houses and from the settlement area. Schofield (1998: 119) has recently suggested about 500 people as a more plausible upper limit for the population of Agia Irini during the Bronze Age.

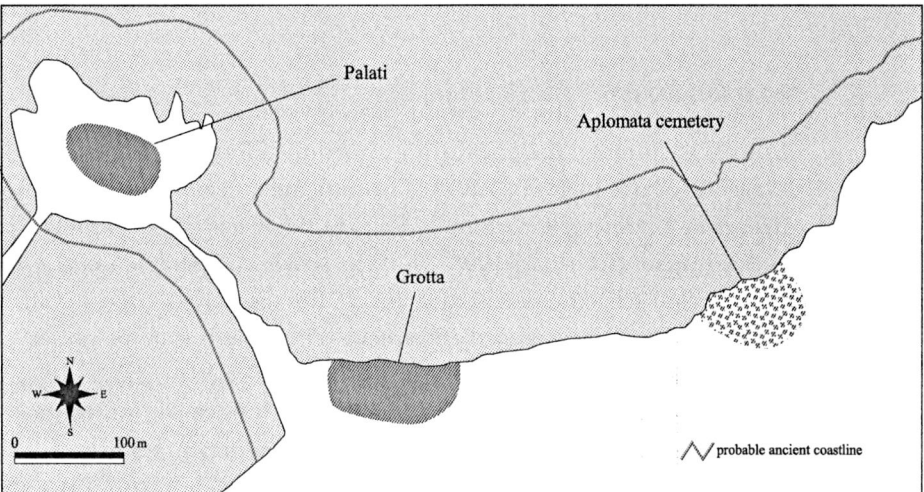

Fig. 66 Grotta-Aplomata. *Above:* view from Aplomata of the coast at Grotta and Palati islet (then a peninsula and now accessed by a causeway). *Below:* plan showing the approximate extent of the ancient shoreline and of the main occupation and burial areas. Plan after Hadjianastasiou 1989: fig. 1.

later disturbance and modern building that hampers excavation of the Neolithic settlement at Grotta. But the settlement was certainly extensive (Hadjianastasiou 1989: 209), and the only open excavation revealed three well-built houses separated by a street (Kontoleon 1949: 112). Aplomata cemetery has the highest density of marble objects per grave in the Cyclades, with forty-two figurines and sixty stone vessels discovered in twenty-seven graves (Getz-Preziosi 1982: 41), including seven rare seated figurines and complex marble vessels such as spool pyxides. The cemetery also contained several silver and lead objects, including a seal, a ladle and diverse jewellery (Kontoleon 1970: plate 195, 1972: plate 143; Marangou 1990: cat. nos. 40, 41). It is unlikely that a small cemetery would contain so many exceptionally material-rich graves and, as Aplomata has suffered much subsequent disturbance, it is probable that the known graves represent a small residue of a substantially larger burial ground. Until the settlement and cemetery material are fully published it remains impossible to assess the evidence for trade in detail, although Renfrew (1972: 155) has identified a mainland frying pan, the only example known in the Cyclades to date. For similar reasons, the case for craft production is also tentative, but Aplomata has produced the longest obsidian blade known in the Aegean, at 21 cm a not inconsiderable knapping achievement (Carter 1998: table 4.4), and the lavish use of lead for a variety of purposes may also hint at local cupellation for silver.

Skarkos and other EB II candidates

Skarkos is currently under excavation, and therefore only preliminary information is available (Marthari 1990, 1997). The settlement occupies a low hill, set inland from the sea in a fertile valley running down to the major bay of northern Ios. At slightly over a hectare (Marthari 1997: 363), its size is comparable to Agia Irini and to the unexcavated Chalandriani settlement. It was densely occupied, with large, regular orthogonal houses separated by streets. The superb state of preservation provides clear evidence for upper storeys. At densities equivalent to those cited above, Skarkos' population should have numbered about 200–300 people. At the moment, there are no data to suggest an investment in prestige production, trade and consumption at a level equivalent to the evidence from the other communities set out above, although it should be noted that no cemetery at Starkos has yet been investigated. Skarkos also differs from Chalandriani-Kastri, Agia Irini and Grotta-Aplomata in being set back from the coast. Ongoing excavations are certain to amplify the picture, but even with the currently available information there are grounds for arguing that Skarkos may represent the first, and therefore a particularly intriguing, example of another variety of village-level community, and may have owed its existence to somewhat different combinations of social and locational circumstances.

Although claims of substantial size have been made for a number of other EB II sites, notably Phylakopi on Melos, Paroikia on Greater Paros and Akrotiri on Thera

(Davis 1987: 20–1; Sotirakopoulou 1990: 41), these cannot be effectively confirmed or denied from the investigations undertaken so far. Renfrew (1982a: 36–7) considers that Phylakopi in fact only became distinct from other Melian communities in terms of size and status at the very end of the EBA (see chapter 10), although the soundings below the later Bronze Age town have been so limited in extent that no firm conclusion can at present be drawn. In the case of Akrotiri, most early sherds come from LBA building debris, and the size of the settlement during the EBA cannot therefore be gauged – although other indices, such as the large number of EBA figurines accumulated at the site, could suggest an important role (Sotirakopoulou 1998). This is not to deny that other large Cycladic EB II communities may have existed, but for the present the most viable strategy is to document the definite examples, and deploy models in an interrogative manner to assess the likelihood that there were other such communities elsewhere in the islands.

Did the large EB II settlements have precursors?

To date, only one earlier site displays several of the characteristics outlined above, and even these in a less pronounced form. This site is the Agrilia cemetery on the arid island of Epano Kouphonisi, one of the smallest members of the Erimonisia (Zapheiropoulou 1983, 1984). The tombs are cut into the soft local rock. The grave goods date to the EB I–II transition, and comprise the largest range of Kampos group material known in the Cyclades (including early frying pans, pedestalled bowls, bottles, and a great variety of amphiconical and truncated-conical pyxides). Metal finds include the earliest long, mid-ribbed daggers known in the islands. Seventy-two graves were excavated after at least a further twenty had been robbed. The original size of the cemetery may sadly never be ascertained, for there are strong rumours of extensive prior robbing in the same area. The minimum figure of ninety-two graves in itself places this cemetery fairly high up the range for the Cyclades. But unlike the case for other large cemeteries, for which a long usage can be demonstrated, the Kampos group horizon was short, and the burials should therefore have been made over a relatively short period of at most a century or two, and possibly far less. This may imply a relatively large living community, especially if much of the cemetery has been lost to looting. Unfortunately, there is no available information about the associated settlement, but other features mark out this community as exceptional. Several objects deposited in the Agrilia cemetery find parallels as far afield as Poliochni on Lemnos in the north-east Aegean (Doumas and La Rosa 1997; Zapheiropoulou 1984), and (as described in chapter 9) at the Agia Photia cemetery, Pyrgos and Kiparissi burial caves and Poros settlement on the north coast of Crete (Day *et al.* 1998; Warren 1984: 58–60). The unusual rock-cut grave architecture at Agrilia, with pits in front of the burial chamber, is also paralleled at Agia Photia. In summary, this cemetery, situated on one of the tiniest of the Cyclades, displays precocious signs of long-range connections. Its proximity to the slightly later, and still more prominent, EB II site of Daskaleio-Kavos on neighbouring Keros is therefore decidedly thought-provoking.

There is at present no other sign in the Cyclades of major sites prior to EB II. It might therefore be suggested that the conditions that favoured their emergence from the period of the EB I–II transition onwards were absent in EB I. This is a point of some importance, for it will enable us to increase the analytical resolution on how conditions altered after EB I to create the arenas in which such communities were able to emerge. It is nonetheless interesting to note that although no large Grotta-Pelos communities are known to date, this phase did witness a small number of spectacular acts of conspicuous consumption in the funerary sphere. This is attested by graves that are abnormally rich in prestige material, mainly figurines and marble vessels. The best examples are Pyrgos grave 103, Krassades grave 117, Zoumbaria grave 137, Livadi grave 129 and Plastiras grave 9, all on modern Paros, Antiparos and Despotikon (the fragments of Greater Paros), with less marked cases in the Panagia, Drios and Glypha cemeteries on the same island(s), and at Akrotiri on Naxos (Doumas 1977: figs. 39, 40, 44–7). Recent publication of the EBA figurines from Akrotiri on Thera has revealed another large concentration of some twenty-seven figurines of diverse Grotta-Pelos culture types, but as all these derive from later Bronze Age levels, their original deposition contexts cannot be ascertained (Sotirakopoulou 1998). The high concentration seen in the richest graves on Greater Paros is brought out by the fact that Pyrgos grave 103, Krassades grave 117 and Livadi grave 129 between them held thirty out of the forty-eight figurines found by Tsountas in 233 unplundered graves on modern Paros, Antiparos and Despotikon (Getz-Preziosi 1987a: 27). The figurine counts for each of the first two graves (fourteen and thirteen figurines respectively) rival the richest graves in the EB II Aplomata cemetery.

Three features of this early phenomenon are noteworthy. One is the focus of such behaviour on Greater Paros, and particularly its south-western part, including the now-remote island of Despotikon. An important role for this region might be inferred also from the traces of metal-working at the sites of Cheiromylos and Avyssos (Renfrew 1967: 4; Tsountas 1898: 176) and the find of a possible Cretan EBA foot amulet on Despotikon (Davis 1987: 42 fn. 62). This contrasts remarkably with the low funerary profile on Greater Paros in EB II, a fact that calls for explanation. Another interesting feature is that, within the context of their individual cemeteries, each of these deposition acts is an isolated phenomenon, in contrast to the number of material-rich graves in the Chalandriani and Aplomata cemeteries, and the similar pattern that will be inferred below at Daskaleio-Kavos. Put another way, there was sufficient spatial drift in the location of these acts to prevent any one community's cemetery from building up a cumulative profile. A final intriguing point is that this first horizon of rich burials in the southern Cyclades coincides with the cessation of prestige material accumulation at the cave of Zas.

Interpreting Daskaleio-Kavos: a comparative perspective

The site's location and the evidence for a settlement

Daskaleio-Kavos lies at the barren western extremity of the small and environmentally marginal island of Keros, at a location devoid of evidence for earlier or later occupation (fig. 67). Like Chalandriani-Kastri, it comprises several foci, the major division being between the Kavos area, a low coastal shelf on Keros itself, and the little conical islet of Daskaleio opposite, which could then have been joined to Kavos by a slender isthmus. Following investigations during the 1960s, in the aftermath of a major looting episode (Doumas 1964; Fitton 1984: 33–5, 72–4; Renfrew 1972: 178, 531–2; Zapheiropoulou 1967, 1968a, 1968b, 1975), new fieldwork in 1987 undertook intensive surface collection and limited excavation in the Kavos area (*Annual Report 1986–7*: 32–4; Doumas *et al.* nd; Whitelaw nd). The data derived from this latest fieldwork, when combined with the information available concerning material recovered in the 1960s, allow a substantially more secure interpretation of the site to be offered than has hitherto been the case (Broodbank 2000 for a fuller discussion of the ceramic data).[3]

In the central-southern part of Kavos are the remains of an extensive settlement. Doumas (1964: 410) excavated a house here, and several walls and large amounts of coarse pottery extend over an area of about 0.5 ha (Whitelaw nd). On the eastern slope of Daskaleio islet are further remnants of settlement. Here, Doumas excavated another house and identified the line of a thick wall, probably a fortification; debris from collapsed houses and their exposed domestic deposits is dense, but as the recent investigations did not extend to the islet any detailed evidence is lacking. It remains unclear whether these settlement areas were synchronously occupied. Doumas (1972: 163, 170) suggested that the settlement on Daskaleio might date to later EB II, whilst at Kavos sherds of painted sauceboats with precise parallels at EM IIA Knossos and Agia Irini II (Wilson 1985: 358–9, plate 58; Wilson 1999: 78–84, pls. 20–21, 68–9) suggest that activity at the site as a whole had begun earlier in EB II. It is therefore possible that a shift in the focus of settlement occurred at Daskaleio-Kavos during EB II, reminiscent of that at Chalandriani-Kastri, with the Kavos settlement equivalent to Chalandriani settlement, and Daskaleio, like Kastri, reflecting a late EB II relocation to a defendable position.

---

[3] I take this opportunity once again to thank warmly the directors of the 1987 project, Christos Doumas, Lila Marangou and Colin Renfrew, as well as Todd Whitelaw (who designed and supervised the gridded surface collection) and Photeini Zapheiropoulou (then Ephor of Prehistoric and Classical Antiquities for the Cyclades), for inviting me to study the pottery recovered during their investigations. The conclusions concerning the site's interpretation that are presented here have been developed in the course of discussions and museum analysis. They do not necessarily represent the views and opinions of the project members as a whole.

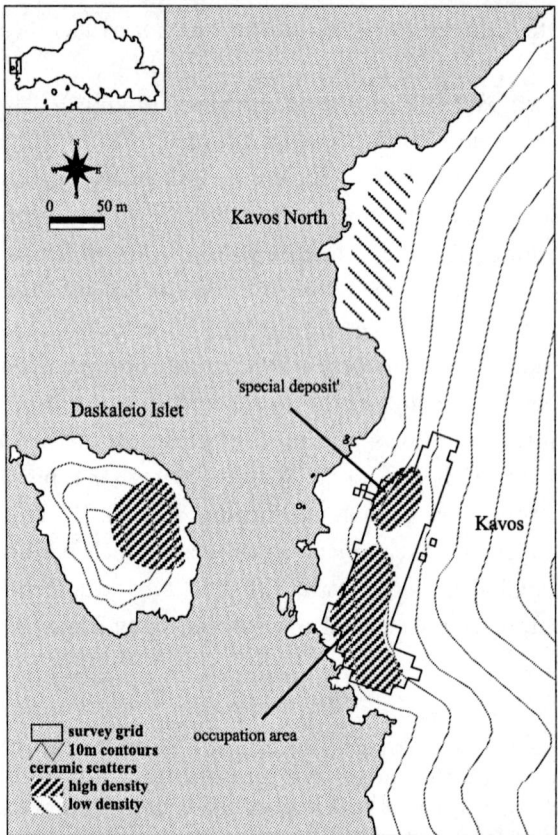

Fig. 67 Daskaleio-Kavos and Kavos North. *Above:* Kavos, Kavos North and Daskaleio islet seen from the sea. *Below:* plan of the same area. Photograph and original plan courtesy of Todd Whitelaw.

The population of Daskaleio-Kavos can only be crudely estimated. The eastern slope of Daskaleio is similar in size to the Kastri settlement, so if these two ostensibly similar settlements were occupied at similar densities, the number of people living on Daskaleio should have been around 100–150 people. At the EBA population densities used so far, the settlement area at Kavos should represent a community of similar size. Depending on the degree of simultaneous occupation in these two areas, the population of the entire site could therefore be anything between 100 and 300 people. This exceeds by a large margin the EBA population of eight to forty-five people for Keros as a whole that was projected on the basis of overall Cycladic EBA population levels (see table 1), as well as the population in the early part of the twentieth century AD, when a few families farmed the only significant patch of arable, at Gerani in north-west Keros. Daskaleio-Kavos therefore represents a highly anomalous build-up of population in the early Cyclades. The anomaly is increased by the absence of arable in the site's immediate vicinity. This would suggest that the community either farmed Gerani (about 40 minutes walk distant), commuted by canoe to fields on the nearest neighbouring islands of the Erimonisia, or traded for at least some of its food supply with communities on other islands.

The case for interpretation of the Kavos special deposit as a cemetery

Remarkable as this settlement is in the context of the EBA Cyclades, Daskaleio-Kavos' reputation has to date been based instead on the material found by illicit and sanctioned excavations of a 'special deposit' just to the north of the Kavos settlement (fig. 8). It is impossible to reconstruct the appearance of this area prior to its looting, because the robbers' activities were so systematic that the entire area now comprises a churned-over matrix of soil, stones and archaeological material. The most notorious body of material that is said to be associated with this deposit is the so-called 'Keros hoard' (fig. 68), a collection of approximately 350 EB II figurine fragments, mainly of folded-arm type, that surfaced on the antiquities market in the 1960s (Getz-Preziosi 1982). In addition, the well-known harpist and flute-player figurines in the National Museum in Athens, which are rumoured to have been found on Keros at the end of the nineteenth century, are sometimes thought to have come from this deposit. Suggestions have also been made that Daskaleio-Kavos was the find-spot of several of the rare large folded-arm figurines (upwards of about 60 cm) that are without a secure provenance (Renfrew 1984b: 29). Some of these associations may be correct, but now only joins with the material legally excavated from the deposit could vindicate them, and the danger of including fakes and contaminating the provenance of individual pieces through error, or wilful association of floating material with a famous site, is obvious (Gill and Chippindale 1993: 621–2).

Fortunately, the archaeological fieldwork in the 1960s amply documented the range and quantity of material in the special deposit (Doumas 1964; Fitton 1984: 72, 74;

Fig. 68 Part of the so-called 'Keros hoard' of looted figurines, now dispersed. Courtesy of the Badisches Landesmuseum.

Getz-Gentle 1996: 101; Renfrew 1972: 531–2; Zapheiropoulou 1968a, 1968b, 1975). This phase of fieldwork recovered some 300 figurine fragments (mainly folded-arm types, but also several bases for more complex standing figurines), and one intact folded-arm figurine. Well over a thousand fragments of marble vessels were found (fig. 69), mainly from shallow bowls, several as much as 50 cm in diameter, as well as elaborate shapes, including large plates with rows of carved birds known as 'dove bowls', pyxides, frying pans, cups and pedestal-based jars. Fragments of intricate vessels in chlorite schist with spiral decoration were also recovered. Other categories of material include obsidian and very large quantities of pottery sherds, including painted, stamped-and-incised, incised and *urfirnis* (dark iridescent slipped) vessels in a range of shapes. Pieces of human bone and one possible grave with a cranium were reported (Zapheiropoulou 1968a: 381). The more recent field-work has fully confirmed these categories of finds (with the exception of the possible grave), and added several others in metal, stone and pottery (Doumas *et al.* nd; Whitelaw nd; Broodbank 2000).

The first archaeologists to visit and excavate this deposit after its devastation by looting reported it as the remains of an exceptionally large, material-rich cemetery perhaps associated with a wealthy trading community (Doumas 1972: 163). But, as alluded to earlier, there has since been speculation that Daskaleio-Kavos was instead a

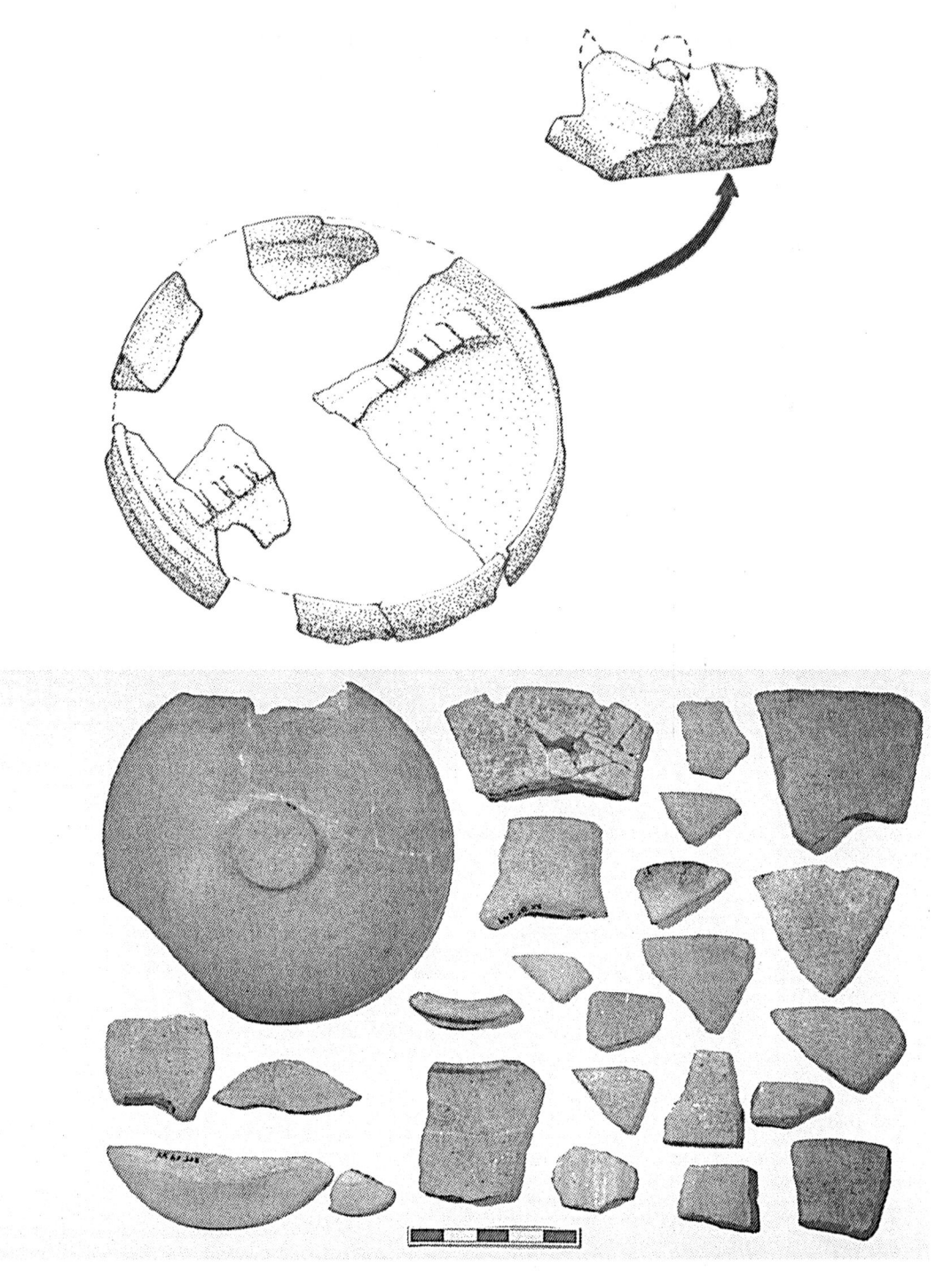

Fig. 69 Marble vessels from sanctioned archaeological work at Daskaleio-Kavos. *Above:* fragments of a large dove bowl from the 1960s excavations. *Below:* vessel fragments, largely from bowls, found in the 1987 investigations. After Zapheiropoulou 1968b: figs. 5–6, and courtesy of Todd Whitelaw, respectively.

pan-Cycladic sanctuary, with the special deposit forming the focus of ritual deposition (Renfrew 1984b: 27–9, 1991: 50, 101, 186). The reasons given in support of this idea rest both on the argument that Keros is so small and remote that nothing other than a sacred role can suffice to explain its huge accumulation of material (Barber 1987: 132; Renfrew 1984b: 28), and on observations about specific features of the special deposit, namely (1) the extreme paucity of identifiable graves, (2) the sheer quantity of prestige material, (3) the unusual nature of certain marble forms (e.g. the dove bowls and large figurines, the latter identified, in a further step, as cult idols) and (4) the fact that most of the marble objects had been smashed in antiquity, presumably during EBA activities at the site, which is not normal practice in Cycladic cemeteries. It might be noted that no structural, spatial or contextual data actually lend any positive support to the sanctuary hypothesis, which emerges largely in claimed default of other explanations. In fact, the arguments against a cemetery interpretation can all be countered.

Regarding the purported remoteness of Keros, we need to recall that the modern patterns of settlement and communication in the Cyclades are misleading templates for understanding the early Cycladic past. In point of fact, several of the sites discussed already in this chapter are located in similar areas, for example Agrilia on Keros' even smaller neighbour Epano Kouphonisi, the Grotta-Pelos cemeteries with material-rich graves on Despotikon and Antiparos, then the extremities of Greater Paros, and indeed Chalandriani-Kastri in terms of its agriculturally marginal location in northern Syros. Moreover, PPA modelling in chapter 6 suggested that the Erimonisia and its surrounding region in fact comprised a coherent interaction zone; and, as will be seen shortly, there are compelling reasons to think that Daskaleio-Kavos, and perhaps earlier Agrilia, lay at the heart of its local maritime network. Lastly, the line of reasoning that identifies Daskaleio-Kavos as a sanctuary because its location is otherwise inexplicable takes no account of the awkward fact that, whatever the nature of the special deposit, the site undoubtedly did also boast one of the largest settlements in the EBA Cyclades. With solid evidence for a large living community at the site, the time has surely come to replace hypotheses that address the problem of the special deposit in isolation with ones that take the overall range of available information about Daskaleio-Kavos into account.

Starting with our knowledge of a large settlement, the problem of the special deposit can in fact be turned on its head. For given the probable size and longevity of the Daskaleio-Kavos community, and the fact that burial in a cemetery adjacent to the settlement is a widely recognised southern Cycladic practice in the EBA, we should in fact anticipate an exceptionally large cemetery close to this settlement. A community of some 100–300 people living at the site for several centuries implies thousands of deaths, indeed more bodies for disposal than even the numbers known at Chalandriani. If the special deposit is not that cemetery, *where is it?* This perspective also casts doubt on Doumas' idea (1990: 95) that the deposit was a burial ground for special individuals from all over the Cyclades. Whilst an intriguing scenario, the number of local dead who need to be accounted for argues no need to import more corpses into our explanations.

The four specific features of the special deposit that are claimed to support the non-funerary interpretation are also more equivocal than they initially seem. Concerning the paucity of graves, local geology does not furnish the schist slabs from which typical Cycladic cist tombs were made (Whitelaw pers. comm.). The hard bedrock equally militates against rock-cut tombs, as are found at Agrilia on the sandstone Kouphonisia (Zapheiropoulou 1983) and later on volcanic Melos (Doumas 1977: 49). Shallow earth-cut pits perhaps with a superstructure of stones are in fact the only option at Daskaleio-Kavos, and this is what Zapheiropoulou's report of the possible tomb that she found seems to describe (1968a: 381). The objection that more graves should have been found does not take account of the deposit's thorough devastation by looters prior to the arrival of the archaeologists, nor of the restricted space available for burial, for Kavos is hemmed by steep soil-barren slopes, gullies and sea on all sides, preventing spatial extension of the burial ground similar to that seen, for example, at Chalandriani. This restriction would have necessitated frequent disturbance of earlier burials as the number and rate of interments grew, and as the community expanded beyond the expectations of the first people to inhabit the site and define the cemetery area. The Kavos cemetery is likely to have evolved into a complex mass of pits and structures built over and into each other, rather than the scatter of discrete graves that is normally encountered, and funerary practices specific to the site could easily have developed in response to unusual conditions. The human bone in the deposit must not be forgotten; whilst it does not necessarily clinch the case for funerary activity, its presence in some quantity, despite likely EBA disturbance, millennia of exposure to the soil and sea-winds, plus recent robbing, is not unsuggestive.

Turning to the material in the deposit, and particularly the fragments of figurines and marble vessels that have occasioned such astonishment, there is no doubt that this does represent the largest accumulation known in the Cyclades. Yet if we think in terms of approximate numbers of original objects, as opposed to fragments, the levels are not beyond those to be expected of a very large cemetery with a number of wealthy graves. The small size of most figurine fragments indicates that even the maximum fragment count of 650 pieces, obtained by combining the legitimately excavated material and the 'Keros hoard', should represent only about 100–200 figurines. Similarly, the total of over a thousand marble vessel fragments should reduce to a vessel total in the low hundreds. Both these figures are much lower than the number of deaths suggested by the size of the community. There should, in other words, have been many more material-poor than material-rich burials at Kavos. Moreover, in the context of a large number of inferred interments, these figures are if anything rather less remarkable than the forty-two figurines and sixty stone vessels documented from the mere twenty-seven excavated tombs at Aplomata (Getz-Preziosi 1982: 41). A comparison with Chalandriani, where figurines and vessels are admittedly rarer

(Getz-Preziosi 1982: 41) must be moderated by the fact that Keros lies in the major marble-working area of the Cyclades, whilst Syros is located on its edge.

The specific nature of the material does not provide any real evidence against the funerary hypothesis either. Dove bowls and outsized figurines (if some of the latter do derive from Daskaleio-Kavos, and this is far from clear) have not been found in *any* other contexts, funerary or other, and for the vast majority of the commoner marble and pottery forms found at Daskaleio-Kavos there are solid comparanda in the cemeteries. All that is necessarily implied by the unusual shapes is that the special deposit was a very unusual cemetery, which can be deduced already from the size of the settlement and the topography of the site. There is, furthermore, no solid reason to presume that the largest figurines were cult idols, not least as they exhibit the same folded-arm posture as the smaller figurines, suggesting that they are actually impressive scaled-up versions of standard types, rather than objects with a different meaning. Finally, the smashing of marble objects is not in itself evidence against the cemetery explanation. It indicates an unusual depositional or post-depositional ritual (perfectly plausible in an unusual cemetery), which was in fact not universal local practice, given the find of one intact figurine (Zapheiropoulou 1968b: fig. 1), possibly as well as the intact harpist and flute-player figurines often associated with Keros. Much of this breakage could have been associated with the treatment of objects from earlier graves as these were disturbed by later interments. An alternative explanation of their destruction as part of a strategy geared towards conspicuous display and value enhancement at the site is, moreover, proposed in chapter 8.

In summary, the sanctuary hypothesis is supported by no compelling evidence, the case against a cemetery is insubstantial, and there is good circumstantial evidence to suggest that the devastated deposit represents the remains of the burial ground of a large village community living at the site, albeit a burial ground in which unusual actions took place. Our task therefore becomes to explain why such features developed within the context of burial, with some answers relating to the spatial circumscription dictated by local geology and topography, but others, notably concerning the diversity and condition of material, requiring specific cultural explanations. In the final assessment, Daskaleio-Kavos represents a uniquely impressive combination and accentuation of features that are attested at other major sites. Its location and community size are not without parallels among the major sites of the EBA Cyclades, and its special deposit can be understood as an extreme yet recognisable version of funerary phenomena seen at Chalandriani (in terms of cemetery size) and Aplomata (in terms of the quantity of prestige objects). With these points now established, further parallels with other major sites can be drawn in terms of skilled production, maritime trade and the conspicuous deposition and consumption of prestige goods. The present analysis focuses on the evidence for craft production and trade, as the special deposit (however interpreted) is a fairly self-evident indication of deposition and consumption on a grand scale.

Fig. 70   Kavos North, showing the low exposed rock-shelf in the foreground.

Evidence for craft production and maritime trade

The case for craft production at Daskaleio-Kavos is strong, despite the site's condition and the relatively small amount of excavation in settlement areas. Pieces of metallurgical debris are found over most of the Kavos area but occur in greater density, accompanied by a thin scatter of obsidian and pottery, at an adjacent location known as Kavos North, a windswept shelf of land that provides ideal conditions for metalworking (fig. 70). Several pieces of slag contain copper prills, although silver-working is not attested. The obsidian industry documents the complete reduction sequence from raw nodules to tools (Whitelaw pers. comm.), and pieces of Naxian emery are known from the site. The discovery of emery, an abrasive, is significant for the debate as to whether some of the marble objects in the special deposit were locally manufactured. Zapheiropoulou (1980: 540) has suggested that Daskaleio-Kavos specialised in marble-working, and a few unfinished marble bowls confirm some local manufacture (Getz-Preziosi 1987a: 151, fn. 109). Objections to this hypothesis have been put forward by Renfrew (1984b: 28) on the grounds that there are no incomplete pieces (published statements are in fact ambiguous) and also Getz-Preziosi (1987a: 140, Getz-Gentle 1996: 173), on the 'common-sensical' grounds that because the best marbles occur on Naxos, the marble objects should also have been manufactured there, as the export of products in Naxian marble from Keros to Naxos would be a case of coals-to-Newcastle.

There is, in fact, good reason to accept the possibility of substantial production of marble objects by people at Daskaleio-Kavos, despite Keros' lack of good marble. First, and as Getz-Gentle herself acknowledges, the weight of raw marble blocks and the danger of hidden faults (only revealed by working) make it likely that objects were roughed out at the marble sources rather than at the settlements (Getz-Gentle 1996: 19). This implies that large quantities of marble chips should not be expected at Daskaleio-Kavos, and therefore that the hypothesis of on-site production cannot be falsified by their absence. The later stages of production involve abrasion (Oustinoff 1984), which requires emery (documented at the site) and generates a fine marble powder that might be at best detectable only by analysis of soil micromorphology. The coals-to-Newcastle objection also has several flaws. It assumes that the purpose of making objects was not to deploy them at Daskaleio-Kavos but to 'sell' them back to Naxos, a quite groundless imposition that neatly reflects the modern concept of these figurines as art objects to be marketed. It is ironic, given that Getz-Preziosi's scholarship exalts the marble-worker's status, that her objection presupposes that access to raw materials, rather than degrees of crafting skill, was the key factor in determining the locus of production. Oustinoff's experiments showed that anyone could in theory create a simple figurine in a few days, but the concentration of extremely complicated marble objects at Daskaleio-Kavos, such as the dove bowls, other elaborate vessels, and complex, standing and large figurines, represents precisely those kinds of object for which greater and more restricted levels of skill can be reasonably posited. In fact, as is suggested in chapters 8 and 9, patterns of skilled manufacture in the early Cyclades may have been determined by social factors (knowledge, experience and mobility) rather than by direct control of the sources of materials. The metal-working and obsidian debris prove that Daskaleio-Kavos imported other materials from distant sources and made things out of them, so there is no reason to reject, and some reason to favour, the idea that many of the marble objects found at Daskaleio-Kavos were also made there, even though there is equally no reason to doubt that many others were finished imports. Several of the clusters of closely comparable figurines that have prompted Getz-Preziosi (1987a) to identify the work of individuals may even reflect some of this community's particular marble-working traditions.

Pottery can also provide crucial insights into Daskaleio-Kavos' significance and role (Broodbank 2000). The case for some degree of local pottery production is equivocal, given our ignorance of clay-beds in the site's vicinity, and the difficulties in deciding whether inclusions common to the geology of both Keros and other areas, including those close enough to have enabled direct access from Daskaleio-Kavos, imply local production. But pottery analysis provides an impressive amount of information about the quantity, provenance and functional range of imported objects at the site, that easily outstrips the potential of any other class of material, including

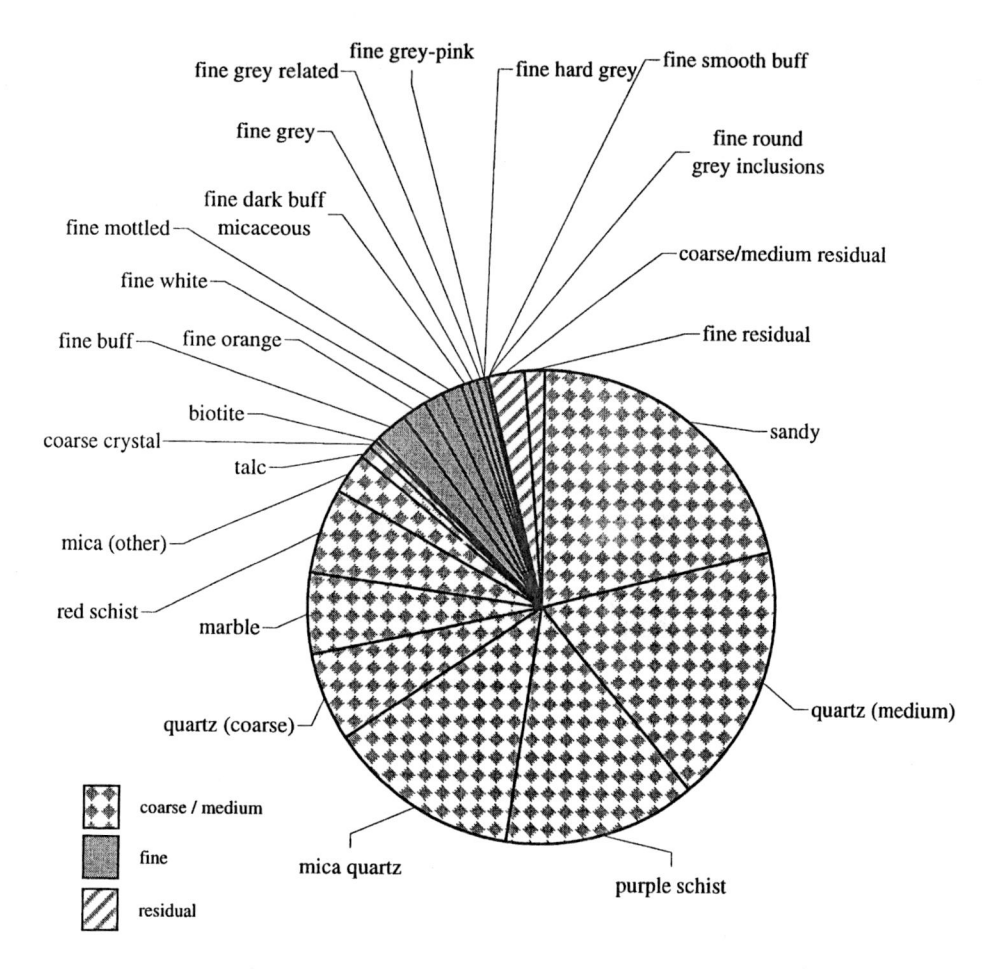

Fig. 71 Quantitative fabric analysis of the surface material collected in 1987 from Daskaleio-Kavos; see further discussion in Broodbank 2000.

the much-vaunted but relatively mute marble figurines and vessels. Fig. 71 summarises the frequencies of fabrics in the 1987 material, showing the complexity of pottery supply to the site. Fig. 72 compares the *minimum* level of imports identified in the 1987 material from the entire Kavos area with data from the contemporary sites of Akrotiri (Sotirakopoulou 1990: 43), Mt Kynthos (MacGillivray 1980), Phylakopi (Renfrew 1982b: 223) and Agia Irini (Wilson 1999). The minimum percentage of imports at Kavos is the highest attested in the early Cyclades. It might be noted, furthermore, that the level of imports is high both in the Kavos settlement area and in the spread deposit, the latter being distinctive rather in terms of the *diversity* of its imports.

Diversity is indeed apparent in the provenance and range of the pottery imports at Daskaleio-Kavos (fig. 73), and the kinds of vessels reaching the site from different areas, as determined by visual comparison of fabrics. Most of the imports derive from nearby islands. From Amorgos the principal shapes were container jars, mostly with

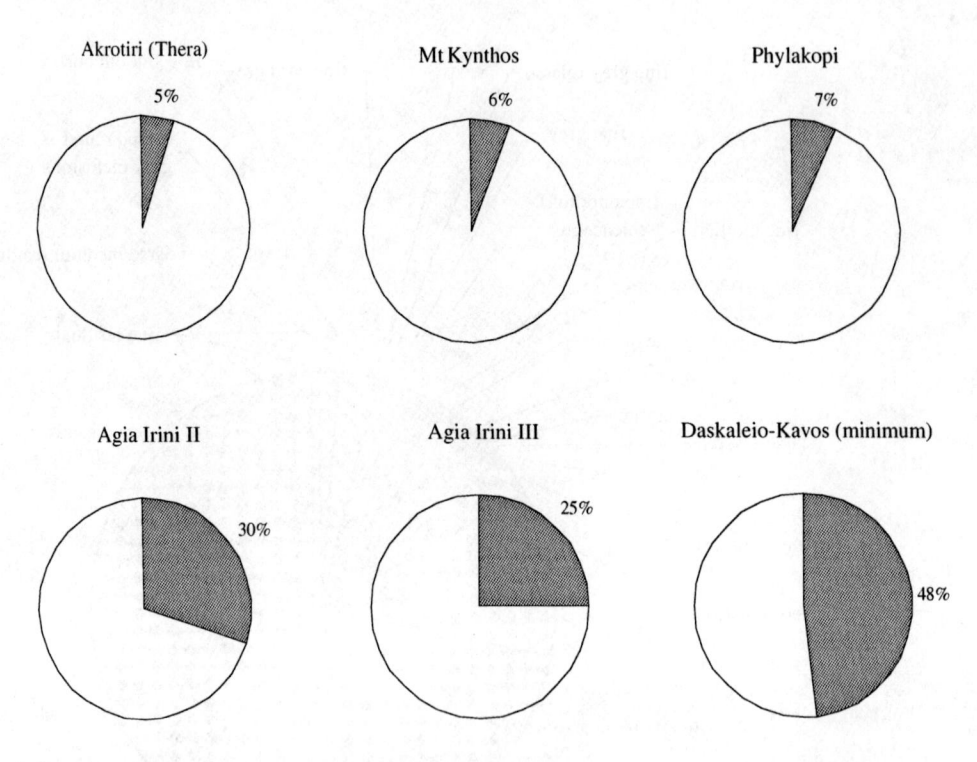

Fig. 72 Pottery import levels at selected Cycladic Early Bronze II sites. The level for Daskaleio-Kavos is a minimum based upon the fabrics that *cannot* be local, i.e. all save for quartz, marble and sandy (the last assuming clay-beds on the Kouphonisia to lie within range of direct access from Keros). Given that some (maybe even all) of the quartz and marble material is in fact likely to be imported from other areas with a similar geology, and that some of the sandy material may also have arrived as imported vessels, the actual level of imports at Daskaleio-Kavos is liable to have been more than 50 per cent, and it could conceivably include all, or almost all, of the pottery found at the site.

upright necks indicating liquid contents, plus a few pouring, eating and drinking shapes, whilst from Naxos came a wider variety of forms. A common sandy fabric, probably from the Kouphonisia, was used primarily for large numbers of pedestal-based jars with incised decoration (cf. fig. 61). The likely contribution from Ios cannot be judged until its EBA fabrics are characterised. The longer-range imports show a much greater predominance of small shapes in fine fabrics, including painted jugs, sauceboats and pyxides (fig. 74), mainly in a white fabric of probable Theran origin, stamped-and-incised pedestal-based jars of Syros type, and a few painted cups that may come from Melos, but also a few larger vessels in a talc fabric tentatively provenanced to Siphnos (see chapter 9). Long-range fine imports from the Greek mainland are represented by sauceboats in a high-fired yellow-blue mottled fabric that have long been considered to be prestigious on the Greek mainland; some of the best-fired sauceboats in a fine buff fabric with *urfirnis* surface may also come from the same

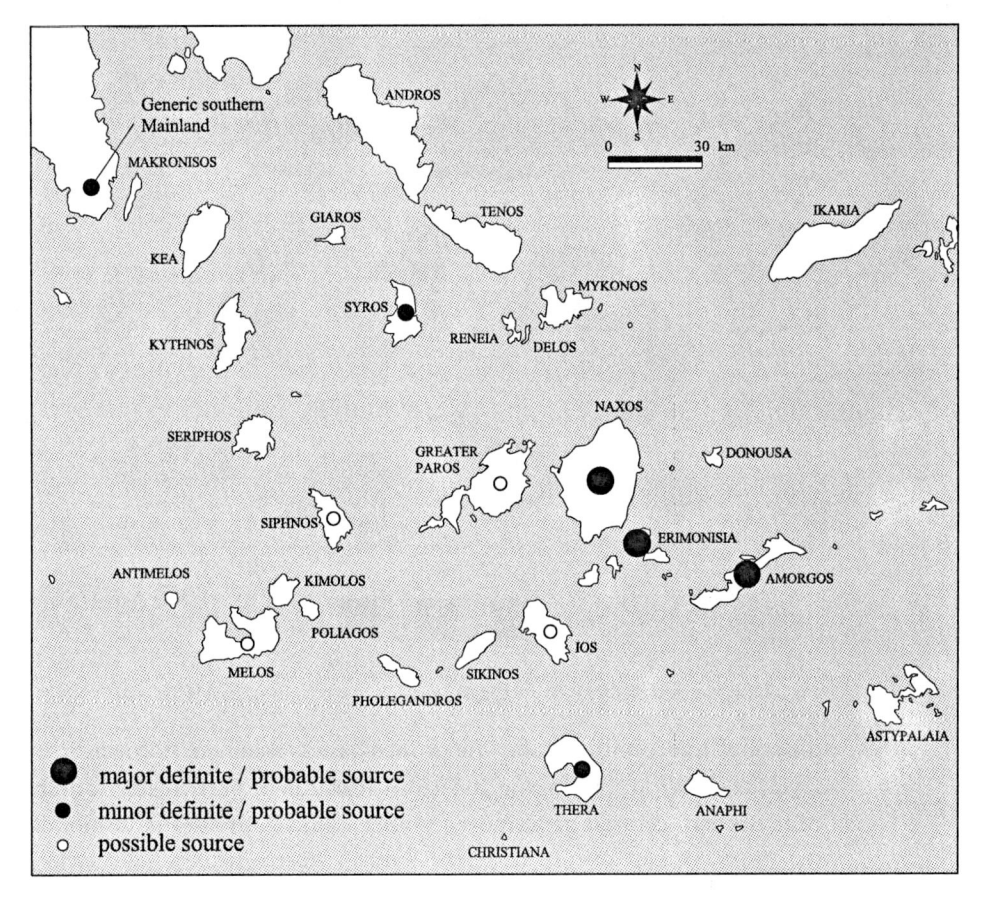

Fig. 73 Provenance of imports at Daskaleio-Kavos. NB dots refer to general areas, not specific archaeological sites.

region. The fact that several fabrics cannot be provenanced indicates that the ceramic relations of Daskaleio-Kavos were probably even more complex than they now appear. The possibility of imports from the east Aegean, whose fabrics are poorly known, must be entertained, but it should be stated that there is no identifiable material from Crete. The nested spheres of pottery importation that are witnessed, grading from a localised zone of abundant import of large and small vessels, to a selective longer-range acquisition of prestigious items, can tell us much about the varying intensity and contexts of different scales of interaction.

Pottery analysis also allows one final touch to be added to the increasingly rich picture of a large community of producers and consumers that is emerging from this reassessment of Daskaleio-Kavos. For the pottery provides clues as to whether objects arrived at the site as a result of non-local people's choices, or whether people resident at the site decided what to acquire from elsewhere in the Cyclades, and indeed beyond. The pottery data strongly favour the latter model, and thereby provide further evidence for local agency at work at Daskaleio-Kavos. One indication of this is the

Fig. 74   Painted pottery from Daskaleio-Kavos collected in 1987.

differing, and quite specific, range of shapes obtained from diverse areas of the Cyclades. This argues for the conscious selection of particularly desirable objects out of the overall ceramic repertoire on other islands. Another indication is the fact that the most popular shapes were obtained in strikingly different ways. For example, whilst most of the pedestal-based jars are either in the Kouphonisia's sandy fabric, the probably Naxian medium quartz group, or the Syros variant's fine grey fabric, sauce-boats exhibit a bewildering range of fine and medium fabrics, and commensurably diverse decoration. Rather than imports arriving on a more or less random basis, this is good evidence for coherent but differentiated ways of obtaining functionally different kinds of vessel, the one through a few focused avenues (possibly including local production), but the other involving very widespread and eclectic networks. A third revealing indication of structure in the assemblage is the fact that the marked rarity of fine pottery bowls and complete absence of pottery frying pans is neatly compensated by the presence of both forms in marble, the former in very large quantities. It is hard to imagine how this process of substitution could have been maintained unless the people at Daskaleio-Kavos played a decisive role in the selection of their material. This selective acquisition could in theory reflect either a process whereby non-local people brought desired objects to the site (i.e. Daskaleio-Kavos acted as a passive centre for pottery exchange), or one whereby people from the site travelled abroad to obtain them (i.e. at least some people at Daskaleio-Kavos were maritime traders themselves). Further light will be shed on this critical question from a series of different perspectives in the course of this and the following chapters.

Centrality in the EBA Cyclades

To consolidate the argument so far, Chalandriani-Kastri, Agia Irini, Grotta-Aplomata and Daskaleio-Kavos share a set of features that differentiate them from the majority of other settlements in the Cyclades. These comprise unusually large population, skilled craft production in several media, marked involvement in maritime trade and high levels of consumption of prestige material culture via funerary deposition. Admittedly, uneven knowledge prevents all these features from being equally securely documented at each site (e.g. evidence for trade at Grotta-Aplomata is elusive, as is that for consumption at Agia Irini). To categorise these sites as a group inviting investigation is not to suggest that they all represented identical communities. Variation in depositional practices has already been discerned, and future research is likely to reveal differences in the relative emphasis on specific kinds of production and trade. How Skarkos stands relative to the above four sites is uncertain, for although it is large, it is not clear that it shares all the other salient features. No additional EB II examples can at present be identified with any confidence. Before EB II, the only community that displays some of the features of the big EB II sites is that known from the cemetery at Agrilia, although conspicuous consumption can be detected in a few Grotta-Pelos graves, mainly on Greater Paros.

We now turn from the archaeology of these communities to the explanation of their locations in the islands. Four main questions need to be addressed. First, why are these communities found where they are? Second, is their distribution as it is currently known fairly complete, or might there be others to be discovered? Third, why do these communities emerge almost exclusively in EB II? Fourth, why was the Grotta-Pelos culture focus of conspicuous deposition on Greater Paros succeeded by an emphasis on different areas, notably the Erimonisia, Syros and Naxos? The thrust of the argument will be that such communities can be demonstrated in almost all cases to have occupied central places in the networks of interaction that linked the Cycladic islanders together. But before investigating this hypothesis in detail, it is as well to ask what other forms of explanation might be forthcoming, and why in the end, they are found wanting.

Control of good arable land does not provide a promising overall explanation for this group of sites, owing to the fact that Daskaleio-Kavos and Chalandriani-Kastri, as well as earlier Agrilia and several of the rich Grotta-Pelos graves, are found in notably poor agricultural areas, and only Grotta-Aplomata, Agia Irini and Skarkos (to the extent that the last site reflects a comparable phenomenon) occupy high-quality agricultural niches. Conversely, this variability argues that community specialisation in production and interaction as a response to an agriculturally marginal, resource-poor location (cf. Rathje 1978 and Allen 1984) is an equally inadequate overall explanation, quite apart from the fact that so much of the Cyclades fits this description that its explanatory power is largely vitiated. Preferential location with regard to mineral resources is unsatisfactory, as none of the confirmed major sites lies close to the obsidian quarries or the metal mines of the western Cyclades – indeed their distance from these areas is well worth noting (unless Phylakopi does belong in this group, and even if it does, Torrence (1982, 1984, 1986) has argued against local control of the quarries). Lastly, the presence or absence of good harbours is less relevant than in later Cycladic history, because canoes could be drawn up on any of the small foreshores that abound in the Cyclades. In fact, the major sites all possess different facilities in this respect: Agia Irini lies on one of the finest anchorages in the Cyclades, Chalandriani-Kastri has only a thin strip of shingle, whilst a small double cove may have existed at Daskaleio-Kavos and a larger double harbour at Grotta-Aplomata, if a spit of land linking Kavos to Daskaleio islet is indeed posited in the former case, and the probable EBA coastline restored in the latter.

So what of centrality, and how is this most fruitfully explored in the Cyclades? Because islandscapes are changeable cultural constructs, they have no intrinsic foci that can be determined simply by examining a map, as indeed the number of central places that have risen and fallen through the long history of the Cyclades amply demonstrates. Equally, because islands in the Cyclades so often dissolve into patchworks of land and sea, especially under the settlement conditions existing in the EBA, centrality needs to be investigated within the skeins of interaction that bound these patchworks together, rather than looking for centres specific to individual islands. In these circumstances it would be quite plausible for at least some centres to be found on the fringes of islands (further implying that the definition of boundaries and margins in the early Cyclades will be fraught with complications). Lastly, it should not be forgotten that not all forms of centrality are likely to operate at the same spatial scales, and it will be necessary to define which scales are appropriate in which cases.

PPA models, which proved informative as simulations of local island networks, can also provide important insights into centrality in the early Cyclades. In theory, two kinds of network centrality could be analysed by PPA. One is the relative *efficiency* of communication enjoyed by each point in the network, as measured by geodesic, short-path links, and the second is the relative *intensity* of communication activity associated with each point, as measured by the number of links to other points (Hunt 1988: 137). The former is a less appropriate measure of centrality for early Cycladic societies, for whilst it is reasonably certain that most islanders did partake in the local interactions that helped to define the centres of intense communication, there is no indication that they all travelled throughout the islands, and some reason to suggest, on the basis of seafaring risks, that many did not. Moreover, whereas the former measurement requires that we define an arbitrary edge to the Cycladic network, when this could in fact be extended to Attica, Euboia and the south-east Aegean (thereby changing the definition of centres), the latter measure highlights local peaks of intensity in networks that could be infinitely extended without affecting each peak's location. The following analysis concentrates on measuring relative intensities of communication (for an

Which islands in the stream? 239

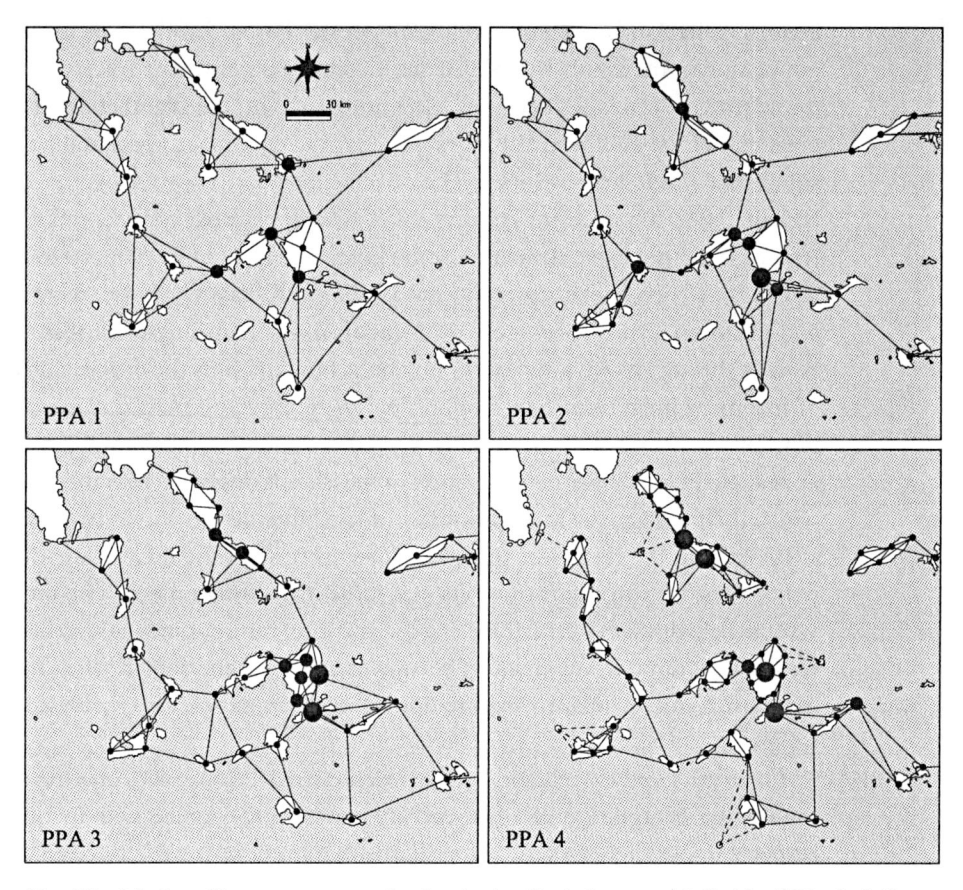

Fig. 75 Nodes of intense communication in the Cyclades as modelled by PPAs 1–4 (five and six linkages only).

examination of communication efficiency via short-path linkage see Broodbank 1996: 147, fig. 6.3, tables 6.1–6.4).

Fig. 75 illustrates the areas of unusually intense communication generated by PPAs 1–4, as defined by points with the maximum attested numbers of connections to other points. The results are revealing. The details of point placement may sometimes be responsible for generating freak results in a single PPA, possible examples being the prominence of Mykonos in PPA 1, Siphnos and southern Andros in PPA 2, and Amorgos in PPA 4. But the trends are clear. In the earlier part of the sequence, Greater Paros and central-to-southern Naxos are the most regularly intensively connected areas, with a major focus emerging in the Erimonisia as soon as they enter the simulation. In PPAs 3–4 Greater Paros' prominence collapses, with high levels of intensity continuing in the Erimonisia and central-to-southern Naxos, and a new focus of communication arising in the north-east on central-to-northern Tenos.

What this tells us is that the changes in local interaction networks resulting from population growth have a fundamental effect on the location of communication centres. What lies behind the decline of Greater Paros, for instance, is the fact that, as population in the south-west Cyclades increases, the former's role as a connection to the south-east Cyclades becomes less important, and the island changes from a principal hub of the southern Cyclades into (variously) a place apart and a margin of the south-east Cycladic networks. The striking position enjoyed by the Erimonisia is largely due to the need for Amorgos to establish external connections to its north; if Amorgos did not exist, the status of the Erimonisia would be reduced to that of minor satellites of Naxos, akin to Donousa. In the north-east Cyclades, what gives central and northern Tenos the edge is its location in the dense network that extends from Andros through to Mykonos as populations built up, plus the crucial additional factor of incoming links from Syros opposite. The complete absence of sustained predictions of local centres in the western Cyclades is no less interesting. The main reason appears to be the linear configuration of the islands, together with their moderate size, which militates against concentrations of local interaction within any one area.[4]

Looking at the results of this predictive exercise in the light of the distribution of major sites, we can claim four hits and three interesting misses. The hits are the rich Grotta-Pelos graves of Greater Paros, and the communities at Agrilia, Daskaleio-Kavos and Grotta-Aplomata. The misses are Chalandriani-Kastri, Agia Irini and Skarkos. A more detailed exploration of each of these cases yields several further insights.

There is a good correlation between rich Grotta-Pelos graves on Greater Paros and the island's centrality under low-density conditions, coupled with its decline in both respects under higher-density conditions. We need, however, to temper this correlation with additional observations. For one thing, we have yet to understand why, if Greater Paros was so central early on, it has not revealed traces of large Grotta-Pelos centres comparable to those of EB II. In short, the increasingly strong differentiation witnessed through the course of the EBA is still not explained. In addition, it would be fair to ask why more rich Grotta-Pelos graves are not known in central and southern Naxos, which is also predicted as an early focus of communication. The first issue cannot really be addressed until the investigation of the location of all major sites in the light of the PPA results is complete. With regard to the second issue, one answer might be that such graves await discovery on Naxos or, more gloomily, that the looters have found them already. But an alternative possibility raised by PPA 1 is that because western Greater Paros was the bottle-neck area through which the south-east and

---

[4] An earlier version of PPA 4 (Broodbank 1993: fig. 3) did predict a centre on eastern Melos, but this was a product of an unrealistic over-representation, in terms of points, of Melos' small satellite islands of Antimelos, Kimolos and Poliagos. It might be noted that although this earlier version similarly over-represented the Erimonisia in the south-east, and Giaros, Delos and Reneia in the north-east, the down-grading of these islands in the present PPA generates almost no substantial changes in the distribution of central places. This serves as a useful confirmation that the main predictions are indeed robust.

south-west Cyclades were connected (much as the Erimonisia link Amorgos and Naxos later in the sequence), currently remote Despotikon and Antiparos formed a communication bridge articulating the main zones of Grotta-Pelos occupation in the southern Cyclades. In comparison, the more open networks on Naxos might have made this region a less effective material trap for circulating Grotta-Pelos prestige objects.

The correlation between both Agrilia's and Daskaleio-Kavos' locations, and the high degree of centrality in the Erimonisia once these islands enter the simulation, obviously merits attention as one of the most informative vindications of the approach. This correlation should dispel any lingering doubts over the reasons for such impressive sites in the Erimonisia. Their existence depended upon a combination of conditions in the south-east Cyclades that has not since been repeated, namely a dispersed settlement pattern (including substantial numbers of communities in southern Naxos), the inhabitation of the Erimonisia themselves, a high degree of dependence on external links on the part of Amorgos, and (it is tempting to add) small-canoe traffic that was less prone to bypass the intervening Erimonisia than later sail-driven ships.

It also renders attractive the hypothesis that Agrilia was in some sense a modest forerunner of Daskaleio-Kavos, with the Erimonisia's central role increasing through the centuries following their colonisation, as its populations became established, and as its people realised the opportunities for mediating relations between communities on the larger islands surrounding them. The shift from Epano Kouphonisi to Keros may hint at an element of serendipity surrounding the precise location of the principal site in this region, with the choice perhaps decided by small-scale, stochastic local factors that are inevitably lost to us. Nonetheless, there is one possible clue as to why a centre emerged at Daskaleio-Kavos, despite the lack of local arable land and the constricted area. For within the Erimonisia the conical islet of Daskaleio is a prominent seamark enjoying a commanding view (fig. 76), and may have acted as a traditional navigational point and stop-over before it developed into a centre of habitation. The first people to settle here, assuredly people attracted more by its prominence than by the greater agricultural potential of the land at Gerani, are unlikely to have predicted the boom that followed. In other words, Daskaleio-Kavos' subsequent spectacular profile may belie its origins and early history; the site probably had modest beginnings, and may have been initially less distinct from Agrilia than it now seems.

What of Naxos, the only island that displays high centrality throughout the PPA sequence? The question of rich early burials was discussed above. For EB II, Grotta-Aplomata on the west coast is well situated as a major centre, being located in a part of Naxos that is regularly predicted to enjoy intense communications, and that links Naxos to Greater Paros. However, the highest degrees of intense communication are predicted to lie further to the east on the island during PPAs 3–4, with other foci shifting across much of central and southern Naxos. It is worth considering whether Naxos

Fig. 76 Islandscape seen from Daskaleio-Kavos, looking north to the Kouphonisia, Schoinousa and the high ground of southern Naxos.

may have boasted at least one other central community. An intriguing possibility is that an inland communication hub developed in the network of valleys at the island's centre, maybe in an area that is now smothered by erosion from the hills. Such a place, at the heart of a terrestrial network, would be of considerable comparative interest as a counter-point to the coastal centres known to date. Other possible areas are the south or east coastal strips. Against this, however, we must ask how many centres could have co-existed in a region of this size, given that any other Naxian centres would be sandwiched between Grotta-Aplomata and Daskaleio-Kavos, which between them probably controlled most of Naxos' external links. In particular, Daskaleio-Kavos dominates the southern and eastern coastline of Naxos, and the successful emergence of a comparable centre here might therefore be doubted. More will be said about the dynamics of Daskaleio-Kavos and its surrounding communities in chapter 8.

Let us now turn to the misses, and first to Chalandriani-Kastri, in the context of the prediction that the focus of communication in the north-east Cyclades should lie not on Syros, but instead across the water on Tenos. The situation is intricate, not least because connections from Syros help to generate the intense levels of communication predicted for Tenos. One viable solution, not least as Tenos remains under-explored, is to conclude that a big centre did exist on this island, probably on the central or northern coast. But an alternative is to interpret Chalandriani-Kastri as this centre for the north-east Cyclades, consciously relocated to Syros. It has been shown that,

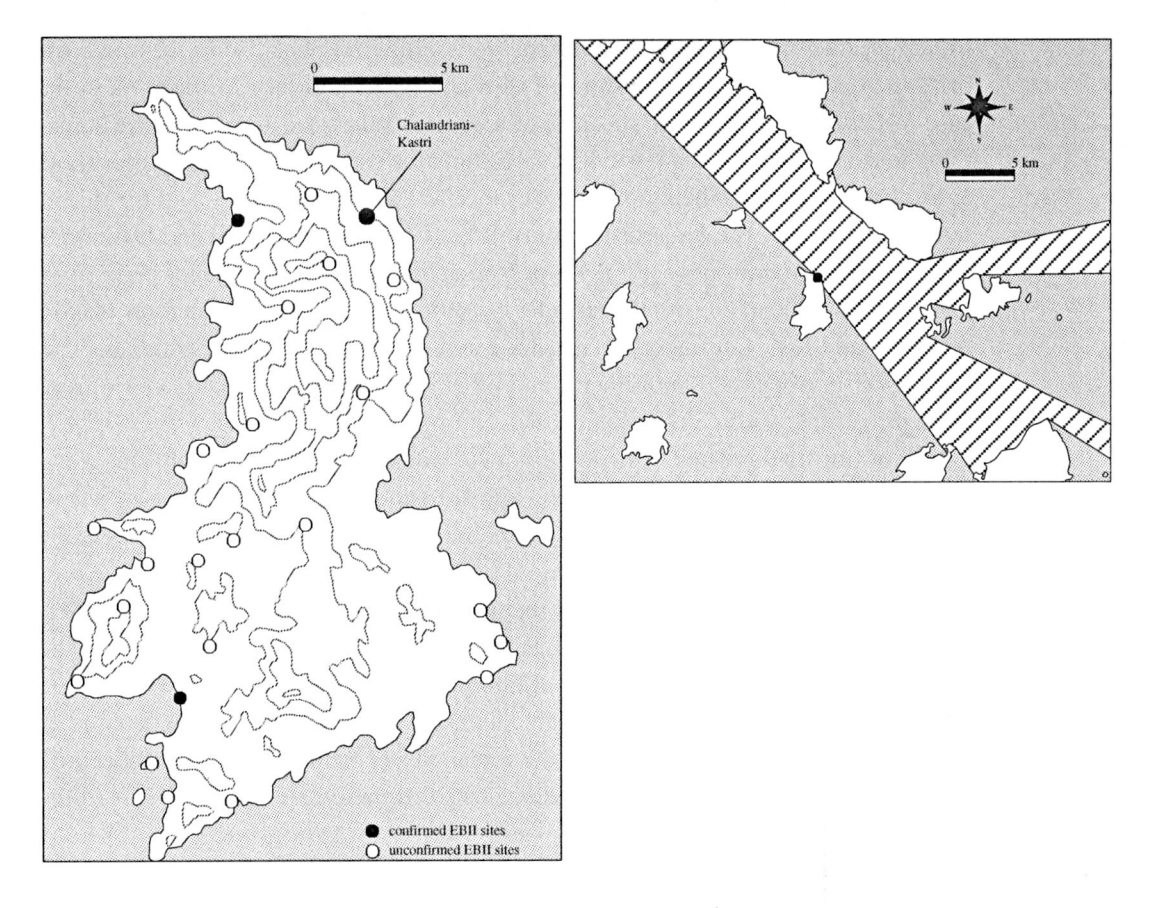

Fig. 77 Syros. *Left:* settlement pattern. *Right:* the view of the north-east Cycladic islandscape seen from Chalandriani-Kastri. Settlement data from Hekman 1994: fig. 8.

although PPA predicted a surprisingly remote status for Syros within the early Cycladic networks, the island's degree of settlement (not least at Chalandriani-Kastri), along with its longboat images, can be read as evidence for an intensification of maritime skills as a strategy for overcoming this condition. This raises questions about the relationship between a large seafaring community at Chalandriani-Kastri and any hypothetical local centre on Tenos, especially if longboats functioned in part as war canoes (see chapter 3). Did people from Chalandriani-Kastri perhaps either suppress the predicted Tenian centre or thwart its emergence and arrogate its role in the north-east Cyclades to their own community? Certainly, the distance of Syros from the rest of the north-east Cyclades would make it an ideal base for raiding, with war canoes able to materialise and vanish with impunity.

Another argument in favour of Chalandriani-Kastri's central role is its location on the high, curving coastline of north-east Syros (fig. 77). This makes little sense in terms of access to good arable land or, equally, a major role within Syros, but it affords a visual territory unrivalled by any other point in the north-east Cyclades, extending in clear weather over the entire islandscape from southern Euboia, down the west coast of Andros and Tenos, past Mykonos, Delos and Reneia, as far as Naxos. As in the case of Daskaleio-Kavos, the specifics of a centre's micro-location may have something to do with occupying positions of prominence within wider islandscapes (note again that the island is therefore an irrelevance as an analytical unit – and the title of this chapter strictly speaking misphrased). What Chalandriani-Kastri and Daskaleio-Kavos sought to control was not Syros or Keros, nor neighbouring islands *per se* (they probably had little to do with the far sides of Andros, Tenos and Mykonos, or Naxos, Amorgos and Ios), but rather the maritime and coastal islandscapes, complete with their traceries of people's movements and other activities, that stretched out in front of them.

One of our three misses is therefore not so wide of the mark, after all, and could indeed be a redirected hit. This leaves Agia Irini and Skarkos, on neither of whose locations PPA sheds any light. At Agia Irini the most likely solution, as intimated by Wilson (1987), is that the site was a central place at a larger, inter-regional scale rather than at the local level, and specifically that it acted as a gateway community in EB II for people travelling between the Cyclades, the metal sources of Lavrion and the important settlements of east Attica and Euboia. A similar role for Kea was proposed during the FN, although at a much less culturally elaborated level. The paradox of Kea is that it is peripheral relative to the remainder of the Cyclades, and yet central for the articulation of sea communications between these islands and regions to the north.

Such perspectives will not, however, explain Skarkos, which stands out as the only large settlement that cannot be convincingly interpreted as a communication hub. Combined with the doubts about its overall similarity to the other major EB II sites, this strengthens the possibility that Skarkos was indeed a different kind of community with different reasons for existing, perhaps a first glimpse of another class of village-sized communities in the EB II Cyclades that has hitherto eluded archaeologists. We can only guess at an explanation, but one possibility is that in the few extended zones of good arable land in the Cyclades (of which the valley around Skarkos is one), localised social factors occasionally created a reversal of the normal tendency to centrifugal dispersal as populations grew. For instance, a community occupying good farmland in an otherwise marginal part of the Cyclades might become, over the long-term, a net gainer by social storage networks, to the extent that neighbours gravitated to it of their own volition or to fulfil otherwise unredeemable obligations (Halstead 1988: 525). This scenario does not imply that large villages are to be predicted in all such areas, for their appearance or non-appearance would depend on how social relations played out (e.g. feuding groups might counteract convergence). But some communities similar to Skarkos, if perhaps not many examples, may be anticipated at other comparable locations in the Cyclades.

By way of drawing this analysis together, to what extent have we answered the four questions posed earlier about the major sites? *Why are they where they are?* They are found in areas of exceptionally intense communication under EBA conditions, with the partial exception of Chalandriani-Kastri, and the clear exception of Skarkos. In the case of Chalandriani-Kastri, the possibility was explored of a predatory community that reworked communication networks to its advantage. Skarkos, however, seems likely to require alternative modes of explanation. An important general point to emerge is that, with the exception of Agia Irini, the crucial scale of centrality has proved to be that of the local networks, suggesting that all these centres, save Agia Irini, emerged through bottom-up processes, rather than as a result of top-down, long-range factors. This need not imply that these centres subsequently confined themselves to the scales of activity to which they owed their origins; indeed long-range imports at Agrilia, Daskaleio-Kavos, Grotta-Aplomata and Chalandriani-Kastri demonstrate the opposite, and Agia Irini may, conversely, have established a local central role for itself within Kea.

Is the distribution of such sites as it is currently known fairly complete or might there be others to be discovered? The likelihood of other villages like Skarkos has been discussed already, but what about centres of communication? The possibility arises in the case of Tenos, although Chalandriani-Kastri may be the predicted centre relocated. Several foci of intense communication were regularly predicted in areas of Naxos, apart from Grotta-Aplomata, and in PPAs 2 and 4 a few other areas made brief appearances whose reliability is hard to assess. There is no current way of telling whether additional centres arose on Naxos, or whether the region was dominated by Grotta-Aplomata and Daskaleio-Kavos. But what can be affirmed with certainty is that under simulated EB II conditions this part of the Cyclades generates an extraordinarily intensive network of communications, without parallels elsewhere in the islands, and a point of some interest when investigating the social and material strategies of people at Daskaleio-Kavos and other communities in its vicinity. As for any other centres of inter-regional linkage on the edges of the Cyclades, in addition to Agia Irini, two plausible areas are Thera and Melos, both articulation points for voyages to Crete and the latter also for voyages to the Peloponnese. If Akrotiri and Phylakopi are ever securely demonstrated to have been large EB II centres, their status could have been associated primarily with long-range interaction. Overall, however, the conclusion seems to be that the number of centres of communication in the EB II Cyclades was probably very limited. Four EB II examples are known (Daskaleio-Kavos, Chalandriani-Kastri, Grotta-Aplomata and Agia Irini), and it is not beyond the bounds of possibility that these were indeed the most prominent centres of their day. Regardless as to whether the future reveals any further examples, this sobering thought should focus attention on making the very most of the substantial amount of data that does lie to hand, not least as one of these centres has been tragically devastated by looting, another's cemetery was largely excavated a century ago, and two more lie partly unrecoverable under later settlements.

Why do these communities emerge almost exclusively in EB II and *why does the focus shift from a promising start on Greater Paros to later emphasis on other areas?* The latter question has been answered by demonstrating that increasing the population of the islands engenders fundamental shifts in local interaction networks. But the former question still begs an answer, and reminds us that locational analysis provides only a partial explanation. It tells us why such sites exist where they do, but it does not give a deeper insight into why they existed in the particular forms that they did. Answers to this question require a rather different kind of investigation of the changing attributes of Cycladic islandscapes and the shifting strategies and actions of the people within them.

8

Paint, paddles and the politics of value

> Stone-faced souls
> peered with their lizard eyes through the pomme-
> Aruac tree,
> then turned from their bonfire. Instantly, like moles
> or mole crickets in the shadow of History,
> the artifacts burrowed deeper into their holes.
> *Omeros,* DEREK WALCOTT

This chapter situates the emergence of the centres analysed in chapter 7 in the context of a change in Cycladic seafaring cultures between EB I and EB II, which magnified the role of well-placed communities and the status of successful seafarers within them. A sustained 'archaeology of the sea' is needed to bring out the extent of this phenomenon. The formulation of a new maritime ideology becomes evident iconographically with the transitional EB I–II Kampos group, and appears to have been further elaborated in EB II, during a period of intensified canoe-based activity at a limited number of locations in the Cyclades. These changes can themselves be related to temporal shifts in the overall incidence of maritime interaction. Moreover, opportunities created by these conditons allow us to understand how people at the main centres deployed material culture in ways that sought differentiation from others. It also offers a means for interpreting the evidence of a conscious manipulation of the regimes of value relating to prestige objects at such places and in their vicinities. By EB II, it will be argued, a major source of social power in the Cycladic islands resided in the practice and proceeds of maritime movement, and in the cultivation of the glory derived from such activities.

It will also become apparent that social power in these islands resided not so much in durable organisational structures, but rather in individuals such as navigators, traders, community heads and perhaps crafters of fine objects, or combinations of these roles, and others unguessed, within a single person. This power is likely to have been personal and achieved, and (often literally) to have accompanied people to the grave. The decisions and deeds of specific islanders must in fact have been fundamental to the creation of the big central communities and their spectacular archaeological signatures. To be sure, the individual islanders behind the artefacts that we recover remain every bit as elusive as Walcott's 'stone-faced souls' of the pre-contact Caribbean. But a growing emphasis on distinguishing and elaborating individuals,

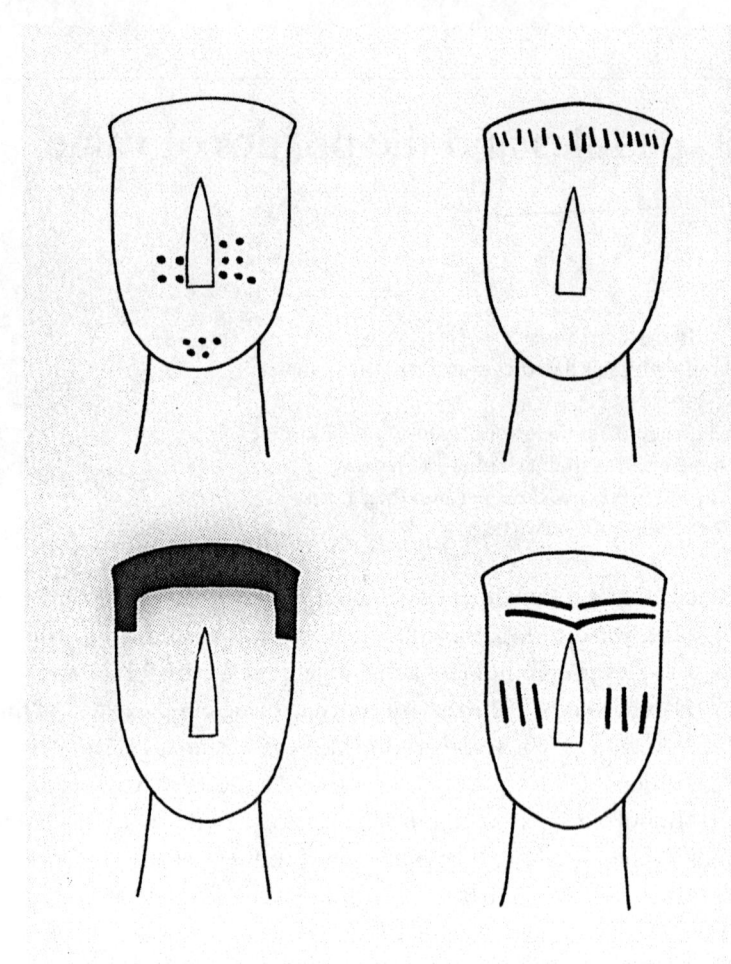

Fig. 78   Similar figurine heads with different decoration. After Getz-Preziosi 1987a: fig. 42.

beyond the predominance of single burial, is attested by the number of finds of apparatus for adorning and framing the human body, beginning in the Kampos horizon but reaching its apogee in EB II, when such finds are often associated with that loose cluster of material known as the 'Keros-Syros' culture.

It is at this time that jewellery in silver first appears in the islands' archaeological record, in the form of bracelets, necklaces, hair-rings, pins and occasionally diadems (Renfrew 1967: 5–6; 1984a). Further echoes of such objects can be picked up, in the form of depictions on the marble figurines (fig. 11) (Getz-Preziosi 1987a: 53–4) and in portrayals of necklace-like chains of lozenges and ovals on sauceboats and jugs, where their location on the vessel's throat is manifestly anthropomorphising. The evidence for tattooing is equally striking. It comprises surviving traces of painted dotted and slashed designs on the figurines' faces (figs. 11, 78), miniature vessels and bone tubes holding azurite and cinnabar pigments, and copper needles, sometimes mounted in finely carved greenstone handles, which probably functioned as tattooing implements (fig. 79). A further form of appearance-altering has been proposed by Carter (1994), who argues that the long pressure-flaked obsidian blades that are found in the Cycladic graves were razors. Alongside the much rarer finds of metal tweezers, these obsidian blades (one of the few obsidian forms still produced in the EBA) indicate a cultural focus on shaving, facial appearance and other kinds of body depilation (Carter in prep.; Nakou 1995: 15).

The precise meanings of such behaviour may escape us, but several interesting points can be noted. These displays are mainly found at the major centres, or else in the richest graves at other sites. For example, pigments saturated Aplomata graves 15 and 23 (Kontoleon 1972: 153) and thirty-five bone tubes came from just thirty graves at the Chalandriani cemetery (Tsountas 1899: 104). They also appear to relate to individual or small group differentiation, perhaps on special occasions, in contrast to the regional styles that were identified in chapter 6. In support of this is the very selective incidence of the equipment for body modification, and the fact that similar figurines can preserve traces of notably different tattooing designs (fig. 78). A nexus of associations between special people, pigments and metallurgy can also be detected (Renfrew 1967: 12), not only in the fact that the pigments found in material-rich graves are associated with ore-bearing minerals, but also because in Agioi Anargyroi grave 5 a fine greenstone handled tattooing tool was found with an example of a small class of greenstone ladles (fig. 80) that have been convincingly interpreted as symbolic crucibles (Getz-Gentle 1996: 187, figs. 103a and 104c). This small thicket of symbols may extend to high-value or socially significant liquids, if the decorated sauceboats and jugs sporting jewellery designs are taken into account. That the people who assiduously cultivated a tattooed, groomed or bejewelled appearance were the same as those who sought fame at sea cannot as yet be proven, and E. S. Sherratt (in press) interprets the adorned women as the prizes rather than the practitioners of maritime activity. Overall, however, there is enough evidence for overlapping incidence to suggest that these personae were indeed closely associated.

Maritime ideology and social power

A new symbolism in the Cyclades

At about the same time as the start of the culture of body modification, material from the islanders' graves reveals the emergence of a nexus of two- and three-dimensional images that represents the earliest iconic information from the Cyclades, apart from the tradition of anthropomorphic figurines. The majority of these images can be read as symbols of the sea, maritime travel or swift movement (fig. 81). In addition to the canoe depictions, these include fish, stars or the sun, birds (most probably doves), and rows or fields of spirals representing waves. Also prominent are female genitalia. Core

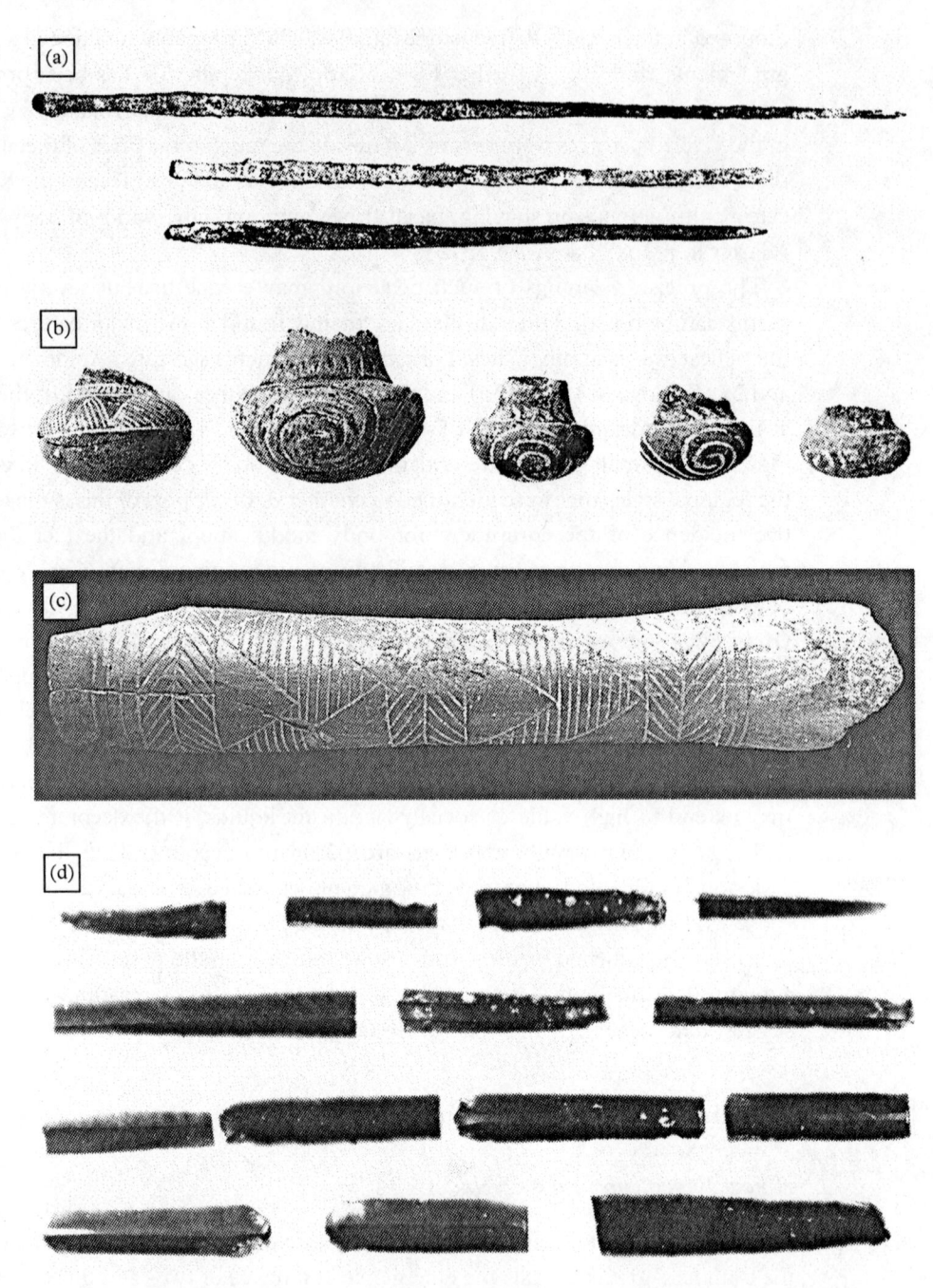

Fig. 79 Equipment for body decoration and modification from burial contexts in the Cyclades (not to scale): (a) needles, (b) miniature pottery pigment containers, (c) incised bone tube containing pigment, (d) pressure-flaked obsidian blades. All courtesy of the National Archaeological Museum, Athens.

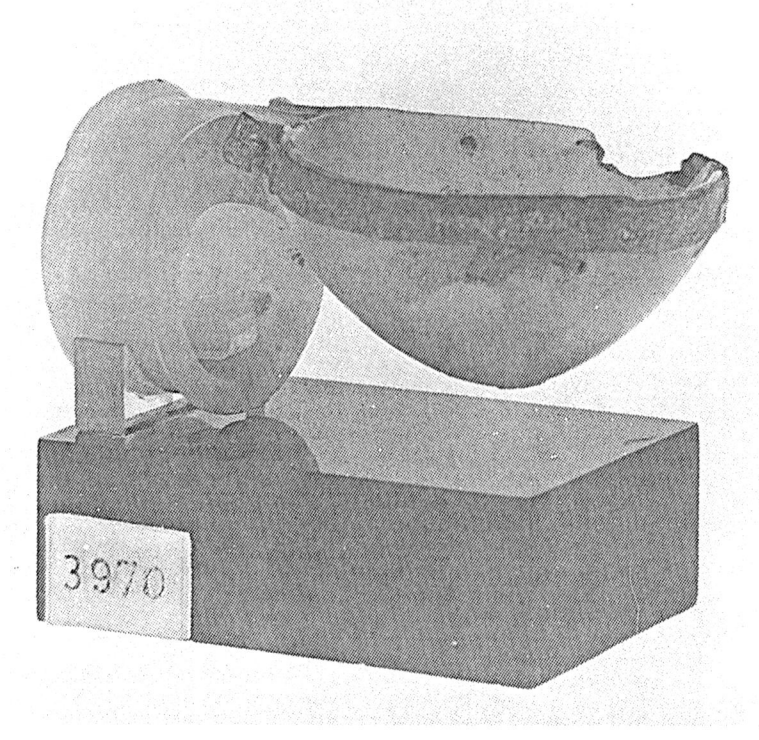

Fig. 80 Greenstone symbolic crucible from Amorgos mended with silver rim band and rivets. Courtesy of the National Archaeological Museum, Athens.

elements of this group – boat, star/sun and sea – remain associated as a complex of maritime symbols into the Aegean later Bronze Age (Morgan 1984). E. S. Sherratt (in press) even makes an intriguing case that this complex can be linked to early Levantine imagery of Astarte as *maris stella*, or at least to the cult of a generic goddess of the sea and sexuality. The most intensive deployment of the new imagery is seen on the frying pans, forms whose function is unknown but which clearly had some ritual or symbolic significance. Other examples occur on prestige objects like marble vessels, fine stone beads, metal pins and diadems. Although a single stone bird pendant comes from the Grotta-Pelos cemetery of Pyrgos on Greater Paros, the first substantial attestation of this complex of images (albeit at this stage lacking canoes) dates to the Kampos group, as is nicely illustrated by the early frying pan from Louros Athalassou grave 26 on Naxos, which is decorated with fish and spirals circling a sundisc; this grave also contained *inter alia* a 200-bead silver necklace, pigment containers, needles and obsidian blades (Papathanasopoulos 1961/2: 132–7; Renfrew 1972: 373). EB II sees the efflorescence of such imagery, much of it concentrated in predicted areas of high connectivity and maritime activity.

It seems very likely that these images are the surviving relics of an ideology of maritime prowess. In a few cases, rather more specific interpretations can be ventured. For

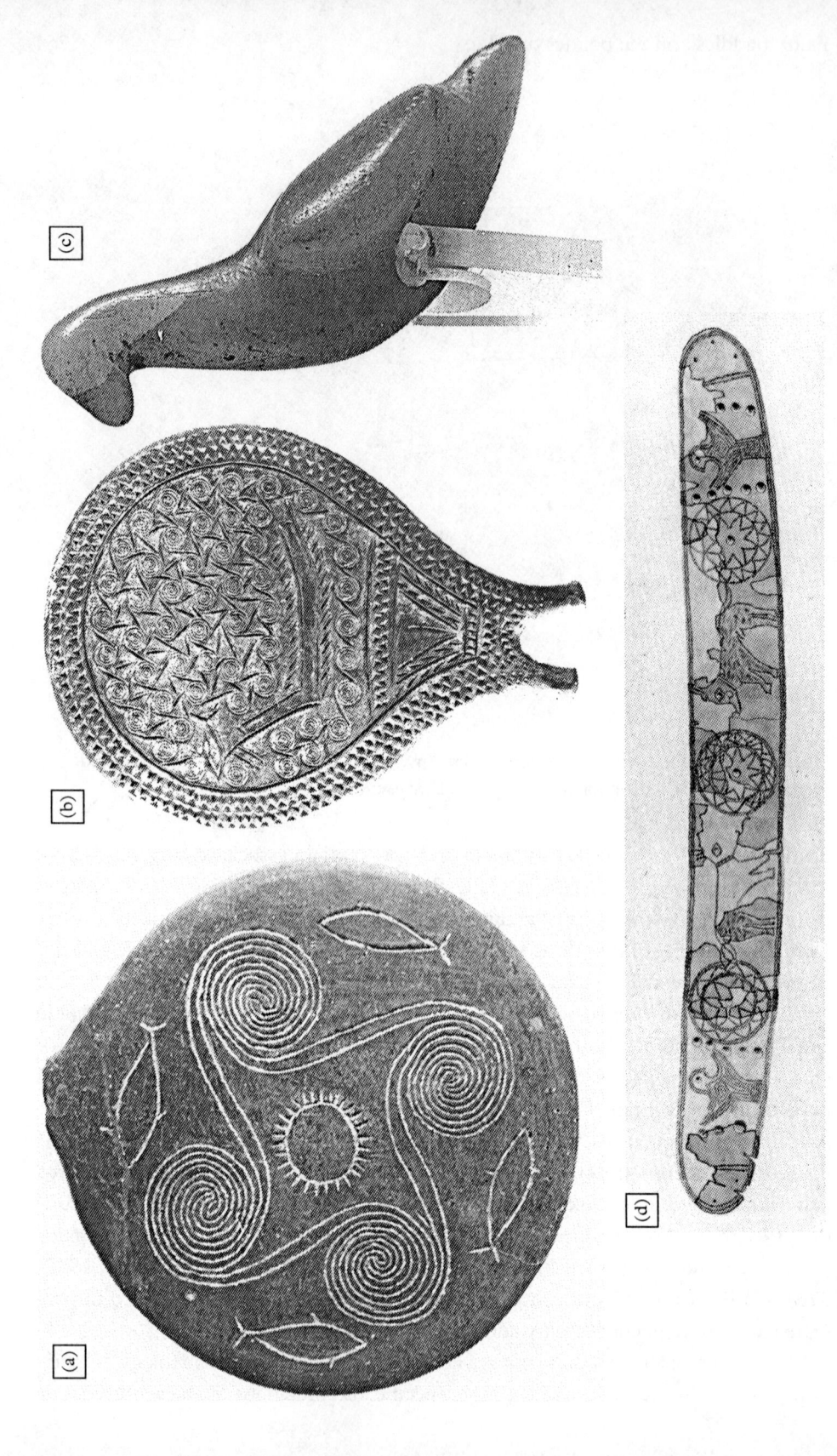

Fig. 81 Symbols of maritime travel, navigation and swiftness (not to scale): (a) fish, sea-spirals and sun on an early frying pan from the Louros Athalassou cemetery, Naxos, (b) longboat, sea-spirals and vulva on a frying pan from the Chalandriani cemetery on Syros, (c) early greenstone dove from the Pyrgos cemetery on Greater Paros, (d) mythical winged creatures, sun/star and collared dogs on a silver diadem from the fortified Kastri settlement on Syros. All courtesy of the National Archaeological Museum, Athens.

example, in the combination of a longboat or star with female genitalia on the frying pans from Chalandriani (fig. 81) it is not hard to discern an association between raiding or long-range navigation and biological reproduction or sexual gratification. Indeed the social and biological reproduction of large maritime communities seem intimately linked in these images. The lack of boat images at Daskaleio-Kavos might be explained by the fact that its frying pans are marble, poorly preserved and as yet not studied for traces of paint; but an alternative is that the depiction of these craft at Chalandriani-Kastri was a result of this centre's exceptional reliance on such boats (see below). Speculatively, a maritime interpretation of the famous harpist figurines of the south-east Cyclades (fig. 82) might also be ventured. Seated on their elaborate chairs, and playing an instrument commonly associated with vocal accompaniment, it is tempting to see these figurines as representations of the experienced seafarer in an authoritative or even mythic role, as the singer of sea-tales and the source of knowledge and stories about distant lands.

Another status domain emerges at this juncture, that of the male warrior armed with a dagger. The significance of this development at an Aegean-wide level is traced by Nakou (1995). There is growing evidence that daggers had existed in the Aegean as early as the FN (Zachos 1996c), but once again it is only in the Kampos horizon, and particularly in EB II, that they start to display a symbolic dimension in the Cyclades. This is attested by their appearance as grave goods (the earliest being long examples in the cemetery at Agrilia on Epano Kouphonisi), their elaboration in several cases with silver rivets and a silvery surface created by arsenic-rich alloys (Marangou 1990: 164, cat. no. 172 for a dagger from Spedos; see further Sherratt in press), and the appearance of a rare class of EB II figurines known as the 'hunter-warrior type', with male sexual characteristics, body sash, and a dagger prominently depicted at the waist (fig. 83). In the early Cyclades fighting must have often involved maritime raids or skirmishes between canoes, and E. S. Sherratt's proposal that the first Aegean spears developed as daggers on thrusting poles for reaching enemies not only behind defensive walls but also on canoes or beaches is certainly attractive (Sherratt in press).

In the Cyclades, the reasons for fighting, besides glorification through combat, are likely to have been the accumulation of prestigious objects, the seizing of animals or crops as a wealth-accruing strategy (or desperate measure in lean years), and the capture of people – maybe often women, given the latter's importance for reproduction in a world of exogamous settlements. E. S. Sherratt (in press) interprets the passive stance and nubile form of the standard female folded-arm figurines of EB II as an indication that a new image of women as sexual possessions was constructed at this time, reworking the more neutral suggestion (in terms of gender relations) that the increasing number of female figurines since the end of the Neolithic reflected the importance of the movement of women between small dispersed communities (chapter 5; Broodbank 1992: 543). In fact, there is likely to have been an often invisibly fine line dividing trading from raiding between island communities. In this sense, Renfrew's

Fig. 82 Marble harpist figurine said to come from Keros. Courtesy of the National Archaeological Museum, Athens.

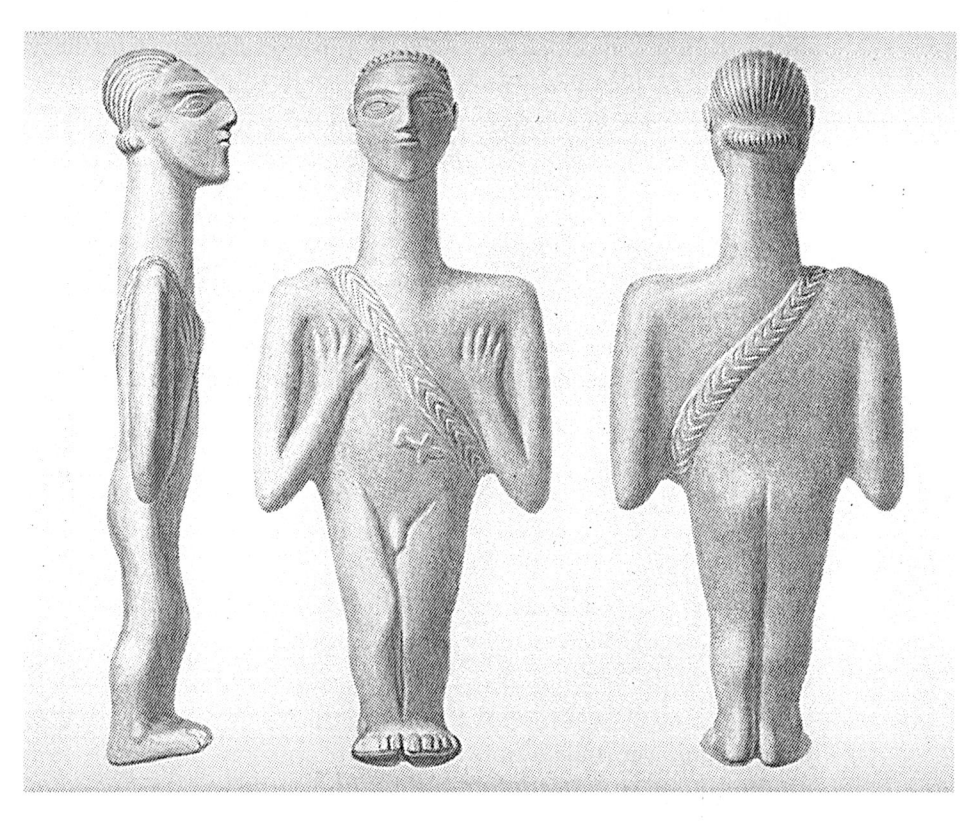

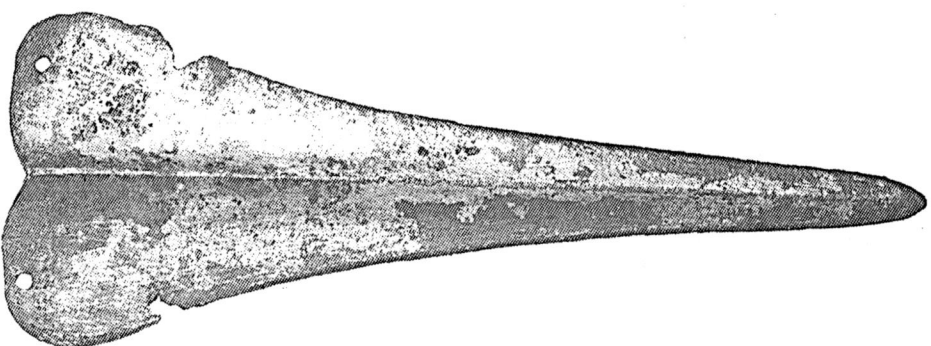

Fig. 83   The ideology of fighting. *Above:* drawing of 'Perditus', a now-lost hunter-warrior figurine. *Below:* 'silvered' dagger. Courtesy of the British Museum and the Ashmolean Museum respectively.

dating of the origins of 'piracy' to the EB II period slightly misses the mark (Renfrew 1972: 398), for piracy can hardly exist without recognised sea-laws, and there must be a strong suspicion that the only sea-laws that existed in the early Cyclades were those that were made and unmade by the practices of powerful island people.

The social dynamics of longboat activity

Building on these symbolic indices of an ideology of seafaring and an associated one of armed male power, we can explore the likely roles of prestigious seafarers in assuring community safety and advancing community power through organising people to build and crew canoes, and especially the large, fast, multi-paddled longboats. Assuming that the minimal longboat crew of roughly twenty-five people estimated in chapter 3 is correct, that the crews were young adults, and that longboat activity was gender-specific (probably male in the case of raiding), a demographic pool of roughly a hundred people would be needed to produce a suitable crew for one of the latter craft. But numbers alone would not suffice without the presence of someone with the authority to attract and mobilise people, either inside or outside of kin group relations. In other words, longboats were probably both indications of a threshold of social organisation and status symbols for those people able to utilise them. Whilst the demographic demands of longboat activity could be met by the handful of larger village settlements in the EB II Cyclades, they far exceeded the labour available in the smaller farmsteads and hamlets that constituted the most common types of island settlement during the EBA. Such communities must have been not only individually unable to deploy longboats, but also often lacking in the skill and knowledge to build them. In order for groups of such communities to cooperate in enabling longboat activity, either for trade purposes or for communal defence, authoritative people would still be needed to mobilise the materials and paddlers (if indeed such inter-community ventures were a practical option).

This prompts some observations on the likely temporal and spatial incidence of longboat activity in the early Cyclades. We asked in chapter 3 if the first iconographic appearance of such seacraft represented a real horizon of innovation, or an ideologically motivated uncloaking of a technology that had been present from an earlier date, similar to the increasing visibility of daggers and indeed to the overall *Metallschock* seen in the EB II Aegean (Nakou 1995). Then, it was pointed out that longboats should have been technologically feasible at least from the FN, when metal tools are first attested, if not earlier in the Neolithic. But if longboats were part of a wider cultural transformation of seafaring activity, it is equally plausible that these boats, and the groups that can be inferred from them, were a social innovation dating to somewhere around the transition to EB II. Even within EB II, when there were more people living in the Cyclades than ever before, the occurrence of longboat activity must have been uneven. Fig. 84 models the plausible foci, determined by the distribution of

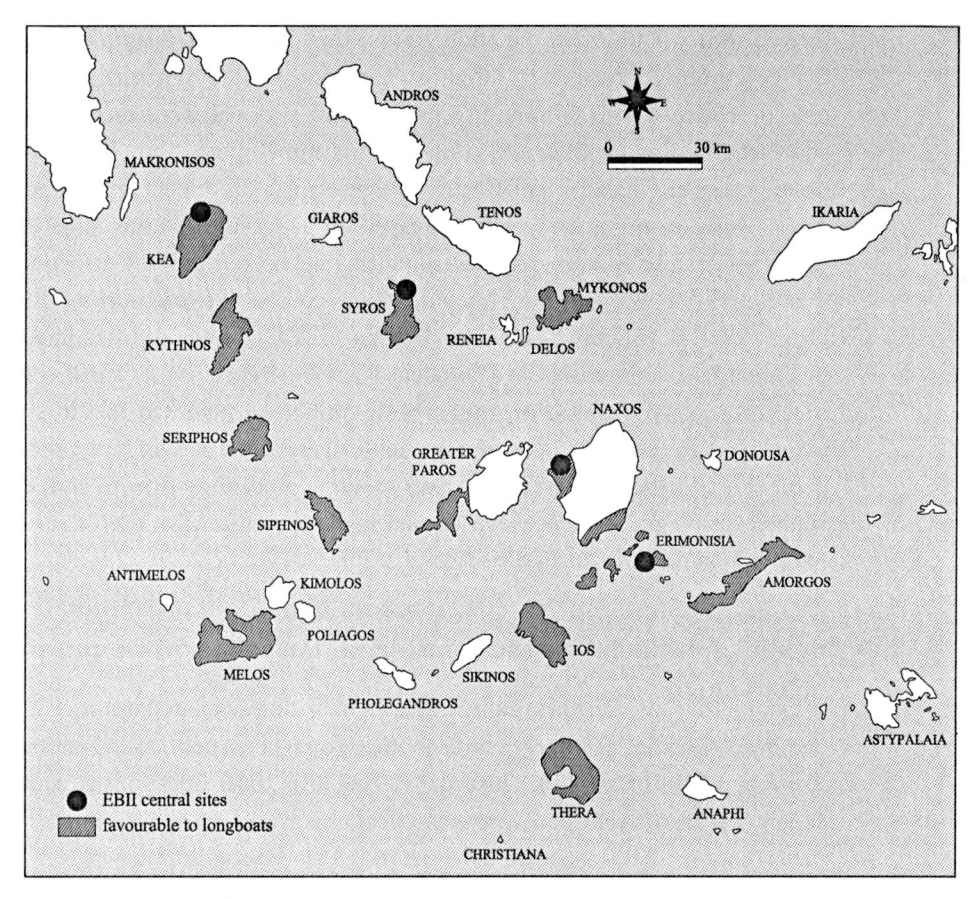

Fig. 84 Areas favourable to the organisation of longboat activity in the Cyclades, as suggested by demography and modelled sea-going orientation in PPAs 3–4.

known large centres and predicted levels of seagoing activity in PPAs 3–4, with the smaller islands in less advantageous positions than the Erimonisia deemed unable to operate such boats, on the grounds that the crew requirements exceeded their human resources. Beyond the large communities, the greatest potential for inter-community mobilisation is seen on medium-sized, fairly maritime-oriented islands like Amorgos, Thera, Mykonos and the western Cyclades. Bearing in mind the additional need for high-status people to put the crews together, however, the actual incidence of longboat activity must have been even patchier.

This is not to belittle the role of longboats, but rather to focus its impact. Among the large central communities, the organisation of canoe activity must have been vital for the promotion of effective maritime trade, further acquisition through fighting, and from time to time suppression of challenges. In certain circumstances it may even have been a crucial element in the centripetal forces that kept a large group of people together in the same place over the long-term. Take, for example, Chalandriani-Kastri, which seems to have owed its prominence to determined agency and to have thrived somewhat against the odds. Rather than proposing a simple equation stating that community size allowed longboat activities, a more dynamic scenario might be considered, in which community growth and survival were recursively related to successful raiding, trading and control of maritime interaction. The actual portrayal of longboats at Chalandriani-Kastri, which forms a unique iconographic peak in the early Cyclades, might in fact have played an active part in this large community's formation, rather than merely signalling that such craft existed. It is not impossible that the grave clusters in the cemetery, which consist of five groups of different sizes, i.e. 65, 75, 108, 158 and 242 tombs (Hekman 1994: table 1), reflect affiliations created by canoe-based activities. At Daskaleio-Kavos, perched on its small rock shelf and islet, and not far from several other well-connected potential foci in southern and eastern Naxos (cf. fig. 75), engaging people in maritime activities of a status-accruing nature could have been essential to promoting community growth and, equally, preventing disintegration. People at Daskaleio-Kavos must have lived their ideology up to the hilt in order to sustain such an extraordinary trajectory.

Spatial approaches to the transformation of maritime culture

Why did this new maritime culture arise? Or (a closely related question), what inhibited the emergence of larger centres in the Grotta-Pelos culture and encouraged them from the EB I–II transition onwards? At one level these questions become inevitably caught up in a cycle of cause-and-effect involving the quickening of interaction throughout the EB II Aegean, in which the Cycladic communities played a major role (see chapter 9). But there are cogent internal reasons for these changes too, in the form of the declining degree of overall seafaring predicted in the Cyclades as populations increased, a process that would paradoxically boost the significance and opportunities afforded by seagoing in those areas that did sustain a maritime orientation. The effects of population growth and increasing demographic self-sufficiency were modelled in chapter 6 (fig. 55), and the result was seen to be a sharp decrease in the general incidence of interaction by sea, with an increasing concentration of such activity in a few areas – in short a substitution of the ubiquitous seafaring of earlier times with a much more variegated pattern.

As communication beyond an island relies on seafaring, this implies a situation in which many people must have gazed far further than they had actually travelled, and others had travelled far further than they could ever see. Conceptions and experience of distance under such circumstances would become increasingly diverse, and knowledge of the world beyond a scrap of lived-in islandscape increasingly filtered by people and places that did maintain seafaring traditions. In such circumstances, Helms' notion of exotic knowledge as a commodity (1988: 118–19), Braudel's concept of news as a luxury import (1972: 365–8) and Renfrew's more archaeologically oriented discussion of 'trade beyond the material' (1993b) are all highly relevant. It can be added that the movement of physical things overseas, including people, objects, and raw materials such as obsidian and metals, might equally be channelled through such areas. At this juncture, let us recall a point made in chapter 6, to the effect that declining levels of generalised seafaring, in combination with increasing overall demands for raw materials as Cycladic populations increased, would have transformed the conditions of procurement, production and distribution. The scope for people living in places that still practised seafaring to a serious degree to manipulate flows to their advantage, in the pursuit of strategies of social power and enhancement of values, is apparent. As a result of such conditions and strategies, the central community within a local network might even have become something of a cosmological focus for the surrounding islanders.

How would some of these trends translate into spatial patterns (cf. figs. 53, 55 and 75)? In the lowest density PPA network (PPA 1), a bottle-neck is identifiable in western Greater Paros, where most of the richest Grotta-Pelos graves are indeed found, but the high levels of seafaring throughout the Cyclades would have made it difficult for people even in this area to maintain the kinds of control outlined above. In EB II, the conditions for the emergence of long-term centres are markedly more favourable. Even in the high-density networks, Syros and the Erimonisia are predicted to retain a strong commitment to maritime links, while most of their neighbours become more terrestrial in orientation, not least as a result of the coincidental presence in both cases of unusually large islands in the vicinity. In the south-east, the Erimonisia are matched in terms of their outgoing maritime links only by a few small and in all cases demonstrably *non-central*, islands, and they are unrivalled throughout the Cyclades in terms of their total maritime connectivity. In the north-east, the only challenges to Syros in this respect are distant, non-central, Mykonos, and northern Tenos (thanks to links over the narrow straits to Andros), an area highlighted in chapter 7 as a predicted communication centre. Again, potential tension is encountered between Syros and Tenos for dominance of the region. The predicted level of maritime activity in western Naxos (i.e. the general area of Grotta-Aplomata), is certainly lower, but this impression is qualified if set in the context of the surrounding network, which is devoid of high-intensity centres with better access to the sea. At least Grotta-Aplomata links the two islands of Greater Paros and Naxos, and would have had more opportunities to control incoming material, people and ideas than a hypothetical inland centre on the latter island. Lastly, the importance of maritime communication at the proposed inter-regional centre of Agia Irini on Kea has to be seen within the wider framework of the increasing amount of longer-range maritime trade in the EB II Aegean, which made this site and any equivalents elsewhere in the Cyclades into nodes in the circulation of material things and information throughout the Aegean.

What else can be inferred about the maritime roles of these centre? Although all are well placed to control sea travel and access to material from across the sea, not all may have been centres of maritime activity in quite the same manner. At Chalandriani-Kastri and Daskaleio-Kavos, a high degree of active seafaring on the community's part seems highly probable, with people from these sites acting as the carriers and traders of both their own and other people's goods. In answer to the question raised in chapter 7 concerning the mechanisms by which the imported pottery reached Daskaleio-Kavos, it now seems likely that much of it was acquired abroad by seafarers resident at the site, although Amorgos' dependency on links with the Erimonisia indicates that other people probably also visited these islands. Despite their similarities, an interesting distinction can also be drawn between maritime activity at Chalandriani-Kastri, which required an investment in range on the part of an otherwise remote area, and at Daskaleio-Kavos, which emerged out of intense network centrality. Forms of maritime activity at Grotta-Aplomata and Agia Irini are difficult to assess, with these sites' potential roles ranging from passive receiving centres, through ferrying points between (respectively) Naxos and Greater Paros, and Kea and Attica, to centres of active seafaring in their own right.

We can also model the extent of the islandscapes within the reach and control of these sites by using the one-day travel ranges established in chapter 3, and assuming for the sake of exploration that all four sites did in fact play an active maritime role (fig. 85). The innermost 10 km range, that for a there-and-back journey in a small canoe or on foot, creates a zone of maximum interaction. The 20 km range, reflecting a one-way journey by such means or a longboat's approximate there-and-back range, might reflect a zone of regular, if less intensive, activity. The 40 km range shows the one-day, one-way range of a longboat (the lower end of the 40–50 km estimate given in chapter 3 is chosen to compensate for the detours around intervening land), and defines a threshold zone between local networks and long-range interaction. Except at the outermost range, the four centres are spatially discrete. Little reason for competition between these centres for local control is therefore evident, although it can be remarked that this would not remain true in the north-east Cyclades if Chalandriani-Kastri did share this islandscape with another centre on Tenos, or indeed in the south-east if other centres were posited in southern or eastern Naxos.

Several other points of interest can be singled out. Daskaleio-Kavos' 10 km and 20 km zones of contact cover the Erimonisia, southern Naxos and (almost) Amorgos, which matches with the range of bulk pottery imports found at the site. The fact that Amorgos and Naxos lay beyond a day's journey of each other increases the likelihood that much interaction between them was mediated via the Erimonisia. At Chalandriani-Kastri and Agia Irini, however, these ranges afford almost no contact with overseas areas (with Tenos lying on the edge of the former's range); as a consequence, more distant activity assumes a major role. At the former site the concentration of longboat images is again cogent, and for the latter site it is likely that any potential involvement in maritime movement comprised fairly extensive activities in the approaches to Lavrion, Attica and Euboia. On a different note, and in sharp contrast to the domination of the eastern and northern Cyclades by a series of maritime centres, most of the western Cyclades lie largely or entirely beyond the

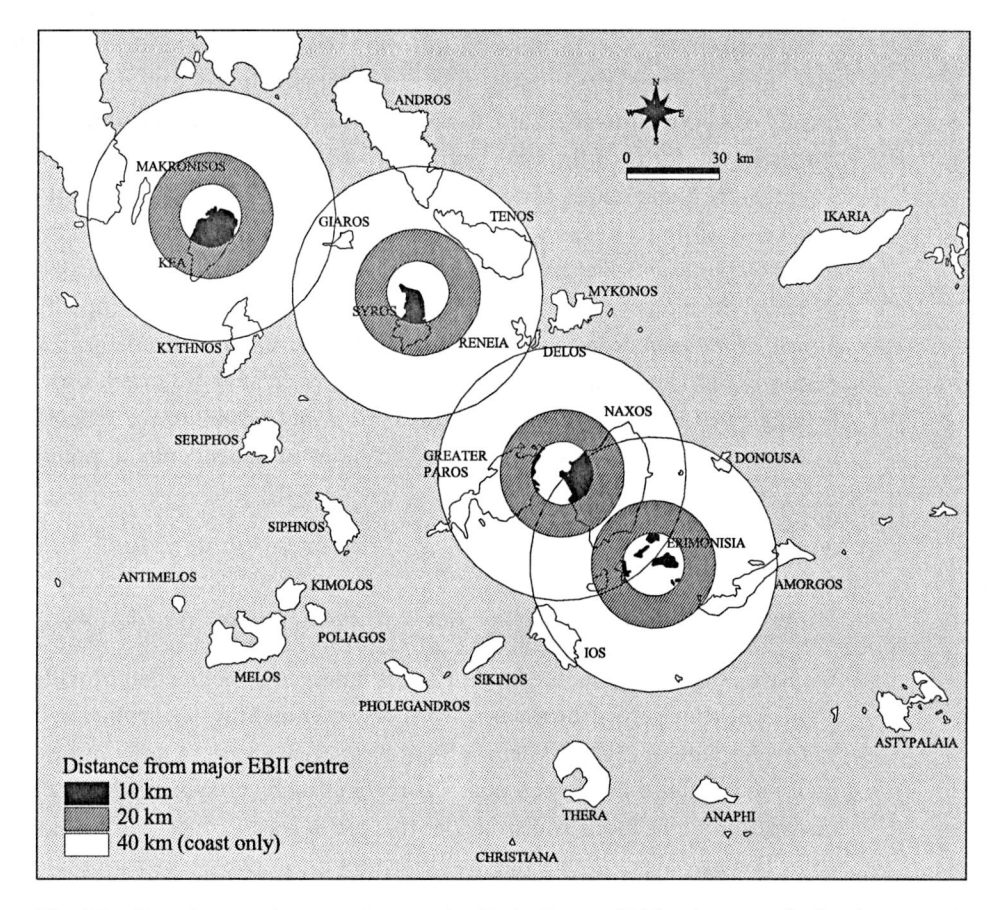

Fig. 85 One-day travel ranges from major Early Bronze II island centres, indicating several zones of interaction that differed in nature and intensity.

zones of activity shown in fig. 85. Unless a major centre awaits discovery here, this encourages us to speculate about the likelihood of rather different kinds of communities and practices in the western islands.

Drawing together several strands of enquiry, we can now better appreciate why Daskaleio-Kavos developed into such a particularly spectacular centre. In addition to the Erimonisia's extremely intense communication networks and unparalleled level of local maritime linkage, one particular opportunity and one potential challenge, both specific to this part of the Cyclades, could have shaped its history. The former is the control of social storage networks, more important in this arid region than in the other areas where centres arose. Controlling such networks in the islandscape extending from southern Naxos to Amorgos effectively entailed the power of life and death over communities. That Daskaleio-Kavos did orchestrate such relations is almost inevitable, given that the site lay at the centre of the networks that sustained them, and that the survival of a large community at this agriculturally inauspicious site would necessitate an active interest in the availability of food. One reason, if not the only one, as we shall shortly see, for the accumulation of prestige material at Daskaleio-Kavos may be that other communities became indebted through its manipulation of the means of survival during hard times. So much for the opportunity; the challenge comes in the form of the PPA predictions of other potential central places in this islandscape. None makes as regular a mark in PPAs 2–4 as do the Erimonisia, and it may be wondered whether another centre was in fact able to take off in the zone dominated by Daskaleio-Kavos. Yet the potential was probably always there, giving an edge to social relations in this region and perhaps exaggerating competition between people. For small communities, the advantages and disadvantages of life in the penumbra of Daskaleio-Kavos must have been delicately balanced, with its presence helping to boost the settlement of this region through intensive articulation of networks, but simultaneously engendering relations of dependency or potential rivalry.

Material culture, social status and the creation of value

Patterns of deposition of prestige goods through burial

We have established that the larger centres emerged at points that provided unusually good opportunities for the manipulation of access and the determination of regimes of value (Appadurai 1986). There is a surprisingly impressive amount of material evidence to suggest that this potential was recognised by the people at these centres, and realised through actions and strategies that are at least in part archaeologically detectable. The investigation that follows concentrates on Daskaleio-Kavos and the sites in its vicinity, not only because of the richness of their data, but also because this region was an exceptionally intense cock-pit of maritime interaction and competition. Several reasons for this amplification were given above, to which will now be added others that enable fresh light to be shed on the region's striking archaeological profile, and not least its rich EB II burials. Much of the case will rest on the treatment of the prestigious or symbolically charged elements of material culture. In contrast to the narrow suite of such objects known in the Grotta-Pelos culture (see chapter 5), in EB II the repertoire of such objects expanded greatly, through internal diversification and the introduction of exotic types from beyond the Cyclades (cf. chapter 9). This combination created the Keros-Syros complex of forms, including painted, incised and stamped-and-incised pottery (e.g. frying pans, pyxides, sauceboats and pedestal-based jars), metal jewellery and weapons, folded-arm and other figurines, and a wide range of marble vessel types.

In the analysis of cultural strategies that follows, three assumptions are made. The first is that throughout the EBA and across most, if not all, of the islands, prestige objects were circulating above ground between people and places, without deposition, in ways and to degrees that are seldom accessible to us. Confirmation of this comes in the form of the occasional settlement finds of figurines, stone vessels, fine pottery and metal items, sometimes demonstrably outside their area of production. These periods of above-ground existence might be long, to judge from the damage, mend-holes and wear on the marble vessels and figurines, as illustrated by the Plastiras type figurine in fig. 51, and also a harpist from Aphendika on Naxos which is so battered that its history may have been as peripatetic as that of its suggested real-life equivalent. Other cases of long-term curation are also apparent, such as a Grotta-Pelos kandila found with EB II material in Spedos grave 12 (Papathanasopoulos 1961/2: 121).

The second assumption is that as such objects circulated or became attached to people, they accumulated individual histories and, in some instances, even fame. These histories culminated with deposition, at which point archaeology intercepts them. The sheer diversity of decoration that survives at least on the pottery and figurines argues that many prestige items were indeed consciously individualised, allowing specific local pieces to be recognised, and exotic imports to stand out even without close inspection.

The third assumption is that the value and meaning of such objects was highly variable, culturally negotiable and mediated by conditions of access and knowledge. A given figurine, for example, could signify something different in different communities, or equally in the same community over time. More specifically, marble objects surely enjoyed a rarity value, other things being equal, on islands such as Melos, Thera, Syros or Kea, where high-quality marbles are scarce or absent, that they lacked in the core area of production in the south-east Cyclades (cf. Davis in Fitton 1984: 34–5).

If these assumptions are accepted, we can start to look at how and why prestige objects came out of above-ground circulation or possession. For although these objects were argued in chapter 5 to have their origins in a culture of exchange tokens created in the Grotta-Pelos culture, even within this horizon their accumulation, possession and withdrawal through funerary deposition was starting to be reworked in a few parts of the Cyclades into a means of defining status or controlling value, an incipient trend that was drastically amplified in EB II. Some general observations help us to contextualise the behaviour at central sites. Signs of an increasing tendency to bury such objects can be seen in the larger absolute quantities of marble figurines, marble vessels and metal objects known from excavation of EB II cemeteries, in contrast to Grotta-Pelos culture ones. The lower frequency of mended figurines in EB II, compared to the earlier types, is also significant. Getz-Preziosi (1987a: 25) argues that the higher incidence of breakage in earlier pieces was due to inferior design, but it is as likely to be a testimony to longer above-ground circulation and exposure to damage. At the risk of simplifying, in EB II substantially more prestige objects were being buried after shorter average life-spans, although some objects still did experience long above-ground lives (e.g. the Aphendika harpist). The only qualifications to this accelerating tendency to disposal are that we cannot assess accurately how it related to levels of above-ground deployment, and that if, in certain parts of the Cyclades, similar aims were achieved by using objects in ways that did not involve burial, we would know next to nothing of it.

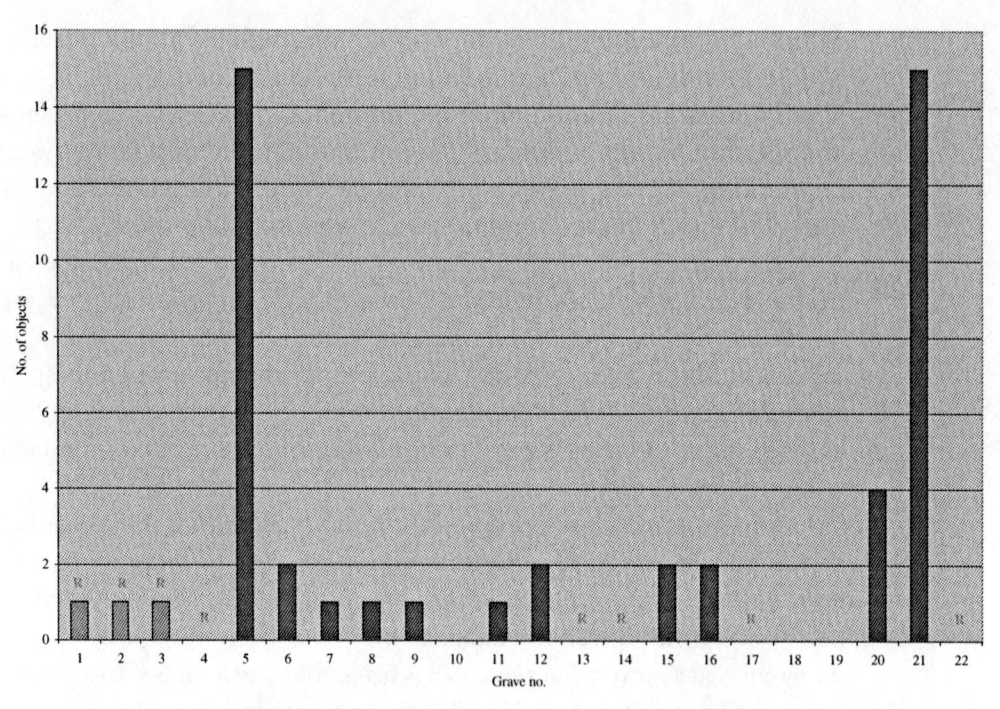

Fig. 86 Number of grave goods per grave in the Agioi Anargyroi cemetery on Naxos. All the unrobbed graves appear to have contained only one or two inhumations, with the exception of the multiple burials found in Grave 21. The spike of deposition in Grave 5 stands out. Data from Doumas 1977.

Although increasing amounts of prestige objects were being buried through the course of the EBA, chapter 7's discussion of the richest Grotta-Pelos graves and the markedly conspicuous deposition at big EB II sites indicated that such deposition acts were concentrated phenomena of far from even incidence. So far, we have focused on the richest cemeteries and individual graves, but it should be stressed that most graves in the Cyclades contained no goods, or only a single item, with a very small number being radically better endowed (Doumas 1977: 58–63; Getz-Gentle 1996: 175; Renfrew 1972: 371–8). This creates a spiky profile in terms of the number of objects per grave in a cemetery, as is illustrated in fig. 86 by the example of Agioi Anargyroi. Because the material-rich spikes correlate with well-built tombs containing a single inhumation (where data are available), a case can be made that they represent important members of the community, and that the death of such people was the occasion for the interment of prestige objects, in other words for the death of the latter as well as the former.

This in turn argues that the materials found in each grave are telling us not really about anything as straightforward as normative burial customs in the islands, but about conscious decisions made at specific times by particular people to take designated items out of circulation. Such events must have occurred quite rarely, as most

Table 10. *Two rich south-east Cycladic burials of Early Bronze II date. Data from Papathanasopoulos 1961/2: 114–19 and Tsountas 1898: 154.*

Spedos grave 10
2 marble folded-arm figurines
3 marble bowls, one spouted
1 marble complex vessel, possibly imitating a lamp
1 pottery pattern-painted triple sauceboat vessel
1 pottery pattern-painted sauceboat
1 pottery pattern-painted jug with skeuomorphic features
1 pottery pattern-painted juglet with skeuomorphic features and traces of silver foil
1 pottery pedestal-based spouted bowl
2 pedestal-based collared jars with incised decoration

Dokathismata grave 14
1 copper/bronze spearhead
1 copper/bronze dagger with silver rivets
1 silver bowl (fragmentary)
2 marble folded-arm figurines
2 marble bowls, one with traces of red pigment
1 pottery jar
1 other pottery vessel (fragmentary)

---

cemeteries have only one or two rich graves, or none at all, and even at Daskaleio-Kavos a comparison between the figurine count (estimated about 100–200 items) and the community lifespan of several centuries suggests that on average a figurine entered the special deposit only every few years, although a tighter concentration of the main deposition phase within a shorter time-span is quite possible. Major acts of deposition must have had an impact in their neighbourhood, especially if the objects involved were well known or coveted.

In those cases where one or two rich graves stand out in a small cemetery, we are probably witnessing the notable yet brief climax of a tiny community, as a result of the achievements of a family head, elder or other local hero who managed to accumulate status symbols and a fragile personal power that did not outlive his or her lifetime. Such phenomena have already been witnessed in a few of the Grotta-Pelos graves on Greater Paros. Kampos group examples include Louros Athalassou grave 26 on Naxos, singled out by Renfrew (1984a: 47–53) as indicative of emergent wealth and status. In EB II, good examples are Dokathismata grave 14 on Amorgos, probably some graves from the Kapros cemetery on the same island, Spedos graves 10 and 13 on Naxos, robbed graves on Naxos such as Aphendika grave 40, from which came the battered harpist (Doumas 1977: 59–60), and others at Phionda (Renfrew 1972: 519), as well as the graves on Ios whose objects were bought by early travellers (Arnott 1990). Table 10 lists two of these accumulations, to illustrate the phenomenon.

A key point to grasp is that what in effect distinguishes the major EB II sites' burial grounds from the above solitary flashes of funerary display is the formers' more

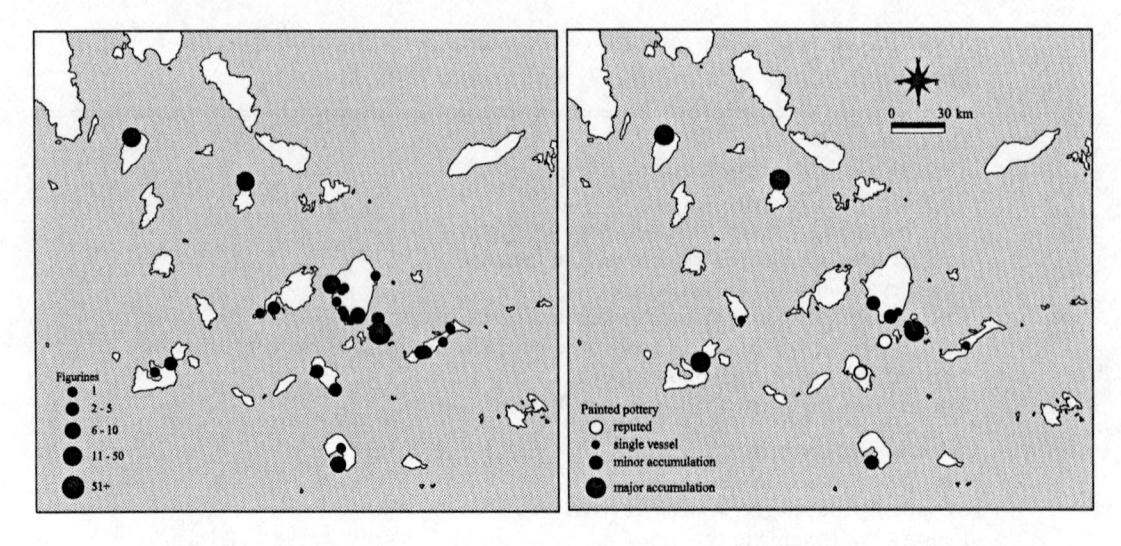

Fig. 87　Early Bronze II Cycladic distributions of (*left*) marble figurines and (*right*) painted pottery.

frequent staging of such actions, which creates the impression of a wealthy cemetery. This can be underlined by considering the group of thirty-plus rich graves out of the hundreds documented at Chalandriani (Renfrew 1972: 373–5), the surviving graves of what was surely originally a bigger cemetery at Aplomata, and Daskaleio-Kavos' special deposit, where even the huge quantity of material is still insufficient to provide material-rich burials for the inferred number of inhumations. In this sense, conspicuous deposition at large sites was a sign not strictly of community wealth, but of the regularity with which such communities produced individuals (or their burying groups) who were capable of major deposition-acts. The relationship between advantageous places, prominent people and the conspicuous disposal of prestige goods was clearly complicated and intricate.

Fig. 87 demonstrates just how successful such people at the central sites were at obtaining prestigious objects and depositing them in the ground, as indicated by plots of securely provenanced EB II figurines and painted pottery.[1] The four major centres

---

[1] In chapter 6 this pottery provided insights into regional styles during EB II, but there is little doubt that it also served as a prestigious class of material in at least some parts of the Cyclades. Reasons include its depiction of maritime imagery, jewellery and possibly textiles. It is absent from most small sites and even if present is always rare. Even at large sites it makes up a small proportion of the entire assemblage. In the few cemetery contexts that allow a detailed comparison with the quantity of marble material, painted pottery is in fact the rarer medium. Thus, for example, there are five painted vessels in the Spedos cemetery, but eight figurines and fourteen marble vessels. Indeed if we put aside the astronomical modern valuations of marble Cycladica, we might infer at least an equivalent early Cycladic value for painted pottery to that of marble objects. The deployment of painted pottery in the EB II Cyclades appears, incidentally, to have been socially controlled in a way that it was not in the Neolithic, when it was a major medium of stylistic communication, nor in EM II Crete, where it is common in large and small settlements (Warren 1972a: 93–4; Wilson 1985: 307–12, 319–30).

account for the majority of the figurines, and even in the figurine-rich south-east, Daskaleio-Kavos accounts for more than all the surrounding sites put together. Depending on the number of figurines that the special deposit at the latter site contained, something like 75–90 per cent of all the figurines with known archaeological contexts in the Cyclades derive from Daskaleio-Kavos, Chalandriani-Kastri, Grotta-Aplomata and Agia Irini, with maybe as much as half this total coming from Daskaleio-Kavos alone. How much this pattern would alter if the find-spots of the unprovenanced figurines in the world's museums and private collections could be reliably ascertained is uncertain, but the changes might not be great. Many of the rumours of illicit finds, such as those surrounding Phionda's looting (Renfrew 1972: 519), together with available data about early purchases, imply a few figurines in each cemetery, in short much the same pattern as the documented find-spots from the richest graves in southern Naxos and Amorgos.

An equally concentrated distribution is revealed by the painted pottery, although here a somewhat surprising feature is the lack of reported material at Grotta-Aplomata and its significant presence at Phylakopi. The former absence, if indeed sustained, may be telling us about the precise chronological horizon of the EB II deposits excavated to date (perhaps very early?). Concerning Phylakopi, one possibility is, of course, that the site was in fact a major centre in EB II. Another is that in parts of the Cyclades less subject to controlled access to prestige goods than in the vicinity of major centres, such material was produced and consumed in different ways. One potential sign that painted pottery could indeed have taken on different meanings on Melos is that only on this island were painted forms other than small, fine fabric shapes manufactured, as demonstrated by the larger broad-streak painted container jars found at Phylakopi and exported to Agia Irini.

Consumption, creation and value at Daskaleio-Kavos

The role of deposition acts in the dynamics of central sites and other communities in their vicinity can be explored by focusing on Daskaleio-Kavos and its neighbours. We have already adduced several reasons why this region might have become a charged arena, including the number of potential centres of communication (in addition to the primary focus in the Erimonisia), and the vital role of social storage for survival. In this volatile context, the material-rich burials dotted across southern Naxos and Amorgos can be interpreted not simply as internalised expressions of status within communities, but also as statements directed outwards, to a wider audience, concerning people whose exploits in life had sought to emulate or challenge the community at Daskaleio-Kavos. Following this line of argument, the wealth of material in the special deposit at the latter site might represent a crescendo of deposition intended to exceed the display capabilities of rivals and, in addition, to remove from circulation quantities of the objects through which status could be acquired by others. Such deposition may, furthermore, have served to underpin the value of prestige objects by ensuring their scarcity. Interpreting the quickening rate of deposition of objects in terms of inflationary spirals certainly runs a risk of anachronism, but there are several reasons to believe that such 'tournaments of value' (Appadurai 1986: 21) did indeed develop in and around Daskaleio-Kavos. Three distinctive cultural traits specific to this region can help to substantiate this claim.

The first comprises the evidence of deliberate destruction of prestige material in the Erimonisia. Naturally, this is best attested by the smashing of the marble objects at Daskaleio-Kavos. Although this is frequently assumed to militate against the funerary interpretation of the special deposit, it should be clear by now that depositional practices in Cycladic graves were strategic rather than normative, and that an unusual community might well deposit in an unusual way. Moreover, a much overlooked piece of evidence confirms that the destruction of objects in a funerary context had wider distribution in these islands. At least one dagger from Epano Kouphonisi had been deliberately 'killed' by the blade being bent back on itself (comment by Zapheiropoulou in Fitton 1984: 35). Several similarly killed daggers in the Apeiranthos museum on Naxos must come from robbed graves in the Erimonisia or southern Naxos. In this context it does not actually greatly matter whether all the smashed marble objects in the Daskaleio-Kavos special deposit accompanied inhumations, or whether a potlatch tradition of conspicuous destruction developed alongside funerary deposition. The condition of the deposit means that we shall probably never know, although two possible cases of figurine deposition outside graves but within cemeteries are known, at Agrilia in the Kouphonisia (Zapheiropoulou 1970: 428) and Aplomata (Kontoleon 1971: 72). Nor is it too great a limitation that we cannot fathom the specific meanings attributed to such acts in the Cyclades (for cross-cultural possibilities see Bradley 1990, Hamilakis 1998 and Treherne 1995). What do matter are the rationale and consequences of destroying marble objects in the south-east Cyclades. For unlike the circumstances on those islands without marble, or with minor sources, it would be impossible for a community in the marble-rich south-east Cyclades to control the overall manufacture of marble objects, forcing strategies of value control to concentrate on capture and removal from circulation. Smashing would achieve this in a spectacular way, impressing other communities that could only occasionally aspire to bury a figurine, destroying the objects' value and power, and perhaps also guaranteeing that such objects could never be extracted for recirculation (a practice that cannot be documented, but which the shallowness of early Cycladic graves might encourage).

The second hint of tournaments of value concerns the production of objects, and reminds us that although Daskaleio-Kavos was a place where the lives of many objects ended, it was equally a place where objects were born. The indications of production at the site were enumerated in chapter 7. The manufacture of objects from non-locally available materials is likely to have created diverse opportunities for value control and enhancement. But again the situation concerning marble objects is especially intriguing. For a complementary strategy to artefact capture and destruction under conditions where access to raw materials could not be controlled would be to increase skills in crafting, enabling the creation of objects that others were unable to emulate. Daskaleio-Kavos' longevity and size would be a substantial advantage in this respect, as it would allow the development of crafting traditions that small sites could seldom match. If anything did make marble-carving the exalted practice that modern enthusiasts assume it to have been, it will have been such extreme demonstrations of virtuosity (cf. Helms 1993). This is an attractive framework for understanding the large and intricate marble objects found at Daskaleio-Kavos, with the limited distribution of such objects elsewhere in the Cyclades being neatly explained if most were both made and consumed at the site. Dove bowls are found nowhere else, marble frying pans are only paralleled at Grotta-Aplomata, as are the extremely delicate pedestal-based jars (with the exception of one at Karvounolakkoi on Naxos), although comparanda from archaeological contexts for the large and complex figurines are too few to allow any firm inferences to be drawn. The parallels at Grotta-Aplomata might suggest that this large site, also in an area of plentiful marble, followed a similar strategy, with its own specialities, or that Daskaleio-Kavos traded for such objects only with a community of equivalent status. Whatever the particulars, this scenario offers an explanation for the boom in the diversity of marble forms witnessed in EB II, as the result of a top-down innovation spiral aiming at social distinction with added bottom-up emulation from aspiring people in other communities.

The third sign of competitive manipulations of value is skeuomorphic imitation of metal objects, and particularly metal vessels. Renfrew (1967, 1969, 1972: plate 19) long ago highlighted Aegean examples of this phenomenon. Some particularly intricate skeuomorphic traits can be detected in the material culture of Daskaleio-Kavos and other sites on southern Naxos and Amorgos. The original metal vessels are rarely found in the Cyclades, as is indeed the case throughout the EBA Aegean, with the exception of Troy (Antonova *et al.* 1996), where a specific horizon of buried 'hoards' late in EB II explains the survival of such objects (Nakou 1997: 635), several of which bear signs of damage and repair suggesting extended above-ground lifespans (Antonova *et al.* 1996: 217–18). Just four metal vessels, all made of silver, are known from the early Cyclades: a cup from Notina on Amorgos (Dümmler 1886: fig. 1.4), two shallow bowls from Kapros and Dokathismata on the same island (Renfrew 1967, plates 1, 10; Tsountas 1898: plate 8 no. 3) and a small juglet from an unrecorded location on Naxos. These sites circle the Erimonisia. As fragile metal objects survive poorly in Daskaleio-Kavos' battered special deposit, any metallic vessels that it did contain have probably been destroyed. Overall, however, the impression remains that such vessels represented an end of Cycladic value spectra that were infrequently deposited in graves, and that are hence all but archaeologically invisible. A chastening implication is that even those items that we term 'prestigious' may not have occupied the ultimate pinnacles of value in the islands, and we can only speculate whether the latter sometimes took the form of metal vessels or other elaborate objects seen by islanders *outside* the Cyclades and only extremely infrequently acquired and brought into the islands, a theme to which we return in the following chapter.

Skeuomorphic features imitative of metal can be seen in several Cycladic object classes that survive, such as the vertical or inset rims set on the flat bases of frying pans and dove bowls – a metal version of the former is known from Alaça Hüyük in central Anatolia (Coleman 1985: 202, 216–17), the ribbed surfaces of several marble bowls and pyxides (Getz-Gentle 1996: 107) and maybe even the angular, planar form of certain of the folded-arm figurines, particularly the Dokathismata type, which have tantalising parallels in metal from central Anatolia (in elaborate form) and the Cyclades themselves (cruder lead objects) (Renfrew 1967: 16, 1969: 31; Thimme 1977: 161, fig. 155). All the above types are encountered in marble at Daskaleio-Kavos, prompting the intriguing observation that even at this commanding site people aspired to objects that they could not get in sufficient quantities, or at least seldom if ever afford to take out of circulation.

But the richest insights into skeuomorphism and value manipulation come from jugs and juglets at Daskaleio-Kavos and in its vicinity. These belong to the social and display-oriented elements of the EB II repertoire, as is shown by their associations with burials, their elaborate decoration, and the fact that a silver example survives. Three varieties of skeuomorphism are attested (fig. 88). The first is the formal imitation of metallic features in clay, notably imitation rivets on the handle-to-body join, handles of a twisted or strap-like form, sharply inset bases and occasionally tubular spouts. Two examples come from Spedos (Papathanasopoulos 1961/2: plates C, 49c–d), and several from Daskaleio-Kavos (Zapheiropoulou 1975: fig. 3b). Such features are otherwise thoroughly rare, if not unknown, in the Cyclades. The second variety is represented by one of the above Spedos juglets, which was first decorated with a painted design and later covered with silver foil, an excellent example of value escalation, given the fact that painted vessels were themselves prestige objects; this is the juglet that is also claimed to have held olive oil (see chapter 3). The third variety of skeuomorphism is attested by a coarse clay jug of common, conical-necked type from Panermos (Marangou 1990: cat. no. 107) on which is incised the image of a different jug with a high columnar neck, long spout and strap handle. This image closely resembles one of the fine painted jugs with rivets and other skeuomorphic features found at Daskaleio-Kavos, and both ultimately reference a metal prototype. This incised image makes an interesting case for a process of imitation from below, in addition to elaboration from above, suggesting that small communities were indeed drawn into the value systems and regimes generated by the larger centres.

Leaving skeuomorphism, there are other instances of bottom-up emulation of high-status symbols. One instance is the fish symbolism on painted jugs at Daskaleio-Kavos and its imitation in an incised form on jars in Amorgian schist fabrics, mostly in fact

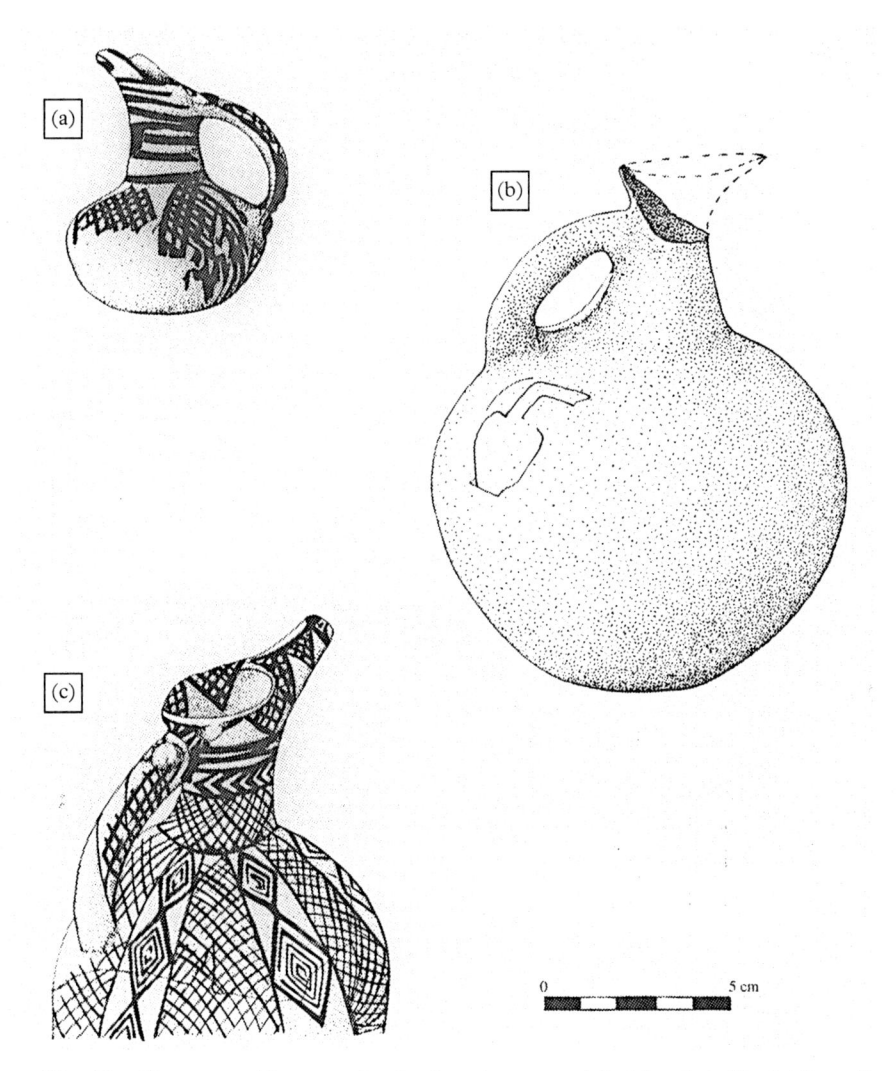

Fig. 88 Skeuomorphism seen in clay jugs (not to scale): (a) painted juglet from Spedos with imitation rivets at the handle/body joins and traces of silver foil on the neck and lower body, (b) plain jug from Panermos with a tall-necked jug incised on the body, (c) painted jug from Spedos with imitation rivets at the handle/body join, twisted handle and tubular spout. (a) and (c) after Papathanasopoulos 1961/2: plates C, 49 c–d; (b) after Marangou 1990: cat. no. 107.

found as imports in the special deposit (Zapheiropoulou 1975: figs. 3i and k). The roughly shaped figurines of the Apeiranthos type might be another example (Renfrew 1969: 14), imitating the fully anthropomorphic folded-arm types, and indeed many of the figurines that are unhelpfully classified as hybrids or stylistic outliers may represent the sporadic creations of small communities seeking to enter the material universe of the handful of sites that could produce appreciable numbers of figurines in well-known forms. In one further case non-preservation (or non-discovery?) at Daskaleio-Kavos has deprived us of the original, but an imitation may lie close to hand. A plainly made drinking animal figurine from Naxos (Marangou 1990: cat. no. 102) is surely a crude version of the hedgehog type (cf. fig. 64) that is known in fine painted pottery at Chalandriani-Kastri and Agia Irini and in carved stone at Manika in Euboia. As finds of these figurines have been forthcoming at most major centres, it would not be surprising if fragments emerge one day from the special deposit, although as the other sites have produced one apiece, the task will be akin to finding the proverbial needle in a haystack.

In summary, the deposition record of the Erimonisia and surrounding islands, now largely destroyed thanks to the actions of tomb robbers and the desires of Western collectors, was the result of a complex social and material universe. It preserves, or at least preserved until tragically recently, many fascinating scraps of a cultural discourse between the people who had forged a competitive, intricately interacting world out of what is now a remote corner of the islands. Similar work in other parts of the Cyclades will only be possible once more archaeological exploration has been undertaken, both to document the major sites in detail and to populate the surrounding islandscapes. There is every chance that the processes that will eventually be clarified in and around Syros will differ from those outlined for the south-east, and this must also hold true for other parts of the early Cyclades, for in no two cases does the combination of opportunities, constraints and insular contexts appear to be quite the same. We may equally discover that the regimes of value in different areas of the islands can be shown to have varied, and triggered quite different material culture trajectories. The potential certainly exists.

Cycladic EBA island traders in comparative perspective

Now that these early Cycladic practices have been delineated in their own terms, we can conclude by drawing parallels and exploring distinctions between the maritime centres described in this and the previous chapter, and the island trader communities known from ethnographic reports elsewhere in the world, and most famously in Melanesia. So far, the temptation to explore such issues and possible analogies has been deliberately resisted, in order to avoid prejudging the nature of the dynamics in the early Cyclades – in much the same way that the ethnographic record was argued in chapter 1 to be a limiting model when exploring the pre-contact Pacific. Now, however, it is rewarding to take a brief look at the ways in which the Cycladic centres join a wider class of island societies, and the extent to which they remain unique.

Comparative data of course supply an almost limitless range of archaeologically invisible products and practices of potential relevance to the early Cycladic centres. To cite two examples, the contact-period Siassi of Melanesia, one of the best-studied island trading societies, traded dances and pigs (Harding 1967: 142–4; Strathern 1983: 76), whilst in recent times the islanders of Arwad off the coast of Syria developed a less illustrious trade in dung (Mallowan 1939). In a different vein, although the sanctuary hypothesis for Daskaleio-Kavos is not empirically supported, and not the best means of explaining the deposits discovered, there are many examples of island trading centres that acquired an aura of sanctity, magical power or cosmological significance, including first-millennium BC Delos, Maya Cozumel, Mailu (Irwin 1974: 270), Chaura in the Nicobar islands (Hutton 1951) and Siassi itself (Strathern 1983: 76–7). It is perfectly possible that via seafaring, production and consumption Daskaleio-Kavos did become a magical, numinous place for other islanders, but it is unlikely that we shall ever know.

More practically, there are certainly some broad parallels to be drawn between the long-term development of trading networks and centrality in the early Cyclades and in Melanesia. The shift identified in the Cyclades, from low-density conditions and open networks of even maritime contact to high-density conditions, regionally focused networks, uneven participation in sea-trade and concentrations of craft production, is also well documented in Melanesia (Allen 1984; Kirch 1990; Spriggs 1997: 152–86). The trading communities of the contact period, such as the people of Siassi, Mailu, Motupore, Tubetube and the Amphletts, are known to possess an ancestry of rather less than a millennium (comparable to the duration of those in the EB II Cyclades) and to have been preceded by different patterns of interaction. Lilley (1988), for example, has shown that in the Lapita period the Siassi islands were relatively unimportant, much as the Erimonisia mattered little in the Neolithic and the period of the Grotta-Pelos culture.

Several other characteristics of the specialised communities in both areas are comparable. Both provide striking examples of high population build-ups in resource-poor areas, implying commuting to fields or trading for foodstuffs, although the early Cyclades cannot match the highest Pacific densities, such as 200 people per sq km on the Torres Strait island of Nagir (Harris 1979: 87–8) and comparable levels on the tiny Siassi islands (Harding 1967: 118). A parallel from the later Aegean is the demography of the Archaic and Classical maritime centre of Aegina (Figueira 1981). Yet in both theatres a central location within specific island networks, rather than environmental marginality *per se*, was the crucial stimulus to the development of a trading role (chapter 7 for the Cyclades; Irwin 1974, 1983, contra Allen 1984, for Melanesia; also Evans 1977 for the Lipari islands of the central Mediterranean). The centralised patterns of connections that both developed, with intensive local links and selective long-range associations, also display general similarities, as is indicated by a comparison of the Siassi networks with those reconstructed for the Erimonisia (fig. 89).

Such parallels can partly be explained by generic properties that the Cycladic and Melanesian islands share in common. These include dense configurations, rugged interiors that encourage maritime links and fragment individual islands, their positions between much larger land-masses (for at least parts of Melanesia), their high levels of environmental micro-diversity, the rich but unevenly distributed mineral resources,

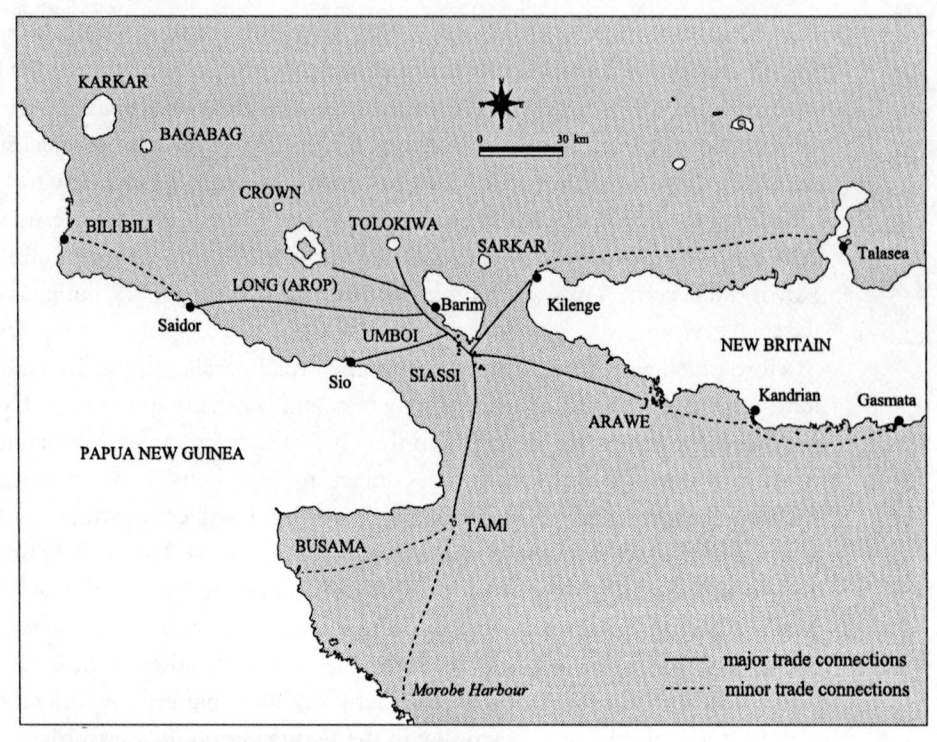

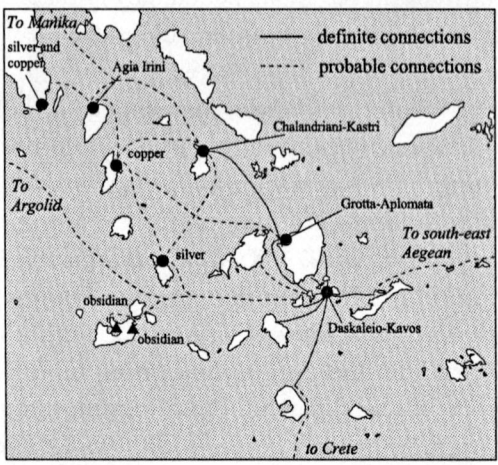

Fig. 89 Two island trading systems compared: the Cycladic Early Bronze II and the ethnohistorically attested Siassi islanders' networks to the same scale. Note that usage of sailing canoes in the latter case qualifies the scalar comparison. Siassi network after Spriggs 1996: fig. 7.3, in turn courtesy of Ian Lilley.

and perhaps, as raised in chapter 2, their locations on the fringe of larger world-systems (South-East Asia and the Near East), the latter a theme to be considered again in chapter 9.

Similarities between more specific economic and cultural practices in the early Cyclades and contact-period Melanesia need to be treated cautiously, however, not least owing to the problem in the latter case of contact-induced change, and equally the recent reworking of several classic components of Melanesian ethnography such as the 'big-man', probably a more contingent phenomenon than once thought (Spriggs 1997: 187, 199, 231; also Godelier and Strathern 1991), and the Trobriand *kula* (Malinowski 1922; Leach and Leach 1983). Elements of Cycladic EB II trade practices can certainly be categorised as prestige goods economies (Friedman 1982), though such economies are far from restricted to island settings. As was the case in the Melanesian systems of the contact period, opportunities existed in the EB II Cyclades too for enhancing status and fame by excelling in maritime prowess (cf. Munn 1987), and for making profits by the skilled negotiation of value, helping to dispel the common misapprehension, prevalent since Malinowski, that island trading systems were simply ring-dances of reciprocity. But the details of social practices more often indicate that circumstances and antecedent history distinguished the Cyclades from contact-period Melanesia, creating different cultural worlds and archaeologies. A fundamental distinction can be drawn between the above-ground domains of display and competition in Melanesia (centred on feasting), which made people of high status all but invisible archaeologically, and the importance of the funerary domain as an arena for display in at least some parts of the Cyclades (although to judge from occasional finds of prestige goods in the settlements, above-ground activities were also important in the Cyclades). This stress on funerary display must be attributed to the cultural role of cemeteries in the early Cyclades since the latest phase of the Neolithic. The early Cyclades and pre-contact Melanesia share, in short, a surprising number of generic features and patterns as island theatres; but their island cultures need to be understood in their own intricate and particular historical contexts.

9

Ulysses without sails

> Thou dost; and think'st it much to tread the ooze
> Of the salt deep;
> To run upon the sharp wind of the north;
> To do me business in the veins o' the earth.
> *The Tempest,* WILLIAM SHAKESPEARE

The preceding three chapters have shown that the dynamics of interaction in the EB I–II Cyclades can be understood to a substantial degree in terms of the local comings and goings of islanders and the social strategies practised at particular places where greater amounts of movement concentrated. But it would be naive to paint an overall image of the Cyclades that omitted the contacts that certain islanders had with other parts of the EBA Aegean and, via that contact, with wider developments and more distant worlds. The role of external contacts has been touched on at several junctures already, examples being the non-Cycladic imports found at the trading sites, the position of Agia Irini II–III as a gateway to regions north of the Cyclades, and the fact that some elements of the Cycladic material, especially Keros-Syros types, match objects known elsewhere in the Aegean. Accordingly, this chapter engages with a cluster of questions surrounding the Cycladic islanders' activities beyond the Cyclades, picking up where the discussion of external connections during the later Neolithic left off in chapter 5. As will become apparent, such connections in the periods of the Kampos group and EB II demonstrate ways of structuring relations with the outside world that differed profoundly from the extensive yet relatively uniform links forged by later Neolithic island communities, and also from the minimal interest in wider horizons during the Grotta-Pelos culture. And even within the former periods, a sequence of changes can be detected in the articulation of such relations that open up larger questions about the integration of Cycladic, Aegean and east Mediterranean history by the second half of the third millennium BC.

The credit for first recognising the evidence for long-range interaction in the EB II Aegean goes to Renfrew (1972: 451–5). A brief outline of his characterisation of this phenomenon can usefully serve to introduce its key features, and acts as a baseline from which to assess subsequent advances. Renfrew contrasted the paucity of evidence for long-range interaction in EB I, excepting a continuing outflow of Melian obsidian, with a burgeoning 'international spirit' that spread across much of the

Aegean in EB II. The latter was documented by the dispersion over several regions of a range of low-bulk but high-value (or at least socially significant) objects. These included mid-ribbed daggers, tweezers and metal jewellery, pottery drinking or pouring vessels such as sauceboats, jugs and in later EB II tankards and depas cups (all having attested metallic versions), folded-arm figurines, and vessels in marble and other stones – in short mainly items associated with the Keros-Syros culture in the Cyclades. The other features identified by Renfrew were (1) the central place of the Cyclades in the distributions of material, (2) the small number of archaeologically visible imports to the Cyclades in comparison to the amount of Cycladic material abroad, (3) the importance of maritime connections (which he associated with a technological innovation in the form of longboats, enabled by metal tools), (4) the virtual exclusion of the land-locked areas of the north and north-west Aegean (although the north-east Aegean islands and western Anatolian coast were considered vital areas) and lastly, and not least presciently, (5) the crucial role of metals as a fluid, desirable medium and a means of acquiring status and fighting power, in generating this pattern of inter-regional linkage. Renfrew made two further good points. First, the international spirit was a fairly thin veneer, a shared vocabulary of forms that overlaid continuing regional traditions. Second, to describe it is not the same as to explain it, and Renfrew accordingly proposed several interaction models, including prestige chains of gift-giving elites and a freelance metals trade by Cycladic islanders.

The essence of this picture has stood the test of time remarkably well, with later analyses largely confirming the prominence of Cycladic activities and ways of doing things (Cherry 1984a: 29–30; Cosmopoulos 1991; Karantzali 1996; Rutter and Zerner 1984: 76). The extent to which Renfrew's picture has required redrawing has primarily been a matter of nuances, albeit not unimportant ones, the infilling of areas necessarily left sketchy in the original rendering, and the addition of new, complementary features.

These developments are variously exemplified by the increasing evidence that long-range interaction took off as early as the EB I/II transitional phase (slightly earlier than Renfrew imagined), some widening of the attested categories of material moving, the vindication by metallurgical investigations and lead isotope analysis of Renfrew's hypothesis that the circulation of metals was a key factor, although one whose impact must be explicitly set in the context of social strategies operating in the Aegean (Nakou 1995, 1997), and the claims put forward, with varying degrees of plausibility, to the effect that several sites beyond the islands can be identified by their material culture and practices as 'colonies' of Cycladic people. Within a wider Aegean framework, whilst the overwhelmingly maritime nature of connections has been reinforced by recent work, it is becoming obvious that the Cycladic islanders were not solely responsible for all the patterns seen. Several maritime networks that do not pass through these islands can be discerned and, in addition, on certain edges of the Cyclades, the distinction between the Cycladic and non-Cycladic worlds is starting to look decidedly negotiable. Moreover, as will be argued, by late EB II such trading patterns had started to change in ways that are not likely to have been to the advantage of traders based in the Cyclades.

These developments, and others besides, are dealt with below. For the moment, we can rehearse a few of the questions that need to be asked of the data. For one thing, it is vital to distinguish wherever possible between imported raw materials, imported objects, rare local copies of imported objects (made from local or imported materials), and shared trans-regional styles whose original locus of development may be hard, if not impossible, to identify. The significance of each of these is, of course, different, as a comparison between imported marble, imported Cycladic figurines, adaptations or copies of such figurines, and distinctive local variants will demonstrate in the case of Crete. Even within the realm of copying, Nakou (1995: 13–14) highlights a distinction in the Aegean daggers between forms of copying that show a merely visual knowledge of the finished product and those that betray an understanding of the manufacturing technique. We would also like to know to what extent an object's cultural associations and specific biography were liable to be transferred with it, and likewise to what extent the objects, practices and symbols that were at home in different regions bore the same associations in each region. For example, it has been cautiously suggested that in the cemetery of Manika in Euboia, frying pans, folded-arm figurines and metal tools are mainly associated with male burials, whilst other objects, including jewellery, pyxides, grinders and containers for colorants correlate mainly with females (Sampson 1985: 385, 1988b: 126). Should this distinction be extrapolated to the almost entirely unsexed Cycladic dead? (The answer in this case is that we simply cannot know.) Developing this point, we must be sensitive to differing regimes of value across the Aegean, amplifying chapter 8's suggestion of variation within the Cyclades. What, for example, should we make of the fact that, despite the quantity of gold objects in the Greek mainland, Crete and the north-east Aegean, all regions that traded with the Cyclades, only a single gold bead has emerged from EBA contexts in the Cyclades, in contrast to the islanders' extensive use of silver? Thinking about value is also rewarding in other respects. *Why*, for instance, were Cycladic things deemed desirable by people living elsewhere, *what* did islanders adopt or import from abroad, and *how much* did status within the Cyclades derive from the practice and proceeds of long-range trade?

In addition, we need a generous spectrum of hypotheses about the mechanisms, modes, durations and periodicities of interaction. These need to extend beyond prestige chains and freelance trade (although both have a part to play) to address the possibilities of direct access, restricted practices, trade partnerships or friendships, creoles, the role of gateways as either neutral or political charged locales, the time-scales and the routes of voyaging, the functions of distance and distant knowledge, and the further range of possibilities raised by the likelihood of extended absence and the diverse social theatres for cross-cultural interaction. And lastly, we need to people these processes. It is not enough to talk about 'the role of the Cycladic islanders', for the last few chapters have made it clear that such a collective never existed. Who exactly were the people doing the moving? Which Cycladic islanders, if any, settled abroad, and how, otherwise, did what look in material terms like Cycladic personae emerge in other parts of the Aegean?

Situating the 'international spirit'

The Aegean in EB II

Effective analysis of such issues requires a slightly fuller picture of the main features of Aegean EB II societies than that provided by the thumbnail sketch in chapter 2. As in the Cyclades, so too in many other parts of the Aegean, the transition from a relatively undifferentiated pattern of small farmsteads and hamlets in EB I to a far more complex scene in EB II is striking (fig. 90). The key developments seen in various parts of the Aegean, beyond intensified long-range interaction and a high profile for metals, include an expansion of settlement, variously measured by numbers of sites or the growth of large communities, usage of the plough, the construction of monumental buildings, new ways of recording or establishing ownership by seals and sealings, indications of vigorous local hierarchies, increased crafting of elaborate objects, often necessitating considerable skills, a spiralling investment in the funerary sphere, and the inception of new drinking practices (probably associated with either the start or the elaboration of wine consumption) attested by an explosion in the range and number of drinking and pouring vessels (Renfrew 1972; Rutter 1993: 758–74, Watrous 1994: 705–17; Wiencke 1989). The communities, social structures, practices and material cultures that developed in different parts of the Aegean varied considerably, however, owing to local strategies and antecedent traditions, selective take-up of innovations, and geographical location.

Before looking at this variation, it is worth affirming and developing Renfrew's observation that many of the key settlements of the period are well placed for access to maritime activity, whether themselves on islands or at key points on the circum-Aegean rim. Good non-Cycladic examples of major sites at nodal points and bottlenecks for local or inter-regional maritime interaction include Manika, at the narrowest point of a corridor of north–south movement passing between Euboia and the mainland (Sampson 1985, 1988b; Sapouna-Sakellaraki 1986, 1987), Limantepe in an equivalent location on the Karaburun isthmus (Erkanal 1996), Troy on the Dardanelles (Blegen *et al*. 1950), centres on inter-regional stepping-stone islands such as Poliochni on Lemnos (Bernabò-Brea 1964, 1976; Doumas and La Rosa 1997), Palamari on Skyros (Theochari and Parlama 1997) or, in later EB II, Kastri on Kythera (Coldstream and Huxley 1972) and lastly, hubs of local maritime activity such as Mochlos in east Crete and Kolonna in Aegina, which acted as central places

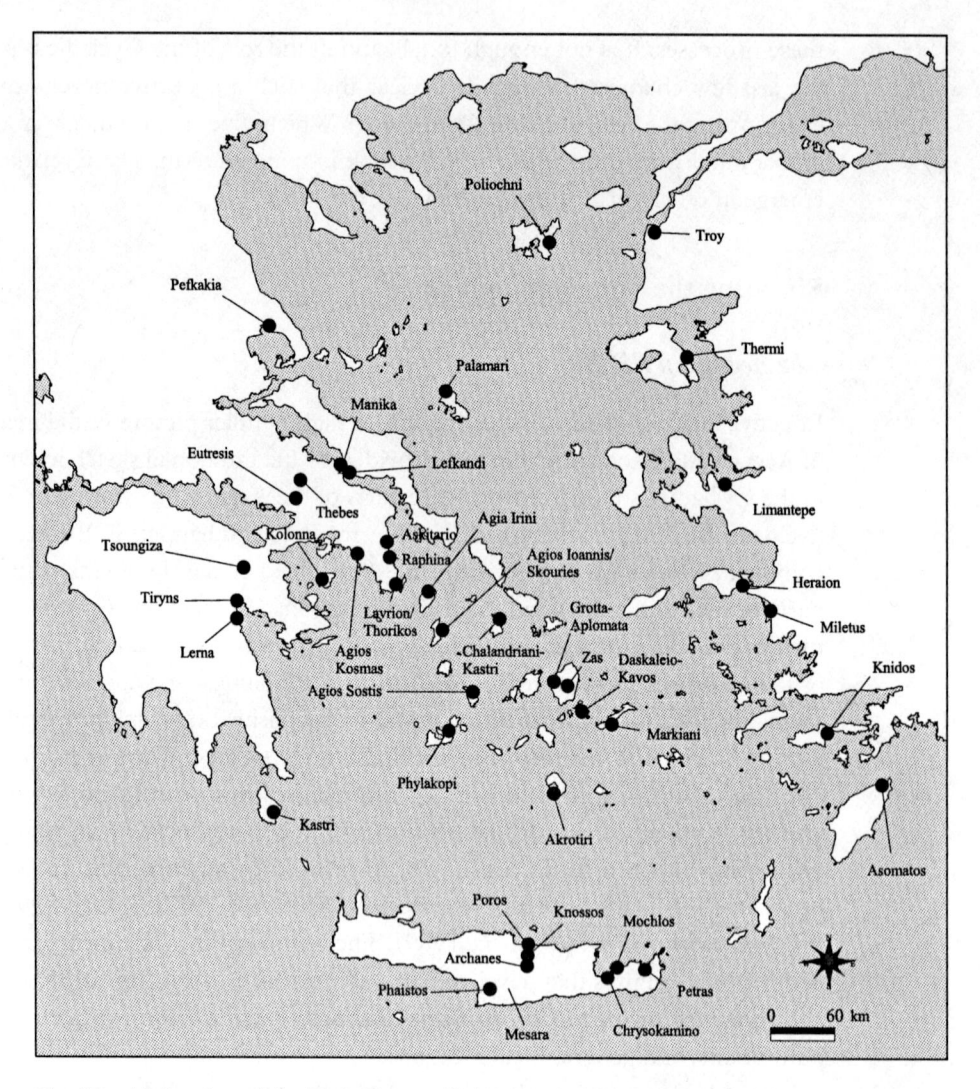

Fig. 90 Major sites of the Early Bronze II Aegean and other sites mentioned in chapter 9.

for the Mirabello and Saronic Gulfs respectively (Branigan 1991; Walter and Felten 1981). Comparable sites must also have existed in the south-east Aegean, a region whose EBA is only now starting to receive the detailed attention that it deserves (Marketou 1990, 1997).

The major mainland settlements that do not occupy such obvious maritime nodal points or bottle-necks are nevertheless typically located on the coast at points that would allow them to control their hinterland communities' access to the sea. Lerna and Tiryns in the Argolid, Askitario and Agios Kosmas in Attica, and Pefkakia at the maritime edge of Thessaly are all examples, and indeed in a Thessalian context Pefkakia is an outpost of the maritime-oriented Aegean in a region otherwise little involved in the activities that concern this chapter (Christmann 1996). A demonstration of what this

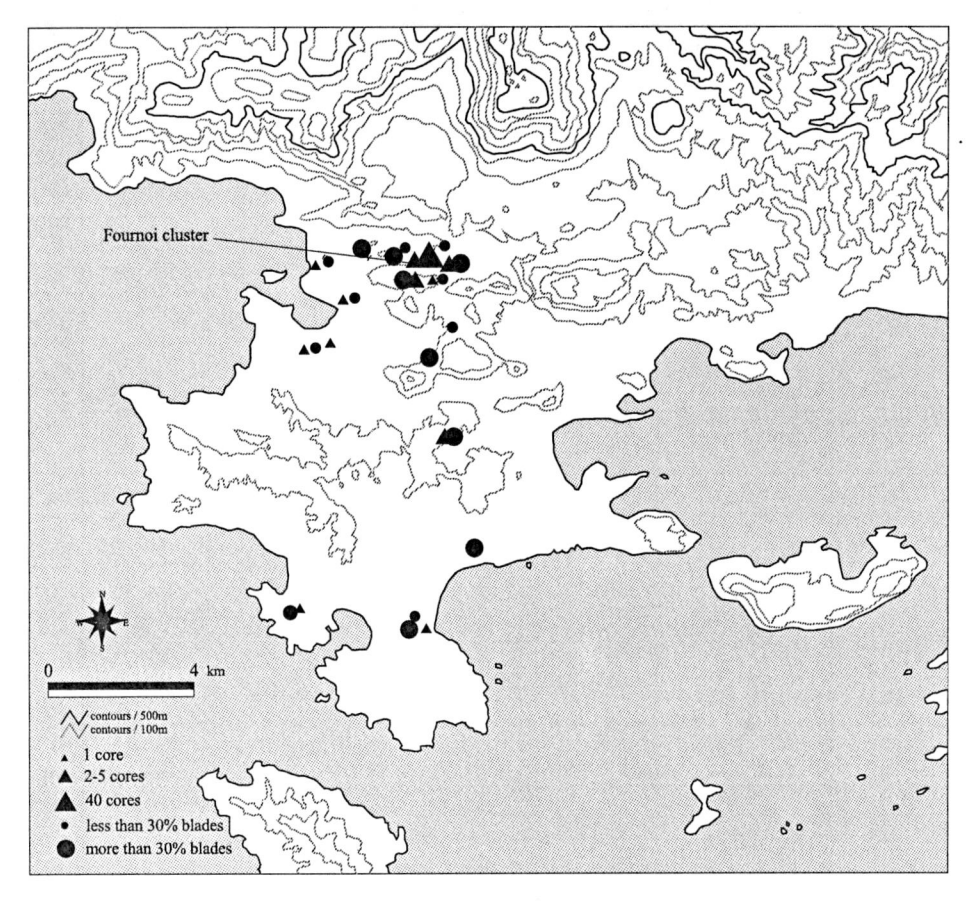

Fig. 91 Distribution of obsidian finds in the southern Argolid, showing differential access to the material and its stages of production. After Jameson *et al.* 1994: fig. 6.13.

could imply in practice is provided by survey data from the southern Argolid (Jameson *et al.* 1994: 356–8), where the distribution of residues from the obsidian reduction sequence argues for restricted access to the raw nodules arriving from Melos (fig. 91). Even in those few instances where major sites occupied large inland tracts of arable land, a link to a nearby coastal community can usually be posited, as is illustrated by Knossos and the maritime settlement of Poros (Dimopoulou 1997). In this sense, the true anomalies are those land-locked areas of the Aegean region that nonetheless do produce evidence of high-profile activity in EB II. One such area is Boiotia, with large settlements at Thebes and Eutresis. Another (in terms of its access to the Aegean sea) is the extensive Mesara plain of southern Crete, with its abundance of large communal tombs, where access to obsidian and other foreign goods was filtered by intervening communities in northern Crete (Carter 1998). These exceptions deserve more searching analysis than they have received, but they do not detract from the fact that across much of the Aegean, and not just within the Cyclades, coastal sites were extremely prominent throughout EB II.

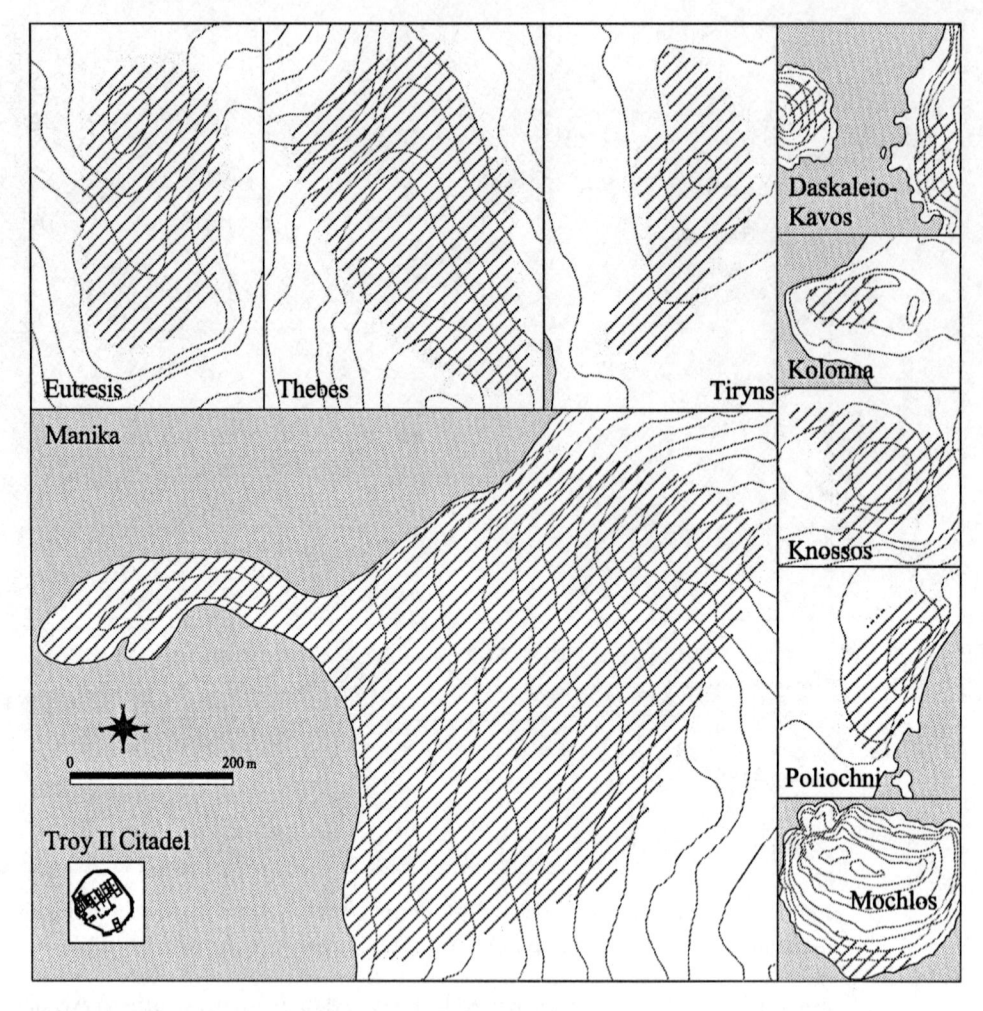

Fig. 92 Selection of large Early Bronze II Aegean settlements to the same scale. After originals by Todd Whitelaw.

So much for placing the Cycladic centres in a broader context. The features that distinguish them from other major settlements dotted around the Aegean, and also such settlements from each other, are just as striking. This becomes clear as soon as we look at the kinds of things going on in different places. For example, whilst Mochlos closely resembles a Cycladic centre (the resemblances include size, boat imagery, rich tombs, and deposition of many stone vessels), sites such as Manika, at an enormous 50–80 ha in area, or Troy II, with its massive fortifications, megaron halls up to about 30 m long, and prodigious metallic wealth, represent very different phenomena. Manika is unique in terms of size, but other settlements dwarf even the largest Cycladic centres (Hägg and Konsola 1986; Whitelaw 1983) (fig. 92). Large buildings are attested in several regions outside the Cyclades by later EB II. The Troy II megara are matched by the 'corridor houses' of the southern Greek mainland, of which

Lerna's House of the Tiles remains the best-known example (Pullen 1986). At Knossos in Crete a big levelling operation, perhaps for an elite quarter, was undertaken at this time, although the later construction of the palatial structures has removed any architectural traces (Wilson 1994: 37). There is, by way of contrast, no evidence to date for monumental buildings in the Cyclades, where large boats took the place of large houses, and where social power operated via the highly individual-oriented if temporally transitory avenues of seafaring and trading.

More ambivalent is the interpretation of seals and sealings (Pullen 1994 for the mainland, Sbonias 1995 for Crete). A few seals have long been known in the Cyclades, and sealings have recently been discovered at Skarkos and Zas cave (Marthari 1997: 375–6; Dousougli-Zachos 1993). Sphragistic activity tends to be interpreted as evidence for administration, but a perceptive reanalysis of the largest known group, from the House of the Tiles at Lerna, questions the scale and sophistication of the system (Weingarten 1997). It seems likely that seals and sealings register an eclectic range of preoccupations within the domain of ownership marking, recording and security, and therefore that the documentation of similar seal designs across the Aegean cannot be easily translated into similar motives for sealing. This last point underlines what is perhaps the key ambiguity noticeable among the societies of the EB II Aegean: the solid evidence for increasingly intense interaction patterns, contrasted with the equally marked evidence for regional divergence and differentiation, the latter trend one that would increase still further in the last centuries of the third millennium BC.

The EB II Aegean and the Near East

In contrast to the wealth of undisputed evidence for internal interaction, the extent of contacts between the Aegean and outside regions, particularly to the east, during EB II remains difficult to characterise. The evidence lies in a rather uneasy limbo between the Neolithic pattern, when the Aegean formed part of a belt of generically similar societies extending from Anatolia to the Balkans, and that of the second millennium BC, when long-range trade between Aegean palatial centres and the east and central Mediterranean is amply attested. As described in chapter 2, debate over the pattern in the EBA defines a field of contention between those who prefer internal models of change (e.g. Renfrew 1972) and proponents of a world-systemic perspective, who affirm that by this juncture Aegean societies and economies had started to be affected by the activities and demands of an expanding Near Eastern core, centred on the Early Dynastic city-states and later Akkadian 'empire' in Mesopotamia, Old Kingdom Egypt and the Levantine city-states, with a crucial, dynamic periphery on the Anatolian plateau (Sherratt and Sherratt 1991).

That some objects, materials and ideas originating in regions to the east reached the Aegean during EB II is hardly deniable (fig. 93). The number of actual imports of orientalia in solid EB II contexts is tiny (so much so that it would hardly crowd a small

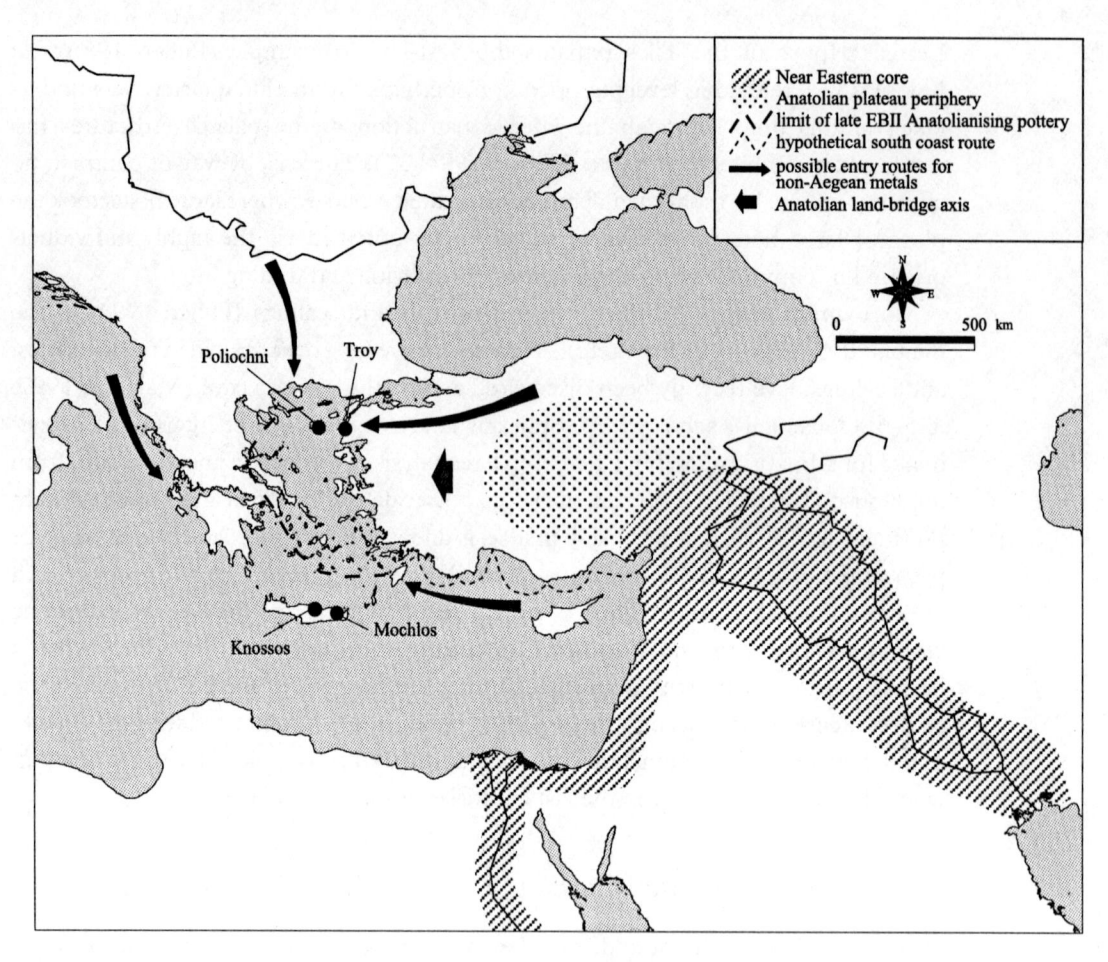

Fig. 93 The Early Bronze II Aegean as a margin of the Near Eastern world system.

coffee-table). Yet there are good reasons to believe that this handful of exotic objects is not fully representative of the inflow and impact of materials, technologies and customs to the Aegean from areas to the east in the EB II period, and especially in late EB II.

Starting with the orientalia themselves, the clearest examples comprise an ivory cylinder seal probably of Anatolian manufacture at Poliochni (Bernabò-Brea 1976: plate 254) a silver one of Syrian type at Mochlos (Aruz 1984), hippopotamus ivory on Crete, including a well-dated tusk fragment at Knossos (Krzyszkowska 1984: 124–5), Levantine faience beads in Chalkidiki, and at Troy, Mochlos and possibly other sites in Crete (Peltenburg 1996: 19 and fig. 2) and (more controversially) fragments of Egyptian stone vases at Knossos (Warren 1995: 1–2; Wilson 1994: 41). Flasks of Syrian type have been found at Troy and Palamari (Theochari et al. 1993: 191 and fig. 3b). Two points about this list can be made straight away. The first is that these objects concentrate at prominent sites, and in several cases at foci of maritime trade. The second is that the majority are found in the interface zones with regions to the east, and none in the Cyclades.[1] Whatever the means by which these objects had entered the Aegean, most therefore seem to have been captured and consumed close to their initial entry points. The inverse of this short list of imported objects is equally relevant: not a single EB II Aegean object has yet been discovered east of a line between Troy and Rhodes. At this stage, Aegean finished artefacts understandably had a minimal appeal within the sophisticated societies of the Anatolian plateau, the Levant and areas beyond.

More impressive is the evidence for Aegean adoptions of external innovations, in particular non-local metals, technologies whose ultimate eastern origin is likely and, at a less tangible level, new ideologies and social customs. The inflow of non-local metals is discussed later; suffice for now to state that tin, the fifth major metal employed in the Bronze Age, and the only one unobtainable within the Aegean, first appeared in the north-east Aegean, from where its incidence expands across much of the Aegean by late EB II (Nakou 1997: 639–42). Several of the cases of transferred technologies also involve metals, notably slotted and tanged spearheads of Levantine or central Anatolian origin with a derivative local sub-type in the Cyclades and north-east Aegean (Nakou 1997: 638, fig. 4) and transportable moulds for casting orientalising trinkets (Canby 1965). Other candidates include the first wheel-made pottery at Troy and in Euboia (Blegen et al. 1950: 219–43; French 1968), found at communities where economies of scale would favour the adoption of this innovation, probably the use of the ox-plough complex, which is first attested by a fragmentary model of yoked oxen in an early EB II context at Tsoungiza (Nemea) in the north-east Peloponnese (Pullen 1992), and possibly the sealing practices at Lerna (Weingarten 1997). A rather earlier ideological transfer is argued by E. S. Sherratt (in press) who sees the Cycladic seafaring ideology that emerged in the Kampos horizon (outlined in chapter 8) and the inlaid eyes and hats of the Plastiras group figurines as features of Levantine derivation. Concerning social customs, in late EB II a horizon of drinking shapes of western Anatolian derivation spread across the Aegean as far as its western seaboard (Rutter 1979; see also below), assuredly the material tracers of Anatolian social drinking practices.

Whatever doubts may still be harboured about specific pieces of evidence, the cumulative image is of an increasing adoption of innovations from the east through EB II, with the most extensive signs dating to later EB II, after c. 2500 BC. In this light, it is best to focus our attention not so much on whether external stimuli were working on Aegean societies at this time (they clearly were) but rather on how they were transferred and what impact they had. Taking the first issue, there is nothing in the current

---

[1] The only Cycladic candidate is a seal said to be from a grave at Kapros on Amorgos, but purchased long ago on the antiquities market. Doubts as to the reliability of this attribution have been expressed for some time (e.g. Renfrew 1984a: 54), and will be confirmed by a definitive publication of the 'Kapros' material (Sherratt in press).

evidence that is incompatible with indirect down-the-line conveyance of eastern objects and ideas via a continuum of communities and high-status individuals across the Anatolian land-bridge, and probably along a southern Anatolian coastal route from the Levant (Mellink 1993). Likely termini for down-the-line movement westward along the river valleys of Anatolia would be places like Troy, Limantepe and similar sites that must exist further south. Troy and other north-eastern centres could, in addition, exploit their proximity to the Balkan/Pontic zone, from where occasional objects, metal-working technologies and perhaps metals filtered into the Aegean (Nakou 1997: 637–8, fig. 3). One terminus for any maritime chain that linked the Levant to the Aegean via the southern Anatolian coast might be the trading centre of Mochlos, although the likelihood of a centre somewhere in the vicinity of Rhodes seems high. The advantage held by people at key locations on the fringes of the Aegean who could intercept and control exotica entering the region must have become increasingly apparent through the course of the third millennium BC.

The feasibility of transfer by down-the-line passage between local communities and prestige chains between elites, combined with the fact that people on the Anatolian plateau were adopting large quantities of 'core culture' by this time, renders the case for a direct Aegean connection to Egypt, Mesopotamia and even the Levant during EB II more or less superfluous. It cannot, of course, be denied that over a period of some 500 years a few Aegean canoes might have been paddled far into the sunrise, or occasional eastern sailors entered the Aegean, given that by this time Sumerian ships were ranging as far as Oman and the Indus (Postgate 1992: 216–18). The point is simply that even if direct voyages in either direction did occur, there is no indication that they had a lasting impact. In other words, by late EB II the Aegean was on the cusp of a major revision of its relations with the outside world, but still lay one crucial step short of the integration that it was to experience within a few centuries. As mentioned in chapter 2, the Aegean finds parallels here with late pre-contact Melanesia and possibly the Caribbean, where islanders' indirect encounters with outlying elements of emergent world-systems may also have started to alter things prior to the first intensive contacts (in the latter theatres in the guise of Europeans) that were so utterly to transform indigenous ways of life.

We therefore need to maintain a fine balance in terms of the explanatory priority attributed to large-scale change, as opposed to local processes, in our interpretations of Aegean and Cycladic histories at this time. If purely internalist interpretations are unable to produce complete accounts, an overly reductive application of world-systems theory will just as assuredly flatten the texture of change, not least because the EBA Aegean is better classified as a distant margin than an integrated periphery. Preferable, therefore, to unsubtle scenarios, such as that of regular fleets of Anatolian merchants processing silver extracted in the western Cyclades at Lerna, with which Weingarten (1997: 159–61) rounds off her otherwise excellent re-evaluation of the Lerna sealings, are ones in which an expanding demand for raw materials in the Near

East gave a slight extra 'kick' to local extraction, circulation and consumption in the Cyclades and neighbouring areas, with an unknown amount of metal possibly trickling east through the same network of Anatolian communities that articulated the more obvious westward-trending routes. In social terms, what we need to consider is how the arrival of orientalia and eastern customs and technologies (their significance much refracted by successive transmissions) made exotic objects, materials and ways of doing things a part of at least some Aegean people's cultural perceptions, thereby widening the repertoire of means for local leaders to advertise status, technological skill and economic power. Unless voyages beyond the Aegean were ventured by Cycladic islanders (and there is no evidence for these), in this part of the Aegean knowledge of the Near East must have been additionally filtered by its location at one remove from the eastern Aegean and western Anatolian contact zone. How this affected the place of the Near East in the islanders' cosmologies is a question that is as intriguing as it is unfortunately impervious to archaeological investigation.

Maritime perspectives on long-range interaction in the EBA Aegean

Voyaging parameters

Unlike local maritime movement, which could take advantage of modest distances and changeable weather conditions to realise most short-range aims, the possibilities under EBA conditions for long-range Aegean voyages would have been more strictly defined by the parameters set out in chapter 3. The Aegean's open season for sea journeys of any length would restrict voyaging to the period between May and September, plus a few uncertain weeks at either end. The requirements of harvesting further confine the 'voyaging window' to risky journeys in April and a longer stretch in August (the month of *meltemia*) and September through to marginal October, unless voyaging communities solved this problem by acquiring food grown by others. In circumstances where a small canoe might cover about 20 km per day and a bigger longboat slightly more than double this, and moreover where experimental archaeology suggests that stormy weather even in the open season would mean on average one day lost for every day or two at sea (cf. fig. 25), journeys of any length were naturally time-consuming ventures. For instance, it was estimated in chapter 3 that at such rates a there-and-back journey across the length of the Cyclades might take about a month in a small canoe, or a fortnight in a longboat. Whether longboats were used for long-range travel, as Renfrew assumed, is uncertain. Their speed, high-status associations and the safety on shore implied by their crew numbers might favour the idea. Against this must be weighed the risk to an entire community in committing so many people to a potentially dangerous venture, and the greater number of voyages in different directions that could be mounted simultaneously by a given number of people in several smaller, if slower, canoes.

The prevailing winds and currents introduce further parameters. For short-range journeys, the high degree of short-term variation has been argued largely to negate the importance of overall trends. This may also be true for long-range voyages that could hug the denser clusters of islands or mainland coasts (although the cumulative amount of time required for what were, in effect, sequences of short-range journeys would still have put pressure on the time-scheduling parameters of voyaging). But for voyages that had to cross stretches of open sea, and therefore relied on steady runs of favourable conditions, prevailing wind and current directions must have been decisive. Particularly important is the dominance of strong winds from the north in the summer months, which would allow a canoe to speed with the wind behind it on a south-bound journey, but virtually prohibit sustained movement northwards across open seas, except for the very rare, unpredictable times when a southern wind blew. East–west movement presents fewer difficulties, thanks to the narrowness of the Aegean in this dimension and the number of cross-currents. These points are brought out by Agouridis' analysis of voyaging parameters (1997), which had fundamental implications for the activities explored in this chapter.

Fig. 94 shows the likely routes for long-range voyaging, including both multi-directional coastal and inter-island routes, and the directional open sea routes permitted by prevailing summer conditions in the Aegean. These are mapped onto an Aegean sea zoned to reveal areas that do not permit land-to-land crossings in a single day in either a small canoe or a longboat, and where steady runs of weather and favourable currents would be vital. This brings out the maritime deserts in the centre of the north Aegean and the broad zone separating the Cyclades from Crete – sea deserts to be crossed with at least one night afloat in canoes with less than a metre's freeboard. Experienced seafarers should have been able to traverse these quite regularly from north to south. To progress northward, however, they would either have needed to wait, probably for months, for a rare wind from the south, or work their way north via the coasts and islands of the Aegean rim, thereby generating long, cyclic routes for outward and return voyaging. For people resident at the southern end of a region, the option of waiting for a favourable shift in the prevailing winds might have been feasible, but for voyagers from the north wanting to return home the cyclic option is likely to have been the most commonly adopted solution. It can be noted that all these cyclic routes pass through or skirt the edges of the Cyclades, suggesting that even if voyaging centres did develop in other regions (see below), the Cyclades should still have enjoyed a unique degree of involvement in movement around the Aegean. People in the northern Cyclades would have had most contact with the northern Aegean circuit, with any Cycladic seafarers in this theatre voyaging northward via Manika and the Euboian straits, or Skyros and the Northern Sporades, or perhaps the east Aegean coasts and islands. Thera and Melos are the most favourable jump-off points for voyages to Crete, with the re-entry areas for returning voyages probably being located in the south-eastern and western Cyclades.

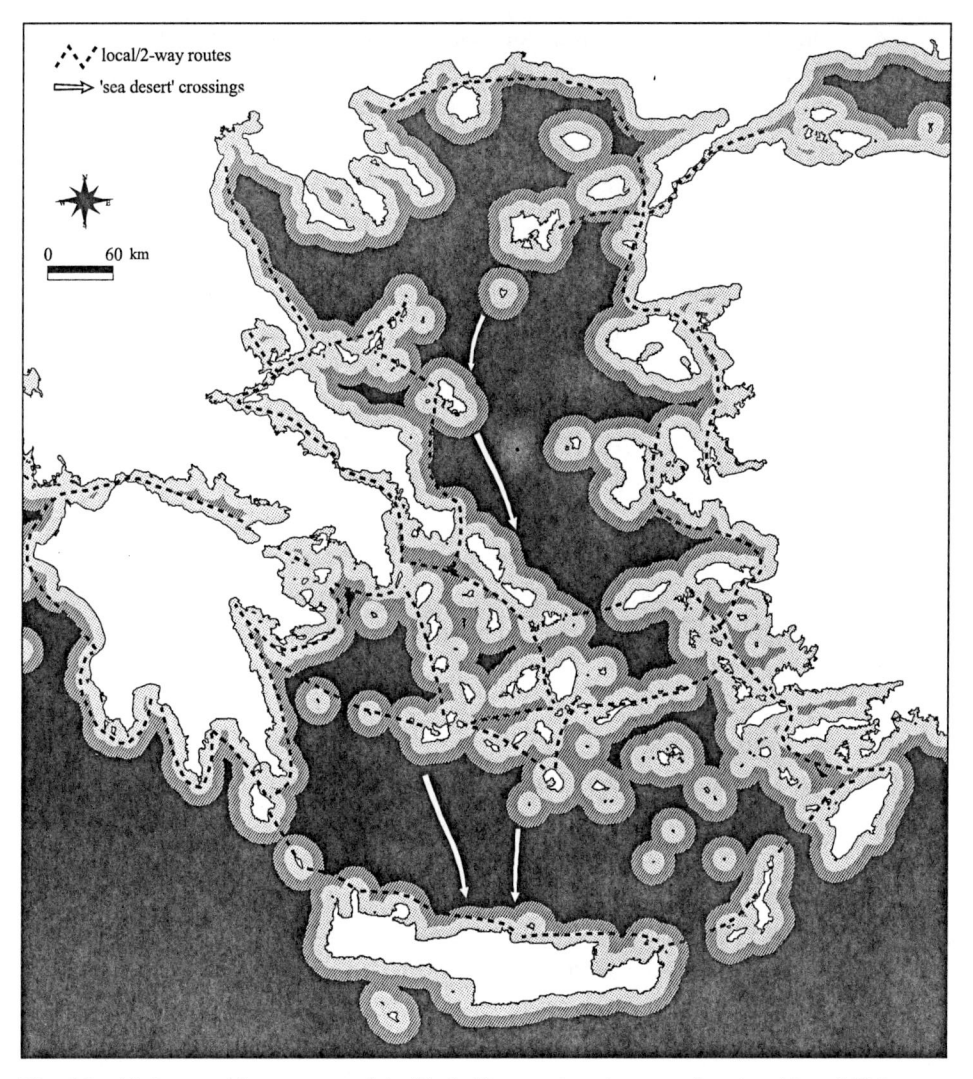

Fig. 94 Major maritime routes of the Early Bronze Age Aegean, showing 10 and 20 km distances from land, the maritime deserts of the northern and southern Aegean, the main networks of two-way voyaging and the directional one-way crossings that imply cyclic voyaging. Routes adapted from Agouridis 1997: fig. 5.

Social and archaeological implications

Once unravelled, these cyclic voyaging routes are extremely long (in the order of 500 km or more, a distance that could in theory take Aegean canoes to Cyprus) and far more time-consuming than earlier estimates suggested (Broodbank 1989: 333–4). They must have exceeded the possibilities for integration with the agricultural calendar, and only communities for which the perceived advantages of voyaging outweighed the problem of making up short-falls in food production are likely to have organised such activities. Equally, in such communities the seasonal absence of part of the population must have been culturally as well as economically acceptable. For all these reasons, and despite the possibilities of inter-community organisation for crewing longboats in various parts of the Cyclades (cf. fig. 84), the major Cycladic participants were surely much the same communities as those identified as centres of local maritime activity in chapters 7 and 8. If long-range voyaging was a lengthy, restricted, relatively infrequent and dangerous business, the rewards must have been commensurate gains in status, power and wealth. It is probably a mistake to imagine these rewards simply in material terms, although the scope for something akin to profit must have been considerable for seafarers based in a centrally placed, metal- and obsidian-rich island group with opportunities to manipulate the value of things abroad. In addition to trade, the practice of long-range voyaging is itself likely to have become a status-accruing activity for those with the skill, knowledge and crew-mobilising power to undertake it, a factor particularly accentuated in the case of voyagers who crossed the Aegean sea deserts and therefore passed between separate worlds. As documented in *Ulysses' Sail*, Helms' classic investigation of pre-modern cultures of long-range movement, the traveller's status tended to become exalted both in the eyes of people encountered abroad, and in the home community where the venture began and ended (Helms 1988).

A second observation is that the patterns of voyaging shown in fig. 94 have implications for the archaeological signatures that we should anticipate (and incidentally for the kinds of continuous or disassociated speech communities that voyagers would have needed to negotiate). Concentrating on the Cyclades' relations with other regions, a distinction can be drawn between long-range movement made up of short-range hops that could operate in both directions, and long-range movement that encouraged cyclic journeys. The former category covers contacts with areas such as Attica, Euboia and the south-east Aegean, highlighted in chapter 4 as staging points for the initial colonisation of the Cyclades. It may also cover another probably very ancient sea-path between the western Cyclades and the Peloponnese via a chain of small stepping-stones, among which Parapola is reported to have EBA pottery (Kyrou 1990: 72–6). In these cases, the signature of interaction should be intense, given that voyages would be on average less drawn out, safer and therefore more frequent, but blurred in cultural terms owing to the easy passage of things in both directions and the lack of sharp borders to the Cyclades.

The latter category (voyaging involving cyclic routes) covers the northern cycles that pass via the Cyclades and – crucially – voyaging from the Cyclades to Crete. As these routes would not generate a single reciprocal exchange followed by a direct homeward passage, but rather ongoing activity around the cycle, the natural corollary is that there would be a turnover in the cargoes and items traded as a voyage progressed. For example, the signature of voyaging from the Cyclades to Crete should be plenty of Cycladic material in Crete, but only the few Cretan objects that were preserved for the remainder of a voyage, alongside more south-east Aegean or Peloponnesian material (depending on the return route) in the Cyclades. If the trade items on some stretches of the voyage were archaeologically invisible (e.g. textiles or human cargoes), the pattern would become even more difficult to detect. Such voyages of changing complexion must have provided seafarers with great opportunities for good trading, and certainly present archaeologists with serious problems, but as seen below, they may also help to explain the archaeological evidence for Cycladic contacts with Crete during the EBA.

Finally, what can we infer about the number of voyaging communities in the EB II Aegean, and the position of Cycladic communities within these? The number of such communities in the Cyclades has been argued to have been restricted by demography and local network conditions. In other regions of the Aegean, where many more village communities are attested, the former factor cannot have been decisive, but nonetheless even at an Aegean-wide level the total number of voyaging communities may not have been high. Many of the coastal settlements for whom open-sea voyaging was not a locationally dictated necessity may have acted as passive, receiving gateways for their hinterlands rather than active centres. Others may have focused on a mixture of short-range traffic and long-range voyaging along the coasts and out into adjacent islands (e.g. possibly Manika, several sites in the Attic-Saronic-Argolid region, plus Troy, Limantepe and other centres on the east Aegean coast). Certain locations on the north coast of Crete might fall into this category, although we will see that the dynamics of long-range interaction with Crete changed repeatedly through the course of the EBA. The only two currently convincing centres for long-range cyclic voyaging, outside the Cyclades, are the widely connected island sites of Poliochni on Lemnos and Palamari on Skyros. If we were to hazard a guess, the total number of major voyaging centres of all varieties in the Aegean may have been in the order of ten to twenty communities, with the ultra-specialised cyclic voyaging in the hands of perhaps as few as half a dozen.

If these orders of magnitude are correct, several interesting points follow. First, the number of people engaged in voyaging must always have been limited. Among this restricted group, many must have known each other and formed trading partnerships. This provides a convincing context for the exchange of prestigious objects as gifts, but also for the cultural convergence of personae. Indeed some aspects of the international spirit must really be about individual traders, rather than regions, talking to each other. Second, the prominence of Cycladic seafarers in the most extended kinds of voyaging makes it unsurprising that many elements of their vocabulary of status were emulated by trading individuals or groups in other regions. Third, at locations in the Aegean that constituted important staging points in cyclic voyages, but where local centres had not emerged, demographic phenomena that we term 'colonies' might very well develop.

Metals and movement

Renfrew's perceptive association of long-range EBA interaction with the movement of metals, often effected by Cycladic traders, was mentioned at the start of this chapter. With the maritime dynamics of long-range voyaging now delineated, a complementary exploration of the means by which metals were accessed and circulated is the next aim. It is as well to affirm from the start that to attribute a key role to metals is emphatically not to propose that other circulating objects travelled on the back of a prosaic resource-oriented trade. For one thing, the conditions of voyaging ensured that most things that travelled over any distance would have become valuable items. But just as importantly, the relatively small-scale metallurgy of the EBA Aegean may itself have been in part a magically charged activity (Budd and Taylor 1995). Indeed, in maritime regions, metal-workers, metal traders, voyagers and perhaps magicians specialising in transformations of weather, ores and metals could have been closely associated people, if not different facets of the same individuals. Another point to stress is that whilst Aegean metals had been moving around since the FN, the degree to which the mechanisms of movement involved an engagement in social relations was highly variable. This reminds us that the international spirit does not correlate with the first circulation of metals, but with a new cultural emphasis on articulating such movement; Nakou (1997) makes a strong case for a further revolution in the significance of metal trading in late EB II (see below). Much the same is true of the various modes of obsidian procurement and circulation, and despite differences between these classes of material, some instructive comparisons can be drawn.

An outline of EBA patterns of metal exploitation and consumption

The distribution of metal sources in the western Cyclades with signs of EBA extraction was discussed in chapter 3, and the uncertain indications of exploitation as early as the FN were touched upon in chapter 5. The islands concerned are Siphnos, mainly if not entirely for silver and lead, and Kythnos for copper, with some copper possibly extracted in Seriphos too; a little to the north lies the polymetallic Lavrion source, with silver, lead and copper. Lead isotope analysis of a large quantity of EBA southern Aegean metal objects shows a strong association with the signatures of the Siphnian, Kythnian and Lavrion sources (Gale and Stos-Gale 1981; Stos-Gale 1989, 1993, 1998; Stos-Gale and Macdonald 1991). Analysis of Cretan artefacts, in particular, suggests that most of the copper entering this major consumption zone came from Kythnos or Lavrion, with only a tiny minority being possibly of local or other origin (Stos-Gale 1993, 1998). On the southern Greek mainland the pattern has yet to be clarified, but there are signs that a similar pattern may obtain, with the one significant difference that Lavrion could be accessed without necessarily involving the Cyclades. Although recent criticisms of such applications of lead isotope analysis in the Aegean urge a degree of caution (Budd *et al.* 1995; Knapp and Cherry 1994; Pernicka 1995), the convergence of such varied forms of data leaves little room for doubt that the Cyclades were supplying a range of metals (gold and, of course, tin excepted) to the southern Aegean during much of the EBA.

The north-east Aegean, with its metal-rich sites at Troy, Poliochni, and Thermi on Lesbos, and connections to non-Aegean metalliferous zones in central Anatolia and possibly the Balkans, presents a complex picture in itself throughout the EBA (Nakou 1997; Pernicka *et al.* 1990; Stos-Gale 1992). Some of its metals may also have derived from the Cyclades, but as a conduit for non-Aegean metals to enter Aegean networks it also played a crucial part in transforming the conditions of metal availability within the Aegean during late EB II. Specifically, the late EB II evidence for increasing circulation of tin and the usage of copper from non-Aegean sources suggests that the internalised patterns of supply hitherto established in the southern Aegean, and probably the social relations tied up with them, were by this time in danger of being undermined. The origins of the tin remain undetermined (Muhly 1993; Yener and Vandiver 1993) but the crucial point is that all the viable sources (i.e. Afghanistan, central Anatolia and Europe) necessarily implied a massive aggregate lengthening of acquisition networks and a competitive edge for places that could control the entry points into the Aegean – places concentrated in the north-east, but maybe also including western gateways from the Adriatic (Nakou 1997: 664). If tin was indeed largely introduced in the pre-alloyed form of tin-bronze, as metallurgical analyses suggest (Nakou 1997: 639; Pernicka *et al.* 1990), knowledge of its properties must have been even more restricted. An emphasis on its acquisition as a status-enhancing strategy gains additional support from the fact that tin-bronze was first used in the Aegean to produce not stronger objects but ones with a brassy sheen, a local distortion of the similarly value-driven stimulus behind its introduction in the Near East, where it seems to have been intended to enhance copper's position within Mesopotamian metal-based regimes of value equivalence (Nakou 1997; Sherratt 1993a: 23).

Metal extraction in the EBA Cyclades: a 'long-range' practice within the islands

Investigation of the means by which the Cycladic sources were exploited furthers our understanding of dynamics within the Cyclades and prepares the way for an exploration of the movement of such metals beyond the islands. The primary smelting of ores was conducted close to the sources. Often smelting took place on the same island, but Stos-Gale (1998: 723–4) makes an interesting case for the transportation of ores for smelting between adjacent islands in the western Cyclades, perhaps owing to the availability of fuel for the smelting operation. Such localised inter-island transport makes sense in a canoe-based system, given that the rich ores that early miners are likely to have found would have weighed little more than the metals that they yielded, whilst the fuel would have been considerably heavier. If this scenario is correct, the large size of the Skouries slag heap on Kythnos, and the number of other slag sites with EBA material now found on the same island, might be attributable to Kythnos' central location within the string of metal sources running from Siphnos to Lavrion, as well as to the dominant role of its own ore deposits. The sites chosen for primary smelting were prominent, windy headlands, usually with little or no trace of permanent settlement in the vicinity (fig. 95). This had a practical dimension, in terms of the regular draught required for smelting, but it also implies that smelting was both segregated from other activity and visible from far – a perhaps deliberate mixture of secrecy and advertisement (Stos-Gale 1993: 125).

In contrast, secondary smelting and the transformation of metals into artefacts seems to be more closely tied to settlements and (as seen in chapter 8) in most cases the central communities of the Cyclades. Moulds are known at some of these communities, yet are absent from the primary smelting sites. On the source islands, knowledge of the different stages of the process, from mining to the making of artefacts, might have been widely disseminated, but on islands without exploited metal sources (i.e. most of the Cyclades), only the final stages would have been knowable to those not involved in the extraction and primary smelting (and even the final stages may have been more hedged around with taboos than the settlement contexts reveal). At least by EB II, when it has been argued that most maritime activity of any range or duration was undertaken by a small number of centres, this implies that most metal procurement outside the source islands is likely to have been the domain of people at these centres, and indeed one of the means by which they established or enhanced their status. Although distances from centres such as Daskaleio-Kavos and Chalandriani-Kastri to the sources in the western Cyclades imply journeys of only a few days, the time needed to extract and process the ores, together with the skills involved, probably rendered procurement expeditions to the western islands equivalent in status to voyages of much longer range.[2]

Such expeditions could well have exploited the ores of the western Cyclades by direct access, and therefore the many circular special-purpose metallurgical installations identified at Skouries on Kythnos (Hadjianastasiou and MacGillivray 1988) could be at least in part built by non-locals. Certainly, although metal production at settlements in the western Cyclades is attested, for example at Akrotiraki on Siphnos (Wagner and Weisgerber 1985: end-map 2), there is no evidence that local communities controlled access to the mines nor that any large settlements in the western Cyclades profited either as passive or active centres for outward conveyance of metals from these islands. An alternative model, however, would be that proposed by

---

[2] Such long-term absences on business within the Cyclades may have occured for other reasons too. In addition to obsidian procurement, discussed later in this chapter, the actual building of longboats must have been a time-consuming process and one often located at some distance from the community, at least in the case of settlements situated in marginal regions that cannot have furnished the stands of large trees required for their construction.

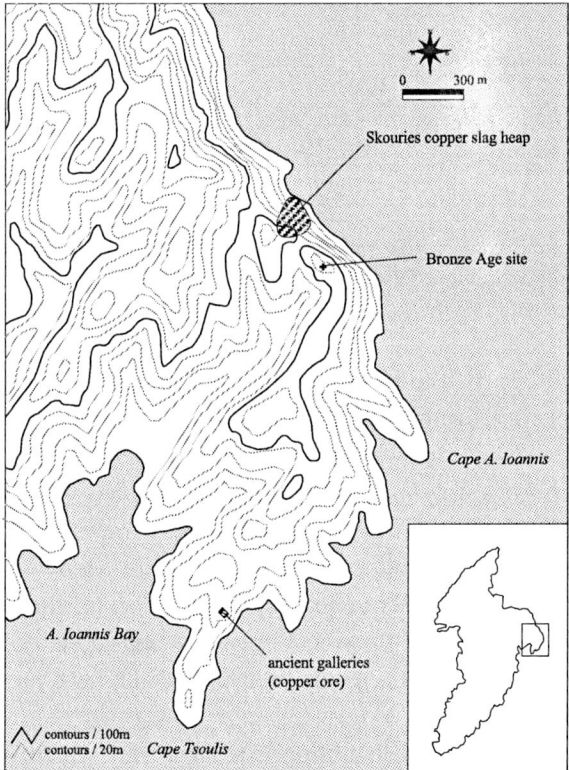

Fig. 95 Two Cycladic metal-processing landscapes. *Above:* the Agios Sostis mining area on Siphnos. *Below:* the Skouries and Agios Ioannis area on Kythnos. Courtesy of Tristan Carter and after Stos-Gale 1998: fig. 2 respectively.

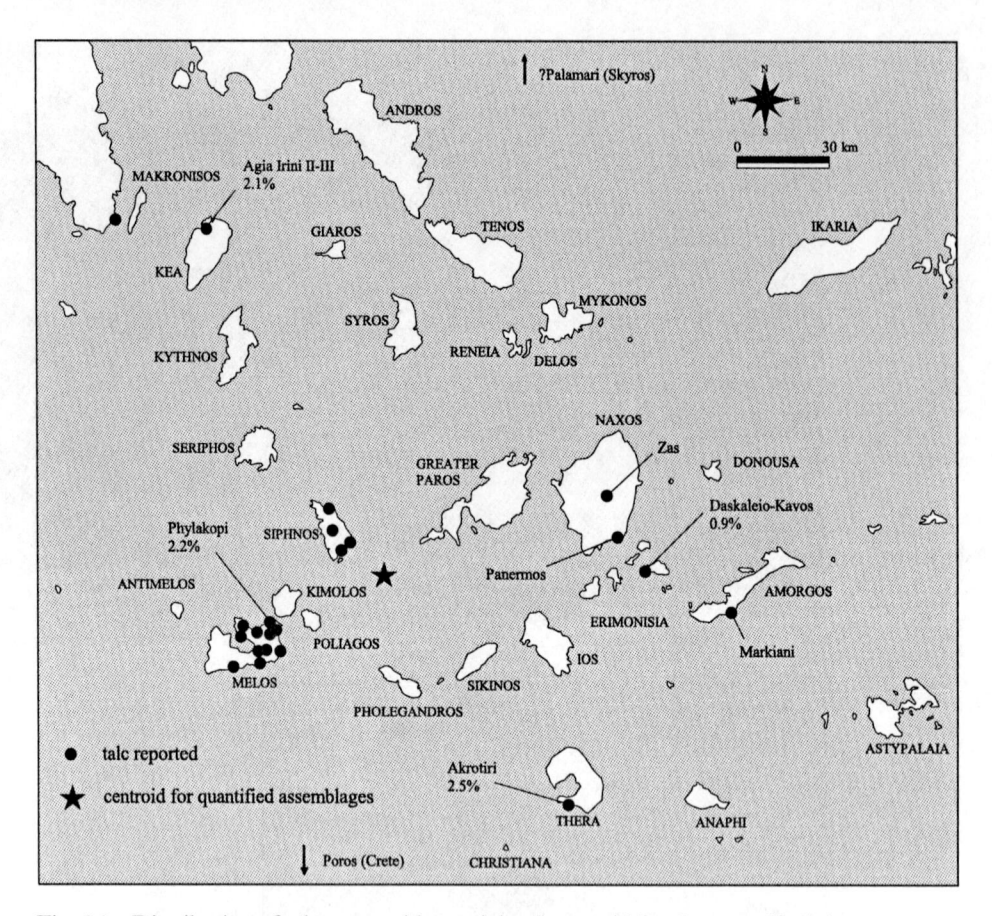

Fig. 96 Distribution of talc ware, with a weighted centroid for the quantified sites. Quantified data from Sotirakopoulou 1990, Wilson 1999, author's research and (for Phylakopi) data made available by the excavator.

Shennan (1999) for the early mining communities of the Mitterberg region in the northern Alps, whereby relatively marginalised miners gained little from their hard work, in comparison to the groups who traded the extracted minerals through wider central European networks. In short, whether they extracted ores themselves or obtained them from local miners, the maritime trading communities of the EB II Cyclades look set to be the major winners. Some contact between non-local metallurgists and local communities is in fact indicated, regardless as to whether it took the form of separate trading activities or procurement by non-locals of metals in an already smelted or semi-smelted state. Evidence is provided by two particularly suggestive pottery distributions.

One of these is the amount of Melian imports at Agia Irini, which Wilson (1987: 44–6, 1999) convincingly connects with north–south traffic between the metalliferous islands of the western Cyclades, extending also to Lavrion. The other is the distribution of a distinctive coarse fabric known as 'talc ware' (fig. 96). Talc ware appears at the end of the Neolithic at Agia Irini I (Wilson 1999: 18), and in late EB I levels at Poros on the north coast of Crete (Day *et al.* 1998: 139), but most of the dated material belongs in EB II. The distribution covers a large number of Cycladic sites, as well as Lavrion, Poros and possibly Palamari on Skyros, though the latter identification is unconfirmed (Vaughan and Wilson 1993). Petrographic analysis has proven inconclusive beyond establishing that the fabric is homogenous (Vaughan and Wilson 1993: 174–6), but as fig. 96 demonstrates, a centroid analysis based on the amounts at the four quantified Cycladic assemblages in which it occurs supports an origin in the vicinity of Siphnos. If a Siphnian origin is correct, the wide but quantitatively uneven distribution of this material could be explained by a mixture of local trade (e.g. with neighbouring Melos) and long-range transportation to more distant central trading communities whose people visited Siphnos for its metals, such people both consuming this pottery at home and dispersing small amounts to other settlements in their local network – as is suggested by the greater quantity of talc ware at Daskaleio-Kavos compared to the minute amounts at other small south-east Cycladic sites like Panermos (Karantzali 1996: 26), Markiani (Whitelaw pers. comm.) and the Zas cave (Vaughan and Wilson 1993: 174).

A comparison with obsidian procurement and circulation

There are certain parallels to be drawn between this model of metal exploitation and the continuing procurement of obsidian. Indeed, the position of Melos just to the south of the metalliferous islands makes it highly plausible that procurement expeditions from afar often collected both obsidian and metals, thereby bringing Melos within the ambit of their activities. Despite likely differences in value between metals and obsidian, there are several underlying similarities in their manners of procurement and distribution.

Torrence (1982, 1984, 1986: 139–217) makes a case for the absence of control of the obsidian quarries, and thus for procurement via direct access rather than interaction with controlling Melian communities. On the other hand, the amount of debris in the EBA 'great obsidian deposit' at Phylakopi, estimated by Torrence (1986: 154) at some 7750 kg even after erosion by the sea, suggests that a substantial amount of obsidian was being processed through Phylakopi and accessed by outsiders by means that imply contact with at least this Melian community. Torrence's calculation that even the great obsidian deposit is too small to prove full-time production throughout the EBA stands (Torrence 1982, 1986: 147–50, 154–63), but Carter's recent reassessment of EBA obsidian procurement and circulation is equally right to point out that episodic production for export might be envisaged, and that the lack of parallels for this deposit elsewhere in the Cyclades does suggest that obsidian was being handled at Phylakopi in an unusual way (Carter 1999). A similar combination of direct access plus a degree of procurement through contact with local communities was suggested above for metals.

Similarities also exist in terms of the means by which control over the materials appears to have been exercised. There is no evidence for direct control of the sources of either metals or obsidian. Instead, it seems that at least by EB II control was achieved by restricting maritime travel to the sources, and by controlling the technological skills of extracting materials and manufacturing objects. The role of remote locations and specialist knowledge in achieving these ends has been highlighted for metallurgy. For obsidian the concentration of the sources on one island served a similar function and, as Carter (1999) argues, the learning process required for knapping fine pressure-flaked blades (as opposed to cruder percussion techniques) may have created a comparable knowledge threshold. Finally, it might be noted that even without invoking restriction, the modest consumption rates for obsidian and metal goods that can be estimated for small farmsteads and hamlets, the length of time involved in procurement journeys, and the difficulty in sustaining transmission of techniques among small groups of people, argue that it may have been more convenient for most communities to obtain finished obsidian and metal products from the nearest trading centre, rather than to procure the raw materials and manufacture artefacts themselves.

From intra-Cycladic to long-range circulation

The movement of Cycladic and Lavrion metals (and perhaps Melian obsidian) beyond the islands can be seen as an extension of the practices attested within the Cyclades. Our combined analyses of long-range voyaging and internal procurement have converged on the key role played by the same handful of Cycladic communities. To what extent long-range procurement and circulation was also undertaken by non-Cycladic voyaging centres is not clear. At least in the case of such communities in Attica and Euboia, there is no good reason to doubt that they too island-hopped through the western Cyclades in search of metals and obsidian, prompting the observation that not all the encounters between long-range traders in different parts of the Aegean need have occurred at each other's communities. Quite what combination of Cycladic, Attic or Peloponnesian voyagers spread metal and obsidian into the Peloponnese is unknown, and on Crete (as discussed below) the situation seems to have altered through the course of the EBA.

Moreover, several further substantial points can be noted. The maritime logic to the pattern seen in the islands is evident too across much of the southern Aegean. In addition to the fact that communities involved in procuring and circulating metals were overwhelmingly coastal (McGeehan Liritzis 1996: fig. 6.6.2.3a), parallels with internal Cycladic practices are starting to emerge, in particular the spatial separation of different stages of the production process. One remarkable example is a small, special-purpose EBA site for copper smelting (probably secondary smelting) at Chrysokamino in north-east Crete (Betancourt *et al.* 1997; Stos-Gale 1993: 124, 1998: 720–1). The site's location on a coastal bluff matches similar sites in the Cyclades

Fig. 97 Chrysokamino and its environs. The metallurgical site is located high on the receding line of cliffs in the distance. Courtesy of Stefie Chlouveraki.

(fig. 97), and reflects a desire for easy access from the sea coupled with seclusion from Cretan communities. Clearly, Chrysokamino represented just one link in the chain of metallurgical activities that ran from ore extraction in the Cyclades to eventual deposition of objects in Crete. The smelting operations at Chrysokamino, the existence of local Cretan dagger forms, and the production of Cycladic-type objects in non-Cycladic materials, argue that most metal reached Crete in the form of primary-smelted material or ingots, rather than as finished objects, and moulds may well have been circulating with (or separately from) the metals and metal-smiths. The identity of such smiths understandably eludes us, but two things are clear. First, many must have been closely associated with voyagers from the Cyclades. Second, the nature of relations between smiths and local communities is sure to have varied with the precise stage of the metallurgical process, the metals being manipulated, and the period in question.

Cycladic long-range trade from the Kampos to Kastri group horizons

We can now explore the extent to which investigation of the conditions of voyaging and mineral extraction enhances our interpretations of the archaeological signatures of long-range interaction involving the Cyclades. Three main phases need to be

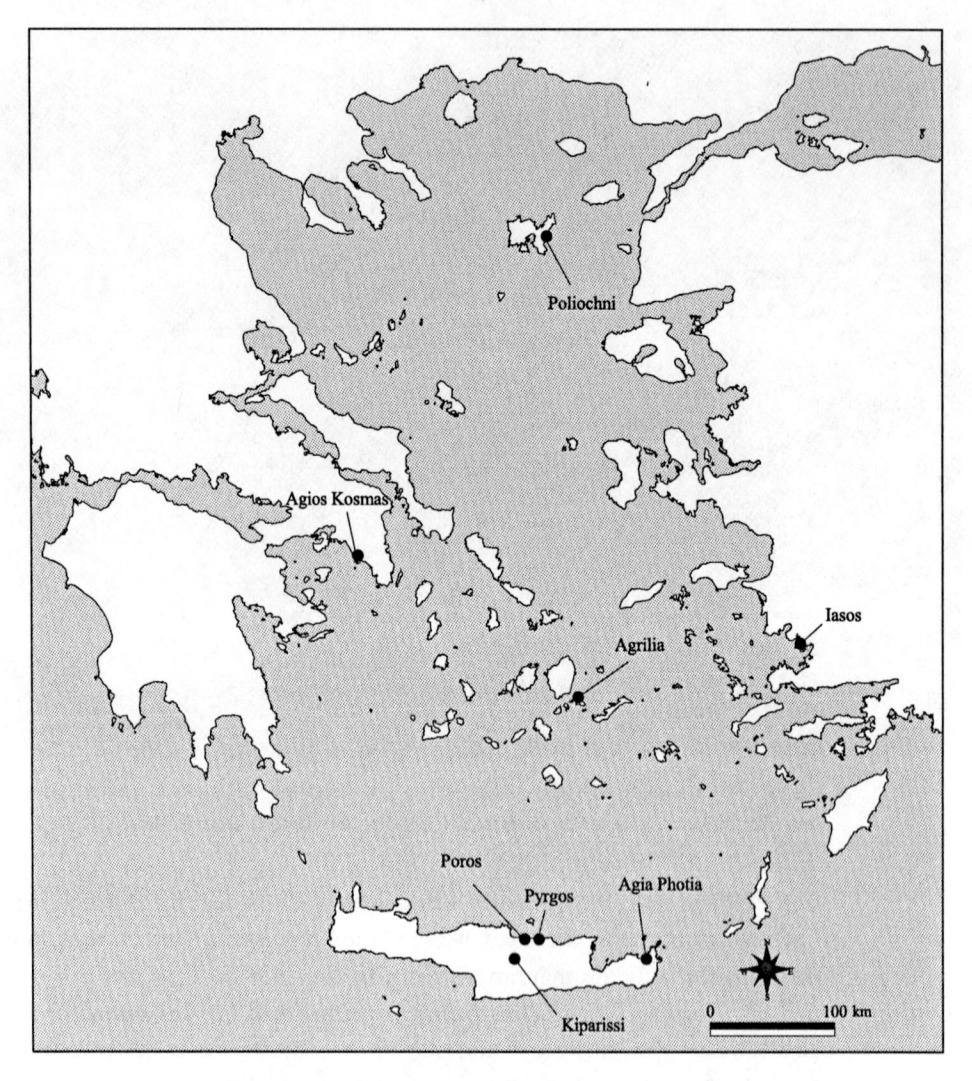

Fig. 98 The main sites involved in long-range Kampos group trade.

distinguished. The first dates to the EB I–II transition, the 'pre-international spirit' phase alluded to early in this chapter (*c.* 2800–2700 BC). The second spans early EB II and includes most of the best-known categories of data (*c.* 2700–2500/2400 BC). The third covers late EB II, commonly associated in the Cyclades with exotic metals, fortified sites and the Anatolian-derived drinking vessels of the Kastri group (*c.* 2500/2400–2200 BC).

Phase 1: The EB I–II transition

Signs of culturally elaborated interaction between the Cyclades and other areas of the southern Aegean by the end of EB I have been apparent for some time (fig. 98). A few

Fig. 99 Kampos group bottle. Courtesy of the British Museum.

Cycladic objects appear in a local cemetery at Iasos on the Anatolian coast (Levi 1961–2, 1965–6). A similar situation obtains at Agios Kosmas in Attica, and the first frying pans are equally at home on mainland Greece and the Cyclades (Coleman 1985: 202–3), an early example of the exchange of symbolic forms between these regions that grows more evident in EB II. In Crete, early excavations found Kampos group shapes among material in the Pyrgos and Kiparissi burial caves on the north coast. The appearance of Kampos group bottles is of particular interest, as this closed form represents the first Aegean shape designed for transport of presumably valued liquids (fig. 99).

Excavations at two further sites on the north coast of Crete are now starting to improve enormously our resolution on the human activities behind this early phase of long-range interaction. For this reason the remainder of this discussion focuses mainly on Crete. The first of these sites is Poros, the coastal settlement due north of Knossos. The study of material from this new site is currently underway, but preliminary reports mention talc ware, metal-working and large amounts of obsidian, all imports from the Cyclades, with local EM I pottery (Day *et al.* 1998: 139, 145; Dimopoulou 1997).

The second site is the cemetery at Agia Photia, near the north-east extremity of Crete (Davaras 1971; Day *et al.* 1998; Carter 1999; Warren 1984; Watrous 1994:

701–3). This large cemetery is a remarkable phenomenon. Dating to late EM I in Cretan terms, it originally comprised about 300 small rock-cut graves with antechambers, alien to Cretan traditions of collective burial, but closely paralleled at the Kampos group cemetery at Agrilia on Epano Kouphonisi, almost 200 km distant. The parallels extend to the burial goods, which include frying pans with star/sun motifs, pyxides and large pedestalled bowls. Recent study of the pottery (Day *et al.* 1998) suggests that out of some 1800 vessels interred, less than 10 per cent are Cretan types, and these mainly imports from Mirabello, north-central Crete and the Mesara. The majority resemble Kampos group shapes, and parallel fabric traditions used in the Cyclades. Save for one imported fabric used for Kampos bottles, it is uncertain whether the vessels are Cycladic imports (Day *et al.*'s preferred option) or represent a Cycladic production tradition active on Crete, but either way, the major fabric matches Cycladic-type fabrics and forms at Poros and the Pyrgos cave, and is not local to the region of the cemetery. Further associations involving materials and technology are the obsidian, knapped following Cycladic rather than Cretan traditions (Carter 1999), objects made of Kythnian copper (Stos-Gale 1993: table 11.1), including midribbed daggers of Cycladic type, and lead of presumably island or Attic origin. Crucibles in the cemetery resemble those at Chalandriani-Kastri and Thermi on Lesbos (Branigan 1988: 239). Two other practices mirror those seen at Agrilia. The first is the 'killing' of daggers (Davaras nd: fig. 10; cf. chapter 8), and the second the burning of organic substances, perhaps aromatics or narcotics, in fenestrated vessels, the latter also seen at Aplomata (Davaras nd: fig. 7; Karantzali 1996: 105). The one note of caution to be injected is that the associated settlement has not been found, owing in all probability to modern building (Tsipopoulou 1989: 97; a similar situation is sadly also true at Agrilia).

In the light of these well-structured and pervasive similarities in the funerary and technological spheres, it is not surprising that Agia Photia is the single candidate for a colony that has found favour with both supporters and sceptics of the identification of Cycladic colonies alike (Doumas 1976b, 1979; Sakellarakis 1977). Despite reservations concerning the social implications of this term (which certainly implies something quite distinct from the primary colonisations of empty islands explored in chapters 4 and 5), and with the proviso that we lack data on the settlement and also physical anthropology, there is much to recommend the hypothesis that the Agia Photia cemetery represents a group of people from the Cyclades, probably from the vicinity of the Erimonisia and perhaps even Agrilia itself, who maintained close links with people back in the islands. To explore this, it is instructive to set out the four basic options that could explain Agia Photia (options that will also be useful when considering later putative colonies):

1 Local people import Cycladic-manufactured objects and imitate practices.
2 Local people imitate Cycladic objects and practices.

3 Cycladic colonists import Cycladic objects and continue practices.
4 Cycladic colonists make Cycladic objects locally and continue practices.

The implications of each option are naturally different. In fact, however, we do have the means to distinguish between the more and less likely options. The fact that the dominant pottery fabric is considered to be non-local argues against 2 and 4 as overall explanations, although the Cycladic metals and obsidian may well have been made into objects at Agia Photia. More generally, the extraordinarily precise nature of the parallels tends to militate against imitation of Cycladic ways of doing things by locals (essential in 2, and necessary also to explain aspects of the phenomenon in 1). For instance, it is hard to see how the specific motor habits involved in knapping blades would have been transferable, or how Cretan communities could have gained knowledge of a style of rock-cut grave that was exceptional even in the Cyclades, being currently known *only* in the Kouphonisia, where it is attributable to the anomalous local geology of sandstone and marl, which prohibited slab-lined cist graves. It therefore looks as if the serendipity of archaeological discovery has revealed two widely separated communities that were intimately connected in terms of culture, customs and trade, and quite plausibly in terms of populations. If it is correct to interpret Agia Photia as a community of Cycladic origin, the spatial overlap between distributions of Cycladic and indigenous material in northern coastal Crete should nonetheless not disguise the fact that indigenous Cretan and intrusive Cycladic identities seem to have remained distinguishable, rather than being eroded by long-range contacts, much as the expanse of intervening sea desert and the difficulty of two-way journeys across it would indeed lead us to predict.

Before summarising what we can say about Cycladic long-range interaction at this juncture, it is worth noting an interesting point that has been overlooked to date in discussions of the significance of Agia Photia. Obviously, if the interpretations offered above are valid, Agia Photia tells us a lot about the activities of Cycladic people abroad. But it also says some suggestive things about processes *within* the Cyclades during the crucial phase that immediately precedes the *floruit* of the large trading communities. It can hardly be coincidental that Agia Photia finds its most thorough-going parallels not with Kampos group sites in general, but with one salient community in the Erimonisia at precisely the time when these islands started to emerge as the focus of intensive local maritime trade in the south-east Cyclades. If the link can be sustained, it implies that long-range voyages, and the forging of links with distant communities, played a part from the very first in the strategies of this emergent centre, and that Aegean voyaging and its accompanying ideologies arose in the context of local efforts at differentiation. The Cycladic mechanisms that created a community in east Crete will remain obscure, but probably involved some form of fissioning within Agrilia or another undiscovered Kampos group centre, triggered by conflict or a conscious decision to expand the community's network. In this context, the demographics of these two quite short-lived communities deserve comparison. With about ninety-two graves, plus an unknown quantity lost to robbing, the Agrilia community was large in Cycladic terms (cf. chapter 7), but it is only a third the size of Agia Photia, where the number of tombs implies a village-level settlement (Day *et al.* 1998: 146). One plausible reason why the community at Agia Photia outgrew its contemporary in the Cyclades could be the better agricultural niche that it occupied. Another might be that an intrusive group in east Crete had to be more self-reliant than one set among a network of similar neighbours.

Stepping back from Agia Photia, this site stands out as one particularly brightly illuminated point amid the diverse evidence for a cycle of long-range voyaging that was based in the south-east Cyclades, took in Crete and probably returned via the south-east Aegean. The first landfall is likely to have been the coast of north-central Crete, a well-populated area and the gateway to the Mesara, after which canoes traded their way east along the coast. In central Crete there is as yet no unambiguous evidence for a Cycladic settlement, although future discoveries may alter this. The Cycladic material is found in an indigenous settlement at Poros and with burials of established Cretan type in the Pyrgos and Kiparissi caves. Moreover, the coast itself was the interface – Kampos group pottery rarely penetrated inland, not even the few kilometres to Knossos (Wilson 1994: 39), although metals and obsidian did percolate across the island via overland networks (Carter 1998; Wilson and Day 1994; Whitelaw *et al.* 1997). In this light, the establishment of a resident Cycladic community in the far east of Crete may reflect the special conditions obtaining in an area probably without its own indigenous centres before EB II, and at a crucial point where canoes had to cease coast-hugging and undertake the open crossing to Kasos and Karpathos (Agouridis 1997: 11). A few eastern Aegean elements in the assemblage of Agia Photia (Haggis 1997: 293–5), plus the varied provenance of the cemetery's Cretan pottery, suggest that this intrusive centre exploited a vacant trading niche between Crete and the south-east Aegean, a niche identified in all probability in the course of voyages along this route. Eastern Aegean parallels at Agrilia itself (Warren 1984: 59–61; Zapheiropoulou 1984: 39) may reflect objects encountered on the last leg of cyclic voyages, and tell us more about an as yet unknown material culture in the EBA south-east Aegean, rather than about contacts with north-east Aegean sites such as Poliochni, as is usually assumed. And, finally, *if* E. S. Sherratt's detection of an echo of Levantine cults and ideologies in the Cyclades at this time is correct, voyages onward from Agia Photia into the south-east Aegean would have provided the best chance for Cycladic seafarers to encounter any ideas filtering west along the southern coast of Anatolia. In this sense, voyaging provides an ideal medium for gathering fragments of exotic ideas, integrating them with local ideology in the home community, and subsequently dispersing them in this revised form through internal Aegean networks.

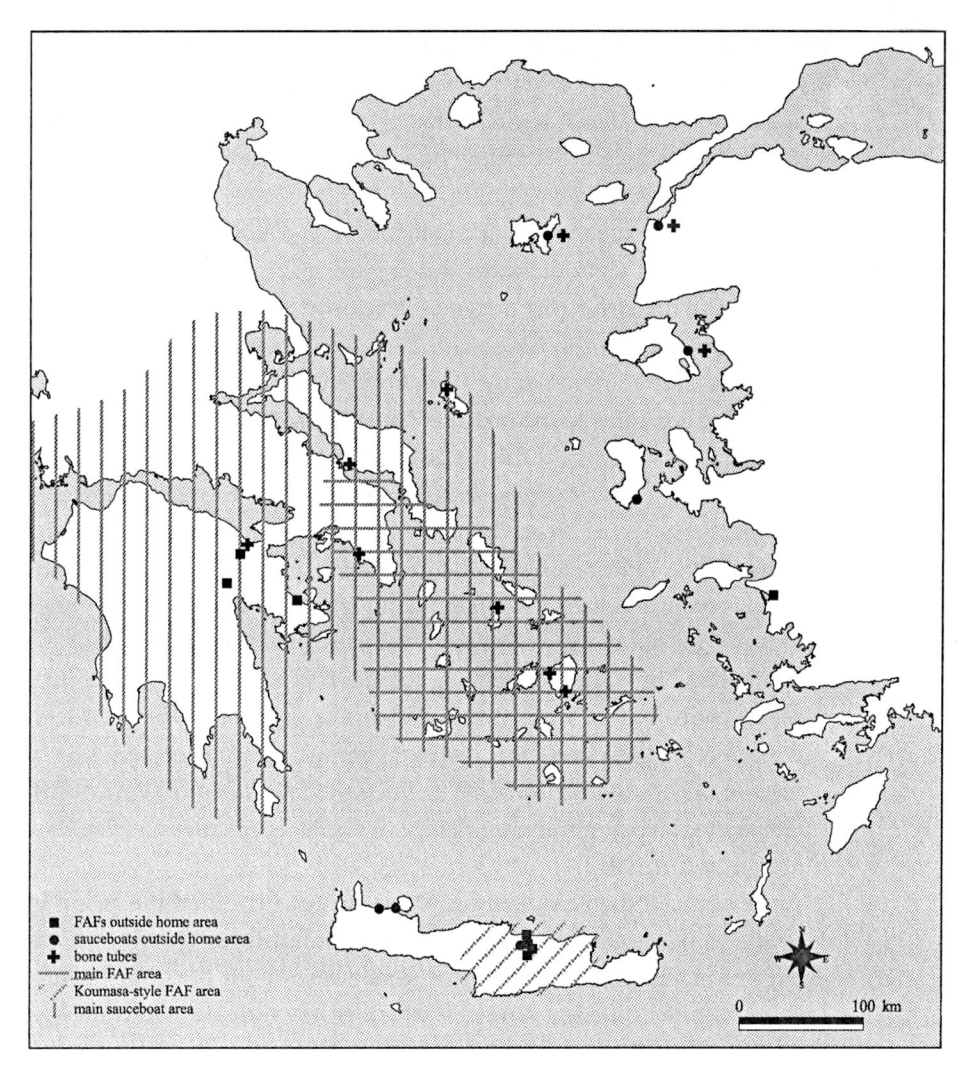

Fig. 100 Distribution of select inter-regional trade objects of earlier Early Bronze II. Data on bone tubes courtesy of Olga Krzyszkowska.

Phase 2: early EB II

To this phase date several of the elements of long-range trade recognised by Renfrew, most notably the movement of sauceboats and folded-arm figurines (fig. 100). A more recently recognised feature is the distribution of medium-sized Cycladic liquid storage jars, with characteristic incised handles, a less specialised but larger replacement for the Kampos bottle. Whilst these jars could be simply discarded water containers from the voyage, their miniature imitation in precious metals as pin finials and pendants in the Cyclades, north-east Aegean and Crete (Branigan 1974: 37; Marangou

1990: 65, cat. no. 42; Sakellarakis and Sapouna-Sakellaraki 1997: fig. 656) suggests that they held a more precious, socially significant and probably alcoholic liquid. This would fit well with the wide circulation of sauceboats, and drinking rituals may therefore have been a means of creating bonds between leading people in widely separated communities.

This phase saw the maximal prominence of Cycladic-based voyaging, and also the social currency of Cycladic ways of doing things at its peak. Presumably building on voyaging and metal-bearing activities developed in the period of the Kampos group, Cycladic traders seem to have made themselves central to long-range movement in the Aegean. The adoption of their symbols (e.g. figurines) and styles (e.g. the fashion for applying colorants to the body) at far-off Aegean sites can be seen as a marker not just of their passage, but of the desire of other prominent individuals or traders to act and look like their Cycladic counterparts, not least to interact effectively with the canoe parties arriving from these islands. The resultant impression of a Cycladic element in the culture of neighbouring areas is responsible for further claims of Cycladic colonies during this phase, although it can be argued that not a single case commands the compelling number of parallels and structural similarities witnessed at Agia Photia. The option of settling abroad, probably only viable if an empty niche existed, seems to have been abandoned at this time; or if island traders did still live and die abroad, their presence has been swamped in archaeological terms by the signatures of the host communities. The purported Cycladic colonies of EB II are rather testimony to the extraordinary prestige of Cycladic practices during the two or three centuries of early EB II.

Links between the Cyclades and Crete, which furnished the fullest image for the preceding phase, now display an altered cultural form (overlaying the continuing import of metals and obsidian) that underscores both the rising status of Cycladic customs and the different terms on which cross-cultural interaction was predicated. Exactly how the Agia Photia community ended remains a mystery, given the lack of settlement data, but a plausible scenario is that it was squeezed out or assimilated, gradually or forcibly, by the expansion of indigenous neighbouring settlements like Petras and the first trading activities of Mochlos. The identification of Cycladic traders at inland Archanes, just south of Knossos in central Crete (Sakellarakis 1977), remains equivocal, because the obsidian, folded-arm figurine fragments and typologically Cycladic metal artefacts are interred in a definitively Cretan communal round tomb at Archanes Phourni cemetery.

The Archanes data in fact contribute important insights into two quite different features of the local treatment of Cycladic objects at this time. The first is that they now penetrated beyond the coastal zone of northern Crete, probably thanks to an improving currency as Aegean prestige goods. The second is that certain kinds of Cycladic imports were both adapted and imitated. Evidence for the former practice is seen in the addition of a mouth (absent in the Cyclades) to the Cycladic figurines at Archanes

Fig. 101 Cycladic imports at Knossos, Crete, in Early Bronze II. *Left:* fragment of a painted sauceboat. *Right:* incised jar handle. Courtesy of David Wilson.

(Papadatos 1999), and for the latter in the derivative Koumasa type of marble figurine, found only on Crete, and Cretan manufacture of figurines in other stones and bone (Branigan 1971; Renfrew 1969; Sakellarakis and Sapouna-Sakellaraki 1997: 703–6). Similar phenomena are seen in the parallels between a class of chlorite schist vessels found in the Cyclades and Crete (Getz-Gentle 1996: 190–204). How the production of Cycladic-type metal objects on Crete was carried out during this phase is unclear; the mid-ribbed dagger, in particular, is almost as much at home in northern Crete as the Cyclades by this time (Papadatos 1999). Interesting as these material dialogues are, it should be noted that their extent was tightly circumscribed to objects in metal and stone. The Cycladic pottery imports of this period stand out as exotic and had no influence upon ceramic production in Crete. The shapes (fig. 101) are mainly richly painted sauceboats, a few *urfirnis* sauceboats of island or mainland origin (if the latter, the mode of conveyance needs to be considered), and the liquid storage jars, several of which seem to be in a Melian fabric (Warren 1972b; Wilson 1994: 39–40).

Relations in early EB II between the Cyclades and the virtually contiguous areas of Attica and Euboia contrast with the patterns seen in Crete. In this theatre, a network of big coastal villages straddled the notional geographical divide, including Agia Irini in Kea, Agios Kosmas, Askitario and Raphina in Attica, and several southern Euboian sites dominated by the 'supernova' settlement of Manika. This resulted in a gradual cline of differing local practices that defies any attempt to draw a hard cultural edge to the Cyclades in this direction. For example, the settlement architecture and local ceramic repertoire of Agia Irini find their best parallels in eastern Attica, with Cycladic imports from further south standing out immediately (Wilson 1987, 1999: 231–2), whilst some Attic and Euboian communities adopted or adapted elements of Cycladic funerary practices and symbolic paraphernalia (Sampson 1988b). This cultural elision is best explained as the result of regular local and longer-range movement along the maritime corridors that link these regions, all busy routes unlike the open passage from the Cyclades to Crete. The character of local traffic must have resembled the intra-Cycladic networks explored in chapter 6, whilst access from a variety of points of origin to the Lavrion and western Cycladic metal sources probably introduced a mixture of long-range voyagers to this cultural melting pot. Such circumstances may argue for the residence of a few islanders in non-Cycladic communities (and maybe vice versa at Agia Irini), but the sheer fuzziness of cultural distinctions and, again, the lack of comprehensive similarities doom any efforts to identify Cycladic colonies. Moreover, specific difficulties attend the two most often cited cases. At Agios Kosmas (Mylonas 1959) only certain graves in the cemetery closely resemble the kinds of constructions of personae in death seen in the Cyclades, and the settlement material is firmly at home on the mainland. The same is true of Manika (Sampson 1985, 1988b; Sapouna-Sakellaraki 1986, 1987), where in addition the site's vast size rules out the colony hypothesis; even at modest occupation densities, and allowing for some temporal drift in the focus of habitation, a settlement of 50–80 ha implies an agglomeration of people that exceeded by a degree of magnitude the populations of even major Cycladic centres – indeed, on the face of it, there could have been as many people living at Manika as on several Cycladic islands put together.

What of the regions to the west and east of the Cyclades? To the west, a scatter of Cycladic artefacts, mainly comprising figurines, extends into the Peloponnese, and incised-handled jars found in Kythera (Coldstream and Huxley 1972: plate 17 nos. 53–6) and Laconia (e.g. Cavanagh *et al.* 1996: fig. 11.6 no. 5) attest to contacts, although the Kytheran jars are largely in a local fabric. In the east, the paucity of EBA data precludes firm conclusions, although a marble bowl reached Asomatos on Rhodes (Marketou 1990) and the recent discovery of a Cycladic figurine on the Anatolian coast at Miletus gives substance to the tantalising hint of similar finds over a century ago in the region of Knidos (Bent 1888). Such data are open to multiple, mutually compatible explanations. They could indicate the return passages of cyclic voyages from the Cyclades to Crete, direct east–west voyages between the Cyclades and such regions, or simply down-the-line radiation of prestige objects through the continuum of southern Aegean networks.

In view of the critical role of north-east Aegean activities in the ensuing, final, phase of Cycladic canoe-based voyaging, a word should be said about the early EB II evidence for Cycladic finds in the north. Apart from the possibility that Cycladic metals reached the north Aegean (Pernicka *et al.* 1990; Stos-Gale 1992), and small amounts of Melian obsidian, the evidence comprises metal artefacts, sauceboat sherds at Troy, Poliochni and Thermi, some Cycladic painted vessels but others of indeterminate island or mainland origin (Renfrew 1972: 209), and bone pigment-containing tubes at all the above sites, as well as Skyros (Krzyszkowska 1981). Given that the northern Aegean voyaging circuit must have grazed the edge of the Cyclades, and that this region could access alternative metal sources, it would be wrong to assume that these objects necessarily demonstrate regular voyaging by Cycladic traders into the northern Aegean. Though this may be the case, all they formally tell us is that at this stage even northern communities were not impervious to the cultural cachet associated with the Cycladic traders. Much as regionally specific cultural, trading and voyaging regimes distinguish the Cycladic interaction with Crete from that with Attica and Euboia, or with the Peloponnese and south-east Aegean, so another set of relations is liable to have obtained in the north. In each case, the articulation between islanders and the 'outside' was structured in distinctive ways that naturally also have implications for the local consumption of different external worlds within the Cyclades.

Some light is shed on this last issue by a few pieces of evidence from within the islands. In the previous section, we suggested that long-range voyaging was a critical element in the emergence of the Cycladic centres. All the signs are that in early EB II the control, use and consumption of exotica continued to play a major role in this respect. One element of such exotica is likely to have remained news of far-off places, coupled with the introduction of foreign tales. But the number of known physical imports that can be associated with voyages to Crete, in particular, remains so low that some non-surviving return cargo may well be postulated, perhaps textiles, or human prizes raided from the south-east Aegean islands or the coast of the southern Peloponnese. The only two well-documented Cretan objects (or memories of such objects) in the Cyclades are, however, suggestive. One, a Cretan bird askos, resonates with Cycladic bird imagery (which we suggested was associated with swift travel) and came from a grave on Epano Kouphonisi in the Erimonisia, a core area for seafaring (Warren 1984: 56; three further EBA Cretan objects from the Cyclades that Warren discusses lack firm contexts but are associated with Melos, Thera and Naxos, all plausible areas of outward or homeward-bound voyaging involving Crete). The second object reflects either a memory, or an as yet undiscovered import: on the lid of a Cycladic marble pyxis from Grotta-Aplomata, also a major island centre, was incised the outline of a recumbent dog that echoes relief-carved dogs on similar pyxides made of chlorite schist and found in east Crete (Getz-Gentle 1996: 196–7). This concentration on the major Cycladic trading sites is matched if we consider the imports from the Greek mainland, for the numerous fragments of fine yellow-blue mottled sauceboats of mainland provenance at Daskaleio-Kavos and Agia Irini (Broodbank 2000; Wilson 1999: 76–7), which are the largest groups of non-Cycladic material known in the islands, represent an accumulation of vessels not attested at smaller island sites. The pieces from Daskaleio-Kavos, in particular, must be fragile goods obtained in distant Attica or the Peloponnese, transformed into status markers in the south-east Cyclades and a nice illustration of how through long-range voyaging a local trading centre might transform itself into a veritable *axis mundi* for its neighbours in the Cyclades.

Phase 3: late EB II and the Kastri group

The last phase of Cycladic long-range canoe-borne trade coincides with further shifts in the dynamics of Aegean EBA interaction, and ones that eventually did much to

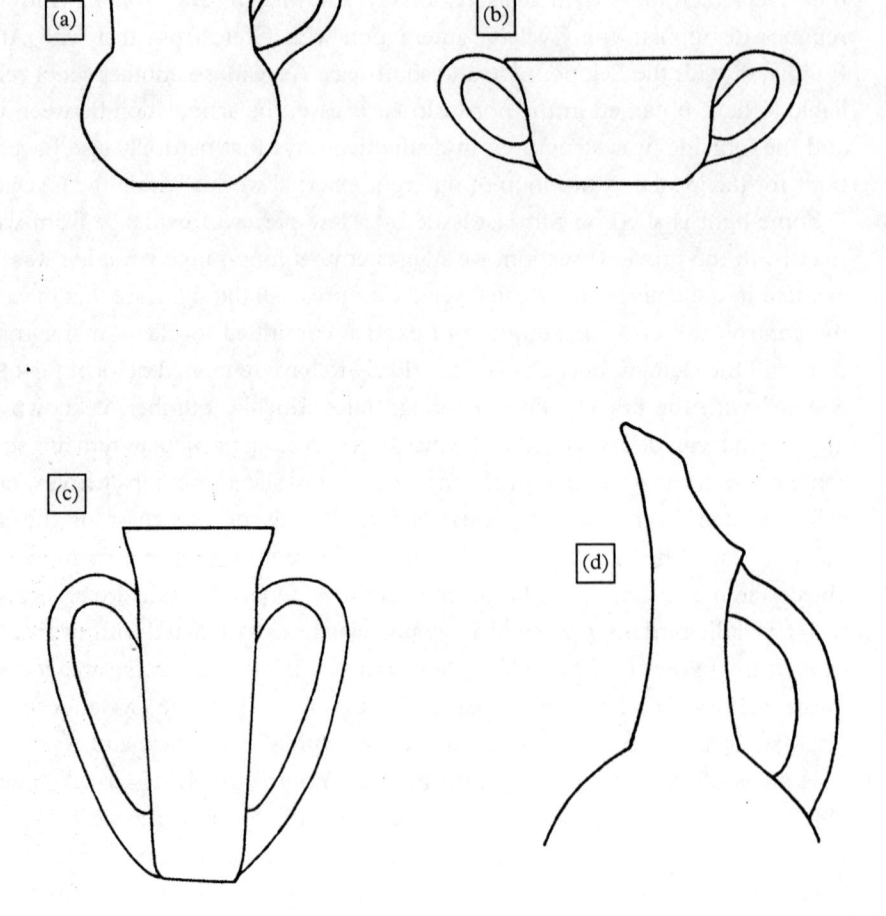

Fig. 102 Principal Kastri group shapes: (a) tankard, (b) bell-shaped cup, (c) depas cup, (d) upright-necked jug with cut-away spout. After Rutter 1979: figs. 1–2.

undercut the strategies through which Cycladic voyagers had established their prestige abroad. In the Cyclades, this phase is commonly defined by the appearance of a loose cluster of Anatolian-derived drinking and pouring shapes with monochrome black through to red-brown burnished surfaces, and clear metallic prototypes. These have been known as the Kastri group since the identification of several examples at Kastri, the fortified settlement above Chalandriani (Renfrew 1972: 533–4; Sotirakopoulou 1993 for a good recent survey). The three key drinking shapes are the tall, double-handled depas cup, a shorter version termed the bell-shaped cup, and the one-handled tankard, to which should be added the upright-necked jug with cut-away spout (fig. 102). These shapes also appear widely on the eastern seaboard of mainland Greece, where they are known as Lefkandi I material, as well as in the eastern

Aegean islands; wheel-made open shapes are found in Lefkandi I assemblages in Euboia but are rare or absent in most of the Cyclades (Wilson 1999: 94, 141–3 for a few imports at Agia Irini).

Rutter (1979) has demonstrated beyond doubt that this horizon falls primarily in late EB II (see chapter 10 for a fuller discussion in the context of the consequent debate over the implications for the late third-millennium EB III period in the Cyclades). This aligns the Kastri group phase in the Cyclades with a substantial period of about 200–300 years, roughly contemporary with the large corridor houses of the Greek mainland, the rich settlements of Troy II and the later levels at Poliochni, the EM IIB phase on Crete, and more generally the centuries during which increasing amounts of exotic metals, technologies and ideas started to filter into the Aegean, especially from regions to the east.

Unfortunately, and despite rapid recent advances in our empirical knowledge of this critical period, the history of the Cyclades in the Kastri group phase continues to be written around an increasingly untenable model of invasion by refugees or conquerors from the east Aegean who swept away most of the islands' communities and customs (Barber 1984: 88, 1987: 28–9, 137–9; Doumas 1988; MacGillivray 1984: 75; Stos-Gale et al. 1984). This model rests on the conflation of separable and in certain instances palpably chronologically disassociated phenomena, namely the appearance of the Kastri group itself, the inflow of eastern metals and metal objects, the numbers of fortified Cycladic settlements encountered in EB II and the desertion of most settlements by the end of the EBA. Until these diverse phenomena are untangled there can be little hope of understanding what was going on. Once this task is accomplished, however, it will be easier to situate the Cycladic islands within late EB II trading patterns, and to build an alternative model to explain the changing nature of the islanders' external relations.

Starting with the appearance of Anatolian drinking and pouring shapes, and the inflow of non-local, probably mainly eastern metals, it should be readily apparent that exotic drinking customs and metals are hardly an adequate reason to postulate external invaders – and indeed in historiographical terms it is striking that no such inference is drawn from the presence of sauceboats from the Greek mainland in the Cyclades, nor of Cycladic sauceboats and metals in Crete. It is also important to resist the temptation to circular reasoning, exemplified by the dominance of the invasionist model in shaping the significance attributed to the identification of tin-bronzes at Kastri itself (Stos-Gale et al. 1984). An explanatory framework for the introduction and circulation of non-Aegean metals, channelled first through centres in the northeast Aegean, was set out earlier in this chapter. Thanks to recent research, a lot more can now also be said about the Kastri group pottery and the specific contexts in which it appears in the Cyclades.

The first point to emphasise is that the Kastri group is not a regularly co-existing suite. Rather, it comprises a series of shapes of thoroughly varied incidence at different

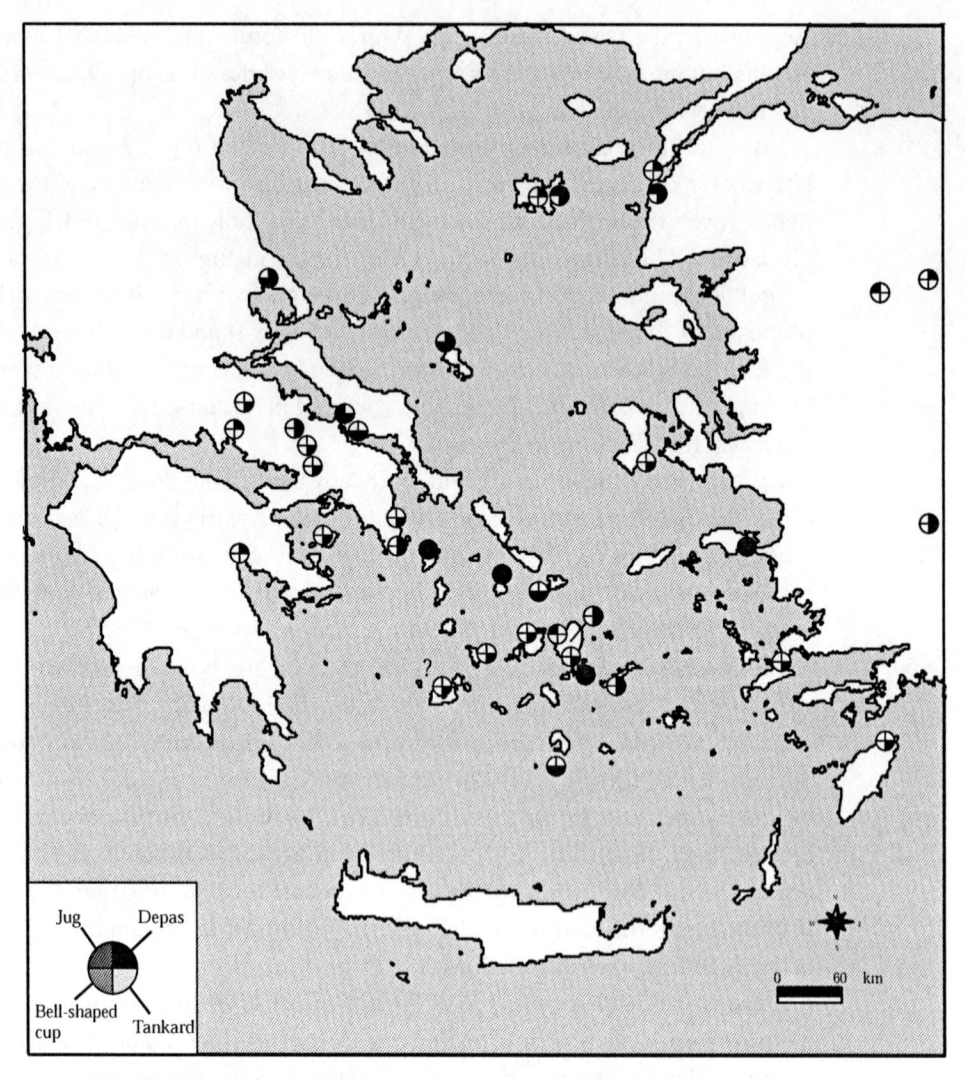

Fig. 103 Distribution of Kastri group pottery in the Aegean. Data from Sotirakopoulou 1993, Wilson 1999 and courtesy of Electra Boli.

sites in and beyond the Cyclades. The overall Aegean distribution of the main shapes illustrates their very uneven uptake (fig. 103). Within the Cyclades, even the drinking shapes do not always occur together. For example, only the tankard and bell-shaped cup are found at Mt Kynthos (MacGillivray 1980: 19–22), only the tankard and depas cup at Markiani (Doumas and Angelopoulou 1997), and the tankard alone at Akrotiraki on Siphnos (Tsountas 1899: plate 9 no. 11). At Agia Irini, where rough quantification can be undertaken, it transpires that the representation of each shape is also uneven: tankards are represented by hundreds of fragments, bell-shaped cups by considerably fewer, and the depas cup is extremely rare (Wilson 1999: 95). Moreover, fabric analysis at Agia Irini, Daskaleio-Kavos and Mt Kynthos argues for different levels of local (or at least nearby) production versus importation for each Kastri group shape (Broodbank 2000; MacGillivray 1980: 19–20; Wilson 1999: tables 3.3, 3.4). In short, the apparent 'group' was in fact brought together to variable degrees, and by a complex shape-specific mixture of local production and external acquisition.

Another insight now provided by the analysis of entire pottery assemblages is that the Kastri group shapes form a statistically minor component that slots into existing repertoires. This should really have been obvious from the start, given the narrow range of functions that these shapes comprise. Once again, Agia Irini demonstrates the point most clearly, with the appearance of the Kastri group shapes around the transition from Agia Irini II to Agia Irini III countered by the overwhelming case for continuity in the overall assemblage; Kastri group shapes make up only about 13 per cent of the total pottery, a figure almost matched by the continuing (though diminished) popularity of sauceboats during late EB II (Wilson 1999: 95, table 3.2). Kastri group shapes make up an even smaller proportion of the Mt Kynthos pottery, and indeed MacGillivray's division of the unstratified material from this site into an early and a late phase may need to be reconsidered in the light of the overlaps now documented at Agia Irini (MacGillivray 1980). Recent reports on the late EB II settlement of Panermos on Naxos, normally considered a typical Kastri group site (e.g. Doumas 1988: 23), mention just *one or two* tankards plus a possible sauceboat sherd among numerous storage jars, cooking pots and bowls (Doumas 1992b: 67; Karantzali 1996: 25–6). In this light, it seems likely that when the pottery assemblage of Kastri itself is fully studied, and compared with material from soundings at the earlier Chalandriani settlement, a similarly nuanced picture will emerge.

Bringing together the Cycladic evidence with the Aegean-wide distribution seen in fig. 103, it looks very much as if the Kastri group shapes in fact spread by trade and adoption through the long-range maritime routes that already existed in the northern and southern Aegean. This would explain the noticeably greater concentration at the central communities in and beyond the Cyclades, with smaller communities often participating to very modest degrees, probably often via a nearby trading centre – very much as was proposed for the dispersion of sauceboats. Likewise, the low incidence of Kastri group shapes in the south-west Cyclades, notably the lack of any definite examples in Melos, makes sense in terms of this area's relative insulation from trading routes that passed through the eastern Aegean. It would also help to circumvent the disagreement as to whether the group's affinities lie principally with north-west or south-west Anatolia (cf. Mellink 1986: 148–9; Sotirakopoulou 1997). For, far from being a package introduced from one region, the Kastri group would reflect the coming together within the trading networks of the Cyclades and the west-central Aegean littoral of shapes that had been borrowed from the diverse coastal Anatolian traditions with which the major centres were in contact.

Such perspectives now allow us to make fairly short shrift of the association of the Kastri group with a horizon of fortification and desertion, in turn used as support for

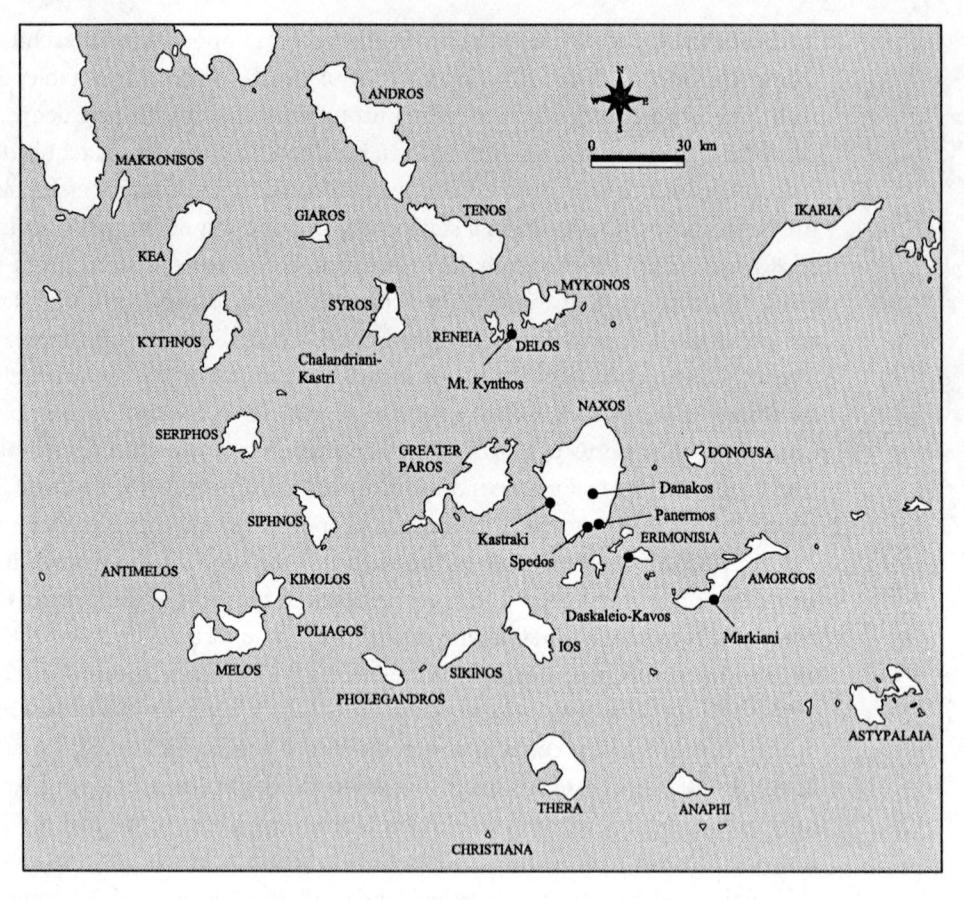

Fig. 104   Distribution of fortified sites in the Cyclades.

the invasion hypothesis. The view that the Kastri group is closely connected with fortified sites in remote, often hitherto unoccupied locations (e.g. Barber 1987: 138; Doumas 1988) is becoming increasingly untenable. It is certainly true that, within late EB II (the vagueness of the phrasing is deliberate), several Cycladic sites were fortified (fig. 104), as one aspect of a broader horizon of fortification across much of the later EBA Aegean. In the Cyclades, fortifications range from imposing free-standing walls with bastions, as at Kastri and maybe Daskaleio-Kavos, through farmsteads or hamlets packed behind a continuous fortified perimeter, as at Panermos, to a simple *ad hoc* restriction of access, as at Mt Kynthos (fig. 105). But the claim that these places occupy new locations cannot be sustained. Those in the south-east Cyclades are at the heart of one of the most densely occupied parts of the Cyclades, and overlie, or are adjacent to, earlier EB II settlements. Kastri in Syros is only some 600 m from the settlement focus at Chalandriani (fig. 63). What is in fact seen is an increasing investment in defence by pre-existing communities, through either on-the-spot building or short-range relocation to more defendable points; it might also be added that at least one major settlement with plenty of Kastri group material, namely Agia Irini, does not

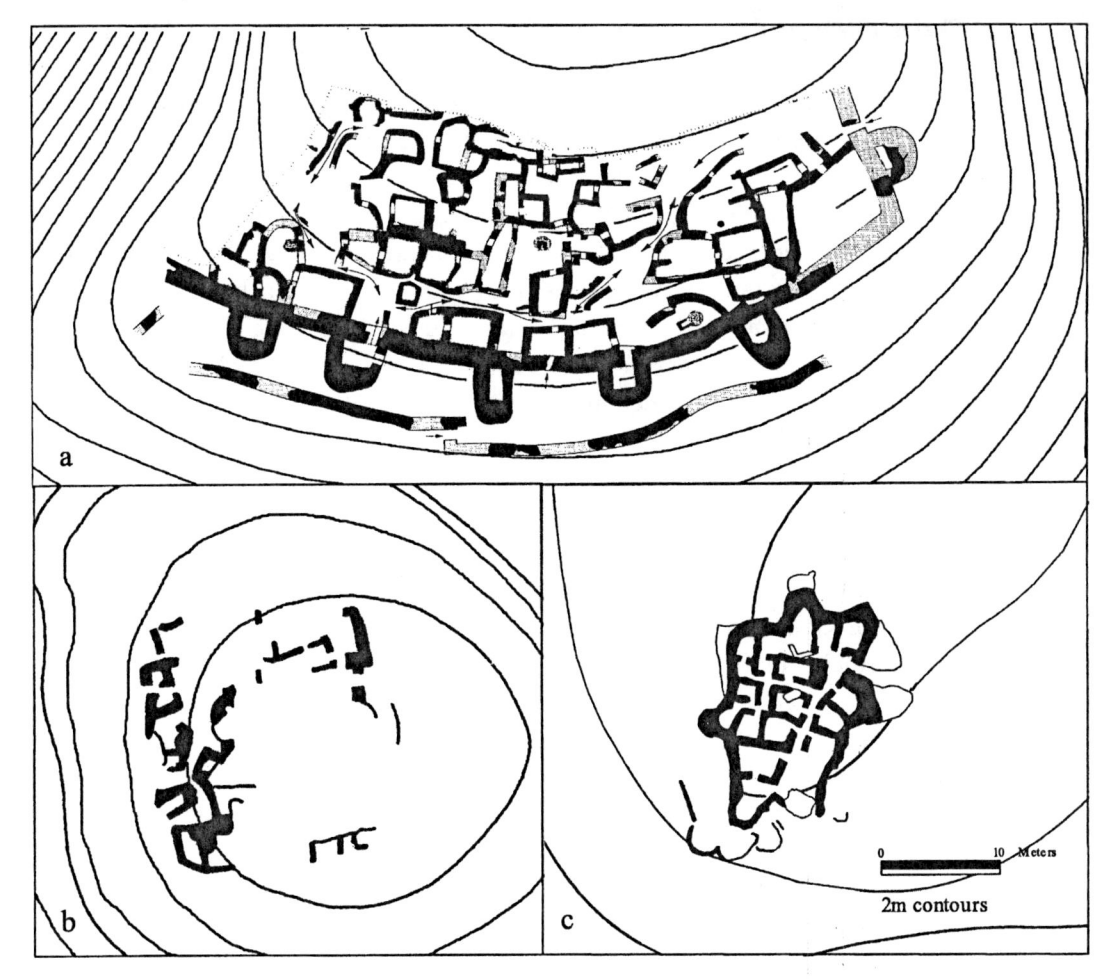

Fig. 105 Fortified settlements: (a) Kastri, (b) Mt Kynthos, (c) Panermos. After originals by Todd Whitelaw.

seem to have been fortified. A further point is that the long duration of late EB II, plus the single-phase nature of the fortified settlements, make it likely that they belong late in the period, and therefore cannot be associated with the earlier introduction of Anatolian shapes. The propensity to fortify in late EB II is important and may tell us something about how EB II ways of life in the Cyclades ended in the late third millennium BC, but to elide it with the arrival of new pottery forms in order to sustain a narrative of invasion is unwarranted.

The association of the Kastri group with a widespread horizon of settlement abandonment definitely, and wrongly, conflates chronologically separate phenomena. As will become apparent in chapter 10, the end of the EBA in the Cyclades did indeed witness the large-scale desertion of sites, but as an ever-increasing number of excavated settlements start to reveal late EB II occupation, it is fast becoming indisputable that this happened well after the introduction of Anatolian shapes and (by definition) after the construction of the subsequently abandoned fortified sites. In this context, it must be stressed that because the small, often numerically rare Kastri group shapes are the only reliable chronological markers that we currently possess for late EB II in the Cyclades, it is quite wrong to assume that surface scatters that fail to produce fragments of these shapes should be dated to a period prior to their appearance. In fact many of the sites dated to EB II from surface material could perfectly well belong late in the period. Despite a trend towards fortification and (as we shall see) major changes in external contacts, the settlement patterns of the early and late EB II Cyclades, and the placement of the principal centres, appear to have remained effectively the same.

So much for a deconstruction of the associations that have built up around the Kastri group. With the accretions stripped away, however, it is worth asking what the Kastri group and other contemporary phenomena in later EB II might actually reveal about changing culture in the Cyclades. One very simple point is also a very important one. In comparison with the strong impression of cultural confidence seen in the elaboration of Cycladic material culture and its dispersion across the Aegean in early EB II, the Kastri group indicates a new degree of deference to outside practices. This goes further than the fact that the new Anatolian shapes are likely to mark the adoption of Anatolian drinking customs (note that their physical manipulation required a different bodily etiquette from anything used earlier). For the monochrome surface of Kastri group vessels provides no field for the ebullient and individualised painted decoration, seen especially on Cycladic sauceboats and jugs. One might not read much into this, were it not that the stratigraphy of Agia Irini reveals that in late EB II painted decoration did decline sharply in quantity, diversity and quality – indeed the only regularly painted late EB II Cycladic shape is the one-handled cup, the fabric of which suggests a Melian origin, and which might be the south-west's response to the tankard (e.g. Tsountas 1899, plate 8 nos. 3–4). A distancing of the Kastri group shapes from the traditional cultural ways of emphasising individual status in the Cyclades is also argued be the fact that the former rarely appear in the cemeteries (Renfrew 1984a: 45). For example, only a few graves at Chalandriani contain Kastri group shapes, despite the occupation of the nearby settlement (Renfrew 1972: 533), and this admittedly tiny sample is negatively associated with frying pans, figurines and pigments, all long-standing symbols of prestige in the islands. There are hints, therefore, that the Kastri group represents not simply an addition to existing Cycladic practices and culture, but a competing ideology that at least partly undermined existing structures. Before we can draw these threads together to construct a new model of change in later EB II, however, we need to survey the overall pattern of evidence for Cycladic voyaging at this time. This reveals some surprising alterations in emphasis.

In a sharp reversal of previous regimes, we have much better evidence in late EB II for what voyagers were bringing in to the Cyclades than for what they were taking out. The inflows of Anatolian pottery forms and non-Cycladic metals have already been discussed; outgoing trade objects and materials are vanishingly rare. In certain areas of the Aegean this might be partly due to the decreased distinctiveness of Cycladic pottery, and especially of any Kastri group exports to the north and east Aegean, although this itself, and the lack of accompanying paraphernalia, argues for the demise of Cycladic objects as an inter-regional vocabulary of prestige. Pottery at Agia Irini III does suggest continuing contacts with Attica and Euboia, as well as the rest of the Cyclades, all areas involved in the adoption of the Anatolian innovations.

But by far the most dramatic change is the complete cessation of material culture evidence for Cycladic trade with Crete (Wilson 1994: 41). This is especially interesting because the continued use of obsidian and probably Cycladic copper in Crete indicates that movement between these two regions was still taking place. We have in effect two options, both of which involve a reversal of the culturally elaborated movement that typified the previous phases. Either Cycladic canoe-loads of raw materials continued to arrive, but without accompanying finished products. Or, for reasons that remain unclear but could be connected with a new assertion of control by Cretan elites in the later pre-palatial centuries, the previous receptiveness to Cycladic traders was rejected in favour of direct exploitation of quarries and mines in the Cyclades by Cretan expeditions that made little or no contact with people in the islands – a reversion to much earlier Cretan strategies, as witnessed by the presence of obsidian at early Neolithic Knossos two millennia before the Cyclades were first settled (Renfrew *et al.* 1965). Cretan voyagers could have moved north along the indirect routes taken by Cycladic canoes on their return routes, and, equally, reaped the benefit of permanent residence in the south by waiting for reversals of the prevailing winds. The first of these explanatory options (i.e. the continuing arrival of Cycladic canoes without finished objects) cannot be ruled out, but the absence of even incised handles from Cycladic containers, and the lack of EM IIB finds in the Cyclades, render it less plausible. In favour of the second option are two other new developments at the southern end of the Aegean. In east Crete, the sea-trading centre of Mochlos experienced a boom in rich burials in EM IIB (Branigan 1991: 97); it also imported copious amounts of obsidian (Carter 1999) but has produced not a single Cycladic artefact. Mochlos may represent a local centre for east Crete that developed its own voyaging tradition around this time. And in the west, it is intriguing to note that later EB II sees the establishment at Kastri on Kythera of a settlement with strong Cretan cultural connections (Coldstream and Huxley 1972: 275–7), a 'colony' phenomenon that could represent the coalescing of west Cretan people at a key point on the indirect northward passage to the western Cyclades.

To summarise, in late EB II two changes that were, at least in proximate terms, unrelated appear to have reduced the scope for Cycladic long-range voyagers to pursue pathways to fame and esteem at a pan-Aegean scale. The first of these was the rise of a new set of strategies at centres on the Aegean rim, in particular the north-east, involving the manipulation and circulation of non-Aegean metals. Through increasing the number of places where metals could be obtained, forcing a dependency on outsiders for access to tin, and perhaps also enhancing interest in gold (the one other metal that the Cyclades did not supply) through the brassy sheen of tin-bronze, this compromised the ability of Cycladic traders to control regimes of metal value. The result seems to have been a new deference to non-Cycladic practices, alongside the adoption of what Nakou (1997: 645) describes as a new ethic of interaction. It is in this context that we need to understand the popularity of Anatolian drinking customs and the decline of several traditional forms of behaviour. The second change was the apparent exclusion of Cycladic traders from the great voyaging circuits that centred on Crete (or at least the collapse of a demand for their prestige goods there), a change that is likely to relate, at some level, to changes in Cretan communities that increased the control of local leaders and generated a sense of cultural exclusivity. The net result was the third distinctive spatial pattern in a temporal sequence that, if now viewed together, illustrates the shifting and contingent nature of Cycladic long-range trading activity through the course of the EBA (fig. 106).

Yet, in concluding this exploration, and with an eye to the next chapter, it must be stated that the implications of the diminished external status of Cycladic voyaging in late EB II for the status of its practitioners *within* the Cyclades may have been relatively slight, a crucial point if in ultimate terms the rewards of voyaging were intended for home consumption. Fortifications at Chalandriani-Kastri, Daskaleio-Kavos and sites in the latter's local sphere of activity could indicate a gathering challenge to existing power groups in the Cyclades, triggered by any number of factors, of which one might be the diminished prestige of Cycladic voyagers abroad. But set against this are the facts that signs of fighting, in the form of dagger burials, have a long antecedent history, at least in the Erimonisia (cf. chapter 8), and that the horizon of fortification in the later EB II Aegean covered a great range of sites, including places like Troy, Poliochni and Lerna that manifestly produced extremely successful individuals or groups. Equally cogent is the point that in terms of local consumption, the essential ability of the Cycladic traders to control access to outside materials, goods and ways of doing things should not have been greatly affected by the fact that the nature of these exotics had changed. That this was the case is suggested by the uneven incidence of the Kastri group shapes within the Cyclades. In this sense, up until the end of EB II dominant people in the Cyclades displayed an impressive ability to incorporate external innovations in ways that allowed them to maintain their pre-eminence inside the world of the islands. Only towards the end of the third millennium BC did the scale of external change in the Aegean theatre surrounding the Cyclades, and in particular the nature of the innovations that were adopted, overwhelm the resilience of established island structures.

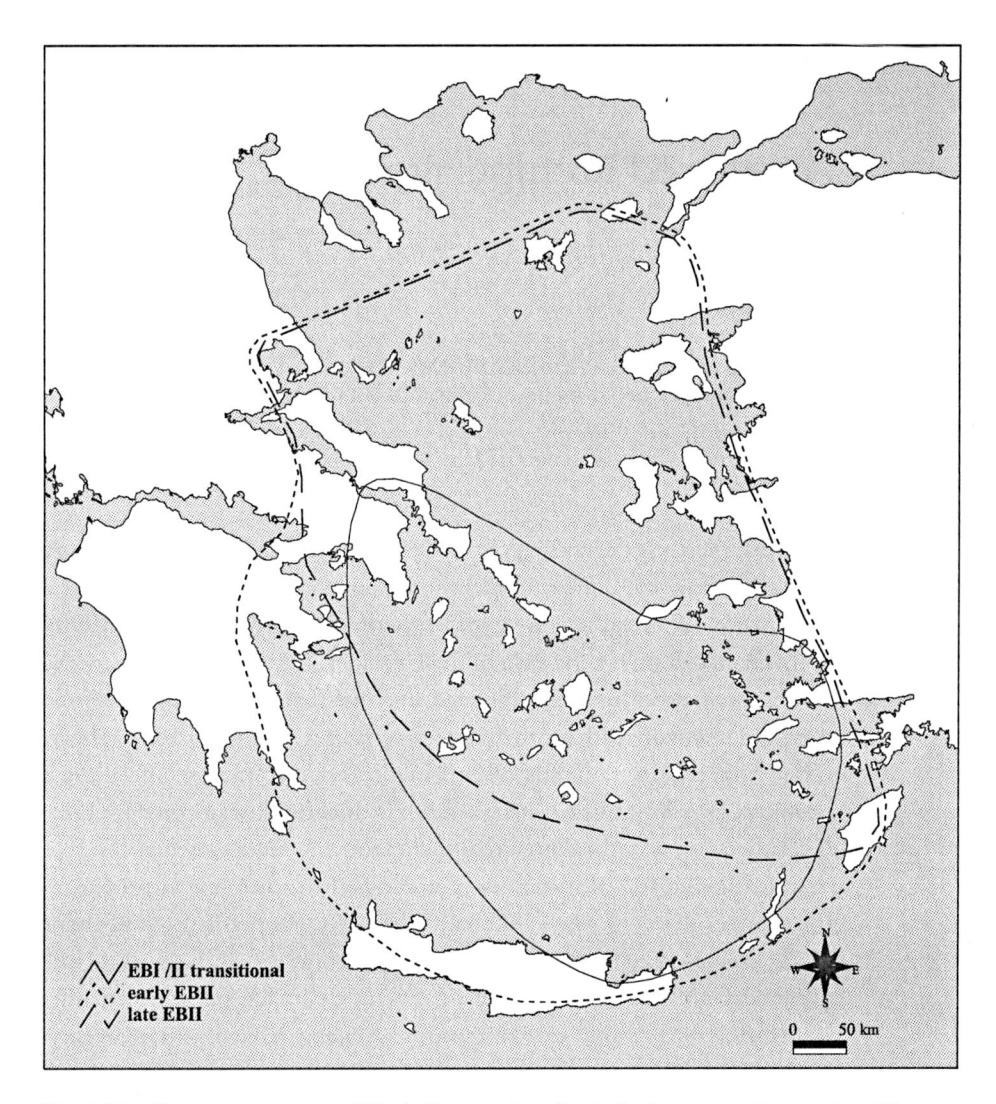

Fig. 106 Changing patterns of Early Bronze Age Cycladic long-range interaction. The spatial extent of activity in each period is an approximation.

10

An altered archipelago

> A people without history
> Is not redeemed from time, for history is a pattern
> Of timeless moments.
> *Four Quartets, Little Gidding,* T. S. ELIOT

Our final theme is the ending of the Cyclades' early history between *c.* 2200 and 1900 BC. There is some danger in identifying an 'ending' in this way, for it can create the expectation of a neat narrative and coherent conclusion (Terrell 1990). But there is scant chance of this in the case of the Cyclades, for the time-span involved has proven an obscure period for archaeologists, and one that also saw the first manifestations of the fundamentally different dynamics of later Cycladic history. Thornier issues are raised concerning the kinds of explanation used to understand these changes. One problem, as will become clear, is that it is uncertain what priority should be given to Cycladic as opposed to inter-regional causes. A second is that the recent history of islands, though full of instances of endings, furnishes few appropriate analogies for the changes that took place in the Cyclades. As was pointed out in chapter 1, the dramatic clashes of culture that typify the encounters over the last 500 years in the Caribbean and Pacific are unlikely to provide parallels for the very differently graded transformations of far earlier periods. Making a virtue of necessity, this second problem can be positively viewed as a stimulus to attempt island archaeological analyses in the Cyclades that will expand our understanding of island worlds under conditions of rapid and fundamental flux.

Before undertaking this, the identification of the changes in the Cyclades at this period as an island ending requires justification. In what respects were they qualitatively different from the antecedent examples that have engaged us? For one thing, the internal evidence of discontinuity and rapid yet profound transformations of island life that will emerge differs by an order of magnitude from the shifts within the EBA that have been identified. But taking a longer-term perspective, the crucial distinction is that during the three millennia that define this book's time-frame, and despite certain compromises by late EB II, the people of the Cyclades interacted with the surrounding world largely on their own terms, and in ways that allowed them to define their insularity and identity. From early in the second millennium BC, regimes of external dominance came increasingly to the fore. The degree of dominance varied in time and space, and seldom excluded island initiatives, as (to take a much later example) Davis' study of Kea and Seriphos under the Ottoman empire reveals (1991), but overall the later Cyclades present a different picture from that depicted in the preceding chapters. By the end of the first century of the new millennium, material from the first established Minoan palace-states on Crete started to appear in the Cyclades, and over the next 500 years Minoan economic, cultural and maybe political influence grew stronger, particularly on Thera, Melos and Kea, prompting an ongoing debate over the existence of Cretan colonies (Branigan 1981; Davis 1979, 1980, 1984b; Hägg and Marinatos 1984; Schofield 1982; Wiener 1990). Similar questions are raised by Mycenaean hegemony during the later second millennium BC (Renfrew 1982a: 41; Schallin 1993). The next millennium saw a Persian sack of Naxos, Cycladic tribute to Classical Athens under the guise of the Delian League, Athens' notorious destruction of Melos (which inspired Thucydides' Melian Dialogue, a classic early discourse on the nature of power), the establishment on Kea of a military base for the Egyptian-based Ptolemaic empire (Cherry and Davis 1991), *proxenoi* (consuls) of Cycladic towns established as far away as Marseilles (Etienne and Dourlot 1996), and the islands' eventual incorporation in the *mare nostrum* of imperial Rome. Roughly three thousand years before 2000 BC, Naxos was in the process of being colonised by Neolithic pioneers; just over three thousand years afterwards, it fell to a Venetian adventurer in the aftermath of the Fourth Crusade.

The archaeological evidence for discontinuities in the Cyclades within the period 2200–1900 BC confirms the identification of a major ending and the beginning of a new order in the islands. This period can be helpfully sub-divided into an earlier phase of internal disruption and transformation of island life, from *c.* 2200 BC, and a later phase marked by the first expansion of Cretan palatial activities into these islands, *c.* 1950–1900 BC. This chapter explores the former process, and chapter 11 the latter.

In late EB II, the general patterns of settlement and activity that had developed in the Cyclades in the course of the third millennium BC were still largely operational. Yet the immediate sequel to this phase, namely EB III (*c.* 2200–2000 BC), is bedevilled by problems of material identification so severe that Rutter (1983, 1984) has argued for a substantial 'gap' between the end of EB II and the start of the MBA. The nature of this gap is evaluated below, but gap or no gap there are ample signs of a transformation of island life. The single feature that has most impressed archaeologists is the very large number of settlements that ceased to exist at this juncture, with some terminated by acts of violence, as at Panermos (Doumas 1992a), but others simply abandoned, as seems to be the case at Markiani (French and Whitelaw 1999: 168). In most cases this cessation was permanent. Moroever, it affected not just farmsteads and hamlets, but also the big, central settlements. Chalandriani-Kastri, Daskaleio-Kavos and Skarkos were emptied forever, a hiatus of several centuries is proven at Agia Irini, and at Grotta-Aplomata there is an absence of evidence for occupation until well into the second millennium BC. In less site-specific terms,

Table 11. *Phylakopi: nomenclature, diagnostics, culture attributions and dates.*

Phylakopi (present)	Phylakopi (original)	Diagnostic material	Culture	Date
Phylakopi 0 A1	Pre-city	Burnished, incised, rolled-rim bowls	Grotta-Pelos	FN/EB I
Phylakopi 0 A2 (or Phylakopi Ii)	City I	Incised, stamped, dark-on-light, sauceboats, frying pans	Keros-Syros	EB II
Phylakopi Iii	City I	Dark faced with incised decoration, dark-on-light lustrous geometric designs, light-on-dark geometric, duck vases, conical pyxides	Phylakopi I	early MBA (+ EB III?)
Phylakopi Iiii	City I	Dark-on-light matt curvilinear designs, light-on-dark	Phylakopi I	early MBA
Phylakopi II	City II	Dark/red burnished, Cycladic white, Middle Minoan imports	None	later MBA

northern Syros, the Erimonisia, southern Naxos and Amorgos lost their former prominence, and entered an extended phase of relative obscurity that in some areas has lasted almost without interruption until the present day.

The next horizon that can be discerned is the Phylakopi I culture, named from large deposits at Phylakopi that overlie earlier EBA material (see table 11 for a summary of the site's stratigraphy, material and nomenclature). Although the Phylakopi I culture is comparatively poorly known, it provides further indications that profound changes were afoot. One of these changes was a shift towards a more nucleated pattern of island settlement. Another was in burial practices, especially on the well-documented island of Melos, where Phylakopi I culture burials are either in elaborate rock-cut tombs designed for multiple inhumations (fig. 107), or jar inhumations within the settlement. There are also innovations in the pottery repertoire. Among the new shapes at this time is the so-called duck vase (fig. 108), a specialised liquid transport vessel of far wider Aegean distribution. Other distinctive pottery in the Phylakopi I levels at the type-site includes conical pyxides with a dark surface and incised decoration (which is also the surface treatment of duck vases at this site), dark-on-light painted bowls, cups, beak-spouted jugs, large barrel jars and elaborate multiple kernoi, as well as a class of light-on-dark pottery (Renfrew 1972: 186–95; Barber 1987: 94–6). Save for a small number of Phylakopi I type figurines of schematic form, the ancient tradition of marble-working effectively ceased. Phylakopi I itself was destroyed some time before *c.* 1900 BC. The next stratum, Phylakopi II, contains the first imports from palatial Crete.

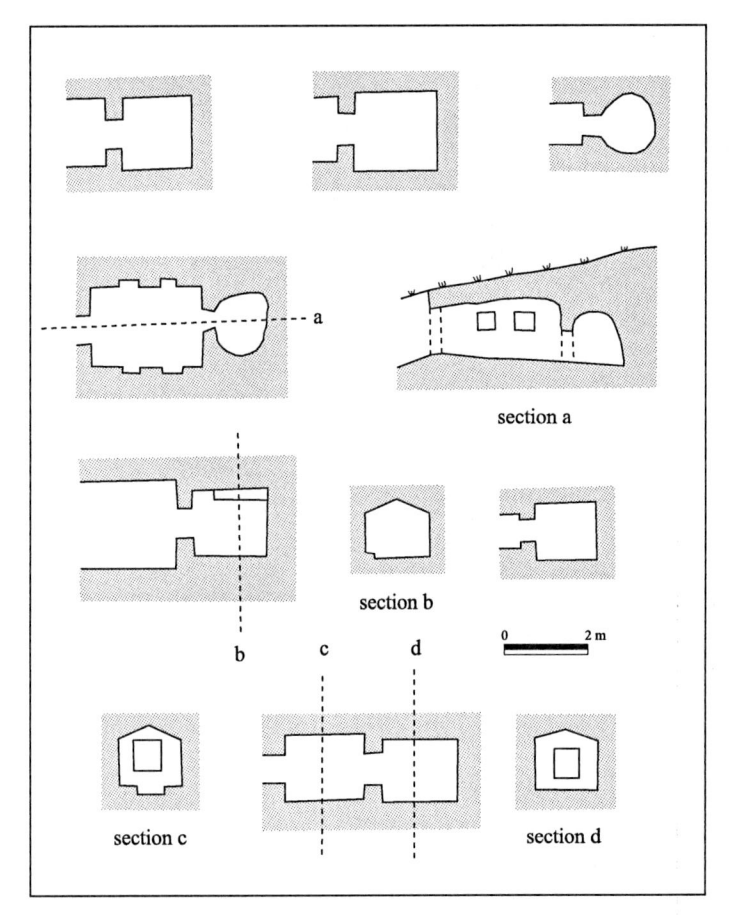

Fig. 107   Phylakopi I culture rock-cut tombs at Phylakopi. After Atkinson *et al.* 1904: fig. 193.

The chronology of the Phylakopi I culture is controversial. The principal phase certainly belongs to the early MBA (*c.* 2000–1900 BC) but much of the debate over the EB III gap revolves around whether its origins might lie earlier. The issue of the gap therefore has implications for the relationship between EB II societies and the Phylakopi I culture that go well beyond matters of chronology. If it reflects a real hiatus in island life, the Phylakopi I culture effectively represents a recolonisation process; but if it can be plugged, Cycladic EB III becomes part of an evolving transformation that stretches from the end of EB II through to the MBA. Either way, the period 2200–1900 BC can be conceptualised as an interstitial one, that displays many of the characteristics typical of the phases that separate more archaeologically accessible and at least ostensibly stable regimes. Careful analysis is required to perceive the structures of such periods, but the rewards, in terms of understanding the working through of change, are commensurate. This chapter and the one that follows suggest that behind the apparent entropy and gaps in the data we can discern a distinct, if

Fig. 108 Duck vase found on Amorgos. Courtesy of the Ashmolean Museum.

ambivalent, patterning that has its own historical significance (if in retrospect a temporally ephemeral one), and which provides insights into the Cycladic islanders' initiatives and responses under rapidly changing conditions.

This chapter's enquiry is structured by three questions. First, what settlement patterns are seen in the Phylakopi I culture and the subsequent MBA Cyclades? Second, is the EB III gap a real feature of early Cycladic history, or a creation of archaeological methods of analysis? Third, can a coherent model of change in the islands be built that illuminates the archaeology of the period $c.$ 2200–1900 BC? The next, and penultimate chapter, looks in more detail at the Phylakopi I culture's trading dynamics and examines how Cycladic ways of doing things became dominated by external, specifically Cretan, interests. The overall conclusion will not be as morally elevating as an 'emergence of civilisation', but the picture that will be sketched, of a ragged ending to traditional EB II island cultures, and a no less uneven start to new maritime initiatives and a new Aegean world, may ring more true in the context of an explicitly insular history of the Cyclades.

The wider context of change in the late third millennium BC

Before starting to address these issues, it is important to acknowledge the wider context of change in the late third millennium BC. The critical period in the Cyclades is roughly contemporary with severe disruption in a swathe of territory stretching from the Tigris and the Nile to the Aegean, including the breakdown of the Akkadian 'empire', the end of Old Kingdom Egypt, and a decline in urbanism in the Levant, followed by an equally rapid recovery by the start of the second millennium (Dalfes *et al.* 1997). It hardly needs to be stated that this dramatic down-swing at the end of a millennium that had witnessed major increases in social complexity in all the above regions, as well as important if less pronounced changes in the Aegean, is a startling phenomenon and one in urgent need of explanation.

In the Aegean, signs of collapse and transformation are widespread (Manning 1997). In addition to the aforementioned evidence in the Cyclades, the southern Greek mainland sees drastic settlement shrinkage, and the end of the corridor houses, as well as of seals and sealings, alongside new pottery types and sharp changes in patterns of trade and material acquisition (Forsén 1992; Runnels 1985b). Not until several centuries later, at the time of the Mycenae Shaft Graves, do indices of social complexity reappear (Dickinson 1977; Graziadio 1991; Voutsaki 1995, 1998). Comparable changes at the end of the third millennium BC occur in the north-east Aegean at sites such as Troy and Poliochni (Mellink 1986). Within this general trend, however, some crucial exceptions can be highlighted. The late third millennium BC witnessed events on Crete that, despite manifest signs of disruption, led to the rapid emergence of the palace-states early in the second millennium (Cadogan 1986; Cherry 1984a; Manning 1994; Warren 1987; Watrous 1994). Several further exceptions can be picked out, all notable for being encountered on islands. At Kolonna on Aegina (Niemeier 1995; Walter and Felten 1981), Palamari on Skyros (Theochari *et al.* 1993) and Heraion on Samos (Milojčić 1961), all thriving settlements, there is a smooth transition from EB II to III; new data from the south-east Aegean suggest a similar state of affairs on Kos and Rhodes (Marketou 1990, 1997).

As this overall horizon can still only be roughly coordinated, it remains difficult to determine whether any common underlying causes should be sought, and, if so, how these might weigh in the balance relative to local factors. Large-scale explanations have traditionally invoked invasion models, in the Aegean associated with the 'coming of the Greeks' (e.g. Blegen and Haley 1928). As the limitations of such explanations become more apparent (Forsén 1992; Morpurgo Davies 1986), other possibilities are emerging. A world-systemic perspective would see widespread interrelated collapse sequences in terms of dislocation caused by shifting emphases in the core areas (Sherratt and Sherratt 1991: 368), although the Aegean's marginal status during the third millennium BC does not suggest that this is an adequate explanation for the depth of the region's disruption. Another hypothesis is of catastrophic land degradation engendered by third-millennium BC over-exploitation, given substance in the Aegean by valley fills in the southern Argolid (Jameson *et al.* 1994: 191, 355) and the erosion of soils at Markiani in the Cyclades (French and Whitelaw 1999). Whilst there is solid documentation of such processes, it is unclear how total an explanation of the temporal focus and geographical extent of the disruption this hypothesis can provide, because the diversity of settlement histories, soils and farming strategies in the Aegean and regions to its east seem to militate against the likelihood of a simultaneous crisis. A third possibility currently hovers tantalisingly short of conclusive proof, but may over the next few years prove to be either decisive or chimerical. This is the apparent evidence for a sudden, brief yet severe increase in climatic aridity across western Asia and surrounding areas (Dalfes *et al.* 1997; Weiss *et al.* 1993). A fourth potential factor that has received less attention than it deserves is an expanding frontier of epidemic propagated in the newly integrated zone of urban communities across the Near East and their outlying regions (McNeill, J. R. 1993: 3; McNeill, W. H. 1976: 78–82). A last, and perfectly plausible, solution is that none of these grand models is correct, or at least had a decisive impact, and that a messier pattern of localised collapse cycles overwhelmed the preceding peaks of sociopolitical complexity. Whatever the validity of the above models (and all have eventually to face the test of explaining the exceptions to their rules), the present task is to integrate such perspectives with data in the Cyclades in order to explore how any of them, singly or in combination, might have worked through in this specific insular context.

Cycladic settlement in the Phylakopi I culture and the later MBA

The first of the three structuring questions set out for this chapter concerned the nature of Cycladic settlement during the period of the Phylakopi I culture and the subsequent middle-to-late (henceforth 'later') MBA. In contrast to the small, dispersed communities of the third millennium BC, plus a handful of villages in EB II, most islanders in the second millennium lived in a small number of larger, nucleated communities, often with one settlement pre-eminent or solitary on a given island (Barber 1978; Wagstaff and Cherry 1982b: 139; Cherry *et al.* 1991: 217–32; Renfrew 1982a: 38). These communities, upward of a hectare in extent, can be considered big villages or modest towns. They controlled extensive arable land, and were usually situated on a good anchorage, either a deep bay or a beach sheltered from prevailing winds, and most had access to nearby perennial fresh water supplies – Phylakopi being situated close to one of the very few such sources on Melos. Substantial terrestrial territories must have been associated with such settlements. This settlement pattern probably generated new perceptions of the Cycladic islandscapes, with the unitary island now acquiring cultural significance as the possession of a dominant community. A second-millennium BC origin might therefore be proposed for the association between an island's name and that of its principal settlement, an association that is textually attested by the next millennium. The mistake that should *not* be made, however, given the modest size of the Cycladic islands, is to regard such combinations of settlements and their hinterlands as comparable to the palatial states of contemporary Crete. In other words, although the Cyclades came under strong external influence in the

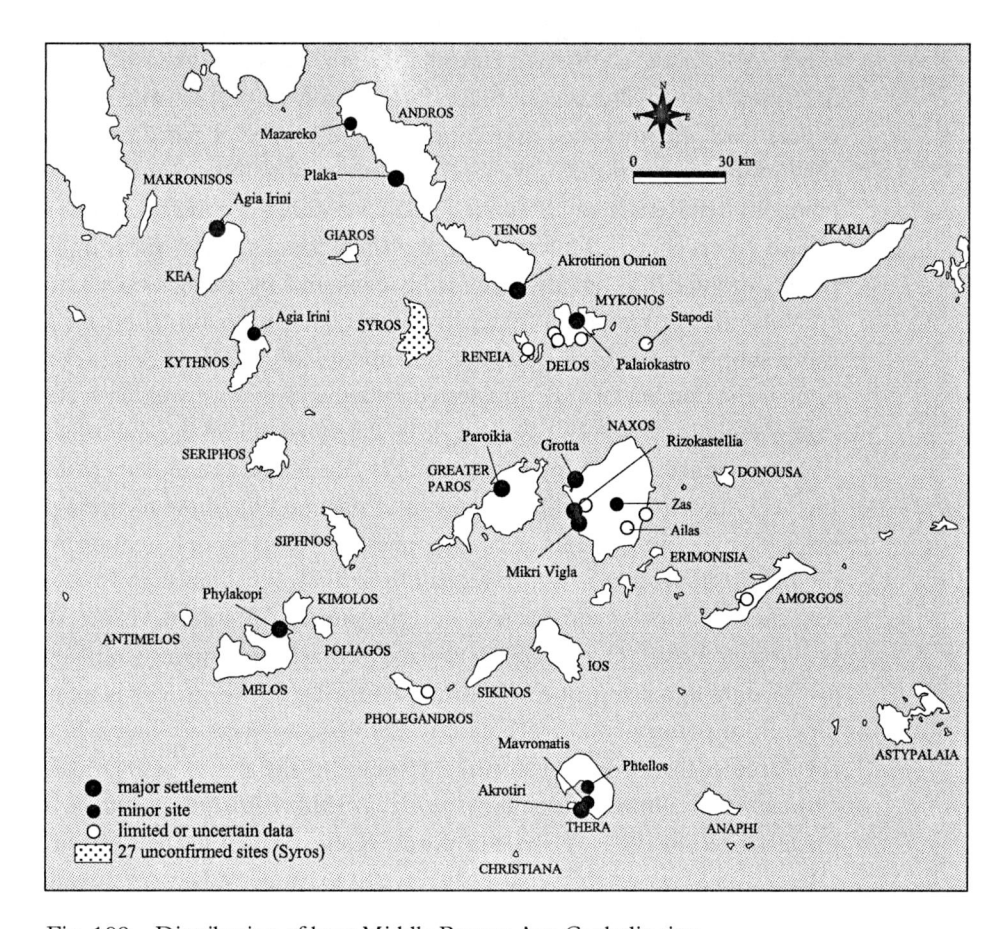

Fig. 109 Distribution of later Middle Bronze Age Cycladic sites.

second millennium BC, the models of political structure used for palatial regions of the Aegean do not make particularly good templates for these islands.

The degree of nucleation in the second-millennium Cyclades varied between islands and periods (Davis and Cherry 1990). The later MBA seems to represent a particularly accentuated phase (fig. 109). Intensive survey on Melos found no traces of occupation outside the settlement of Phylakopi II (Wagstaff and Cherry 1982b: 139), and on several other islands the primacy of a single community is evident, examples being Agia Irini IV–V on Kea, Akrotiri on Thera, Paroikia on Greater Paros, and Akrotirion Ourion on Tenos. Naxos, the largest of the Cyclades, forms a partial exception, with three sizeable nucleated settlements (Grotta, Mikri Vigla and Rizokastellia) spaced out along the fertile west coast, and a final concentration of population at Grotta achieved only in the LBA (Hadjianastasiou 1989, 1993). On Andros a similar pattern might be anticipated; to date the only known large MBA settlement is at Plaka, but a hill-top shrine at Mazareko in the north-west (Koutsoukou 1993: 102–3) may suggest another centre in this part of the island. Unsubstantiated reports of numerous small MBA sites on Syros (Hekman 1994: fig. 9), Mykonos, Reneia and even Mykonos' tiny satellite islet of Stapodi (Sampson 1997: 13–14) could indicate divergences from the nucleated pattern, perhaps indicative of failed nucleation. But until solid support for these identifications is forthcoming, little further can be said, save to point out that Reneia and Stapodi would constitute the only exceptions to the general rule of an absence of settlement on the small islands at this time, in contrast to the pattern in the EBA – an absence readily explained by the lack on such islands of the combinations of resources (extensive arable land, proper anchorages and a regular water supply) prioritised by major settlements in the MBA. A last point to remark upon is the number of MBA nucleated settlements that were either fortified, as in the case of Agia Irini, or located on an easily defended hilltop or peninsula (fig. 110).

The evidence concerning antecedent Phylakopi I culture settlement is less clear cut. Fig. 111 shows the distribution known to date and attempts to distinguish between probable major settlements and minor ones, as well as funerary contexts (discussed in the next section) that have produced Phylakopi I type objects in EBA type cemeteries. The major settlements include the type site itself (Renfrew 1982a: 37–8), Paroikia on Greater Paros (Overbeck 1989a) and Akrotiri on Thera (Sotirakopoulou 1990, 1996), although it must be confessed that the latter two's status is inferred from the amount of pottery and, in the case of Paroikia, architecture found in limited exposures, rather than from any accurate estimate of site size. The status of several other Phylakopi I culture settlements, such as Mikri Vigla on Naxos (Barber and Hadjianastasiou 1989), Plaka on Andros (Koutsoukou 1992) and Kastro on Siphnos (Brock and Mackworth Young 1949) is hard to gauge. Whether other important later MBA settlements, for example Grotta and Akrotirion Ourion, were inhabited at this time is unknown (Hadjianastasiou 1989; Renfrew 1972: 513). One important piece of negative evidence is the certainty that during most of the Phylakopi I phase Agia Irini was not occupied, the start of Agia Irini IV dating to c. 1900 BC on the basis of imported Cretan pottery of early palatial styles (Overbeck 1989b: 1). Overall, a southern bias in the distribution of Phylakopi I culture settlements is apparent, although with the exception of the evidence of absence at Agia Irini, the usual provisos about the under-explored north apply.

Melian data at present provide the only relatively clear insight into settlements of this period. Survey has revealed that the Phylakopi I culture pattern was less dispersed than that of the EBA but less nucleated than that of the MBA. Phylakopi was probably already the largest site, but other settlements are indicated by surface scatters and rock-cut tombs at Asprochorio, Agios Panteleimon, Agios Theodoros and Spathi (Cherry 1982b, Sites 37, 53, 61 and 64). This settlement pattern has been taken to reflect a transitional phase in the shift from EBA to MBA patterns (Renfrew 1982a: 37–8; Wagstaff and Cherry 1982b: 139). This is an attractive hypothesis, but given the potential gap in EB III, we need to demonstrate the plausibility of continued settlement on Melos, and other Cycladic islands, before it can be argued that this

Fig. 110 Two major Middle Bronze Age Cycladic settlements. *Above:* Phylakopi, located on the eroding cliff-top at the centre of the photograph, with the approximate outline of the ancient harbour shown. *Below:* Mikri Vigla, situated on the promontory in the middle distance, overlooking the straits to Greater Paros.

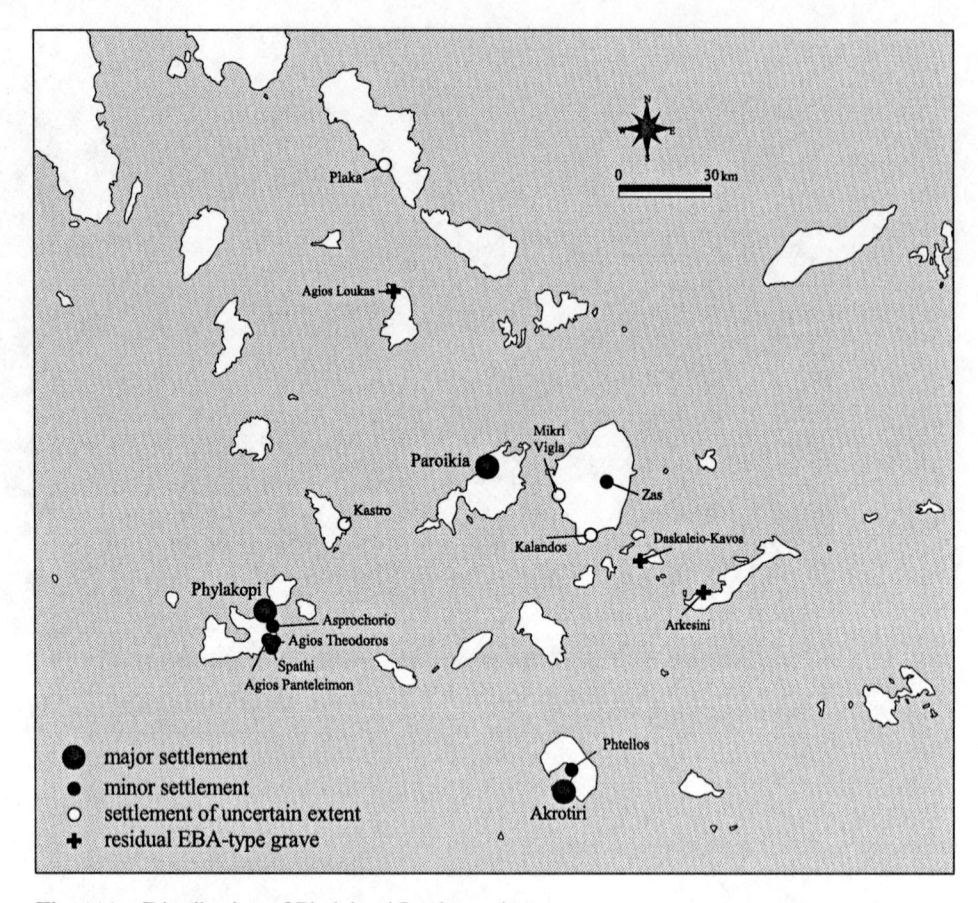

Fig. 111   Distribution of Phylakopi I culture sites.

transitional status represents one point in a process of genuinely ongoing change, rather than a fortuitous half-way house between two historically unrelated ways of ordering settlement.

The settlement area of Phylakopi I itself seems to have been comparable to that of Phylakopi II, estimated at 1.8 ha without the probably substantial part of the site that has been destroyed by coastal erosion (fig. 112). Occupation densities of 200–300 people per hectare generate a population total of 360–540, exclusive of the number that should be added for the area lost to the sea, although as open spaces existed between the houses at this stage these figures may accord better with the later phases of the site and slightly inflate the minimum likely population of Phylakopi I (Doumas 1972: 168; Mackenzie 1904: 35). Analysis of the site's catchment indicates that a population of some 251–855 might be sustainable (Wagstaff *et al.* 1982: 175). Much higher population levels of 1400–2250 people for the similarly sized later MBA and LBA settlements at Phylakopi have been calculated using cross-cultural estimates for the area of floor space occupied per person (Wagstaff and Cherry 1982b: 139–40). The information on Aegean settlement densities that is emerging indicates that these

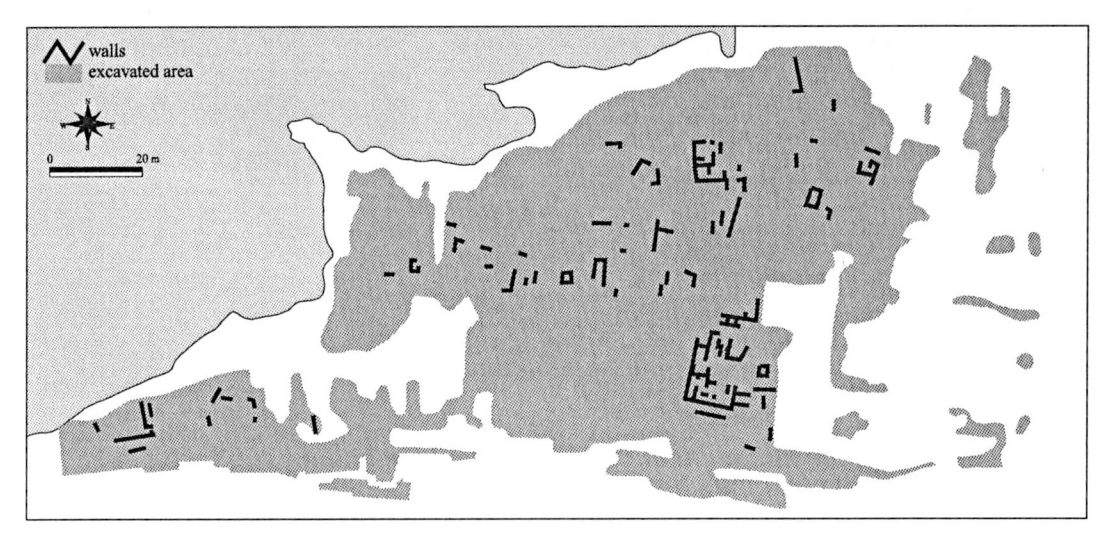

Fig. 112 Phylakopi I. After original by Todd Whitelaw.

levels are too high (they imply densities of around 750–1250 people per hectare, approximately four times the densities advocated here). The discrepancy suggests that the latter calculations over-estimated the proportion of living space in each house, as opposed to storage areas and yards, and the proportion of the settlement taken up by simultaneously inhabited houses. Whatever the truth concerning Phylakopi I's exact population, and allowing for some loss to the sea, it is likely that the settlement was bigger than anything known in the earlier Cyclades.

The architecture of Phylakopi I is poorly preserved, but it anticipates the regular alignments of houses and streets seen in Phylakopi II, and fragments of houses can be discerned that similarly resemble Phylakopi II's substantial houses (Renfrew 1982a: 37–8). In contrast to the prominent central buildings encountered at LBA Phylakopi, however, there is no evidence of differentiation or concentration of power in Phylakopi I, or indeed II. Instead, we might hazard a guess that the community was structured around a network of big, stable households. Additional evidence for an emphasis on such households is the new burial types, both the jar inhumations under house-floors, which may indicate the long-term identification of a burying group with a particular plot in the settlement, and the rock-cut tombs for multiple burials, which are well suited to family-sized groups and which would serve to define each group more fixedly than the loose clusters of individual graves in the earlier EBA cemeteries.

The EB III gap: historical caesura or artefact of archaeology?

The difficulty that has just been encountered in determining in what sense the Phylakopi I culture settlement pattern on Melos is transitional underlines the fact that until the issue of the EB III gap is resolved, only limited progress can be made towards

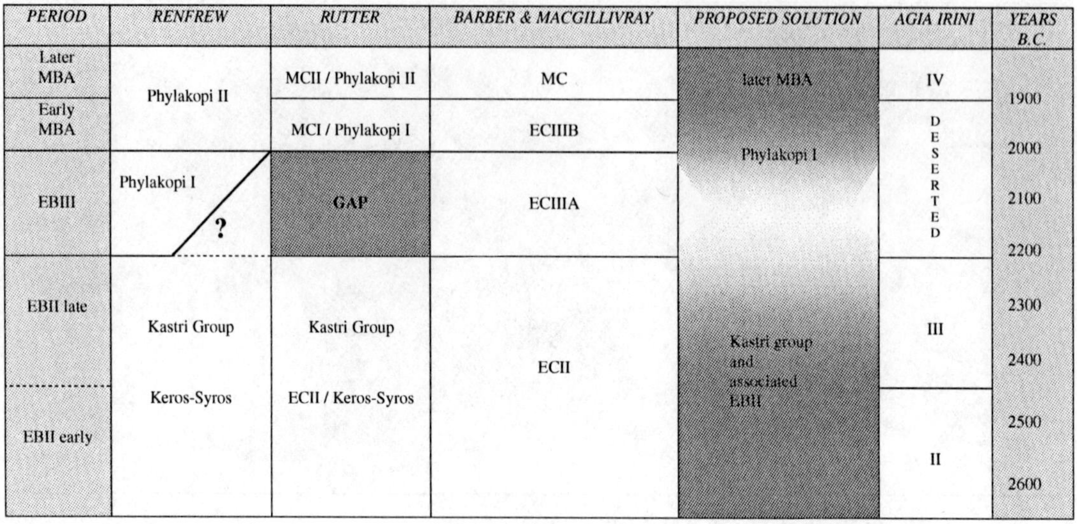

PERIOD	RENFREW	RUTTER	BARBER & MACGILLIVRAY	PROPOSED SOLUTION	AGIA IRINI	YEARS B.C.
Later MBA	Phylakopi II	MCII / Phylakopi II	MC	later MBA	IV	
Early MBA		MCI / Phylakopi I	ECIIIB	Phylakopi I	D E S E R T E D	1900
						2000
EBIII	Phylakopi I ?	GAP	ECIIIA			2100
						2200
EBII late	Kastri Group	Kastri Group	ECII	Kastri group and associated EBII	III	2300
						2400
	Keros-Syros	ECII / Keros-Syros				2500
EBII early					II	2600

Fig. 113 The Early Bronze III 'gap': a simplified summary of the main positions and terminologies, and proposed solution. The absolute chronology provided is that used throughout this book, and can only be a best fit relative to the specific variants advocated by different scholars in the 'gap' debate.

understanding island dynamics at the end of the third millennium BC. When Renfrew first established a culture sequence and chronology for the early Cyclades, he regarded the Phylakopi I culture as belonging in EB III (Renfrew 1972: table 13.2). The possibility of a gap was first raised through Rutter's meticulous comparisons of Aegean ceramic sequences in the later EBA (Rutter 1979, 1983, 1984). These confirmed the Kastri group as late EB II in date, but highlighted the fact that most exports of Phylakopi I culture material at non-Cycladic sites were found in contexts dating to the early MBA rather than EB III (fig. 113 summarises the gap controversy). Given that the Cycladic archaeological record has revealed no unbroken stratified sequence running from late EB II to the early MBA, this apparently rendered EB III in the islands devoid of assemblages. Depending on the length of time assigned to EB III, the resultant gap spans some 150–200 years. Rutter (1984) has set out the implications of this gap, which he is careful to define as first and foremost one in our knowledge. In terms of island occupation he sees the gap as an absence of clear evidence of continuity, rather than as a solid proof of a total abandonment, although it certainly contributes to the image of disruption derived from discontinuities in other varieties of data. In the present context, a full rehearsal of the controversy that has ensued cannot be presented, but it is essential to highlight some salient factors, and substantiate the solution that will be offered here.

The gap hypothesis relies on a clean-cut division of time into short, neat periods typified by discrete assemblages. The feasibility of defining such precise parcels of time and material culture at this stage in Cycladic history is, however, questionable. It seems more appropriate to the second millennium BC, when fast stylistic turn-overs of imported Minoan and Mycenaean pottery and its imitations allow the confident identification of phases of a century, or even less, than to the longer, fuzzier time-periods that comprise all that we have for the earlier Cyclades. Doubts of this variety are implicit in several responses to Rutter's case. MacGillivray (1984) has suggested that part of the gap can be closed by allowing the Kastri group, and assemblages dated by it, to continue in the Cyclades into early EB III. Manning (1995: 66–72) supports this, and likewise argues for a backward extension of the start of the Phylakopi I culture into EB III. Barber and MacGillivray's alternative Cycladic terminology (which assigns the Kastri group to 'EC IIIA' and the Phylakopi I culture to 'EC IIIB') skirts the archaeological problem rather than solving it (Barber and MacGillivray 1980, 1984; Barber 1983, 1984; MacGillivray 1983, 1984), but they do make the important point that bringing the end of the Kastri group and the start of Phylakopi I into the short EB III period raises the possibility of a partial overlap between elements of these assemblages (Barber and MacGillivray 1980: 151, fn. 86; also Doumas 1988: 24). Put another way, if we substitute neat divisions with notional tapering 'battleship-curves' as our means of conceptualising distributions of early Cycladic material culture traits through time, the arguments underpinning the EB III gap will inevitably weaken, and indeed the intrinsic likelihood of our being able to isolate such a brief phenomenon (even if it did exist) appears correspondingly slighter.

Other arguments that have been used in attempts to fill the gap divide into (1) the intra-Cycladic case against a break between the Kastri group and Phylakopi I culture (including claimed identifications of both EB III contexts and similarities between EB II and MBA material that must indicate continuous production), and (2) external evidence of a small number of Phylakopi I culture objects in EB III contexts elsewhere in the Aegean. The evidence against the gap as a historical phenomenon is slowly becoming stronger, although to date it remains a critical distance short of conclusive proof.

It should be stressed that the permanent abandonment of innumerable dispersed EBA sites by the end of the third millennium, in conjunction with the more concentrated Phylakopi I culture pattern, makes it inevitable that arguments concerning occupational continuity or interruption focus on a small number of sites occupied on both sides of the divide. The sample is reduced further by the fact that conclusive proof either way can only be furnished by excavated sequences. In practice this means that this aspect of the debate narrows to a mere six excavated sites, of which three have stratified sequences, only one of which is decisive. At Phylakopi, the stratigraphy of the first excavations was not recorded in sufficient detail, and the 1970s investigations did not encounter the earliest Phylakopi I levels (Evans and Renfrew 1984: 66); the dearth of Kastri group shapes also makes it hard to determine where within EB II the material underlying the Phylakopi I levels belongs. At Zas cave the stratigraphy of the EBA–MBA transition is still under analysis (Zachos 1994). At Grotta the limited extent of excavations, the lack of a master stratigraphy and the fact that a substantial part of the MBA appears to be missing, ensure that this site's present contribution is minimal, and at Paroikia the relationship between the Kastri group and Phylakopi I culture material was not recorded (Overbeck 1989a: 20). At Akrotiri, the typological attribution of material found together in closed contexts to both sides of the gap has been claimed as evidence for continuity and EB III activity (Sotirakopoulou 1996). This may indeed be so, but the reliance on attribution of material to the highly problematic 'Amorgos group', and the lack of key Kastri group diagnostics in these contexts, mean that the case cannot yet be clinched.[1] In fact, the only indisputable stratigraphically confirmed hiatus remains that between Agia Irini III and IV, and even this is a special case, as the abandonment continued into the early MBA and therefore included the main period of the Phylakopi I culture.

In addition to the excavated settlement data, there are a few graves of EBA types that contain material of the Phylakopi I culture (see fig. 111). One good example is an EB II-type corbelled grave at Agios Loukas on Syros, which held a Phylakopi I culture pyxis and jug, a mainland bowl of EB III–MBA date, and an EB II pyxis fragment (Barber 1981). Several cist graves at Arkesini and other sites on Amorgos contained Phylakopi I culture shapes (including duck vases) and an eclectic range of late EBA or early MBA weaponry (Bossert 1954; Branigan 1974: fig. 10; Renfrew 1972: 534). Renfrew's report of a few duck vase fragments in the Daskaleio-Kavos special deposit is also of interest in this context (Renfrew 1972: 194), though parallels were not found during the recent investigations. The most plausible explanation of this phenomenon is some slight continuation of burial at a few EBA cemeteries (and therefore habitation at their associated settlements) into a period when Phylakopi I culture objects were already circulating, rather than the reuse of EBA tombs after an abandonment of the Cyclades. Chronologically, such deposition should belong within a Cycladic EB III.[2] The cultural implications of this phenomenon are, as we shall see later, decidedly intriguing.

Other internal evidence for continuity, noted even before the eruption of the gap controversy, includes a few close similarities between elements of EB II and Phylakopi I pottery, that constitute a modest but suggestive counter-point to the

---

[1] On the resolution of the Akrotiri sequence must hang the dating of a floating group of material from Thera's tiny satellite of Christiana (Doumas 1976a). Some of the finds from this island are EB II in date (Sotirakopoulou 1993: 16–17), but salient elements of the 'Christiana group' material are several jugs bearing ribbed decoration. Rutter (1983: 71) places this group early in the MBA on the basis of parallels at Kolonna on Aegina, but taking account of Christiana's remote location and utter dependency on Thera, its material culture needs to be understood primarily in relation to the latter island, and only stratified deposits at Akrotiri are likely to resolve satisfactorily the date of the later material in the Christiana group. Certainly, the inhabitation of this tiny island fits better with what we know of third- rather than second-millennium island settlement patterns.

[2] The only traces of renewed activity after a definite break at an EBA cemetery are a series of MBA cups from the Aïlas cemetery on Naxos (Hadjianastasiou 1989: 206).

overall impression of disruption (Barber 1984; Renfrew 1972: 194–5). The most striking example is the duck vase, one of the best-known Phylakopi I culture shapes. Duck vases are certainly attested elsewhere in the Aegean during EB III. Moreover, several small, side-spouted globular vessels found in the abandonment debris at Kastri can hardly be other than prototypes (Bossert 1967: fig. 5 nos. 1–2; Rutter 1985: 17), and the leaf-shaped spouts of the full-sized vases are already seen on some Kastri group jugs. Other hints include the white infill used to highlight incised decoration on Phylakopi I culture dark-faced pottery, a technique also widely used in EB II, and the tradition of complex dark-on-light decoration used on both sides of the divide.

The second major form of argument against the gap rests on evidence external to the Cyclades. Although no less significant, it can be more summarily dealt with. Rutter himself collated the available evidence for Phylakopi I-type objects, or the prototypes of such objects, in EB III contexts beyond the islands. Rutter's 'certainly Cycladic' group comprised imported pieces in good EB III contexts on Aegina and the Greek mainland (Rutter 1984: 99–100). Since then, two additional finds have expanded the extent of Cycladic EB III external links. One is a Phylakopi I culture jug in association with late EBA material overlying a floor with Kastri group pottery at Palamari on Skyros (Theochari et al. 1993). The other draws Crete into the ambit of island interaction, however slightly, and takes the form of a Phylakopi I culture jar handle in Theran or Melian clay in an EM III level at Knossos (Momigliano and Wilson 1996: 44). Such finds naturally imply pottery production in the EB III Cyclades, as well as the trade mechanisms to export overseas.

In summary, Rutter was undoubtedly right to draw attention to the problematic nature of our knowledge of EB III in the Cyclades, and the sharp discontinuities in island life between EB II and the MBA, but there seems little doubt that at least some islands continued to be inhabited in the last centuries of the third millennium BC. From this point onwards in the analysis, a degree of ongoing activity in the Cyclades during EB III is therefore assumed. It may one day be proven that the origins of the major Phylakopi I settlements lie within EB III, and there is certainly no definitive stratigraphical evidence against this hypothesis. Furthermore, taking the finds of Cycladic material on the Greek mainland, Aegina, Skyros and Crete into account, island connections in EB III seem to be little less wide ranging (if maybe less intensive) than in EB II or the early MBA (see chapter 11). This intriguing and uneven picture of the end of the third millennium in the Cyclades issues us with two challenges. The first is to document the transition through the archaeological investigation of early Phylakopi I culture levels and other potential contexts. The second, more immediately realisable challenge, is to generate explanatory models to explore the patterns that we are starting to discern. Such models need to shed light on why this brief period witnesses, on the one hand, the end of many EB II sites (including all the major centres) and other aspects of traditional Cycladic life, and, on the other hand, the start of new ways of living and new forms of island culture.

Models for the late third-millennium transformation of the Cyclades

If the second challenge is to be addressed, two basic questions about the transformation at the end of the third millennium BC will demand analysis. First, *why* did the antecedent EB II regime of a limited number of seafaring centres dominating networks of small, dispersed communities end? Second, and this is not simply an inversion of the first point, *why* did an overall shift towards settlement nucleation get underway? Although longer-term perspectives can shed considerable light on the fluctuations between nucleated and dispersed settlement in the Cyclades (Cherry *et al.* 1991: 458–62, 473–6; Wagstaff and Cherry 1982b), the changes at the end of the third millennium BC should not be taken for granted as part of an inevitable trajectory towards urbanism (let alone statehood) in the Cyclades. Instead, they reward investigation as specific processes that corresponded to particular circumstances in these islands during the late third millennium, processes that should stimulate us to produce equally specific and contextual explanations.

The importance of the change in settlement pattern is demonstrated by the fact that it provides a framework for explaining several of the other indices of radical change as its fairly predictable correlates, rather than as surprising or inexplicable occurrences. This is particularly true of the desertion of so many of the EB II settlements, for this would be, of course, an inevitable feature of a trend towards nucleation. The population estimates generated over the last few chapters suggest that large numbers of small EB II settlements would have to empty out in order to form a major Phylakopi I culture or later MBA settlement. Indeed, despite the ostensible evidence for island depopulation, if continued inhabitation of the EB III Cyclades is accepted, ongoing demographic growth through EB III could theoretically be posited, albeit growth disguised by an increasing concentration of people in a small number of as yet underinvestigated big settlements.

Moreover, the decline of the EBA settlement regime and the movement towards nucleation must have had implications for burial practices and prestige material culture, given that the symbolism of both these was intimately related to specific ways of living, interacting and defining status. A shift in the significance of burials was argued above in the case of the community at Phylakopi I. Concerning island material culture, it might likewise be expected that many traditional objects and practices would vanish, or alter in meaning and form, and new ones emerge. The disappearance of the EBA repertoire of prestige goods must surely reflect the redundancy of inter-community demographic and social storage networks as the gradual shift towards nucleation transformed inter-group relations and subsistence strategies. It may also reflect the collapse of the EB II centres that had produced and consumed much of this material, and fashioned the physical and ideological contexts for its deployment. New forms, expressive of different communal identities (e.g. the Phylakopi I culture kernoi?) or different kinds of interaction (e.g. duck vases) should come as no surprise. In short, if we can explain changes in where people lived in the Cyclades, we will in fact be explaining a lot of other things besides.

Models of large-scale change

So what kinds of models might bring us closer to understanding why the distribution of people in the islands altered? Let us start by looking at the explanations that have been proposed for the widespread changes in the Aegean and Near East during the late third millennium BC, as set out earlier in this chapter. Several could indeed have potential validity in the Cyclades, although none in isolation can make full sense of the spatial and temporal variation in patterns of settlement and culture that is actually attested.

Although *external invasion* is seldom now regarded as a viable explanation for the overall disruption in the late third millennium Aegean, it has recently been resurrected by Doumas (1988) to explain the changes seen in the Cyclades and other islands. In the form of the hypothesis of invasion from the north-east Aegean as an explanation for the Kastri group, this model was encountered in the previous chapter. Its relevance at the present juncture is that Doumas uses the model to explain the differences between sites with Kastri group and Phylakopi I culture material, and the fact that, as he observes, these two sets of material may have overlapped slightly in EB III. Doumas explains these differences in terms of two different groups of people inhabiting the Cyclades, the former material relating to northern invaders and the latter to the indigenous population. This observation of a potential overlap has much to recommend it, although it will be suggested below that the differences in material relate to two different kinds of island lifestyles rather than to radically different ethnic groups. But at a general level, the basic problem with the invasion hypothesis is the familiar one, namely that it assumes modes of explanation for phenomena such as cultural change and violent destructions whose veracity cannot in fact be properly demonstrated. More specific problems include the increasing signs of inter-penetration in the distributions of the two sets of cultural traits in the southern Cyclades, the need to invoke further, very particularistic arguments in order to accommodate the precise site histories that are attested, and the limited ability to explain why the end result should have been nucleation, save as a defensive measure.

The main problem with *world-systemic disruption* is that the impact on Aegean societies of changes in the core regions will remain hard to assess until it can be decided to how significant an extent the Aegean was integrated in east Mediterranean structures at this juncture. On present evidence it seems doubtful whether change at the core could trigger such intense local disruption in as far a margin as the Cyclades. At a more local level, given that the Aegean EB II system as a whole certainly did experience disruption (whether through predominantly internal or world systemic processes), the collapse of many of the non-Cycladic centres that had been the destinations of long-range voyaging by Cycladic islanders might well have damaged trading ideology, to the detriment of the island centres that participated in such activities – although this is to rephrase, rather than solve, the fundamental question. Towards the end of this chapter, an alternative model of change that involves the selective adoption in the Cyclades of a key element of Near Eastern maritime technology will be proposed, but that is a rather different matter.

The *degradation of land* through over-exploitation by farming or grazing may have played a part in triggering some desertion episodes, and perhaps also encouraged a concentration of settlement close to the larger lowland areas that benefited from hillslope soil loss (French and Whitelaw 1999: 178). It also has the virtue of being demonstrable in one Cycladic context, namely the soil profiles at Markiani on Amorgos. But the very variable settlement histories of different parts of the Cyclades, and the diverse relief and soils of the islands, make it unlikely that conditions would radically worsen throughout the islands within a sufficiently tight time-span to explain the extent of the change at the end of the EBA. Certainly in the Pacific islands, where anthropogenic degradation is well attested, its temporal incidence varies greatly (Kirch and Hunt 1997).

As was noted earlier, a *sudden climatic snap involving a high level of aridity* is currently something of a joker in the pack. If such an event did indeed occur, it is ostensibly easy to envisage how it might have swatted many of the small settlements in one of the most water-poor areas of the Aegean – in fact it is hard to see how it could have failed to have catastrophic implications for parts of the Cyclades. The problem is that the attested pattern of abandonment and nucleation shows little sign of favouring the better-watered islands. The one definite hiatus in a stratigraphic sequence is demonstrated at Agia Irini, located beside a spring on well-watered Kea, whilst two major Phylakopi I culture centres are located on the dry islands of Melos and Thera, and the best candidates for closed EB III contexts likewise come from water-poor Thera and Amorgos. This tends to suggest that even if the putative climatic change is confirmed, a lot more detailed information will be needed concerning its severity, extent and duration before its putative effects can be modelled with any accuracy in the Cyclades.

A *wave of epidemic* is no more than a speculative hypothesis at present, if an event that might well be anticipated, given textual references to virulent diseases in the disease-generating urban centres of the third millennium Near East (McNeill 1976: 79–80), the fact that, by the second half of this millennium, chains of people and places had started to link the Aegean to this area, and the general point that disease has been a major killer of islanders under conditions of increasing contact with distant urban areas since appropriate records have existed. As the Cyclades and the majority of the Aegean lacked concentrations of population sufficient to harbour such diseases in the long-term and thereby develop immunities, the expectation would be brief episodes of devastating fatalities, with the communication nodes and their dependent communities probably the first and worst affected, and a stochastic hit-and-miss pattern obtaining in other areas of the islands. The emptying of large sites as well as

An altered archipelago

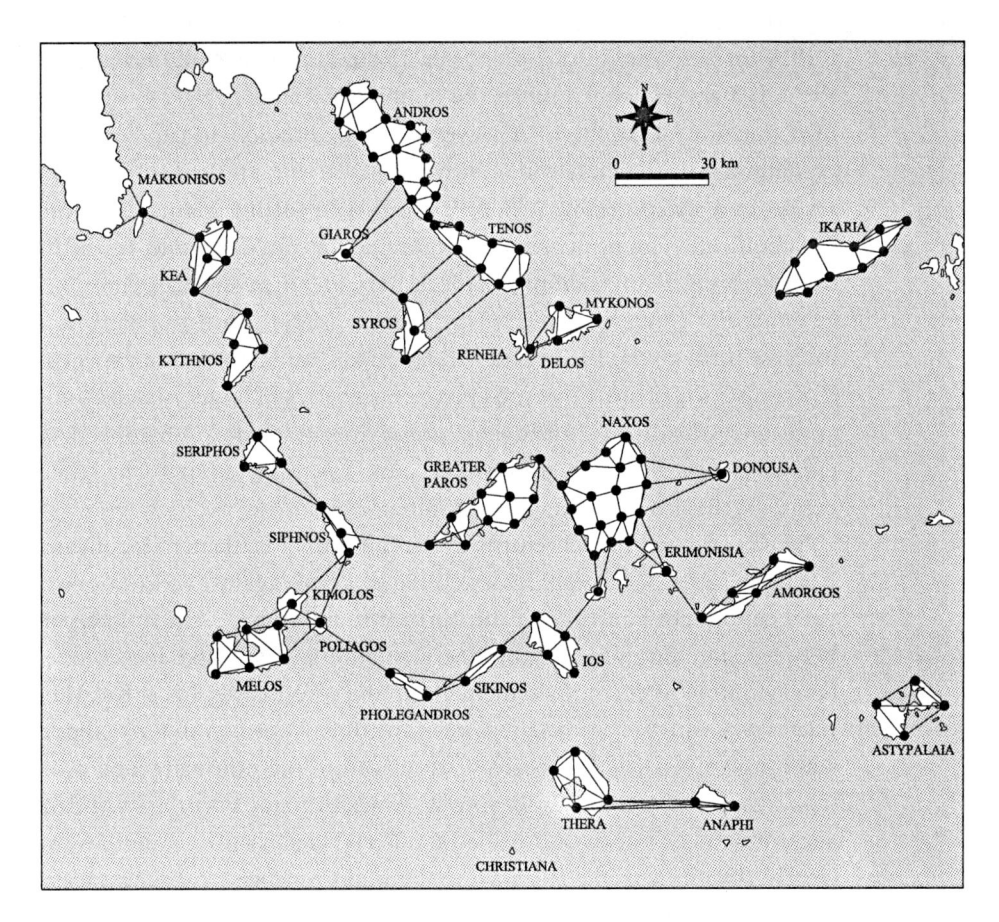

Fig. 114 Proximal Point Analysis 5.

many minor ones, and the collapse of formal funerary rituals as burying groups disintegrated would be some likely results. Moreover, the aftermath of such horizons has often seen the survivors espouse cultural and ideological change (McNeill 1976). This model might explain elements of the discontinuity that is attested, although it is not clear how island populations could have recovered so quickly by the MBA. The retort to the criticism that supporting evidence for this hypothesis is entirely lacking is, quite simply, that the residues of epidemic are not ones that we are yet prepared to detect in the Cycladic archaeological record.

Two models of internal change

Alternatives to the large-scale models outlined above are localised intra-Cycladic models of change. Two can be proposed, one being demographically driven, the other based on conflictual conditions. Both provide intriguing perspectives, although like the large-scale models, they fall short of a complete explanation. The former explores continuing population growth and its impact on interaction networks. Fig. 114 shows a PPA for a density of one point per 25 sq. km. This continues the sequence from PPAs 1–4 and roughly doubles the number of points in PPA 4, simulating a take-off of population late in the EBA. Several striking predictions can be made. Many more medium-sized islands become fairly self-sufficient. In the south-east Cyclades, this results in a sharp decline of the Erimonisia to satellite status. New centres of local communication intensity join the continuing foci on Naxos and Tenos. In all instances these are located on medium to large islands, and in several cases most of the links that generate the centre are internal to a single island. So if populations continued to increase through the EB III and MBA periods, we might in fact expect a centre in the Erimonisia to fail and others to emerge on a series of larger islands, sometimes in circumstances that would make them island-specific nodes. What this does not in itself explain is why the shift towards nucleation was triggered, nor why other major EB II centres were also abandoned at this time.

The conflictual model returns to the horizon of settlement fortification in the late EB II Cyclades. Chapter 9 reviewed the evidence against an invasionist explanation, yet a case might be made for the horizon representing a rise in internal competition between communities that degenerated into warfare and localised collapse. The concentration of defended settlements in the south-east, plus at Kastri on Syros, correlates well with the predicted zones of maximal inter-community competition. In the south-east Cyclades this receives support from the unusually high profile of burials with weapons, from the earlier Agrilia cemetery to the later tombs of Amorgos. It also accords with the fate of the fortified southern Naxian site of Panermos, whose end was clearly violent, with the entrance to the building burnt and slingstones and a spearhead in the debris (Doumas 1992a). Parallels might be sought in the influential models of boom-to-bust cycles of a few centuries' duration that have been developed for island trader systems in Melanesia (Allen 1977, 1984), although as the Melanesian past becomes better known, such cyclic models may be replaced by ones of ongoing, cumulative change to different structures, similar to those proposed here for the Cyclades. Certainly, the fortification horizon can be interpreted as evidence of a crisis within the internal networks in certain parts of the Cyclades, but like the model of demographic growth it cannot really explain the overall transformation, not least with regard to the spatial extent of change across the Cyclades, including areas of less evidently acute competition during EB II.

What both of these models remind us is that, as at any moment in island history, localised shifts in population and social strategies ensured that constellations of activity could never remain indefinitely static, however much ideologies or traditional ways of doing things might try to eternalise a contingent pattern. Although the precise manner in which these constellations might shift is hard to predict, one point of interest is that both models hinted that the ascendancy of Daskaleio-Kavos and its regime in the south-east Cyclades might be prone to failure at some point, perhaps with the ascendancy moving to other centres on (and principally for) some of the larger members of the Cyclades. To summarise so far, there is no lack of convincing models that could explain parts of the pattern seen between 2200 and 1900 BC in the Cyclades. Which are in fact close to the mark, and how they might be combined into more complex scenarios, is hard to assess for the present, but collectively they give us ample reasons to anticipate change.

A maritime and insular model of transformation in the Cyclades

The rest of this chapter proposes an explicitly maritime, insular model for explaining the changing lifestyles of the EB III to early MBA Cyclades. This model is compatible with elements of several of those outlined above, but concentrates on a feature of change at the end of third millennium BC that has not so far been discussed. This is the appearance in the Aegean at around this time of a radically new seafaring technology in the form of the first deep-hulled sailing ships. The fact that the first appearance of these ships is closely associated with increasing evidence of contact between Crete and the east Mediterranean during the period of Minoan state formation reminds us that, in distinction to the largely negative models of change proposed above, the transition from the third to the second millennium saw a rapid *increase* in social complexity in one major region of the Aegean (Cherry 1984a; Manning 1994; Watrous 1994: 721–36). Sailing ships transformed interaction between the Aegean and areas to the east. Previously, innovations or objects originating in the Near East probably moved west via down-the-line passage across the Anatolian land-bridge or along its southern shore, being so heavily filtered and repackaged for small-scale societies *en route* that there can seldom have been much difficulty, once they arrived, in slotting them into existing socio-economic structures. From now onwards, however, innovations and objects from the Near East could be directly transferred from their core areas of deployment. This might well have served the legitimising strategies of the emerging elites on immediately pre-palatial Crete, but could have provided critical problems of incorporation for traditional people and practices elsewhere in the Aegean.

In essence, the maritime model proposes that the take-up of sailing technology in the Cyclades entailed a revolution in the islanders' seafaring ideology and dynamics. Unlike the late EB II arrival of tin and Anatolian drinking customs, which altered island practices but could ultimately be incorporated within existing intra-Cycladic systems, it will be suggested that the availability and selective adoption of this maritime innovation spelt the end of traditional ways of living and opened up a different set of opportunities and risks in island life. During a transitional period, however, traditional and innovating maritime cultures may have briefly co-existed among diverse groups of islanders. If this link between seacraft and a transformation of island life can be sustained, the result will be an insight into how a crucial shift in the Aegean's place within the wider world first started to affect the patterns of insular history in the

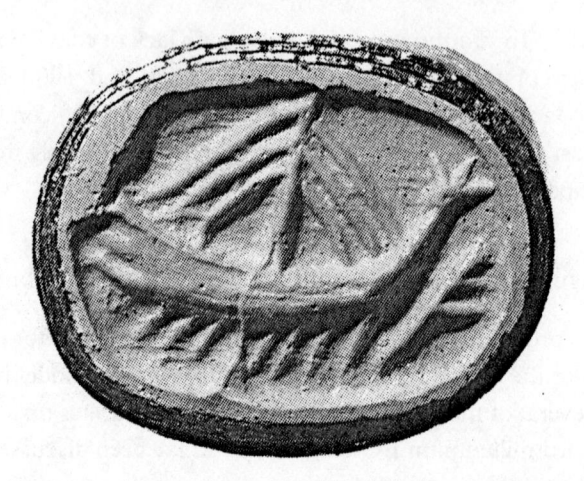

Fig. 115 Design on a Minoan seal illustrating a sailing ship. Courtesy of the Ashmolean Museum.

Cyclades. In order to validate this model's explanatory potential, we first need to review the empirical evidence for the introduction of the new shipping at this time, and to consider the technical mechanisms through which such an innovation may have been realised. We will also have to explore how sailing craft presented a different set of maritime options to the antecedent canoes. Only then can we examine the impact of such an innovation on Cycladic communities as they existed by the end of EB II, and demonstrate how it favoured new ways of living and new centres of activity, to the long-term detriment of existing practices and places.

The introduction of sailing ships into the Aegean dates to *c.* 2200–1950 BC, to judge from depictions on Minoan seals of EM III–MM IA and MM IB date (fig. 115) (Betts 1971; Wachsmann 1998: 99; Yule 1980: 165–6), plus the contemporary rise in the incidence of long-range contacts, attested by the first transfers of pots between Crete and Cyprus (Catling and Karageorghis 1960; Catling and MacGillivray 1983) and the increasing importation of oriental objects, materials, technologies and images to Crete by MM IA (Krzyszkowska 1983: 168–9; Warren 1995: 2; Watrous 1994: 734–6, 1998). The first Minoan depictions show vessels with a deep, curving, clearly plank-built hull, oars, mast and rigging, all a far remove from dug-out canoes or elaborations of such designs. The first actual illustration of a sail dates slightly later, but the presence of the mast on the antecedent images manifestly indicates the usage of sails.

Such ships resemble the so-called 'Byblos ships' that had plied routes between the Nile delta and the Levantine coast since the middle of the third millennium BC, forging a maritime link between the urban centres and resources of the Levant and the colossal vortex of consumption that was Old Kingdom Egypt (Marcus 1998: 35–58; Sherratt 1992; Wachsmann 1998: 9–18). The fact that the sail seems to have been invented only two or three times in human history (in the south-west Asian and

Egyptian sphere, the Indo-Pacific, and the west coast of South America, if the last case was not triggered by Polynesian contacts), combined with the overall similarity of the first Aegean boats to Levantine types, makes the likelihood of an indigenous Aegean invention vanishingly remote. The exact mode, medium and locus of the Aegean's learning process may never be known, with a major uncertainty being whether occasional ships of this type visited the Aegean earlier in the third millennium BC. If they did, Crete is a plausible landfall. Regardless, however, the seal depictions and evidence for direct contacts between Crete and the east make Crete a likely point for the initial adoption of the new technology. In the Cyclades, conversely, we shall have reason to doubt whether the main EB II centres played a particularly positive role, despite their long-range voyaging activities.

What is the evidence for such vessels in the Cyclades, bearing in mind that EM III–MM IA is contemporary with Cycladic EB III and the earliest MBA? The published material comprises two depictions on sherds from the old excavations at Phylakopi (fig. 116). One, in a diagnostic Phylakopi I culture incised style, shows a curving hull with oars or paddles, a huge steering blade and a helmsman. As luck would (not) have it, the sherd is broken where the mast might be expected to be, but the steering oar (absent on the longboat depictions) makes best sense on a sail-driven craft. The other depiction, in the painted style of either Phylakopi I or II, shows a slender, masted vessel with oars or paddles. The differences between these depictions and those in Crete might indicate a degree of adaptation of local canoe-building technologies in the Cyclades, albeit in the context of a knowledge of the new types. But the Cycladic boats are emphatically more than simply longboats with a small sail mounted, as was attested among the Maori (Best 1925: fig. 91) and in the Pacific North-West after contact with Westerners (Drucker 1951: 85–6; de Laguna 1972: 341). The curved hull argues for a fundamentally different construction, and the tall mast, seen in one image and implied in the other, could only be stabilised by adding out-riggers to a canoe (the Pacific solution, which is not attested in the Mediterranean) or broadening the hull beyond the limits of canoe design to create a stable platform. Moreover, as McGrail (1991: 87) states, the hull stresses on craft driven by a large sail demand fundamental changes in boat design.[3]

---

[3] The most famous images of ships in the later Bronze Age Cyclades are those of mid-second-millennium BC date in the wallpaintings of the West House at Akrotiri on Thera, in the last settlement on the site before the great eruption of the Thera volcano (Doumas 1992b: figs. 35–43; Morgan 1988; Televantou 1990). The sea-going vessels that are depicted are all descendants of the new ships that entered the Aegean at the end of the third millennium BC. One detail of the excellently preserved 'ship procession' scene is of particular interest. Most of the ships (which have their sails down, are festooned with elaborate decorations, and bear high-status passengers) are being propelled over what is clearly a short distance by swarms of paddlers (not rowers) in a manner similar to the technique required for an EBA longboat some 500 or more years earlier (Morgan 1988: 127). This depiction of a reduntant form of locomotion in a ceremonial context raises interesting questions about the curation of archaisms in the long-term memories and ceremonial practices of the Cycladic islanders, or alternatively about the conscious reinvention of an island tradition that had lapsed in the interim.

Fig. 116 Images of the new shipping in the Cyclades found at Phylakopi. Courtesy of the National Archaeological Museum, Athens.

Table 12. *Comparative boat performance for canoes and sailing ships.*

Criterion	Canoe	Sailing ship
Day's range	About 20–40/50 km	About 100–150 km
Overall range	Short hops/intra-Aegean	Short hops to pan-Mediterranean
Directional freedom	Moderate (low to windward)	Moderate (tacking to windward)
Wave tolerance	Moderate	High
Cargo capacity	Small	Larger
Harbour facilities	Minimal	Protected anchorage
Crew	Small (but longboat large)	Small (but many if rowed)
Skilled crew	Navigator	Navigator and sail operators
Construction	Simple carpentry	Complex joinery and sail-making
Main materials	Wood	Wood and linen sails
Coercive potential	Longboat high	High if heavily manned

Even if the introduction of this maritime technology from the east Mediterranean was more filtered in the Cyclades than in Crete, the result was a seacraft different from anything that had hitherto existed in these islands. Table 12 contrasts the main features of canoes and early sailing vessels under Aegean conditions (cf. Casson 1971; Georgiou 1991, 1993). Some enduring continuities are seen, for example both require high degrees of skill on the part of a few people, utilise variable numbers of crew, and can be made suitable for warfare. But a series of more fundamental distinctions are also brought out. Setting aside differing constructional requirements (including more intensive labour-input for the new ships), it emerges that four performance-related factors had the potential to revolutionise island life in the Cyclades.

The first of these is *speed of travel*. Sailing ships must have drastically shrunk maritime space both in and beyond the Aegean. For instance, in fair conditions a four-day voyage could take a longboat from the middle of the Cyclades to Crete, whilst a similar period in a sailing ship could cover the distance from Crete to Egypt (Casson 1971: 282–8). One result of this would have been partly to demystify internal Aegean distance, and therefore also Aegean things, with Near Eastern exotica (at least on Crete) usurping the role of inter-regional Aegean imports in the preceding EBA and Neolithic. A no less important corollary would be the relative ease with which outside groups deploying the new maritime technology could penetrate the Cyclades, thereby profoundly reducing the islanders' ability to control their external contacts and making their islands more dangerous places in which to live. The impact of both these changes on Cycladic maritime-based ideologies must have been considerable. The social prestige of longboat voyaging would have been reduced, and the ability of dominant centres in the islands to maintain locally universalised regimes of value and truth critically undermined.

The second factor concerns the *greater flexibility of travel direction under any given conditions afforded by sailing ships*. Examination of sail rigs suggests that early Aegean sailing ships could make considerable headway against the wind (Gifford and Gifford 1997). Some ability to do so would have been crucial for northward expansion up the Levantine coast against prevailing winds, and the development of a sophisticated set of skills may be assumed by the time that such ships were taken up in the Aegean. The emphasis on the rigging and ancillary oars on the Cretan depictions may therefore be relevant as iconographic signifiers of manoeuvrability as well as speed. The impact of this enhanced directional freedom of movement would have been least at the level of localised travel, where all seacraft could take advantage of short-term fluctuations in the wind, yet decisive for long-range travel, for which canoes demanded steady tail winds. In the Aegean, sailing ships will have revolutionised the potential for direct northward movement across open sea and against the prevailing winds, obviating the earlier need for long-range traffic in this direction either to wait months for a southern wind or to claw its way north using circuitous routes. For the Cyclades, this spelled an end to the preceding travel conditions that had favoured islanders' journeys to Crete but hindered travel in the opposite direction. Ostensibly, this might seem to work to the islanders' advantage, rendering long return journeys unnecessary. But the converse was that the Cyclades now lay within easy reach of Cretan seafarers, and – equally significantly – of the now emerging palatial communities and elites that lay behind them.

The third factor is *cargo capacity*, with the new harnessing of wind-power as a substitute for, or addition to, muscle-power transforming the potential for the transport of bulk goods overseas. For example, the excavation of the fourteenth century BC Uluburun shipwreck off the southern Anatolian coast has revealed a ship comparable in length to a longboat, yet its contents comprised more than 20 tonnes of material, far more than a longboat's plausible cargo capacity (Bass 1987; Bass *et al.* 1989). One result would have been to facilitate the large-scale movement of cargo such as metals, textiles and processed products, but a no less important consequence for island life would have been the new possibility for major transfers of bulk staples between islands in the event of harvest failure. One 20 tonne cargo of grain could, for example, feed roughly a hundred people for a year or several hundred people for a shorter period of dearth, and be transported under safer conditions (as well as more easily) in the hull of a sailing ship than in even a flotilla of canoes. In terms of survival strategies, this meant that a third option could be added to the previous choice between location in a prime arable niche with augmentation of the food supply by wild resources (the proposed Saliagos culture model), and small-scale arable and herding settlement linked together by social storage networks (the strategy favoured from the end of the Neolithic and through most of the EBA). This third option can be summarised as settlement nucleation, necessarily close to extensive arable land, and the bulk import of staples by sea, potentially over a substantial distance, in the event of a bad harvest. This option, which was to become fundamental to the dynamics of Mediterranean urbanism throughout later antiquity, first became viable in the Cyclades with the advent of the sail.

This brings us to our fourth and final factor, the *necessity of proper anchorages* for the new shipping. Whilst canoes could be drawn up on a small foreshore, and thus centres of canoe-based maritime interaction might develop at almost any point along the coasts of the Cyclades, this would not be the case with sailing vessels, which (contrary to popular wisdom) cannot be drawn out of the water unless completely unloaded, and therefore require sheltered anchorages (Georgiou 1993). As there are relatively few such natural harbours in the Cyclades, the location of centres of sailing vessel activity would be subject to topographic constraints that were previously unfelt. Interestingly, Ambrose (1997: 533) has recently proposed that the changeover from paddled to sailing canoes in Melanesia imposed similar locational constraints and created a suite of further social, cultural and environmental implications for island settlement patterns.

Taken together, these factors add up to a transformation of Cycladic maritime dynamics, and given the extent to which island societies appear to have been structured by these dynamics, the ramifications must have been extensive. Chalandriani-Kastri and (to a lesser degree) Daskaleio-Kavos are poorly endowed with sheltered harbours, and would be unsuitable centres for sailing ships. Moreover, if there was as much invested in canoe-based activity as has been argued, such centres are very likely to have been too socially and ideologically locked in to canoe-oriented practices to accept innovations (cf. Lemonnier 1993), despite the probability that new craft with superior performance, combined with the concomitant shrinking of Aegean maritime space, undercut the basis of their pre-eminence in the eyes of other islanders. In terms of harbours, the same is not true for Grotta-Aplomata and Agia Irini, but an ideological commitment to older ways might have been no less important; in the former case what happened at the end of the EBA is not known, and the latter site only developed into a centre of sailing traffic after a break of several centuries. For all the hints of fighting at or around some of these sites, it is quite possible that, in the end, the EB II central communities simply melted away as the prestige-oriented seafaring activities that had held them together lost their power. This fits the picture of abandonment rather than a violent ending that is indicated by the excavation of the latest EBA occupation areas at Agia Irini III and Chalandriani-Kastri.

In contrast, the new nucleated settlements possess excellent harbours. Paroikia lies on a deep bay, reconstruction of Thera before the second-millennium eruption indicates a fine harbour in the earlier caldera (Heiken and McCoy 1984) in addition to the inlet at Akrotiri itself, and Phylakopi possessed a small, now alluviated, harbour at the site (fig. 110), as well as an excellent anchorage at nearby Pollonia (Davidson *et al.* 1976; Georgiou 1993). The maritime factors encouraging a trend towards nucleation at such sites are likely to have included the expanded possibilities for bulk transport of staples by sea, security in numbers in the face of increased vulnerability to long-range sea-raids by external groups, and a desire to be associated with new forms of seafaring.

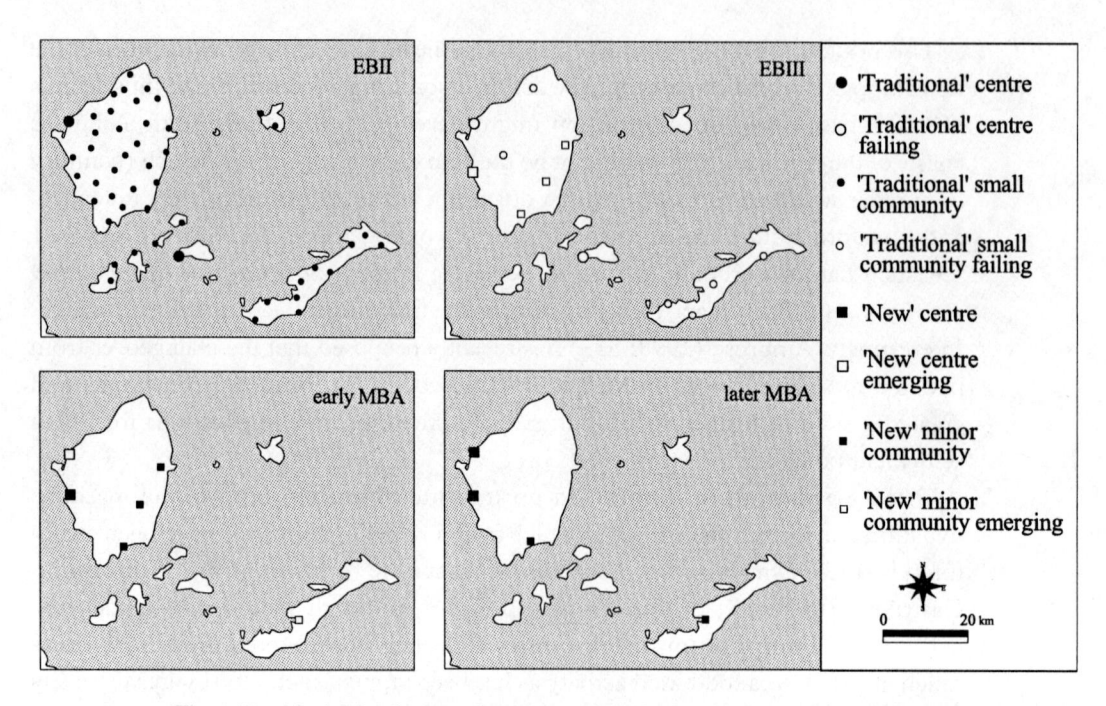

Fig: 117 Model for the transformation of settlement in the south-east Cyclades from the end of EB II to the MBA. Note that although the locations of the major sites match known examples, the minor sites are not intended to represent specific archaeological sites but rather reflect the overall patterns of change.

In conclusion, what we may be seeing in the Cycladic archaeological record in EB III and the early MBA is the playing out of these changes, crudely speaking with the Kastri group as the last cultural expression associated with the canoe-based networks, and the Phylakopi I culture associated with the emerging nucleated pattern and the new technology of maritime movement. The spatially differentiated distribution of old and new centres and assemblages may reflect the different demands and opportunities of the new ships, plus ideological resistance to innovation in focal areas of traditional canoe activity. If the Phylakopi I culture centres really are a southern Cycladic development, this might be explained in terms of the most likely entry points of the new technology.

Fig. 117 illustrates how this transformation from EB II to the MBA might have reworked one islandscape, that of the south-east Cyclades. The varied rate of up-take of innovation would have created a mosaic of traditional and innovating communities and their associated material cultures, probably with several overlap areas, and within the EB III period a few generations of islanders probably experienced a phase of uneasy co-existence between two maritime cultures, prior to the demise of the older way of life as a result of technological out-competition and ideological failure. This scenario in fact provides a rather attractive explanation for the residual activity at a few EBA cemeteries, involving the deposition of Phylakopi I culture objects. All the

Fig: 118   Phylakopi I culture pyxis from the Agios Loukas cemetery on Syros. Courtesy of the National Archaeological Museum, Athens.

known examples of such activity, on Syros, Amorgos and possibly Keros, correlate with areas that were heavily involved in canoe-borne traffic, but which have no signs of major Phylakopi I culture settlements. What we are probably witnessing is the interment of new circulating trade goods, captured by the last traditional conspicuous burial acts in conservative areas of the Cyclades. The prominence of Amorgos in this respect indicates an enduring streak of conservatism, which enabled its cist graves to act as material traps much later than was common in the Cyclades. It may also be relevant that the bays along the island's north coast provide shelter for boats moving between the southern Cyclades and the south-east Aegean, a route that (as will shortly become clear) formed a major axis of movement at this time. As a final indication of the cultural ambiguity evinced in this period, however, we can close with the example of the Phylakopi I culture pyxis in a late grave at Agios Loukas on Syros (fig. 118). Incised on its lid is the same star/sun symbol as that earlier employed as an alternative to the longboat motif on frying pans at Chalandriani-Kastri, the latter a lonely spot by the time the pyxis was deposited, but just an hour's walk away over the hills – and perhaps equally close in local memory.

11

The emergence of Minoan dominance

> Little islands out at sea, on the horizon
> keep suddenly showing a whiteness, a flash and a furl, a hail
> of something coming, ships a-sail from over the rim of the sea.
>
> And every time, it is ships, it is ships,
> it is ships of Cnossos coming . . .
>   *The Greeks Are Coming,* D. H. LAWRENCE

In the previous chapter we looked at how the disruption and change in the Cyclades at the end of the third millennium BC might best be understood. A series of large-scale and local models were shown to have potential relevance to understanding these processes. Although it remains unclear in most, if not all, cases how widespread or serious the impact of the circumstances that these models explore might actually have been, their collective message is that an horizon of major change in the Cyclades during this period should come as no surprise. And regardless of these current imponderables, a maritime and insular model demonstrated that the iconographically attested introduction of a new type of seacraft at this time would have added a further, and perhaps decisive, element to the complex of factors working against the survival of EB II ways of living and in favour of a thorough transformation of island life. But, as was also intimated in chapter 10, this complex of factors does not in itself offer a full explanation of the island ending between *c.* 2200 and 1900 BC. For the other decisive factor in this respect, and one that marked Aegean history's switch to new pathways, was the irruption of palatial Cretan activity into the Cyclades and neighbouring areas from *c.* 1950–1900 BC. This oriented the islands towards a major external power for the first time, and made them in effect a periphery zone of the Minoan palaces, with Crete's position shifting from its pre-palatial status as the southern edge of an Aegean region centred on the Cyclades, to that of the Aegean's first 'core' and its main point of articulation with lands to the east.

The aims of this brief penultimate chapter are therefore twofold. The first is to look in more detail at the trading dynamics of the Phylakopi I culture, in other words at that short but extremely interesting period of island history, of perhaps 200–300 years' duration, that followed the collapse of the canoe-based systems, but pre-dated the first Minoan palatial activity in the Cyclades. In that period can be discerned the traces of a distinctive pattern of insular relations that, if external factors had not soon impinged, might have become the next long-term structure in the Cyclades. The contemporary period in Crete, defined by the EM III and MM IA phases, comprises the centuries of state formation that culminated during MM IB in the massive mobilisation of resources and statements of power represented by the construction of the first palaces at Knossos, Phaistos and Mallia, events taken to denote the start of the palatial age in the Aegean. This chapter's second aim is to examine how Cretan palatial activities and power were first manifested in the Cyclades, bringing to a close the early island history that has been the subject of this book.

Maritime interaction zones of the late pre-palatial period

A Phylakopi I culture trading system?

So far, we have looked at the archaeology of the Phylakopi I culture mainly in terms of its settlements, and in order to answer questions concerning its chronological position. By the end of the last chapter, however, it was clear that the Phylakopi I culture could also be associated with something of a revolution in Cycladic maritime activity. In fact, the archaeology of Phylakopi I culture trading activities confirms the existence at this period of an impressive, if transitory, configuration of maritime interconnections, quite different in extent and kind from anything seen so far, and equally distinct, too, from the dendritic routes that would radiate from palatial Crete into the southern Aegean.

Fig. 119 shows the distribution of duck vases, the most diagnostic trade item of the EB III and early MBA period. It reveals that the Cyclades, and the southern islands in particular, lay at the centre of an extensive arc of island-based production, stretching from Kolonna on Aegina to the south-east Aegean, with production centres on Aegina, Melos, Greater Paros and Samos, and possibly others on Naxos, Thera and among the south-east Aegean islands; exported duck vases are found on the Greek mainland and in western Anatolia, and imitations appear at Beycesultan, probably Troy and even Cyprus (Misch 1992; Rutter 1985). The only parts of the Aegean that lie outside this distribution are Crete, the southern Peloponnese and most of the northern Aegean. This informs us, first, that island centres were crucial to southern Aegean trade at this time (in which context the fact that sites like Aegina and the newly discovered south-east-Aegean settlements produce little sign of disruption in EB III is significant), and, secondly, that the main Cycladic settlements need to be understood as part of a wider swathe of island nodes. Once again, the framework of analysis cannot be realistically restricted to the Cyclades.

This configuration of trade, and the possible forms of trading culture behind it, deserve further exploration. Spatially, the distribution is just as impressive as that of the sauceboats or folded-arm figurines in the 'international spirit'. Other parallels with

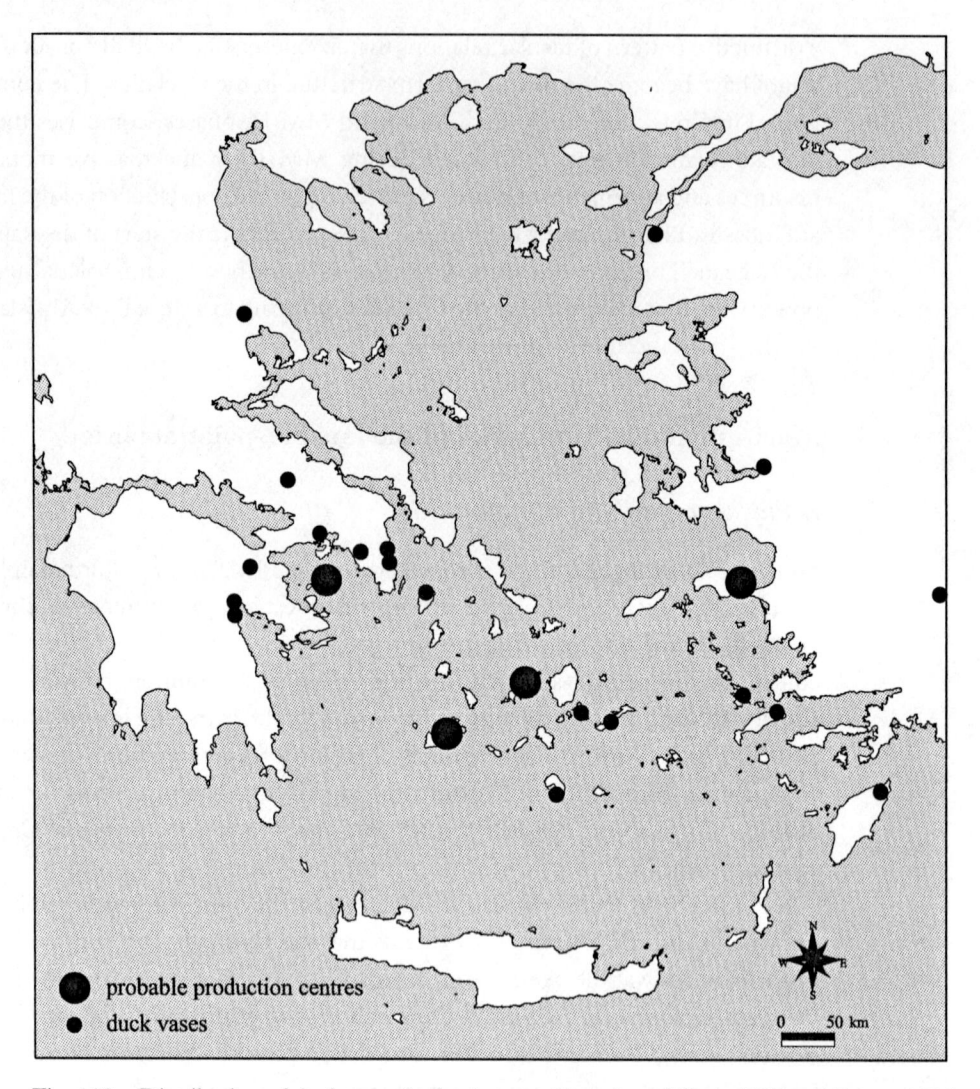

Fig. 119 Distribution of duck vases in the Aegean. Data from Misch 1992 and Rutter 1985.

EB II include the fact that both were horizontal networks created by a series of independent centres, rather than by a single unified organisation. But in the place of the symbolically charged trade of EB II, so rich in prestige objects and symbols, the emphasis was now exclusively on what can be regarded as commodity-oriented activity, shorn of elaborate social associations. Particularly interesting is the evidence for trade in liquid products, attested by the development of specialised liquid transport vessels, like the duck vase and other rarer, but functionally analogous, shapes from Thera and Melos, such as ring vases, animal 'rhyta' and basket-handled askoi (Rutter 1985). These represent the Aegean's first vessels specially designed for moving liquids overseas, save for the brief appearance of the Kampos group bottles half a millennium earlier. They are without functional equivalents in the Cretan and mainland repertoires until the development of the well-known stirrup-jar several centuries later (Betancourt 1985: 105; Rutter 1985: 20). Olive oil is surely the most likely contents of such vessels, given the leaf-shaped spout for carefully pouring a viscous substance.[1] Indeed, the duck vase and associated forms could well reflect a link between increased agricultural production and processing, and a growing long-range maritime trade in agricultural products, favoured by the combination of sailing ships and settlement concentration in good arable areas.

In this respect, the distinctive incised or painted designs that can be tentatively associated with the duck vases from each production centre (Rutter 1985: 17), and the visually striking nature of the related container forms, may indicate deliberate efforts to distinguish the products of different communities, and perhaps be seen as something akin to a ploy to attract consumers. A further sign of changing practices in production and trade is the suddenly high incidence of pot-marks attested at Phylakopi (Edgar 1904), Kolonna (Walter and Felten 1981: 125–6) and, at a slightly later date, a resettled Agia Irini (Bikaki 1984: 7–21, 42–3). Exactly how this production and trading system was organised within islands and island communities is uncertain, although the most likely social units are households, or groups of households working in concert. In distinction to Niemeier's proposal that the first non-Cretan Aegean state emerged during the MBA on Aegina (an island of only 83 sq km in area) what is really interesting about the island centres of the earlier second millennium BC is that they indicate an alternative, apparently highly effective, means of organising agricultural production and export that did *not* require the centralised systems and modes of operation that are associated with the early Cretan states.

Moreover, it is likely that the duck vase distribution does not tell the whole story. The possibility of a trade in textiles is raised by a boom in the amount of painted Phylakopi I culture pottery, several of the designs on which resemble textile patterns; Rutter (1988) argues the same for basketry with regard to mainland EH III pottery. But it is equally likely that the centres of the Phylakopi I culture Cyclades were engaged in metal procurement, production and trade, and that the arc of island interaction revealed by the duck vases may hint at such activities, perhaps pointing towards Anatolia. Given the demonstrated links between the circulation of metals and distributions of pottery in both the preceding EB II period (chapter 9) and the later MBA

---

[1] This naturally raises the question as to whether, or to what extent, olive oil was being produced in the EBA, as discussed in chapters 2 and 3. For those who favour little or no production before the end of the third millennium BC, the duck vases could reflect the first circulation of a new substance. For those who affirm that olive oil was being produced in the EBA, the appearance of the duck vases might relate either to new, more refined or perfumed kinds of oil, or to a change in status to a regular commodity for maritime exchange. Whatever the correct answer, the fact that miniature proto-duck vases and small jugs with leaf-shaped spouts had both appeared by the end of the Kastri group would suggest that a substance similar to that held by the full-sized duck vases was already starting to circulate slightly earlier (cf. further discussion in Rutter 1985, where fish-paste is put forward as another possible contents for these vessels).

and LBA periods (see below), this is an intrinsically not unreasonable assumption, despite the low visibility of metals at this time, which is due largely to the fact that few intact funerary contexts of this date are known. In fact, where the evidence does survive, glimpses are afforded of a heavy involvement in metal-working. At Phylakopi I, crucibles and copper production waste were discovered (Atkinson *et al.* 1904: 191, fig. 59), at Kolonna and Heraion there are plentiful signs of metal-working (Branigan 1974: 204–5; Milojčić 1961), and the late tombs of Amorgos trapped a range of artefacts that provide a rare glimpse of the period's finished metal objects (Branigan 1974: fig. 10; Nakou 1997: fig. 4).

The provenance of the metals circulated by island communities at this time is very poorly known. At the time of the late EB II Kastri group, Cycladic communities were already procuring metals that originated from a wider range of sources than those of Kythnos, Siphnos and Lavrion. By the later MBA, exploitation of the Cycladic ores had effectively ceased, with Lavrion and non-Aegean sources taking over, probably because the palatial economies of Crete demanded larger scales of extraction than the Cycladic sources could provide (Gale and Stos-Gale 1984). This switch is well illustrated by comparison between the metals at Agia Irini II–III and Agia Irini IV–V (Gale *et al.* 1984: 394), but even here the transitional period is missing, and we have therefore little means of finding out precisely when and how the change-over in sources took place.

The Phylakopi I culture trading system and contemporary Cretan maritime activity

The island-based network described above was one of three principal EB III to early MBA zones of Aegean maritime interaction (fig. 120). North of the major belt of island activity was a zone embracing north-west Anatolia, Macedonia, Thessaly, Euboia and the mainland opposite (Rutter 1979: 13, 1988). To the south-west lay a third zone, smaller in extent but of more immediate relevance in the present context, defined by finds of Cretan MM IA pottery or its local imitations on Kythera, where the 'colony' at Kastri mentioned in chapter 9 continues (Coldstream and Huxley 1972: 277–8) and the coastal Peloponnesian sites of Lerna, Agios Stephanos and Asine, with a few examples of MM IA pottery travelling as far as Kolonna, Athens and Eutresis (Hiller 1993: 197; Rutter and Zerner 1984: 77–9). The signature of this Cretan activity in the south-west Aegean is different from that of the arc of island-based trade centred on the Cyclades. In terms of pottery, whilst the latter reflects a network concentrating on liquid transport vessels, the former represents the transfer of elements of Cretan-derived social ideology and way of life, attested by imports and imitations of cups and bridge-spouted pouring jars as well as container shapes. At Lerna, moreover, a Cretan type of loom appears to have been introduced, and at around this time (the exact date is not yet established) a peak sanctuary cult of indisputably Cretan type was established

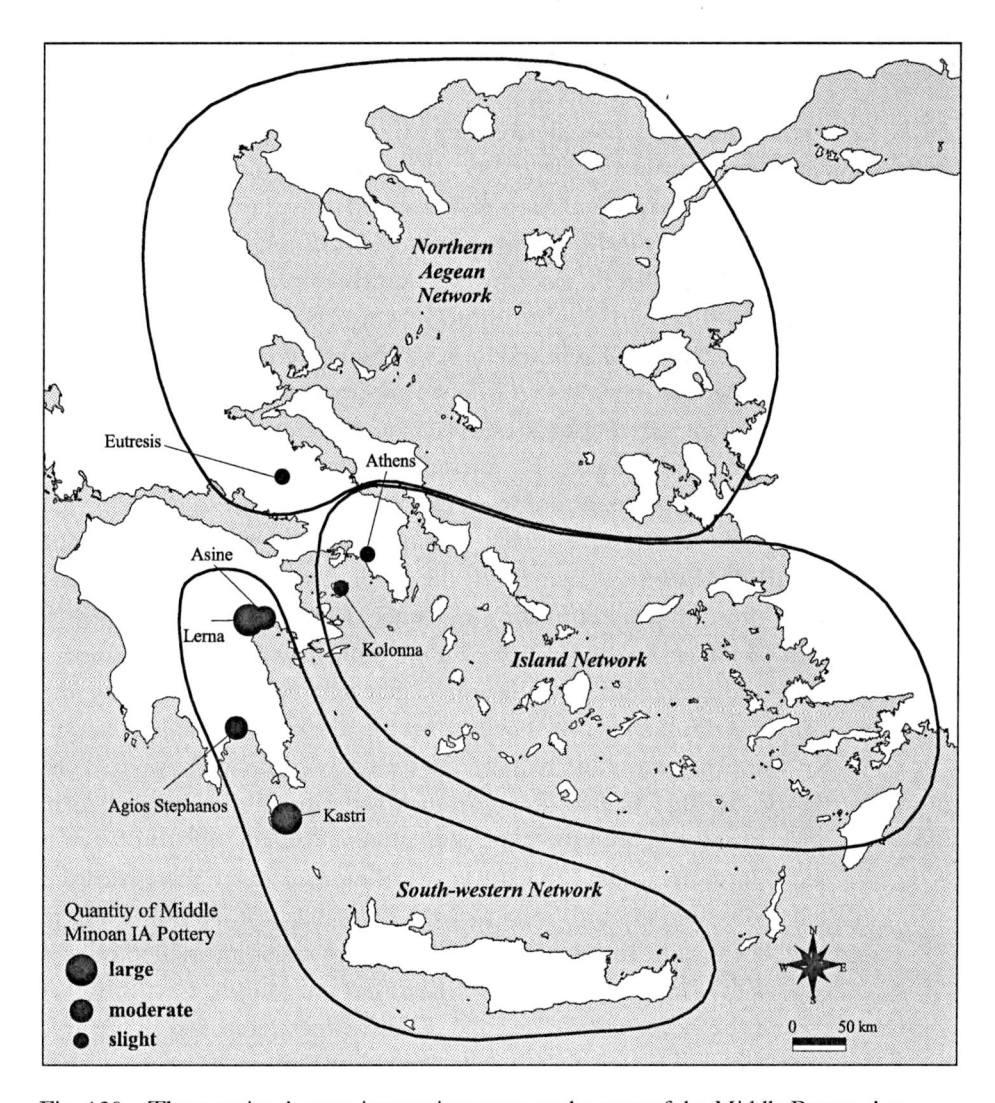

Fig. 120 Three major Aegean interaction zones at the start of the Middle Bronze Age.

overlooking Kastri on Kythera (Sakellarakis 1996). To what extent this south-west Aegean horizon reflects colonisation and Cretan enclaves is uncertain, but it is tempting to infer the first demonstrations of external control or cultural domination by Cretan elites based at one or more of the centres of the then-emerging Minoan states.

The very limited overlap between the distributions of the Cycladic-centred island system and the zone of MM IA activity is striking. Only a few sites in the Saronic gulf, Boiotia and the north-east Peloponnese have produced examples of both duck vases and MM IA pottery. Furthermore, contacts between the islands and Crete itself throughout EB III and the earlier MBA appear, on the basis of ceramics, to be minimal. No MM IA pottery has been found in a clear Phylakopi I culture level in the Cyclades, which makes the prominent profile of MM IA activity in the south-west

Aegean all the more striking. Only a few pieces occur at Kolonna (Hiller 1993) and one at Heraion (MacGillivray 1984: 74). Imports from the Cyclades to Crete are also rare, comprising a few sherds in EM III and MM IA contexts (MacGillivray 1984: 73; Momigliano and Wilson 1996: 44); petrographic analysis has now suggested a non-Cycladic origin for a class of dark-faced incised pottery at Knossos that was once held to be Cycladic (MacGillivray *et al.* 1988; cf. MacGillivray 1984: 73). Imports to Crete from mainland Greece are even rarer, comprising just two examples at Knossos (Rutter and Zerner 1984: 81; MacGillivray 1984: 73). To set this image for limited interaction between Crete and most other areas of the Aegean in a wider, contrasting context, MM IA saw the first Minoan pottery reach Cyprus, and the first substantial horizon of imported oriental objects, materials and images on Crete (Watrous 1998).

This minimal evidence for interaction between Crete and the islands to its north requires explanation. At one level, of course, it continues a trend begun in later EB II, when the level of visible exchange between the two areas drops off abruptly, and in EM III–MM IA (as in later EB II) the continuing consumption of Melian obsidian on Crete presents an interpretative challenge. Rutter's proposed reasons for the lack of MM IA pottery in the Cyclades are not ultimately convincing (Rutter 1983: 73). As he indeed recognises, the suggestion that only western Crete was interested in sea trading at this time is belied by the fact that the known mainland imports come from Knossos. His alternative, namely that the Cycladic networks were so disrupted by the EB III gap that Cretan seafarers took some time to rediscover them, seems also unlikely in the light of the reinterpretation of Cycladic EB III offered in chapter 10, and it furthermore fails to explain why Kolonna, where there is certainly no gap in activity, is also all but devoid of MM IA pottery. An attractive alternative solution would be that the social dynamics of these two major interaction zones were different enough to be incompatible and perhaps even antagonistic. Certainly, there is a marked contrast between, on the one hand, Crete's export of its way of life to the south-west Aegean and its preference for cultivating Near Eastern connections, and, on the other hand, the commodity-oriented networks generated by the villages or small towns of the Cyclades and adjacent islands.

The end of early Cycladic history

The Cretan dendritic system

For a brief period, therefore, an island-based network running east–west from Aegina through the Cyclades to the south-east Aegean flourished as an alternative system for structuring southern Aegean maritime interaction to the dendritic, north–south oriented system focused on palatial Crete that was to overlay and dominate other networks for the next half-millennium. The strange fact is that, save for expansion in the south-west Aegean, Crete's hegemony, though in temporal terms imminent, was at

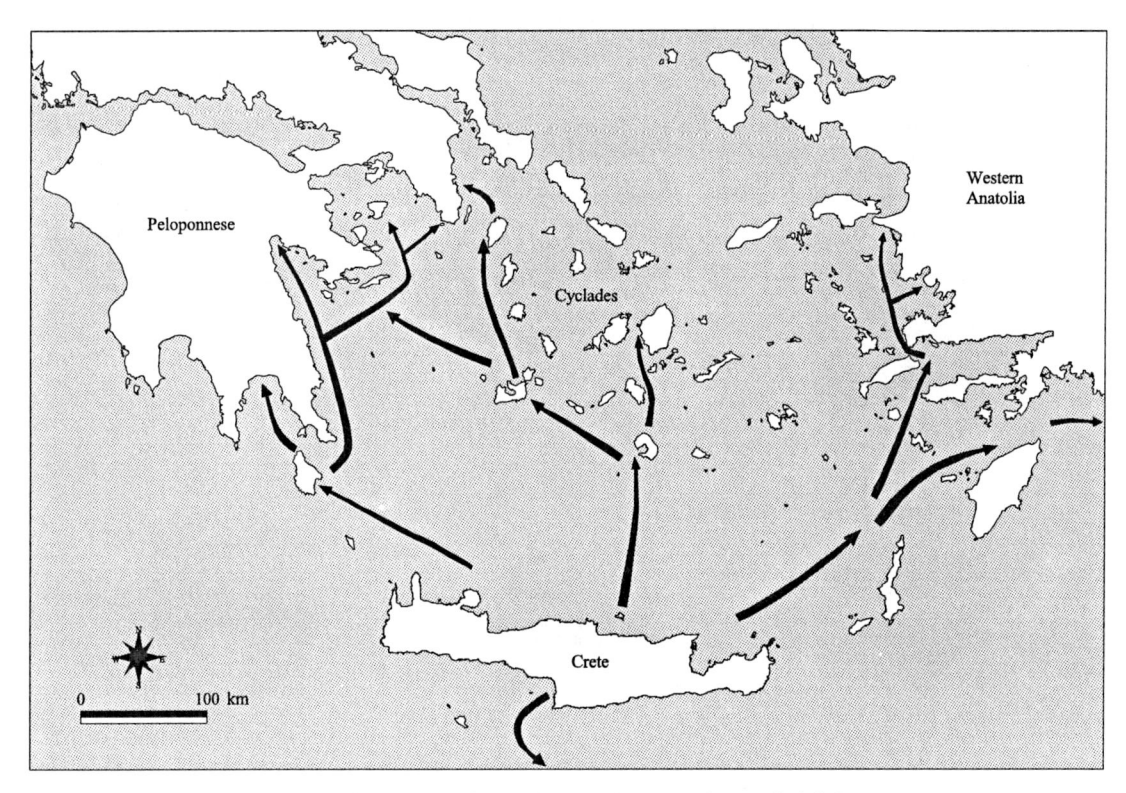

Fig. 121 Dendritic pattern of maritime trade centred on palatial Crete.

this juncture still far from apparent. If we do want to identify the moment at which the early history of the Cyclades ended (and admitting the simplifications inherent in this desire), it was perhaps less the point in time when the EB II world began to unravel, than that when the Phylakopi I culture island-based system surrendered its maritime primacy to sea-routes radiating out from palatial Crete. What is the evidence for this change, and what does it tell us about the processes by which Minoan domination became established?

Cretan pottery of palatial styles starts to appear in the later MBA Cyclades from MM IB in Cretan terms. Its appearance forms one part of a process by which the already established string of Cretan-influenced sites in the south-west Aegean was augmented by a further string through the Cyclades, and another transecting the islands and coastal zone of the south-east Aegean (fig. 121). This dendritic pattern has been widely, and surely correctly, regarded as a reflection of the routes by which materials, in particular metals, reached the Cretan production and consumption centres from what was now, in effect, a southern Aegean periphery (Davis 1979; Gale and Stos-Gale 1984; Wiener 1990). At Phylakopi II, the Cretan imports comprise 2–3 per cent of the total pottery (fig. 122) (Renfrew 1982b: 223), and local 'minoanising' pottery is much in evidence (Barber 1978). Agia Irini was reoccupied at around this juncture, non-coincidentally at a time when the north–south routes that this site served

Fig. 122 Middle Minoan imports from palatial Crete found at Phylakopi. Courtesy of the Ashmolean Museum.

regained their prominence; at Agia Irini IV, plentiful Cretan imports and local imitations are found (Overbeck 1984, 1989b: 11–12). Imports are also known from soundings at Akrotiri (Papagiannopoulou 1991: 51–4), as well as Kolonna (Hiller 1993) and several sites in the south-east Aegean islands and the facing Anatolian coast (Davis 1982b: 38–9). Much of the pottery consists of fine shapes associated with drinking and pouring, much as was the case with the MM IA pottery in the southern and eastern Peloponnese, and suggests an ideological adoption of Cretan customs by non-Cretan communities.

The dendritic pattern remained in place throughout the age of the Minoan palace-states, with the principal Cycladic nodes (Phylakopi, Agia Irini and, until its volcanic destruction, Akrotiri) spaced a day's sail apart. Debate continues over the interpretation of the steadily growing Cretan influence on material culture, economy, administration, architecture and cult in the Cyclades, with opinions split between the rather tired options of political control from Crete (known as the 'thalassocracy of Minos' in later Greek tradition) and the cultural minoanisation of independent island communities (e.g. Hägg and Marinatos 1984). Internal trade within the Cyclades and between them and their other island neighbours was, it should be stressed, not stifled. The best archaeological tracer of internal trade in the later MBA is the pale Melian fabric found on Kea and Naxos (Barber 1987: 156). Early LBA links with the southeast Aegean have been identified at both Agia Irini and Akrotiri (Davis *et al.* 1983; Marthari *et al.* 1990), and a few pieces of Cypriot pottery at Akrotiri (Cline 1994: 185–6) may imply some direct connection to the east Mediterranean. Moreover, Naxos continued to be an important settlement focus and also received imported pottery, not least from Crete, even though it does not seem to have lain on the major trans-Cycladic route (Barber and Hadjianastasiou 1989: 140; Hadjianastasiou 1989). But although the picture of Cretan dominance should therefore not be overdrawn, the new regime of interaction in the southern Aegean, and the role of the Cycladic communities in such networks, delineate a fundamentally altered world.[2]

A final model: early palatial aggression in the southern Cyclades?

Is it possible to explore how this change was initially effected? At least at a speculative level, it is worth exploring the possibility that the cessation of the Phylakopi I system and the establishment of Creto-centric routes through these islands were not simply successive processes, but causally related ones in so far as the demise of the Phylakopi I system was the result of a long-range exercise of Cretan power, contemporary with, or just after, the building of the palaces. Two complementary motives might be proposed. One is the success of the island system, and its apparent non-integration with Cretan ways of doing things; as an alternative southern Aegean network for acquiring and circulating desirable goods and materials, it may have been simply too dynamic to be left intact, in addition to the fact that the imitation duck vases on Cyprus could indicate that islanders were reaching a part of the Mediterranean to which the Cretan centres wished to control access. The other motive is that the Phylakopi I culture settlements, and the east–west network that they articulated, lay directly across what was to become the central route from Crete to Lavrion. Access to Lavrion must have been crucial, given the value attributed to precious metals among the east Mediterranean complex societies that Cretan elites aspired to imitate. While a series of Cretan-influenced sites was established in the south-west Aegean in MM IA, thereby allowing access to the Peloponnese, the central route seems to have been essentially closed at this time, and indeed the Kytheran and Peloponnesian sites with MM IA material might well reflect an earlier, circuitous route towards Lavrion that avoided the Cyclades. A more direct route required that

---

[2] Broadly comparable regimes, albeit involving different centres and routes, existed in the later second millennium BC, when Mycenaean palatial centres dominated the Greek mainland (Schallin 1993). A brief return to a less externally regulated and perhaps more entrepreneurial system was to occur in the islands in the twelfth century BC, following the collapse of the Mycenaean palaces. Uncanny parallels exist between this phase and that of the Phylakopi I culture, not the least being the fact that in both periods island-specific liquid transport containers emerge as prominent elements in the material culture of trade.

the main nodes in the intervening island-based network become amenable to trade with Crete.

A scenario of early palatially organised attacks against off-island communities is compatible with the defensive stance taken at smaller Cretan settlements away from the emerging palace centres in the centuries on either side of the end of the third millennium BC. In east Crete, for example, where the first definite evidence for a palace building, at Petras, dates to a late phase of MM II (Tsipopoulou 1999), a considerable time after the foundation of the first palaces in the centre of the island, defensive sites include Kastri at Palaikastro (Sackett *et al.* 1965: 269–99), Chamaizi (Davaras 1972), Agia Photia Kouphota (Tsipopoulou 1988) and possibly Gournia and Vasiliki (Watrous 1994: 721). Seager (1909: 275, 1912: 101–2) reported a destruction horizon followed by reduced occupation at the hitherto flourishing settlement of Mochlos, the reduction in occupation being further confirmed by recent investigations at the site (Soles and Davaras 1992: 417, 426–7). One significant difference between the outlying areas of Crete and the islands to the north is, of course, that any intervention in the latter necessarily involved maritime action, and the use of the new shipping to compromise the islands' independence and effectively dictate the terms of their insularity. In this context, it is interesting to consider that the same technological introduction may have had a different impact in the islands and Crete. In the former area sailing ships were used as a vehicle for enhanced trade between independent if perhaps competing island centres. In the case of Crete, too, they were used for trade, but also to build a bridge to the east for the transfer of ideologies and technologies, and within the Aegean, as an instrument for the projection of economic or political dominance.

This model actually fits the current data from the Cyclades relatively well. Then, as later, Phylakopi and Akrotiri must have been the two crucial centres for controlling access to the Cyclades from Crete. The end of Phylakopi I itself came in the form of a destruction that razed the settlement. This was possibly followed by a period of desertion (Barber 1978: 368), before a reoccupation by a community with different pottery traditions, that concentrated the island's population at the site and enjoyed close contacts with Crete. Barber postulates an earthquake as the cause of the destruction, but this does not explain the hiatus in cultural traditions and possibly in time. Enemy action is, in the circumstances, a very plausible alternative. Phylakopi II's material culture is Cycladic enough to preclude any argument for Cretan reoccupants, but the duck vases and many other Phylakopi I traits disappear. At Akrotiri a sufficient MBA exposure has not been opened to enable a comparison with the sequence at Phylakopi. But Paroikia, a major Phylakopi I culture settlement that lay off the main route from Crete to Lavrion, sharply declined as the dendritic pattern became established (Davis 1979: 144; Overbeck 1989a: 20–1), and on Naxos the MBA centres at Mikri Vigla and Rizokastellia are on defendable hill-tops. On Amorgos and the remainder of the south-eastern Cyclades, a zone far from the main Cretan routes, the archaeological profile is now very low.

Further north, and further from Crete, the picture at Agia Irini IV is different. Cycladic duck vases and incised pottery are found in the new fortified settlement, well after production of such types had terminated at Phylakopi, along with large amounts of Cretan and minoanising material. A similar continuation of the duck vase tradition is seen at Kolonna, which was also fortified and has produced a unique iconography of boats bristling with warriors and spears (Siedentopf 1991: plates 35–8). It seems to be likely, therefore, that northern island communities, although realigning both spatially and culturally to exploit the new Cretan trade routes, maintained certain island traditions longer than did people in the south, and that they were also more successfully resistive to attempts at coercion by Cretan palaces. This distinction may help to explain why the later MBA cultural sequences of Phylakopi II and Agia Irini IV have proved so hard to integrate (Barber 1987: 143–4; Overbeck and Overbeck 1979). For as ever, the Cyclades were operating not as a cultural unit, but as a tangle of island communities pursuing converging and diverging pathways through history. But the vital difference this time, and not for the last time, was that the directions taken by those pathways had ceased to be primarily of the islanders' own making.

12

Cycladic archaeology as island archaeology

> Look, stranger, on this island now
> The leaping light for your delight discovers,
> Stand stable here
> And silent be,
> That through the channels of the ear
> May wander like a river
> The swaying sound of the sea.
>   *On this island,* W. H. AUDEN

Two interwoven aims have shaped this book. The first has been to write a history of the early Cyclades through an archaeology that is more specific, more general and more convincingly explanatory than its predecessors. That archaeology, it has been argued, must be an island archaeology. And the second aim has been to advocate change within the field of island archaeology itself, using the early Cyclades to illustrate the potential, challenge and rewards of different ways of understanding islands and island people in the past. These aims cannot, of course, be fully realised within the scope of an essay such as this. In the Cyclades, there remain spatial and temporal gaps in our knowledge, as well as limitations to the extent to which we can penetrate the significance of material culture. Likewise, the outline of a new island archaeology that was set out in chapter 1, and which the remaining chapters have tried to exemplify, requires far wider application and development in other island theatres before its overall relevance can be assessed. Yet despite these limits, we have seen that an island archaeological approach can shed light on the distant history of the Cyclades in ways that satisfy the complex archaeology of this specific island group, and enable us to view these islands in a wider comparative context. Ways of living in the early Cyclades were radically different from those of later history, let alone the present, but that does not mean that they need be incomprehensible to us. Once we decide what questions to ask, we start to appreciate that there is a great deal of sense (if a peculiarly *insular* sense) in the data, and that in a few cases we may in fact know more than we thought we did. And even where lacunae still predominate, we can better understand why this should be so, and start to establish the boundaries of our ignorance and uncertainty in ways that may enable us to transcend them in future. In closing, let us draw together, and briefly reflect upon, some of the major points that have emerged through the course of this exploration.

The island archaeology that has been advocated here views islands as prisms that refract human practices and desires in varied ways, creating people who are neither entirely different from the rest of the world nor yet wholly similar. Islands, it has been argued, are places rich in history and culture, and islanders' activities and ideas do just as much to remake islands, physically and in terms of the definition of their insularity, as an island's environment does to fashion island life. Insularity is, in short, a dynamic condition. Consequently, island archaeology must seek to discern the forms of ancient islandscapes (and abandon the expectation that discrete islands are necessarily useful analytical units), to practice an archaeology of the sea that is more than an archaeology of boats, to search for traces of sea-paths and modes of maritime interaction, movement and trade, and to engage with the detailed attributes and distributions of island material culture. Although island biogeography and island archaeology remain natural partners in investigating island worlds, the former cannot provide, and in fairness should not be expected to provide, an overall agenda for the history of islanders.

If these kinds of perspectives can indeed enrich our understanding of islands, the Cyclades and other Mediterranean insular regions should be destined to play a major role in the development of a new generation of island archaeology, rather than merely comprising case studies distant from the Pacific hub of research. For although no other theatre can match the Pacific in terms of size (even taking scaling factors into account), sheer numbers of islands and (in outer Oceania) perseverance for over a millennium as a world (almost) without continents, even the best-known parts of the Pacific, and equally the Caribbean, cannot match the density and diversity of archaeological data that have been encountered in just one small Mediterranean island group. In the archaeology of island societies across the world there can be very few, if any, examples that provide insights into the dynamics of island life as eloquent as those afforded by the Cyclades.

What are the main features of the island history that we have delineated for the early Cyclades? It is worth reminding ourselves that this is a very ancient history, one indeed that came to an end before the start of the Lapita phase in the Pacific, and which predates most knowledge of the pre-Columbian Caribbean. This implies that although serious parallels can be identified between the early Cyclades and other island societies, there may be basic differences with regard to the position of islands in the world as whole. For instance, although the period 2200–1900 BC in the Cyclades saw one of the earliest island endings, a distant premonition of the later fate of most islands, we have just seen that the processes by which this was worked through are unlikely to find close parallels in the history of recent centuries, after the break-out of the Western navigators, their world-system and its out-riders into the Atlantic, Indian and Pacific oceans.

As history, this exploration has been short on events. In the three millennia that have concerned us, there is no equivalent to the dramatic vulcanism or relatively recent mythistorical events that punctuate one recent account of Melanesian history (Spriggs 1997). In contrast, the second-millennium BC Aegean produces examples of both, in the form of a massive eruption of the Thera volcano, and the ideology of early Mycenaean Greece as it is distantly reflected in Homeric epic (Sherratt 1990). Instead, our island history has taken shape through comparison of changing patterns and practices in space and time, with the time-frames growing shorter through this book. Formally, it has also been lacking in identifiable individuals, although archaeological evidence and theoretical modelling have both indicated that individuals mattered a lot in the arenas of the islands, and we have come tantalisingly close to glimpsing personae and projections of identities at various junctures. One reason for the extraordinary diversity that has been seen in the preceding chapters may be the comparatively generous opportunities for individual or small-group initiatives afforded by a very small-scale demography acting in combination with the openings afforded by maritime incentives. This book has also affirmed that there is no intrinsic contradiction between reticulate history and long-term perspectives, and equally that bottom-up and top-down approaches will both be needed if we want to understand the local texture of the early Cycladic past and to place these islands appropriately in the Aegean and east Mediterranean worlds.

We can also highlight a few of the salient themes of early Cycladic history, that collectively take us some way towards understanding the richness of Cycladic material culture and its manifold ways of being deployed. One is the alteration of islandscapes through time. As acknowledged from chapter 3 onwards, the Cyclades are a somewhat fuzzy analytical set, and we have no assurance that they were recognised as a coherent group during the Neolithic and EBA. Much of the evidence from cultural distributions and modelled networks suggests that at certain levels they were not, with pan-Cycladic identities ('We, the Cycladic islanders') lost in a range of alignments encompassing more localised and wider affiliations. If we are correct in this, the Cyclades and early Cycladic culture are later inventions, the former dating to the era of the *kyklos* around Delos and the latter a creation of nineteenth-century archaeologists and twentieth-century aesthetes.

Within these islands, cultural islandscapes made up of patchworks of land and sea were the vital structuring factors in island life, with unitary islands commonly of limited importance prior to nucleation of settlement in the second millennium BC. Within these islandscapes, local sea-paths were defined by points that people wished to move between rather than by the patterns of winds and currents. At different times, different extents of these islandscapes were settled, with the latest Neolithic and EBA marking the peak of dispersion, and the preceding Neolithic and the MBA seeing more selective inhabitation (although each differed in its distribution and ways of exploiting the remaining areas). At particular points in these islandscapes that were advantaged environmentally (e.g. the niches occupied by some Saliagos culture villages) or in terms of intensity of communications (e.g. the EB II centres), and at times when the cultural conditions were favourable, people coalesced and created places with some long-term locational gravity amid a skein of shifting patterns. From the ultra long-term perspective that we enjoy, however, even these places and the regimes of island life that they constructed around them were transient, and one of the most exacting challenges has been to explain the rise and fall in cultural prominence of different areas, by asking what mattered when, where and why. It is interesting to reflect upon the differences between areas like the Erimonisia or Syros, which enjoyed a spectacular but limited period of glory dependent on a fairly precise set of conditions, and the regular prominence of much of Naxos, which seem to have been at the centre of things, albeit for changing reasons, from the earliest landfalls to the second millennium BC. Such high-profile areas can be contrasted with others that must also have possessed significance, but which were not culturally elaborated in ways that are now archaeologically visible, such as the obsidian and metal sources of the western Cyclades, or with certain archaeologically lower-profile areas in the islands, which might reflect different lifestyles as well as simply a lack of looking.

Movement, and particularly movement over the sea, has been a recurrent theme of this island archaeology of the early Cyclades, whether movement of people, animals, foodstuffs, objects, materials, customs or ideas, and with motives ranging from hunger to the pursuit of fame. There has been no sign of the alternating orientation towards exchange and monument-building that is suggested for Malta (Stoddart *et al.* 1993), nor of an esoteric efflorescence of culture even in the few relatively involuted areas of the Cyclades. But instead, we have seen astonishing variability between places and periods in the kinds of movement and interaction going on. What was moving? Over what distances? Between what places and people? Who did the moving? Why were they moving things? How frequently was movement effected? It is in fact through trying to answer these questions that we have come closest to explaining the changing dynamics of Cycladic societies. For example, to take just a single transect through this variability, long-range movement was a recurrent feature in the history of the early Cyclades, yet there was all the difference in the world between exploration and resource acquisition by visiting hunter-gatherers, the extensive but undifferentiated stylistic communication between Saliagos villages, the markedly low investment in long-range links during the Grotta-Pelos culture, the intensive, asymmetrical, symbolically laden voyaging of EB II, the commodity-oriented Phylakopi I culture activity, and the dendritic axes of maritime power established by early palatial Crete. Even this transect simply catches one highly visible variety of movement. If we instead oriented our transect across early Cycladic space at any point, we would discover endless variability between people and places in the degrees, purposes and motives for movement, albeit with certain phases displaying more differentiation than others. To underline the dominant type is therefore to miss the diversity. To illustrate this point, it is worth recalling that in EB II, a period best known for its inter-regional trade, people still had to find spouses, herd animals, buffer against harvest failures, and replenish material supplies, and that it was precisely such ongoing needs, set against the ever-altering conditions within which they had to be fulfilled, that generated the cross-cutting grains of activity out of which emerged the specific structures of power, forms of material culture, and dichotomies between open and closed cultural horizons that are seen in the islands at this time. The early history of the Cyclades is therefore, at one level, that of its islanders' movements, and if we over-simplify the latter, the former is sure to be the poorer for it.

A third recurrent theme of this book has been the relationship between a cluster of islands and the world beyond. In chapter 1, it was stressed that in all island theatres a degree of linkage with the outside world can be discerned, even if it is a faint hint like the dispersal of an American domesticated plant across the Pacific, or scraps of South-East Asian bronze in Melanesia. But external links played a particularly important role in the early Cyclades, as indeed in most of the Mediterranean islands, and contributed a distinctive element to island histories in this region. We have explored the relationships between the Cyclades and other areas at two levels. One has been the empirical tracing of routes, connections and inflows and exports of things, customs and ideas, which has allowed us to comprehend how people in the Cyclades established their islands' centrality in the Aegean and, equally, how objects or practices of exotic origin were incorporated into island culture. This has provided many insights into the complexities of the early material in the Cyclades, with island culture at several periods including a reworking of things derived from all over the Aegean, and possibly regions beyond.

The other level of exploration of external links has been more conceptual, and has concerned the role of external change (most immediately within the Aegean but also involving the Near East and east Mediterranean), in determining the overall history of the Cyclades. From the period of the Cretan palaces onwards, external influences were undoubtedly strong, but in the period that has concerned us for most of this book a more delicate balance has had to be struck between internal initiatives and the impact of external change. The subtleties of this balance have been most obvious in discussions of the period leading up to and during EB II, when we have had to integrate bottom-up approaches to the location and strategies of maritime centres with top-down processes, including an expanding Near Eastern world-system and associated phenomena such as exotic drinking styles and new metals. But it is implicit also in earlier shifts such as the change in community size and subsistence strategies at the end of the Neolithic, and in later issues such as the introduction of sailing vessels. The relative emphasis placed on local versus external processes at different places and points in time is certain to require fine-tuning, and in some cases perhaps more drastic revision. What can be stated with confidence, however, is that early Cycladic history as a whole must neither be reduced to an entirely reticulate or narrowly autonomous process, nor portrayed as a matter of mere details that were to be swamped in the long-term by world-systemic expansion.

Finally, what are the future prospects for an archaeology of the early Cyclades? At the empirical level, archaeological data will continue to emerge, and we only need to look at a site like Skarkos on Ios, whose finely preserved houses are currently being revealed, to remind ourselves that there are sure to be surprises in store. Other surprises are likely to be encountered in re-examination and republication of old data. But while certain categories of information look set to become better understood, others represent a more immediately finite, threatened resource. Of the latter, the cemeteries are the most alarming example, with looting and under-recorded early excavations probably having destroyed most of the funerary record in some parts of the Cyclades. More fieldwork is undoubtedly needed, not least in unknown areas. Recently developed scientific techniques are also certain to have a role to play. For example, the provenancing of material is an enormous yet rewarding task that still has a long way to go. An intensive programme of environmental sampling is also clearly essential, and in the more distant future we can imagine a role for DNA investigations of human bone that might dramatically advance understanding of the distributions of people in these islands. But now, as we conclude the centenary celebrations of the pioneering excavations at the end of the nineteenth century, and contemplate the prospect of a second hundred years of early Cycladic archaeology, we must recognise the overwhelming need for a strong research agenda and a coherent intellectual focus, as well as more fieldwork and better science. The development of a new island archaeology and the exploration of a first island history give us exactly that.

REFERENCES

Abu-Lughod, J. L. 1989. *Before European Hegemony: The World System A.D. 1250–1350.* Oxford: Oxford University Press.

Adams, J. and A. B. Kasakoff 1976. 'Factors underlying endogamous group size', in C. A. Smith (ed.), *Regional Analysis II: Social Systems*, 149–73. London: Academic Press.

Agouridis, C. 1997. 'Sea routes and navigation in the third millennium Aegean', *Oxford Journal of Archaeology* 16: 1–24.

Alden, J. R. 1979. 'A reconstruction of Toltec period political units in the Valley of Mexico', in A. C. Renfrew and K. L. Cooke (eds.), *Transformations: Mathematical Approaches to Culture Change*, 169–200. New York: Academic Press.

Alegría, R. E. 1983. *Ball Courts and Ceremonial Plazas in the West Indies* (Yale University Publications in Anthropology 79). New Haven: Department of Anthropology, Yale University.

Algaze, G. 1993. *The Uruk World System: The Dynamics of Expansion of Early Mesopotamian Civilization.* Chicago: University of Chicago Press.

Allen, J. 1977. 'Sea traffic, trade and expanding horizons', in J. Allen, J. Golson and R. Jones (eds.), *Sunda and Sahul: Prehistoric Studies in Southeast Asia, Melanesia and Australia*, 387–417. Canberra: Australian National University Press.

1984. 'Pots and poor princes: a multi-dimensional approach to the role of pottery trading in coastal Papua', in S. E. van der Leeuw and A. C. Pritchard (eds.), *The Many Dimensions of Pottery: Ceramics in Archaeology and Anthropology* (Cingula 7), 407–63. Amsterdam: University of Amsterdam.

Allen, J. and C. Gosden (eds.) 1991. *Report of the Lapita Homeland Project* (Occasional Papers in Prehistory 20). Canberra: Australian National University.

Ambrose, W. R. 1988. 'An early bronze artefact from Papua New Guinea', *Antiquity* 62: 483–91.

1997. 'Contradictions in Lapita pottery, a composite clone', *Antiquity* 71: 525–38.

Amorosi, T., P. Buckland, A. Dugmore, J. H. Ingimundarson and T. H. McGovern 1997. 'Raiding the landscape: human impact in the Scandinavian north Atlantic', *Human Ecology* 25: 491–518.

Andreou, S., M. Fotiades and K. Kotsakis 1996. 'Review of Aegean prehistory V: the Neolithic and Bronze Age of northern Greece', *American Journal of Archaeology* 100: 537–97.

Annual Report of the Managing Committee of the British School at Athens, 1986–7.

Anthony, D. W. 1990. 'Migration in archaeology: the baby and the bathwater', *American Anthropologist* 92: 895–914.

1996. 'V. G. Childe's world system and the daggers of the Early Bronze Age', in B. Wailes (ed.), *Craft Specialization and Social Evolution: In Memory of V. Gordon Childe* (University Museum Monograph 93/University Museum Symposium Series 6), 47–66. Philadelphia: University Museum of Archaeology and Anthropology.

References

Antonova, I., V. Tolstikov and M. Treister 1996. *The Gold of Troy: Searching for Homer's Fabled City*. London: Thames and Hudson.

Appadurai, A. 1986. 'Introduction: commodities and the politics of value', in A. Appadurai (ed.), *The Social Life of Things: Commodities in Cultural Perspective*, 3–63. Cambridge: Cambridge University Press.

Arnott, R. 1990. 'Early Cycladic objects from Ios formerly in the Finlay collection', *Annual of the British School at Athens* 85: 1–14.

Aron, F. 1979. *Ptyches tis archaias Syrou*. Athens.

Aruz, J. 1984. 'The silver cylinder seal from Mochlos', *Kadmos* 23: 186–8.

Atkinson, T. D., R. C. Bosanquet, C. C. Edgar, A. J. Evans, D. G. Hogarth, D. Mackenzie, C. Smith and F. B. Welch 1904. *Excavations at Phylakopi in Melos* (Society for the Promotion of Hellenic Studies Supplement 4). London: Macmillan.

Bahn, P. and J. Flenley 1992. *Easter Island Earth Island: A Message from our Past for the Future of our Planet*. London: Thames and Hudson.

Baladié, R. 1980. *Le Peloponnèse de Strabon: étude de géographie historique*. Paris: Société d'Edition 'Les Belles Lettres'.

Barber, R. L. N. 1978. 'The Cyclades in the Middle Bronze Age', in C. G. Doumas (ed.) *Thera and the Aegean World I*, 367–79. London: Thera and the Aegean World.

1981. 'A tomb at Ayios Loukas, Syros: some thoughts on early-middle Cycladic chronology', *Journal of Mediterranean Archaeology and Anthropology* 1: 167–70.

1983. 'The definition of the Middle Cycladic period', *American Journal of Archaeology* 87: 76–9.

1984. 'The pottery of Phylakopi, First City, Phase ii (I-ii)', in MacGillivray and Barber (eds.), 88–94.

1987. *The Cyclades in the Bronze Age*. London: Duckworth.

Barber, R. L. N. and O. Hadjianastasiou 1989. 'Mikre Vigla: a Bronze Age settlement on Naxos', *Annual of the British School at Athens* 84: 63–162.

Barber, R. L. N. and J. A. MacGillivray 1980. 'The Early Cycladic period: matters of definition and terminology', *American Journal of Archaeology* 84: 141–57.

1984. 'The prehistoric Cyclades: a summary', in MacGillivray and Barber (eds.), 296–302.

Basch, L. 1987. *Le musée imaginaire de la marine antique*. Athens: Hellenic Institute for the Preservation of Nautical Traditions.

Bass, B. 1998. 'Early Neolithic offshore accounts: remote islands, maritime exploitations, and the trans-Adriatic cultural network', *Journal of Mediterranean Archaeology* 11: 165–90.

Bass, G. 1987. 'Splendors of the Bronze Age', *National Geographic Magazine* 172: 693–732.

Bass, G., C. Pulak, D. Collon and J. Weinstein 1989. 'The Bronze Age shipwreck at Ulu Burun: 1986 campaign', *American Journal of Archaeology* 83: 1–29.

Beckett, J. 1988. *Torres Strait Islanders: Custom and Colonialism*. Cambridge: Cambridge University Press.

Bellard, C. G. 1995. 'The first colonization of Ibiza and Formentera (Balearic Islands, Spain): some more islands out of the stream?', *World Archaeology* 26: 442–55.

Bellwood, P. 1987. *The Polynesians: Prehistory of an Island People* (revised edition). London: Thames and Hudson.

1996. 'Phylogeny *vs* reticulation in prehistory', *Antiquity* 70: 881–90.

Bellwood, P. and P. Koon 1989. '"Lapita colonists leave boats unburned!": the question of Lapita links with island southeast Asia', *Antiquity*: 63: 613–22.

Belmont, J. S. and A. C. Renfrew 1964. 'Two prehistoric sites in Mykonos', *American Journal of Archaeology* 68: 395–400.

Bender, B. (ed.) 1993. *Landscape: Politics and Perspectives.* Providence: Berg.
Bennet, J. 1997. 'Homer and the Bronze Age', in I. Morris and B. Powell (eds.), *A New Companion to Homer,* 511–34. Leiden: Brill.
Bennet, J. and S. Voutsaki 1991. 'A synopsis and analysis of travelers' accounts of Keos (to 1821)', in Cherry, Davis and Mantzourani, 365–82.
Bent, J. T. 1884. 'Researches among the Cyclades', *Journal of Hellenic Studies* 5: 42–58.
  1888. 'Discoveries in Asia Minor', *Journal of Hellenic Studies* 9: 82–7.
Bernabò-Brea, L. 1964. *Poliochni: città preistorica nell'isola di Lemnos* (Volume I). Rome: L'"Erma' di Bretschneider.
  1976 *Poliochni: città preistorica nell'isola di Lemnos* (Volume II). Rome: L'"Erma' di Bretschneider.
Best, E. 1925. *The Maori Canoe* (Dominion Museum Bulletin 7). Wellington: W. A. G. Skinner.
Betancourt, P. 1985. *The History of Minoan Pottery.* Princeton: Princeton University Press.
Betancourt, P., C. R. Floyd and J. D. Muhly 1997. 'Excavations at Chrysokamino, Crete, 1996', *American Journal of Archaeology* 101: 374–5 (abstract).
Betts, J. 1971. 'Ships on Minoan seals', in D. J. Blackman (ed.), *Marine Archaeology* (Colston Papers V.23), 325–38. London: Butterworths.
Bikaki, A. H. 1984. *Keos IV. Ayia Irini: The Potter's Marks.* Mainz on Rhine: Philipp von Zabern.
Bintliff, J. L. 1977a. *Natural Environment and Human Settlement in Prehistoric Greece* (British Archaeological Reports Supplementary Series 28). Oxford: British Archaeological Reports.
  1977b. 'Appendix 2: the number of burials in the Mesara tholoi', in D. Blackman and K. Branigan, 'An archaeological survey of the lower catchment of the Ayiofarango valley', *Annual of the British School at Athens* 72: 13–84.
Birdsell, J. B. 1977. 'The recalibration of a paradigm for the first peopling of Greater Australia', in J. Allen, J. Golson and R. Jones (eds.), *Sunda and Sahul: Prehistoric Studies in Southeast Asia, Melanesia and Australia,* 113–67. Canberra: Australian National University Press.
Black, S. J. 1978. 'Polynesian outliers: a study in the survival of small populations', in I. Hodder (ed.) *Simulation Studies in Archaeology,* 63–76. Cambridge: Cambridge University Press.
  1980. 'Demographic models and island colonisation in the Pacific', *New Zealand Journal of Archaeology* 2: 51–64.
Blegen, C. W., J. L. Caskey, M. Rawson and J. Sperling 1950. *Troy I. General Introduction, the First and Second Settlements.* Princeton: Princeton University Press.
Blegen, C. W. and J. Haley 1928. 'The coming of the Greeks', *American Journal of Archaeology* 32: 141–54.
Bökönyi, S. 1986. 'Faunal remains', in A. C. Renfrew, M. Gimbutas and E. S. Elster (eds.), *Excavations at Sitagroi: A Prehistoric Village in Northeast Greece* (UCLA Institute of Archaeology Monumenta Archaeologica 13), 63–96. Los Angeles: UCLA Institute of Archaeology.
Bosanquet, R. C. 1904. 'The obsidian trade', in Atkinson *et al.*, 216–33.
Bossert, E.-M. 1954. 'Zur Datierung der Gräber von Arkesine auf Amorgos', in W. Kimmig (ed.), *Festschrift für Peter Goessler,* 23–34. Stuttgart: Kohlhammer.
  1960. 'Die gestempelten Verzierungen auf frühbronzezeitlichen Gefässen der Ägäis', *Jahrbuch des deutschen archäologischen Instituts* 75: 1–16.
  1967. 'Kastri auf Syros: Vorbericht über eine Untersuchung der prähistorischen Siedlung', *Archaiologikon Deltion* (Meletai) 22: 53–76.
Bourdieu, P. 1977. *Outline of a Theory of Practice.* Cambridge: Cambridge University Press (English translation of French original published in 1972).

Bowdler, S. 1995. 'Offshore islands and maritime explorations in Australian prehistory', *Antiquity* 69: 945–58.

Bradley, R. 1990. *The Passage of Arms: An Archaeological Analysis of Prehistoric Hoards and Votive Deposits*. Cambridge: Cambridge University Press.

1993. *Altering the Earth: The Origins of Monuments in Britain and Continental Europe* (Society of Antiquaries of Scotland Monograph Series 8). Edinburgh: Society of Antiquaries of Scotland.

Branigan, K. 1970. *The Tombs of Mesara*. London: Duckworth.

1971. 'Cycladic figurines and their derivatives in Crete', *Annual of the British School at Athens* 66: 57–78.

1974. *Aegean Metalwork of the Early and Middle Bronze Age*. Oxford: Clarendon Press.

1981. 'Minoan colonialism', *Annual of the British School at Athens* 76: 23–33.

1988. *Pre-Palatial. The Foundations of Palatial Crete: A Survey of Crete in the Early Bronze Age*. Amsterdam: Adolf M. Hakkert.

1991. 'Mochlos: an early Aegean "gateway community"?', in R. Laffineur and L. Basch (eds.), *Thalassa: L'Egée préhistorique et la mer* (Aegaeum 7), 97–105. Liège: Université de Liège.

1993. *Dancing with Death: Life and Death in Southern Crete, c. 3000–2000 BC*. Amsterdam: Adolf M. Hakkert.

1998a. 'Prehistoric and early historic settlement in the Ziros region, eastern Crete', *Annual of the British School at Athens* 93: 23–90.

1998b. 'The nearness of you: proximity and distance in early Minoan funerary landscapes', in K. Branigan (ed.), *Cemetery and Society in the Aegean Bronze Age* (Sheffield Studies in Aegean Archaeology 1), 13–26. Sheffield: Sheffield Academic Press.

Braudel, F. 1949. *La Méditerranée et le monde méditerranéen à l'époque de Phillippe II*. Paris: Armand Colin.

1972. *The Mediterranean and the Mediterranean World in the Age of Philip II*. London: Collins (English translation of French original published in 1949).

Briois, F., B. Gratuze and J. Guilaine 1997. 'Obsidiennes du site néolithique précéramique de *Shillourokambos* (Chypre)', *Paléorient* 23: 95–112.

Brock, J. K. and G. Mackworth Young 1949. 'Excavations in Siphnos', *Annual of the British School at Athens* 44: 1–92.

Broodbank, C. 1989. 'The longboat and society in the Cyclades in the Keros-Syros culture', *American Journal of Archaeology* 93: 319–37.

1992. 'The spirit is willing', *Antiquity* 66: 542–6.

1993. 'Ulysses without sails: trade, distance, knowledge and power in the early Cyclades', *World Archaeology* 24: 315–31.

1996. 'This small world the great: an island archaeology of the early Cyclades'. PhD dissertation, University of Cambridge.

1999. 'Colonization and configuration in the insular Neolithic of the Aegean', in P. Halstead (ed.), *Neolithic Society in Greece* (Sheffield Studies in Aegean Archaeology 2), 15–41. Sheffield: Sheffield Academic Press.

2000. 'Perspectives on an Early Bronze Age island centre: an analysis of pottery from Daskaleio-Kavos (Keros) in the Cyclades', *Oxford Journal of Archaeology* 19.

Broodbank, C. and T. F. Strasser 1991. 'Migrant farmers and the Neolithic colonization of Crete', *Antiquity* 65: 233–45.

Brookfield, H. C. with D. Hart 1971. *Melanesia: A Geographical Interpretation of an Island World*. London: Methuen.

Brotherston, G. 1992. *Book of the Fourth World: Reading the Native Americas Through Their Literature*. Cambridge: Cambridge University Press.

Brown, J. H. and A. Kodric-Brown 1977. 'Turnover rates in insular biogeography: effect of immigration on extinction', *Ecology* 58: 630–4.

Budd, P., A. M. Pollard, B. Scaife and R. G. Thomas 1995. 'Oxhide ingots, recycling and the Mediterranean metals trade', *Journal of Mediterranean Archaeology* 8: 1–32.

Budd, P. and T. Taylor 1995. 'The faerie smith meets the bronze industry: magic versus science in the interpretation of prehistoric metal-making', *World Archaeology* 27: 133–43.

Burney, D. A. 1997. 'Tropical islands as paleoecological laboratories: gauging the consequences of human arrival', *Human Ecology* 25: 437–57.

Cadogan, G. 1986. 'Why was Crete different?', in G. Cadogan (ed.), *The End of the Early Bronze Age in the Aegean*, 153–71. Leiden: Brill.

Canby, J. V. 1965. 'Early Bronze Age trinket moulds', *Iraq* 27: 42–61.

Cann, J. R., J. E. Dixon and A. C. Renfrew 1968. 'Appendix IV: the sources of the Saliagos obsidian', in Evans and Renfrew, 105–7.

Carter, T. 1994. 'Southern Aegean fashion victims: an overlooked aspect of Early Bronze Age burial practices', in N. Ashton and A. David (eds.), *Stories in Stone*, 127–44. London: Lithic Studies Society.

1998. 'Reverberations of the international spirit: thoughts upon "Cycladica" in the Mesara', in K. Branigan (ed.), *Cemetery and Society in the Aegean Bronze Age* (Sheffield Studies in Aegean Archaeology 1), 59–77. Sheffield: Sheffield Academic Press.

1999. 'Through a glass darkly: obsidian and society in the southern Aegean Early Bronze Age'. PhD dissertation, University of London.

in prep. 'Cinnabar and the Cyclades: body modification and political structure in the late EB I Aegean', in H. Erkanal (ed.), *The Aegean in the Neolithic, Chalcolithic and Early Bronze Age*.

Carter, T. and M. Ydo 1996. 'The chipped and ground stone', in Cavanagh *et al.*, 141–82.

Case, H. 1969. 'Neolithic explanations', *Antiquity* 43: 176–86.

Caskey, J. L. 1964. 'Greece, Crete and the Aegean islands in the Early Bronze Age', in *The Cambridge Ancient History* (Volume I.2; 3rd edition), 771–807. Cambridge: Cambridge University Press.

1971a. 'Investigations in Keos, part I: excavations and explorations, 1966–1970', *Hesperia* 40: 358–96.

1971b. 'Marble figurines from Ayia Irini, Keos', *Hesperia* 40: 113–26.

1972. 'Investigations in Keos, part II: a conspectus of the pottery', *Hesperia* 41: 357–401.

1974. 'Addenda to the marble figurines from Ayia Irini', *Hesperia* 43: 77–9.

Casson, L. 1971. *Ships and Seamanship in the Ancient World*. Princeton: Princeton University Press.

1989. *The Periplous Maris Erythraei*. Princeton: Princeton University Press.

Catling, H. W. and V. Karageorghis 1960. 'Minoika in Cyprus', *Annual of the British School at Athens* 55: 109–27.

Catling, H. W. and J. A. MacGillivray 1983. 'An Early Cypriote III vase from the palace at Knossos', *Annual of the British School at Athens* 78: 1–8.

Cavanagh, W. G., J. H. Crouwel, R. W. V. Catling and G. Shipley 1996. *Continuity and Change in a Greek Rural Landscape: The Laconia Survey. II. Archaeological Data* (British School at Athens Supplementary Volume 27). London: British School at Athens.

Cavanagh, W. G. and C. Mee 1998. *A Private Place: Death in Prehistoric Greece* (Studies in Mediterranean Archaeology 125). Jonsered: Paul Åströms Förlag.

Chapman, R. 1990. *Emerging Complexity: The Later Prehistory of South-East Spain, Iberia and the West Mediterranean.* Cambridge: Cambridge University Press.

Chaudhuri, K. N. 1985. *Trade and Civilisation in the Indian Ocean: An Economic History from the Rise of Islam to 1750.* Cambridge: Cambridge University Press.

  1990. *Asia before Europe: Economy and Civilisation of the Indian Ocean from the Rise of Islam to 1750.* Cambridge: Cambridge University Press.

Chaunu, P. 1979. *European Expansion in the Later Middle Ages.* Amsterdam: North Holland.

Chernykh, E. N. 1992. *Ancient Metallurgy in the USSR.* Cambridge: Cambridge University Press.

Cherry, J. F. 1979. 'Four problems in Cycladic prehistory', in Davis and Cherry (eds.), 22–47.

  1981. 'Pattern and process in the earliest colonization of the Mediterranean islands', *Proceedings of the Prehistoric Society* 47: 41–68.

  1982a. 'A preliminary definition of site distribution on Melos', in Renfrew and Wagstaff (eds.), 10–23.

  1982b. 'Appendix A: register of archaeological sites on Melos', in Renfrew and Wagstaff (eds.), 291–309.

  1983. 'Evolution, revolution and the origins of complex society in Minoan Crete', in O. Krzyszkowska and L. Nixon (eds.), *Minoan Society*, 33–45. Bristol: Bristol Classical Press.

  1984a. 'The emergence of the state in the prehistoric Aegean', *Proceedings of the Cambridge Philological Society* 30: 18–48

  1984b. 'The initial colonization of the West Mediterranean islands in the light of island biogeography and paleogeography', in W. H. Waldren, R. Chapman, J. Lewthwaite and R.-C. Kennard (eds.), *The Deyà Conference of Prehistory: Early Settlement in the Western Mediterranean Islands and the Peripheral Areas* (British Archaeological Reports International Series 229), 7–23. Oxford: British Archaeological Reports.

  1985. 'Islands out of the stream: isolation and interaction in early east Mediterranean insular prehistory', in A. B. Knapp and T. Stech (eds.), *Prehistoric Production and Exchange: The Aegean and Eastern Mediterranean* (UCLA Institute of Archaeology Monograph 25), 12–29. Los Angeles: UCLA Institute of Archaeology.

  1987. 'Island origins: the early prehistoric Cyclades', in B. Cunliffe (ed.), *Origins: The Roots of European Civilisation*, 15–29. London: BBC Books.

  1988. 'Pastoralism and the role of animals in the pre- and protohistoric economies of the Aegean', in C. R. Whittaker (ed.), *Pastoral Economies in Classical Antiquity* (Cambridge Philological Society Supplementary Volume 14), 6–34. Cambridge: Cambridge Philological Society.

  1990. 'The first colonization of the Mediterranean islands: a review of recent research', *Journal of Mediterranean Archaeology* 3: 145–221.

  1992a. 'Beazley in the Bronze Age? Reflections on attribution studies in Aegean prehistory', in R. Laffineur and J. L. Crowley (eds.), *Eikon: Aegean Bronze Age Iconography: Shaping a Methodology* (Aegaeum 8), 123–44. Liège: Université de Liège.

  1992b. 'Palaeolithic Sardinians? Some questions of evidence and method', in R. H. Tykot and T. K. Andrews (eds.), *Sardinia in the Mediterranean: A Footprint in the Sea* (Monographs in Mediterranean Archaeology 3), 28–39. Sheffield: Sheffield Academic Press.

Cherry, J. F. (ed.) 1995. *Colonization of Islands* (*World Archaeology* 26). London: Routledge.

Cherry, J. F. and J. L. Davis 1991. 'The Ptolemaic base at Koressos on Keos', *Annual of the British School at Athens* 86: 9–28.

References

Cherry, J. F., J. L. Davis and E. Mantzourani 1991. *Landscape Archaeology as Long-Term History: Northern Keos in the Cycladic Islands from Earliest Settlement to Modern Times* (UCLA Institute of Archaeology Monumenta Archaeologica 16). Los Angeles: UCLA Institute of Archaeology.

Cherry, J. F. and R. Torrence 1982. 'The earliest prehistory of Melos', in Renfrew and Wagstaff (eds.), 24–34.

  1984. 'The typology and chronology of chipped stone assemblages in the prehistoric Cyclades', in MacGillivray and Barber (eds.), 12–25.

Childe, V. G. 1957. *The Dawn of European Civilization* (6th edition). London: Routledge and Kegan Paul.

Chippindale, C. 1993. 'Editorial', *Antiquity* 67: 699–708.

Christmann, E. 1996. *Die frühe Bronzezeit: Die deutsche Ausgrabungen auf der Pefkakia-Magula in Thessalien 2*. (Beitrage zur ur- und frühgeschichtlichen Archäologie des Mittelmeer-Kulturraumes 29). Bonn: R. Habelt.

Cline, E. H. 1994. *Sailing the Wine-dark Sea: International Trade in the Late Bronze Age Aegean* (British Archaeological Reports International Series 591). Oxford: Tempus Reparatum.

Clutton-Brock, J. 1982. 'The animal bones', in M. S. F. Hood, *Excavations in Chios 1938–1955: Prehistoric Emporio and Ayio Gala II* (British School at Athens Supplementary Volume 16), 678–97. London: British School at Athens.

Coldstream, J. N. and G. L. Huxley (eds.), 1972. *Kythera: Excavations and Studies*. London: Faber and Faber.

Coleman, J. E. 1977. *Keos I. Kephala: A Late Neolithic Settlement and Cemetery*. Princeton: Princeton University Press.

  1979a. 'Chronological and cultural divisions of the Early Cycladic period: a critical appraisal', in Davis and Cherry (eds.), 48–50.

  1979b. 'Remarks on "Terminology and beyond"', in Davis and Cherry (eds.), 64–5.

  1985. '"Frying pans" of the Early Bronze Age Aegean', *American Journal of Archaeology* 89: 191–219.

  1992. 'Greece and the Aegean', in R.W. Ehrich (ed.), *Chronologies in Old World Archaeology* (3rd edition), 247–88. Chicago: University of Chicago Press.

Columbus, C. 1492. *Journal of the First Voyage* (edited and translated by B. W. Ife 1990). Warminster: Aris and Phillips.

Conkey, M. W. and C. A. Hastorf (eds.), 1990. *The Uses of Style in Archaeology*. Cambridge: Cambridge University Press.

Corbett, D. G., C. Lefevre and D. Siegel-Causey 1997. 'The western Aleutians: cultural isolation and environmental change', *Human Ecology* 25: 459–79.

Cosgrove, D. E. 1984. *Social Formation and Symbolic Landscape*. London: Croom Helm.

Cosmopoulos, M. B. 1991. *The Early Bronze 2 in the Aegean* (Studies in Mediterranean Archaeology 97). Jonsered. Paul Åströms Förlag.

Coy, J. P. 1977. 'Animal remains', in Coleman, 129–32.

Crosby, A. W. 1986. *Ecological Imperialism: The Biological Expansion of Europe, 900–1900*. Cambridge: Cambridge University Press.

Crouwel, J. H. 1981. *Chariots and Other Means of Land Transport in Bronze Age Greece*. Amsterdam: Allard Pierson.

Dalfes, H. N., G. Kukla and H. Weiss (eds.), 1997. *Third Millennium BC Climate Change and Old World Collapse*. Berlin: Springer.

Dalongeville, R. and J. Renault-Miskovsky 1993. 'Paysages passés et actuels de l'île de Naxos', in R. Dalongeville and G. Rougemont (eds.), *Recherches dans les Cyclades*, 9–57. Lyons: Maison de l'Orient Méditerranéen.

Darwin, C. 1859. *On the Origin of Species by Means of Natural Selection*. London: John Murray.

Davaras, C. 1971. 'Protominoikon nekrotapheion Agias Photias Siteias', *Athens Annals of Archaeology* 4: 392–7.

  1972. 'The oval house at Chamaizi reconsidered', *Athens Annals of Archaeology* 5: 283–8.

  nd. *Hagios Nikolaos Museum*. Athens: Editions Hannibal.

Davidson, D. A., C. Renfrew and C. Tasker 1976. 'Erosion and prehistory in Melos: a preliminary note', *Journal of Archaeological Science* 3: 219–27.

Davis, J. L. 1979. 'Minos and Dexithea: Crete and the Cyclades in the later Bronze Age', in Davis and Cherry (eds.), 143–57.

  1980. 'Minoans and minoanization at Ayia Irini, Keos', in C. G. Doumas (ed.), *Thera and the Aegean World II*, 257–60. London: Thera and the Aegean World.

  1982a. 'Thoughts on prehistoric and Archaic Delos', *Temple University Aegean Symposium* 7: 23–33.

  1982b. 'The earliest Minoans in the southeast Aegean: a reconsideration of the evidence', *Anatolian Studies* 32: 33–41.

  1984a. 'A Cycladic figure in Chicago and the non-funereal use of Cycladic marble figures', in Fitton (ed.), 15–21.

  1984b. 'Cultural innovation and the Minoan thalassocracy at Ayia Irini, Keos', in Hägg and Marinatos (eds.), 159–66.

  1987. 'Perspectives on the prehistoric Cyclades: an archaeological introduction', in Getz-Preziosi 1987b, 4–45.

  1991. 'Contributions to a Mediterranean rural archaeology: historical case studies from the Ottoman Cyclades', *Journal of Mediterranean Archaeology* 4: 131–216.

  1992. 'Review of Aegean prehistory I: the islands of the Aegean', *American Journal of Archaeology* 96: 699–756.

  2000. 'Review of Aegean prehistory I: the islands of the Aegean' (revised and updated), in T. Cullen (ed.), *A Review of Aegean Prehistory* (American Journal of Archaeology Supplement 1). Boston: Archaeological Institute of America.

Davis, J. L. and J. F. Cherry 1990. 'Spatial and temporal uniformitarianism in Late Cycladic I: perspectives from Kea and Milos on the prehistory of Akrotiri', in D. A. Hardy, C. G. Doumas, J. A. Sakellarakis and P. M. Warren (eds.), *Thera and the Aegean World III. I. Archaeology*, 185–200. London: Thera Foundation.

Davis, J. L. and J. F. Cherry (eds.), 1979. *Papers in Cycladic Prehistory* (UCLA Institute of Archaeology Monograph 14). Los Angeles: UCLA Institute of Archaeology.

Davis, J. L., E. Schofield, R. Torrence and D. F. Williams 1983. 'Keos and the eastern Aegean: the Cretan connection', *Hesperia* 52: 361–6.

Day, P. M., D. E. Wilson and E. Kiriatzi 1998. 'Pots, labels and people: burying ethnicity in the cemetery at Aghia Photia, Siteias', in K. Branigan (ed.), *Cemetery and Society in the Aegean Bronze Age* (Sheffield Studies in Aegean Archaeology 1), 133–49. Sheffield: Sheffield Academic Press.

Deagan, K. (ed.), 1995. *Puerto Real: The Archaeology of a Sixteenth-Century Spanish Town in Hispaniola*. Gainesville: University Press of Florida.

de Angelis, F. 1998. 'Ancient past, imperial present: the British Empire in T. J. Dunbabin's *The Western Greeks*', *Antiquity* 72: 539–49.

Deetz, J. 1991. 'Introduction: archaeological evidence of sixteenth- and seventeenth-century encounters', in L. Falk (ed.), *Historical Archaeology in Global Perspective*, 1–9. Washington: Smithsonian Institution Press.

de Laguna, F. 1972. *Under Mount Saint Elias: The History and Culture of the Yakutat Tlingit*. Washington: Smithsonian Institute Press.

Demoule, J.-P. and C. Perlès 1993. 'The Greek Neolithic: a new review', *Journal of World Prehistory* 7: 355–416.

Denoon, D. 1997. 'Land, labour and independent development', in D. Denoon (ed.), *The Cambridge History of the Pacific Islanders*, 152–84. Cambridge: Cambridge University Press.

Dermitzakis, M. D. and P. Y. Sondaar 1978. 'The importance of fossil mammals in reconstructing paleogeography with special reference to the Pleistocene Aegean archipelago', *Annales Géologiques des Pays Helléniques* 29: 808–40.

Dewar, R. E. 1995. 'Of nets and trees: untangling the reticulate and dendritic in Madagascar's prehistory', *World Archaeology* 26: 301–18.

 1997. 'Does it matter that Madagascar is an island?', *Human Ecology* 25: 481–9.

Diamant, S. 1977. 'A barbed and tanged obsidian point from Marathon', *Journal of Field Archaeology* 4: 381–6.

Diamond, J. M. 1972. 'Biogeographic kinetics: estimation of relaxation times for avifaunas of southwest Pacific islands', *Proceedings of the National Academy of Sciences, USA* 69: 3199–203.

 1974. 'Colonization of exploded volcanic islands by birds: the super-tramp strategy', *Science* 184: 803–6.

 1977. 'Colonization cycles in man and beasts', *World Archaeology* 8: 249–61.

Diamond, J. M. and W. F. Keegan 1984. 'Supertramps at sea', *Nature* 311: 704–5.

Diamond, J. M. and E. Mayr 1976. 'Species–area relation for birds of the Solomon archipelago', *Proceedings of the National Academy of Sciences, USA* 73: 262–6.

Dickinson, O. T. P. K. 1977. *The Origins of Mycenaean Civilisation* (Studies in Mediterranean Archaeology 49). Göteborg: Paul Åströms Förlag.

Dimopoulou, N. 1997. 'Workshops and craftsmen in the harbour town of Knossos at Poros-Katsambas', in R. Laffineur and P. P. Betancourt (eds.), *TEXNH: Craftsmen, Craftswomen and Craftsmanship in the Aegean Bronze Age* (Aegaeum 16), 433–8. Liège: University of Liège.

Doumas, C. G. 1964. 'Archaiotites kai mnimeia Kykladon', *Archaiologikon Deltion* (Chronika) 19: 409–12.

 1965. 'Korphi t'Aroniou', *Archaiologikon Deltion* (Meletai) 20: 41–64.

 1972. 'Notes on Cycladic architecture', *Archäologischer Anzeiger* 87: 151–70.

 1976a. 'Protokykladiki kerameiki apo ta Christiana Theras', *Archaiologiki Ephimeris* 1976: 1–11.

 1976b. 'Proïstorikoi Kykladites stin Kriti', *Athens Annals of Archaeology* 9: 69–80.

 1977. *Early Bronze Age Burial Habits in the Cyclades* (Studies in Mediterranean Archaeology 48). Göteborg: Paul Åströms Förlag.

 1979. 'Proïstorikoi Kykladites stin Kriti', *Athens Annals of Archaeology* 12: 104–9.

 1983a. *Cycladic Art: Ancient Sculpture and Pottery from the N. P. Goulandris Collection*. London: British Museum Press.

 1983b. *Thera: Pompeii of the Ancient Aegean*. London: Thames and Hudson.

 1988. 'EBA in the Cyclades: continuity or discontinuity?', in E. B. French and K. A. Wardle (eds.), *Problems in Greek Prehistory*, 21–9. Bristol: Bristol Classical Press.

References

1990. 'Death', in Marangou (ed.), 93–5.

1992a. *The Wall-Paintings of Thera*. Athens: Kapon.

1992b. 'An early Cycladic "hooked-tang" spearhead from Naxos', in G. K. Ioannidis (ed.), *Studies in Honour of Vassos Karageorghis* (Kypriakai Spoudai 54–5), 67–8. Lefkosia: Etaireia Kypriakon Spoudon.

Doumas, C. G. and N. Angelopoulou 1997. 'Oi vasikoi keramikoi typoi tis Poliochnis kai i diadosi tous sto Aigaio kata tin Proimi Epochi tou Chalkou', in Doumas and La Rosa (eds.), 543–55.

Doumas, C. G. and V. La Rosa (eds.), 1997. *I Poliochni kai i Proimi Epochi tou Chalkou sto Voreio Aigaio/Poliochni e l'Antica Età del Bronzo nell'Egeo Settentrionale*. Athens: Panepistimio Athinon Tomeas Archaiologias kai Istorias tis Technis/Scuola Archeologica Italiana di Atene.

Doumas, C. G., A. C. Renfrew and L. Marangou nd. 'Radiocarbon dates from Keros (Dhaskaleio Kavos)' (manuscript).

Dousougli-Zachos, A. 1993. 'Sas-Höhle', in I. Pini (ed.), *Corpus der minoischen und mykenischen Siegeln* 5, Supplement 1B, 103–9. Berlin: Mann.

Drucker, P. 1951. *The Northern and Central Nootkan Tribes* (Smithsonian Institution Bureau of American Ethnology Bulletin 144). Washington: Government Printing Office.

Dugit, E. 1874. *Naxos et les établissements Latins de l'Archipel*. Paris.

Dümmler, F. 1886. 'Mitteilungen von den griechischen Inseln', *Mitteilungen des deutschen archäologischen Instituts: Athenische Abteilung* 2: 15–46.

Edgar, C. C. 1904. 'The pottery marks. A: occurrence of the marks', in Atkinson *et al.*, 177–80.

Edwards, N. 1990. *The Archaeology of Early Medieval Ireland*. London: Batsford.

Efstratiou, N. 1985. *Ayios Petros: A Neolithic Site in the Northern Sporades* (British Archaeological Reports International Series 241). Oxford: British Archaeological Reports.

Elia, R. J. 1993. 'A seductive and troubling work', *Archaeology* 46: 64–9.

Erard-Cerceau, I., V. Fotou, O. Psychogos and R. Treuil 1993. 'Prospection archéologique à Naxos (région nord-ouest)', in R. Dalongeville and G. Rougemont (eds.), *Recherches dans les Cyclades* (Collection de la Maison de l'Orient Méditerranéen 23), 59–96. Lyons: Maison de l'Orient Méditerranéen.

Eriksen, T. H. 1993. 'In which sense do cultural islands exist?', *Social Anthropology* 1: 133–47.

Erkanal, H. 1996. 'Early Bronze Age urbanization in the coastal region of western Anatolia', in Y. Sey (ed.), *Housing and Settlement in Anatolia: A Historical Perspective*, 70–82. Istanbul: Türkiye Ekonomik ve Toplumsal Tarih Vakfi.

Etienne, R. and E. Dourlot 1996. 'Les Cyclades', in E. Lanzillotta and D. Schilardi (eds.), *I Cicladi ed il mondo Egeo*, 21–31. Rome: University of Rome 'Tor Vergala'.

Evans, J. D. 1973. 'Islands as laboratories for the study of culture process', in A. C. Renfrew (ed.), *The Explanation of Culture Change: Models in Prehistory*, 517–20. London: Duckworth.

1977. 'Island archaeology in the Mediterranean: problems and opportunities', *World Archaeology* 9: 12–26.

1994. 'The early millennia: continuity and change in a farming settlement', in D. Evely, H. Hughes-Brock and N. Momigliano (eds.), *Knossos: A Labyrinth of History. Papers in Honour of Sinclair Hood*, 1–20. Oxford: British School at Athens.

Evans, J. D. and A. C. Renfrew 1968. *Excavations at Saliagos near Antiparos* (British School at Athens Supplementary Volume 5). London: British School at Athens.

Evans, R. K. and A. C. Renfrew 1984. 'The earlier Bronze Age at Phylakopi', in MacGillivray and Barber (eds.), 63–9.

Fagan, B. M. 1998. *Clash of Cultures* (2nd edition). London: Sage Publications.

Fairbanks, R. G. 1989. 'A 17,000 year-old glacio-eustatic sea level record: influence of glacial melting rates on the Younger Dryas event and deep ocean circulation', *Nature* 342: 637–42.

Figueira, T. J. 1981. *Aegina: Society and Politics*. New York: Arno Press.

Finney, B. 1994. *Voyage of Rediscovery: A Cultural Odyssey through Polynesia*. Berkeley: University of California Press.

Firth, R. 1936. *We, the Tikopia*. London: George Allen and Unwin.

Fischer, S. R. 1997. *Rongorongo – The Easter Island Script: History, Traditions, Texts*. Oxford: Oxford University Press.

Fitton, J. L. (ed.), 1984. *Cycladica: Studies in Memory of N. P. Goulandris*. London: British Museum Publications.

Fitzhugh, B. and T. L. Hunt 1997. 'Introduction: islands as laboratories: archaeological research in comparative perspective', *Human Ecology* 25: 379–83.

Fitzhugh, W. 1997. 'Biogeographical archaeology in the eastern North American Arctic', *Human Ecology* 25: 385–418.

Flannery, T. F. 1994. *The Future Eaters: An Ecological History of the Australasian Lands and People*. London: Secker and Warburg.

Flannery, T. F. and J. P. White 1991. 'Animal translocation', *National Geographic Research and Exploration* 7: 96–113.

Flood, J. 1995. *Archaeology of the Dreamtime: The Story of Prehistoric Australia and its People*. Sydney: Angus and Robertson.

Forbes, H. 1976. '"We have a little of everything": the ecological basis of some agricultural practices in Methana, Trizinia', *Annals of the New York Aacademy of Sciences* 268: 236–50.

Forge, A. 1972. 'Normative factors in the settlement size of Neolithic cultivators (New Guinea)', in P. J. Ucko, R. Tringham and G. W. Dimbleby (eds.), *Man, Settlement and Urbanism*, 363–76. London: Duckworth.

Forsén, J. 1992. *The Twilight of the Early Helladics: A Study of the Disturbances in East-Central and Southern Greece towards the End of the Early Bronze Age* (Studies in Mediterranean Archaeology and Literature Pocket-book 116). Jonsered: Paul Åströms Förlag.

Fosberg, F. R. (ed.), 1963. *Man's Place in the Island Ecosystem*. Honolulu: Bishop Museum.

Fotou, V. 1983. 'Les sites de l'époque néolithique et de l'âge du bronze à Naxos (recherches archéologiques jusqu'en 1980)', in G. Rougemont (ed.), *Les Cyclades: matériaux pour une étude de géographie historique*, 15–57. Paris: Editions du Centre National de la Recherche Scientifique.

Foucault, M. 1986. 'Of other spaces', *Diacritics* 16: 22–7.

Frake, C. 1985. 'Cognitive maps of time and tide among medieval seafarers', *Man* N.S. 20: 254–70.

Frank, A. G. and B. Gills 1993. *The World System: 500 Years or 5000?* London: Routledge.

Fraser, P. M. and G. E. Bean 1954. *The Rhodian Peraea and Islands*. Oxford: Oxford University Press.

French, C. A. I. and T. M. Whitelaw 1999. 'Soil erosion, agricultural terracing and site formation processes at Markiani, Amorgos, Greece: the micromorphological perspective', *Geoarchaeology* 14: 151–89.

French, D. H. 1968. 'The pottery', in M. R. Popham and L. H. Sackett (eds.), *Excavations at Lefkandi, Euboia 1964–6: A Preliminary Report*, 9. London: British School of Archaeology in Athens and Thames and Hudson.

Friedman, J. 1982 'Catastrophe and continuity in social evolution', in A. C. Renfrew, M. Rowlands and B. Seagraves (eds.), *Theory and Explanation in Archaeology*, 175–96. New York: Academic Press.

Furness, A. 1956. 'Some early pottery of Samos, Kalimnos and Chios', *Proceedings of the Prehistoric Society* 22: 173–212.

Galani, G., L. G. Mendoni and H. Papageorgiadou 1987. 'Epiphaneiaki erevna stin Kea', *Archaiognosia* 3: 237–44.

Gale, N. H. 1998. 'The role of Kea in metal production and trade in the Late Bronze Age', in Mendoni and Mazarakis Ainian (eds.), 737–58.

Gale, N. H. and Z. A. Stos-Gale 1981. 'Cycladic lead and silver metallurgy', *Annual of the British School at Athens* 76: 169–224.

1984. 'Cycladic metallurgy', in MacGillivray and Barber (eds.), 255–76.

Gale, N. H., Z. A. Stos-Gale and J. L. Davis 1984. 'The provenance of lead used at Ayia Irini, Keos', *Hesperia* 53: 389–406.

Gale, N. H., Z.A. Stos-Gale and A. Papastamataki 1988. 'An Early Bronze Age copper smelting site on the Aegean island of Kythnos, part I: scientific evidence', in J. Ellis Jones (ed.), *Aspects of Ancient Metallurgy and Mining*, 23–30. Bangor: Department of Classics, University of North Wales.

Gallant, T. W. 1985. *A Fisherman's Tale: An Analysis of the Potential Productivity of Fishing in the Ancient World* (Miscellanea Graeca 7). Brussels: University of Ghent.

1991. *Risk and Survival in Ancient Greece: Reconstructing the Rural Domestic Economy.* Cambridge: Polity Press.

Gamble, C. S. 1979. 'Surplus and self-sufficiency in the Cycladic subsistence economy', in Davis and Cherry (eds.), 122–34.

1982. 'Animal husbandry, population and urbanisation', in Renfrew and Wagstaff (eds.), 161–71.

1993. *Timewalkers: The Prehistory of Global Colonization.* Stroud: Alan Sutton.

Garanger, J. 1972. *Archéologie des Nouvelles Hébrides* (Publications de la Société des Océanistes 30). Paris: Musée de l'Homme.

Geertz, C. 1975. 'Common sense as a cultural system', *Antioch Review* 33; reprinted in C. Geertz (1983), *Local Knowledge: Further Essays in Interpretive Anthropology*, 73–93. New York: Basic Books.

Gejvall, N.-J. 1969. *Lerna: A Preclassical Site in the Argolid. I. The Fauna.* Princeton: American School of Classical Studies in Athens.

Georgiou, H. 1991. 'Bronze Age ships and rigging', in R. Laffineur and L. Basch (eds.), *Thalassa: L'Egée préhistorique et la mer* (Aegaeum 7), 61–71. Liège: University of Liège.

1993. 'A sea approach to trade in the Aegean Bronze Age', in C. W. Zerner (ed.), *Wace and Blegen: Pottery as Evidence for Trade in the Aegean Bronze Age 1939–1989*, 353–64. Amsterdam: J. C. Gieben.

Georgiou, H. and N. Faraklas 1985. 'Ancient habitation patterns of Keos: locations and nature of sites on the northwest part of the island', *Ariadne* 3: 207–66.

1993. 'Archaia katoikisi stin Kea: to voreio tmima tis anatolikis plevras tou nisiou', *Ariadne* 6: 7–57.

Getz-Gentle, P. 1996. *Stone Vessels of the Cyclades in the Early Bronze Age.* University Park: Pennsylvania State University Press.

Getz-Preziosi, P. 1977. 'Cycladic sculptors and their methods', in Thimme (ed.), 71–91.

1987a. *Sculptors of the Cyclades: Individual and Tradition in the Third Millennium BC.* Ann Arbor: University of Michigan Press.

1987b. *Early Cycladic Art in North American Collections.* Seattle: University of Washington Press.

1982. '"The Keros hoard": introduction to an Early Cycladic enigma', in D. Metzler and B. Otto (eds.), *Antidoron: Festschrift für Jürgen Thimme*, 37–44. Karlsruhe: C. F. Müller.

Gifford, E. and J. Gifford 1997. 'The probable sailing capabilities of Middle Minoan Aegean ships', *The Mariner's Mirror* 83: 199–206.

Gill, D. W. J. and C. Chippindale 1993. 'Material and intellectual consequences of esteem for Cycladic figures', *American Journal of Archaeology* 97: 601–59.

Gladwin, T. 1970. *East is a Big Bird*. Cambridge, Mass.: Harvard University Press.

Glazier, S. D. 1991. 'Impressions of aboriginal technology: the Caribbean canoe', in E. N. Ayubi and J. B. Haviser (eds.), *Proceedings of the Thirteenth International Congress for Caribbean Archaeology* (Reports of the Archaeological-Anthropological Institute of the Netherlands Antilles 9). Curaçao.

Godelier, M. and M. Strathern (eds.), 1991. *Big Men and Great Men: Personifications of Power in Melanesia*. Cambridge: Cambridge University Press.

Goldman, I. 1957. 'Variations in Polynesian social organization', *Journal of the Polynesian Society* 66: 374–90.

Goodenough, W. H. 1957. 'Oceania and the problem of controls in the study of cultural and human evolution', *Journal of the Polynesian Society* 66: 146–55.

Gosden, C. 1993. *Social Being and Time*. Oxford: Blackwells.

Gosden, C., J. Allen, W. Ambrose, D. Anson, J. Golson, R. Green, P. Kirch, I. Lilley, J. Specht and M. Spriggs 1989. 'Lapita sites of the Bismarck archipelago', *Antiquity* 63: 561–86.

Gosden, C. and L. Head 1994. 'Landscape: a usefully ambiguous concept', *Archaeology in Oceania* 29: 113–16.

Gosden, C. and C. Pavlides 1994. 'Are islands insular? Landscape vs. seascape in the case of the Arawe islands, Papua New Guinea', *Archaeology in Oceania* 29: 162–71.

Graves, M. W. and D. J. Addison 1995. 'The Polynesian settlement of the Hawaiian archipelago: integrating models and methods in archaeological interpretation', *World Archaeology* 26: 380–99.

Graziadio, G. 1991. 'The process of social stratification at Mycenae in the Shaft Grave period: a comparative examination of the evidence', *American Journal of Archaeology* 95: 403–40.

Greenblatt, S. 1991. *Marvelous Possessions: The Wonder of the New World*. Oxford: Clarendon Press.

Gropengiesser, H. 1987. 'Siphnos, Kap Agios Sostis: keramische prähistorische Zeugnisse aus dem Gruben- und Hüttenrevier II', *Mitteilungen des deutschen archäologischen Instituts (Athenische Abteilung)* 102: 1–54.

Grove, R. H. 1995. *Green Imperialism: Colonial Expansion, Tropical Island Edens and the Origins of Environmentalism, 1600–1860*. Cambridge: Cambridge University Press.

Guilaine, J., F. Briois, J. Coularou and I. Carrère 1995. 'L'établissement néolithique de Shillourokambos (Parekklisha, Chypre): premiers résultats', *Report of the Department of Antiquities, Cyprus* 1995: 11–31.

Haddon, A. C. and J. Hornell 1936–8. *Canoes of Oceania* (B. P. Bishop Museum Special Publications 27–9). Honolulu: Bishop Museum.

Hadjianastasiou, O. 1988. 'A Late Neolithic settlement at Grotta, Naxos', in E. B. French and K. A. Wardle (eds.), *Problems in Greek Prehistory*, 11–20. Bristol: Bristol Classical Press.

1989. 'Some hints of Naxian external connections in the earlier Late Bronze Age', *Annual of the British School at Athens* 84: 205–15.

1993. 'Naxian pottery and external relations in Late Cycladic I–II', in C. W. Zerner (ed.), *Wace and Blegen: Pottery as Evidence for Trade in the Aegean Bronze Age 1939–1989*, 257–62. Amsterdam: J. C. Gieben.

References

1996. 'Kastellos: mia proïstoriki thesi sti Pholegandro', *I Kathimerini* 28/7/1996 (supplement): 4.

1998. 'Simeioseis apo tin Kythno', in Mendoni and Mazarakis Ainian (eds.), 259–73.

Hadjianastasiou, O. and J. A. MacGillivray 1988. 'An Early Bronze Age copper smelting site on the Aegean island of Kythnos, part II: archaeological evidence', in J. Ellis Jones (ed.), *Aspects of Ancient Metallurgy and Mining*, 31–4. Bangor: Department of Classics, University of North Wales.

Hage, P. and F. Harary 1991. *Exchange in Oceania: A Graph Theoretical Analysis*. Oxford: Clarendon Press.

1996. *Island Networks: Communication, Kinship, and Classification Structures in Oceania* (Structural Analysis in the Social Sciences 11). Cambridge: Cambridge University Press.

Hägg, R. and D. Konsola (eds.), 1986. *Early Helladic Architecture and Urbanization* (Studies in Mediterranean Archaeology 76). Göteborg: Paul Åströms Förlag.

Hägg, R. and N. Marinatos (eds.), 1984. *The Minoan Thalassocracy: Myth and Reality*. Stockholm: Paul Åströms Förlag.

Haggis, D. 1997. 'The typology of the Early Minoan I chalice and the cultural implications of form and style in Early Bronze Age ceramics', in R. Laffineur and P. P. Betancourt (eds.), *TEXNH: Craftsmen, Craftswomen and Craftsmanship in the Aegean Bronze Age* (Aegaeum 16), 291–9. Liège: University of Liège.

Halstead, P. 1981a. 'From determinism to uncertainty: social storage and the rise of the Minoan palace', in A. Sheridan and G. Bailey (eds.), *Economic Archaeology: Towards an Integration of Ecological and Social Approaches* (British Archaeological Reports International Series 96), 187–213. Oxford: British Archaeological Reports.

1981b. 'Counting sheep in Neolithic and Bronze Age Greece', in I. Hodder, G. Isaac and N. Hammond (eds.), *Pattern of the Past: Studies in Memory of David Clarke*, 307–39. Cambridge: Cambridge University Press.

1987a. 'Traditional and ancient rural economy in Mediterranean Europe: *plus ça change?*', *Journal of Hellenic Studies* 107: 77–87.

1987b. 'Man and other animals in later Greek prehistory', *Annual of the British School at Athens* 82: 71–83.

1988. 'On redistribution and the origin of Minoan-Mycenaean palatial economies', in E. B. French and K. A. Wardle (eds.), *Problems in Greek Prehistory*, 519–28. Bristol: Bristol Classical Press.

1989. 'The economy has a normal surplus: economic stability and social change among early farming communities of Thessaly, Greece', in P. Halstead and J. O'Shea (eds.), *Bad Year Economics*, 68–80. Cambridge: Cambridge University Press.

1994. 'The north–south divide: regional paths to complexity in prehistoric Greece', in C. Mathers and S. Stoddart (eds.), *Development and Decline in the Mediterranean Bronze Age* (Sheffield Archaeological Monographs 8), 195–219. Sheffield: J. R. Collis Publications.

1996a. 'The development of agriculture and pastoralism in Greece: when, how, who and what?', in D. R. Harris (ed.), *The Origins and Spread of Agriculture and Pastoralism in Eurasia*, 296–309. London: UCL Press.

1996b. 'Pastoralism or household herding? Problems of scale and specialization in early Greek animal husbandry', *World Archaeology* 28: 20–42.

1998. 'Mortality models and milking: problems of uniformitarianism, optimality and equifinality reconsidered', *Anthropozoologica* 27: 320.

in prep. 'Pastoralism and marginal colonisation: LN–EC3 animal exploitation at the cave of Zas, Naxos' (manuscript).

Halstead, P. and G. Jones 1987. 'Bioarchaeological remains from Kalythies cave', in Sampson, 135–52.

    1989. 'Agrarian ecology in the Greek islands: time, stress, scale and risk', *Journal of Hellenic Studies* 109: 41–55.

Halstead, P. and J. O'Shea 1982. 'A friend in need is a friend indeed: social storage and the origins of social ranking', in A. C. Renfrew and S. Shennan (eds.), *Ranking, Resource and Exchange*, 92–9. Cambridge: Cambridge University Press.

Hamilakis, Y. 1996. 'Wine, oil and the dialectics of power in Bronze Age Crete: a review of the evidence', *Oxford Journal of Archaeology* 15: 1–32.

    1998. 'Eating the dead: mortuary feasting and the politics of memory in the Aegean Bronze Age societies', in K. Branigan (ed.), *Cemetery and Society in the Aegean Bronze Age* (Sheffield Studies in Aegean Archaeology 1), 115–32. Sheffield: Sheffield Academic Press.

Hansen, J. M. 1988. 'Agriculture in the prehistoric Aegean: data versus speculation', *American Journal of Archaeology* 92: 39–52.

Harding, T. G. 1967. *Voyagers of the Vitiaz Strait*. Seattle: University of Washington Press.

Harris, D. R. 1979. 'Foragers and farmers in the western Torres Strait islands: an historical analysis of economic, demographic, and spatial differentiation', in P. C. Burnham and R. F. Ellen (eds.), *Social and Ecological Systems* (Association of Social Anthropologists Monograph 18), 75–109. London: Academic Press.

Hassan, F. 1981. *Demographic Archaeology*. New York: Academic Press.

Hather, J. and P. V. Kirch 1991. 'Prehistoric sweet potato (*Ipomoea batatas*) from Mangaia Island, central Polynesia', *Antiquity* 65: 887–93.

Hau'ofa, E. 1993. 'Our sea of islands', in E. Waddell, V. Naidu and E. Hau'ofa (eds.), *A New Oceania: Rediscovering Our Sea of Islands*, 2–16. Fiji: University of the South Pacific Press.

Heiken, G. and F. McCoy 1984. 'Caldera development during the Minoan eruption, Thera, Cyclades, Greece', *Journal of Geophysical Research* 89: 8441–62.

Hekman, J. J. 1994. 'Chalandriani on Syros: an Early Bronze Age cemetery in the Cyclades', *Archaiologiki Ephemeris* 133: 47–74.

Held, S. O. 1989a. 'Colonization cycles on Cyprus, 1: the biogeographic and palaeontological foundations of early prehistoric settlement', *Report of the Department of Antiquities, Cyprus* 1989: 7–28.

    1989b. 'Early prehistoric island archaeology in Cyprus: configurations of formative culture growth from the Pleistocene/Holocene boundary to the mid-3rd millennium BC'. PhD dissertation, Institute of Archaeology, University College London.

Helms, M. W. 1988. *Ulysses' Sail: An Ethnographic Odyssey of Power, Knowledge, and Geographical Distance*. Princeton: Princeton University Press.

    1993. *Craft and the Kingly Ideal: Art, Trade and Power*. Austin: University of Texas Press.

Hendrix, E. 1998. 'Painted ladies of the Early Bronze Age', *Metropolitan Museum of Art Bulletin* 55: 4–15.

Herz, N. and C. Doumas 1991. 'Marble sources in the Aegean Early Bronze Age', in E. Pernicka and G. A. Wagner (eds.), *Archaeometry '90*, 425–34. Basel: Birkhäuser Verlag.

Heyerdahl, T. 1952. *American Indians in the Pacific*. Chicago: Rand McNally.

Higgs, E. S., I. M. Clegg and I. A. Kinnes 1968. 'Appendix VII: Saliagos animal bones', in Evans and Renfrew, 114–17.

Hill, J. N. and J. Gunn (eds.), 1977. *The Individual in Prehistory: Studies of Variability in Style in Prehistoric Technologies*. London: Academic Press.

Hiller, S. 1993. 'Minoan and minoanizing pottery on Aegina', in C. W. Zerner (ed.), *Wace and Blegen: Pottery as Evidence for Trade in the Aegean Bronze Age 1939–1989*, 197–9. Amsterdam. J. C. Gieben.

Hodder, I. 1990. *The Domestication of Europe: Structure and Contingency in Neolithic Societies*. Oxford: Basil Blackwell.

Honea, K. 1975. 'Prehistoric remains on the island of Kythnos', *American Journal of Archaeology* 79: 277–9.

Hope Simpson, R. and O. T. P. K. Dickinson 1979. *A Gazetteer of Aegean Civilisation in the Bronze Age. I. The Mainland and Islands* (Studies in Mediterranean Archaeology 52). Göteborg. Paul Åströms Förlag.

Hunt, T. L. 1988. 'Graph theoretical network models for Lapita exchange: a trial application', in Kirch and Hunt (eds.), 135–55.

Hutton, J. H. 1951. 'Less familiar aspects of primitive trade', *Proceedings of the Prehistoric Society* 7: 171–6.

Immerwahr, S. A. 1971. *The Athenian Agora: Results of Excavations Conducted by the American School of Classical Studies at Athens. XIII. The Neolithic and Bronze Ages*. Princeton: Princeton University Press.

Irwin, G. 1974. 'The emergence of a central place in coastal Papuan prehistory: a theoretical approach', *Mankind* 9: 268–72.

  1977. 'Pots and entrepots: a study of settlement, trade and the development of economic specialization in Papuan prehistory', *World Archaeology* 9: 299–319.

  1983. 'Chieftainship, kula and trade in Massim prehistory', in Leach and Leach (eds.), 29–72.

  1985. *The Emergence of Mailu* (Terra Australis 10). Canberra: Australian National University.

  1989. 'Against, across and down the wind: a case for the systematic exploration of the remote Pacific islands', *Journal of the Polynesian Society* 98: 167–206.

  1992. *The Prehistoric Exploration and Colonisation of the Pacific*. Cambridge: Cambridge University Press.

Irwin, G., S. H. Bickler and P. Quirke 1990. 'Voyaging by canoe and computer: experiments in the settlement of the Pacific', *Antiquity* 64: 34–50.

Jameson, M. H., C. N. Runnels and T. H. van Andel 1994. *A Greek Countryside: The Southern Argolid from Prehistory to the Present Day*. Stanford: Stanford University Press.

Jarman, M. R. 1996. 'Human influence in the development of the Cretan mammalian fauna', in Reese (ed.), 211–29.

Jarman, M. R. and H. N. Jarman 1968. 'The fauna and economy of Early Neolithic Knossos', in P. M. Warren, M. R. and H. N. Jarman, N. J. Shackleton and J. D. Evans, 'Knossos Neolithic, Part II', *Annual of the British School at Athens* 63: 239–85.

Johnson, M. 1996. 'Water, animals and agricultural technology: a study of settlement patterns and economic change in Neolithic southern Greece', *Oxford Journal of Archaeology* 15: 167–95.

Johnston, P. F. 1985. *Ship and Boat Models in Ancient Greece*. Annapolis: Naval Institute Press.

Johnstone, P. 1988. *The Sea-Craft of Prehistory* (2nd edition). London: Routledge.

Jones, R. 1976. 'Tasmania: aquatic machines and offshore islands', in G. de G. Sieveking, I. H. Longworth and K. E. Wilson (eds.), *Problems in Economic and Social Archaeology*, 235–63. London: Duckworth.

  1977. 'Man as an element of a continental fauna: the case of the sundering of the Bassian bridge', in J. Allen, J. Golson and R. Jones (eds.), *Sunda and Sahul: Prehistoric Studies in Southeast Asia, Melanesia and Australia*, 317–86. Canberra: Australian National University Press.

Joukowsky, M. S. 1996. *Early Turkey: Anatolian Archaeology from Prehistory through the Lydian Period*. Dubuque: Kendall/Hunt.

Kambouroglou, E., H. Maroukian and A. Sampson 1988. 'Coastal evolution and archaeology north and south of Khalkis (Euboia) in the last 5000 years', in A. Raban (ed.), *Archaeology of Coastal Changes: Proceedings of the First International Symposium 'Cities on the Sea – Past and Present'* (British Archaeological Report International Series 404), 71–9. Oxford: British Archaeological Reports.

Karantzali, E. 1996. *Le Bronze Ancien dans les Cyclades et en Crète: les relations entre les deux régions; influence de la Grèce continentale* (British Archaeological Reports International Series 631). Oxford: Tempus Reparatum.

Karo, G. 1930. 'Archäologische Funde aus dem Jahre 1929 under der ersten Hälfte in 1930: Griechenland und Dodekanes', *Archäologischer Anzeiger* 45: 88–167.

Kavvadias, G. 1984. *I Palaiolithiki Kephallonia: o politismos tou Physkardou*. Athens: Phytraki.

Keegan, W. F. 1985. 'Dynamic horticulturalists: population expansion in the prehistoric Bahamas'. PhD dissertation, University of California, Los Angeles.

  1992. *The People Who Discovered Columbus: The Prehistory of the Bahamas*. Gainesville: University of Florida Press.

  1995. 'Modeling dispersal in the prehistoric West Indies', *World Archaeology* 26: 400–20.

Keegan, W. F. and J. M. Diamond 1987. 'Colonization of islands by humans: a biogeographical perspective', in M. Schiffer (ed.), *Advances in Archaeological Method and Theory* 10, 49–92. New York: Academic Press.

Keller, D. R. 1982. 'Final Neolithic pottery from Plakari, Karystos', in P. Spitaels (ed.), *Studies in Southern Attica I* (Miscellanea Graeca 5), 47–67. Ghent: Belgian Archaeological Mission in Greece.

Keller, D. R. and T. Cullen 1992. 'Prehistoric occupation of the Paximadhi peninsula, southern Euboia', *American Journal of Archaeology* 96: 341 (abstract).

Kirch, P. V. 1984. *The Evolution of the Polynesian Chiefdoms*. Cambridge: Cambridge University Press.

  1986. 'Exchange systems and inter-island contact in the transformation of an island society: the Tikopia case', in P. V. Kirch (ed.), *Island Societies: Archaeological Approaches to Evolution and Transformation*, 33–41. Cambridge: Cambridge University Press.

  1988. 'Long-distance exchange and island colonization: the Lapita case', *Norwegian Archaeological Review* 21: 103–17.

  1990. 'Specialization and exchange in the Lapita complex of Oceania (1600–500 BC)', *Asian Perspectives* 29: 117–33.

Kirch, P. V. and J. Ellison 1994. 'Palaeoenvironmental evidence for human colonization of remote Oceanic islands', *Antiquity* 68: 310–21.

Kirch, P. V. and R. C. Green 1987. 'History, phylogeny, and evolution in Polynesia', *Current Anthropology* 28: 431–56.

Kirch, P. V. and T. L. Hunt 1988. *Archaeology of the Lapita Cultural Complex: A Critical Review* (Thomas Burke Memorial Washington State Museum Research Report 5). Seattle.

Kirch, P. V. and T. L. Hunt (eds.), 1997. *Historical Ecology in the Pacific Islands: Prehistoric Environmental and Landscape Change*. New Haven: Yale University Press.

Kirch, P. V. and M. D. Sahlins 1992. *Anahulu: The Anthropology of History in the Kingdom of Hawaii*. Chicago: University of Chicago Press.

Kirch, P. V. and D. E. Yen 1982. *Tikopia: The Prehistory and Ecology of a Polynesian Outlier* (B. P. Bishop Museum Bulletin 238). Honolulu: Bishop Museum.

Knapp, A. B. 1990. 'Paradise gained and paradise lost: intensification, specialization, complexity, collapse', *Asian Perspectives* 28: 179–214.

Knapp, A. B. (ed.), 1996. *Sources for the History of Cyprus II: Near Eastern and Aegean Texts from the Third to the First Millennia BC*. Altamont: Greece and Cyprus Research Center.

Knapp, A. B. and J. F. Cherry 1994. *Provenience Studies and Bronze Age Cyprus: Production, Exchange and Politico-economic Change* (Monographs in World Archaeology 21). Madison: Prehistory Press.

Knapp, A. B. and L. Meskell 1997. 'Bodies of evidence on prehistoric Cyprus', *Cambridge Archaeological Journal* 7: 183–204.

Kontoleon, N. M. 1949. 'Anaskaphai en Naxou', *Praktika tis en Athinais Archaiologikis Etaireias* 1949: 112–22.

1970. 'Anaskaphai Naxou', *Praktika tis en Athinais Archaiologikis Etaireias* 1970: 146–55.

1971. 'Anaskaphai Naxou', *Praktika tis en Athinais Archaiologikis Etaireias* 1971: 172–80.

1972. 'Anaskaphai Naxou', *Praktika tis en Athinais Archaiologikis Etaireias* 1972: 143–55.

Kopytoff, I. 1986. 'The cultural biography of things: commoditization as process', in A. Appadurai (ed.), *The Social Life of Things: Commodities in Cultural Perspective*, 64–91. Cambridge: Cambridge University Press.,

Koutsoukou, A. 1992. 'An archaeological survey in NW Andros, Cyclades'. Ph.D dissertation, University of Edinburgh.

1993. 'Archaiologiki epiphaneiaki erevna stin voreioditiki Andro', *Andriaka Chronika* 21: 99–110.

Krzyszkowska, O. 1981. 'The bone and ivory industries of the Aegean Bronze Age: a technological study'. PhD dissertation, University of Bristol.

1983. 'Wealth and prosperity in pre-palatial Crete: the case of ivory', in O. Krzyszkowska and L. Nixon (eds.), *Minoan Society*, 163–70. Bristol: Bristol Classical Press.

1984. 'Ivory from hippopotamus tusk in the Aegean Bronze Age', *Antiquity* 48: 123–5.

Küchler, S. 1993. 'Landscape as memory: the mapping of process and its representation in a Melanesian society', in Bender (ed.), 85–106.

Kuklick, H. 1996. 'Islands in the Pacific: Darwinian biogeography and British anthropology', *American Ethnologist* 23: 611–38.

Kyrou, A. K. 1990. *Sto stavrodromi tou Argolikou*. Athens: Photosyn Abee.

Lambeck, K. 1996. 'Sea-level change and shore-line evolution in Aegean Greece since Upper Palaeolithic time', *Antiquity* 70: 588–611.

Lambert, N. 1973. 'Vestiges préhistoriques dans l'île de Makronissos', *Athens Annals of Archaeology* 6: 1–12.

1981. *La grotte préhistorique de Kitsos (Attique), missions 1968–78. I. l'occupation néolithique, les vestiges des temps paléolithiques, de l'antiquité et de l'histoire récente*. Paris: ADPF – Ecole Française d'Athènes.

Lambrinoudakis, V. 1979. 'Anaskaphes Naxou', *Praktika tis en Athinais Archaiologikis Etaireias* 1979: 249–58.

1990. 'Archaeological research on the Early Cycladic period in Naxos', in Marangou (ed.), 25–6.

Las Casas, B. de 1951. *Historia de las Indias* (ed. A. Millares Carlo). Mexico City.

Lax, E. and T. F. Strasser 1992. 'Early Holocene extinctions on Crete: the search for the cause', *Journal of Mediterranean Archaeology* 5: 203–24.

Leach, J. W. and E. Leach (eds.), 1983. *The Kula: New Perspectives on Massim Exchange*. Cambridge: Cambridge University Press.

Lemonnier, P. (ed.), 1993. *Technological Choices: Transformations in Material Cultures since the Neolithic*. London: Routledge.

Levi, D. 1925–6. 'La necropoli Geometrica di Kardiani a Tinos', *Annuario della regia scuola archeologica di Atene e della missioni Italiane in oriente* 8–9: 203–34.

   1961–2. 'Le due prime campagne di scavo a Iasos (1960–1), *Annuario della scuola archeologica di Atene e della missioni Italiane in oriente* N.S. 23–4: 504–71.

   1965–6. 'Le campagne 1962–4 a Iasos', *Annuario della scuola archeologica di Atene e della missioni Italiane in oriente* N.S. 27–8: 401–56.

Levison, M., R. G. Ward and J. W. Webb 1973. *The Settlement of Polynesia: A Computer Simulation*. Minneapolis: University of Minnesota Press.

Lewis, D. 1972. *We, the Navigators*. Canberra: Australian National University Press.

Lilley, I. 1988. 'Prehistoric exchange across the Vitiaz Strait, Papua New Guinea', *Current Anthropology* 29: 513–16.

Linnekin, J. 1997. 'Contending approaches', in D. Denoon (ed.), *The Cambridge History of the Pacific Islanders*, 3–31. Cambridge: Cambridge University Press.

Lohmann, H. 1993. *Atene: Forschungen zu Siedlungs- und Wirtschaftsstruktur des Klassischen Attica*. Cologne: Böhlau Verlag.

McArthur, N., I. W. Saunders and R. L. Tweedie 1976. 'Small population isolates: a microsimulation study', *Journal of the Polynesian Society* 85: 307–26.

MacArthur, R. H. and E. O. Wilson 1967. *The Theory of Island Biogeography*. Princeton: Princeton University Press.

MacCluer, J. N. and B. Dyke 1976. 'On the minimum size of endogamous populations', *Social Biology* 23: 1–12.

McGeehan Liritzis, V. 1988. 'Seafaring, craft and cultural contact in the Aegean during the 3rd millennium BC', *International Journal of Nautical Archaeology* 17: 237–56.

   1996. *The Role and Development of Metallurgy in the Late Neolithic and Early Bronze Age* (Studies in Mediterranean Archaeology and Literature Pocket-book 122). Angered: Paul Åströms Förlag.

MacGillivray, J. A. 1980. 'Mount Kynthos in Delos: the Early Cycladic settlement', *Bulletin de Correspondance Héllenique* 104: 3–45.

   1983. 'On the relative chronologies of Early Cycladic IIIA and Early Helladic III', *American Journal of Archaeology* 87: 81–3.

   1984. 'The relative chronology of Early Cycladic III', in MacGillivray and Barber (eds.), 70–7.

MacGillivray, J. A. and R. L. N. Barber (eds.), 1984. *The Prehistoric Cyclades: Contributions to a Workshop on Cycladic Chronology*. Edinburgh: Department of Classical Archaeology, University of Edinburgh.

MacGillivray, J. A., P. M. Day and R. E. Jones 1988. 'Dark-faced incised pyxides and lids from Knossos: problems of date and origin', in E. B. French and K. A. Wardle (eds.), *Problems in Greek Prehistory*, 91–4. Bristol: Bristol Classical Press.

McGrail, S. 1988. 'Assessing the performance of an ancient boat – the Hasholme logboat', *Oxford Journal of Archaeology* 7: 35–46.

   1990. 'The theoretical performance of a hypothetical reconstruction of the Clapton logboat', *International Journal of Nautical Archaeology* 19: 129–33.

   1991. 'Bronze Age seafaring in the Mediterranean: a view from N.W. Europe', in N. H. Gale (ed.), *Bronze Age Trade in the Mediterranean* (Studies in Mediterranean Archaeology 90), 83–91. Jonsered: Paul Åströms Förlag.

Mackenzie, D. 1904. 'The successive settlements at Phylakopi in the Aegeo-Cretan relations', in Atkinson *et al.*, 238–72.

McNeill, J. R. 1993. Comment on A. G. Frank 'Bronze Age world system cycles', *Current Anthropology* 34: 417.

McNeill, W. H. 1976. *Plagues and Peoples*. London: Penguin Books.

Malinowski, B. 1922. *Argonauts of the Western Pacific*. London: Routledge and Kegan Paul.

Mallowan, M. E. L. 1939. 'Phoenician carrying trade, Syria', *Antiquity* 13: 86–7.

Malone, C. 1999. 'Processes of colonisation in the central Mediterranean', in E. Herring, R. Whitehouse and J. Wilkins (eds.), *Accordia Research Papers* 7: 37–57.

Manning, S. W. 1994. 'The emergence of divergence: development and decline on Bronze Age Crete and the Cyclades', in C. Mathers and S. Stoddart (eds.), *Development and Decline in the Mediterranean Bronze Age* (Sheffield Archaeological Monographs 8), 221–70. Sheffield: John Collis Publications.

　1995. *The Absolute Chronology of the Aegean Early Bronze Age: Archaeology, Radiocarbon and History* (Monographs in Mediterranean Archaeology 1). Sheffield: Sheffield Academic Press.

　1997. 'Cultural change in the Aegean c.2200 BC', in Dalfes, Kukla and Weiss (eds.), 147–71.

Manti, V. 1993. 'Prosdiorismos tis proelevsis tou marmarou archaion mnimeion me tis technikes tou ilektronikou paramagnitikou syntonismou kai tis netronikes energopoiisis'. PhD dissertation, University of Athens.

Maran, J. 1998. *Kulturwandel auf dem griechischen Festland und den Kykladen im späten 3. Jahrtausend v. Chr: Studien zu den kulturellen Verhältnissen in Südosteuropa und dem zentralen sowie östlichen Mittelmeerraum in der späten Kupfer- und frühen Bronzezeit*. Bonn: Dr Rudolf Habelt.

Marangou, C. 1991. 'Maquettes d'embarcations: les débuts', in R. Laffineur and L. Basch (eds.), *Thalassa: L'Egée préhistorique et la mer* (Aegaeum 7), 21–42. Liège: Université de Liège.

Marangou, L. 1984. 'Evidence for the Early Cycladic period on Amorgos', in Fitton (ed.), 99–115.

　1994. 'Nees martyries gia ton Kykladiko politismo stin Amorgo', in X. Tzouvara-Souli, A. Vlachopoulou-Oikonomou and K. Gravani-Katsiki (eds.), *Phygos: timitikos tomos gia ton Kathigiti Sotiri Dakari*, 467–88. Ioannina: University of Ioannina.

Marangou, L. (ed.), 1990. *Cycladic Culture: Naxos in the 3rd Millennium BC*. Athens: Nicholas P. Goulandris Foundation – Museum of Cycladic Art.

Marck, J. C. 1986. 'Micronesian dialects and the overnight voyage', *Journal of the Polynesian Society* 95: 253–8.

Marcus, E. 1998. 'Maritime trade in the southern Levant from earliest times through the Middle Bronze IIA period'. DPhil dissertation, University of Oxford.

Marfoe, L. 1987. 'Cedar forest to silver mountain: social change and the development of long-distance trade in early Near Eastern societies', in M. Rowlands, M. Larsen and K. Kristiansen (eds.), *Centre and Periphery in the Ancient World*, 25–35. Cambridge: Cambridge University Press.

Marketou, T. 1990. 'Asomatos and Seraglio: EBA production and interconnections', *Hydra* 7: 40–8.

　1997. 'Asomatos Rodou: ta megaroschima ktiria kai oi scheseis tous me to voreioanatoliko Aigaio', in Doumas and La Rosa (eds.), 395–413.

Marthari, M. 1990. 'Skarkos: enas protokykladikos oikismos stin Io', *Idryma N. P. Goulandri, Mouseio Kykladikis Technis, Dialexeis 1986–1989*, 97–100. Athens: Nicholas P. Goulandris Foundation – Museum of Cycladic Art.

1997. 'Apo ton Skarko stin Poliochni: paratiriseis gia tin koinoniko-oikonomiki anaptyxi ton oikismon tis Proimis Epochis tou Chalkou stis Kyklades kai sta nisia tou voreioanatolikou Aigaiou', in Doumas and La Rosa (eds.), 362–82.

1998. *Syros Chalandriani Kastri: apo tin erevna kai tin prostasia stin anadeixi tou archaiologiko chorou – Syros Chalandriani Kastri: From the Investigation and Protection to the Presentation of an Archaeological Site*. Athens: Ministry of the Aegean.

1999. *To archaiologiko mouseio tis Iou*. Athens: Ministry of the Aegean/KA'Ephorate of Prehistoric and Classical Antiquities.

Marthari, M., T. Marketou and R. E. Jones 1990. 'LB I ceramic connections between Thera and Kos', in D. A. Hardy, C. G. Doumas, J. A. Sakellarakis and P. M. Warren (eds.), *Thera and the Aegean World III. I. Archaeology*, 171–84. London: Thera Foundation.

Mayr, E. 1954. 'Change of genetic environment and evolution', in J. S. Huxley, A. C. Hardy and E. B. Ford (eds.), *Evolution as a Process*, 156–80. London: Allen and Unwin.

Mead, M. 1928. *Coming of Age in Samoa*. New York: William Morrow.

Mee, C. and G. Taylor 1997. 'Prehistoric Methana', in C. Mee and H. Forbes (eds.), *A Rough and Rocky Place: The Landscape and Settlement History of the Methana Peninsula, Greece*, 42–56. Liverpool: Liverpool University Press.

Melas, E. M. 1985. *The Islands of Karpathos, Saros and Kasos in the Neolithic and Bronze Age* (Studies in Mediterranean Archaeology 67). Göteborg: Paul Åströms Förlag.

Meleisea, M. and P. Schoeffel 1997. 'Discovering outsiders', in D. Denoon (ed.), *The Cambridge History of the Pacific Islanders*, 119–51. Cambridge: Cambridge University Press.

Mellink, M. 1986. 'The Early Bronze Age in west Anatolia: Aegean and Asiatic correlations', in G. Cadogan (ed.), *The End of the Early Bronze Age in the Aegean*, 139–52. Leiden: E. J. Brill.

1993. 'The Anatolian south coast in the Early Bronze Age: the Cilician perspective', in M. Frangipane, H. Hauptmann, M. Liverani, P. Matthiae and M. Mellink (eds.), *Between the Rivers and Over the Mountains: Archaeologica Anatolica et Mesopotamica Alba Palmieri Dedicata*, 495–508. Rome: University of Rome 'La Sapienza'.

Mendoni, L. G. and A. Mazarakis Ainian (eds.), 1998. *Kea-Kythnos: History and Archaeology – Kea-Kythnos: istoria kai archaiologia* (Meletimata 27). Athens: Research Centre for Greek and Roman Antiquity – National Hellenic Research Foundation.

Merrillees, R. S. 1995. 'The archaeological background to the Cypro-Minoan script', *Bulletin of the Institute of Classical Studies* 40: 263–4.

Milojčić, V. 1961. *Samos I. Die prähistorische Siedlung under dem Heraion: Grabung 1953 und 1955*. Bonn: Dr Rodolf Habelt Verlag.

Misch, P. 1992. *Die Askoi in der Bronzezeit: eine typologische Studie zur Entwicklung askoider Gefässformen in der Bronze- und Eisenzeit Greichenlands und angrenzender Gebiete* (Studies in Mediterranean Archaeology and Literature Pocket-book 100). Jonsered: Paul Åströms Förlag.

Momigliano, N. and D. E. Wilson 1996. 'Knossos 1993: excavations outside the south front of the palace', *Annual of the British School at Athens* 91: 1–57.

Morgan, L. 1984. 'Morphology, syntax and the issue of chronology', in MacGillivray and Barber (eds.), 165–78.

1988. *The Miniature Wall Paintings of Thera: A Study in Aegean Culture and Iconography*. Cambridge: Cambridge University Press.

Morpurgo Davies, A. 1986. 'The linguistic evidence: is there any?', in G. Cadogan (ed.), *The End of the Early Bronze Age in the Aegean*, 93–123. Leiden: E. J. Brill.

Morris, C. 1993. 'Hands up for the individual! The role of attribution studies in Aegean prehistory', *Cambridge Archaeological Journal* 3: 41–66.

Morrison, I. A. 1968. 'Appendix I: relative sea-level change in the Saliagos area since Neolithic times', in Evans and Renfrew, 92–8.
Moya Pons, F. 1992. 'The politics of forced Indian labour in La Española 1493–1520', *Antiquity* 66: 130–9.
Muckelroy, K. 1978. *Maritime Archaeology*. Cambridge: Cambridge University Press.
Muhly, J. D. 1993. 'Early Bronze Age tin and the Taurus', *American Journal of Archaeology* 97: 239–53.
Munn, N. D. 1987. *The Fame of Gawa: A Symbolic Study of Value Transformation in a Massim (Papua New Guinea) Society*. Cambridge: Cambridge University Press.
Mylonas, G. E. 1959. *Aghios Kosmas: An Early Bronze Age Settlement and Cemetery in Attica*. Princeton: Princeton University Press.
Myres, J. L. 1941. 'The islands of the Aegean', *Geographical Journal* 97: 137–57.
Nakou, G. 1995. 'The cutting edge: a new look at early Aegean metallurgy', *Journal of Mediterranean Archaeology* 8: 1–32.
  1997. 'The role of Poliochni and the north Aegean in the development of Aegean metallurgy', in Doumas and La Rosa (eds.), 634–48.
  2000. 'The end of the Early Bronze Age in the Aegean: material culture and history'. DPhil dissertation, University of Oxford.
Naval Intelligence Division 1945. *Greece. III. Regional Geography* (Geographical Handbook Series). London: Naval Intelligence Division.
Nero, K. 1997. 'The end of insularity', in D. Denoon (ed.), *The Cambridge History of the Pacific Islanders*, 439–67. Cambridge: Cambridge University Press.
Nevett, L. 1988. 'An island's polities'. M.Phil dissertation, University of Cambridge.
Niemeier, W.-D. 1995. 'Aegina – first Aegean state outside of Crete?', in R. Laffineur and W.-D. Niemeier (eds.), *Politeia: Society and State in the Aegean Bronze Age* (Aegaeum 12), 73–80. Liège: University of Liège.
Obeyesekere, G. 1992. *The Apotheosis of Captain Cook: European Mythmaking in the Pacific*. Princeton: Princeton University Press.
Olivier, J.-P. 1986. 'Cretan writing in the second millennium BC', *World Archaeology* 17: 377–89.
Oustinoff, E. 1984. 'The manufacture of Cycladic figurines: a practical approach', in Fitton (ed.), 38–47.
Overbeck, J. C. 1984. 'Stratigraphy and ceramic sequence in Middle Cycladic Ayia Irini, Kea', in MacGillivray and Barber (eds.), 108–13.
  1989a. *The Bronze Age Pottery from the Kastro at Paros* (Studies in Mediterranean Archaeology and Literature Pocket-book 78). Jonsered: Paul Åströms Förlag.
  1989b. *Keos VII. Ayia Irini Period IV: The Stratigraphy and the Find Deposits*. Mainz on Rhine: Philipp von Zabern.
Overbeck, J. C. and G. F. Overbeck 1979. 'Consistency and diversity in the Middle Cycladic era', in Davis and Cherry (eds.), 106–12.
Papadatos, Y. 1999. 'Mortuary practices and their importance for the reconstruction of Prepalatial society and life: the evidence from Tholos Gamma, in Archanes-Phourni'. PhD dissertation, University of Sheffield.
Papadopoulos, G. C. 1862. 'Notice sur quelques antiquités de l'île de Syra', *Revue Archéologique* 6: 224–8.
Papagiannopoulou, A. 1991. *The Influence of Middle Minoan Pottery on the Cyclades* (Studies in Mediterranean Archaeology and Literature Pocket-book 96). Göteborg: Paul Åströms Förlag.

Papalas, A. J. 1992. *Ancient Icaria*. Wauconda: Bolchazy-Carducci.
Papathanasopoulos, G. A. 1961/2. 'Kykladika Naxou', *Archaiologikon Deltion* (Meletai) 17: 104–51.
  1976. 'To protoelladiko navagio tis nisou Dokou', *Athens Annals of Archaeology* 9: 17–23.
  1981. 'Naxos: ypovrychia archaiologiki erevna', *Praktika tis en Athinais Archaiologikis Etaireias* 1981: 298–302.
  1990. 'Dokos excavation 1989: the Early Helladic wreck and the prehistoric settlement', *Enalia* 1: 34–7.
Papathanasopoulos, G. A., Y. Vichos, E. Hatzidaki and Y. Lolos 1992. 'Dokos: 1990 campaign', *Enalia* 2: 6–23.
Patton, M. 1991. 'Stones axes in the Channel Islands: Neolithic exchange in an insular context', *Oxford Journal of Archaeology* 10: 33–43.
  1996. *Islands in Time: Island Sociogeography and Mediterranean Prehistory*. London: Routledge.
Payne, S. 1975. 'Faunal change at Franchthi cave from 20,000–3000 BC', in A. T. Clason (ed.), *Zooarchaeological Studies*, 120–31. Amsterdam: North-Holland.
Peebles, C. and S. Kus 1977. 'Some archaeological correlates of ranked societies', *American Antiquity* 42: 421–8.
Peltenburg, E. 1996. 'From isolation to state formation in Cyprus, c. 3500–1500 BC', in V. Karageorghis and D. Michaelides (eds.), *The Development of the Cypriot Economy from the Prehistoric Period to the Present Day*, 17–44. Nicosia: University of Cyprus/Bank of Cyprus.
Perec, G. 1987. *Life: A User's Manual*. London: Harvill Press.
Perlès, C. 1987. *Les industries lithiques taillées de Franchthi (Argolide, Grèce). I. Présentation générale et industries paléolithiques* (Excavations at Franchthi Cave, Greece, Fascicle 3). Bloomington: Indiana University Press.
  1990a. *Les industries lithiques taillées de Franchthi (Argolide, Grèce). II. Les industries du Mésolithique et du Néolithique initial* (Excavations at Franchthi Cave, Greece, Fascicle 5). Bloomington: Indiana University Press.
  1990b. 'L'outillage de pierre taillée néolithique en Grèce: approvisionnement et exploitation des matières premières', *Bulletin de Correspondance Hellénique* 114: 1–42.
  1992. 'Systems of exchange and organization of production in Neolithic Greece', *Journal of Mediterranean Archaeology* 5: 115–64.
Pernicka, E. 1995. 'Crisis or catharsis in lead isotope analysis', *Journal of Mediterranean Archaeology* 8: 59–64.
Pernicka, E., F. Begemann, S. Schmitt-Strecker and A. P. Grimanis 1990. 'On the composition and provenance of metal artefacts from Poliochni on Lemnos', *Oxford Journal of Archaeology* 9: 263–98.
Pétrequin, P. 1993. 'North wind, south wind: Neolithic technical choices in the Jura mountains, 3700–2400 BC', in Lemonnier (ed.), 36–76.
Postgate, J. N. 1992. *Early Mesopotamia: Society and Economy at the Dawn of History*. London: Routledge.
Powell, J. 1996. *Fishing in the Prehistoric Aegean* (Studies in Mediterranean Archaeology and Literature Pocket-book 137). Jonsered: Paul Åströms Förlag.
Price, R. P. S. 1993. 'The west Pontic "maritime interaction sphere": a long-term structure in Balkan prehistory?', *Oxford Journal of Archaeology* 12: 175–96.
Price, S. 1989. *Primitive Art in Civilized Places*. Chicago: University of Chicago Press.
Price, T. D. and J. A. Brown (eds.), 1985. *Prehistoric Hunter-Gatherers: The Emergence of Cultural Complexity*. Orlando: Academic Press.

Pullen, D. J. 1986. 'A "House of the Tiles" at Zygouries? The function of monumental Early Helladic architecture', in Hägg and Konsola (eds.), 73–8.
    1992. 'Ox and plow in the Early Bronze Age Aegean', *American Journal of Archaeology* 96: 45–54.
    1994. 'A lead seal from Tsoungiza, Ancient Nemea, and Early Bronze Age sealing systems', *American Journal of Archaeology* 98: 35–52.
Purcell, N. 1990. 'Mobility and the *polis*', in O. Murray and S. Price (eds.), *The Greek City: From Homer to Alexander*, 29–58. Oxford: Clarendon Press.
Quammen, D. 1996. *The Song of the Dodo: Island Biogeography in an Age of Mass Extinctions*. London: Hutchinson.
Rackham, O. 1972. 'Charcoal and plaster impressions', in Warren, 299–304.
    1978. 'The flora and vegetation of Thera and Crete before and after the great eruption', in C. G. Doumas (ed.), *Thera and the Aegean World I*, 755–64. London: Thera and the Aegean World.
Rackham, O. and J. Moody 1996. *The Making of the Cretan Landscape*. Manchester: Manchester University Press.
Rathje, W. L. 1978. 'Melanesian and Australian exchange systems: a view from Mesoamerica', *Mankind* 11: 165–74.
Redman, C. 1977. 'The "analytical individual" and prehistoric style variability', in Hill and Gunn (eds.), 41–53.
Reese, D. S. (ed.), 1996. *Pleistocene and Holocene Fauna of Crete and Its First Settlers* (Monographs in World Archaeology 28), 211–29. Madison: Prehistory Press.
Renfrew, A. C. 1965. 'The Neolithic and Early Bronze Age cultures of the Cyclades and their external relations'. PhD dissertation, University of Cambridge.
    1967. 'Cycladic metallurgy and the Aegean Early Bronze Age', *American Journal of Archaeology* 71: 1–20.
    1969. 'The development and chronology of the Early Cycladic figurines', *American Journal of Archaeology* 73: 1–32.
    1972. *The Emergence of Civilisation: The Cyclades and the Aegean in the Third Millennium BC*. London: Methuen.
    1973a. *Before Civilisation: The Radiocarbon Revolution and Prehistoric Europe*. London: Jonathan Cape.
    1973b. 'Monuments, mobilization and social organization in Neolithic Wessex', in A. C. Renfrew (ed.), *The Explanation of Culture Change: Models in Prehistory*, 539–58. London: Duckworth.
    1979. 'Terminology and beyond', in Davis and Cherry (eds.), 51–63.
    1982a. 'Bronze Age Melos', in Renfrew and Wagstaff (eds.), 35–44.
    1982b. 'Prehistoric exchange', in Renfrew and Wagstaff (eds.), 222–7.
    1984a. 'From Pelos to Syros: Kapros grave D and the Kampos group', in MacGillivray and Barber (eds.), 41–54.
    1984b. 'Speculations on the use of Early Cycladic sculpture', in Fitton (ed.), 24–30.
    1986. 'Varna and the emergence of wealth in prehistoric Europe', in A. Appadurai (ed.), *The Social Life of Things: Commodities in Cultural Perspective*, 141–8. Cambridge: Cambridge University Press.
    1989. 'Introduction', in Y. Maniatis (ed.), *Archaeometry: Proceedings of the 25th International Symposium*, 677–8. Amsterdam: Elsevier.
    1991. *The Cycladic Spirit: Masterpieces from the Nicholas P. Goulandris Collection*. London: Thames and Hudson.

1993a. 'Collectors are the real looters', *Archaeology* 46: 16–17.

1993b. 'Trade beyond the material', in C. Scarre and F. Healy (eds.), *Trade and Exchange in Prehistoric Europe* (Oxbow Monograph 33), 5–16. Oxford: Oxbow.

1994. 'Preface', in C. Mathers and S. Stoddart (eds.), *Development and Decline in the Mediterranean Bronze Age* (Sheffield Archaeological Monographs 8), 5–11. Sheffield: J. R. Collis Publications.

1998. 'Word of Minos: the Minoan contribution to Mycenaean Greek and the linguistic geography of the Bronze Age Aegean', *Cambridge Archaeological Journal* 8: 239–64.

Renfrew, A. C. and A. Aspinall 1990. 'Aegean obsidian and Franchthi cave', in Perlès, 257–70.

Renfrew, A. C., J. R. Cann and J. E. Dixon 1965. 'Obsidian in the Aegean', *Annual of the British School at Athens* 60: 225–47.

Renfrew, A. C. and M. Wagstaff 1982a. 'Introduction: an initial perspective', in Renfrew and Wagstaff (eds.), 1–8.

Renfrew, A. C. and M. Wagstaff (eds.), 1982b. *An Island Polity: The Archaeology of Exploitation in Melos*. Cambridge: Cambridge University Press.

Renfrew, J. M. 1968. 'Appendix X: the cereal remains', in Evans and Renfrew, 139–41.

1977. 'Appendix 3: seeds from area K', in Coleman, 127–8.

1982. 'Early agriculture in Melos', in Renfrew and Wagstaff (eds.), 156–60.

Renfrew, J. M., P. H. Greenwood and P. J. Whitehead 1968. 'Appendix VIII: the fish-bones', in Evans and Renfrew, 118–21.

Roberts, O. T. P. 1987. 'Wind-power and the boats from the Cyclades', *International Journal of Nautical Archaeology* 16: 309–11.

Rose, M. J. 1986. 'Neolithic fishing in the Aegean: new evidence from Franchthi cave', *American Journal of Archaeology* 90: 177 (abstract).

Rougemont, G. 1990. 'Géographie historique des Cyclades: l'homme et le milieu dans l'archipel', *Journal des Savants* 1990: 199–220.

Rouse, I. 1977. 'Pattern and process in West Indian archaeology', *World Archaeology* 9: 1–11.

Runnels, C. N. 1985a. 'Trade and the demand for mill-stones in southern Greece in the Neolithic and Early Bronze Age', in A. B. Knapp and T. Stech (eds.), *Prehistoric Production and Exchange: The Aegean and Eastern Mediterranean* (UCLA Institute of Archaeology Monograph 25), 30–43. Los Angeles: UCLA Institute of Archaeology.

1985b. 'The Bronze Age flaked-stone industries from Lerna: a preliminary report', *Hesperia* 54: 357–91.

1995. 'Review of Aegean prehistory IV: the Stone Age of Greece from the Palaeolithic to the advent of the Neolithic', *American Journal of Archaeology* 99: 699–728.

Runnels, C. N. and J. M. Hansen 1986. 'The olive in the prehistoric Aegean: the evidence for domestication in the Early Bronze Age', *Oxford Journal of Archaeology* 5: 299–308.

Rutter, J. B. 1979. *Ceramic Change in the Aegean Early Bronze Age* (UCLA Institute of Archaeology Occasional Paper 5). Los Angeles: UCLA Institute of Archaeology.

1983. 'Some observations on the Cyclades in the later third and early second millennia BC', *American Journal of Archaeology* 87: 69–76.

1984. 'The Early Cycladic III gap: what it is and how to go about filling it without making it go away', in MacGillivray and Barber (eds.), 95–107.

1985. 'An exercise in form vs. function: the significance of the duck vase', *Temple University Aegean Symposium* 10: 16–41.

1988. 'Early Helladic III vasepainting, ceramic regionalism, and the influence of basketry', in E. B. French and K. A. Wardle (eds.), *Problems in Greek Prehistory*, 73–89. Bristol: Bristol Classical Press.

References

1993. Review of Aegean prehistory II: the prepalatial Bronze Age of the southern and central Greek mainland', *American Journal of Archaeology* 97: 745–97.

Rutter, J. B. and C. W. Zerner 1984. 'Early Hellado-Minoan contacts', in Hägg and Marinatos (eds.), 75–83.

Ryan, W. and W. Pitman 1998. *Noah's Flood: The New Scientific Discoveries about the Event that Changed History.* New York: Simon and Schuster.

Sackett, L. H., M. R. Popham and P. M. Warren 1965. 'Excavations at Palaikastro, VI', *Annual of the British School at Athens* 60: 248–314.

Sahlins, M. D. 1955. 'Esoteric efflorescence in Easter Island', *American Anthropologist* 57: 1045–52.

1957. 'Differentiation by adaptation in Polynesian societies', *Journal of the Polynesian Society* 66: 291–300.

1972. *Stone Age Economics.* Chicago: Aldine.

1985. *Islands of History.* Chicago: University of Chicago Press.

1995. *How 'Natives' Think: About Captain Cook, For Example.* Chicago: University of Chicago Press.

Sakellarakis, J. A. 1977. 'Ta Kykladika stoicheia ton Archanon', *Athens Annals of Archaeology* 10: 93–115.

1996. 'Minoan religious influence in the Aegean: the case of Kythera', *Annual of the British School at Athens* 91: 81–99.

Sakellarakis, J. A. and E. Sapouna-Sakellaraki 1997. *Archanes: Minoan Crete in a New Light.* Athens: Ammos.

Sampson, A. 1981. *I Neolithiki kai i Protoelladiki I stin Evvoia.* Athens: Etaireia Evvoïkon Spoudon.

1984. 'The Neolithic of the Dodecanese and Aegean Neolithic culture', *Annual of the British School at Athens* 79: 239–49.

1985. *Manika: mia Protoelladiki poli sti Chalkida.* Athens: Etaireia Evvoïkon Spoudon.

1987. *I Neolithiki periodos sta Dodekanisa.* Athens: Tameio Archaiologikon Poron kai Apallotriosion.

1988a. *I Neolithiki katoikisi sto Gyali tis Nisyrou.* Athens: Euboïki Archaiophilos Etaireia.

1988b. *Manika II: o Protoelladikos oikismos kai to nekrotapheio.* Athens: Ekdosi Dimou Chalkidion.

1992. 'Late Neolithic remains at Tharrounia, Euboia: a model for the seasonal use of settlements and caves', *Annual of the British School at Athens* 87: 61–101.

1993. *Skoteini Tharrounion: to spilaio, o oikismos kai to nekrotapheio.* Athens: Department of Palaeoanthropology and Speleology.

1996. 'Excavation at the cave of Cyclope on Youra, Alonnessos', in E. Alram-Stern (ed.), *Die Ägäische Frühzeit. 2. Serie Forschungsbericht 1975–1993. 1. Band: Das Neolithikum in Greichenland mit Ausnahme von Kreta und Zypern*, 507–20. Vienna: Austrian Academy of Sciences.

1997. *Mykonos: O Neolithikos oikismos tis Phtelias kai i proïstoriki katoikisi sto nisi.* Athens: 21st Ephorate of Antiquities of the Cyclades.

1998. 'The Neolithic and Mesolithic occupation of the cave of Cyclope, Youra Alonnessos, Greece', *Annual of the British School at Athens* 93: 1–22.

Sapouna-Sakellaraki, E. 1986. 'Stromatographiki ereuvna sti Manika Chalkidas', *Archaiologikon Deltion* (Meletes) 41: 101–270.

1987. 'New evidence from the Early Bronze Age cemetery of Manika, Chalkis', *Annual of the British School at Athens* 82: 233–64.

1991. Manika Chalkidas: Stromatographiki erevna ston oikismo (Oikopedo Zousi)', *Archaiologikon Deltion* (Meletes) 41: 101–270.

Sbonias, K. 1995. *Frühkretische Siegel: Ansätze für eine Interpretation der sozial-politischen Entwicklung auf Kreta während der Frühbronzezeit* (British Archaeological Reports International Series 620). Oxford: Tempus Reparatum.

Schallin, A.-L. 1993. *Islands under Influence: The Cyclades in the Late Bronze Age and the Nature of Mycenaean Presence* (Studies in Mediterranean Archaeology 111). Jonsered: Paul Åströms Förlag.

Schama, S. 1995. *Landscape and Memory*. London: Fontana Press.

Schilardi, D. 1990. 'Paros', *To Ergon tis Archaiologikis Etaireias* 37: 104–8.

1991. 'Paros' *To Ergon tis Archaiologikis Etaireias* 38: 81–3.

Schofield, E. 1982. 'The western Cyclades and Crete: a special relationship', *Oxford Journal of Archaeology* 1: 9–25.

1998. 'Town planning at Ayia Irini, Kea', in Mendoni and Mazarakis Ainian (eds.), 117–22.

Schüle, W. 1993. 'Mammals, vegetation and the initial human settlement of the Mediterranean islands: a palaeoecological approach', *Journal of Biogeography* 20: 399–411.

Seager, R. B. 1909. 'Excavations on the island of Mochlos, Crete, in 1908', *American Journal of Archaeology* 13: 273–303.

1912. *Explorations on the Island of Mochlos*. Boston: American School of Classical Studies in Athens.

Shackleton, N. J. 1968. 'Appendix IX: The mollusca, the crustacea, the echinodermata', in Evans and Renfrew, 122–38.

Shelmerdine, C. W. 1985. *The Perfume Industry of Mycenaean Pylos* (Studies in Mediterranean Archaeology Pocket-book 34). Göteborg: Paul Åströms Förlag.

Shennan, S. J. 1999. 'Cost, benefit and value in the organization of early European copper production', *Antiquity* 73: 352–63.

Sherratt, A. G. 1981. 'Plough and pastoralism: aspects of the secondary products revolution', in I. Hodder, G. Isaac and N. Hammond (eds.), *Pattern of the Past: Studies in Honour of David Clarke*, 261–305. Cambridge: Cambridge University Press.

1992. 'The first European sailing ships', *The Ashmolean* 1: 12–14.

1993a. 'What would a Bronze-Age world system look like? Relations between temperate Europe and the Mediterranean in later prehistory', *Journal of European Archaeology* 1: 1–57.

1993b. 'Who are you calling peripheral? Dependence and independence in European prehistory', in C. Scarre and F. Healy (eds.), *Trade and Exchange in Prehistoric Europe*, 245–55. Oxford: Oxbow.

1995. 'Reviving the grand narrative: archaeology and long-term change' (2nd David L. Clarke Memorial Lecture), *Journal of European Archaeology* 3: 1–32.

Sherratt, A. G. and E. S. Sherratt 1991. 'From luxuries to commodities: the nature of Mediterranean Bronze Age trading systems', in N. H. Gale (ed.), *Bronze Age Trade in the Mediterranean* (Studies in Mediterranean Archaeology 90), 351–86. Jonsered: Paul Åströms Förlag.

Sherratt, E. S. 1990. '"Reading the texts": archaeology and the Homeric question', *Antiquity* 64: 807–24.

in press. *The Captive Spirit: A Catalogue of Cycladica in the Ashmolean Museum, Oxford*. Oxford: Oxford University Press.

Shipley, G. 1987. *A History of Samos, 800–188 BC*. Oxford: Clarendon Press.

Siedentopf, H. B. 1991. *Alt-Ägina IV.2. Mattbemalte Keramik der Mittleren Bronzezeit*. Mainz on Rhine: Philipp von Zabern.

Simberloff, D. and B. Levin 1985. 'Predictable sequences of species loss with decreasing island area – land birds in two archipelagoes', *New Zealand Journal of Ecology* 8: 11–20.

Simmons, A. H. 1991. 'Humans, island colonization and Pleistocene extinctions in the Mediterranean: the view from Akrotiri *Aetokremnos*, Cyprus', *Antiquity* 65: 857–69.

 1998. 'Of tiny hippos, large cows and early colonists in Cyprus', *Journal of Mediterranean Archaeology* 11: 232–41.

 1999. *Faunal Extinction in an Island Society: Pygmy Hippopotamus Hunters of Cyprus*. New York: Kluwer Academic/Plenum.

Sinos, S. 1971. *Die vorklassische Hausformen in der Ägäis*. Mainz on Rhine: Philipp von Zabern.

Smith, A. 1995. 'The need for Lapita: explaining change in the Late Holocene Pacific archaeological record', *World Archaeology* 26: 366–79.

Snodgrass, A. M. 1987. *An Archaeology of Greece: The Present State and Future Scope of a Discipline* (Sather Classical Lectures 53). Berkeley: University of California Press.

Soja, E. W. 1989. *Postmodern Geographies: The Reassertion of Space in Critical Social Theory*. London: Verso.

Soles, J. S. and C. Davaras 1992. 'Excavations at Mochlos, 1989', *Hesperia* 61: 413–48.

Sopher, D. E. 1965. *The Sea Nomads: A Study Based on the Literature of the Maritime Boat People of Southeast Asia* (Memoirs of the National Museum, Singapore 5). Singapore: Lim Bian Han.

Sotirakopoulou, P. 1986. 'Early Cycladic pottery from Akrotiri', *Annual of the British School at Athens* 81: 297–312.

 1990. 'The earliest history of Akrotiri: the Late Neolithic and Early Bronze Age phases', in D. A. Hardy and A. C. Renfrew (eds.), *Thera and the Aegean World III. III. Chronology*, 41–7. London: Thera Foundation.

 1993. 'The chronology of the "Kastri group" reconsidered', *Annual of the British School at Athens* 88: 5–20.

 1996. 'The dating of the late Phylakopi I as evidenced at Akrotiri on Thera', *Annual of the British School at Athens* 91: 113–36.

 1997. 'Kyklades kai voreio Aigaio: oi scheseis tous kata to devtero imisi tis 3is chilietias p.ch.', in Doumas and La Rosa (eds.), 522–42.

 1998. 'The Early Bronze Age stone figurines from Akrotiri on Thera and their significance for the early Cycladic settlement', *Annual of the British School at Athens* 93: 107–65.

 1999. *Akrotiri Thiras: I Neolithiki kai i proimi epochi tou chalkou epi ti basi tis keramikis* (Bibliothiki tis en Athinais Archaiologikis Etaireias 191). Athens: Archaeological Society of Athens.

Spitaels, P. 1982a. 'Provatsa on Makronisos', *Athens Annals of Archaeology* 15: 155–8.

 1982b. 'Final Neolithic pottery from Thorikos', in P. Spitaels (ed.), *Studies in Southern Attica I* (Miscellanea Graeca 5), 9–44. Ghent: Belgian Archaeological Mission in Greece.

 1984. 'The Early Helladic period in mine no. 3 (Theatre Sector)', *Thorikos* 8: 151–74.

Spriggs, M. 1997. *The Island Melanesians*. Oxford: Blackwell.

Spriggs, M. (ed.), 1990. *Lapita Design, Form and Composition* (Occasional Papers in Prehistory 19). Canberra: Department of Prehistory, Australian National University.

Stanley Price, N. P. 1977. 'Colonisation and continuity in the early prehistory of Cyprus', *World Archaeology* 9: 27–41.

Steadman, D. 1995. 'Prehistoric extinctions of Pacific island birds: biodiversity meets zooarchaeology', *Science* 267: 1123–31.

Steiner, C. B. 1994. *African Art in Transit*. Cambridge: Cambridge University Press.

Stephanos, K. 1906. 'Anaskaphai en Naxo', *Praktika tis en Athinais Archaiologikis Etaireias* 1906: 86–9.

Stoddart, S. 1999. 'Contrasting political strategies in the islands of the southern central Mediterranean', in E. Herring, R. Whitehouse and J. Wilkins (eds.), *Accordia Research Papers* 7: 59–73.

Stoddart, S., A. Bonanno, T. Gouder, C. Malone and D. Trump 1993. 'Cult in an island society: prehistoric Malta in the Tarxien period', *Cambridge Archaeological Journal* 3: 3–19.

Stos-Gale, Z. A. 1989. 'Cycladic copper metallurgy', in A. Hauptmann, E. Pernicka and G. A. Wagner (eds.), *Archäometallurgie der Alten Welt/Old World Metallurgy* (Der Anschnitt 7), 279–91. Bochum: Deutschen Bergbau-Museum.

1992. 'The origin of metal objects from the Early Bronze Age site of Thermi on the island of Lesbos', *Oxford Journal of Archaeology* 11: 155–78.

1993. 'The origin of metal used for making weapons in Early and Middle Minoan Crete', in C. Scarre and F. Healy (eds.), *Trade and Exchange in Prehistoric Europe*, 115–29. Oxford: Oxbow.

1998. 'The role of Kythnos and other Cycladic islands in the origins of Early Minoan metallurgy', in Mendoni and Mazarakis Ainian (eds.), 717–35.

Stos-Gale, Z. A., N. Gale and G. R. Gilmore 1984. 'Early Bronze Age Trojan metal sources and Anatolians in the Cyclades', *Oxford Journal of Archaeology* 3: 23–53.

Stos-Gale, Z. A. and C. F. Macdonald 1991. 'Sources of metals and trade in the Bronze Age Aegean', in N. H. Gale (ed.), *Bronze Age Trade in the Mediterranean* (Studies in Mediterranean Archaeology 90), 249–88. Jonsered: Paul Åströms Förlag.

Strathern, A. J. 1983. 'The kula in comparative perspective', in Leach and Leach (eds.), 73–88.

Talalay, L. E. 1983. 'Neolithic figurines of southern Greece: their form and function'. PhD dissertation, Indiana University.

1991. 'Body imagery of the ancient Aegean', *Archaeology* 44: 46–9.

1993. *Deities, Dolls and Devices: Neolithic Figurines from Franchthi Cave, Greece* (Excavations at Franchthi Cave, Greece, Fascicle 9). Bloomington: Indiana University Press.

Televantou, C. 1990. 'New light on the West House wall-paintings', in D. A. Hardy, C. G. Doumas, J. A. Sakellarakis and P. M. Warren (eds.), *Thera and the Aegean World III. I. Archaeology*, 309–24. London: Thera Foundation.

Terrell, J. E. 1977a. 'Geographic systems and human diversity in the North Solomons', *World Archaeology* 9: 62–81.

1977b. *Human Biogeography in the Solomon Islands* (Fieldiana: Anthropology 68.1). Chicago: Field Museum of Natural History.

1981. 'Linguistics and the peopling of the Pacific islands', *Journal of the Polynesian Society* 90: 225–58.

1986. *Prehistory in the Pacific Islands*. Cambridge: Cambridge University Press.

1988. 'History as a family tree, history as an entangled bank: constructing images and interpretations of prehistory in the South Pacific', *Antiquity* 62: 642–57.

1989. 'Commentary: what Lapita is and what Lapita isn't', *Antiquity* 63: 623–6.

1990. 'Storytelling and prehistory', *Archaeological Method and Theory* 2: 1–27.

1998. 'The prehistoric Pacific', *Archaeology* 51: 56–63.

Terrell, J. E., T. L. Hunt and C. Gosden 1997. 'The dimensions of social life in the Pacific: human diversity and the myth of the primitive isolate', *Current Anthropology* 38: 155–95.

Terrell, J. E. and R. L. Welsch 1997. 'Lapita and the temporal geography of prehistory', *Antiquity* 71: 548–72.

Theochari, M. D. and L. Parlama 1997. 'Palamari Skyrou: i oxyromeni poli tis Proimis Chalkokratias', in Doumas and La Rosa (eds.), 344–56.

Theochari, M. D., L. Parlama and E. Hatzipouliou 1993. 'Kerameiki tis Proimis Chalkokratias III apo to Palamari tis Skyrou', in C. W. Zerner (ed.), *Wace and Blegen: Pottery as Evidence for Trade in the Aegean Bronze Age 1939–1989*, 187–93. Amsterdam. J. C. Gieben.

Theocharis, D. R. 1953/4. 'Askitario: protoelladiki akropolis para tin Raphinan', *Archaiologiki Ephimeris* 1953/4 (Volume III): 59–76.

Thiel, B. 1987. 'Early settlement of the Philippines, eastern Indonesia and Australia–New Guinea: a new hypothesis', *Current Anthropology* 28: 236–40.

Thimme, J. (ed.), 1977. *Art and Culture of the Cyclades*. Karlsruhe: C. F. Müller.

Tichy, R. nd. Report of the Society for the Expedition Monoxylon.

Tilley, C. 1994. *A Phenomenology of Landscape: Places, Paths and Monuments*. Oxford: Berg.

Torrence, R. 1979. 'A technological approach to Cycladic blade industries', in Davis and Cherry (eds.), 66–86.

   1982. 'The obsidian quarries and their use', in Renfrew and Wagstaff (eds.), 193–221.

   1984. 'Monopoly or direct access? Industrial organization at the Melos obsidian quarries', in J. E. Ericson and B. A. Purdy (eds.), *Prehistoric Quarries and Lithic Production*, 49–64. Cambridge: Cambridge University Press.

   1986. *Production and Exchange of Stone Tools: Prehistoric Obsidian in the Aegean*. Cambridge: Cambridge University Press.

   1991. 'The chipped stone', in Cherry, Davis and Mantzourani, 173–98.

   1993. 'Ethnoarchaeology, museum collections and prehistoric exchange: obsidian-tipped artifacts from the Admiralty Islands', *World Archaeology* 24: 467–81.

Treherne, P. 1995. 'The warrior's beauty: the masculine body and self-identity in Bronze Age Europe', *Journal of European Archaeology* 3: 105–44.

Tsakos, K. 1992. 'Mia proïstoriki thesi sti Mykono: o "tymbos" tis Phtelias – taphos tou Aiantos?', *Archaiognosia* 6: 121–32.

Tsipopoulou, M. 1988. 'Agia Photia Siteias: to neo evrima', in E. B. French and K. A. Wardle (eds.), *Problems in Greek Prehistory*, 31–47. Bristol: Bristol Classical Press.

   1989. *Archaeological Survey at Aghia Photia, Siteia* (Studies in Mediterranean Archaeology and Literature Pocket-book 76). Partille: Paul Åströms Förlag.

   1999. 'Petras, Siteia: from an Early Minoan II settlement to a palatial centre', *Bulletin of the Institute of Classical Studies* 43.

Tsountas, C. 1898. 'Kykladika', *Archaiologiki Ephimeris* 1898: 137–212.

   1899. 'Kykladika II', *Archaiologiki Ephimeris* 1899: 73–134.

Tzala, C. 1989. 'O dromos tou opsidianou me ena papyrenio skaphos stis Kyklades', *Archaiologia* 32: 11–20.

van Andel, T. H. 1989. 'Late Quaternary sea-level change and archaeology', *Antiquity* 63: 733–45.

   1990. 'Addendum to "Late Quaternary sea-level change and archaeology"', *Antiquity* 64: 151–2.

van Andel, T. H. and C. N. Runnels 1988. 'An essay on the "emergence of civilization" in the Aegean world', *Antiquity* 62: 234–47.

   1995. 'The earliest farmers in Europe', *Antiquity* 69: 481–500.

van Andel, T. H. and J. C. Shackleton 1982. 'Late Paleolithic and Mesolithic coastlines of Greece and the Aegean', *Journal of Field Archaeology* 9: 445–54.

van der Leeuw, S. E. and R. Torrence (eds.), 1989. *What's New? A Closer Look at the Process of Innovation* (One World Archaeology). London: Unwin Hyman.

van Leur, J. C. 1955. *Indonesian Trade and Society*. The Hague: W. van Hoeve.

Vaughan, S. J. 1989. 'Appendix II: petrographic analysis of Mikre Vigla wares', *Annual of the British School at Athens* 84: 150–62.

  1990. 'Petrographic analysis of the Early Cycladic wares from Akrotiri, Thera', in D. A. Hardy, C. G. Doumas, J. A. Sakellarakis and P. M. Warren (eds.), *Thera and the Aegean World III. I. Archaeology*, 470–87. London: Thera Foundation.

Vaughan, S. J. and D. E. Wilson 1993. 'Interregional contacts in the Aegean in Early Bronze II: the talc ware connection', in C. W. Zerner (ed.), *Wace and Blegen: Pottery as Evidence for Trade in the Aegean Bronze Age 1939–1989*, 169–86. Amsterdam: J. C. Gieben.

Vayda, A. P. and R. A. Rappaport 1963. 'Island cultures', in F. R. Fosberg (ed.), *Man's Place in the Island Ecosystem*, 133–44. Honolulu: Bishop Museum.

Vermeule, E. 1964. *Greece in the Bronze Age*. Chicago: University of Chicago Press.

Veth, P. M. 1993. *Islands of the Interior: The Dynamics of Prehistoric Adaptations within the Arid Zone of Australia* (International Monographs in Prehistory AS-3). Ann Arbor: University of Michigan Press.

Vigne, J.-D. 1987. 'L'extinction holocène du fonds de peuplement mammalien indigène des îles de Méditerranée occidentale', *Mémoires de la société géologique de France* N.S. 150: 167–77.

Vitelli, K. D. 1993. *Franchthi Neolithic Pottery 1: Classification and Ceramic Phases 1 and 2* (Excavations at Franchthi Cave, Greece, Fascicle 8). Bloomington: Indiana University Press.

von den Driesch, A. and J. Boessneck 1990. 'Die Tierreste von der mykenischen Burg Tiryns bei Nafplion/Peloponnes', in H.-J. Weisshaar, I. Weber-Hiden, A. von den Driesch, J. Boessneck, A. Rieger and W. Böser, *Tiryns: Forschungen und Berichte 11*, 87–164. Mainz on Rhine: Philipp von Zabern.

Voutsaki, S. 1995. 'Social and political processes in the Mycenaean Argolid: the evidence from the mortuary practices', in R. Laffineur and W.-D. Niemeier (eds), *Politeia: Society and State in the Aegean Bronze Age* (Aegaeum 12), 55–66. Liège: University of Liège.

  1998. 'Mortuary evidence, symbolic meanings and social change: a comparison between Messenia and the Argolid in the Mycenaean period', in K. Branigan (ed.), *Cemetery and Society in the Aegean Bronze Age* (Sheffield Studies in Aegean Archaeology 1), 41–58. Sheffield: Sheffield Academic Press.

Wachsmann, S. 1998. *Seagoing Ships and Seamanship in the Bronze Age Levant*. College Station: Texas A&M University Press.

Wagner, G. A., W. Gentner, H. Gropengiesser and N. H. Gale 1980. 'Early Bronze Age lead-silver mining and metallurgy in the Aegean: the ancient workings at Siphnos', in P. T. Craddock (ed.), *Scientific Studies in Early Mining and Extractive Metallurgy* (British Museum Occasional Paper 20), 63–85. London: British Museum Research Laboratory.

Wagner, G. A and G. Weisgerber (eds.), 1985. *Silber, Blei und Gold auf Sifnos: prähistorische und antike Metallproduktion* (Der Anschnitt 3). Bochum: Deutsches Bergbau-Museum.

Wagstaff, M. and S. Augustson 1982. 'Traditional land use', in Renfrew and Wagstaff (eds.), 106–33.

Wagstaff, M., S. Augustson and C. Gamble 1982. 'Alternative subsistence strategies', in Renfrew and Wagstaff (eds.), 172–80.

Wagstaff, M. and J. F. Cherry 1982a. 'Settlement and resources', in Renfrew and Wagstaff (eds.), 246–63.

  1982b. 'Settlement and population change', in Renfrew and Wagstaff (eds.), 136–55.

Wagstaff, M. and C. Gamble 1982. 'Island resources and their limitations', in Renfrew and Wagstaff (eds.), 95–105.

Waldren, W. 1994. *Survival and Extinction:* Myotragus balearicus, *an Endemic Pleistocene Antelope from the Island of Mallorca* (DAMARC 27). Oxford: Donald Baden-Powell Quaternary Research Centre, Pitt Rivers Museum, University of Oxford and Baleares, Spain: Deìa Archaeological Museum and Research Centre, Deìa, Mallorca.

Walsh, J. 1993. 'Foreward', in *The Getty Kouros Colloquium*, 7. Athens: Kapon Editions.

Walter, H. and F. Felten 1981. *Alt-Ägina III.1. Die vorgeschichtliche Stadt: Befestigungen, Häuser, Funde.* Mainz on Rhine: Philipp von Zabern.

Warren, P. M. 1972a. *Myrtos: An Early Bronze Age Settlement in Crete* (British School at Athens Supplementary Volume 7). London: Thames and Hudson.

1972b. 'Knossos and the Greek mainland in the third millennium BC', *Athens Annals of Archaeology* 5: 392–8.

1984. 'Early Minoan–Early Cycladic chronological correlations', in MacGillivray and Barber (eds.), 55–62.

1987. 'The genesis of the Minoan palace', in Hägg and Marinatos (eds.), 47–56.

1995. 'Minoan Crete and pharaonic Egypt', in W. V. Davies and L. Schofield (eds.), *Egypt, the Aegean and the Levant: Interconnections in the Second Millennium BC*, 1–18. London: British Museum Press.

Warren, P. M. and V. Hankey 1989. *Aegean Bronze Age Chronology.* Bristol: Bristol Classical Press.

Washburn, D. K. 1983. 'Symmetry analysis of ceramic design: two tests of the method on Neolithic material from Greece and the Aegean', in D. K. Washburn (ed.), *Structure and Cognition in Art*, 138–64. Cambridge: Cambridge University Press.

Waterman, T. T. and G. Coffin 1920. *Types of Canoes on Puget Sound.* New York: Museum of the American Indian.

Watrous, L. V. 1994. 'Review of Aegean prehistory III: Crete from the earliest prehistory through the protopalatial period', *American Journal of Archaeology* 98: 695–753.

1998. 'Egypt and Crete in the early Middle Bronze Age: a case of trade and cultural diffusion', in E. H. Cline and D. Harris-Cline (eds.), *The Aegean and the Orient in the Second Millennium* (Aegaeum 18), 19–28. Liège: University of Liège.

Watson, G. E. 1964. 'Ecology and evolution of passerine birds on the islands of the Aegean Sea'. PhD dissertation, University of Yale.

Watters, D. R. 1997. 'Maritime trade in the prehistoric eastern Caribbean', in S. M. Wilson (ed.), *The Indigenous People of the Carribean*, 88–99. Gainesville: University Press of Florida.

Weinberg, S. S. 1951. 'Neolithic figurines and Aegean interrelations', *American Journal of Archaeology* 55: 121–33.

Weingarten, J. 1997. 'Another look at Lerna: an EHIIB trading post?', *Oxford Journal of Archaeology* 16: 147–66.

Weiss, H., M. A. Courty, W. Wetterstrom, F. Guichard, L. Senior, R. Meadow and A. Curnow 1993. 'The genesis and collapse of third millennium north Mesopotamian civilization', *Science* 261: 995–1004.

Whitelaw, T. M. 1983. 'The settlement at Fournou Korifi, Myrtos and aspects of Early Minoan social organization', in O. Krzyszkowska and L. Nixon (eds.), *Minoan Society*, 323–45. Bristol: Bristol Classical Press.

1991a. 'Investigations at the Neolithic sites of Kephala and Paoura', in Cherry, Davis and Mantzourani, 199–216.

1991b. 'The ethnoarchaeology of recent rural settlement and land use in northwest Kea', in Cherry, Davis and Mantzourani, 403–54.

1998. 'Colonisation and competition in the polis of Koressos: the development of settlement in north-west Kea from the Archaic to the late Roman periods', in Mendoni and Mazarakis Ainian (eds.), 227–57.

nd. 'Preliminary analysis of the surface data from the 1987 season at Dhaskalio Kavos, Keros' (manuscript).

Whitelaw, T. M., P. M. Day, E. Kiriatzi, V. Kilikoglou and D. E. Wilson 1997. 'Ceramic traditions at EMIIB Myrtos Fournou Korifi', in R. Laffineur and P. P. Betancourt (eds.), *TEXNH: Craftsmen, Craftswomen and Craftsmanship in the Aegean Bronze Age* (Aegaeum 16), 265–74. Liège: University of Liège.

Whittaker, R. J. 1998. *Island Biogeography: Ecology, Evolution and Conservation.* Oxford: Oxford University Press.

Whittle, A. W. R. 1996. *Europe in the Neolithic: The Creation of New Worlds.* Cambridge: Cambridge University Press.

Wickler, S. 1990. 'Prehistoric Melanesian exchange and interaction: recent evidence from the Northern Solomon Islands', *Asian Perspectives* 29: 135–54.

Wiencke, M. H. 1986. 'Art and the world of the Early Bronze Age', in G. Cadogan (ed.), *The End of the Early Bronze Age in the Aegean,* 69–92. Leiden: E. J. Brill.

1989. 'Change in Early Helladic II', *American Journal of Archaeology* 93: 495–509.

Wiener, M. 1990. 'The isles of Crete? The Minoan thalassocracy revisited', in D. A. Hardy, C. G. Doumas, J. A. Sakellarakis and P. M. Warren (eds.), *Thera and the Aegean World III. I. Archaeology,* 128–61. London: Thera Foundation.

Williamson, I. and M. D. Sabath 1984. 'Small population instability and island settlement patterns', *Human Ecology* 12: 21–34.

Williamson, M. 1981. *Island Populations.* Oxford: Oxford University Press.

Wilson, D. E. 1985. 'The pottery and architecture of the EM IIA West Court House at Knossos', *Annual of the British School at Athens* 80: 281–364.

1987. 'Kea and east Attike in Early Bronze II: beyond pottery typology', in J. M. Fossey (ed.), *Syneisphora McGill 1: Papers in Greek Archaeology and History in Memory of Colin D. Gordon,* 35–49. Amsterdam: J. C. Gieben.

1994. 'Knossos before the palaces: an overview of the Early Bronze Age (EM I–III)', in D. Evely, H. Hughes-Brock and N. Momigliano (eds.), *Knossos: A Labyrinth of History,* 23–44. Oxford: British School at Athens.

1999. *Keos IX. Ayia Irini Periods I–III; The Neolithic and Early Bronze Age Settlements. Part I: The Pottery and Small Finds.* Mainz on Rhine: Philipp von Zabern.

Wilson, D. E. and P. M. Day 1994. 'Ceramic regionalism in Prepalatial central Crete: the Mesara imports at EM I to EM IIA Knossos' (with a contribution by V. Kilikoglou), *Annual of the British School at Athens* 89: 1–87.

Wilson, D. E. and M. Eliot 1984. 'Ayia Irini, Period III: the last phase of occupation at the EBA settlement', in MacGillivray and Barber (eds.), 78–87.

Wobst, M. 1974. 'Boundary conditions for Paleolithic social systems: a simulation approach', *American Antiquity* 39: 147–78.

Wolf, E. R. 1982. *Europe and the People Without History.* Berkeley: University of California Press.

Yener, K. A. and P. B. Vandiver 1993. 'Tin processing at Göltepe, an Early Bronze Age site in Anatolia', *American Journal of Archaeology* 97: 207–38.

Yule, P. 1980. *Early Cretan Seals: A Study of Chronology* (Marburger Studien zur Vor- und Frühgeschichte 4). Mainz on Rhine: Philipp von Zabern.

Zachos, K. L. 1990. 'The Neolithic period in Naxos', in Marangou (ed.), 29–32.
    1994. 'Archaiologikes erevnes sto spilaio tou Za Naxou', in *I Naxos dia mesou ton Aionon*, 99–113. Athens.
    1996a. 'Metallurgy', in G. A. Papathanasopoulos (ed.), *Neolithic Culture in Greece*, 140–3. Athens: Nicholas P. Goulandris Foundation – Museum of Cycladic Art.
    1996b. 'The Zas cave', in G. A. Papathanasopoulos (ed.), *Neolithic Culture in Greece*, 88–9. Athens: Nicholas P. Goulandris Foundation – Museum of Cycladic Art.
    1996c. 'Metal jewellery', in G. A. Papathanasopoulos (ed.), *Neolithic Culture in Greece*, 166–7. Athens: Nicholas P. Goulandris Foundation – Museum of Cycladic Art.
    1996d. 'Anthropomorphic figurines: the Aegean islands', in G. A. Papathanasopoulos (ed.), *Neolithic Culture in Greece*, 156–7. Athens: Nicholas P. Goulandris Foundation – Museum of Cycladic Art.
    1999. 'Zas cave on Naxos and the role of caves in the Aegean Late Neolithic', in P. Halstead (ed.), *Neolithic Society in Greece* (Sheffield Studies in Aegean Archaeology 2), 153–63. Sheffield: Sheffield Academic Press.
Zapheiropoulou, P. 1967. 'Archaiotites kai mnimeia Samou kai Kykladon: Keros', *Archaiologikon Deltion* (Chronika) 22: 466.
    1968a. 'Kyklades: anaskaphikai erevnai – periodeiai: Keros', *Archaiologikon Deltion* (Chronika) 23: 381.
    1968b. 'Cycladic finds from Keros', *Athens Annals of Archaeology* 1: 97–100.
    1970. 'Archaiotites kai mnimeia Kykladon: Kouphonisi', *Archaiologikon Deltion* (Chronika) 25: 428–30.
    1975. 'Ostraka ek Kerou', *Athens Annals of Archaeology* 8: 79–85.
    1980. 'Protokykladika eidolia tis Naxou', in *Stele: tomos eis mnimin Nikolaou Kontoleontos*, 532–40. Athens: Somateio oi Philoi tou Nikolaou Kontoleontas.
    1983. 'Un cimetière du Cycladique ancien à Epano Kouphonissi', in C. and G. Rougement (eds.), *Les Cyclades: matériaux pour une étude de géographie historique*, 81–6. Paris: Editions du Centre National de la Recherche Scientifique.
    1984. 'The chronology of the Kampos group', in MacGillivray and Barber (eds.), 31–40.
    1990. 'Naxos', in Marangou (ed.), 21–4.
Zervos, C. 1957. *L'art des Cyclades du début à la fin de l'Age du Bronze, 2500–1100 avant notre ère*. Paris: Cahiers d'Art.

INDEX

Admiralty Islands 14
Adriatic Sea 30, 41, 44
Aegean, north-east 46, 162, 221, 277, 278, 285–6, 293, 304, 305, 308–9, 311, 316–18, 325, 337
Aegean, south-east 117, 141–2, 145, 149, 160, 162, 164, 238, 280, 290–1, 304, 309, 325, 349, 351, 356–9, 361
   as jumping-off region 131–3, 136–9
Aegina 133, 273, 335, 351, 353
Agia Irini (Kea) 50, 88, 149, 183, 198, 202, 216, 220, 223, 237–8, 240, 244, 259–60, 266–7, 272, 307–9, 316, 321, 338, 347, 358–9
   Agia Irini I 123, 126, 139, 155, 159, 296–7
   Agia Irini II 223
   Agia Irini II–III 139, 179, 201, 204–7, 216–218, 312–14
   Agia Irini IV–V 327, 334, 353, 357, 361
   agricultural land at 237
   centrality in EB II 244–5
   figurines 218
   as gateway 244
   metalworking 218
   pottery 218
   pottery imports 233, fig. 72
   settlement 216–18, fig. 65
   stratigraphy 218
Agia Photia (Crete) 221, 301–4, 306
Agia Photia Kouphota (Crete) 360
Agioi Anargyroi (Naxos) 179, 264, fig. 86
   grave 5 249
Agios Ioannis (Kythnos) fig. 95; *see also* Skouries
Agios Kosmas (Attica) 200, 280, 301, 307–8
Agios Loukas (Syros) 178, 334, 349, fig. 118
Agios Panteleimon (Melos) 328
Agios Petros (Kyra Panagia, Northern Sporades) 82
Agios Sostis (Siphnos) 123, 159, fig. 95
Agios Stephanos (Peloponnese) 354
Agios Theodoros (Melos) 328
agriculture 44, 94–6, 108, fig. 22
   LN to FN shift 155
   see also animals, domestic; polyculture, Mediterranean; storage; subsistence
Agrilia (Epano Kouphonisi) 177, 212, 221–2, 228–9, 240, 340
   agricultural marginality 237
   contacts 302–4
   daggers 253, 268
   as forerunner to Daskaleio-Kavos 241, 245
Agrilia (Melos) 118, 124–5, 140, 145, 237
Ailas cemetery (Naxos) 334
Akkadian 'empire' 283, 325
Akrotiraki (Siphnos) 171, 312
Akrotiri (Naxos) 197
   conspicuous consumption 222
Akrotiri (Thera) 50, 52, 71, 100, 123, 146, 201, 202, 206, 327–8, 347, 358–60
   as possible EB II centre 245
   EBA extent of 220–1
   figurines 221, 222
   pottery imports 233, fig. 72
   stratigraphy 334 n.1
   West House wall-paintings 100, 343 n.3
Akrotirion Ourion (Tenos) 327–8
Alaça Hüyük (Anatolia) 270
Alaska 9
Aleutian Islands 9
Amorgos 23, 49, 51, 69–70, 74–5, 87, 111–12, 117, 125–6, 132–3, 135, 137–8, 140–2, 177–8, 188, 195, 204, 207–10, 233–4, 239–41, 244, 257, 260–1, 267, 269, 338, 340, 349, 354, figs. 13, 108
Amorgos group 53, 55
   deconstruction of 209

Index

Amphletts 273
Anaphi 69, 79, 103, 111, 192, 195–6
Anatolia
   colonisation from 140
   drinking shapes 285, 300, 310, 311, 313, 315–18, 341
   EB I–II contact 301
   EB II contact 308
   EB III contact 351
   exchange mechanisms with 285–6
   MBA trade 354, 358
   metals trade 285, 293, 317, 341
   Neolithic 283
   plateau and Near Eastern world-system 47, 283, 285, 286
   seal 284
   skeuomorphism 270
   trade routes with 286, 304
   west coast, configuration of 132
anchorages
   and sailing technology 347
   facilities for EB II centres 238, 347
   lack of at Chalandriani-Kastri 238, 347
   EB III to MBA role 326, 347
Andros 3, 41, 49, 74, 78, 123, 125, 131, 132, 135, 139–42, 176, 186–7, 193–5, 197–8, 239, 240, 244, 259, fig. 13
animals, domestic 82–3, fig. 20; *see also* colonisation, animal transportation; equids; ox-plough complex; pastoralism; secondary products
Antikeri 74, 89, 207
Antimelos 185, 192, 195–6, 240 n.4
Antiparos 71, 113, 209, 222, 228, 241
Aphendika (Naxos) 178, 214, 263
   grave 40 265
Aplomata *see* Grotta-Aplomata
Aravissos (Macedonia) 160
archaeology, island 1–5, 362–7
   and biogeography 28–32, 33
   early Cycladic contribution to 36–8
   expanding horizons 32–5
   first generation Cycladic 65–7
   as island history 12–15
   Pacific 15
   see also history, island
'archaeology of the sea' 34, 58, 247, 363
Archanes (Crete) 306
   Phourni cemetery 306
Argolid 114, 131, 133, 281, 325
Argo-Saronic Islands 41
Arkesini (Amorgos) 334

arsenic 45
   silvering 253, fig. 83
Arwad (Syria) 272
Ashmolean Museum 50, 98 n.4
Asia, late EBA climatic aridity in west 326
Asia, south-west 342
Asine 354
Askitario (Attica) 204, 280, 307
Asomatos (Rhodes) 308
Asprochorio (Melos) 328
Astarte, 251
Astypalaia 131–3, 135, 137, 164, 185, 192
Athens 321, 354
Atlantic Ocean 363
Attica 41, 68, 80, 114, 130–1, 132–3, 139, 142, 162–4, 185–6, 198, 201, 204, 207, 218, 238, 244, 260, 290, 309, 317, fig. 38
Australia 19
autocatalysis 31–2, 131–2, 137
Avdeli (Naxos) 177
Avyssos (Greater Paros) 169
Aztec 13

Bahamas 32, 48, 91
Bahrain 12, 43
Balearics 8, 18, 41
Bali 20
Balkans 45, 159, 160, 279, 293
   Balkan/Pontic zone 46, 162, 286
Barber, R. L. N. 56, 190, 332; *see also Cyclades in the Bronze Age, The*
Bent, T. J. 48
Beycesultan (Anatolia) 351
Bikini 6
biogeography, island 6, 8, 22, 33, 89, 141, 143–4, 363
   as analogy 31–2
   influence on island archaeology 28–9
   people vs. island flora/fauna 8, 29–30
   scale of analysis 31–2
   see also colonisation; laboratories, island
Black Sea 47, 115, 160
body modification 248–9, 306, figs. 11, 78–9
   and metalworking 249, fig. 80
Boiotia 355
Borneo 38
Bougainville, Louis Antoine, Comte de 14
Bougainville island 23
Braudel, F. 6, 16, 19, 38, 65, 96, 175, 258
   longue durée 5
'Byblos ships' 342

canoes 91–101, 215–16, 247, 251, 293, 304, 348, 350, fig. 23
   sails on 99
   see also longboats; seacraft, seafaring
Caribbean 8–9, 13, 15, 23, 30, 34, 38–40, 99, 105–6, 108, 247, 286, 320, 363, fig. 3
Carteret, Philip, voyage of 14
cemeteries
   Aplomata (Naxos) 220
   burial, individual 170–4
   Chalandriani (Syros) 214–15, 266, fig. 64
   Kavos (Keros) 228–30
   EB I–II 221–2
   EBII 177–9, 199–200, fig. 58, table 5
   FN appearance of 150, fig. 42
   Greek mainland 308
   Grotta-Pelos culture 152–3, 222, 228, 237, 240, 249, fig. 44
   Kampos group 221, 300–4
   Kastri group 316
   location 171
   overview of research 48–9, 51
   Phylakopi I culture 334, 348–9, fig. 118
   prestige goods deposition in 262–72, fig. 86, table 10
   significance 153, 170–1, 222, 264–7, fig. 86, table 10
   tomb types 198–200, 221, 229, 303, 323, 334, fig. 107
   see also demography
centrality 365
   Agrilia and Daskaleio-Kavos 241
   as bottom-up process 245
   communication 245, 364
   definition 238
   EB I–II shift 237, 239–40, 246
   in the EB II 237–46
   irrelevance of island as unit 241–2, 244
   maritime role of centres 258–62, fig. 85
   see also proximal point analysis
Ceylon 12, 16
Chalandriani-Kastri (Syros) 54, 178–9, 196–8, 201, 202, 204–5, 223, 237–8, 240, 242–4, 252–3, 272, 294, 321, 347, 349, figs. 58, 60, 63–4, 81
   agricultural marginality of 228, 237, 243
   centrality in EB II 242–5, 257–60
   Chalandriani cemetery 214–15, 266, 222, 229–30, 249, 253, 266–7, 316, figs. 64, 81
   Chalandriani settlement 220
   craft production at 215
   Kastri settlement 214–15, 314–16, 302, 310, 314, 318, 335, 340, figs. 104–5
   settlement relocation 223
   as vantage point 243–4
   and voyaging 99–100, 215–16, fig. 23
Chalkidiki 41, 284
Chamaizi (Crete) 360
Chaura (Nicobar Islands) 273
cheese-pots 83, 150, 154
Cheiromylos (Greater Paros) 169
Cherry, J. F. 29, 37, 51, 56, 60, 65–6, 81, 87–8, 89, 107–8, 109, 112, 114, 120, 124, 128, 130, 185–6
Childe, V. G. 46, 53, 54
Chios 70, 131, 135
Christiana 74, 103, 185, 188, 192, 195–6, 334 n.1
Christiana group 334 n.1
chronology 53–5, 311, fig. 1
   culture system of 53–4, 332
   see also EB III 'gap'; radiocarbon
Chrysokamino (Crete) 298, 299, fig. 97
'civilisation' 1, 2, 64–5
climate 38–40, 77–8, 89, 132, 133, 193
   abrupt change, late EBA 326, 338
   Neolithic and EBA 77–8, 154–5, 176–7
collapse 4–5, 46
   Aegean 324–6, 336–41
   Near Eastern 324–5, 326, 337
   see also EB III
'colonies' 277, 291, 300–4, 306–8, 317, 354
colonisation 30–1, 107, 117, fig. 30
   animal transportation 96–7, 108, 365
   axes of entry 133–7, fig. 36
   Cherry model of 107–8, 125
   configurational perspective 129–33, 141–3, fig. 36, table 4
   definition 108–10, fig. 26
   expansion model, central-west Aegean 135, fig. 38
   expansion model, south-east Aegean 137–41, fig. 40
   motivational models 126–9
   nurseries, island 131–3
   pre-colonisation phase 110–17
   site distribution pattern 125–6
   see also autocatalysis, Neolithic
Columbus, Christopher 8–9, 13, 17, 91, 102
Cook, Captain James 8, 14
   Sahlins on Hawaiian encounter 9
Cook Islands 23

configuration
  Aegean 41
  conceptions of 21–5, fig. 2
  Cycladic 41–2, 68–76, fig. 12–16
  historical 68–70
  island unit 22–3, 26–7
  Mediterranean 38–41
  and Near Eastern macro-history 43–4, 46–8
copper 45, 99, 165, 169, 215, 231, 292, 293, 302, 317, 354
  sources 79–80, 292–7, 354
  see also metal
Corsica 41
Cozumel (Central America) 273
Crete 19, 41, 92, 131, 145, 171, 288
  colonisation 96–7, 108, 113
  East Mediterranean trade 284
  EB I–II 55, 300–4
  EB II, early 278, 281, 305–9
  EB III Cycladic import 335
  EB III disruption of trade 317
  EM III–MM IA ceramic zone 354–6, fig. 120
  Minoan expansion 43–4, 317–18, 321–2, 345, 350–1, 359–61, 365
  Minoan palace-state, emergence of 321, 325–6, 351
  MM palatial dendritic system 356–61, 365, figs. 121–2
  Neolithic 162–3, 317
  sail 342–4, fig. 115
  traded items 290–1
cup, bell-shaped 310, 312, figs. 102–3; *see also* Kastri group
Cyclades in the Bronze Age, The 56
  critique of 56–8
  see also Barber, R. L. N.
Cycladia 73–4, 110–14
Cycladic archaeology
  current knowledge 48–53
  frameworks of explanation, 1–5, 55–67
  as island archaeology, 2–5, 36–8
Cyclops cave (Gioura) 116
Cyprus 12, 41, 43, 342, 346, 359
  aceramic Neolithic 20–1
  Akrotiri-Aetokremnos 113

daggers 221, 253, 268, 277, 278, 299, 302, 307, 318, fig. 83
  'killed' 268, 302
dairy products 45, 82–3

Daskaleio-Kavos (Keros) 50, 54, 64, 70, 179, 201, 207–9, 212, 215, 253, 273, 297, 314, 318, 321, 334, 340, 347, figs. 62, 67, 70
  agricultural marginality of 237–8, 241, 261
  and Agrilia (Epano Kouphonisi) 222, 241
  cemetery 222, 225–30, fig. 69
  centrality in EB II 239–42, 244–6, 258–62
  as commuter settlement 225
  consumption at 265–71
  craft production at 230, 231–2
  demography 225, 228
  Daskaleio as navigation-point 241, 244
  Daskaleio islet settlement 223
  exchange 233–6, figs. 71–4
  habitation area 223–5, fig. 67
  Kavos North 231, fig. 70
  'Keros hoard' 225, 229, fig. 68
  looting 51, 223, 225
  pottery assemblage 202, 204–7, 232–6, 309, figs. 71–4
  sanctuary hypothesis 227–8
  settlement relocation 223
  'special deposit' 225–30, fig. 69
  and voyaging 260–2
Darwin, Charles 10, 26
Davis, J. L. 65–6, 182, 218; see also *Papers in Cycladic Prehistory*
Delos 23, 65–6, 69, 71, 74, 112, 179, 182, 185, 195, 240 n.4, 244, 273, 364
Demenegaki (Melos) 79
demography 87–9, 153–6, 291, 364, table 1
  Agia Irini 216–18
  Chalandriani-Kastri 212–16
  Daskaleio-Kavos 225, 228–9
  EB II population growth 176–9
  EB III–MBA 336, 339–40, fig. 114
  Grotta-Pelos culture 152–3
  Kampos group 303–4
  Kephala culture 149–51
  and local interaction 177–80, 339–40, fig. 114
  Manika 307–8
  MBA 327, 331
  occupation densities 146 n.1, 217 n.2, 308, 330–1
  Phylakopi I 326–31
  Saliagos culture 145–6
  see also cemeteries; nucleation; settlement
  and voyaging 256–7, fig. 84

Index

depas cup 277, 310, 312, figs. 102–3; *see also* Kastri group
Despotikon 71, 222, 228, 241
Dodecanese 43, 69, 133, 149
Dokathismata (Amorgos) 269–70
   grave 14, 265, table 10
Dokos wreck (Argolid) 97
Donousa 74, 89, 185, 192, 195–6, 240, fig. 13
Dorak 97, n.3
Doumas, C. G. 48, 51, 53, 214, 228, 335
drinking customs 83–4, 167, 279, 285, 306, 311, 316, 318, 341
Drios (Greater Paros), conspicuous consumption 222
duck vase 322, 334–7, 351, 352–3, figs. 108, 119
Dümmler, E. 48

Easter Island 8, 12, 19, 27, 131
EB I *see* Grotta-Pelos culture, Plastiras group
EB I–II *see* Kampos group
EB II
   end of 320–1
   general features 279–83, figs. 90–1
   material culture 200–7
   see also Keros-Syros culture
EB III
   'gap' 321–2, 324, 331–5, fig. 113
   models of change 336–49, figs. 114–18
   see also collapse; Phylakopi I culture
Egadi Islands 41
Egypt 44, 47, 286, 342, 345
   Old Kingdom 283, 325
   Ptolemaic 321
Elba island group 41
Emergence of Civilisation, The 45
   critique of 56
   see also Renfrew, A. C.
emery 79, 231–2
Emporio (Chios) 82
environment
   anthropogenic alteration of 7–8, 28–9, 87
   see also resources, environmental; soil degradation
epidemic 326, 338–9
equids 57, 92
equilibrium, edenic 7–8
Erimonisia 49, 74, 87, 150, 177, 179, 185, 195, 207–8, 210, 225, 228, 260–2, 267–9, 273, 302–3, 309, 318, 340, 365, fig. 16
   centrality in EB II 237, 239–41, 240 n.4

Euboia 41, 68, 74, 130–1, 132–3, 139, 142, 159, 162–4, 185–6, 198, 218, 238, 244, 260, 285, 290, 308, 313, 317, 354, fig. 38
Eutresis (Boiotia) 281, 354
Evans, J. D. 17, 26, 27, 38, 112, 117
exchange *see* trade
exogamy 86, 91, 153, 173
exploration, index of 51–3, fig. 7

fauna, endemic 112, 113
figurine(s), anthropomorphic 51, 54, 166, 214, 226, 262–3, 277, 285, 306, 308, 351
   above-ground use of 262–3
   Agia Irini 218
   Akrotiri 221, 222
   Apeiranthos type 271
   Aplomata 220
   art-historical study of 60–3, fig. 10
   complex 220, 225, 232
   Daskaleio-Kavos 225, 226, 229–30, fig. 68
   deposition 230, 262–8
   distribution 266–7, 306, 308
   and EB I conspicuous consumption 222
   EB II 200–1, 266–7, fig. 87
   FN to EB I changes 171–3, fig. 51
   and gender 173, 251, 253
   Grotta-Pelos culture 171–3, fig. 51
   harpist 225, 230, 253, 263, 265, fig. 82
   hunter-warrior 253, fig. 83
   Koumasa type 278, 307
   large 225, 230, 232
   Louros type 173
   metallic parallels 270
   modern valuation 58–60, 64–5, fig. 9
   Neolithic 171, fig. 51; symbolism 253
   painting on 63–4, 248, figs. 11, 78
   Phylakopi I type 322
   Plastiras type 171–3, 263, 285, fig. 51
   provenances, reputed 51, 58–60, 225
   Type C (Neolithic) 161–2, fig. 46
   violin-shaped 171–3, fig. 51
   see also marble
figurine(s), hedgehog 215, 272, fig. 64
Firth, R. 14
fishing *see* resources, marine; tunny
'founder effect' 20
Franchthi cave (Argolid) 44, 110–11, 114, 115, 127, 129

Index

frying-pan(s) 54, 97–9, 214, 215, 221, 226, 251, 253, 262, 269, 270, 278, 301, 302, fig. 23
   marble 253, 269
   metal 270

geology, Cycladic 73–4, 78–80, fig. 19
Gerani (Keros) 225, 241
Getz-Preziosi (also Getz-Gentle), P. 51, 57, 60–3, 190, 200, 231–2, fig. 10; *see also* figurines
Giali 160
Giaros 74, 103, 135, 185, 192–3, 195–6, 240 n.4
Glypha (Greater Paros), conspicuous consumption 222
gold 45, 79, 159–60, 165, 278, 293, 318
Gournia (Crete) 360
Grotta-Aplomata (Naxos) 50, 123, 125, 145, 179, 201, 212, 218–20, 237–8, 240, 259–60, 267–9, 309, 321, 347
   agricultural land at 237
   Aplomata cemetery 220, 222, 249, 266, 302, fig. 66
   centrality in EB II 241, 245
   Grotta settlement 220, 327–8, fig. 66
Grotta-Pelos culture 53, 54, 120, 123, 124, 125, 126, 144–5, 162, 166–7, 177–9, 197, 237, 241, 258, 262
   cemeteries 152–3, 222, 228, fig. 44
   distribution 198, fig. 57
   exchange 156–74
   EB I centrality 240–1
   FN–EB I date 120
   rich cemeteries 222, 228, 237, 240, 259, 264–5
   settlements 150–2, 153–6
Guam 14

Hambledon Hill, Neolithic enclosure 16
harbours *see* anchorages
Hawaii 8, 14–15, 23
Helms, M. 23, 258–9, 290
Heraion (Samos) 325, 354, 356
Herodotos 8, 17
history, island 2–3, 7–9, 362–7
   contact/ethnographic sources for 13–15
   and literacy 12–13
   nature of 9–11
   oral 12
   'prehistory' 2, 11
   reticulate vs. linear models of 10–11, 19
   see also archaeology, island

Iasos (Anatolia) 301
iconography, maritime
   celestial symbols 249–53, 302
   longboat and canoe 97–100, 215–16, 256–8, fig. 23, table 2
   sailing ships 99, 342–4, figs. 115–16
   West House wall-paintings 100, 343 n.1
ideology, maritime 94, 247–56, 258–72, 290, 294, 304, 306, 309, 347
   Levantine cult 251, 285, 304
   see also body decoration
Idra 18
Ikaria 78, 131, 132–3, 135, 137, 149, 164, 185–6, fig. 37
Inca 13
Indian Ocean 9, 20–1, 38, 363
individuals, visibility of 170–4, 247, 249, 264–6, 316, 318, 364
Indo-Pacific region 343
Indus 286
insularity 33, 363
   analytical islands 16
   as cultural construct 17–18, 19–21
   definition 16–17
   habitat islands 16, 26, 75
   matchbox continents 16–17
   perceived islands 16
   seafaring skills and 21
   stereotypes of 18–21
   see also biogeography, island; equilibrium; isolation; seclusion
interaction, local 175–6, 365
   demographic model of 177–8
   PPA results 181–95, 239–40
'international spirit' 210, 276–7, 279–87, 292, 351; *see also Emergence of Civilisation, The*; exchange; Renfrew
intervisibility
   Cycladic 71–3
   Mediterranean 40, fig. 4
invasion, models of 311, 313–14, 337
Ios 49, 69, 74, 87, 137, 178, 191, 195, 204, 207, 210, 234, 244
Irakleia 72, 207
islandscape(s) 21–3, 33, 36, 57, 66, 70, 113, 146, 153, 156, 171, 211, 238, 243–4, 261, 363, fig. 13; *see also* topography
isolation 191–4
   parochial areas 191, 193, 195, 197, fig. 56
   remote areas 191–3, 194, 196, 216, 243, 260, fig. 56
   stereotype of 8–9, 18–21

Japan, 16
jar, incised-handle 305–6, 308, 317, fig. 101
  representations of 305–6
jar, pedestal-based 54, 202–4, 205, 214, 215, 226, 234, 236, 262, figs. 60–1
jewellery 248, 251, 266 n.1
  metal 54, 214, 215, 262, 277, 305–6

Kallimachos 69
Kalymnos 131, 149
Kalythies cave (Rhodes) 82, 157, 162
Kampos group 53, 55, 159, 178, 221, 247, 251, 265, 276, 285, 299, 305, 306, 352
  beginning of long-range interaction 277
  bottle 221, 301–4, 305, fig. 99
  cemeteries 300–4, fig. 98
  Cretan links 300–4
Kampos tis Makris (Naxos) 152, 178
Kapros (Amorgos) 177, 269, 285 n.1
Karpathos 133, 137, 149, 304
Karvounolakkoi (Naxos) 178, 269
Karystos cave (Euboia) 133
Kasos 304
Kastellorizo 18
Kastri (Kythera) 279, 317, 354–5
Kastri, Palaikastro (Crete) 360
Kastri (Syros) *see* Chalandriani-Kastri
Kastri group 53, 55, 309–19, 332–3, figs. 102–6; *see also* EB III
Kastro (Siphnos) 328
Kea 23, 49, 65–6, 74, 76, 78, 80, 87, 111, 123, 125, 131–2, 135, 137, 139–40, 142, 149, 159, 164, 167, 183, 186, 192, 194, 198, 244, 260, 263, 307, 321, 338, 359
Kea Survey 66, 177
Kephala (Kea) 118, 123, 126, 149–50, 154–5, 158–9, 163–4, 171–3, figs. 32, 42
  faunal assemblage 81–2, fig. 20
Kephala culture 53, 54, 120, 145, 198
  exchange 156–74
  settlement 149–50, 153–6
Kephallonia 111, 113
Keros 51, 74, 89, 201, 207, 228, 230, 241, 349, figs. 13, 82
Keros-Syros culture 53, 54–5, 248, 262, 276, 277
  as prestige culture 54–5
  material culture 249–56, 262–72
  regionalism 198–9, 207
Kimolos 185, 194, 195, 240 n.4

Kinaros 68, 131
Kiparissi cave (Crete) 221, 301, 304
Kitsos cave (Attica) 133, 157
Knidos (Anatolia) 308
Knossos (Crete) 44, 45, 82, 88, 163, 281, 283–4, 317, 335, 351, 356, fig. 101
  EM IIA links with Kavos settlement 223
Kolonna (Aegina) 325, 334 n.1, 353–4, 356, 358, 361
Korphi t'Aroniou (Naxos) 177
  carvings 97, 127, fig. 23
Kos 131, 132, 137
Koukounaries (Greater Paros) 123
Kouphi (Melos) 124–5, 140, 145
Kouphonisia 50, 209, 234
  Epano 74, 207, 241, 309, fig. 13
  Kato 74, 207
Krassades (Greater Paros) 152, 178
  grave 117 and conspicuous consumption 222
Kythera 24–5, 41, 308, 359, fig. 2
Kythnos 49, 74, 111, 127–8, 139, 192, 194, fig. 13
  metal sources 50, 79, 292, 354

laboratories, island 33
  in Cycladic archaeology 66
  history of concept 6, 26
  phylogenetic approach 10, 17
  see also biogeography, island; seclusion; insularity
Laconia 308
La Houe Bie (Jersey) 23
Lakkoudes (Naxos) fig. 44
Lapita 34, 35, 36, 38, 48, 54, 105, 163, 180, 363
Las Casas, history of the Caribbean 13
Lavrion (Attica) 80, 159, 244, 260, 292, 294, 296–7, 308, 354, 359–60, fig. 25
lead 79, 220
Lefkandi I group *see* Kastri group
Lelu 8
Lemnos 70
Lerna (Argolid) 45, 280, 283, 285, 318, 354
Leros 131
Lesbos 41
Levant 47, 96, 283, 285, 286, 325
Levitha 68, 131
Limantepe (Anatolia) 279, 290
Lipari 41
lithics 50, 57; *see also* obsidian
Livadi (Greater Paros)

grave 129 and conspicuous consumption 222
longboats 97–101, 101, fig. 23
  building 256–8
  Chalandriani representations of 97–101, 215–16, 253, fig. 23, table 2
  cargo limitation 101–2
  lead models of 97 n.4
  and long-range travel 287
  social implications of 256–8, fig. 84
  travel range 260–1, 287, fig. 85
  see also seacraft; seafaring
looting 51, 367
  Daskaleio-Kavos 58–9, 223, 225, figs. 8, 68
  Phionda 267
Louros Athalassou (Naxos), grave 26 251, 265, fig. 81

MacArthur, R. H. & E. O. Wilson 22, 28
Macedonia 354
Madagascar 10, 16–17
Mailu 14, 180, 182, 273
Makronisos 49, 74, 111, 135, 142, 185, 195
Malea, Cape 131
Malinowski, B. 14–15, 275
Mallia (Crete) 44, 351
Malta island group 19–21, 23, 27, 41, 194, 365
Mangaia 8
Manika (Euboia) 45, 272, 278–9, 282, 288, 291, 307–8
Manus 111
Maori 99–100, 343
maps 23, 33
marble 201, 214, 215, 263
  Daskaleio-Kavos 226, 229–32, 251, 253, 268, fig. 69
  working 231–2, 268–9
  sources 78, 79, 231–2
  value 263, 268–9, 278
  see also figurines; vessels, marble
Markiani (Amorgos) 50, 71, 76, 151, 179, 201, 209, 297, 312, 321, 325, 338
Maroula (Kythnos) 116
Marquesas 23
Marseilles 321
Mauritius 8, 17
Mavrispilia (Mykonos) 117, 145–6
Mazareko (Andros) 327
MBA
  demography 327, 331, 336, 339–40, fig. 114
  settlement 326–33, 347–9, figs. 109–14, 117
  trade, 356–61, figs. 120–2
Mead, M. 14
Melanesia 9, 14, 17, 29, 38, 48, 105, 111, 181, 275, 286, 340, 347, 363, 366
Melos 44, 49, 65–6, 74, 84, 87–8, 117, 131, 151, 167, 178, 192, 194, 205, 209, 218, 229, 240 n.4, 263, 281, 288, 309, 313, 321, 322, 326, 327–8, 331, 338, 351–2, figs. 13, 21, 25
  obsidian sources 79, 111–12, 114, 120, 123–6, 157–8, 297, fig. 18
Melos Survey 66, 87, 120, 153, 177, 327, 328
meltemia 92–4, 95, 287
Mesara plain (Crete) 281, 302
Mesolithic 44, 115–16, fig. 29
Mesopotamia 47, 286
metal 45, 50, 97, 99, 214, 215, 226, 259–62, 279, 282, 291
  circulation, long range 277, 285, 286–7, 292–3, 298–9, 308, 311, 317–18
  Crete 298–9, 302, 306–7
  Daskaleio-Kavos 231, fig. 7
  FN acquisition and consumption 159, 169, fig. 45
  jewellery 54, 214, 215
  lead isotope analysis 50, 292–3
  Neolithic 45
  Phylakopi I culture 353–4
  as possible motive for colonisation 127, 128
  sources, smelting and mining 50, 79–80, 292–7, 244
  vessels 269–70
  working 50, 159, 169, 215, 218, 220, 231–2, 293–4, 298–9, 301, 302, 354, fig. 95
  see also arsenic; copper; dagger(s); gold; lead; silver; spearhead(s); tin
Methana 133
Micronesia 8, 14, 176
Mikri Vigla (Naxos) 327–8, 360, fig. 110
Miletus (Anatolia) 308
Minoa (Amorgos) 123, 146, 208
Mirabello gulf (Crete) 280
Mitterberg (Alps) 296
mobility 89–91, 365–6
  terrestrial 91–2
  see also exchange; interaction, local; proximal point analysis; seafaring

Mochlos (Crete) 48
monumental buildings 279
  corridor house 282–3
  lack of in Cyclades 283
  megaron 282
Motupore 273
Mount Kynthos (Delos) 50, 177, 198, 312–14
  pottery imports 233, fig. 72
Mycenae (Argolid) 325
Mycenaean 259, 364
Mykonos 49, 74, 111, 123, 126, 135, 137–8, 140–2, 163, 191, 195, 199, 239–40, 244, fig. 16

Nagir (Torres Straits) 273
Naxos 41, 49–50, 70–4, 77–9, 88–9, 111–12, 117, 125–6, 133, 135, 137–43, 147, 149, 154, 176–8, 185, 187, 193, 195, 197, 201, 202, 204, 207–8, 210, 231–2, 234, 240–1, 244, 259–61, 265, 267, 269, 272, 309, 340, 359, 365, figs. 13, 16, 37
  centrality in EB I–II 237, 239, 241–2
  Persian sack of 321
  terrestrial communications 242
Near East
  contacts with 5, 326, 335, 338, 366
  literacy 12
  orientalia 283–5, 286, 287, 293
  and sailing technology 341–3, 345, 348–9
  technological innovations 285, 287, 293, 317, 318
  see also Kastri group
Neolithic, Aegean 44–5
Neolithic, Cycladic fig. 34
  history of research 117–25
  surrounding settlement pattern 133–5
  subsistence 81–2, 85
  see also colonisation; Grotta-Pelos culture; Kephala culture; Saliagos culture
New Zealand 31, 99–100
Nile 325
Notina (Amorgos) 269
nucleation 326–31, 336
  and sail technology 346–7

obsidian 57, 96, 105, 165, 226, 231, 251, 259, 301, 306, 308, 317
  Aplomata 220

Crete 301–2, 306, 317
  and depilation 249
  EBA procurement and distribution 281, 297–8, fig. 91
  EM III–MM IA 356
  FN industries 120, 123–4, fig. 33
  FN procurement and consumption 157–9
  Giali 160
  Kavos North 231–2
  as possible motive for colonisation 114–16, 127, 128
  pre-Neolithic 110–11, 116
  projectile points 161, fig. 46
  sources, Melian 79, 114, 157, fig. 28
  see also lithics
Oceania
  far 29
  south-west 38–40, 105–6
  see also Pacific
Oinousses 18
olive 45, 57, 82, 83
  oil 83, 270, 353 n.1
Oman 286
On the Origin of Species 26
orientalia 284–5
Ottoman Empire 321
ox-plough complex 45–6, 82, 279, 285

Pacific 27, 36, 37, 38, 99, 102, 105–6, 108, 137, 320, 338, 363, 366, fig. 3; see also Oceania
Pacific Northwest 99, 100, 343
Palaeolithic
  Middle 111, 113
  Upper 44, 110
Palaikastro (Crete) 360
Palamari (Skyros) 279, 284, 291, 297, 325, 335
Panagia, conspicuous consumption 222
Panermos (Naxos) 177, 209, 270, 297, 313, 321, 340, fig. 88
Pantelleria-Lampedusa island group 41
Paoura (Kea) 123, 126, 149, 158–9
Papers in Cycladic Prehistory 65
Papua New Guinea 29
papyrella 102, 105, 116, fig. 25; see also seacraft, seafaring
Parapola 290
Paroikia (Greater Paros) 221, 327–8, 334, 360
Paros 71, 222

Greater 71–4, 79, 111, 117–18, 125–6, 137, 139–41, 154, 178, 187, 191, 195, 198, 204, 222, 228, 241, 259–60, 265, 351, figs. 14, 16
  centrality in EB I 237, 239–40
  decline in EB II 240, 246
pastoralism 82–3
  as motive for colonisation 127–8, 129
  FN–EB I increase 154
Patmos 131
Pefkakia (Thessaly) 280
Peloponnese 41, 285, 290, 308–9, 351, 358–9
Pelos (Melos) fig. 13
periplous tradition 13, 23
Petras (Crete) 306, 360
Phaistos (Crete) 44, 351
phenomenology 33
Phionda (Naxos) 265, 267
Pholegandros 49, 179, 192, 195–6
Phtelia (Mykonos) 50, 81, 123, 125, 145–6, 154, 173
  faunal assemblage 85
Phylakopi (Melos) 48, 50, 57, 85, 201, 202, 205
  EBA extent of 220–1
  EB II–MBA 326–31
  faunal assemblage 81–2, fig. 20
  and obsidian 297–8
  as possible EB II centre 245
  pottery imports 233, fig. 72
  stratigraphy 322, 333, table 11
Phylakopi I culture 53, 55, 322–4, figs. 107–8
  chronology 331–5, fig. 113
  graves 334
  settlement 328–31, figs. 111–12
  trading system 351–4, 365, figs. 119–20
  see also duck vase(s); EB III; MBA
Phyrroges (Naxos) 178
Pitcairn Island 29
Plaka (Andros) 327–8
plants, cultivated 82
  grain residues in kandila 65
  see also olive; vine
Plastiras (Greater Paros), grave 9 and conspicuous consumption 222
Plastiras group 53, 55
  conspicuous consumption 222, 228, 237
Pleistocene 4, 15, 16, 44, 73, 81, 110–14, 116
  fauna 112–13

Pohnpei 8
Poliagos 185, 194–5, 240 n.4
Poliochni (Lemnos) 48, 279, 284, 291, 293, 308, 311, 318, 325
  Kampos group connections 221
Pollonia (Melos) 347
polyculture, Mediterranean 45; *see also* olive; vine
Polynesia 9–10, 20, 23, 27, 31
Pontic zone *see* Black Sea
Poros (Crete) 221, 281, 297, 301, 302, 304
Poros island 23
potmarks 353
pottery 50, 213, 262–3
  Cypriot 359
  Daskaleio-Kavos acquisition model 235–6
  Daskaleio-Kavos assemblage 232–6, figs. 71–4
  EB I–II exchange 301–2
  EB II 201–7, 307, 308, figs. 60–1, tables 7–9
  EB II–Phylakopi I similarities 334–5
  fabric 50, 204, 233, 234, 270, 296, 302, 303, 308, fig. 71
  imports, as proportion of assemblage 232–6, 262–7, 302–3, 307, 311–13, 357–9, figs. 71–2
  incised (EB II) 4, 202–4, 209, 226, 234, 262, 270–1, figs. 60–1, table 7
  incised (Grotta-Pelos) 167
  incised (Neolithic) 163
  incised (Phylakopi I) 322, 335, 343, 361, fig. 116
  light-on-dark (Neolithic) 162, 167, fig. 47
  light-on-dark (Phylakopi I) 323
  MM IA 354–6, 359
  MM IB 357–9, fig. 122
  Neolithic stylistic interaction 160, 162–3, 167–9
  painted 167, 202–7, 223, 234, 262, 266 n.1, 267, 270–2, 307, 308, 316, figs. 60–1, 74, 87, 88, 101, tables 7–9
  pattern-burnished 118, 122, 123, 125, 154, 163, 167
  red crusted 154, 164
  stamped-and-incised 202–4, 207, 215, 226, 234, 262, figs. 61–2, table 8
  symmetry studies 163
  talc ware 234, 296–7, 301, 334, fig. 96
  urfirnis 226, 234, 301, 307
  wheel-made 285, 311

presentation, cartographic *see* maps
Provatsa (Makronisos) 129
proximal point analysis (PPA)
   and centrality 238–46, 257, 259, 262, figs. 75, 77, 84
      Cycladic 183–95, figs. 53–6, table 6
      EBII to MBA change 339–40, fig. 114
      methodology 180–3
      Pacific 180, fig. 52
Pyrgos cave (Crete) 221, 301–4
Pyrgos (Greater Paros) 152, 178, 251, fig. 81
   grave 103 and conspicuous consumption 222
pyxis 169, 201, 205, 220, 221, 234, 262, 278, 302, 322, 349, figs. 49, 118
   chlorite schist 226, 307, 309

radiocarbon, Saliagos 118, 146
rainfall 77–8, 338, figs. 17–18
Raphina (Attica) 307
Reneia 74, 123, 185, 195, 240 n.4, 244, 328
Renfrew, A. C. 44, 45, 46, 47, 49, 50, 53, 54, 55, 86, 87, 117, 127, 163, 175, 209, 220, 231, 256, 258, 265, 269, 276, 287, 292, 305, 332, 334
   'craft specialisation/wealth' model 46
   culture sequence 53–4, fig. 113
   material culture 175
   'subsistence/redistribution' model 46
   see also Emergence of Civilisation, The
resources 76–80, 346
   arable land 77, 87, 237, 281, 326
   arable land, lack of at EB II centres 237–8
   fresh-water 77–8, 147–8, 326, figs. 17–18
   marine 44, 85, 127, 148–9
   mineral 78–80, 127, 238, figs. 19
   wild 85–6
Rhodes 23, 41, 85, 131, 133, 137, 285–6
Rizokastellia (Naxos) 327, 360
rolled-rim bowl 122, 154, 162
Rome 321

Sahlins, M. 9, 14–15, 19
Sahul 111
sailing ships 341–2
   advantages of 345–8, table 12
   empirical evidence for 96–7, 342–4, figs. 115–16
   see also seacraft, seafaring
St Helena 8
Saliagos (Greater Paros) 81, 107, 118, 125, 145–6, 154, 158, 160, 162–3, 171, 364–5, fig. 31
   faunal assemblage 84–5, 147
Saliagos culture 53, 54, 117, 120, 126, 130, 137–41, 150, 164, 167, 169, 198, 208, 364–5
   exchange 156–74
   settlement 145–9, 153–6
   subsistence 148
Samoa 14
Samos 23, 78, 131, 133, 135, 149, 163, 351, fig. 37
Sardinia 41
Saronic gulf 280–355
sauceboats 54, 205, 214, 223, 234, 248, 262, 277, 305, 307, 308, 311, 313, 316, 351, fig. 60
   painted 307, fig. 101
   urfirnis 307
   yellow-blue mottled 234, 309
Schoinousa 74, 207
seacraft 96
   construction 256–8, 294 n.1, 343–5 n.1
   iconography 96–100, fig. 23, table 2
   indirect evidence 96–7
   performance 101–2, table 3
   wrecks, possible 97
   see also canoes; longboats; *papyrella*
seafaring
   cyclic voyages 288–91, 304, 308, 345–6
   degrees of 258–62
   different views of 57–8
   EB II transformation 256–62, fig. 85
   long-range 287–91, 307–8, fig. 94
   PPA insights into 188–91, 193–5, table 6
   pre-Neolithic 114–17
   scope 102–6, figs. 24–5
   sea conditions 92–6, figs. 21–2
   voyaging calendar 94–6, 289–90, fig. 22
   winds 92–4, 100, 105, 135, 136, 183, 288, 317, 326, 346, 364, 287, fig. 21
   see also 'archaeology of the sea'; harbours; longboats; sailing ships; seacraft
sea-level, changes in 40, 70–1, 111, 127, fig. 27
   submergence, localised 71 n.1
   see Cycladia
seals and sealings 279, 283, 285, 286
   cylinder seals 284
seclusion, pristine 7, 8–9
secondary products 45, 47, 83; *see also* ox-plough complex; pastoralism
Seriphos 53, 74, 75, 80, 111, 112, 191, 194
settlement 57, 291, 364–5
   Agia Irini 216–17

Chalandriani-Kastri 212–16
  EB II 177, 178–9, 220–1, 245–6, 279
  EB II, late 277–8, 315–16
  EB II, non-Cycladic 279–83, 291, figs. 90, 92
  EB III discontinuity 311, 313, 321–2, 333–4, 337–8
  FN 149–50
  FN–EB I variability 153–6
  fortified 311, 313–16, 318, 340, 361, figs. 104–5
  Grotta 218–20
  Grotta-Pelos culture 150
  MBA 326–33, 347–9, figs. 109–12, 117
  overview of research 49–50
  Phylakopi I 326–31
  and sail technology 346–9, fig. 117
  types 86–7
  see also demography; topography; villages
Siassi traders 11, 18, 272, 279, fig. 89
Sicily 17, 23, 41
Sikinos 195
silver 45, 79, 159, 215, 217, 248, 251, 253, 270, 286, 292
  cupellation 218, 220
Siphnos 74, 75, 111, 127, 128, 139, 194, 239
  metal sources 50, 79–80, 218, 292, 294, 297, 354
Skarkos (Ios) 50, 51, 179, 201, 209, 212, 237, 240, 367
  agricultural land at 237, 244
  centrality in EB II 244–5
  inland location of 220
  settlement 220–1
  as village community 244
skeuomorphism 269–70, 310, fig. 88
Skouries (Kythnos) 294, 321, fig. 95; *see also* Agios Ioannis
Skyros 111, 113, 288, 335
soil degradation 71, 176, 325–6, 338
Solomon Islands 105, 137, 180–1, fig. 52
South America 9, 343
South-East Asia, Island 9, 13, 16, 19, 48, 131, 366
Spathi (Melos) 328
spearhead(s)
  metal 253, 285
  obsidian 165
Spedos (Naxos) 205–6, 209, 263, 265, 270, figs. 60, 88
  graves 10 and 13 265, table 10
  juglet 83, 270

Spondylus shell 45, 160
Sporades
  Northern 43, 117
  Southern 69
Sta Nychia (Melos) 79
Stapodi (Nr Mykonos) 328
storage 81, 83–4
  physical 84
  and sail technology 346
  social 83–4, 91, 166–7, 244, 261–2
style 34–5, 162–3, 166–9
subsistence 81–4
  FN–EB I 154
  Saliagos culture 148
  wild resources 85
Sumatra 38
Syros 49, 71, 74, 75, 77, 87, 103, 135, 139, 178, 193, 196, 198–9, 201, 207, 218, 230, 240, 259, 263, 272, 328, 349, 365
  centrality in EB II 237, 242–3

tankard, one-handled 277, 310, 312, 313, 316, figs. 102–3; *see also* Kastri group
target/distance (T/D) analysis 136–7, fig. 39
Tenos 53, 74, 78, 117, 135, 139–40, 176, 193, 195, 199, 244, 259–60, 340
  predicted centrality in EB II 239–40, 242–3, 245
terminology 53–5, 321–4, 331–3, fig. 113, table 11
textiles 291, 309, 353
  loom 354
  weaving equipment 163
Tharrounia (Euboia) 150
Thasos 41
Thebes (Boiotia) 281
Theory of Island Biogeography, The 22
Thera 65, 69, 71, 74, 75, 78, 79, 103, 111, 126, 137, 140, 167, 192, 195, 207, 234, 256, 263, 288, 309, 321, 338, 352, fig. 14
  volcanic erruption 343, 347, 364
Thermi (Lesbos) 293, 302, 308
Thessaly 44, 146, 354
Tigris 325
Tikopia 14
tin 45, 215, 285, 293, 311, 318, 341
tin-bronze *see* tin
Tiryns (Argolid) 280
Torres Strait Islands 11, 89
trade 34, 45, 89–91, 97, 365
  bulk transport 346

Index

trade (cont.)
  Daskaleio-Kavos pottery acquisition model 233–6, figs. 71–4
  EB I–II 277, 300–4, figs. 98–9
  EB II 279–83, figs. 90–1
  and EB II changes in mobility 259
  EB II, early 305–9, fig. 100
  EB II, late 309–19, figs. 102–6
  EB III–MBA 341–2, 345, 354–6, 356–61, figs. 120–2
  ethnographic analogies 272–5, fig. 89
  LN–FN 156–74, figs. 45–7, 49–51
  long-range 47–8, 276–9, 365–6
  Near East 283–7, fig. 93
  in perishable goods 48, 205, 291, 301, 306, 309, 353–4
  Phylakopi I culture 350–6, fig. 120
  voyaging parameters 287–91, fig. 94
  see also ideology, maritime; 'international spirit'; seafaring
tramping and supertramping 31, 156
Troad 163
Trobriand Islands 14, 275
Troy 45, 269, 279, 282, 284, 285, 291, 293, 311, 318, 325
Tsoungiza (Argolid) 285
Tsountas, C. 48, 97 n.4, 214, 215
Tuamotu Islands 23
tubes, bone 248, 249, 305, 308, fig. 100
Tubetube 273
tunny 115–16, 148–9
  as motive for colonisation 127, 129
Tyrrhenian Sea 40, 41, 44

Uluburun wreck 346
Ulysses' Sail 290; see also Helms, M.

value
  above-ground circulation 263
  burial 263–7, 275, fig. 86, table 10
  destruction 268
  tournaments of 262–72
  see also skeuomorphism
Vanuatu 12, 137
  'graves' of Roy Mata and retinue, Garanger's excavation 12
Varna (Bulgaria) 160
Vasiliki (Crete) 360
vegetation, natural 71
  woodland, recent 71 n.2
Vermeule, E. 1, 2, 3–4, 207

vessels, marble 161–2, 167–9, 198, 214, 220, 262, 266 n.1, figs. 46, 49, 69
  beaker 167, fig. 49
  beaker, pointed-based (FN) 161, fig. 46
  bowl 167, 201, 215, 226, 231, 270, 308
  dove-bowl 226, 228, 230, 277, 232, 269, 270, fig. 69
  frying-pan 269
  kandila 167, 263, fig. 49
  palette 167
  pyxis 270
villages 178
  Neolithic 44, 145–6, 148, 149, 153–6, 158, 166, 170, 173–4, 364, 365
  EB II 86, 87, 89, 183, 211, 212, 216, 229, 230, 245, 256, 291, 304
  EB III–MBA 291, 326–31, 356
vine 45, 57, 82, 83
wine 279
  see also drinking customs
Vouni (Greater Paros) 118, 124, 145
voyaging nurseries 111, 131

warfare
  and EB III collapse 321, 340–1
  fortifications see settlement, fortified
  iconography of 253, fig. 83
  and Minoan expansion 359–61
  raiding 100, 159, 215–16, 243, 253, 255, 258, 347
  see also daggers
'western string' model 65
wheel and cart 92
world-systems 11, 46–8, 283, 286, 366
  EBA–MBA transition 325–6, 337–9
  relevance to Cycladic archaeology 66–7, 366
  Sherratt's ideas concerning 46, 47

Xylokeratidi (Amorgos) 209

Zas (Naxos)
  archaeobotanical assemblage 85
  cave 50, 81–2, 99, 113, 122–3, 125, 126, 139, 146, 154, 159–60, 163, 173, 297, fig. 45
  faunal assemblage 81–2, 85
  Mount 74, 137, 165, 207, fig. 48
  as regional focus 164–5
  stratigraphy 122–3, 333–4
Zoumbaria (Greater Paros), grave 137; and conspicuous consumption 222